PERFECTLY INNOCENT - The Wrongful Conviction of Alfred Trenkler

ISBN-13 9780983798538

ALFRED TRENKLER INNOCENT COMMITTEE
P.O. Box 870111, Milton Village, MA 02187-0111
www.alfredtrenklerinnocent.org

10 October 2007

Dear Reader of Version 9 of the Manuscript Edition of *Perfectly Innocent*:

Thank you for reading this book, which is one small step in the effort to find and publicize the truth about the Roslindale Bomb case. This version is available online, until the next version is created and an few copies will be printed in looseleaf manuscript form because we need more time and help to find and present additional facts and truth in this case. Its format emphasizes our ability to make changes in the book. It is not bound and sealed. One hundred copies of Version 8 were printed.

The manuscript is the latest version of copies which are being sent to people affected by, or involved in, the Roslindale Bomb case, including the trials of Tom Shay and Alfred Trenkler. They are being brought or sent to the families of Jeremiah Hurley and Francis Foley and to the judges, prosecutors, witnesses and investigators. To the extent possible, they are being brought or sent to the jurors in both trials. As is noted in Chapter 13, "Campaign for Justice for Alfred Trenkler," we believe that everyone can help secure justice in this case and that includes especially those who contributed mistakenly and unknowingly to the wrongful convictions. In other professions, mistakes are corrected, as they should be here.

The book was written primarily using public documents and newspaper articles, most of which are available on Alfred's website. As we already had a strong point of view when the writing began, that Alfred Trenkler was perfectly innocent and Tom Shay, too, it was decided to complete the manuscript first so that there would be no surprise about the book's perspective. With manuscript in electronic or hard copy print, we hope that you, the readers, will now provide feedback which will include additional facts and viewpoints, corrections and criticisms, too. As much as possible, and unless requested otherwise, that feedback will be posted on the website verbatim, and then included as faithfully as possible in the book. We will incorporate that feedback, regardless of where it leads, into the final edition which will hopefully be published as a commercial book. It is our belief that the truth will set Alfred Trenkler free, and will clean Tom Shay's record, and we welcome any and all efforts to present the truth in this case.

Sincerely,

Morrison Bonpasse
P.O. Box 390
Newcastle, ME 04553-0390
207-586-6078
morrison@alfredtrenklerinnocent.org

Alfred Trenkler
19377-038
USP Allenwood
P.O. Box 3000
White Deer, PA 17887

TABLE OF CONTENTS

PREFACE

"Justice is but Truth in Action"[1]
Louis D. Brandeis

On 8 March 1994, Alfred Trenkler[2] was sentenced to two life terms in Federal prison for building a bomb in 1991 that killed a Boston policeman and severely wounded another. The prosecution's theory was that the bomb was intended for the father of Tom Shay, an acquaintance of Alfred's. Through a series of tragic mistakes and some lies, Alfred and Tom Shay were wrongly convicted.

On Friday, 24 March 2006, Alfred's half-brother, David Wallace, called me to ask me to establish a website for Alfred, who, David said, had been wrongly convicted of building a bomb which killed a Boston police officer. David called me because I had built a website for Maine's best known wrongfully convicted person, Dennis Dechaine. David didn't know about my other work for Dennis, and my philosophy that efforts on behalf of a wrongfully convicted person should be pursued as a combined educational, legal, political and public relations campaign. Among the corollaries to that philosophy is the view that every citizen, including the friends and families of victims, and each former member of a jury, has an obligation to pursue justice and, when necessary, to correct injustice. I presume, unless proven otherwise, that everyone, especially members of the law enforcement community, seeks to fulfill that obligation. It's the work of a campaign for a wrongfully convicted person to bring to the public's attention the need to correct an injustice; for if the people do not know about a wrongful conviction, it is less likely to be corrected. We live in a democracy, and the police, prosecutors and judges do pay attention to the views of the people. The ever increasing number of exonerations, most clearly achieved through DNA testing, shows that for too long the police, prosecutors and judges thought that the public was more interested in punishment than in justice. With 2 million Americans behind bars, a 1% wrongful conviction rate would mean that 20,000 innocent people are in U.S. prisons and jails.

David and I met shortly after our telephone call at a restaurant in Bath, Maine, halfway between our homes, and I began to absorb his vast knowledge about Alfred's case. It didn't take long to suspect that a gross miscarriage of justice had occurred and after five weeks, I was 99.9% convinced that Alfred Trenkler was totally innocent of any involvement in the crimes for which he was wrongfully convicted.

But what about that .1%? Everyone who works on behalf of a person s/he believes to be wrongly convicted must wonder, "But what about that .1%?" Sometimes I think, "but what about what 'X' said, as compared to what Alfred said?" And following that comes the question, "**Could** Alfred have done it?" Well, it's **possible**, which is why the 99.9% is not 100% - but still very unlikely. Anyway, that's not the standard to use. For a person to be found guilty and sent to prison, there must be a finding of guilt beyond a reasonable doubt, and not whether he **could have** done it. He didn't, and there is no piece of convincing evidence that he did.

Soon, I came to believe that Thomas A. Shay[3] is entirely innocent, too, of any involvement in the building of the 1991 bomb. Given what's related in this book, it's very hard to conceive how Thomas A. Shay could have built and placed the bomb by himself or worked with anyone else. Not impossible, but highly improbable.

However, he was a free man shortly after I started on this road, and the need to fully explore his case was less pressing than for Alfred. Tom Shay is now back in prison for 33 months for violating the terms of his probation. He was excoriated in the newspapers for his conduct while on probation, but the government's conviction of an innocent man trumps those mistakes. Were there no wrongful conviction, there would have been no probation and no probation violations. He has read this manuscript and provided helpful clarifications and careful proofreading edits, and has completed his "Testimony" in Appendix B.

The website, **www.alfredtrenklerinnocent.org**, was initiated in early April, 2006, about the same time as began my weekly one or two fifteen-minute phone calls with Alfred. Although neither of us noted the milestone at the time, the total time of our conversations passed the 8.5 hour mark some time in September. That was longer than the total length of time Alfred Trenkler was in the presence of Tom Shay, in the summer of 1991, and twice as long as the total length of their conversational time.

Fortunately for me, and hopefully Alfred too, my relationship with Alfred has gone forward and we have become close friends. Alfred's acquaintance with Tom Shay did not go further than those few hours, mostly spent listening to music on the car radio, and that is one of the core facts of this book that the jury did not understand. The acquaintance was short and short-lived.

Until Alfred's 4 April 2007 resentencing I had not had the privilege of meeting him face-to-face because of a Bureau of Prisons rule which forbids visits to inmates by friends if such friendships did not precede the inmate's incarceration. The irrationality of the rule becomes apparent when one considers the likely circles of friends of most inmates before their incarceration. The Allenwood warden, Jonathan Miner, is permitted by the Rule to allow exceptions to the friends' visitation prohibition when consistent with the security and good order of the prison, but he has chosen, so far, and without further explanation, to affirm his subordinates' decisions. As this book is being written, the denial stands, despite my and Alfred's efforts.

This isn't the place to present a detailed chronology of my efforts since then, which have included requests to my Congressman, Tom Allen. Suffice to say that our efforts have been unsuccessful so far. The effect of the denial of visits has been to impair the search for truth, and to frustrate the Bureau of Prisons' own stated goals for visits to inmates which include the maintenance of ties to the outside community.

Two significant changes in April may persuade Warden Miner to allow me to visit Alfred. First, he was resentenced to 37 years instead of his previous double-life term. As it is now probable that Alfred will live to see his release, he now has more of a need for friends on the outside. Second, while Alfred was in the custody of the U.S. Marshal Service after his 4 April resentencing, I visited him seven times at the Donald Wyatt Detention Center in Central Falls, Rhode Island.

Around the world, Amnesty International fights for the ability to obtain access to forgotten prisoners, and here in the U.S. I'm unable to visit Alfred Trenkler who currently gets between two to three visits a year by his family and none, so far, from any of his friends. No reason for the denial has been given so far, other than that the Bureau of Prisons has the power to deny my visits, so visits it will deny. This book is part of the effort to speak truth to power in general, and the effort to visit Alfred is a rightful part of that effort.

Is it a coincidence that it's been so difficult for me to visit a man who has claimed his innocence from the beginning? Or does it mean something more intentional is at work? Generally, as this book shows, in the absence of clear evidence, I try to see only mistakes and errors where others may see intent and conspiracy; but it would be naive not to wonder, sometimes.

"Coincidence" is a phenomenon that's much referenced in this book, as you, the reader, will be asked rhetorically, or will ask yourself, whether the simultaneity of two or more events was a coincidence, *i.e.* happening entirely by chance, or whether there was some human intent involved. I've long been intrigued by the concept of coincidence and once wrote an essay for a local newspaper in Maine to capture the coincidences at play upon our purchase of a home in Maine. For example, it was a coincidence that a family friend from Duxbury, Mass. lived five houses down the road in Maine from us, and that another neighbor went to college with my mother. During the writing of this book, we learned that a friend here in Maine is writing a book about her daughter's correspondence with the Pakistani who killed a randomly selected motorist who was driving to work in Virginia's Washington, D.C. suburbs in 1993. The killer was executed and the daughter's correspondence morphed into a long term correspondence between her mother and the widow of the Pakistani. The man he killed was a friend of my parents in Duxbury, where he was a general practitioner M.D. until joining the State Department and then the CIA.

Sometimes, such coincidences are known as "small world" stories. After Alfred's resentencing on 4 April 2007, he was in the Metropolitan Detention Center in Brooklyn, New York where he met a recently sentenced "Ponzi Scheme" operator, Blake Prater. Alfred soon discovered that Prater was a supporter of a single global currency, after having read my book, "*The Single Global Currency - Common Cents for the World.*"

Prior to this year's involvement, I did know two other participants in this story. At Boston University Law School, I took a legal writing course from Nancy Gertner from which I remember her positive personality, her dramatic hand gestures, and the beautiful moonrises over the Charles River basin. She was Tom Shay's attorney and is now a Federal District Court judge.

I also know my prep school and college classmate, Judge Doug Woodlook, who was the judge of the David Lindholm case, and who reduced Lindholm's sentence by 55 months after his incriminating testimony against Alfred Trenkler. At that time, Doug could not have known the full background of the U.S. Government's request for a reduced sentence, and I haven't yet determined the best way to bring it to his attention. Maybe he will read this book. Another prep school classmate once did a state-funded psychological examination of one of Tom Shay's sisters. Other acquaintances include a judge at one of Tom Shay's municipal hearings, a lawyer who participated in Tom Shay's deposition in his father's civil suit, the first lawyer for Alfred, the art dealer for David Lindholm in the 1980s, and one of the

U.S. Attorneys for Massachusetts whose name is in several of the appellate filings in the case. There are not many degrees of separation among the people of Boston and the people involved in the case, as listed in "Who's Who?" in Appendix C. It's safe to say that everyone in Boston knows someone who knows at least one one of those people in Appendix C.

I spent my childhood in Duxbury, and there I and my family knew many friends of the Wallace family, but we never met until David's call. One family friend of the Wallaces grew up in Winchester where his parents were the closest friends of my grandparents, and where it was hoped he or his brother would marry my mother or one of her sisters. I've since visited his home which previously had been visited by Alfred and his parents and my mother and her parents.

One coincidental connection that did not occur was that both Alfred and I could have used the auto body repair services of Thomas L. Shay and his brother Arthur. The condition of Alfred's 1979 Toyota Celica is described in the book. When Arthur Shay saw in 2007 the condition of my 1993 Honda Accord with its 579,000 miles, he said, "*I'd like to do some work on your car.*"

The campaign for the exoneration of Dennis Dechaine began immediately after his 1989 conviction in Maine for murder. Years of efforts by his dedicated support group, "Trial and Error," came up short and the campaign languished until the publication of the book, *Human Sacrifice,* by James Moore in 2002. A retired ATF agent, Moore began investigating the Dechaine case as an unpaid volunteer in June 1992. He began his investigation with the assumption, arising from his ATF work, that the legal system usually arrests and correctly convicts criminals. However, he soon realized that the case was badly investigated and prosecuted, and that Dechaine was very likely innocent. Further investigation into the time of the victim's death revealed that it likely occurred when Dechaine was being questioned and in the custody of, or under surveillance by, the police. The realization confirmed his views about Dechaine's inncoence. Moore relentlessly sought to obtain the government's documents about the case and every time that unseen documents were found, and almost literally unearthed, they supported Dechaine's claims of innocence. Now, Moore and thousands of others are 99.9% certain of Dennis's total innocence of any involvement in that horrible crime. Still, Dennis awaits justice in Maine.

I had became involved in "Trial and Error" upon reading *Human Sacrifice* at the urging of a friend, Bill Bunting, in early 2002 and have been convinced ever since of the power of a book to present a coherent view of injustice and to motivate people to join or support a campaign to correct that injustice.

Thus came the awareness that the campaign for Alfred Trenkler also needed a book. After the failure of several efforts to find an author for this book, and after Dennis' encouragement, I decided to start writing it myself.

This edition is called the "Manuscript Edition," meaning that it's the test, or even trial, edition. It was limited by time and resources, and thus does not show the benefits of interviews with participants and observers. Instead, it relies almost entirely upon the written legal record and media reports, and upon correspondence and short conversations with Alfred. The one or two weekly phone calls with Alfred are limited to 15 minutes each, so there has not been much opportunity for extended interviews. As I came to the writing after I had formed most of my opinions of the case, interviewees would have been cautious to share with me their views. Now, however, with the publication of this "Manuscript Edition," potential interviewees will see what's been written so far and they can contribute to the search for the truth as they wish. The packaging as looseleaf pages bound in string should reinforce the perspective that it's a work-in-progress.

There is no hidden agenda. When Joseph McGuiness was asked to write what became his book about the Jeffrey McDonald case, _Fatal Vision_, there was an assumption that he would conclude that McDonald was innocent. However, the book presented the other view. That will not be the case here unless new evidence points in that direction, and in the 14 years since Alfred's conviction, the new or rediscovered evidence has all pointed toward his innocence.

I believe that everything stated in this book as fact is true. Any reader who finds an inaccuracy, or gap in information, or a need to provide any other feedback, is welcome to let me know and a correction will be posted on Alfred's website at **www.alfredtrenklerinnocent.org**, where the entire "Manuscript Edition" also will be posted. Changes will be made in the book as soon as possible. After several months, it's hoped that a more polished and accurate paperback edition will be published and distributed through normal channels with a planned publication date of 28 October 2007, 16 years after the Roslindale Bomb explosion.

Corrections are especially welcome, as a major goal of Alfred's campaign for justice is truth. In my work with Alfred, nothing that I have read by him or that he has told me has been shown to be false by reference to other reliable sources, such as documents. Where there are assumptions or deductions, readers are welcome to weigh them against his/her own, and send me email or U.S. mail.

Copies will be sent to most of the people named in Appendix C, to the extent that their addresses can be found. Hopefully, some will accept email copies to keep costs down. Hopefully, too, some people will purchase a "Manuscript Edition" copy, to assist our efforts. All proceeds from the sale of this manuscript, and subsequent editions, will go initially to pay for printing costs, with any remaining balances to go to the Alfred Trenkler Innocent Committee, and its campaign for the exoneration of Alfred Trenkler and Tom Shay.

Also, it's hoped by circulating these "Manuscript Edition" copies to as many people as possible, including those who believe that justice already has been done, that communications can be opened among members of the law enforcement community, and Alfred's supporters and members of the victims' families. Every member of each group has a common interest in truth and justice, and the correction of injustice when they see it.

One of the themes of this book is that the adversarial criminal trial process is not a good method for determining truth. It is hoped that the writing of this book, and its subsequent editions, will be more effective in determining that truth, or possible truths.

The title, _Perfectly Innocent_, comes from a statement made to the press by Alfred's lawyer, Terry Segal, in 1992 at Alfred's bizarre arraignment on a bounced check charge from Rhode Island. He said in reference to the Roslindale Bomb case, "_My client maintains he is perfectly innocent in that matter._"[4]

Of course, many people will find it hard to believe Alfred Trenkler and the conclusions of this book, but that's not the same as proving that anything written here is false. Remember that Alfred was convicted by a jury of twelve people who believed the charges and a set of claimed facts to be true beyond a reasonable doubt. The minimum goal for this book is to convince readers to doubt, or even strongly doubt, the truth of the charges against Alfred Trenkler, for that should be enough to support the effort to set him free, or obtain a new trial. No one should be in prison unless there are crimes correctly attributed to them beyond a reasonable doubt. Raising substantial doubt, not to mention total innocence, should be available to every convicted inmate. The State of North Carolina has recently established a non-judicial Actual Innocence Commission where such claims can be made. Every state, and the Federal Government, should have such a commission.

Realistically, reaching that minimum goal of raising doubt is not enough to swing the prison doors open, so this book aims to present the truth, and that truth turns the jury's verdict on its head and shows Alfred's **innocence** beyond a reasonable doubt. It is the truth which should and shall set him free.[5]

This book focuses on the evidence presented at the trials of Thomas A. Shay and Alfred Trenkler. During the investigation of both men, there were many twists and turns that were interesting examples of truth and deception, generosity and greed, and honor and dishonor; but their presentation will do little to explain why two juries of twelve convicted Thomas A. Shay and Alfred W. Trenkler.

The best example of Alfred's stated views is his Pre-Sentencing Statement which he presented orally to Judge Rya Zobel and attending visitors to her court on 8 March 1994. Unfortunately, his attorney had advised Alfred not to take the stand in his own defense, but when given the chance to proclaim his total innocence, he did so. Everything he said on that day was true then, and remains true now. It was too late for the jury to hear or consider, but it could be considered the beginning of the campaign for public support for the exoneration of Alfred Trenkler.

Almost all of the source documents for this book are posted on Alfred's website. Thus, the endnotes for chapters are abbreviated, but they give enough information to get interested readers to the correct document in the website, **www.aftredtrenklerinnocent.org**. References to the transcripts of the trial of Thomas A. Shay will have a "T" for "transcript" and "S" for Shay, and the page number, e.g. (TS 2-24), and similarly for the Trenkler trial, e.g. (TT 2-25). When sources other than the website are utilized, they are cited where appropriate with standard references.

Graphically, the main text of the book is set in Bookman Old Style. Alfred's documents and statements are presented in *Verdana Italic*, and the prosecutors' and ATF and police documents and statements are in Verdana. All other quotes are in *Bookman Old Style Italic*.

Perhaps more than in other similar books, the original documents and statements are quoted extensively here, as this book is intended to be both a narrative story and a collection of the important documents or references to them. Original documents, rather than hearsay, should be more effective than my own prose or opinion. I've used many of Alfred Trenkler's own written statements so the reader can get as good a sense as possible of his character and dilemma. This book seeks to add to his voice, so it can be heard for the first comprehensive time. He wasn't heard by the grand jury, or at the detention hearing, the suppression hearings, or Tom Shay's trial, or even at his own trial. He was defined by others in the courtroom and by the media outside the courtroom with whom he was forbidden to communicate.

One difficulty in the writing of this book, especially during Chapters 5 and 7 about the two trials, is that it was difficult to separate my own observations from those of the witnesses and the lawyers. Hopefully, the reader will recognize the difference.

Another difficulty was that the book is arranged relentlessly chronologically, but sometimes it made for a better narrative to present a fact out of order, such as when that fact was revealed to the jury through a witness's testimony rather then when it occurred. Thus, because of that practice and my own comments, the book doesn't show exactly what the members of the jury knew when they went into their deliberations; but it hopefully comes close. The point of the book is not just to explain why two juries mistakenly convicted Thomas A. Shay and Alfred W. Trenkler, but also to show that the two men are completely innocent. Sometimes, "not guilty" and "actual innocence" are not the same thing.

The two cases present webs of lies that were spun, puzzles created to be solved, and games set up to be played. The result was a tight web that left puzzles unsolved and the losers of the games to pay the price.

The public Campaign for Alfred Trenkler accelerated in April 2006 with the creation of a website and the establishment of the Alfred Trenkler Innocent Committee. It is time for the public to become involved in correcting at least one severe injustice. Even members of each jury can help as their public voices of doubt or concern would be very powerful. At the end of the Thomas A. Shay trial, Judge Rya Zobel said to the jurors, "*You are now free to talk about this case if you choose to do so.*" (TS 21-6) Even though she then urged jurors not to discuss the case for unspecified reasons, their rights to do so are undiminished. What is the problem with talking about truth and justice?

Jurors are like temporary employees as they are hired to do a job for a short period of time, with no experience necessary. Indeed, jurors are paid on a daily basis for their work at trials. If we can question the work done by other short term temporary workers, why not that of jurors?

Readers will ask themselves ask themselves during their reading whether Alfred Trenkler is guilty or innocent....and Tom Shay, too. To find someone guilty of a crime, it's not enough to think that someone **might have done** something; a jury must be convinced beyond a reasonable doubt. Below are two charts showing the range of innocence to guilt in numbers and words.

The first is a scale of involvement in the Roslindale Bomb, or innocence expressed as a percentage.

Percent (%) of certainty of involvement
```
0--.1--1--10---20---30---40---50---60---70---80---90--99--99.9--100
|-----------------------NOT GUILTY----------------------------||GTY|
```

The second uses words to go with the percentages. Lawyers and judges and legal writers are reluctant to affix a number to the phrase "beyond a reasonable doubt." They seem to prefer maintaining a level of mystery, which also makes a jury verdict less appealable. Below are explanations of the percentages of non-involvement expressed as the completed segment of the sentence beginning with: "Alfred Trenkler....."

0%	- did not build the "Roslindale Bomb" with total certainty. NOT GUILTY
.1%	- did not build the "Roslindale Bomb" w/ near total certainty. NOT GUILTY
1.0%	- did not build the "Roslindale Bomb" with much certainty. NOT GUILTY
10%	- very likely did not build the "Roslindale Bomb". NOT GUILTY
20%	- probably did not build the "Roslindale Bomb". NOT GUILTY
30%	- might not have built the "Roslindale Bomb". NOT GUILTY
40%	- possibly did not build the "Roslindale Bomb". NOT GUILTY
50%	- undecided. Don't have an opinion. NOT GUILTY
60%	- possibly did build the "Roslindale Bomb". NOT GUILTY
70%	- might have built the "Roslindale Bomb". NOT GUILTY
80%	- probably did build the "Roslindale Bomb". NOT GUILTY
90%	- very likely did build the "Roslindale Bomb". NOT GUILTY
99%	- did build the "Roslindale Bomb", with much certainty. NOT GUILTY
99.9%	- did build the "Roslindale Bomb", beyond a reasonable doubt. **GUILTY**
100%	- did build the "Roslindale Bomb", absolutely, with total certainty. **GUILTY**

Where are you, the reader, on this chart as you start this book, and where will you be throughout your reading and at the end? Please keep asking the same question.

Someday, the Campaign for Alfred will be able to "*melt* [the] *bars*"[6] which imprison him, to use his uncle William Barnum's words, and emerge a free man.

Morrison Bonpasse
Vice-President
Alfred Trenkler Innocent Committee
P.O. Box 870111
Milton Village, MA 02187-0111

home
P.O. Box 390
Newcastle, ME 04553-0390
morrison@alfredtrenklerinnocent.org

END NOTES
---

1. Louis D. Brandeis. 1914. This quote is set in stone in the lobby of the United States John Moakley Courthouse in Boston.
2. Alfred W. Trenkler is referenced here as Alfred W. Trenkler or Alfred Trenkler or Alfred or Trenkler. His friends since childhood have called him Al, but his family calls him Alfred. He was 35 years old when the 1991 Roslindale Bomb exploded, and is called Alfred here.
3. Thomas Arthur Shay is referenced in this book as either Thomas A. Shay or Tom/Tommy Shay. His father is Thomas Leroy Shay who is referenced as either Thomas L. Shay or Mr. Shay. During the investigation, the shorthand was used of calling Tom Shay, "Shay, Jr.", and Thomas L. Shay, "Shay, Sr." However, Thomas L. Shay named his only son Thomas Arthur Shay, and not Thomas Leroy Shay, Jr. "Arthur" was his father's as well as his brother's name. In any case, Thomas A.

Shay was never a "Jr.," and his father never a "Sr." The only "Jr." in this tragic story is Jeremiah J. Hurley, Jr., whose proud father was also a Boston policeman.

4. "Lawyer for Milton man denies link to bombing," by John Ellement, _Boston Globe_, 23 April 1992.

5. The expression ,"*The truth shall set you free*" comes from the Bible. The full expression from the Book of John, Chapter 8, Verse 32 is "You shall know the truth and the truth shall set you free."

6. William J. Barnum, _Of Rare Design, A collection of Poetry_. Natick, Mass., 1999.

INTRODUCTION

*"It is thus essential in this science-related area
that the courts administer the Federal Rules...
so that the truth may be ascertained."*[1]
Justice Stephen Breyer

On 28 October 1991 a bomb exploded at the home of Thomas L. Shay of 39 Eastbourne Street[2], Roslindale, a neighborhood in Boston, Massachusetts. [For a map of metropolitan Boston with case-related sites, see Appendix D.] The explosion killed not the apparent target, Thomas L. Shay, but a Boston Policeman, Jeremiah J. Hurley, Jr., and severely injured his partner, Francis X. Foley. The Boston Police Department immediately began its investigation and pursued several theories about the identity of the person called in this book, the "Bomb Maker." One possibility was that the defendants in a civil suit filed by Thomas L. Shay may have sought to either intimidate Shay or kill him. Another was that Shay may have had the bomb built by someone he knew, perhaps his brother, Arthur, and then had it planted underneath his car to make it appear that someone else was trying to intimidate or kill him. A third theory was that someone was sending a message to Mr. Shay about the need to pay his gambling debts. A fourth theory was that Thomas L. Shay's 19 year old son, Thomas A. Shay, sought to kill his father in revenge for his institutionalized upbringing and/or to gain through inheritance his share of his father's expected windfall from the civil lawsuit.

Alfred Trenkler had never met Mr. Thomas L. Shay, but he did meet his son, Thomas A. Shay, in June 1991 when Shay was asking passersby for a ride home to Roslindale from a 24-hour convenience store in Back Bay, Boston. Alfred gave him a ride, and subsequently met him, by chance, on five other occasions, and gave him rides four of those five times during June and July. The last contact was a final chance meeting in August 1991. None of those contacts was planned beforehand by Alfred Trenkler. There has been no contact since, except voice contact when they were placed in neighboring jail cells, on both sides of a cell adjoining each of their cells, in the Federal Court lockup on 25 June 1993, just prior to Tom Shay's trial. Alfred did not plan that contact either.

Thomas A. Shay was openly gay, or bisexual, and he recorded the names of some people he knew in an address book, but there were heterosexuals in that address book, too, such as his father and his father's lawyer, Alan Pransky. He added Alfred's name to that list without any indication of sexual preference. The phone number came from Alfred's business card which Tom Shay tricked Alfred into giving to him. When Tom Shay was arrested on other charges, after the 28 October 1991 bomb explosion, called the "Roslindale Bomb" here, the police began contacting everyone in that address book. Whether assuming it from the appearance in the address book, or whether from other sources, the investigators soon guessed that Alfred Trenkler was also gay, and that it was somehow relevant and important; but they never asked him. Not once. If they had, he would have said that his sexual preference was a private matter and was none of their business.

Immediately after the explosion, the Quincy, Massachusetts Police Dept. contacted the Boston Police Department with the independent information that

Alfred Trenkler had detonated a military artillery simulator on a truck in Quincy in 1986 and that the similarity with the circumstances of the "Roslindale Bomb" explosion might warrant further investigation. It was a long shot, but....

When the Boston Police came upon a receipt from a purchase by a Mr. "S A H Y" at a Boston Radio Shack store for items that might have been included in the Roslindale Bomb, it appeared to them that Thomas A. Shay and Alfred Trenkler were the sources of the bomb.

However, the meager evidence developed by the Boston Police was not enough for a successful prosecution, or, in the view of one Boston detective for even getting an indictment. The U.S. Bureau of Alcohol Tobacco and Firearms (ATF) felt it could do better and took over the investigation. Also, the Boston-based U.S. Attorney for Massachusetts assumed a significant role in the case, including pre-trial investigative interviews. Together, they focused on Alfred Trenkler and Thomas A. Shay and paid scant attention to other theories about the case.

The two men were indicted on 16 December 1992, and in early 1993, the U.S. Attorney's office notified Trenkler's attorney that a witness had come forward with a claim that Alfred Trenkler had admitted to him during pre-trial incarceration that Alfred had admitted his involvement in the bombing.

Thomas A. Shay's trial was held in July, 1993. He was found guilty on two of the three counts, and sentenced to 15 years 8 months in Federal prison.

Alfred Trenkler's trial was held in November 1993 and he was found guilty on all three counts on 29 November. He was sentenced on 9 March 1994 to two concurrent life terms in prison, and he has so far, through 26 August 2007, served 13 years, 9 months of that sentence. When his 231 days of pretrial incarceration is added, the total is a 14 years and 5 months. Alfred Trenkler has always maintained his innocence to all who would listen.

On 4 April 2007 Alfred Trenkler was returned to Boston to be resentenced, after he had successfully shown the court that his original sentence did not comply with the jury-recommention requirements of the law at that time. He was resentenced to 37 years, which was his approximate life expectancy when originally sentenced in 1994. With time off for good behavior, he can expect to be released in 2025 at the age of 69, unless he is exonerated beforehand.

The conviction of Thomas A. Shay was reversed on appeal on 8 April 1998 because of the judge's error in declining to admit the testimony of an expert witness who was expected to testify that Shay had a psychological disorder of a strong propensity to lie. His conviction was vacated, and a retrial was anticipated. The prosecution had publicly announced it was ready to retry the case, but behind the scenes the victims' families were very reluctant to go through a third trial.

Thus, a plea-bargain agreement was struck. By that agreement Shay was resentenced on 29 October 1998 to 12 years in prison, including the six years already served, and including the pre-trial confinement in 1992-93. He was released on 30 August 2002 and into five years of supervised release. In 2005, he was returned to prison for six months for violating his supervised release, and on 24 July 2007 he was sentenced to an additional 33 months in prison for again violating the terms of his supervised release.

END NOTES

1. Justice Stephen Breyer, concurring opinion in <u>General Electric v. Joiner</u>, 118 S.Ct. 512, 520 (1997), citing <u>Federal Rule of Evidence</u> 102.

2. Coincidenally, in the Summer of 2006 the author met the mother of Tom Hunt, the author of *Cliffs of Despair*, which is the story of suicides from the English Channel cliffs in Eastbourne. The site is among the most popular suicide locations in the world. In September, the author leaned that his cousin's husband worked in Eastbourne as a druggist for a number of years.

Chapter 1. Explosion-1991

"Because one of the main sources of our national unity is our belief in equal justice ... we need to make doubly sure no person is held to account for a crime he or she did not commit...."
George W. Bush, State of the Union Address, 2 February 2005.

On 28 October 1991 shortly after noon, in a residential driveway in the Roslindale section of Boston, Massachusetts, Francis X. Foley said to his Boston Police Dept. Bomb Disposal Unit partner, Jeremiah J. Hurley, Jr., *"Jerry, is that a servo?"* They were examining a mysterious black box, and a servo is an arm of a remote control device, as Foley knew from his training in explosives. (TS 16-88) As Foley spoke, and he saw the servo moving, both he and Jeremiah Hurley knew, for a few desperate, fear-stricken moments, what would likely come - and it did: an explosion of two or three sticks worth, or 2-4 pounds, of dynamite, which tore off much of Officer Hurley's left hand, broke his right knee, and left a large 10 inch laceration in his left leg. The explosion left Officer Foley with a mangled face. Incredibly, both men survived the initial blast, but they both thought they were dying, and told the other officers nearby to tell their families and their wives that they loved them. They also selflessly told the others to be careful because there may still be in the vicinity unexploded and dangerous remnants of the bomb.

Emergency vehicles arrived shortly and took the still-conscious men away to Brigham and Women's Hospital, draped in household towels to absorb the blood. In the effort to save him at the hospital, Jeremiah Hurley's left hand was amputated; but it was to no avail. He died at 7:22 that evening. Most of Frank Foley's body recovered, except for his left eye which was replaced with a prosthesis. He was unable to return to work, and retired on disability.

At that explosive instant the lives of six men intersected forever: Francis X. Foley, Jeremiah Hurley, Jr., the Bomb Maker, Thomas A. Shay, Thomas L. Shay and Alfred W. Trenkler.

Officers Foley and Hurley had been called at about 11:50 a.m. to go to 39 Eastbourne Street, Roslindale to investigate a possible bomb. (For two ATF and Boston Police drawings of the neighborhood and the Shay lot with the locations of the cars and bomb, see Appendix D.)

Nineteen ninety-one was the 5th year the two policemen had been together in the Boston Bomb Disposal Unit, nicknamed the "Bomb Squad." The year began with the world knowing that the 1990 invasion of Kuwait by Iraq, a result of a series of mistaken calculations, would be corrected in some way. On 12 January 1991, the U.S. Congress authorized military action by the United States and its U.N.-authorized international coalition, and on 16 January the war began. By 27 February it was over. Correcting the mistakes of the Roslindale Bomb investigation and prosecution would take much longer.

On 4 March 1991, the earliest version of the World Wide Web was launched and on 17 April, the Dow Jones Industrial Average closed above 3,000 for the first time.

In August, Bruce Nelson became the fourth man to be exonerated by DNA, as listed by the Innocence Project. He had been convicted in 1982 of rape and murder, with the primary evidence in the case being the confession of a co-defendant in a botched robbery. Nelson was also claimed by the prosecution to have confessed when he confronted the already confessed partner, "*What did you tell them?*"[1] The overeager prosecution mistook, intentionally or unintentionally, the apparently admitted role in the robbery for the denied role in the rape and murder of the unexpected female intruder.

On 12 June 1991, Boris Yeltsin was elected the President of the Russian Republic and by the end of August, the Soviet Union was no more. During those last 80 days of the Soviet Union, an acquaintance between two of the six men, Tom Shay and Alfred Trenkler, started, stalled and stopped in Boston.

Francis X. Foley

The first of the six men, alphabetically, was Francis X. Foley, who was 49 years old on 28 October and the divorced father of three daughters and a son. He joined the Boston Police Department in 1967 after four years in the U.S. Air Force. He spent ten years Boston's well-regarded horse-mounted unit before joining the Bomb Squad in 1986. In 1987, he went to the FBI explosives school in Huntsville, Alabama and was certified as an explosives technician.

In his 5-6 years on the 13-member Bomb Squad, he had investigated 50-60 bomb cases, or about ten per year, which was about one-tenth of the entire Squad's work. None of Foley's cases ever involved a remote control detonation system, but he had been trained to know how they worked.

Foley and his partner had a system to alternate the responsibility of directly handling the device by agreeing that the driver of their Ford Bronco for the day would be the officer to handle the suspected device on that day. If there was more than one suspected device during one day, the other officer would handle the next device. This practice ensured fair sharing of the deadly responsibility and risks.

Frank Foley and Jerry Hurley had been paired as team members since Foley joined the Squad. Every week, two of his four work days were with Jeremiah Hurley.

Jeremiah J. Hurley, Jr.

Officer Jeremiah Hurley, Badge number 1772, was a handsome, hazel-eyed, 240 pound, 6 foot 3 inch, 50 year-old man. He had just reached that half-century mark only a month before the explosion, and 28 October was his first day back at work after a week's vacation in the Caribbean with his wife, Cynthia. He had joined the Boston Police Dept. in 1968 and had been in the horse-mounted unit before Frank Foley. Hurley joined the Bomb Squad in 1985. Jeremiah Hurley was known for his wit according to a long-time friend, Angelo Scaccia, who said in a newspaper article, "*He was a raconteur*," and he had the ability to make one laugh so hard tears rolled down your face. Mayor Raymond Flynn met with members of the Hurley family on the night of the explosion and later said to the media, "*The City of Boston has lost one of its finest sons tonight.*" Reporting on the funeral, the *Worcester Telegram* reported that Governor Weld had attended Hurley's wake the previous night. The article continued, "*Police Commissioner Francis Roache, his voice breaking several times throughout the eulogy, remembered Hurley as a man 'slow to anger, quick to be kind and forgiving.' The Rev. Arthur Driscoll, the former pastor of St. Anne's, recalled seeing Hurley at many church functions. 'Often he was still there after everyone else had left, with a broom cleaning up,' Driscoll recalled. 'When you thanked him, the response was always same, 'Someone has do it.' Likewise, when Driscoll asked Hurley why a man with a wife and four children would join the bomb squad, the officer replied: 'Someone has to do it.' ' "*

Jeremiah Hurley left his wife, Cynthia, and two stepsons and two daughters. One stepson, David Powell, was a Boston Police officer, the first of the third generation of Hurley's family to serve in the Boston Police Department. Later, one of Hurley's daughters, Leanne, would also join, and by 2007, three of his children were serving in the Boston Police Dept.

Boston's Cardinal Bernard Law presided at Jeremiah's Hurley's funeral, which was held at St. Anne's Church on West Milton Drive in Readville, Boston. Three thousand policemen from 125 police departments attended the ceremony. Flags on all Boston Police Dept. buildings continued to fly at half-mast until 28 November.

The Bomb Maker

We can surmise that he was male, as there have been few women bomb builders. After that, we can surmise little. Probably he was from Boston. Maybe he knew Mr. Thomas L. Shay, maybe not. He had some knowledge of how to handle explosives, as he removed the brown and identifiable paper covering before placing the equivalent of 2-3 sticks of dynamite into the carefully crafted wooden box. Showing that he was a better woodworker than electrician, he carefully drew ballpoint penned straight edging lines for his power saw cuts. This craftsmanship made more sense than his wiring the six 9-volt batteries in a series. The resulting wiring produced a 45 volt charge instead of the necessary 1.5 volts. One 9-volt battery, or even one 1.5 volt "D" battery would have been sufficient. Such wiring showed that the Bomb Maker was almost certainly not an electrical engineer. The Bomb Maker did have one exclusive piece of knowledge, however. As Alfred Trenkler wrote in 2007, *"There are two parties on this earth that know for a fact that I had nothing whatsoever to do with this bombing, me and the actual Bomb Builder(s)."*

If the Bomb Maker intended that the bomb actually explode, and harm Mr. Thomas L. Shay, he failed. If the detonation was planned to be triggered by a Futaba transmitter, that, too must have failed because it's unlikely that someone would have intentionally sent a radio signal while a policeman was holding the device, unless the person holding a transmitter was not able to see that the officers were with the Bomb when it was detonated. They may have been obscured by the parked cars or by other objects. Alternatively, it may have been ignited by a stray radio signal, perhaps amplified by Jeremiah Hurley acting as a human antenna, or by a foreign-made radio with a radio frequency not authorized by the FCC or by some other mishap. One problem with theories of how the explosion occurred is the need to explain why the bomb did not explode during the period since its discovery by Mr. Thomas L. Shay on Sunday, 27 October.

Thomas A. Shay (Tom)

When Thomas A. Shay met Alfred Trenkler, he was an articulate but troubled and emotionally wounded 19-year-old survivor of a dysfunctional family, government social service agencies and foster homes since he was five years old.

The son of Thomas Leroy Shay and Nancy Peters Shay, Thomas Arthur Shay was born on 3 November 1971, about two months after Alfred Trenkler began his ninth grade year at Thayer Academy in Braintree, Massachusetts. Tom's middle name came from his grandfather, Arthur Shay, or his uncle, Arthur James Shay, or both. The grandfather Arthur died in 1969, before Tom was born, and his grandmother, Rose, was still alive in 1991. Tom's mother, Nancy, had two daughters, Jeanne(1963) and Amy (1965) by previous husbands, and she and Thomas L. Shay had their first child, Nancy, in 1967 and Paula followed in 1968. Tom was born on 3 November 1971.

In February 1977, when Tom was five and one-half and shortly after his parents' separation, he had 15 teeth removed due to periodontal infection. Mrs. Shay and her children were living in a two floor apartment in the Alston public housing projects. On 26 March 1977 Tom caused a destructive fire when playing with matches upstairs in his room while attempting to set afire his Teddy Bear. He was missing for several minutes and was later found hiding in the refrigerator room of the local variety store.

The family was forced to seek temporary housing and government assistance. Seeking psychological help for Tom's behavior, his mother, Nancy Shay, took him to Metropolitan State Hospital in Waltham for what was expected to be a 10-day evaluation. At the expiration of that period, the doctors would not release him for another five months, as they insisted that he required considerable psychological care. That was the beginning of approximately 30 years of state-provided care and institutionalization for Tom Shay. His sisters, Nancy and Paula, also received services from the Massachusetts Dept. of Social Services (DSS).

After his "Met State" evaluation, Tom Shay was in and out of special residential schools, and was referred to many psychologists. One characteristic behavior was lying, perhaps to get attention. At one school he charged a teacher with sexual abuse, and at another, Tom told the teachers, and then the police, that there was a handgun at his residential school.

From time to time, he would come home to live with his mother at 26 Belvoir Road in Milton, only 1.5 miles from Whitelawn Ave. home of the Wallaces, the mother and stepfather of Alfred Trenkler. That wasn't far geographically, but they were on different sides of the proverbial railroad tracks and no member of either family had met a member of the other, until June 1991. There are never too many degrees of separation, however, and one social link between the families was that a close male friend of Alfred was a friend of one of Tom Shay's older half-sisters in the late 1970's.

In May 1979, Tom's mother took him to the Milton Police Dept. to seek help for his firesetting behavior, and in September 1980, the nine year-old Tommy Shay was arrested for pulling fire alarms in the Blue Hills Reservation area of Milton. The next month, while at the Wollaston Bowladrome, he notified police that a person was drowning at Wollaston Beach in Quincy. After many hours of searching with boats and a helicopter, the police were informed that Tom Shay sometimes made up stories. It was on the television news, which was an attraction for Tommy. In November, he was knocked unconscious in a rock fight with other boys and required hospitalization.

Trouble at home was a source of Tom Shay's difficulties. His father's beatings of his mother led her to seek a temporary restraining order on 12 November 1981, and the father, Thomas L. Shay, was ordered to vacate the family home on 17 November 1979.

In December 1981, Tommy Shay claimed to be the victim of a robbery at the Jordan Marsh department store in Boston. A subsequent Milton Police visit to his home found that no parents were living with Tommy, age 10 and his teen-aged sisters. In January, 1982, he stole jewelry and other items from the neighbors in the downstairs apartment, and later that month he was admitted for residential care at the Nazareth Child Care Center in Jamaica Plain. Once, he took his half-sister's MBTA cap and, while she was looking for it in order to get to work, he was outside directing traffic as if he were a policeman. When Tom was at home, his life could sometimes seem quite normal. He set up a lemonade stand, and had a short stint with a newspaper route. His oldest half-sister, Jeanne, took him camping and other trips. At the age of 11, he had a "crush" on a girl named Elizabeth and purchased a Valentine's Day gift for her.

At Nazareth his problems with the staff involved his telling of lies, which seemed to result from his saying what he thought people wanted to hear. He often asked, "*Do you still like me?*" At Nazareth, Tom contracted gonnorhea and/or syphillis among other effects of sexual abuse, and that was not a lie from Tommy. The lies in that instance came when DSS persuaded Thomas L. and Nancy Shay not to file a complaint or otherwise press charges arising from the sexual abuse. It wasn't only the Boston Archdiocese that was covering up sexual abuse of children in Boston.

In May 1984, he was admitted to Bournewood Hospital in Brookline and stayed until discharged in October into the custody of his father. In November, Tommy Shay was placed with the secure Spaulding Youth Center in Tilton, New Hampshire. Patriotism joined his menu of emotions as he painted an authorized mural-sized American flag on the wall of his residential Colcord Cottage, and led an effort to raise money to replace the school's tattered outdoor flag. He lived there for almost two years until his discharge on 25 July 1986, which followed an arrest in Concord, New Hampshire in a stolen Jeep. While noting his emotional growth during his stay, Spaulding nonetheless recommended that he be placed in a more secure locked facility.

Next, Tom Shay was evaluated at the Gaebler Unit for children at the Metropolitan State Hospital in Waltham, and was then placed in August 1986 at the Fuller Memorial Hospital in South Attleboro for another evaluation. Finally in October, he was placed at the Baird Center in Plymouth where he stayed for a year, until October, 1987, when his father regained custody. There, among other lies, he once reported that he had seen a gun, which led to a police investigation. On another occasion, he reported that a staff member had inappropriately touched him.

The good news at Baird was that Tom's father "*has been very involved with Tommy's program,*" which led to his subsequent placement at his father's home. Also in October 1987, Tom was visiting his father at his auto body shop at the Dedham Service Center in Dedham when someone threw a large firecracker into a barrel making a loud noise. Both Mr. Shay and his son, Tom, were nearby.

While living at home with his father, in Hyde Park, he attended an alternative high school, the Compass School in Jamaica Plain, from December 1987 through June 1988, which overlapped his moving with his father to 39 Eastbourne Street, Roslindale.

In late May 1988 Thomas L. Shay and Tom moved to the home of Mr. Shay's woman friend, Mary Alice Flanagan, 27. Mary's mother, who owned and lived in the house with Mary and Kristen, died in April, and Mr. Shay's divorce from Nancy Shay became final on 5 May. Unhappy with having to share his father with Mary, who was about the same age as his oldest half-sister, and unhappy with the rules of his new home after only a few days, Tom stole $300 in June from the home. Later, that theft was forgiven and he returned for one day. Then he stole his father's coin collection, and bars of silver and many items of Mary Flanagan's jewelry that she had inherited from her mother. He fled to Florida with $6-10,000 in cash and valuables, and was discharged from the Compass School program. Upon his return in September, he was admitted for an evaluation to the Psychiatric Center at the University of Mass. Medical Center in Westboro. That led to placement in the Boston Cluster Program of the New England Home for Little Wanderers, a quaintly named organization providing help for disturbed children. There, he earned his GED, or equivalency high school diploma. In November, Tom was arrested in Manchester, New Hampshire for auto theft.

After the summer of 1988, Tom lived away from home and was actively gay, sometimes working as a male prostitute. In December 1988, Tom's social worker and legal guardian, Ron Payne, reported to the Boston Police that Tom was missing.

During the years 1989 through 1991, Tom traveled the country and was believed to be at times in Florida and the State of Washington. He sometimes earned legitimate money, even if under-the-table, by doing massage work. In February 1989, he was arrested in Boston for prostitution, and in March Ron Payne applied, on Tom's behalf, for a placement with the U.S. Job Corps. That application was unsuccessful.

In May 1989 the 17 year-old Tom Shay was arrested for auto theft in Milton and was sent to the Norfolk County Jail in Dedham. There, a psychologist recommended a commitment to the Bridgewater State Hospital because of Shay's suicidal tendencies, stating that he "attempted to open door on airplane and jump out," and that he "is a danger to himself and others." The Jail's medical director confirmed the recommendation saying, "This man is seriously depressed and a psychiatric examination is of paramount importance." On 25 May, the Quincy District Court ordered Tom Shay to be committed to Bridgewater State Hospital for a 30-day mental health evaluation.

On 20 June 1989, Dr. Charles Forbes, completed his evaluation of Tom Shay. He noted that it was Shay's first such evaluation at Bridgewater and that Shay had not received any psychiatric medications while at the hospital. Forbes interviewed Shay for a total of three hours, and also discussed his case with members of the Bridgewater staff and with Ronald Payne, Shay's legal guardian at the DSS. There were two in-house incident reports in Shay's file considered by Dr. Forbes. One stated that on 10 June, "Patient was very upset and acted as if he did not know what was going on. Patient was placed in four point restraints per Dr. Patel for the safety of patient Shay and the Safety of medical unit.... No use of force." On 20 June, one staffer reported, that Tom Shay, "became aggressive and threatening towards the staff, stating, 'I don't have to listen to any of you.' Repeated attempts to get Shay to comply with ward officer directives were fruitless. At this point it was determined that Shay was a danger to himself and others on Medical. He was at this point escorted to ITU by CO Medeiros and myself without incident, injury or use of force." Without referring to these incident reports, Dr. Forbes found Shay to be "generally pleasant, appropriate and cooperative. His thought processes are coherent and goal directed....Mood and affect are appropriate to the situation... is showing no evidence of major mental illness... he presents, however,... gender identity issues of longstanding duration... His behavior may at times also appear to be provocative to others. This may make him vulnerable to ridicule or abuse by others. He has, however, experienced no major difficulties in this regard while at Bridgewater State Hospital. At this time, he is requesting to be returned to the Dedham House of Correction for adjudication of his charges." Regarding criminal responsibility, Dr. Forbes concluded that, "Mr. Shay can be returned to the Dedham House of Correction to await trial on the charges against him."

On 2 July 1989 Shay was arrested in Boston for being a "common nightwalker," and again on 5 July. Back in court, his criminal sentence was six months in jail, suspended, and he was released.

On 19 March 1990, the Quincy District Court issued an arrest warrant for Tom for violating his probation by failing to maintain contact with his probation officer. Given the still minimal level of interstate communication of police data, the Quincy Probation Office did not know about other arrests and convictions outside of Massachusetts. The original charge was possession of a stolen motor vehicle.

In April 1990, Tom was arrested for driving without compulsory insurance and for giving a false name to a Milton police officer. He was fined $500 and sentenced to probation. It was for this offense and violation of probation that a default warrant for his arrest was issued on 10 February 1992.

Eighteen year old Thomas A. Shay appeared on 18 June 1990 on the Boston television program, "*People are Talking*," hosted by Tom Bergeron. This segment of the show concerned the issue of being a gay teenager. His mother was on the program, but Shay stated on camera that his father would learn about his sexual orientation only if he watched the program, as a family member advised him to do. Mr. Thomas L. Shay and Mary Flanagan did watch the program, and subsequently, the father and son did not discuss it. In 2006 Bergeron became the host of the national program, "*Dancing with the Stars.*"

On 28 August 1990, Tom Shay was implicated in the theft of valuables and cash from the home of a Mr. M. Turner in Los Angeles. Turner had befriended Shay and allowed him to live in his home, but when Turner returned from a trip, both Shay and $16,000 worth of valuables and cash were gone. Shay was arrested in Seattle on 23 September for possession of stolen property in September, but the case was dismissed on 20 November, perhaps because Tom had left the state.

Back in the Back Bay, he was arrested on 13 November 1990 for making a bomb threat at the Back Bay MBTA Station.

On 28 February 1991, Thomas A. Shay was arrested for making a false report of rape and kidnapping after a consensual, but dispute-ridden, sexual encounter in Broward County, Florida. On the 27th he had reported to the police that four men had kidnapped him and taken him to a warehouse where he was forced to witness a murder. Later he changed his story to one of kidnapping and rape, resulting in the arrest of two individuals. Later he recanted all allegations and acknowledged that his sexual contact with the men was consensual, and that the stories were false. During the investigation, the police telephoned Mr. Thomas L. Shay, who told them that his son had filed a similar false report in another state within the past year. The police report in Florida noted that "over nine hours of police man power were wasted because of defendant's lies." Fortunately, those two men were not convicted because of Shay's web. He was convicted on 1 March 1991 for making a false police report. Perhaps because of that conviction or because he was out-of-state, the Quincy District Court issued an arrest warrant for violating probation for that previous driving-without-insurance violation.

In June 1991, he was staying with his mother, who was then living at 200 Falls Boulevard, in Quincy, which was, again coincidentally, only 4.3 miles from the apartment of roommates John Cates and Alfred Trenkler. As is described below, he met Alfred Trenkler in June. Tom Shay stated later in a deposition that he had lived for a month over July/August in New York with a man named Bill Smith on Fifth Avenue, and later in Dartmouth, Mass. with Russ Bonanno.

The defendants in Tom's father's lawsuit had been seeking in 1991 to depose Tom Shay, but he was difficult to pin down for a deposition. Finally, on 13 September, his father's attorney, Alan Pransky, picked Tom up at his mother, Nancy's home and drove him to the Charlestown offices of the opposing lawyers. Such careful handholding was required because earlier in the year Mr. Thomas L. Shay had driven to Derry, New Hampshire and brought Tom Shay back to Boston for a deposition the next day; but he didn't appear - to the consternation of several lawyers and the frustration of Mr. Shay. Hence, in September, Alan Pransky provided secure transportation.

In the 157 page deposition, Tom Shay stated under oath that he had previously worked for his father in the auto body business, which wasn't true. He stated that before the explosion, he had seen fireworks, M-80's and Roman candles, in the backseat of a Ford Bronco, and that he knew what they were because he had seen them during his family's trips to the South where they purchased fireworks. That was another lie, according to his mother who said the family did not make trips South. Tom Shay said in the deposition he saw Jeff Berry with fireworks in his hand and then the explosion occurred. Early in the deposition, he had been advised of the possible criminal penalties for perjury in a deposition.

He said he was living with Russ Bonanno, but planned to move in with a "Scott," a Massachusetts State Policeman who was never later identified.

Mr. Thomas L. Shay was probably relieved that Tom's deposition finally occurred after one or two false starts earlier in the year. Their relationship seemed to be improving. Tom was asked by attorney Richard Zucker in his deposition, "*Tell me about your relationship with your father before October 30, 1987*," and Tom replied, "*We had a good relationship; we still do.*" Mr. Zucker responded, "*That hasn't changed at all?*" and Tom replied, "*No.*" (page 51 of Transcript)

In September, Mr. Shay took Tom to a card playing gathering in Boston. On 12 October, Mr. Shay and some friends had rented a bus to take them to the Seabrook, New Hampshire dog racing track and Mr. Shay invited Tom to come along. Afterwards, they returned to Mr. Shay's club in the South End. So moved was Tom by his father's fatherliness, that he wrote a note to him, "*Dad, thanks for a real fun time. I hope that we can do this more often....*" Mr. Shay read a few words, and put it into his car ashtray. Perhaps the expressed emotion was too much. The next week, Mr. Thomas Shay gave Tom $120 for a dental appointment that he needed, but Tom never appeared for the appointment and spent the money.

Tom's older sister, Nancy (called in case papers, "Nancy, Jr."), lived in Somerville, Mass, just north of Boston and she has said that Tom visited her almost every day at her job at "Everything Yogurt" at South Station during the three months before the bombing. She felt that she was closer to Tom than her other siblings and believed that Tom would have mentioned Alfred Trenkler to her if he had any kind of a friendship with him. Knowing that her brother had a hard time keeping secrets, Nancy, Jr. said that if Tom had any idea of whatever bomb effort was brewing by him and/or anyone else, Tom would have told her.

On Friday 25 October, Tom Shay met Scott Critcher at a "Store 24" in Quincy where Critcher worked the 4-to-midnight shift. They exchanged address information, and Shay went to Critcher's annual Halloween party on the following Saturday night.

On Monday, 28 October, Tom was at his mother's home with her man friend, David Shilalis, watching television, until he saw a story on the 6:00 O'clock News.

Thomas L. Shay (Mr. Shay)

Thomas Leroy Shay is the father of Thomas Arthur Shay and he was likely the intended target of the Roslindale Bomb. Aged 47 in 1991, he lived at 39 Eastbourne Street, Roslindale with his woman friend, Mary Alice Flanagan, and their five-year old daughter, Kristen Elizabeth Flanagan. He worked as an auto body mechanic, first with his own shop in Allston, and later in rented spaces and at home. Mr. Thomas L. Shay had a brother, Arthur, who also worked in the auto body or auto repair business.

Mr. Shay dropped out of high school after 10th grade and was in the Army National Guard from 1961 to 1967, from the age of 18 to 24. The Massachusetts National Guard was descended from the Massachusetts Militia which defeated, on 3 February 1787, the rebellion known as Shay's rebellion. Mr. Shay has stated that he is descended from Daniel Shay for whom the rebellion was named.

Mr. Thomas L. Shay married Nancy Peters Cargle in 1966 and became the stepfather of the three-year-old Jeanne and one-year-old Amy who were given his surname. Nancy's mother, Florence Peters, was a court reporter in Middlesex County.

In the early 1970's Mr. Shay started an auto body repair business in Allston with his father and brother, Arthur James Shay. When they worked on the same cars, Arthur's expertise was the body filler, and Thomas L. Shay did the painting. One indication that starting a family business wasn't easy was the 1973 lawsuit against Thomas L. Shay and his brother, Arthur, for repayment of a $6,800 loan from the

Consumers Credit Union. Approximately in 1973-74, his daughter Nancy was injured by a door at a Burger King and Mr. Shay sued and collected for damages.

In the late 1970's Mr. Shay separated from Mrs. Shay after many years of jealous, controlling behavior and physical abuse to her, which was witnessed by the children.

In 1982, Thomas L. Shay was involved in an automobile accident and received a settlement of $100,000. In October 1986 he was in another car accident which resulted in a settlement of $22,000. These were two of several law cases resulting in legal settlements for him.

On 5 March 1987 the Boston Municipal Court dismissed Mr. Shay's claim for state compensation for victims of violent crime, because Thomas Shay did not respond to the Interrogatories from the Office of the Attorney General about the claim. Shay originally filed a claim on 16 July 1984 for $4,949.24 because of an alleged assault by a "*black man*" at Symphony Station on the MBTA trolley system's Green Line.

Since the mid-1980's Mr. Shay and his brother had moved their auto body shop from Allston to rented space at the Dedham Service Center in Dedham, Mass, about 2 1/2 miles from Eastbourne Street. Shay's brother, Arthur, operated an auto repair business at the Center, too. The Dedham Service Center was owned by Jeffrey Berry and Louis Giammarco through their corporation, Ber-Giam. Thomas L. Shay's daughter, Nancy, sometimes worked there with him, but not his son, Tom. On 30 October 1987 Tom was visiting and someone tossed a large firecracker, like an M-80, into a trash barrel, making a deafening noise. Later, it was thought to have been a quarter-stick or half-stick of dynamite, or equivalent. Shortly thereafter, Mr. Thomas L. Shay went to the Faulkner Hospital complaining of ringing in his ears and flashes of light in his eyes.

On 24 November 1987 Mr. Shay filed for divorce from Mrs. Nancy Shay.

Over the next two years, Mr. Shay claimed that the ringing in his ears and light flashes and other symptoms from that blast were worsening and quit his work in 1989. Probably not coincidentally, the rent was raised prior to his departure, and he was not happy about it.

On 23 October 1989 a truckload of spare auto body parts was dumped in the driveway at 39 Eastbourne, as Mr. Giammarco had Mr. Shay's debris removed from his former tenancy at the Dedham Service Center and taken to his house. Despite its apparent source and his assumed knowledge that the dumped materials were his own property, Mr. Shay filed a police complaint.

Ten months later, in August 1990, Mr. Shay filed a lawsuit against the two owners of the Service Center. Tom Shay, the son, was slightly injured in the blast, but he never joined the lawsuit; and no one ever alleged that he had a role in causing the explosion. The lawsuit was for unspecified monetary damages. Later, it became known that the defendants had insurance with a maximum coverage of $400,000, and it was mistakenly thought by some that that was the value of the lawsuit.

Also, Mr. Shay qualified for Social Security disability payments, and began receiving monthly payments of about $600.

In March 1991, Mr. Shay said to a psychiatrist retained by the insurance company of the defendants Berry/Giammarco/Ber-Giam, Dr. Robert Weiner that he was concerned that people were trying to kill him, and he was increasingly fearful in general. Subsequently, he told Dr. Weiner many times that he was afraid that the defendants would try to kill him. He had erected a motion-sensitive security light system at home and had blocked the opening of the windows and the door to the basement with removable boards. Mary Flannagan had told Dr. Weiner of Thomas L. Shay's paranoia, exemplified by his locking windows and by regularly checking underneath his car for a bomb before leaving the home.

In April 1991 Shay's lawyer, Alan Pransky, filed an amendment to Shay's claim against Berry and Giammarco for a loss of companionship claim by Shay's daughter, Kristen Flanagan.

On 13 May, Mr. Shay reported to the Boston Police that a car was following him, and he gave the police the license plate number. That car was later traced to a Mark Griffin of Brookline, but the purpose of Griffin's surveillance, if any, was not known at the time. Subsequent trial discovery from the insurance company defending Berry and Giammarco led to the sharing of reports by a private detective who had put Thomas L. Shay under surveillance on that day, and on 9 May and 10 April as well.

On 14 October Mr. Shay exchanged his 1986 Buick Century with the 1990 Buick owned by Louis and Roselyn Rotman of Randolph, so he could do auto body repair work on the Rotman's car. In addition to doing the repair work, Shay had been using the Rotman's car for personal use until 11:00 a.m. on Friday morning, 25 October, when he drove to Randolph and re-exchanged the vehicles.

Also on the 14th his attorney, Alan Pransky, told Mr. Shay that his civil lawsuit was not going well, because the defendants were refusing to settle and they had developed an affirmative defense that Mr. Shay was faking his injuries. It would have been logical for Mr. Shay to start thinking about what could be done to strengthen his case against the people who caused the 1987 explosion.

On Friday afternoon, 25 October, Thomas L. Shay went to the Ringling Brothers, Barnum and Bailey circus with Mary Flanagan and daughter Kristen, in Mary's car, a Lincoln Town Car. On Saturday evening, Shay drove his 1986 Buick to his club, or the Waltham Tavern or Franklin Cafe, in the South End where he double parked on Shawmut Avenue and watched friends play whist. He left the South End and drove to Brookline to pick up Chinese food and then returned to Roslindale and parked on Eastbourne Street around 9:30. The next morning he drove the Buick approximately 40 miles around metropolitan Boston on errands, including a visit to either "Burger King" or "McDonalds" in the Fenway area where many cars, without bombs underneath, bottom out with scraping at the speed bumps; and then returned home in late morning. Backing into the driveway, Mr. Shay heard a scraping sound underneath the car when he parked in the driveway, but thought little of it.

Mary and Kristen Flanagan went to their church's 9:30 a.m. Mass., and then returned to their neighborhood to collect contributions for their church. Around 1:00, when Mary and Kristen left in Mary's car to a Halloween party in West Roxbury, Mr. Shay moved the Buick out to the street and heard more scraping as the car moved out the driveway. After parking the car, he saw a black object in the driveway and "picked it up and examined it. Finally he threw it against the house," according to the report by Detectives George Bishop and John Messia.

Then, Mr. Shay went inside to watch television. The report continued, "Going inside, he had second thoughts [and] came out [and] picked it up again and threw it under the front of the car." Thus, the object was left in the space between his vintage Pontiac GTO and his utility van, and was close to being underneath the front of the GTO, which was turned in the direction of the street. Mary and Kristen Flanagan returned home around 6:00 p.m. and Mr. Shay said nothing to them about the black box.

The next morning he drove his Buick, or a neighbor's gray Mazda on which he was about to do some auto body work, to take his daughter to school, and then to his brother's garage in South Boston, and then to a "Z-lock" store, where Mary Flanagan had a "kill switch" installed for her car; and then headed home. The uncertainty about which car he drove on these morning travels was just one of the puzzling uncertainties in the case. Then he drove to the District E-5 police station in the Mazda.

Alfred W. Trenkler

Alfred was born on 6 February 1956 to "Ice Capades"[2] clown Alfred Maximillian "Freddie" Trenkler, and Josephine Barnum Trenkler. She was descended from Phineas Taylor (P.T.) Barnum's brother William, and thus had an association with the Ringling Brothers, Barnum & Bailey Circus. While it probably would not have been a complete coincidence that Alfred was taken to that circus when he was a child, it surely was a complete coincidence that it was to that same circus that Thomas L. Shay and Mary Flanagan took their daughter Kristen on Friday, 25 October. Josephine Barnum was from Milton, Massachusetts, which bordered Quincy and Boston. She had won a national figure skating championship and then joined the "Ice Capades" where she met Austrian-born Freddie, who first toured with the ice revue in 1940, after three years with another revue, the "Gay Blades." In 1958 his act was on the Ed Sullivan Show, televised from Madison Square Garden, where he had a famous accidental collision with a spectator. When not touring with the ice variety show, the Trenklers lived at 239 Central Avenue in Milton, just a few miles from the birthplace of former President George Herbert Walker Bush. In July 2007, *Money* Magazine ranked Milton as the seventh best place to live in the entire country.

The stress of a show business marriage was too much for the Trenkler marriage, and they divorced in 1960. Freddie married another skater from the "Ice Capades," Gigi Jelberte and moved to California and had two daughters. Josephine (Jo) married John (Jack) Wallace in 1961 and in July 1962 they moved to 7 Whitelawn Avenue in Milton, and lived in that house for 43 years until moving to a smaller one-level home in 2006. David Johnson Wallace was born in 1962.

Alfred's first school was kindergarten at Milton Academy from which his mother graduated in 1947 and where she taught ice skating. Other graduates from Milton include T.S. Eliot (1906) and Buckminster Fuller (1923). Politically well-known graduates of Milton include Eliot Richardson (1937), Robert F. Kennedy (1942), Senator Edward Kennedy (1950) and the newly elected Governor of Massachusetts, Deval Patrick (1974).

Alfred's early interest in theater and electronics was already showing at Milton, where he managed the sound system for a school play in 1969. A sixth grade teacher Roy Patterson, known affectionately as "Sir Patterson," wrote to Alfred, "*I have more time now and want to tell you how very much I appreciated your expert help* [with the sound system]... *Do keep up your interest in the subject* [electronics], *learn all you can about it, and who knows what success you may achieve one day!*"

Alfred transferred to the Park School in Brookline, the birthplace of President John Kennedy, and earned certificates in baseball, wrestling and soccer. He graduated in 1971 and then entered Thayer Academy in Braintree, Mass. for his 9th through 12th grade high school years. Braintree was the birthplace of President John Adams and Thayer's graduates include the current congressman for Boston's South Shore, William Delahunt, class of 1959, and Alfred's half-brother, David Wallace, in 1981. Author John Cheever was expelled from Thayer in the 1920's for smoking, and another notable graduate was on the 1980 U.S. Olympic hockey team which won the gold medal game against the Soviet team. The Thayer Academy "misson" is "*to inspire a diverse community of students to moral, intellectual, aesthetic, and physical excellence so that each may rise to honorable achievement and contribute to the common good.*"[3]

While at Thayer, Alfred's interests in friends, (to whom he was known as Al), his car and electronics outweighed his interest in academic subjects and much of his energy was focused outside of school. In 1974, he began his long-term interest in fire and rescue, and completed an American Red Cross "Standard First Aid and Personal Safety" course. The course was provided by the Milton Police Department. In his senior year, his mother shared in carpool driving duties, but sometimes Alfred borrowed the family car for the seven miles to school. Alfred's other interests included the lights and sound operations for the annual variety show at the Milton Hoosic Club in Milton to which his family belonged. There, he also played tennis and golf. At home, his interest in electronics led to a radio connection with a childhood friend and neighbor, Kip Draper. His summer job in 1973 and 1974 was, as he puts it in his resume, "Hobart Aquatic Engineer" at the Wollaston Country Club in Quincy where he washed dishes, using the Hobart dishwashing machine.

Alfred graduated in 1975 and his yearbook entry reads, "*To some people the only way to have a good time is to do it and try not to get caught, and to others a good time can be had without worrying about being caught, and to me a mixture, in the right proportion results in a good time.*" For most readers, this balanced statement was the expression of a thoughtful adolescent boy, but to others it documented the genesis of a terrorist Bomb Maker. That summer he landed a job doing electrical and other maintenance work at the Harborview Hotel in Edgartown on Martha's Vineyard, and he returned there for the summer of 1976.

Socially, Alfred had many friends and his friendship was valued. Wrote his friend Paul Ochs in a presentencing letter to Judge Zobel, "*Alfred was like an older brother to many of us in the neighborhood and provided a positive role model, especially where his technical abilities were concerned.*" The issue of defining his sexual preference was not a significant issue for him in high school where he escorted female friends at dances and other dates.

Nearly every graduate of Thayer goes on to college, and Alfred's interest in electronics led him to a two year program at Wentworth Institute in Boston, to which he commuted from the family home on Whitelawn Ave. 8 1/2 miles away. As Wentworth was a small college with few non-academic activities, his social life included hanging out with friends at their Boston apartments. He earned an Associates Degree in Electronic Engineering in 1977.

Alfred was known as a kind young man who would help anyone. In fact, this entire story of his wrongful conviction can be said to have begun with two such friendly acts. First came the detonation of the 1986 device at the request of a friend, and second came the 1991 provision of a ride, and then four more rides) at the request of Tom Shay. Both arose from the inclination to assist others.

During the 5-8 February 1978 Massachusetts "Blizzard of '78" Alfred drove his car, with friends, up and down Boston's older Route 128 beltway to provide water, food, rides and other assistance to stranded motorists.

His first full-time, non-summer, job was at Analog Devices, a high-tech company in Norwood, Mass, where he was an analog and repair test technician. There, he told his friends that his ambition was to set out on his own, and some years later his customer list included Analog Devices. From experienced managers within his extended family, he had learned of Eric Hoffer, who believed that individual effort was the source of creative energy. Hoffer wrote, "*When we are in competition with ourselves, and match our todays against our yesterdays, we derive encouragement from past misfortunes.*"[4] In December 1979, he completed a course at Northeastern University on microprocessors.

In 1980 he began work for the Catholic Archdiocese of Boston which had an ambitious regional communications system including broadcast facilities atop Boston's Prudential Building. Alfred helped construct the electronic connection to the Cardinal's residence and performed his work so well that he was temporarily dispatched to a diocese in Long Island, New York to troubleshoot an ITFS (Instruction Television Fixed Service) microwave communications problem there.

After five years of building confidence and skills, Alfred established his own company, AWT Associates in 1986. Its corporate organizational meeting was conducted by attorney Gregory Galvin and Alfred Trenkler on 14 August 1986. From his resume, Alfred notes "*Installed ITFS receiver systems for Northeastern University and Boston University and at the many businesses that subscribed to the college courses being offered as part of the remote viewing and learning programs for in-house off-campus learning in eastern Mass. Installations completed for Raytheon, Draper Labs, Digital Equipment Corporation, BBN, LTX, AT&T, Northrup, Texas Instruments, Polaroid, Analog Devices, Avco Systems, Textron and, following a thirty day waiting period for an extensive security check by the CIA, FBI and NSA, I was permitted to enter a top secret project area in order to complete an installation* [for Mitre Corporation] *in Billerica, Mass.*"

His major partner or associate was Richard Brown whose father was Dwight "Chip" Brown, a chief aide to a Fire Chief in the Boston Fire Department in charge of Ladder 13 near Wentworth Institute. One of Mr. Brown's close friends was another fire department officer, Paul Davies, who was also a chief aide to a Fire Chief and may have had a liaison role with the Boston Bomb Squad.

During these years just after college, Alfred Trenkler had what one of his friend's mother called in 2007, "*fun, fun, fun.*"

In late August, early September 1986 Alfred participated in Quincy in what he describes as a *"prank gone too far."* His friend, Donna Shea, the wife of a Milton childhood friend, John Shea, was in a tiff with her former employers, Walter and James Wojtasinski, owners of the Capeway Fish Market. Donna asked Alfred Trenkler to help her throw a scare into the Wojtasinski's by detonating a military artillery simulator, later identified as an M21 Hoffman, at the Wojtasinski's home. Not knowing how powerful the M21 would be, Alfred said that the safest way to detonate it would be with a remote control. Later, Alfred described the background, acquisition and building of the device,

"During one of Bob's [Craig] and my visits to Donna's house she voiced her anger at the owners of the fish company and wanted to get back at them, or at least scare them the same way they scared Donna's kids. Donna then went to the back room of her basement and showed Bob and I the flash simulator, which she had showed Bob and I before, and asked how it could be set off. I told her I had never seen anything like that before and had no idea how to set it off. At this point the discussion was dropped. This was probably a month or so before I became involved.

About a week or so before I made the device, Donna told me she had spoken to 'Peg Leg' [David Noonan, father of Todd Leach, whose mother, MaryAnn Leach, was Donna Leach Shea's sister] *who she said had originally given her the simulator. She told me that he said that the simulator was set off by attaching 12 volts to the wires that came out of the top of the white plastic container. She then asked me how would we go about setting this off without getting caught. At this point I told her that I had no idea, other than carrying a battery with long wires and a switch. She told me to think about it, how to set this thing off, which at the time I did not take her seriously.*

Subsequent to the above visit, Bob and I were again at Donna's house. Donna kept on prodding me for an answer on how to set off the simulator from a distance. I then said it could probably be done by remote control but I did not have any experience with that sort of thing. This had now become an obsession of Donna's and every other topic had to do with setting off this simulator....

On Wednesday prior to the 1st [of September, i.e. 27 August] *Donna Shea came to my office at 197 Quincy Ave in Braintree and wanted to get the remote control car that we had spoken about a few days earlier. Donna and I went to the Radio Shack on Quincy Ave in Quincy and bought a $20.00 dollar remote control car. It was the type that would have a 50 to 100 foot range. Both Donna and I went into the store, picked the first cheap remote control car that we saw (since I was not sure I could even make something out of the remote car system and had mentioned this to Donna, she did not want to spend a lot of money on something that may or may not work.) We both went up to the counter, Donna handed the clerk the money to purchase the car....*

Donna then took me back to my office and said she was going home, me taking the model car. After that I went back to 35 Union Street from my office in Braintree. When I got home, Bob [Craig] was there and he wanted to play with the toy car, so he put the batteries in the model car and Bob and I played with it that evening. A Bill Miller was one of the people who played with it... This went on for a couple of nights.

On Sunday around 12:00 noon Donna called on the phone and invited Bob Craig and I to a cookout and she told me to bring the remote control car.

When we arrived, around 2:00 pm, Donna was upset that I had not built the controller. Bob and I played with the car in the driveway for a while. Donna then demanded that I start building the remote so that the device could be set off.

At this point, around 2:30 pm, my car parked in the parking lot, next to Donna's house, on the hood of my car, next to where everyone was sitting, I broke apart the car to gain access to the remote control circuit board, leaving all the wires connected to whatever they controlled so that I could take voltage readings as I activated the remote control transmitter. Todd Leach watched and asked what he could do to help.

Todd Leach was watching me while everyone else was sitting about twenty feet away including Bob Craig.

I found a couple of wires that would have no voltage if the transmitter control button was not pressed and voltage if the transmitter control button was pressed. However, I was told by Donna, who said that her friend, Peg Leg, told her that the simulator needed 12 volts to set it off. The voltage coming out of the receiver was only about three volts. I then told Donna that I would not be able to make this work. She asked me what would be needed and I told her that I may be able to hook up a relay but I would need another power source to make up the 12 volts. She asked if a camera battery would be enough power because her batteries for her camera were 6 volts. I told her that we would need two of them to make it work. But first I told her that I had to make sure that I could even control a relay with the remote control.

At this point I looked through my spare parts supply, which I had in my car from a previous job, and found a relay. I then loosely attached the wires from the receiver unit to the relay, then, using clip leads, attached my volt ohm meter (in the 200 ohm range-resistance) to the switched part of the relay to see if the receiver would cause the relay to activate. This worked. Both Bob and Todd were watching me.

The next thing I did was to see how far the transmitter would work from the receiver after adding a long length of wire (since playing with the car it only seemed to work about 50 to 70 feet away). I then handed the transmitter to Todd Leach and told him to walk away to the end of the parking lot and press the transmitter. This would barely work at a 100 foot distance. But then the next problem was that the relay would switch without anyone pressing the transmitter.

I then took a light bulb from my spare parts supply and connected it to the relay so that I could monitor how many times the receiver would go off by itself and see how far I could walk away from the receiver and still be able to control it. Also, since the false receiver action was so quick, my volt meter had a difficult time reading such a quick on-off-on action. This enabled me to be around 50 feet away and monitor the results. I told Donna that I made it work but that it was not reliable and that if we hooked up the simulator it could go off at any time.

Donna told me that the simulator would not go off unless the safety cap was pulled. So with this in mind, combined with the fact that the wires that were attached to the simulator were almost 20 inches long, the safety cap could be pulled from a safe distance (should the simulator go off).

I needed my soldering iron so I borrowed an extension cord from John Shea. He plugged it at his house and ran the cord out to where I was by the hood of the car. I then plugged my soldering iron in. I then started to solder the wires from the receiver to the relay. (Bob and Todd were watching off and on.) Donna went to the camera store to get the two 6 volt batteries. When she arrived she gave me the two batteries. When I saw them I realized that I would now have to solder the wires to the battery since the batteries only had surface contacts. So now I got some scraps of wire that I had in my car and soldered wires to the relay and to the batteries.

At this point I connected my volt ohm meter to the battery/relay circuit to make sure that it worked when the transmitter button was pressed. It worked. Again, Todd was standing next to me, watching my every move.

At this point I was ready for the simulator. Donna handed me the simulator. I then stripped some of the insulation off of the simulator leads and attached and soldered the wires from the relay/battery circuit to the simulator.

I wanted to make sure that there was no way for the simulator to go off accidentally since the safety cap on the simulator was loose. I then found a toggle switch in my spare parts collection and soldered more wire scraps to the switch contacts. Then I soldered the other ends of the wires to the two simulator wires so that when the switch was in the 'on' position it would act as a short, backing up the shorting cap, should it fall off.

Now all the connections I taped with electrical tape.

Now was the problem of attaching the device to a metal surface. The only way we could figure was a magnet. Well, in the parking lot was a discarded speaker. It could not be used in the form that I saw it so I told Todd Leach to break the magnet apart from the rest of the speaker.

(It was a car stereo speaker, I remember it was a Jenson speaker, a very common car stereo speaker).

After Todd broke apart the speaker he handed it to me. I then had to insulate the bottom of the receiver circuit board from the metal surface of the magnet. I took some duct tape and layered on one side of the magnet. I put the circuit board, (containing 4 AA size Ray-O-Vac batteries in the Tyco battery compartment), on top of the tape, on top of the magnet then put the two camera batteries next to the receiver circuit board, then put the relay next to the two 6 volt batteries then put the simulator on top of the receiver and batteries and wrapped this whole mess with duct tape. At this point Bob Craig was helping me tape the device, leaving the toggle switch hanging out of the assembly as well as the wires from the simulator with the shorting cap on the end, also leaving an access to the slide switch of the receiver.

I then went over how the device worked with John [Shea], and Donna with Bob Craig and Todd Leach all watching.

At this point Donna got a cardboard box and put the device in it and put it in her car so that the kids could not get at it.

It took me all of an hour and a half to put this whole thing together. We all sat down and ate.

Bob and I left and went back to 35 Union Street for what we thought was the night.

As for Bob's participation, the only thing he helped me with was wrapping the device with tape and observing some of the steps of me testing the device basically wanting nothing to do with the thing.

Todd Leach was very interested in what I was doing asking to help whenever he could. The only part he had in the building of the device was breaking apart the magnet for me and pressing the remote control transmitter at a short distance. He was never in my car at any point of that day or any other day for that matter.

As for my part, the only things that had to be purchased were, the remote control model car, which Donna Shea and I purchased the previous Wednesday and the two Duracell camera batteries that Donna purchased on the afternoon on my making of this device. The other parts, wire, relay, toggle switch, electrical tape and duct tape, were all parts that I carried around with me in my tool boxes in my car. I never had to go to a store to get any further items for this device."

Present at the picnic that Sunday, 31 August, were Alfred, Bob, Donna and John Shea and their two daughters, Jennifer (age 10-11) and Nicole (1-2), and MaryAnn Leach and son Todd (11) and Donna and MaryAnn's mother. Also there were some other neighbors. It was a Sunday afternoon party.

Coincidentally, the M21 Hoffman, used by National Guard units to simulate battle noises, originally came from the Wojtasinski's who had given it to David Noonan, the father of Todd Leach, who had given it to Donna Leach Shea, the sister of Todd's mother, MaryAnn Leach. The Leach's lived next door to the Shea's in Weymouth. Another numeric coincidence was that Alfred's office was at 197 Quincy Ave in Quincy, and the 18 October 1991 purchase was at the Radio Shack Store at 197 Mass. Ave in Boston. It was pure coincidence, and nothing could be made of it.

Alfred's recounting continued, *"Around 11:30 pm Donna and John Shea came by our apartment and wanted us to go with them for drinks at the Sun Tuey restaurant on Cambridge Street in Boston. On the way Donna had John go by Willard Street where the Capeway Fish owner lived to show everyone where they lived and to see if the truck was parked there. It was. We did not stop. We just went by and went to town. We returned from town around 1:30 am and John was in the process of dropping Bob and I off at our apartment. Donna, at this point, asked who would stick the device on the fish truck. We all said "No." Donna went ballistic. John got in his car and spun his tires in reverse and started to make a real scene with Donna. She would not stop. I told Donna to shut up and I would go do it. John and Donna calmed down and went in with Bob to our apartment.*

I then went to Willard Street where the truck was parked. I parked around the corner. I got out and went to the side of the truck. I put the device on the outside of the frame, in front of the left rear wheel and away from the gas tank or any fuel lines. (The area was well lit). I threw the toggle switch then ran back to my car and drove away, pressing the remote control button as I drove by, but nothing happened. Then I remembered that I had forgotten to pull the shorting cap.

I went back to the apartment and told Donna that it did not work because I had forgotten to pull the shorting cap. I said that I had to go back to set it off. I then went back, parked my car in the same spot, went up to the truck and pulled the shorting cap (shunt) and quickly walked away. By the time I got 75 feet away, the device went off and I did not even have the remote control transmitter with me. It was in the car.

I then left and went back to my apartment.

Alfred later described to a friend the circumstances of the 1986 incident with fewer details, "*At a picnic at Donna Shea's house I broke apart the receiver unit and Rube Golberged together the receiver, simulator and a speaker that John Shea had recently discarded, with the necessary batteries and used duct tape to hold the contrivance together. Later that night Donna Shea wanted someone to go and set this thing off on or near the fish company owner's fish delivery truck. Donna made a big scene and demanded that someone better set this thing off and, since I had built it I was elected. I stuck it on the side of the back of the fish truck and set it off sometime around 2:00 a.m. There was no damage done and none intended and no injuries, none intended, simply a loud noise, just like a firecracker.*"

The resulting explosion was upsetting to the Wojtasinski's, who called the police, but it caused no damage to the truck, nor to any person.

As the Quincy Police report of the incident said, "Something peculiar about this is that the victim [Wojtasinski] seems to know an awfully lot about the bomb, type in what [sic] it was made from. The deputy of the fire department feels that the victim may have done it himself."

The police investigation soon led to Alfred Trenkler who acknowledged his role after an initial denial. He described the device for Detective Lanergan as having 2 AA batteries for the radio receiver unit, or fusing circuit, and 2 6-volt batteries connected in series for a 12-volt charge in the firing circuit to detonate the M21 Hoffman. A small lightbulb was used to test the one of the circuits, and a toggle switch was used to disable fusing circuit until the device was in place. A round magnet from a loudspeaker was taped to the device so the entire device could be attached to the truck. The device was roughly circular with a six inch diameter, the size of the magnet, and three to four inches thick. It was the size of a large ashtray or about twice the size of an ice hockey puck.

A criminal complaint was issued for "possession of an infernal machine," on 7 January 1987. The charge was dismissed in Quincy District Court on 3 December

1987, after one year's probation, at the request of the Norfolk County District Attorney's office.

In a self-described "*break from the rat race*," Alfred left the hi-tech world and drove a cab for Quincy Cab Co. in 1988 to 1989, and he maintained that company's two-way radio system. Also, he worked with, and for, friends in the Greenview Lanscaping Company.

From 1989 through 1990, he worked for Ashley Telecommunications Company (ATEL) in South Boston which was headed by Sharpless Jones. He had obtained that job after Sharpless's brother, Edward, had come to sell two-way radios to Greenview. Alfred talked with Edward and realized that for an electrical engineer, mowing lawns and resurfacing blacktop driveways was not a profitable combination. Soon after beginning work for ATEL, he moved into in a room above the ATEL office from March to October, 1990. Also living there was Edward Jones and Tommy Leonard, who was famous in Boston for tending a bar at the end of the Boston Marathon. At ATEL, Alfred resumed hi-tech two-way radio engineering work and radio support for such customers as the Massachusetts Capitol Police and the Perini Corporation. From time to time, members of the Boston Police Department would bring their motorcycle and car radios for a quick repair, rather than taking the time for them to be repaired at the Police Dept's motor vehicle facilities. If Jeremiah Hurley and/or Francis Foley had had a problem with their radios, they might have brought them to Alfred Trenkler.

On 26 June 1990, an ATEL customer, Ray Collins from Telewave in Mountain View, Calif., wrote Alfred a complimentary response to a business proposal. It begins, "*I am satisfied that you have done your home work, and have an excellent concept on what is required for a good system design.*" In September 1990 Alfred learned about a large project at the Christian Science Publishing Society, an arm of the Christian Science Church, which was headquartered in Boston.and began working on that project for ATEL. The ATEL president, Sharpless Jones, did not appreciate its importance; so Alfred left ATEL in February 1991, and worked on a 30-day project for the MBTA and then a consulting project with Global Tech Research Corp.

During this time, Alfred provided technical consulting to Fidelity Investments as that company was acquiring newspapers and communications companies.

In June 1991 at the age of 35 and with an eye to returning to the Christian Science project, he established Advanced Research Communications (ARCOMM) with partner, Richard Brown, and his career seemed ready to take off. ARCOMM's primary business was mounting microwave antenna dishes on existing towers and buildings and building towers, too. His first contract, for $6,000, was in July 1991 for Marcus Communications in Connecticut to install a temporary tower, and give an estimate for moving two towers, and building a 500 foot tower. In August, his former employer, ATEL, hired him and ARCOMM to replace a Boston Police Dept. radio tower in South Boston. That summer, ARCOMM landed the coveted project with the Christian Science Church. It was to be ARCOMM's biggest microwave antenna installation contract.

When preparing for the 1993 trial, Alfred compiled a list (See Appendix D) of projects proposed by his major customers for AWT Assoc/ARCOMM/ATNS[5] for the years 1991-92. The value of the contracts totaled $553,000, of which $46,000 was completed prior to October 1991, and another $26,000 worth was completed by December 1992. In another list, he estimated that ARCOMM had a good chance of winning new contracts with a total value of $704,000. According to ARCOMM's October bank statement from Shawmut Bank, the average daily balance had been $7,008 and there were 82 checks written in the month.

Financial success finally seemed to be coming Alfred's way, but it wasn't the only goal. Wrote his friend Paul Ochs in 1994, "*Whereas financial motivation has been known to alter the scruples of many, Alfred was never that interested in financial success. He has good values and is perhaps a little over-relaxed where financial matters are concerned. He has possessed since a very young age great earning potential on which he has felt no overwhelming need to capitalize. As critical as we are of this behavior in this money-centric society, it is not a bad thing to be without greed.*"

On Monday, 10 June 1991 Alfred returned from a business trip to Connecticut. Later that evening, he met Thomas A. Shay at a "White Hen Pantry" 24-hour convenience store at 1252 Boylston Street in Boston's Fenway area. It is now the site of the "Home Run Deli." The building is a few blocks south of the Boston Red Sox's baseball field, Fenway Park. In Alfred's own words:

"Earlier in the day I was in Connecticut inspecting a tower site for Bruce Marcus of Marcus Communications. He wanted me to move two radio towers from one location to another and wanted an estimate. On the way back I stopped to eat at the Red Lobster - there was no Red Lobster in 1991 in Mass. I left and drove back through Boston and stopped by Pat's Tow in Allston to shoot the breeze. They were customers of Atel's when I worked at Atel. I had become friends with them. I left there and drove to Ed's Tow on Boylston Street. It just happened they were having some problem with one of their tow trucks' two way radios. Since I had my tools on me I repaired the radio. By the time I was done, it was 2 a.m. I left there to grab a snack at the White Hen and to see if my Fenway Community Watch friend, Tom Tompson, was around...

Tom Tompson was then in his 70's and liked to stop and socialize in front of the White Hen store. I had met Tompson in 1977 while staying with classmates from Wentworth Institute on Peterborough Street and had started a community watch program in 1978 with Tompson and neighbors living on Peterborough, Queensberry, Jersey, Kilmarnock and Park Drive. There were two nightclubs on the same block of Boylston Street, "Herbies" of Boston next door to the White Hen Pantry on Boylston Street and the 1270 Club on the other end of the building catering to the alternative lifestyle. After the clubs close, 20-30 people congregate around the White Hen.

Amongst the people hanging around was Tom Shay who stood almost half a foot taller than everyone else. Shay Jr. was asking people around him for a ride to Dorchester, a town I had to drive through to get to Quincy. Someone there commented that that was Tom Shay who recently appeared on Tom Bergeron's talk show, <u>People Are Talking</u>. I remembered seeing a snippet of the show and knew that Shay was from Milton, Mass, my hometown. I offered Shay a ride to Dorchester - simply doing a favor for someone that didn't require me to go out of my way. I had driven a cab for Quincy Cab in 1988 and was used to giving *strangers rides. On the way back to Dorchester Shay told me he forgot his dad was having a late night party with some biker friends and when they were around his father was embarrassed/ashamed to have Shay Jr. around because of Shay Jr.'s recent appearance on the talk show where he announced he was gay. He said he could not go home yet, now 2:30-2:45 a.m. I ask where I could drop him off since I have an early meeting and need to get some sleep. He asks if he could wait at my place for a few hours. I tell him he can't, it's not my place. As if on cue, it began to rain. I tell him ok, but at 6 a.m. I'm driving him to Dorchester, rain or shine.*

The apartment I was staying in at 133 Atlantic Street in Quincy, Mass., just over the Boston line, belonged to my friend John Cates. He was on vacation in England for 10 days in June of 1991. I had moved into Cates' apartment in October of 1990 one month after buying my white 1979 Toyota Celica.

I must have dozed off, at 6:30 a.m. my business partner, Rich Brown called on the phone and said he was on the way over to pick me up for our 7 a.m. meeting with Spector Steel in Holbrook, Mass. Rich lived about a mile away also in Quincy. I told Rich Brown I would drive to his house because I had to give someone a ride to Dorchester. Rich said that instead he would come over and give the person a ride on the way to the meeting at Spector Steel - We were submitting plans for the Christian Science project and seeking an estimate from different fabricators. Rich Brown arrived a few minutes later. Shay Jr. asked Rich if he was a cop, whereupon Rich produced his Boston Police Special Badge he had retained from his job at the World Trade Center, Boston. In turn, Shay Jr. produced an EMT badge, then produced a security police badge and said he was a security cop at Bloomingdales. (I had done some work for Bloomingdales security force, but there were no connections to Shay.) He then said he was an MBTA cop - very doubtful. Rich Brown and I had worked at the MBTA Police and Shay Jr. did not fit the mold. Shay Jr. asked what we did for work and we told him we did microwave tower work for TV, radio, police and fire two-way radio work. After the bragging session, Rich, Tom Shay and I got into Rich's car; Rich drove at Shay Jr.'s direction to Richmond Street or Ave. in Dorchester near Baker's Chocolate Factory. Shay Jr. claimed this was his father's house, a three decker house. Rich Brown and I continued to our Holbrook meeting."

During Alfred's first encounter with Thomas A. Shay he was warily exposed to Shay's propensity to lie as with Shay's claim to have worked for the MBTA (Mass. Bay Transportation Authority), and Bloomingdales department store as a security guard. His MBTA claim may have arisen from his older half-sister's, Jeanne's, employment with the MBTA.

Later in June, Alfred met Thomas A. Shay for the second time, when Shay was hanging around on Boylston Street.

"John Cates returned from his vacation. We returned to the normal schedule; in the morning I would drive Cates to work at Fleet Bank on Boylston Street by the Prudential Center, Boston, dropping him off at 7 a.m. and picking him up, my schedule permitting, at 5-6 p.m. I had given John Cates a hand held UHF two-way radio, the same type that police and firemen carried, in order to call me to arrange his ride home. Rich Brown and I carried two way portable radios not

only to stay in contact with each other but to monitor our tow truck clients. If they had a problem, they could call us directly. We used the same repeaters that gave us a 15-20 mile radius coverage around Boston.

As usual, I dropped John Cates at his place of work at Fleet Bank on Boylston Street by the Prudential Center, Boston at 7 a.m. I headed back to Quincy to meet my business partner, Rich Brown, to look for office space for ARCOMM. As I approached the stoplight at Park Square on Boylston Street by Boston Common, Tom Shay came to my window and asked where I was headed. I told him I was going to Quincy on business. He asked if he could have a ride to Quincy Center. It seemed as if no matter where I was going, he had a reason to go with me to meet someone he knew or just needed to go. On the way he told me that his mother had moved from Milton to the Falls condo complex in Quincy where, it turned out, he was actually going. I dropped him off there."

Later that month, and still during the period of time that John Cates was in London from 9 to 18 June, Alfred Trenkler ran into Tom Shay a third time, or, rather, Tom Shay found him, as Alfred relates:

"At around 7 a.m. I received a radio call from Pat's Towing in Allston, Mass. They needed a repair on a two way radio in one of their flatbed tow trucks. I told them I would be there at 8 a.m. I finished around 10:30 a.m. I used their phone and called Tom Tompson of Peterborough Street to meet him for lunch at McDonald's on Boylston Street, across from Fenway Park. Later in the day I had an afternoon site survey in Providence, Rhode Island. Around 11:30 I left the McDonald's building and headed to my car in the parking lot.

Sitting on the hood of my Toyota was Tom Shay, Jr. He asked what I was up to. I told him I was headed to Rhode Island on business. He said, 'Wait a minute,' and ran to the bank of pay phones adjacent to the parking lot, made a call, ran back to my car and asked if I was driving down Route 95. I said yes, he ran back to the pay phones; then again returned and asked me if I would drop him off at a friend of Shay Jr.'s store in Attleboro, Mass. At first I told him, 'No', but Shay retorted with apologizing about the first time we met and that he was sorry for putting me out of my way by going to my apartment and that he truly forgot his father's friends were around the morning I gave him a ride. I admonished Shay Jr. that he best be sure of his destination because no matter what, I had to be at my meeting and he could not come to the meeting and sure enough, he directed me to the back of a clothing store and introduced me to his friend, apparently the owner, Randal Stoller. He, Stoller, joked by asking how he (Shay, Jr.) roped me into giving Shay Jr. a ride. Stoller and I traded business stories. Then I left for my survey."

The fourth encounter with Tom Shay occurred while John Cates was still away. Alfred saw Tom Shay at the "White Hen Pantry" on Boylston Street, and Tom asked for a ride to a party in Nahant, a seaside town just north of Boston's Logan Airport. Wrote Alfred, "Evidently, Shay had lied to me about the party in Nahant. Upon arriving with Shay, the owner of the condo became very angry at Shay and told Shay to stay away and never return or else he would call the security force to arrest Shay for trespassing. The man apologized to me and warned me that Shay was trouble. He accused Shay of taking the man's telephone number from *earlier in the day. Though I was mad at Shay I figured it was best I take him back to Boston to drop him off. I ended up driving Shay to the Falls condo in Quincy. I was invited in to see the condo. I ended up falling asleep - dozing really - on a couch only to wake up to a dark haired woman* [It was Tom's sister, Paula] *saying hello to me and launching into a heated argument with Shay Jr., something about being told to stay away from the condo since all Shay did was to cause trouble for everyone around him. The woman was definitely not Shay's mother, Nancy Shay. The woman I met looked nothing like Nancy Shay*[who was and is blonde] *that testified at my trial. Nancy Shay, the mother, testified that she had never met me before."*

On 27 June, Alfred and his roommate and friend, John Cates, were injured in a car accident in Richard Brown's car, and they soon thereafter began weekly Wednesday chiropractic treatments for their backs.

Alfred's fifth encounter with Thomas A. Shay was in July 1991, on Boylston Street. He wrote, *"On my way to pick up my roommate, John Cates, at his place of work, Fleet Bank on Boylston Street, across the street from the Prudential Center, Boston, Shay Jr., waves me over in front of the Hynes Convention Center also on Boylston Street. He jumped into the passenger seat and asks where I'm going. I tell him he is a nutcase and I'm picking up my roommate and we were going somewhere. I drive him toward the Fleet Bank* [about 1/4 mile] *and pull over to where my roommate, John Cates, was standing. Shay Jr. jumps out and John gets in. Cates and I both agree that Shay Jr. is off-the-wall and can be a pain in the neck.* [John Cates had met Tom Shay before, but Alfred did not know that.] *He wants so desperately to be accepted and tries to be friends with everyone he meets and gets overbearing. Cates knew of Shay Jr.'s exploits from friends of his and was unaware that I had met Shay. Cates told me that Shay was a thief, a liar and a bullshit artist. Nuff said. I was not going to argue."*

In 2007 Alfred described more generally the circumstances in the summer of 1991 of his encounters with Tom Shay. *"Sometime around June of '91 Shay, Jr. had been brought back to Boston for his father's depositions. On Boylston Street from Fenway Park to Boston Commons Shay Jr. would walk back and forth meeting whoever would talk to him night and day. By coincidence I had clients also on Boylston Street: Ed's Towing by Fenway Park, informal "neighborhood watch" with Tom Tompson on Boylston, Peterborough, Queensbury, Jersey, Kilmark and Park Drive, installations on the John Hancock building and the Prudential Building, visits to Boston Public Library for research, and bring my ill[6] roommate, John Cates, to and from work at Fleet Bank also on Boylston Street. Plus I patronized the "White Hen Pantry" on Boylston Street. Since Shay basically lived on Boylston Street the chances he would "bump" into me were great. Just driving Cates to and from work put me on Boylston Street 10 times a week. On the weekends and whenever in the area on business, I would drop by to check up on my friend Tom Tompson. During the day, if I was in the area I would take lunch at McDonalds on Boylston Street."*

The earliest possible date for the building of the 1991 Roslindale Bomb is established by the presence in the bomb of a fragment of at least one page of the July 1991 issue of Robert Kennedy's *Musclemag International* (no relation to the late U.S. Senator and U.S. Attorney General). The paper was used to wrap the dynamite. Although interested in being physically fit, Alfred Trenkler has never subscribed to that or any other similar magazine, and had never read nor even heard of _Musclemag International_ before the presence of that page in the bomb was revealed. No prosecutor nor ATF nor Boston Police investigator ever asked him about that magazine.

In August, Alfred encountered Thomas A. Shay, face-to-face, for the sixth and last time. He wrote, _"The Christian Science Monitor microwave project had been approved by the church and a notice of intent had been sent to ARCOMM. We used Rich Brown's Quincy address prior to renting our 82 Broad Street, Weymouth office in October of 1991._

Sometime in the first two weeks of August around 11 p.m. John Cates and I were in front of the "White Hen Pantry" store on Boylston Street across from Staples Office Supply and Fenway Park, the same White Hen I had met Shay Jr. for the first time in June of '91. I was visiting with my friend Tom Tompson. John Cates was talking with some friends of his. Shay Jr. appeared and tells me about an alleged engineer friend of his that worked at the radio station across the street, WBCN, that was looking for a company to do some antenna work for the station. At this point I was not turning away any possible business no matter what or who the referral came from. Legitimate work, that is. I handed Shay Jr. one of my business cards with my new voice mail pager number on it [and] instructed Shay Jr. to give the card to his engineer friend. I also told Shay Jr. that if the job came my way I [would] pay out [a] 5% finder's fee. After a few days went by with no call from WBCN, I called to inquire about the alleged antenna work only to be told there was no work being farmed out and that I was misinformed.

It turned out to be a typical ruse by Shay Jr. to get someone's phone number, in this case a phone number attached to me. Apparently, Shay Jr. would end up at someone's house or apartment, typically by invitation to a party, and hunt for the phone number to enter into his phone book to later call and establish some kind of friendship. See, for example, ATF interviews of . . . Adams and Zimmerman."

After that August meeting, along with John Cates, Alfred did not talk with Thomas A. Shay again, until they shared a cell block without eye-to-eye contact in the Federal Courthouse on 25 June 1993. Thus, his non-sexual acquaintance with Tom Shay from June through August 1991 was for five rides and one chance meeting over a period or about 7 1/2 hours. In an 8 August 2007 letter, Tom Shay recalled four meetings over about 12 hours, although his recollection of the locations differs from Alfred's.

In August or September 1991 Alfred Trenkler called the Quincy Police Department about a _"suspicious person sitting in a car for almost one week peering toward the 133 Atlantic Ave. house John Cates and I were living in with binoculars and taking pictures with a large telephoto lens. Later that day the police were driving around the neighborhood and told me that the man in the car was a private investigator doing surveillance on a house next to 133 Atlantic relating to Immigration and Naturalization Service violations."_

Below, Alfred relates Thomas A. Shay's efforts in August and September 1991 to contact him by phone. Also included are a few details of his work chronology through October.

"The way my voice mail pager service operated, one would call my voice mail phone number, leave a brief audio voice message, then hang up. Within minutes my pager would "beep" simply indicating that I had a voice mail message waiting. Until I took the time to find a [pay] phone [or other reliable phone] I would have no idea who it was who called or the content of the message. Being as the only way to reach my business was via my voice mail pager service, I would make a concerted effort to get to a phone as soon as possible. A missed call might be missed business. My pager was not used for personal calls.

August 1991

Amongst the legitimate business related voice mail messages I received, I had received multiple calls from Shay Jr. from different phone numbers asking for rides from different locations in the Boston area. After a week or more of retrieving non-business related messages from Shay Jr. asking for rides or simply asking 'what's up?' I became upset that this was beginning to take me away from my work. I made it a point to call Shay Jr. back to tell him to stop calling. The first few attempts revealed numbers that would not accept incoming calls, most likely pay phones, or phone numbers that would ring with no answer. When I finally reached Shay Jr., I told him how upset I was at his wasting my time calling my pager. I was not a taxi service. I said I was mad at Shay Jr. for lying to me about his alleged friend at WBCN, my pager voice mail was for business only followed by me hanging up on Shay Jr.

September 1991

Christian Science's Scott Davis signs the contract with ARCOMM to install the 3 site microwave system for the World Monitor News.

The Comptroller, Scott Davis, cuts a check for $12,500 down payment. We give the go ahead to all parties to prepare for the installation, coordinating with fabricators, installers, Wiggins Airways, laborers, CSM Security, Boston Police, Boston Fire, and Stone and Webster engineers, equipment vendors and more. For the next 4 weeks we were working 6-7 days a week. In our spare time we were looking for office space.

Shay Jr. continued to leave voice mail messages but a bit less frequently than August. I refused to answer any of his calls. I figured he would eventually give up. One of his messages was Shay Jr. inviting me to some kind of all day all night party in Methuen so he could introduce me to some friends of his. In a glimmer of brilliance, Shay Jr. pulled a ruse. I received a page from someone requesting I call about some kind of antenna work. Potential work. Of course, I call the number and the party asked me to hold a moment. The next thing I know, Shay Jr. is on the phone laughing. I hung up. This kid was a genuine pain in the neck.

October 1991

Others than some caller(s) that called my voice mail without leaving any message, the only call I received [in October] from Shay Jr. was on October 25 when Shay Jr. invited me and my friend (John Cates?) to some Halloween party in Quincy. I replayed the message for John Cates. He testified to this fact, also to the fact that I did not return the call. Cates and I were already invited to a party at David Millette's house in Dorchester, never mind the fact that we would not have gone in the first place even if there was nothing else to do."

Again, after the August 1991 accidental meeting, there was no other contact between Alfred W. Trenkler and Thomas A. Shay before the 28 October 1991 explosion. Since then, the only other contact through 2007 came when they were temporarily within talking distance, but not able to see each other, in the same Boston Federal lockup in the U.S. Courthouse two years later, on 25 June 1993.

No physical evidence exists to corroborate Tom Shay's few inconsistent statements which indicated he had known Alfred Trenkler prior to June 1991. There are no receipts, no photographs, and no letters. At Alfred Trenkler's trial, three men, Richard Brown, Edward Carrion and Paul Nutting said that they saw the two together prior to June 1991, but Brown wavered on his recollection, and the other two were simply wrong or mistaken or lying. At the time of each of those sightings, the witnesses knew only Shay or Trenkler but not both. The identification of the other person was made later.

Alfred's major projects that Fall were to find an office for the newly formed ARCOMM and to prepare for the September/October antenna installations for the Christian Science contract. He located a storefront office at 82 Broad Street, Weymouth which was owned by Tom Peters of Milton, who had no known relation to Nancy Peters Shay, mother of Tom Shay, who lived in Milton in the 1980's.

The opening of the new office symbolized the progress that ARCOMM and Alfred Trenkler had made. From June through September, the company had grossed about $60,000. In addition to the satellite dish work, ARCOMM *"provided sales service and installation of Two Way radio systems for various Boston area towing companies, oil companies, construction companies, fleet dispatch services, answering services, police and fire departments"* all of which had generated about $10,000 through September. The company had no debt and was entirely funded by customer payments, and the receivables looked good.

On Sunday 29 September and Sunday 13 October, ARCOMM completed two dramatic helicopter lifts of the antennas and related structures to the roof of the Christian Science buildings in Boston. The work was done on Sundays to minimize interference with workday traffic. For those two flights, Wiggins Airways billed ARCOMM $1,849.

The weekend of 26-27 October was quiet for John Cates and Alfred Trenkler. Alfred drove John to work Saturday morning and Alfred went to Weymouth to work on preparing the new office for business. That night, they went to a dinner party at the Dorchester home of David Millette and were joined by several others. Alfred describes Sunday, *"Spent day with John Cates. We left house around 12:00 p.m. to eat at the 'Egg and I' where I saw, and said hello to, Officer Lanergan of the Quincy Police Department who was also dining. We left there and went shopping at Stop & Shop in Quincy. Then went to the laundromat. After laundry we took the dog for a walk. Then spent the duration at home."* It was an ordinary Sunday for Alfred Trenkler.

By Monday, 28 October, he had almost completed the large contract with the Christian Science Church to install microwave antennas on its Boston headquarters. Below is his schedule for the 28th.

7:15   AM *LEAVE JOHN CATES HOUSE WITH JOHN*
7:18   AM *ARRIVE PJ'S MINI MART-COFFEE/CIGARETTES*
7:23   AM *LEAVE PJ'S MINI MART WITH JOHN*
7:45   AM *ARRIVE ST JAMES STREET-DROP JOHN OFF*
7:46   AM *LEAVE ST JAMES STREET*
8:10   AM *ARRIVE AT 82 BROAD STREET WEYMOUTH OFFICE*
           ORGANIZE OFFICE-DO PAPER WORK
9:00   AM *START PHONE CALLS*
9:30   AM *NURDAN ARRIVES AND HELPS CLEAN-NO CHARGE AND*
           ANSWERS PHONES AND TALKS TO RICH AND I ON TWO WAY
           RADIO FOR PRACTICE
10:00 AM *RICH BROWN ARRIVES CALL BOB PERRIGO @ DIRECT CELL*
           RICH CALLS ROB DAVIDSON @ DAVIDSON DISTRIBUTING
10:30 AM *RICH AND I LEAVE TO GO TO DAVIDSON DISTRIBUTING*
           (CK # 1143 FOR ANTENNA)
11:15 AM *RICH AND I LEAVE DAVIDSON @ GO TO*
           DIRECT CELL, TO ORDER FLIP PHONE AND PICK UP
           FLYERS

Elsewhere in the city at 11:50 a.m., Officers Jeremiah Hurley and Francis Foley received a call to go to 39 Eastbourne Street, Roslindale to deal with a black object found in his driveway by the owner. [See Appendix D for a 2007 drawing of the "Roslindale Bomb."] After arriving, they quickly learned that the owner, Thomas L. Shay, had discovered the device a day or two before, so they assumed that the device was not on a timer detonation switch. Also, Mr. Shay told them that he had moved the device twice before leaving it in its current location on the ground underneath his GTO. The officers assumed that the device, if a bomb at all, did not have an "anti-disturbance" trigger which would have been already set off by Mr. Thomas Shay's handling of the device. They didn't bring the Bomb Squad's larger vehicle with the trailing "bomb pot," because it was thought to be too cumbersome for the roughly two cases per day for the squad. If a preliminary evaluation had determined that they needed it, it would have been brought to the scene and they would have suited up with protective gear.

They approached the device and Jeremiah Hurley said to Francis Foley, "*This looks machine made,*" and also that it had a switch. He said nothing about any damage to the box, which would have occurred from being scraped from the bottom of Mr. Shay's car or from being tossed to the ground. Frank Foley said "*Jerry, is that a servo?*" and saw that the servo, a remote control mechanism, was moving....

END NOTES

---

1. See Summary of case of Bruce Nelson at Innocence Project website at http://www.innocenceproject.org/case/display_profile.php?id=13. See also the summary of his

case at the website for the President's DNA Initiative at
http://www.dna.gov/case_studies/convicted_exonerated/nelson

2. The "Ice Capades" was a traveling revue on ice, and its main competitor was the "Ice Follies." From 1963 to 1986, the "Ice Capades" was owned by John W. Kluge, who was identified by _Forbes_ magazine in 1989 as the richest man in the United States. In 1989 he sponsored a reunion in Santa Monica for over 700 current and former members of the "Ice Capades" family, including Freddie Trenkler.

3. Website of Thayer Academy, www.thayer.org.

4. www.worldofquotes.com Eric Hoffer.

5. ATNS, for Advanced Telecommunications Network Systems, was formed in February 1992, after the difficulties with his ARCOMM partner, Richard Brown, and the pressure of the Roslindale Bomb investigation led to Alfred's departure from ARCOMM. Learning from previous efforts at starting small businesses with partners, Alfred formed ATNS on his own.

6. John Cates was suffering from the after effects of hepatitis B, from which he later died in 2005.

Chapter 2: EARLY INVESTIGATION: 28 OCTOBER 1991 TO 16 APRIL 1992

"White lies always introduce others of a darker complexion."
William Paley[1]

The investigation into what became known as the 1991 Roslindale Bomb began a few minutes before the explosion, as Francis Foley, Jeremiah Hurley, Denise Kraft and Sergeant Thomas Creavin arrived on the scene and began asking Thomas L. Shay questions. Mr. Shay recognized Denise Kraft because she recorded the report that Shay had filed about being followed on 13 May 1991. Apparently, he still didn't know that it was a private detective hired by the insurance company defending Berry and Giammarco against Mr. Shay's civil lawsuit arising from the 1987 explosion at the Dedham Service Center. If he had known, he would have told Kraft and perhaps been a little less paranoid, too.

Eighty law enforcement people came to 39 Eastbourne on the 28th: 2 Superintendents, 4 Deputy Superintendents, 2 Captains, 3 Lieutenants, 7 Sergeants, 21 Detectives, 26 Patrolmen, 2 EMT's, 2 Mass. State policemen, 2 County Asst. District Attorneys, 2 from the Boston Crime Lab, 3 from the Boston Fire Dept., and four agents from the U.S. Bureau of Alcohol Tobacco and Firearms (ATF).[2] The investigation was a joint effort by the City of Boston and the Federal Government.

Initially, the Boston Police Dept Homicide division was responsible for the investigation, and detectives immediately began interviewing every possible person. They cordoned off as much as possible of the site at 39 Eastbourne, and requested that the ATF do a complete analysis of the bomb site and debris.

ATF had investigated 25 bomb incidents in Massachusetts in 1990, out of 1,573 reported nationwide, an increase of about 50% over the previous five years. About one-fifth of the bomb incidents involved automobiles as targets.

The ATF's Northeast Region National Response Team, headed by Daniel Boeh, began arriving Monday night and began its full inquiry Tuesday morning with a briefing at the Area E Police HQ in West Roxbury. ATF Special Agent Jeff Kerr, from the Boston Office, was designated as the case agent, and the two other lead ATF agents were Dennis Leahy and Thomas D'Ambrosio. Dennis Leahy was on the case early, and personally, as he was present at the autopsy of Jeremiah Hurley.

The National Response team meticulously searched the entire neighborhood for fragments of the bomb. Magnets were used to attract metal parts. Photographs were taken of the scene and of parts recovered. X-rays showed that parts of the bomb, including a piece of a blasting cap, were in Officer Hurley's body, and they were removed during the autopsy on the night of the 28th.

Boston Police began the interviewing process and ATF initially focused on the physical evidence and the science. At 1:00 p.m. Officer Diane Culhane talked briefly with Mary Flanagan. Asked if she could help with information about the explosion, Mary responded at one point, *"What if he* [Mr. Shay] *told me not to?"*

The Boston detectives asked Mr. Shay who might want to harm him and Shay gave them a few names, but the list has not been seen by the author, and there have been no references elsewhere to the names on that list. Two people likely on the list were Jeffrey Berry and Richard Louis Giammarco, two of the defendants in

Mr. Shay's civil lawsuit for the 1987 "1/4 stick dynamite" explosion at the Dedham Service Center. Was it a coincidence that the 1991 Roslindale Bomb exploded at Noon almost exactly four years after the noontime 30 October 1987 Dedham Service Center explosion?

Berry and Giammarco were interviewed separately on the 28th by Officers Dwyer, Flynn, Molloy and Spellman. Louis Giammarco described the 1987 firecracker incident and Mr. Thomas L. Shay's subsequent departure as a tenant after a rent increase two years later in 1989. Mr. Shay sued in August 1990 for damages from the 1987 incident, just two months inside the three year statute of limitations deadline. Mr. Giammarco acknowledged having a collection of auto body parts removed from the section rented by Mr. Shay and delivered to Mr. Shay's home in 1989, but said he bore Mr. Shay no ill will. The latest flareup in relations occurred when Mary Flanagan had work done on her car at the Dedham Service Center and had not paid the bill, which was later settled in Small Claims Court when Mr. Shay gave them $12.00 in cash and later sent a check for about $270.

Mr. Thomas Shay wasn't on his own list either, but he was a logical suspect from the beginning of being involved with building the Roslindale Bomb. The theory of his involvement was that he might have placed the bomb underneath his car to make it appear that someone was trying to harm or kill him. In particular, his lawsuit was not going well, with the insurance company aggressively pursuing the view that Shay was faking his injuries and his claims of paranoia. His psychologist, Dr. Chengalis, had been deposed on Wednesday, 23 October, and his hearing doctor was scheduled for a deposition on 28 October, the day of the explosion. According to the theory, if it appeared that the Dedham Service Center defendants were trying to kill him, perhaps the momentum in his lawsuit might shift in his favor and the insurance company might be willing to settle. Mr. Thomas L. Shay had had many sessions with psychiatrists retained by Ber-Giam's insurance company and Shay had generally expressed his concern to them that Jeff Berry and Louis Giammarco were intending him harm or death, and that one scenario included placing a bomb underneath Mr. Shay's car or underneath the driver's seat.

Neither Alfred Trenkler nor Thomas (Tom) A. Shay was on Mr. Shay's list, either. Mr. Shay had never heard of Alfred Trenkler, and he and his son, Tom, had several get-togethers in the fall, and seemed to be getting along well. Tom had never threatened any kind of violence against his father, nor against other family members nor others.

On Monday afternoon, Alfred Trenkler continued his afternoon, 28 October business activities schedule.

12:15 AM RICH AND I LEAVE DIRECT CELL AND GO
BACK TO OFFICE
12:40 PM RICH AND I ARRIVE BACK AT OFFICE
12:45+PM NURDAN AND I LEAVE FOR CH 68 (RICH WRITES CK)
1:00 PM NURDAN AND I ARRIVE @ S BOSTON CHECK CASHING
NURDAN CASHES CHECK # 1 1 4 5 FOR $200.00, $40 FOR
NURDAN AND $80 RICH $80 AL (WE TAKE LUNCH)
1:30 PM NURDAN AND I LEAVE FOR CH 68 (LUNCH OVER)
1:45 PM NURDAN AND I ARRIVE AT CHANNEL 68 TO UNPACK DISH

> *AND ASSEMBLE MOUNT, DISH, AND RADOME. ALSO BREAK*
> *APART SHIPPING CRATE AND DISCARD*
> *4:30   PM   NURDAN AND I LEAVE CHANNEL 68 AND HEAD BACK TO*
> *OFFICE*
> *5:15   PM   NURDAN AND I ARRIVE AT WEYMOUTH OFFICE*
> *5:30   PM   I LEAVE TO PICK UP JOHN CATES ON BOYLSTON ST,*
> *BOSTON*

Tom Shay's 28 October began at his mother's Quincy condo, rising typically late. His mother's man friend, David Shilalis, was unemployed and was home all day watching television and Tom joined him. At 6:00 p.m. the local news carried the story of the noon bomb explosion at 39 Eastbourne and Tom Shay was described by Shilalis as being as shocked as he, Shilalis, was. Tom's half-sister, Jeannie, learned about the bomb from a friend who worked at the Post Office with Mary Flannagan. When she called her mother's home and talked with David, she could hear Tom's expressions of shock and surprise over the telephone. David and Tom both drove to pick up his mother, Nancy Shay, at the T station. Then Tom decided to hitchhike to his father's house to see what he could do to either learn more or to help or both. Perhaps he thought it could be another precious chance to get closer to his father.

He arrived around 12:30 a.m. on the 29th at the home, which was cordoned off by police crime scene tape, and was advised by the officers guarding the scene to go to the Area E police station to learn more. He arrived at the police station, and Officer Bridgeforth drove him to the office of the Homicide Division in South Boston. Tom Shay was interviewed in a room where he could see through a window a remote control toy truck, which for some unknown reason was on a table in the next room. After Tom Shay's interview there, Bridgeforth drove him back to Mrs. Nancy Shay's home in Quincy.

On Tuesday, 29 October Boston Police detectives Diane Culhane and Peter O'Malley interviewed Mary Flanagan and Thomas L. Shay at 39 Eastbourne. Diane Culhane's report stated that she discussed with Flanagan her relationship with Thomas L. Shay and Culhane reported the following:

"*After Tom* [Mr. Thomas L. Shay] *moved in* [1987] *he became increasingly paranoid. At first Mary thought he was just careful. Always double checking locks on doors and generally suspicious that someone might get in. Within the first year he boarded up some windows (I am not sure if this is a reference to the sticks or if this is a separate incident.) He installed locks on the front windows w/i the first year of moving in and put sticks behind the locks of all the windows. Mary eventually removed these. Most recently he added a motion detector. He is constantly worried that someone might be after him.*"

Mr. Shay's fear of being harmed by others was expressed many times in medical reports available to the police at the time. It was said that he had predicted a bomb being placed under his Buick and even that he drew a diagram of it for his psychiatrists, or that a psychiatrist drew a diagram based on his description. Due to his lawyer's oversight the medical reports for Mr. Shay in the civil case against Jeffrey Berry and Louis Giammarco were available to the public until the media discovered them after the 28 October explosion. Then, Shay's attorney, F. Jay Flynn, filed a motion to have the records sealed.

At some point in the interviews of Mary Flanagan, she was thought to have said that she had recently assisted Mr. Thomas L. Shay by giving him the money to pay his gambling debts. If true, the repayment enabled Mr. Shay to be able to say at the trials that in October 1991 he had no gambling debts. Other Shay family members believe that the payoff was in the range of $25,000, which was significantly larger than earlier thought. Obtaining such a large amount of money was thought by other family members to require Mary Flanagan to borrow from her retirement savings. The subsequent transfer of the 1986 Buick was also thought to be in satisfaction of gambling debts.

Later on the 29th, Thomas L. Shay and Peter O'Malley finished their interview, and Mr. Shay joined Officer Culhane and Mary Flanagan. Reported Culhane, *"Tom [Mr. Thomas L. Shay] then related the incidents of the day by describing what he did in great detail. At the point in his story where the explosion occurred he no longer mentioned his own activities. He spoke only of the activities of the police officers and in very vague terms with little detail.*
I asked him what he did when the bomb exploded. **answer** *The officer wanted towels.*
I asked him again what he did. **answer.** *He answered by telling about the condition of the female officer after she went back to see what happened.*
I asked him what he did when he heard the explosion. **answer** *He told me how upset he was and how he hoped it was not a real bomb.*
During the conversation in the evening Tom repeatedly and emphatically said he feared for Mary and; would we check her car, would we let him have a carpenter board up the cellar window, what kind of protection would they have, when are the police leaving the area.
Tom kept repeatedly stated[sic], 'I don't want to think who would do this. I don't want to suspect that someone would want to do this. This shouldn't have happened.'"

Also during this interview, the neighbors across the street, Jim and Eleanor McKernan, came over and spoke to the police. Eleanor said that *"she had come home just before the explosion and remembers because Tom Shay [Mr. Thomas L. Shay] had parked a car in a way that made it difficult for her to access her driveway. She was looking around to see where he was because of the parked car when she noticed him standing in his driveway with a black box in his hand."*

On Tuesday, 29 October, the Boston Police obtained search warrants for the house and premises at 39 Eastbourne and for adjoining premises as well, in order to permit searches by the ATF for bomb fragments and other evidence. However, not all the rooms in Mr. Shay's house were searched, nor were there seizures of items possibly related to bombmaking, such as were seized later at Alfred Trenkler's locations. There were many samples of wood, paint and nails at 39 Eastbourne, but none was seized.

That afternoon, Tom Shay called his friend Russ Bonanno, who lived in North Dartmouth, Mass. and asked if he could stay with him for a few days. It took a special request, because Bonanno had ejected Tom Shay from his home in September after about two weeks into a visit, because Shay acquired two kittens, perhaps for his mother, while in North Dartmouth and animals were prohibited in Bonanno's University of Mass. housing units. Bonanno worked there as a housing coordinator, and before that as an Ambulance and EMT dispatcher for the Belmont, Mass. police.

To get to Russ's home on that Tuesday, Shay called another friend, Randy Stoller, and asked him to give him a ride from his mother's in Quincy to Bonanno's home. (Back in June, the second of the four rides Alfred Trenkler had given Tom Shay was to Stoller's place of work, a clothing store, in Attleboro.) Stoller later told the ATF that he took Tom Shay to a bookstore in Providence. Such requests for rides made his five-ride acquaintance with Alfred Trenkler more believable.

On Wednesday afternoon, 30 October, Alfred Trenkler and his roommate, John Cates, were waiting for their weekly chiropractor $58.00 treatments at the office of Daly Chiropractic in Quincy. The therapy was needed to treat injuries they received from the accident in Richard Brown's car the previous June. Initially, they were receiving treatments on Mondays and Wednesdays, but physical improvement had led to the reduction to weekly visits on Wednesdays. One of the men saw an article about the Roslindale Bomb at the home of Thomas L. Shay. It may have been the article on the first page of that day's "*Metro*" section, "*MOTIVE FOR ROSLINDALE BOMBING SOUGHT.*" Or, as is often the case in doctors' reception areas, it could have been the article from the previous day, Tuesday, 29 October, also on page 1 of the "Metro" section, "*ROSLINDALE BOMB KILLS OFFICER, HURTS PARTNER - 2 WERE CHECKING SUSPICIOUS BOX LEFT IN DRIVEWAY.*"

In Wednesday's *Boston Globe* article, Tom (Thomas A.) Shay was quoted extensively from a press conference he called at his mother's Quincy home on Tuesday, where he said he was "*speaking on behalf of his four sisters.*" Said Tom at this first of several press conferences, "*My father is a very nice guy. He's not into any criminal activity. He's never, ever done anything wrong.*" Shay continued, "*My father is not a criminal guy. He's not involved with the IRA... He's never done drugs. He's never bet on a game in his life. He goes to church twice a month.*" The article reported that Tom Shay went to see his father after hearing of the bombing, but complained that police were blocking him from seeing his father.

Tom Shay's statement that his father didn't bet on sports was the most blatant of the lies he told that day. By itself, it was not important, but the spinning and weaving of lies had begun.

While reading the article, Cates and Trenkler said to each other that the bombing was about as crazy as Tom Shay appeared to be. They didn't take the article with them nor make a copy nor go out and purchase another copy of the newspaper so as to preserve the article. It was just another footnote in a story about a strange kid they both knew, minimally and warily.

The next time they heard about the bombing was when they learned that a friend of Cates had been called by the police because his name had been in Tom Shay's address book. Alfred then expected that he might get a call, too, because of his acquaintance with Tom Shay, and because Tom had his pager number, after tricking Alfred into giving him an ARCOMM business card.

On Wednesday, 30 October, Tom Shay called Stoller again for another ride, this time to Russ Bonanno's in North Dartmouth. Shay arrived at Russ Bonanno's late Wednesday night and stayed until Thursday evening when Bonanno took him to the Trailways bus station in New Bedford around 6:00 p.m. Upon his arrival at the Boston Trailways Bus Station, Tom Shay held his second press conference, to which he had alerted the press by phone from North Dartmouth. Despite his lack of a steady job, Tom was able to dress relatively well, thanks to gifts of clothes from Randy Stoller.

After the Roslindale explosion, Officer Thomas Tierney at the Quincy Police Department thought that the Roslindale Bomb had one or more characteristics similar to the M21 Hoffman Artillery simulator device which was exploded on the Capeway Fish Market truck in Quincy in 1986. Perhaps it was the remote control, or perhaps the siting of the bomb underneath or on the vehicle which caught his attention, even though he knew that the 1986 device was detonated on the side of the Capeway Fish Market truck. For whatever reason, Tierney sent his personal copy of the 1986 incident to the Boston Police Dept. on Thursday, 31 October, because the Quincy Police Dept.'s copies could not be found or had been discarded. His fellow detective, William Lanergan, who shared the investigation of the 1986 M21 Hoffman incident with Tierney, did not believe that there was any connection between the two events. Of the two officers, Lanergan knew Alfred Trenkler, and had just seen him, and shared greetings, the previous Sunday at a restaurant in Quincy.

By the end of that same Thursday, the ATF's National Response Team's investigation at 39 Eastbourne Street was completed, and a final briefing was held for interested local police. The ATF forensic chemist on the team, Cynthia Wallace, handwrote some preliminary information the next day about the contents of the bomb and gave "search suggestions" for the detectives. Her notes said that the bomb contained:

"- Magnets - two types	-----> Adhesive & wood on both types of magnets indicates that they were originally glued to box.
- Blasting caps 2 Austin Rockstars	-----> A connection between 2 yellow copper wires was wrapped with white tape. Bolsters theory that one detonator was placed on each dynamite cartridge.[3]

- Explosive - dynamite
- Batteries - 9 volt and AA
- Radio control - Futaba unit
  found fragments of servo unit, receiver and
  battery holder (for AA batteries)
- Page from weight lifting/muscle magazine
- Tape - 3 types recovered
        - 3/4" black electrical tape
        - fiber reinforced silver duct tape
        - white plastic tape
- Box was constructed of wood panelling
- Paint - black spray paint
- Adhesive - hard clear or yellowish clear adhesive"

The Boston Police report on that day found that there were 17 different fingerprints on Mr. Shay's Buick, but it was never revealed which, if any, were identified. Twelve prints were found on the outside body, and five on the undercarriage. The prints were lifted "using the cyanocrylate fuming method (superglue)." The name of this method was coincidental as it was later determined that the adhesive used to bind bomb parts within the black box was a type of "superglue" with the more scientific name of cyanocrylate. Presumably, some prints on the outside body belonged to Mr. Thomas L. Shay, but none to Tom Shay nor Alfred Trenkler. None of the prints underneath the car should have belonged to Mr. Thomas Shay because he said that he did not touch the undercarriage. If any of the prints had been helpful to convict the new priority suspects, they would have been disclosed and used. As our fingerprints do not change over time, it's not too late to search for the owners of those prints.

Also on the 31st, the _Boston Globe_ reported that Terrence McArdle, Special Agent in charge of the Boston ATF office, had stated that enough fragments of the bomb had been recovered to "_satisfactorily identify it_" and determine where its constituent parts had been acquired. The article, "_ENOUGH OF BOMB FOUND TO TRACE DEVICE_," also divulged information about Mr. Thomas L. Shay's mental and physical health, from documents publicly available from his Dedham Service Center case. Both Thomas L. Shay and Mary Flanagan said they had been asked by the police not to speak to reporters, but the police denied making such a request.

Below are presented excerpts from Tom Shay's Trailways press conference in the evening of the 31st, attended by several reporters, including "Karen" (perhaps Karen Marinella from Channel 56), and several Boston Policemen in civilian clothes. The excerpts are presented in [S]hay and [R]eporter format.

S Opening statement: "_Two days ago the Boston Police told me to leave town because they thought that - my father - my father's and my name was_ [sic] _the same, and that I would be in danger so I left, but today the federal police had gone to my house and asked my mother to find me and get me back in town. The police don't think the bomb was meant for my father, and I, myself don't think it was meant for my father. I think - the bomb was meant for myself. I'm in debt to a man, who is here in Boston, for $50,000, but that was the past - it was two years ago - that I borrowed the money, and, ah like I said, my dad is not a criminal. He's not into any drugs, gambling, or anything like that. So, other than the man that he's suing for $400,000, I think that the bomb was meant for me. The insurance company said they'd pay the $400,000... Any questions?_

R "_If you think the bomb was meant for you, why would they put it under your father's car?_"

S _Well, because I was living at that address two years ago, and - ah - and the guy knew that I was living at that address, and his car is registered in Thomas Shay. I am Thomas Shay, also._"

R "_Are you junior?..._"

S "_No, Thomas A. Shay, Jr. but I'm_ [not] _a junior._"...

R "_Tom, have you had a chance to talk to your family?_"

S "_Well, just that I talked to a guy over the phone, and they said that they found pieces in the truck that may have - that looked like part of the bomb, but lawyers think that somebody is trying to either frame me or frame my father for the bomb._"...

R "_Why didn't you do that_ [talk with the person you owed $50,000] _before?_

S "...the $50,000 isn't actually, in money. It was, a car for $20,000 and I had smashed it; and $30,000 that I had borrowed within a six month period."

R "...Are you fearful for your life?"

S "I don't want my family and - if - if - there is a crazy guy out there who wants my death, he can have my death; but stay away from my family. Tomorrow I'm going to walk in the Boston Common. Now, I hope he sees us on the air tonight or tomorrow. I'm going to walk around there all day tomorrow and tomorrow night. If there is a man out there that wants my death, that's where I'll be, walking around by myself, without any police around."

R "Why would police ask you to leave one day and then tell you to come back two days later? I mean, your story is - seems difficult to believe."

S "Well, they want the guy out of there. They want - the - the police want to draw this man that has killed an officer, injured one more; and I want to draw him out because he shocked my family, put my family in a very depressed ... state."

R "How would someone else be able to put material into your father's truck?"

S "Well, I don't know that... The truck was open and I guess they found stuff that you could find in the bomb, but they also said, you could find this in anybody's household.... like wires and little pieces of something. They didn't say exactly say what it was... "

R "Tommy, did this guy [the police]...question you about the bombing? In terms of being a suspect?"

S "If they are, where are they? I don't - I don't - I didn't think that. No."

R "Now, why - why would this man give you a $20,000 car unsecured and then $30,000 in a six-month period?"

S "Well, we were very good friends..."

R "What did you do with the money?"

S "I gambled it away."

R "So in the two year period there has been no contact with him, until about two...weeks ago?

S "That's right... None at all."

R "$50,000 and there has been no contact at all?"

S "None"

R "Can you tell us anything more about this guy...?

S "His name is Ralph P. Pace. He lives at 23 Jefferson Court, Stoughton, Massachusetts."

R "And you think he planted that bomb?"

S "I think he wants his money back; and if he's desperate enough, he'd - he'd be out to kill one for it."

R "Do you think maybe he was trying to send a message to you through your father?"

S "Maybe... maybe he tried to kill my father, and then he came back and that's telling me that, you know, if I don't pay this $50,000 that he'd kill me too."

R "Tom what can you tell us about your father's arrest, in regards to the bomb threat in Milton earlier this year? ...Do you know anything about your father's arrest earlier this year in connection with the bomb threat in the MBTA station?"

S "No, I do not." [This was one example of the confusion caused by the similarity of the names of Tom Shay and his father. The MBTA bomb threat was made by Tom

Shay, the son, but he did not clarify the distinction when answering the question.]

R *"Can you give us more to go on? I mean, your story just seems so hard to believe."*

S *"Hard to believe?... What do you mean?... Well, actually, I told him I'd pay him back at some point..."*

R *"What happened to the car?"*

S *"Well, it was a 1989 Monte Carlo and I got in an accident with it, and had no insurance.... totaled it."*

R *"Fifty thousand dollars? ...."*

S *"Well, I guess he had been working a long time. He had about $65,000 in the bank. First it was $20,000, and then I asked him to borrow money from him so I could start my own business and then pay him back."*

R *"Did you tell the police this gentleman's name?..."*

S *"No, I haven't - I haven't talked to the police about this guy yet."*

R *"And why are you coming back again, then?"*

S *"Well, the police - the police want to draw either the sicko or somebody out that has put this bomb under my father's car...what I'm basically saying is if he wants me, he can have me, but leave my family alone."*

R *"What exactly did they [the police] tell you, in terms of whether you should return?"*

S *"They said, if I come in contact - any contact myself, they wouldn't want me to go out and take the chance of being killed; but if I find out the guy that has done this - and I want to find out who has done this - then I will - will talk to the guy, go in the Common or whatever. I'll pick the spot. I'll go out there. If he comes to me, and they'll put him away."*

R *"I thought you hadn't actually talked to the police, though?"*

S *"Well, I actually talked to them through my mother."*

R *"You don't give someone a car....."*

S *"He lent me the car for the day, and I smashed it up in... you can call the Manchester [New Hampshire] police up... in '89"*

R *"You guys [you and your father] been in contact?"*

S *"Well, we talked on the phone, but they [the police] won't let me see him."*

R *"Did you tell him [your father] this story?"*

S *"No. I didn't want to get him involved."*

R *"Who is 'they' that won't let you see your father?"*

S *"The Boston - see the Boston Police on Tuesday, at 1:00 p.m. [sic] in the morning tricked me into going over to the E Area Police Station, asking me questions like does my father know how to build a remote control; does he take off [unintelligible]; what does he watch for sports- and all kinds of questions."*

R *"When did you speak with him [your father]?"*

S *"Yesterday morning... He just said that - well, my father is in shock. He didn't say too many words. He said about five words through the whole conversation... I said, 'I love you, Dad.' He said, 'Hello, I'm worried. I'm scared. I can't talk now. Goodbye. So basically, somebody has ruined my father's life. Ruined an officer's life. Ruined his family's life. Ruined, you know, Officer Foley's life."*

R *"Did you drive your father's car?"* [Mr. Thomas L. Shay stated to the ATF that Tom never drove one of his cars. At least one reason was that Tom Shay never obtained a driver's license.]

S "Sometimes I drove his car."

R "So you didn't see any...."

S "He [Ralph Pace] knew my mother and my... sisters."

R "So, why wouldn't he [Pace] just, you know, come find you and deal with you, as opposed to - I mean... it just seems kind of skippy .. He didn't make any collection efforts? You know, just not make contact with someone and then bomb their car, Do you?"

S "Well... the guy at 106 Washington [Jeffrey Berry and Louis Giammarco] he has no reason. The insurance company is willing to pay the $400,000. We didn't - I didn't know this on the ... day after the explosion. I never knew abut the insurance company not paying the $400,000, but now they are willing to pay it."

R "Pay who?"

S "My father because he has a lawsuit against these people [decribed the 1987 explosion]."

R "Tom, your records show that you've been in several different psychiatric hospitals - including Gaebler and some of the others. Are you still under doctor's supervision?"

S "No, I'm not. I haven't been for five years. Where did you get that information, if I may ask?"

R "From court records."

S "Court records? Huh."

R "If someone were to say you were considered a suspect in all of this, what would you say?"

S "I'd say, get me the proof. Prove I'm guilty, and here I am. But I did not, and I do not have the technique to build a bomb. I didn't even graduate high school. I work with my hands on bodies, not, you know, electrical equipment."

R "You have no reason to even consider killing your own father?"

S "Me and my father love each other. We go out to the games together. You know, baseball games. We go over [to] his friend's house where they play football. You know, we're father and son. Even when my parents got - were divorced, we've been father and son since I was born. You know, I have no reason to kill anybody."

R "So if somebody were to suggest this, are you shocked or are you angry? What is your reaction to the suggestion?"

S "I'd be, ah - I'd say that's outrageous. It's BS. That's what that is. For anybody to think that I - I could actually build a bomb, one, or ah - or - or kill somebody is - that's - that's BS."

R "Are there any close friends of yourself that - that you feel may be angry at you for some reason, other than this man, Mr. Pace, that you have mentioned?"

S "No, I don't... hang around those type of people. I'm a quite [sic, quiet?], kind of guy. I keep to myself. I have two or three friends."

R "Tom, why are you coming forward to us with this information rather than the Boston Police Department?"

S "Well, you see, I was told - well, my mother told me over the phone today that the Boston Police didn't want me to say anything. See, I'm telling you this because, you know, the first interview I had with, ah, the news - the news people, [on Tuesday at his mother's condo] ah, my words didn't get out like I wanted them to. You know, I said, you know, that my father wasn't a criminal man. It came out in

The _Herald_. That was good. Like I wanted to - like, today I want to say to this guy, if you're out there, meet me in the Common tomorrow... Come and get me."

R "Well, ... you know where he lives. You could go to him. You could knock on his door and say, well, here I am if you - Yes? No?"

S "No. That wouldn't be...."

R "Do you know who made the bomb?"

S "I don't know anybody that could make a bomb. In general, I don't know anybody that could - I can't even make the model car myself."

R "But they [the Boston Police] didn't say why they were looking for you?"

S "They want to question me. They think this guy is after me. I think this guy is after me.... My father is not a criminal. I'm not a criminal. I'm not into anything criminal, but this guy I owe $50,000."

R "And he loaned you this money two years ago, right?"

S "That's correct... It [the car] had no insurance."

R "A 33 year-old accountant had a car with no insurance?"

S "He didn't get any money back, he told me, after I ruined it. I've been doing massage for, like, four years now. I make about six or seven hundred bucks a week. You know, I told him to lend me some money so I can get my business going again. I kept on, you know, going to the track gambling and trying to win all the money back so I could pay him, but it didn't happen that way."

R "And what was your relationship with this guy?..."

S "He was my best friend... Father and son [relationship]. Well, you know, father and son, like going out and doing things. Okay. I'd mean like, ah, when he was not working, we'd go... to the movies and ... ball games."

R "... Seventeen year old guy, thirty-three year old guy have a relationship... That almost sounds sexual to me. Was it..?"

S "No.... He expected it [the money] back when my money started coming in. I had him thinking that, ah, I had a big business going. I was hiring ten masseurs and - "

R "At seventeen?"

S "I made $600 a week. At one point, before I met this guy, I had gold jewelry, you know, my own car and everything. You know, ... I was even going to apply for a Visa card..."

R "Was he one of your customers?"

S "Yes, he was..."

R "Are you a licensed masseur?"

S "No, I'm not."

R "How were you going to start a business without having a license?"

S "Illegally.... It's not really illegal though-. "

R "When was the last time you drove your father's car?...."

S "... About five months ago..."

R "So he [Ralph Pace] called you... and asked you where the money was?"

S "Yes... I said I didn't have it. Goodbye."

R "Tom, why should we believe this story?..."

S "You want information that's true. You'll only get it from me, because none of my other family members are going to speak on the news. I got the information from the grapevine. Nobody else wants to speak. I'm not going to name them but one of my sisters is a lawyer at a law firm here in Boston. One works for the MBTA. One is becoming a cop, and one has got her own business. They won't - they don't want to get involved because, you know, ah, they could lose their job."

R "[Channel 7 not here.] I'm Channel 4... can you shed some light on ...your psychiatric treatment?

S "When I was 12 years old, I was out in Milton. I fell asleep in the snow. You know, I was tired all day. So I - laid back and some cop found me and they put me in the Department of Social Services thinking my father and mother weren't taking care of me properly. That's how it all started. "

R "... it's just - these are unbelievable charges that - that you're making to us... We're all listening but it just seems hard to believe."

S "Not exactly to this Ralph P. Pace. You know, I'm saying if there is a sicko out to get, you know, my family, take me..."

R "Are they [your family] angry with you?"

S "Well, there are two sides to the family. There is the Flanagan side, there is the Shay side; there is the Peters side. Peters is my mother. Flanagan is Mary Flanagan, the girlfriend of the kids in the family, and then there is my father and his family."

[Then Tom Shay called Ralph Pace during the press
conference with a cell phone and a reporter talked with Mr. Pace.]

R "Tom, he doesn't deny that he knows you. He says that you stole his car... three or four years ago. That you have a history of stealing cars, and you had been in the Dedham Jail, the Bridgewater jail. He said, quote 'You're a habitual liar.' He said that he once attempted - had considered being a foster parent for you. He tried to help you. He tried getting you a job. That you, in his words, are a troubled young man."

S "I'm telling you that he's the liar. He's backing off, because, you know - I'm gonna go over there and talk to the guy myself, and you, you know he - did he deny that he called on the phone two weeks ago, too?"

R "He said that if you ever come to his house, he'd have you arrested..."

S "Well, legally he can't do that unless there is a warrant."

R "Oh, oh, I forgot. Thank you. He did say there was a warrant for your arrest. I forgot that one. Sorry."

S "... I stole a car, but I didn't actually steal it. I was just one of the guys in the car."

R "Were you convicted of stealing a car?"

S ".. five days. So I said, ah - I said that I was gonna commit suicide so I could go to Bridgewater, because I heard it was like a country club there. I went there, and I did like five days...."

R "I thought you did 30 days."

S "No five days...."

R "But you just...."

S "Excuse me. Ah. excuse me...." [Shay walked away and left the bus station.]

The press conference had lasted 40-50 minutes. Shay's comments contained nothing new about the investigation and the information he released could have come from his collection of newspaper articles. For example, his statements about the police finding materials in his father's van or truck closely track the applicable section of the previous day's *Boston Globe* article, "MOTIVE FOR ROSLINDALE

BOMBING SOUGHT," which said, "*Investigators spent a great deal of time yesterday searching a large white truck parked in the driveway, very close to where the bomb exploded. A source said several items 'consistent with what was in the bomb' were taken from inside the truck. Investigators, however, were cautious about the significance of the confiscated items because they might be found at anyone's home.*"

After the press conference, Boston Police Detective Dennis Harris asked Tom Shay if he would go with him voluntarily to the Homicide offices, again, and then drove him to that South Boston office where Shay had been briefly interviewed the previous Tuesday morning.

At Homicide, he was interviewed by Detectives Miller Thomas, Peter O'Malley, William Fogerty and ATF Agent Tom Bowen. Tom Shay told them that he wanted to take a lie detector test and that all he knew about the case came from the television and from his sister.

At the conclusion of the interview, Tom Shay was arrested on an outstanding warrant from the Milton Police Dept, arising from a conviction for receipt of stolen goods. As part of the arrest process, William Fogerty searched Shay and his belongings, among which was Shay's address book. Fogerty photocopied each page, and later returned the address book to Tom Shay, who was then sent to the Norfolk County Jail in Dedham as Milton is part of Norfolk County. The next day, the 1 November *Boston Globe* reported in its article, "*SON SAYS BOMB MEANT FOR HIM,*" that Ralph Pace had said that Shay didn't owe him anything; and that the car which was totaled in an accident was not borrowed by the unlicensed Tom Shay. It was stolen. Also on 1 November, Shay was arrested on another charge, of failing to attend a court hearing on a 1989 charge in Boston of streetwalking.

Tom Shay's arraignment on the pending arrest warrants was scheduled for Monday, 4 November, the day after his 20th birthday, but he was arraigned in Quincy District Court on Friday, 1 November for violating terms of his probation.

In a 1 November article, "BOMB SUIT APPRAISAL CHALLENGED," the *Boston Globe* opened up a sensitive issue about the precautions taken by Officers Hurley and Foley prior to the explosion and whether donning a special Kevlar-cloth suit would have saved their lives. Deputy Police Superintendent Edward Eagar was quoted as saying that the suit would not have helped, but the head of the U.S. Army's "armor" section at the Natick Development Lab in Natick where the special suit was developed, said that "*Something is better than nothing.*"

About other precautions, the Boston Police Dept. explained the usual procedure for a bomb incident which is for the investigating officers to make a preliminary assessment and then decide what protective gear to wear. It was during that preliminary assessment at 39 Eastbourne that the bomb exploded. The timing was close. As Francis Foley said in a newspaper article, "*I walked back to Jerry to see... whether we should suit up or X-ray the device. Then it went off.*"

Later, the controversy evolved into the volatile question of whether the two officers were responsible for the extent of their own injuries. The ATF reported that Mrs. Nancy Shay, said in her 31 January 1992 interview, that the officers should have been more careful and that they were, at least in part, responsible. Tom Shay said the same thing in his 28 March 1992 *Herald* story. The ATF's 13 January 1993 report of the interview with William David Lindholm carried his allegation that Alfred Trenkler said it, too. The issue was about as sensitive as blaming

Princess Diana for her death because she was not wearing a seat belt. That disease is called here the "Princess Diana Blame Disease (PDBD)"

The 2 November _Boston Globe_ story was "_SELF-PROFESSED BOMB TARGET HAS LONG HISTORY OF PROBLEMS._" Tom's sister, Paula Shay, denied that Tom would want to kill their father, but summed up years of psychological evaluations by saying, "_but he would say anything._" This five word comment was one of the core truths of the entire case. The _Globe_ article reported that when four years old, Shay and his older sisters saw their father beat their mother so severely that she required hospitalization.

The _Boston Globe_ headline for 3 November was "_LEGAL TROUBLE FOR MAN WHO SAYS HE WAS BOMB TARGET._" At the arraignment, he was also "_arrested_" for failure to attend a court hearing on a charge of communicating yet another false bomb threat.

An _Associated Press_ article in the _Worcester Telegram_ quoted Shay's new attorney whom he had met on 1 November, William McPhee, who "_said his client had 'absolutely nothing' to do with the explosion Monday. 'He's not a danger to himself. He is not a danger to others,' McPhee said. 'He is not involved in that Roslindale situation and unfortunately he finds himself caught up in an investigation that he knows nothing about.'_ " While William McPhee believed that media relations was a necessary part of this case, he was increasingly frustrated that Tom Shay would not follow his advice and stop contacting the media on his own.

Early the next week, probably on Monday, 4 November, ATF Special Agent Thomas D'Ambrosio looked at the Quincy report of the 1986 M21 Hoffman incident and then wondered if anyone who participated in that incident was in Thomas Shay's address book. The first name listed alphabetically by first name was "Al Trenkler." The investigators must have thought they had hit the jackpot, and began searching for more information about Alfred Trenkler and the 1986 device. For Alfred Trenkler, it was a complete coincidence that the name of a person who had detonated a small remote controlled device five years previous was in the address book of a young man whose father appeared to be the target of a deadly bomb. The police didn't think it was a coincidence, and the investigation began turning toward Tom Shay and Alfred Trenkler and away from Mr. Thomas L. Shay and his possible enemies.

Because of this turn toward Tom Shay and Alfred Trenkler, the police did not search, nor chemically sniff, the Mazda on which Mr. Thomas L. Shay was planning to do auto body repairs on the week of the 28th. There was to be no search, nor chemical sniffing, of Louis Rotman's car which Mr. Thomas Shay had been driving for the ten days prior to the Friday, 25 October return of his own car. The Rolling Wrench Garage, where he and his brother, Arthur, worked, was not seriously searched.

On Sunday 3 November, Randy Stoller, who was listed in Tom Shay's address book was invited to come to the Homicide Dept. office. He told them about his giving Tom Shay a ride to No. Dartmouth the previous Tuesday, and that Tom said he needed the ride because his lawyers, not the police, had recommended he leave the city. He said he first met Tom Shay at the Blue Hills Reservation, where Shay needed a battery boost and neither man was sufficiently proficient in electronics to understand the need to connect the positive terminal to a positive terminal, etc.

Also, when asked about Shay's unusual habits, Stoller said that Shay would write notes when he was having a hard time expressing emotion, and that he did not know how to properly hold a knife, fork and spoon.

On Monday, 4 November, detectives Peter O'Malley and Miller Thomas went to the Dedham Service Center and asked Jeffrey Berry and Louis Giammarco to take lie detector tests and both agreed and even said their lawyers had agreed. The polygraph examination for Louis Giammarco was scheduled to be administered by ATF on Wednesday, 6 November.

The ATF reported on 4 November that over 200 interviews had taken place thus far with demolition companies, hobby shops and others, though most of them had not been reported in formal form. Forty-five exhibits had been retrieved from 39 Eastbourne. Also, ATF Agent Sandra LaCourse sent a copy of Tom Shay's Trailways bus terminal press conference video and copies of newspaper clippings to Special Agent Philip Horbert, Chief of the Explosives division in Washington, in order that a "personality assessment" could be done on Tom Shay. The results of that assessment, assuming that it was done, have not been released.

During this week, Tom Shay wrote to Randy Stoller, surely without knowing that Randy had met with the homicide detectives on Sunday, Tom's birthday. "*Dear Randy, Hello Randy, I'm in jail now. They think I built the Bomb. You probably saw me in the Globe or the Herald or the Ledger or on the news. I turned 20 last Sunday. There are no cute boys in here. Just a bunch of black or older gentlemen. By the time I get out, I will have no warrants. They will all be taken care of. When I get out, I can start nice and fresh. I was thinking of starting my own houseboy service. 24 hr. Service with my beeper and a couple of friends. I will get SSI for sure now. My lawyer said. Welfare is in my future, he said. Then I can buy all the supplies I need. My mother said I am welcome home, and that she is there if I need her. I miss you Randy. No matter what happens I will never forget you. Please write to me to pass the time ok. Write it to my house and my mother will give it to me. Thomas A. Shay... P.S. Do some cruising for me, ok. And tell the guy in RI I said hello.*" Was this letter written by a young man who just conspired to kill his father? Or who was responsible for the killing of a policeman?

On Tuesday, 5 November, around noon, Thomas D'Ambrosio and Dennis Leahy interviewed Donna Shea, as she had been at the center of the 1986 Quincy Artillery Simulator incident. They reported that she told them that her husband, John Shea, was a partner with Alfred Trenkler in the former firm, AWT Associates. Also, she said that Alfred was "doing cocaine and young boys." The report continued, "Ms. Shea said that Trinkler [sic] frequented the Blue Hills and rest area's, picking up 14-15 year old gays," and that Alfred Trenkler " 'rigged up' his Jack Coyle's [his roommate] stereo so that when Coyle brought back gay partners for sex, Trenkler could listen to their conversations and sex acts." Donna Shea's friendship with Alfred Trenkler had its ups and downs over the years, and the ATF apparently found her at one of the down times. These untruths henceforth dominated the ATF's and prosecutors' perceptions of Alfred Trenkler, and the prosecutors sought, but failed, to present them to the Trenkler jury the next year. She also told D'Ambrosio and Leahy about Trenkler's acquaintance with Michael Coady, who did testify for the prosecution at the 1993 Trenkler trial.

Also on Tuesday, the Boston Police began looking for Alfred Trenkler and went to the South Boston offices of ATEL, where Sharpless Jones told them about ARCOMM. Then they went to ARCOMM's Weymouth office and the secretary, Judy Fredette, said that Richard Brown and Alfred Trenkler would be returning shortly. The officers left and put the office under surveillance. They followed Richard Brown's car to several locations, and finally at about 8:15 p.m. to Trenkler's apartment at 133 Atlantic Street, Quincy, which he shared with John Cates.

At about 11:00 that evening, 5 November, the police knocked on the door of Cates' apartment. Quincy Police Dept. Detective Thomas Tierney was with the search team and he identified Alfred Trenkler. ATF Special Agent Thomas D'Ambrosio talked with Alfred Trenkler and later described him as cooperative. Not yet familiar with the roles being played by the Boston Police and the ATF in the Roslindale Bomb investigation, Alfred asked Dennis Leahy if the visit by the police was in response to his call to the Quincy Police Dept. in August or September about suspicious people in the neighborhood. ATF Agent Leahy responded that he did not know anything about that call, and that this visit was about the Roslindale Bomb.

Boston Police detectives William Fogerty, Dennis Harris and Timothy Murray interviewed John Cates outside the apartment, while the others stayed inside with Trenkler. Fogerty reported that both Cates and Trenkler knew Tom Shay, and that Cates did not know of any interest by Trenkler in bombs. Cates said that Alfred had seen Tom Shay a few times and that they had discussed the Roslindale Bombing after seeing a reference to it in the media. In his report, Tim Murray wrote, "Mr. Cates seemed hurt and disappointed when we floated the scenario that "Tom" had been observed going into Mr. Cates's apartment."

Although the "consent" was later disputed, the police conducted a "consent search" which was unrestricted as to scope, and then several officers drove Trenkler to his ARCOMM office for another consent search, and then to his parents' in Milton. Finally, according to the ATF report, in the early hours of Wednesday, 6 November, they searched Trenkler's car on Mechanic Street, Quincy, disabled due to a broken water pump, and cut a 4" X 4" carpet sample from the trunk to test for traces of dynamite. (Alfred recalls the sequence differently, that they went from Cates' and his apartment to his disabled car and then to the ARCOMM office.) After taking Alfred to a store where he purchased a pack of cigarettes, they drove him home. Late in the evening, in a conversation with Boston Detective Peter O'Malley, Trenkler had agreed to take a lie detector test and O'Malley gave him a card with a phone number to call the next day to schedule a polygraph examination.

The search at 133 Atlantic Street and the suspicion of his involvement in the Roslindale Bomb explosion was not Alfred's first experience with police mistakes. When he was a teenager around 1973, he was walking to his Milton home from Brigham's Ice Cream in "Lower Mills." He was approached by a Boston Police Officer who hit him with his flashlight and took Alfred to the nearest police station. Then, the policeman realized that he had mistaken Alfred for someone else and Alfred agreed to sign a release to ease the officer's fear of being sued for false arrest. The police mistakes surrounding the Roslindale Bomb would not be resolved so easily nor so quickly.

Seventy-three days after the 5 November 1991 searches, on 17 January 1992, ATF Special Agent Dennis Leahy wrote a more complete, though belated report of the evening's work. He wrote:

"With Alfred W. Trenkler, on November 6, 1991, at 133 Atlantic Avenue.... Mr. Trenkler said that he resides at 133 Atlantic Ave., Quincy with his [roommate] John Alan Cates and has lived there with Cates for approximately eight months. Mr. Trenkler and Mr. Cates allowed a consent search of this apartment in the basement of 133 Atlantic street. Observed in the apartment was an exposed speaker with speaker magnet attached on a shelf near the kitchen. The speaker was not attached to a stereo, television or other electronic device. Also observed was a book on "Dirty Tricks" containing information on how to get even with people. Mr. Trenkler was noticeably shaken and asked how we located him....

Mr. Trenkler said that he had nothing to hide and also agreed to accompany us to ARCOMM, Inc. ... Mr. Trenkler admitted building a remote control bomb in 1986 for John and Donna Shea and placing the bomb on a truck in Quincy, Massachusetts....

Mr. Trenkler also discussed his construction and building procedures of the bomb that he was arrested for in Quincy in detail to include drawing a diagram of the internal components and electrical wiring system. Mr. Trenkler also, when asked how he would build and wire the internal components of the bomb that had killed Boston Police Officer Jerry Hurley, drew a diagram of an electrical circuit with an electrical detonator (blasting cap) to each stick of dynamite; showing two sticks of dynamite and two electrical detonators in the bomb.

Mr. Trenkler said that he had all the tools to build a bomb at ARCOMM as he was in the communications business. Mr. Trenkler said that he knew Thomas A. Shay and had given him a ride several times and approximately four times had stopped by 133 Atlantic Ave., Quincy with Thomas A. Shay, but that Shay had never been inside his and Cates apartment. Trenkler said that he ... met Thomas A. Shay at or near a White Hen located on Boylston Street, Boston, Massachusetts.... Trenkler said that he gave Thomas A. Shay his business card."

Alfred Trenkler's contemporaneous recollection of that night was less antiseptic. He wrote:

" ... We heard what sounded like many people coming down the basement stairs. Next was a knocking at the door to the apartment. I got up and stood by the door and asked who it was. A voice said, 'Open up, we want to talk with you.'...Then Peter O'Malley said, 'You got away with it in 86. You're not getting away with it this time.' Almost immediately, Dennis Leahy moved between myself and Peter O'Malley. I said to O'Malley, 'I don't know what you're talking about.' O'Malley said, 'You're an asshole, I know you did this for fucking Shay.' I said, 'I've done nothing.'

Jeff Kerr or Dennis Leahy told John Cates to come outside with them while they asked me some questions...

...When John was still in the apartment the agents (Dennis Leahy) asked me if I ever had (Jr.) in the apartment and at this time I had said no. After John was taken outside I had told Dennis Leahy that I did bring Jr. to John Cates apartment once on the night I met him for a few hours but never told John Cates because I promised him that I would not bring anyone there during his (Cates) vacation and that the reason that I never mentioned it was because I discovered that Tom (Jr.) was a nit wit, I did not want John Cates to know that I had a nit wit in his apartment. Plus it was only for a few hours since Jr. told me he could not go home until later in the morning.

I was then escorted out of John Cates house by, I believe, Dennis Leahy or Jeff Kerr and told to sit in the back of the unmarked car. What was strange was that there was a black bag (sports bag) that contained various guns and ammunition rite [sic] next to me (on my right).... and we proceeded to 82 Broad Street.

... two or three other people came in, Victor Palaza bringing coffee, one for me. Dennis then said, 'You see, we're not that bad!'

They had selected [for seizure] diagonal cutters, plyers [sic], needle nose plyiers [sic], wire strippers and crimpers. They showed me the tools at which point I told them that some of the tools that they had belonged to Rich Brown. They then told me that they had to take the tools to the lab for analysis. I said, 'You can't take these tools, I need them on the job site tomorrow.' Dennis Leahy said, 'Well Al, we have to check everything out. You know, these tools will be on the way to Florida by the time we get to Whitelawn Ave.' I said, 'but what about me, I need these tools tomorrow morning, I won't even have time to replace them.' Dennis said, 'You'll get them back.' I asked when and he said he was not sure. He said not to worry and that he would give me a receipt for them. I said that would not help me. He (Leahy) then said his famous statement, 'Al, if you have nothing to do with this you have nothing to worry about.' I again said that I had nothing to hide, and had nothing to do with this incident.

Dennis then said, 'I'm interested in this 86 device. Would you care to sketch it here for me' and then he turned a pad of paper toward me and placed an onyx pen on the pad. I said that I did not remember exactly and he said just basically from memory. I said again that it is public knowledge and drew a very basic block diagram. Dennis Leahy then said that my drawing was very similar to Shay's drawing. I did not answer and immediately tore off that drawing and the next few pages and got up and shredded it. Dennis had only viewed the drawing from the other side of the desk and did not attempt to stop me from getting up and crossing the room and shredding the drawing.

Dennis Leahy then asked what I knew about dynamite and I said that I knew absolutely nothing. He asked what I knew about blasting caps and I said that I knew nothing about them either. I said that I have only seen these things on TV and thought that blasting caps set of [sic, off] dynamite but other than that I have never seen either dynamite or blasting caps in person nor knew anyone that used them....

Dennis Leahy asked where I had met him [Shay] and I said near a White Hen Pantry next to the Fenway. Dennis asked if this was near the Ramrod,... and I said it was next door but that I never went in because I don't drink and generally do not go to bars....

At this point it was about 12:15 to 12:30 a.m. I said to Dennis Leahy that it was a bit late to be going to my parents' house and that it would upset them if we were to go there at this hour....

Dennis Leahy said that he would call my parents the next day and tell them what transpired tonight/this morning. I said, 'just what are you going to tell my parents when they wake up at 1:00 a.m. in the morning?' Dennis said, 'We'll tell them [a white lie that] *we work for you and we have an early job tomorrow and we have to look for something in the garage.' I said, 'without a search warrant?' Dennis then said, 'You let us search the office and your apartment, you've got nothing to hide you have nothing to worry about.'...*

On the way back [to Quincy] *I had said, 'I don't know what to say to you guys except that I have nothing to do with this whole affair, all I did was give this Shay kid a few rides and that's it, he never talked to me about his family matters, he just wanted me as a friend but he was not my kind of friend, he was a nit wit.' O'Malley said, 'I'd choose my friends a little more carefully.' The rest of the ride was in silence....*

The first stop[of the evening] *was at 25 Mechanic Street* [Nurdan Cagdus' home, and location of his car disabled with a broken water pump, where he had left it on the afternoon of 5 November after returning from work on the Channel 68 tower in Brighton] *Leahy said that he had to take a sample of my carpet and told me it was because if I had dynamite in my car that there would be traces of it in the carpet. I said that if it would clear me, by all means take it."*

Alfred continues to insist that the agents never asked him about his physical relationship with John Cates. If they had, he or John would have told them that John was being ravaged by the effects of Hepatitis B, and because of that, the two men did not have a physical relationship. Cates would die from the disease in 2005. Trenkler maintains that he never said that he had the tools to build a bomb and he never said that he had brought Tom Shay to 133 Atlantic four times. Most importantly, he never drew a diagram of what the Roslindale Bomb might look like if he built it.

That night of 5-6 December was the first face-to-face contact between Alfred Trenkler and the investigators seeking to solve the Roslindale bomb case. There were conversations between Alfred and investigators, but there was never any serious formal questioning. There were never any questions, for example, about Alfred's whereabouts on Monday, 28 October and over the previous weekend. There were never any written questions, akin to interrogatories in civil lawsuits. There was never a request to Alfred to come to the Boston Police Dept. for a serious, sit-down interview, with his lawyer present. The omission of such an interview led one Boston Policeman in 2007 to ask, *"Why didn't he tell us he had an alibi for that weekend?"* One answer is that Alfred wasn't asked. Perhaps the police assumed that Alfred's attorney would object to any such questioning, just as did Louis Giammarco's attorney and other attorneys in similar circumstances.

Unlike other inquiries into truth such as scientific research, the investigative process is not conducive to interactive communications. The police just could not pick up the phone and ask Alfred some questions, or ask him to come down to the police station for a chat. Similarly, even though he was a suspect, Alfred was not permitted to examine any of the evidence against him. Those are the rules. That would remain true until his indictment, after which he was imprisoned.

Thus, all of the subsequently recollected conversations between Alfred Trenkler and investigators came as by-products to other activities such as searches, or retrievals of property. As the police developed their theories of the crime and their suspicion of Alfred Trenkler, they filled in the gaps of their knowledge with hunches rather than with answers to specific questions directed to Alfred.

The police might have asked, for example about the unattached speaker seen by Agent Leahy at 133 Atlantic. John Cates had found it in the trash outside his apartment before Alfred moved in, and Cates thought he might be able to use it. The book _Dirty Tricks,_ which Leahy spotted and from which suspicion evolved, did not belong to Trenkler either. Cates' landlord, Mike Green, who lived upstairs, later told the ATF that he had left the book in the apartment's utility closet, and that it belonged to his brother, George Green, who also lived upstairs in the two-family home at 133 Atlantic Street. Alfred doesn't remember looking at the book, but it might have been about the Nixon presidency.

Later on Wednesday, 6 November, Special Agent Jeff Kerr forwarded another 14 exhibits obtained from the Trenkler searches, to the ATF National Laboratory in Maryland. The laboratory determined that none of the items matched anything in the Roslindale Bomb.

On 6 November, the polygraph examination for Louis Giammarco was performed by Special Agent David Filion and Mr. Giammarco was asked three questions:

1. Did you plan with anyone to cause that explosion?

2. Did you plan, with anyone to cause that explosion in Roslindale, on October 28?

3. Do you know for sure who made that explosive device?"

Giammarco answered "No" to each of the three questions and the examiner determined that "The examinee was deceptive in his responses to the above relevant questions."

The polygraph examination for Jeffrey Berry was never conducted.

Also on 6 November, the police received the first of several communications from fellow inmates of Tom Shay with whom Shay had discussed various aspects of the Roslindale Bomb. Dan Goldrick wrote that Shay, "mentioned to me on two occasions that his uncle and him used to make bombs all the time. He said to me that his uncle was a bomb suspect [sic] in the service." He closed by saying, "I don't know if this helps, but it's a dam [sic] shame when anyone dies (for something so stupid)." Dan Goldrick did not testify at Shay's trial.

Interviews were conducted with all the people named in Tom Shay's address book. On 7 November, one ATF report concerned three: Abraxas Adams, Charles Helyer and Dan Zimmerman. Adams was a roommate of Zimmerman's, and who brought Tom Shay home about a month previous. Adams barely knew Tom Shay and didn't know why his name was in Shay's book. Dave Zimmerman met Shay at the Ramrod Club in Boston and brought Shay home, and apparently expressed interest in purchasing a kitten Shay had for sale, as Shay called back a week later and talked to Adams about it. Zimmerman allegedly described Shay as "immature and self-centered" and definitely didn't want to give him his phone number, but Shay must have taken it from a phone set in the apartment. The third was Charles

Helyer who worked at Greyhound, where Shay would hang out. He exchanged phone numbers with Tom Shay and that was it. None of the three had ever heard of Alfred Trenkler and none heard Tom Shay say anything about explosives. It didn't take much to have your name entered into Tom Shay's address book. It's not known if ATF contacted "Jennifer," the one woman listed in the book.

By 7 November the investigation continued to focus on Tom Shay and Alfred Trenkler, but also on Louis Giammarco after his failed polygraph exam. ATF wanted to interview Giammarco to try to ascertain the reason for the "extremely deceptive" answers, according to Jeff Kerr's report, but Giammarco called and said he would decline all further tests and all interviews on the advice of his lawyer. Alfred Trenkler also told the ATF the previous day that he was taking the advice of his lawyer, Martin Cosgrove of Quincy, not to take a polygraph exam. Unfortunately, Alfred disregarded another part of Cosgrove's advice, and he continued to be cooperative and conversational with the police and ATF and his words were to be twisted against him. His mistake was not in being cooperative, as law-abiding citizens should be when asked questions by the police, but in failing to have a friendly witness with him, or a recording device, to vouch for his statements. Alfred met with Attorney Martin Cosgrove on the 7th.

One paragraph of Jeff Kerr's 7 November report contained the primary ingredients of the Government's ultimate case against Alfred Trenkler:

"Continuing investigative efforts have disclosed that one Thomas A. Shay, the son of Thomas L. Shay, has engaged in homosexual relations with one Alfred Trenkler, of 7 Whitelawn Ave., Milton, MA. Trenkler was arrested in 1986 by the Quincy Mass. Police Dept. for construction of a destructive device which utilized many of the same components as the device which detonated on October 28, 1991 killing Officer Hurley."

One wonders about those "continuing investigative efforts" as Trenkler never said he had had a sexual relationship with Tom Shay. Was Tom Shay the only source? If he was, it's not reported in any ATF nor Boston Police reports. Nor should it have been relevant in a criminal trial, but it seemed important to the ATF as did other matters sexual. In an August 2007 letter, Tom Shay confirmed what Alfred Trenkler has always maintained, which was that there was never any sexual relationship between them.

On 8 November Tom Shay was sentenced by Quincy District Court Judge James F.X. Dineen to 30 days in jail for violating a probation agreement arising out of the 1989 case of operating a stolen car. Given credit for time served, he had 23 days to go. That same day, The Boston Police and ATF conducted a test at 39 Eastbourne with a mockup of the bomb and Mr. Shay's Buick. The mockup was viewed by Mr. Thomas L. Shay and Denise Kraft and it was thought to be the same thickness of the actual bomb, including the little square box with the switch. The mockup was attached to the bottom of the car and then the car was put through a series of "back ups" and "drive outs" in order to recreate the moments when, according to Mr. Shay, the actual bomb scraped the driveway twice, and fell off the second time. A videotape, and many photographs were taken of the recreation. The mockup neither scraped the driveway nor fell off.

On 11 November, the Boston Police Patrolmen's Association, together with the U.S. Bureau of Alcohol, Tobacco and Firearms (ATF) announced a $50,000 reward

($25,000 from each organization) for the "arrest and conviction of the individual or individuals responsible for the manufacture and placing of the bomb which took the life of Boston Police Officer Jeremiah J. Hurley." The ATF contribution of $25,000 was one of the highest ever offered by that organization, with its usual contribution being $5,000. Said ATF chief Terrence McArdle in the _Boston Herald_ article, "*The case isn't as viable as it was a week ago. We want help.... We're not at a dead end. Could it be solved without the reward? Yes,*" but the reward could lead to a breakthrough sooner. Later, in January 1992, that reward was increased by $10,000 from the Governor of Massachusetts, William Weld, and by $5,000 from the Boston City Council for a total of $65,000.[4]

Also on 11 November, Jeff Kerr prepared a report of the components and design of the Roslindale Bomb for distribution to over 3,000 members of the International Association of Bomb Technicians and Investigators in the hope that someone might recognize a pattern of bomb building. The listed parts were the same as in Cindy Wallace's 1 November handwritten notes, except for the crucial added information that the toggle switch was a Radio Shack Model #275-602, and the Futaba information was expanded to "1 Futaba Switch, 1 Futaba Radio Control and 1 Futaba Servo (FSH-6E), 1 Futaba Receiver and 1 Futaba battery holder." He wrote, "The aforementioned components were encased in a 12 3/4" X 5 1/4" X 1 1/2" box made from wood paneling. Attached to the box were approximately 10-15 General Hardware 372C button hole magnets each measuring 1" in diameter and 5/8" in thickness. Also, 2 large doughnut shaped magnets, approximately 3/12" in diameter and 5/8" in thickness."

The ATF interviewed Alfred's mother, Josephine Wallace, on 19 November and the importance of labels was apparent. Agents Paolillo and Muniz called the 1986 device a "bomb" and she called it a "firecracker." In any case, said Mrs. Wallace, Alfred had not been in any trouble since 1986. The judicial grinder of that case was deterrent enough for Alfred. The next day the same agents interviewed Russ Bonanno and seized a section of ubiquitous black electrical tape and a dispenser. They went to ARCOMM's offices and interviewed Richard Brown and left with a Black and Decker cordless glue gun, in the hope that it was the dispenser of the glue in the Roslindale Bomb. It wasn't.

Wrote Alfred Trenkler in 2007, "*Black and Decker glue gun, Hell, I had that lying around since the 80's, purchased for repairing tears in the plastic windows of my wrag* [sic] *top C57 Jeep. This was simply another case of an otherwise common household item, but in my hands a potential bomb component. Why was the glue gun at Shay Sr.'s house a common household item. Of course, it really doesn't matter, anyway, hot melt glue was not mentioned as being used in the '91 device, and there was no glue whatsoever in the '86 device. Hot melt glue is not unusual to have.*"

Also on 19 November 1991 Special Agents Edmond Cronin and Dennis Leahy interviewed William Cody of Dexter Corporation about the magnets used in the Roslindale Bomb. Wrote Leahy in his report: "Mr. Cody stated the Dexter Corporation sells magnets to the Defense Industry and the Central Intelligence Agency. Cody stated that the holding power of a magnet is measured in pounds and that it is also a function of the thickness of the steel of the car body. Cody stated one of the magnets in question was an Eclipse Button magnet catalogue number E821. He related that the Button magnets are very brittle and hard. He stated the composition of the magnet is aluminum, nickel and cobalt known in the industry as Alnico. Cody stated that the steel on the underside of an automobile would show scrape marks before any scrapes would show up in the magnets. Cody related the magnets would break away from a surface they were glued to before a magnet would snap.

Cody related that no U.S. manufacturer cuts bevels into Button Magnets. The only manufacturer that cuts magnets is Eclipse Magnets, Vulcan Road, Sheffield S9 LEW, England, and that they are a division of James Neil Tools Ltd. Cody related that Button Magnets that are blue in color are distributed only by the Edmunds Scientific Company, 101 E. Gloucester Pike, Barrington, N.J. USA 08007-1380."

Alfred Trenkler understands that the ATF did a followup investigation with Edmund Scientific as it did with Radio Shack, but has never seen any report of such an effort. ATF could have, for example, asked Edmund Scientific for a list of all New England purchasers over the past five years of such magnets, with a similar request as it made to Radio Shack's corporate offices.

Unlike the author, Alfred Trenkler has never purchased any items from Edmund Scientific.

On 21 November 1991 Richard Brown was interviewed by Dennis Leahy and Thomas D'Ambrosio and Boston Detective Miller Thomas. Brown told them that he was 80% sure that he had seen Tom Shay in a "Store 24" across the street from the ARCOMM office in Weymouth and that he had seen Tom Shay with Alfred Trenkler the previous year at the ATEL office in South Boston. In a supplemental report of that same interview, but written 13 months later, on 10 December 1992, D'Ambrosio wrote that Brown said "that he now wasn't sure Shay was the person he gave a ride to, from ATEL in Boston to the 'T'. He also stated that Trenkler made a statement to him to the effect that the only way he would talk about confessing is with a written deal through an attorney." While no facts were revealed here, the dangerous part of Brown's alleged statements was the implication of Alfred Trenkler's admission of guilt. It was like blood to sharks.

On 21 November, Tom Shay was ordered to Bridgewater State Hospital for a 30-day stay to evaluate whether he was competent to stand trial for the charges of making a false bomb threat and being a common streetwalker. The evaluation was completed on 23 December by Paul Nestor, Ph.D., who noted that Tom Shay was advised at the outset that whatever he said could be included in a report, and Shay responded, "there is nothing I could share with you that could incriminate myself." Mr. Nestor also noted that "Upon admission, Mr. Shay was described as belligerent and threatening and required four-point restraints on the Intensive Treatment Unit. He soon, however, stabilized, and was transferred to minimum security unit, where he has had no significant difficulties. He has not been prescribed any psychopharmacological medication."

Nestor reported that Tom Shay had told him "that he has worked on a volunteer basis for an ambulance company... that he witnessed the death of his lover in what he describes as a gay bashing incident in 1989. He is a recent father of a baby girl." None of those claims was true. When Shay denied, "any history of head injuries and/or seizures," he may simply have forgotten his being knocked unconscious in a rock fight as a child. Nestor wrote that Shay was dismissive of the evaluation and thought it a waste of taxpayers' money, and that he brought with him several newspaper clippings about himself; and that

"Notwithstanding his apparent disdain for much of the evaluation, Mr. Shay presents as a likeable young man, who clearly appears to enjoy and crave the attention inherent in the one-on-one clinical interviews. In fact, he seems to relish attention and publicity; for example, he often boasts about how news organizations have offered him financial inducements for his story and, on other occasions, he shows the evaluator professional cards of Boston news reporters, whom, he claims, were eager to talk to him. Beneath his apparent attention-craving and somewhat lighthearted veneer is a more serious and sad side, evident when he discusses his childhood and his family. He speaks with feeling about some of the losses and apparent rejections he has experienced in the past." Nestor also wrote,

"...his thinking is clear and organized; reality testing is intact. His mood, however, is elevated and inappropriate, particularly in light of his claim that he is a suspect in the death of a Boston Police officer in a bomb explosion. Indeed, he seems childish, self-centered, and egocentric, almost as if he were basking in the limelight of a tragic event. This elevated and grossly inappropriate mood, though, is not a product of a mental illness, but rather is more indicative of a poorly-developed, immature, and longstanding personality and/or characterological structure that appears to be driven by an insatiable need for attention. He denies any suicidal and/or homicidal ideation."

Getting to the question of competency, Mr. Nestor said that Tom Shay understood the court system and "claims that his attorney [William McPhee] is a well-experienced and high-priced litigator, who apparently is taking his case pro bono. In short, Mr. Shay is, in my opinion, competent to stand trial."

Mr. Nestor continued,

"Indeed, he is so utterly taken by his perceived notoriety that he often had difficulty addressing substantive questions of this evaluation. The borderline traits are evident by his apparent long history of interpersonal difficulties, emotional instability, and his reported identity problems. Also evident is a decidedly manipulative quality, as he states, for example, that he is not mentally ill now, but if he is sentenced he will be mentally ill because he cannot tolerate confinement in a cell. He then goes on to demonstrate how he would make believe that he is talking to imaginary people in an attempt to feign mental illness. The critical point here is that his gross immaturity, his histrionics, and his emotional instability do not fulfill the criteria for a mental illness, as defined by Chapter 123." Mr. Nestor recommended that when Tom Shay is returned to the community that he receive outpatient counseling or some type of mental health treatment.

One theory of the detonation of the Roslindale Bomb was that other radio signals in the area may have been picked up by the Futaba receiver and set the Servo in motion. In a 25 November report, ATF Agent Seref McDowell stated that the

Futaba receivers used four frequencies, 75 megaherz (MHZ) and 72, 52 and rarely 27. The nearby NYNEX facilities transmitted at frequencies all over 5,900 Mhz, and Cablevision's were over 13 "Giga Hz."

ATF Agents D'Ambrosio and Leahy went to the Christian Science work site of the ARCOMM antenna installation and retrieved pieces of wood and electrical tape for analysis by Cindy Wallace back in Maryland. There was no connection found to the Roslindale Bomb.

The search for samples of black electrical tape found its way into Tom Shay's fantasy web of distortion and lies. He wrote to Russ Bonanno,

"This letter is very important. I am in jail right now and I am scared and depressed. The police think I built the bomb or I had something to do with it. We both know that I don't. You know that black tape I got at your house. They are going to try to use it against me in court. My attorney is going to need you to bring you [sic] and that tape down to his office. He is William McPhee [retained on 1 November 1991, as Shay's court appointed lawyer]....*He is a real nice guy. Call him and explain our relationship as Friends. How we met, what you do for work. When I came over [to] your house and when that black tape came into my hands. That black tape is a Big part of this court case. It is probably the only lead the police have. Get IT to my lawyer and your statement, OK?"* Tom Shay didn't know that the ATF had already seized a sample of Bonanno's black electrical tape.

On 3 December, D'Ambrosio and Leahy interviewed John Cates at his place of work and Cates maintained that Alfred Trenkler had nothing to do with the Roslindale Bomb. Stated the report, "Mr. Cates was adamant that Trenkler had heeded his advice and has not spent any time with Shay. Mr. Cates stated that he was not aware of the fact that Trenkler had previously made a remote control explosive device. He said that he was told by Trenkler that he (Trenkler) had made a fireworks type of device in the past."

Under the strain of the intense criminal investigation, the partnership between Richard Brown and Alfred Trenkler was collapsing. The ATF seemed to be intentionally or unintentionally intimidating ARCOMM's customers, but the customers continued to work with Alfred as his skills were valuable. The ATF visits to the ARCOMM office also intimidated secretary Judy Fredette. At the 18 October meeting with accountant Mark Ramboli, Alfred had been alerted to irregularities, such as Rich Brown's writing checks for equipment, with no receipts to back them up, and then selling that equipment for cash, after little or no ARCOMM use. Alfred writes of the last meeting between the partners in early December:

"I met with Rich Brown and told him I wanted to split up ARCOMM into two divisions, one for the microwave and radio tower consulting and installation service which was my expertise and which I would manage and the other division, two-way radios, cellular phones and pagers would be for Rich Brown to manage. I would even help him with any engineering questions that came up. My plan was to have separate bank accounts and simply pay our share of the rent and operating expenses. I thought it was more than fair. We would each earn a living based on the work each actually did.

Rich Brown would not hear of it and I was tired of him riding on my coattails, all the way to the bank. He reacted violently. You can probably see the impression in the wall where Rich Brown tried to push me through. Combined

with Rich Brown's paranoia of the ATF and the fact that he held a checkbook with 29 thousand dollars, Rich Brown left ARCOMM." He pursued his interests with girlfriend Jennifer Powers in Cohasset and Vermont and she was later subpoenaed to the grand jury. The $29,000 in the checking account constituted ARCOMM's profit for its July-December operations, but Rich Brown took the checkbook, receipts, sales figures and other records. The next time Alfred saw Richard Brown was at his October-November 1993 trial where Brown was a witness for the prosecution. Sometime after the trial, Alfred discovered another coincidence: that Richard Brown had been arrested several years before 1991 for detonating a large firecracker in a telephone booth, and that he was afraid that the ATF would try to tie him into the Roslindale Bomb case because of that earlier incident. In early 1992, he had seen what the ATF was doing with Alfred's own 1986 incident.

On 16 December 1991 Anthony Giammarco filed an Answer to Mr. Thomas L. Shay's Amended complaint in the case of Thomas L. Shay against Jeffrey Berry and Louis Giammarco (individually and as trustees of Ber-Giam Realty Trust), Ber-Giam, Inc., and Anthony Giammarco. He denied, or denied sufficient knowledge to give an answer, to 37 of the complaint's paragraphs. He admitted only one: that Thomas L. Shay was at the Dedham Service Center on 30 October 1987, the day of the M-80 explosion in a trash barrel. Importantly, Mr. Giammarco stated six "affirmative defenses" and asked that the lawsuit be dismissed and that he be awarded attorneys' fees. The first "*Affirmative Defense*" stated that Mr. Shay continued to operate his auto body shop for two years after the 30 October 1987 incident and that "*the plaintiff has not been medically disabled from his occupational endeavors, and therefore the co-defendant, Anthony Giammarco, now owes the plaintiff nothing.*" The "*Fifth Affirmative Defense*" stated, "*As the plaintiff concedes that he allowed the alleged explosion to occur (Amended Complaint, para. 30), the plaintiff is responsible for any damages that he inflicted upon himself.*" Thus, while the Boston newspapers had often stated that Tom Shay sought to inherit a portion of what might have been a $400,000 (the limit of the defendants' insurance policy), legal victory, the reality of the case was that it was barely a legitimate case, and would likely only be settled, if at all, for its nuisance value. That is, the defendants would likely make the calculation that it would be cheaper to settle the case for a few tens of thousands of dollars than it would be to run up huge legal fees defending against it.

On 18 December, the Massachusetts House of Representatives gave a standing ovation to Officer Francis Foley and a one-minute period of silence in honor of Jeremiah Hurley. The Roslindale Bomb case continued to have high public interest and thus high pressure on the ATF and Boston police to solve it.

Mr. Thomas L. Shay had not been forgotten, and he provided a wood sample with black paint on it for ATF analysis.

On 3 January 1992 Tom Shay was released on bail from the Suffolk County jail where he was being held for his alleged November 1990 MBTA bomb threat. One of the conditions of his release was to report daily to Ms. Moy, a Boston Municipal Court probation officer. Also, he was to meet weekly with her, and to attend daily an Alcohol Anonymous meeting and to apply to the Quincy Mental Health Center for out-patient treatment.

In early January ATF agents and Boston Police detectives discussed what needed to be done in the overall investigation and Boston Detectives Peter O'Malley and Lt. McNeely proposed to Special Agents Dennis Leahy and Jeff Kerr that the ATF become the lead agency and take over the investigation. On 10 January, the ATF agents, together with ATF supervisor Victor Palaza and Special Agent Thomas D'Ambrosio, met with Assistant U.S. Attorneys Paul V. Kelly and Frank A. Libby, Jr., to update them on the progress of the investigation, and to consider how such a transfer of responsibility might be accomplished. On 14 January the Suffolk County District Attorney, Newman Flanagan, agreed with the decision to seek Federal prosecution of the Roslindale Bomb case, and on the 16th, the agreement was formalized.

The news of the changed responsibility was not publicized until 2 March. The *Boston Globe* headline read, *"EXPLOSION CASE PUT IN FEDERAL BAILIWICK,"* and said that Federal resources would more likely lead to success. The article summarized the status of the case, but was limited to off-the-record *"sources familiar with the investigation."* As an example of the official reluctance to discuss the case, it could not be confirmed on-the-record that the Federal grand jury had begun hearing testimony from *"friends, acquaintances and enemies"* of Mr. Thomas L. Shay and his son, Tom. A source revealed that the names of two witnesses had come from Tom's address book but there was no mention of Alfred Trenkler.

The article did not reveal that the ATF had already zeroed in on the 197 Mass. Ave. Radio Shack store, and said that the $65,000 reward had failed to generate sufficient evidence. The article noted that the Boston Police had renamed their Special Operations Building to be the Jeremiah Hurley, Jr. building, and that Francis Foley retired from the Boston Police Dept on 1 March.

The first fruits of the ATF's new lead role were plans for wiretaps and Federal search warrants of Alfred Trenkler's home and work areas.

On 14 January, James Keough, the father of Paula Shay's son, and living with Paula at Mrs. Nancy Shay's, tried to kill himself with a knife after a dispute with Paula. The family turmoil on that day caused Tom Shay to miss his daily report to his probation officer, which was the third failure to report in two weeks. When Keough returned from the hospital on the 17th, he was told that Tom Shay had taken his National Guard ID and some clothing and left the state, apparently fearing that his three failures to report to his probation officer would lead to his re-incarceration.

Another result of the change to ATF responsibility was the discovery that no report had been written by the Boston Police about the 5 and 6 November interviews with Alfred Trenkler and the four consent searches. Thus, Dennis Leahy wrote on 17 January 1992 the full report described above for the events 73 days earlier.

Perhaps most importantly, Assistant U.S. Attorney (AUSA) Paul Kelly began to take a personal interest in the case. It's rare for an AUSA to get involved in the investigation stage of an ATF investigation, but he shared the interviewing of Russ Bonanno on 22 January with Jeff Kerr, Case Agent for the entire case; and they traveled to Dartmouth, Mass. to meet him. The five page report concerned Shay's two stays with Bonanno, in September and then late October, and Shay's many lies. Bonanno told Kelly and Kerr how he had introduced Tom Shay to David

Hanbury, a gay high school student from Needham, Mass. whom Bonanno had known through BAGLY [Bi-Sexual Alliance of Gay and Lesbian Youths] There was no mention of Alfred Trenkler nor anything substantive about the Roslindale Bomb.

Bonanno agreed to use a cassette tape recorder he was given to record any calls which might subsequently come in from Tom Shay.

The highly ranked interview team of AUSA Paul Kelly and Jeff Kerr were joined by ATF Supervisor Victor Palaza when they went on 28 January to a "Roy Rogers" restaurant in Needham to meet with David Hanbury, a junior at Needham High School.

Hanbury described a bizarre weekend the previous Fall when Russ Bonanno drove to Needham and brought Hanbury to Quincy where they picked up Tom Shay and drove to Dartmouth to get Shay acquainted with Hanbury. The gathering went poorly and Bonanno decided to drive the young men home, but Shay insisted on going to a hospital because he was feeling suicidal and then to various homes of friends, none of whom was home. Finally, they returned to his mother's in Quincy where Shay was left.

Subsequently, Hanbury received several strange calls from Shay and a person purporting to be a District Attorney investigating gay harassment. Hanbury was concerned that he would be forced to "come out" to his friends in Needham, as he had not yet done so. All very odd for an AUSA, an ATF Senior Supervisor and an ATF Special Agent to be asking and recording. There was nothing in the report of the interview about the Roslindale Bomb, nor Alfred Trenkler. Hanbury gave them a letter Shay had written to him. They must have concluded that Tom Shay was a crazy kid, but crazy like a bomber rather than the more accurate crazy like a mixed-up false confessor. Shay's letter says, in part:

"I'm so sorry on the way we met. I wish I could had [sic] *been a little more suddle* [sic]. *You are a very handsome young man and I wish that someday we can become good friends. Boyfriends. Lovers, etc. My heart goes out to you. I wish we were together right now. I'm not home right now, so don't bother to call. I'm in a* [facility?] *Help me get undepressed. But I would like for you to write me a nice long letter about who you have told so far. and how life is treating you, and I will write you right back. Write me at home and my mother will bring it to me...."*

Despite his conversational openness and journeys into the den of the ATF, Alfred Trenkler was not unaware of the risks and approaching danger. After several family discussions and recommendations, Alfred chose a new law firm, Segal and Feinberg of Boston, to represent him, and his parents would pay for it. Terry Segal was a well-known lawyer, and former Assistant U.S. Attorney. His father had been a Boston lawyer, too, and had, for a period of time, represented the Boston Police Department, but Alfred did not know this then, or whether Segal's loyalties might be divided. Alfred's step-uncle, attorney Philip Suter,[5] a long-time partner at the Boston firm, Sullivan and Worcester, recommended Segal. The choice of lawyer was fateful, but who could have predicted that the result would be a sentence for two life terms in prison? Who knew that the Wallaces would drain their life savings and retirement plans of approximately $650,000 over the next 14 years on different lawyers. Who knew that a person claiming indigency, as Alfred could have done, could retain the services of a lawyer as good as Nancy Gertner, who was initially authorized to bill the Federal Government $200 per hour? Hindsight, hopefully like the analysis in this book, is often 20/20.

On 28 January, AUSA Paul Kelly applied for a 30-day court order for electronic surveillance of Alfred Trenkler's pager and thereby his communications with Thomas A. Shay, John Cates, Richard Brown and others yet unknown about the Roslindale Bombing. The application included a 23 page affidavit by Special Agent Jeff Kerr. Paul Kelly stated in the application,

"...a. There is probable cause to believe that Alfred W. Trenkler has committed violations of the Federal explosives laws...

b. There is probable cause to believe that particular electronic communications of Alfred W. Trenkler and others as yet unknown, concerning, and in furtherance of, concealment of the above-described offenses will be intercepted over a digital display paging device assigned telephone number (617-553-0778). In particular, there is probable cause to believe that the communications to be intercepted will concern the telephone numbers subscribed to or used by associates and confederates of Alfred W. Trenkler, and the dates and times of communications between such persons and Trenkler, thereby helping to identify the co-conspirators and aiders and abettors of Alfred W. Trenkler. These communications are expected to constitute admissible evidence of the above described offenses.

c. Normal investigative techniques have been pursued and continue to be pursued, yet appear to be effectively exhausted, particularly with respect to establishing the identities of all associates and confederates of the foregoing conspiracy to conceal the above-described violations of federal law. In addition, continued pursuit of non-electronic investigative techniques may jeopardize the likelihood of reaching a successful conclusion to this investigation."

Jeff Kerr's affidavit repeated Paul Kelly's claims of probable cause and reviewed the history of the investigation of the Roslindale Bomb, and stated that "a motor vehicle (truck) was destroyed as a result of the detonation [of] an infernal device, i.e. bomb.... [which Alfred W. Trenkler] designed to be triggered by radio remote control, at the request of a friend, who paid him for his efforts."

In fact, the Quincy Police report, by Officer Peter Turowski, Badge #133, said there was "no visible damage to truck." Also, Alfred was not paid by Donna Shea to assemble the device, using the M21 Hoffman artillery simulator which she contributed. Kerr also repeated the information about the unattached speaker in John Cates' apartment and the presence of the book, "*Dirty Tricks*, containing information on how to get even with people." To give some balance, it must be noted that Kerr stated that Alfred Trenkler had told his partner, Richard Brown, that he had nothing to do with the Roslindale Bomb - as Alfred has told everyone since November 1991.

Kerr also said that Richard Brown had stated that Tom Shay had spent a weekend with Trenkler at ATEL. Kerr wrote that "Trenkler and many of his associates are gay, often moving in tightly-knit circles that include only other gay males. This creates manifest difficulties in effectively maintaining an uninterrupted covert surveillance, ..." This report shows the ATF bias and lack of gay agents and lack of familiarity with gay people. Alfred Trenkler has never acknowledged that he is gay, and most of his associates were heterosexuals, who often moved in tightly-knit circles that include only other heterosexuals.

Jeff Kerr said one reason for the electronic surveillance was that subpoenaing the targets of the investigation to testify before the grand jury would not be likely to help. He wrote, "the targets and subjects of this investigation, should they be called before the grand jury, would most likely be uncooperative and invoke their Fifth Amendment privilege not to testify.... Additionally, the service of grand jury subpoenas upon associates of Alfred Trenkler or other subjects would likely only serve to alert the target and subjects of the focus of this investigation, thereby causing them to be more cautious in their activities, to flee to avoid further investigation or prosecution, or to otherwise compromise this investigation. Obviously, serving Trenkler himself with a subpoena would serve no useful purpose."

On the other side, Terry Segal and the new defense team had decided not to offer Alfred Trenkler's testimony to the grand jury. Alfred recalled in 2007 the reasoning, "*With the lax rules governing federal grand juries AUSA Paul Kelly would be allowed to ask any and all inflammatory questions without restraint. A visit to the grand jury would only help Paul Kelly indict me faster. Any possible benefits would be severely outweighed by the negatives. It was decided that it would be best if I not testify at the grand jury.*"

The criminal justice cannot be working well if an innocent defendant does not feel that going to a grand jury would be helpful. It's unfortunate that no one laid out the "benefits" and "negatives" on a simple piece of paper. If they had been reasonably presented, and even if they had known the terrible results which might be coming, and which might be caused in part by such non-testimony, the testimony decision might have been different. Below is such a comparison:

Benefits	Negatives
-Get his side of the story into print	-If make an error in recollection, can be later used to show untruthfulness.
-Get the truth to the prosecutors who, to that point were relying upon reports.	-Prosecutors may not be listening, and may twist what they hear.
-Present an image to friends and others that you have nothing to hide.	-Prosecutors may twist and twist information, and twist again.
-Can make a statement, even without a prosecutor question.	-Prosecutors can ask questions for which they know the answer is negative, just
-May be able to return to the grand jury to answer more questions after grand jurors were able to hear others.	to have the grand jurors hear the question.
-May be able to avoid indictment, and prosecution, trial and chance of a wrongful conviction.	-Prosecutors can present their theories as fact to inflame the grand jury.

In 2007 a grand juror in Maine told me how one defendant came to the grand jury before the prosecution's case had been presented and she made an impressive case for her innocence. The grand juror voted against the subsequent indictment, but without her appearance, the indictment would likely have been unaminous.

Kerr's information about the upcoming grand jury subpoenas was inaccurate as several of Trenkler's friends and associates were, in fact, called to the grand jury. Also, Alfred Trenkler knew he was a suspect and he was desperately trying to convince the investigators that they were making a big mistake, and also trying to keep his business together.

Most importantly, Alfred Trenkler would have wanted to testify before the grand jury, but that desire might have been thwarted by his lawyers. Who knows what would have happened if the grand jury and Paul Kelly and Frank Libby did actually speak with and listen to Alfred W. Trenkler. If they had, and not heard about him through the ears of ATF agents and people with biases against him; the grand jury and the Assistant U.S. Attorneys would likely have viewed Alfred William Trenkler quite differently. Suppose, for example, and looking ahead, Trenkler had said to them exactly what he said to Judge Zobel in his pre-sentencing statement in 1994?

Finally, Kerr stated that the phones of John Cates, ARCOMM and Thomas L. Shay were already being monitored by obtaining the phone numbers of incoming and outgoing calls.

The court order was requested to be issued to Alfred's paging company, "Metro Media Paging" in Brighton and that the existence of the order be secret and that Paul Kelly report back to the U.S. District Court judge every 10 days on the status of the electronic surveillance. ARCOMM was a "re-dealer" for Metro Media Paging as well as being a customer.

The request for the court order was approved by U.S. District Court Judge Edward Harrington on 30 January 1992.

In another important development on 28 January, the U.S. Attorney's office applied for Search Warrants for three Alfred Trenkler locations: his home at 133 Atlantic St., his company office, ARCOMM at 62 Broad Street in Weymouth and his parents' garage at 7 Whitelawn Ave in Milton. This application was made despite, or perhaps because of, having found nothing of value during the consented, and therefore unrestricted, searches on the night of 5/6 November 1991. The supporting Affidavit by Special Agent Thomas D'Ambrosio said the warrants were required to look for, in summary, anything which might look like a component of a bomb similar to the Roslindale Bomb and anything which might show an association between Alfred Trenkler and Tom Shay, and between Trenkler and Mr. Thomas L. Shay, too.

In paragraph 11 of D'Ambrosio's affidavit he stated,

"During the interview [on 31 October at the Homicide Unit] Shay Jr. described the workings of a remote controlled model car and drew a diagram of a remote control transmitter. Shay Jr. stated that he knew several gay law enforcement officers, and he provided the detectives with names. Shay Jr. denied having anything to do with the making or setting of the explosive device that killed Officer Hurley."

A copy of Shay's diagram is shown in Appendix D. That a diagram looking like something from a 1st grade drawing class could be used to convince a Federal judge to approve search warrants for an acquaintance of the drawer of the diagram might shock some. It's not known why Tom Shay's knowing the names of gay police officers had any relevance to such a request for search warrants.

Special Agent D'Ambrosio's affidavit stated in paragraph 15 that Robert Evans, a fellow inmate of Shay's at the Norfolk County House of Correction, told Boston detectives William Fogerty, Peter O'Malley, and Miller Thomas that "he [Shay] was not smart enough to make a bomb, but that he 'bought it off a guy who made it and stuck it over there.' Evans further stated that he asked Shay Jr. if his father would bail him out? Shay Jr. replied, 'What, are you crazy? After what I tried to do to him?' "[6]

In paragraph 18, Special Agent D'Ambrosio cited the presence of the unhooked speaker at 133 Atlantic Street and the copy of the book *Dirty Tricks*, despite John Cates' explanations for the presence of both those items to the search team. Neither item belonged to Alfred Trenkler, who was described as the "roommate" of John Cates.

Paragraph 20 stated that "Trenkler admitted he was gay and that he knew Shay, Jr...." The word "admitted" means more to a law enforcement person that it does to laypeople. It means to acknowledge that you have done something wrong. Further, Alfred Trenkler says that he was never asked about his sexual preference. In his 1994 presentencing statement, he said it was "*interesting,*" and there was no need to know more. Nowhere in the voluminous record of the case is there a statement that anyone "*admitted*" that s/he was heterosexual. No one was asked, either, if s/he were heterosexual.

In paragraph 22, D'Ambrosio said that ATF Agents Sandra LaCourse and Dennis Leahy had interviewed Richard Brown on 20 November and that "Brown stated that Trenkler paid to have sex with younger males, and that he enjoyed taking photographs of sex acts." Usually a charge that someone has taken photographs is accompanied by the obvious evidence: a photograph. Despite searches, there was no evidence of such photographs nor even a mention of a camera, even though ARCOMM did use a camera to document its work. There is a report that Dennis Leahy and Thomas D'Ambrosio talked with Richard Brown on 20 November, but it made no mention of a charge that Alfred Trenkler paid for sex with younger males. Both officers talked with Richard Brown on 4 December, too, without such a reference.

Finally, in paragraph 23, the Affidavit said that Richard Brown "... also stated that Trenkler recent produced a 'glue gun' from the back room of the business, and that this bothered him because they did not use glue guns in their business."

The Warrants were issued by U.S. Magistrate Judge Marianne Bowler and a team was assembled, including 15 Boston policemen who were deputized as U.S. Marshals for one day, 31 January, so they could participate in the Federal search. The 15 included Francis Armstrong, William Fogerty, Peter O'Malley and Miller Thomas who had previously worked on the case.

On 29 January, an ATF form ("Personal History/TECS Input") was completed by someone with the handwritten initials "bw" for entry into an apparent ATF database, TECS, for Thomas Arthur Shay. The "Armed and Dangerous" box was checked "Yes." He was described further as, "the X-lover of Alfred Trenkler, history of mental health problems. Love/hate relationship with father Thomas L." Again, where was the evidence that ATF used to state that Tom Shay was ever the lover of Alfred Trenkler? Did any of the ATF agents and managers and even an

Assistant U.S. Attorney think it was reasonable to get involved, or become a lover, with Thomas A. Shay? What happened to that 4 November 1991 ATF request for a personality assessment of Tom Shay?

According to ATF reports, Alfred Trenkler came under surveillance of ATF Special Agent Henry Moniz and Boston Police detective Robert Ahearn on 31 January when Trenkler and John Cates left their apartment at 7:00 a.m. to drive Cates to work in Boston. He returned at 7:30 and then left for his parents' house at 8:10, as he was told his parents had requested. The search of Alfred's parents' garage began at 9:00 and Dennis Leahy wrote the report of the search and his conversations with Alfred Trenkler, who talked with Leahy despite his acknowledgement that his lawyer advised against it. Leahy wrote that Trenkler described difficulties in his work relationship with Richard Brown. Trenkler said that he had made Radio Shack purchases in the past, including at the Mass. Ave. store in Boston. The report continued,

'Trenkler also said that Shay hated his father, and that Trenkler had given rides from Boston on several occasions, once to Shay's father's house. Trenkler also admitted that he and Shay may have spent the weekend together at ATEL and that he had forgotten to tell us that before. Trenkler said that he had two theories on how the bombing had happened; one was that the guys from where Shay (Sr.) worked did it and the second was that Shay (Jr.) did it. Trenkler said that he was concerned the 'feds' would fabricate evidence against him."

Alfred Trenkler's account of the morning and his conversation with Dennis Leahy differs substantially. Wrote Alfred in May 2006,

"On January 31, 1992 I had driven my roommate, John Cates, to his job at Fleet Bank on Boylston Street in Boston, leaving him at 8 a.m. I left and was driving back to the 133 Atlantic Street Apartment to make some phone calls. Some of my clients had called my pager voice mail. On the way back I remembered that a communications company down the street from John Cates' apartment had moved. I wanted the phone number of the landlord to discuss rental details. I drove by Cates' apartment and stopped next to the building, took my mini-tape recorder out of my briefcase and dictated the phone number. I returned to Cates' apartment, briefcase in hand and upon entering noticed a slew of agents in the basement apartment. I was told by Agent Kerr that they were executing search warrants at the apartment, my parents' and my ARCOMM office. Agent Kerr told me that my parents had requested I return to their house in Milton so I could lock up after the search was done there. I turned to leave with briefcase in hand and Agent Kerr demanded I open it to be searched. I told him I just came in with it. He told me, 'No,' it was there when they came in. I said, I'm not an idiot, I just opened it to get my tape recorder in my car. I told Kerr he was welcome to look in it, it was just business records. Instead he took out all my folders and told me they would give me back copies later. I told him they were plans and designs for current jobs and it would interfere with my business if I did not have them. A short discussion about using a copy machine down the street was nixed by Kerr.

Frustrated, I turned to leave. An agent stopped me on the way out and expressed his dismay at what the ATF was putting me through, that he had seen many cases; and this was the first where some viewed me as having no involvement in this case. I asked, knowing the answer, if he would put that in writing for my attorney. He said, 'Are you kidding me? They'd throw me in jail.'

I left and drove to my parents' house in Milton. Upon arrival I saw a utility type van and 2 Crown Victoria's in my parents' driveway and more across the street. I parked just at the end of the driveway. I went into the house to see my parents. They told me they had to leave for work which they did. I went back outside to see if they [the agents] were getting close to finishing. Around 9:10 a.m. Dennis Leahy had me sign a consent waiver to search my Toyota and have some newly developed gas chromatograph spectrum analyzer developed, ironically by MIT, a "sniffer" by layman's terms, sample the air inside my car. The device pulls in air and analyzes particles given off, in this case, nitrates associated with ammonia dynamite. It was said that I had used my Toyota to transport ammonia dynamite, further, that this device would detect the presence of nitrates for up to six months. January was 3 months from the time I allegedly transported dynamite. Not to mention the fact that on November 6 at 12:30 a.m. Agent D'Ambrosio took, with my permission, an 8" by 8" square piece of carpet from my car which also tested negative for explosive residue. I then moved my car to the street since the agents were getting ready to wrap up their search.

While I was waiting, Peter O'Malley, who had recently been removed as lead Boston Police Detective in this case, pulls up, gets out of his car, and has a brief discussion with Officer Fogerty. There was some kind of disagreement. O'Malley left in a huff.

Dennis Leahy, who was in front of my parents' garage yells over to me, 'Hey, could you come over here and give me a comment on some of this stuff?' He had a table with piles of items on it.

William Fogerty said, 'Trenkler, stay away from Leahy, you have an attorney and don't have to talk to him.'

Leahy in response said, 'Al, all I need you for is to tell me what stuff is yours, what's your brother's [David Wallace] and what's your parents'. Then, 'Al, we don't convict innocent people. If you have nothing to do with this you have nothing to worry about. I will only help clear your name if you speak with us.' A ruse by Leahy to start a conversation with me.

I did say that I was having problems with Rich Brown, [and] that Brown was bouncing checks all over town, that he had met some coke whore he was spending money on like a drunken sailor and had started selling equipment out the back door. I went on that I had severed relations with Brown and had a new business partner from Hull.

Since it was already public knowledge, I had admitted to putting together the '86 prank device, that I had done a Rube Goldberg assembly out of old parts and a $20 toy remote control good for a 50 foot range.

Here's where Dennis Leahy got extremely creative. Leahy asked me if I knew was a shunt was. I told him it was something in first year electronics taught at Wentworth, that it was a diverter of current typically used in building analog meters. Leahy then asked if I thought a wire could act as an antenna. I told him that was basic communication physics and seen in the wire antenna in the windshield of a car or a ham radio receiver or AM radio antenna. He asked if I've ever been near a blasting site. I told him I've driven by construction sites where they do blasting. I said that I can remember driving by construction sites where there are signs posted, 'Blasting area, turn off all two way radios.' Leahy asked what I thought that was. I said I guess because it might accidentally set off the explosives if someone with enough transmit power got too close while transmitting. Who hasn't seen one of those signs? Leahy then asked what would I think would happen if someone set off dynamite next to other dynamite. I said that logically I would think it might cause the unexploded dynamite to explode, like the match in the fireworks factory joke, as well as basic physics, called heat transferable like heat sinks for transistors. Leahy went on to ask where I have seen dynamite. I said the only time I've ever seen explosives is on TV or in the movies like the Road runner or Clint Eastwood. - Who hasn't? -

Tom Tierney of the Quincy Police, who had, unbeknownst to me, called the Boston Police concerning the 1986 incident, had seen me in a store down the street from John Cates house and had said to me he had heard that the '91 bomb exploded when a female patrol officer keyed her portable radio at the scene of the bomb discovery.

Leahy asked me if cheap remote control toys were reliable devices. I told him I've seen the cheap toys with minds of their own that make turns or moves without being commanded.

Leahy asked if I was ever at the Radio Shack across from Christian Science Monitor. I told him I was there during Wentworth during the '70's, while I worked at ATEL and to pick up a part for my car sound system....

I said to Leahy that, from what I remembered, Tom L. Shay, the father was mad at Tom A. Shay the son because of the "People are Talking" show where Tom A. Shay told the country he was gay.[7] I did say that I had given Tom A. Shay rides on a few occasions, once to Richmond Street or Ave. in Dorchester that Tom A. Shay said was his father's house, but obviously was a lie since Tom L. Shay's house was on Eastbourne Street in Roslindale. I did not say that Tom A. Shay spent the weekend with me at ATEL. I stopped living at ATEL in September of '90 when I moved with Cates and had quit ATEL in February of '91, and did not meet Tom A. Shay until June of '91.

Leahy asked me what my theory was on the bombing. I said one was that Shay the father did it for his lawsuit or that the guys he was suing did it. Leahy substitutes Tom A. Shay, the son, for what I said, Tom L. Shay the father. Leahy had a habit of hearing the way he wants to hear.

I did say that I was concerned that the "Feds" would fabricate evidence against me. Leahy responded with his standard response that 'we don't arrest innocent citizens.' I said, 'You keep on saying that, and yet here you are searching my office, apartment and parents' house.'

I was carrying a cellular phone in expectation of a call from a contact involved with the Nigerian Government and I mentioned it was a rental phone at $1.00 a minute. My pager had gone off but my phone was dead. I asked Fogerty if I could use a cellular phone they had since I could not miss an important call. I *was literally on standby for a call from my contact in Nigeria. I called the page. It turned out to be my new business partner from his house in Hull. I didn't have the keys to my folks' house; I had inadvertently left them at Cates' house and my folks had left for work.*

<u>*Creativity of Dennis Leahy*</u>

Because I knew that a shunt diverts current in electronics and that a wire can act as an antenna, both topics taught at Wentworth and other engineering schools, and that I had seen signs at construction sites that said 'Blasting Area, Turn Off All Two Way Radios', this demonstrated that I knew all about <u>blasting caps,</u> <u>leg wires</u> and <u>leg wire shunts</u>. Of course, this would also include every electronic engineering student in the City of Boston.

That I guessed, logically, if someone set off dynamite next to other dynamite the unlit dynamite might explode, this demonstrated to Dennis Leahy that I knew all about <u>sympathetic detonation</u> - a term used in the explosives field. That I said the only place I've seen dynamite was on TV in Road Runner cartoons and Clint Eastwood movies translated, in Dennis Leahy's mind, that I learned all about <u>dynamite</u> and <u>explosives</u> on TV.

To sum up, because Alfred Trenkler studied electronics, guessed that unlit dynamite would possibly explode next to lit dynamite and watched Road Runner and Clint Eastwood movies makes Alfred Trenkler an expert in explosives."

A total of 36 items, some of them with multiple pieces, were seized during the three searches and were sent to the ATF laboratory in Maryland. None was determined to have any connection to the Roslindale Bomb, except for a lame effort at Alfred Trenkler's trial to link his roll of duct tape to the bomb because it had been torn lengthwise, as had pieces of duct tape found amidst the debris. However, the width of those pieces was different from that of the pieces seized at Alfred Trenkler's parents' garage.

Among the items taken from Jack and Josephine Wallace's garage was a small wooden box. At 6:00 p.m. that night, Special Agent Dennis Leahy received a call, as requested, from Alfred's half-brother, David Wallace, who explained the function of the box. Leahy wrote,

"Mr. Wallace said that he was going to use it for target practice as he practices shooting in Maine, and that the black circles on the box were bullseyes for target practice. Mr. Wallace said that he spoke with Al Trenkler before he telephoned ATF. Mr. Wallace described the box as grey primer, made of plywood, (3/8" or 1/2") and that he put it together with sheetrock screws. Mr. Wallace said that the left side of the garage was his and that Al Trenkler used the right hand side of the garage."

Interestingly, the investigators did not take, or perhaps did not even notice, any of what Alfred calls the "*vast variety of toggle switches from a wide range of sources*" which were in boxes in the garage. Alfred had accumulated them over the years when disassembling appliances. If he needed a toggle switch, he did not need to go any further than his own garage to get one. Of course, it would have been far more prudent to acquire parts for an illegal bomb from a used collection rather than a new purchase with a receipt. However, even that reasoning was unnecessary because Alfred likely would not have used a toggle switch at all. It would have been far easier to use an electronic relay between the fusing circuit and the firing circuit, rather than an electromechanical movement of a sliding bar which then would physically move a toggle switch. Alfred's situation was as if he were a race car driver and the government had found a receipt for horseshoes and was arguing that Alfred had arranged for the purchase as he planned to use a horse as a getaway vehicle.

Also on 31 January, ATF agents interviewed Mrs. Nancy Shay who was reported to have said that no one knew her son, Tom, as well as she did. She knew the names of a few of Tom's friends, but had never heard the name of Trenkler.

On 3 February, Alfred Trenkler called the ATF office to inquire about the return of the documents taken from his briefcase on the 31st, and talked with Dennis Leahy. This was the only time that Alfred Trenkler ever called any person involved in the Roslindale Bomb investigation. Leahy's report stated, "Trenkler also said that he gave Shay (Jr.) several rides from Boston, once to his father's house on Richmond St., Boston and Shay (Jr.) said that he had to wait till his father left the house before he (Shay Jr.) could go in." Leahy must have confused the facts of the first day's acquaintance with Tom Shay where Alfred took him to 133 Atlantic Street because he couldn't go to his father's house, and then later the same morning, Trenkler and Richard Brown took Shay to Richmond Street, where Shay's mother used to live.

On the 4th, Trenkler went to the ATF office where he talked with several agents. Dennis Leahy wrote a report of his conversation with Trenkler and ATF Agent Sandra LaCourse. Besides recording conversation that repeated previous statements, Leahy said that Alfred Trenkler offered to "talk to Shay (Jr) for the government." Also, wrote Leahy, "Trenkler denied having sex with Shay (Jr.)..." This was the first and only time any law enforcement person had claimed to discuss that issue directly with Trenkler. However, Alfred insists that even that claimed posing of the question did not occur. Despite the claimed denial of a sexual relationship betwen Shay and Trenkler, and the lack of any credible evidence to the contrary, the Government, with the media behind it, continued pushing its theory of a lover relationship between Trenkler and Tom Shay.

On 6 February, Alfred Trenkler turned 36, but ATF wasn't giving him a gift of the return of his documents, so Scott Lopez of the firm, Segal and Feinberg, called AUSA Paul Kelly to seek his assistance in obtaining the return to Trenkler of the business documents taken from his briefcase on 31 January by Special Agent Jeff Kerr. The followup letter threatened a lawsuit for damages if copies of the documents were not made available by 2 p.m. the next day.

Alfred Trenkler prepared on 6 February 1992 an Affidavit in support of the anticipated Motion for Return of Property. He stated in the first official document in this case containing his own words:

"... 3. I am an Electronics Communication Engineer/Consultant doing business as Advanced Telecommunication Network Systems Research & Development (hereinafter ATNS R&D). My hourly rate is presently $150.00 per hour.

4. On January 31, 1992, my home, office and the apartment of a friend was the subject of a search and seizure...

5. During the search of 133 Atlantic Street, Quincy, MA, an apartment owned by John Cates, the agents opened and searched the closed briefcase in my

possession and seized business records identified in the return to the search warrant as 'paperwork to include 3 notebooks, loose papers and twelve files.' ...

6. This paperwork is absolutely essential to my ongoing business relationships with various clients, including but not limited to, the Christian Science Church and Massachusetts Institute of Technology....

10. Specifically, I cannot continue the performance of the Christian Science Air System contract until I obtain my calculations for the system which are contained within this paperwork. This paperwork contains work product that took numerous hours to produce and cannot be reproduced without a similar effort. ...

11. Without this paperwork I can not even send out bills for services I have completed or pay my creditors the money I owe them because the documents contained my financial records....

18. In essence, the seizure of this paperwork has effectively put me out of business. Every day that goes by without this paperwork deprives me of my property, of running my business, of earning a living and of performing my business contracts."

Thursday, the 6th of February was a significant day, too, because the grand jury heard its first witnesses on the case: Richard Brown, John Cates and Mary Flanagan. A week later, Nancy Shay, mother of Tom Shay, and Robert Craig, former roommate of Alfred Trenkler, and Donna Shay testified. Grand jury testimony is secret, except that witnesses may see the transcripts of their own testimony, and prosecutors and defense counsel may see them too. Also, a witness may disclose a summary of what s/he said, but not the actual questions and answers.

On 7 February, Jeff Kerr wrote a report summarizing recent developments in the case and said that it was believed Tom Shay was in San Francisco. On 26 February, Tom Shay called his attorney, William McPhee, from Canada and said he was afraid to return.

On 10 February, Agents Thomas D'Ambrosio and Jeff Kerr interviewed Christopher Punis, a friend of Alfred Trenkler. Punis told the agent that he first met Trenkler when working for Greenview Landscaping Co. in 1987, and they were later roommates for a short time in Hull, Massachusetts. Most recently, Punis was hired by ARCOMM to help with the Christian Science Church project.

Also on 10 February, AUSA Paul Kelly sent his first 10-day report of the wiretap on Alfred Trenkler's pager to Judge Harrington as required by the implementation order. Kelly wrote, "The clone pager has not been as productive as we had hoped." In short, nothing was learned. Kelly explained that Trenkler uses his multi-option pager for its "voice mail" option more often than for displaying the display messages from callers, such as "Call Chris" which was the information that Judge Harrington's surveillance order was designed to capture. There were 7 messages and 89 voicemail calls. Of the seven, five were business calls, one was from Trenkler's friend and part-time employee, Chris Punis, and one was from Donna Shea. Paul Kelly said the U.S. Attorney's office was considering whether to ask for additional authorization to capture Trenkler's voicemail. The second 10-day report was filed on 20 February and showed similar results, as did the third and final report on 2 March; and the 30-day surveillance order lapsed.

One piece of information about Alfred Trenkler's pager number (617-553-0778) was that he acquired it in July 1991, and thus Tom Shay's entry in his address book with that phone number could not have been entered any sooner than that date. Such evidence, if presented at trial, would have supported Trenkler's defense that his acquaintance with Tom Shay began in June of 1991 and he gave him an ARCOMM business card with Alfred's pager number in July 1991.

On 9 February 1992 the fugitive Tom Shay called his friend Russ Bonanno and told him that he was "thirty two hundred miles away," which led the police to believe that Shay was on the West Coast.

On 11 February, Mr. Thomas L. Shay gave a 225 page deposition in his lawsuit against Jeffrey Berry, individually and together with Louis Giammarco as trustees of Ber-Giam Realty Trust, Ber-Giam, Inc., and Anthony Giammarco. The attending lawyers were Jay Flynn for Thomas L. Shay and John Finnerty, Richard Zucker, and Thomas J. Freedman for the defendants and their corporate entities. There were few questions relating to the 28 October 1991 explosion. On the issue of the claimed partial loss of Mr. Shay's hearing, Attorney Finnerty asked Mr. Shay if he had heard the 28 October explosion, and Mr. Thomas L. Shay said, "*Yes*," in a definite understatement. There were no further comments about that question. He confirmed that the gross receipts for Shay Auto Body were $86,000, $180,000, $206,000 and $140,000 for the years 1986-1989. He didn't recall the receipts for 1990, but they were substantially less, as he had stopped working regularly. In 1989 a new Massachusetts law had been implemented that required independent appraisers to estimate the cost of auto repairs, and that change reduced the profit margins of auto body shops across the state.

Oddly, on 11 March, the U.S. Assistant Attorney General Robert Mueller III, Chief of the Criminal Division in Washington, D.C., authorized through Deputy Asst. Atty Gen John Keeney, the application to a Federal judge for the electronic surveillance of Alfred Trenkler. Then, Keeney wrote to Wayne Budd, U.S. Attorney for Massachusetts and advised that the Boston U.S. Attorney's office could go ahead with the application to a Federal judge - 42 days after the first application by AUSA Paul Kelly to the judge. Robert Mueller was an Assistant U.S. Attorney in Boston in the 1980's before moving to the Justice Dept. in Washington, and in September, 2001, became the Director of the FBI, the position he now holds.

On the 12th of February, the grand jury heard testimony from John James Doering, the owner of the "Rolling Wrench Garage," where Arthur Shay and Thomas L. Shay sometimes worked, and from Paula Shay, sister of Tom Shay, and from Todd Leach, the teen-aged nephew of Donna Shea. The previous week, Richard Brown had returned to testify for a second time.

Although the investigation was now centered on Alfred Trenkler, investigators continued pursuing other theories, and put Thomas L. Shay under surveillance from time to time. On 13 February, ATF Special Agents John Paolillo and Ed Cronin were following Mr. Thomas L. Shay beginning at 8:30 a.m. Shay traveled through Newton and Belmont where he apparently suspected he was being followed. He drove in a few circles and returned to the Brighton section of Boston where he pulled up to a Boston policeman at a construction site. The policeman then motion to the unmarked ATF vehicle to pull over. An unmarked Boston police car then pulled up and said that the driver of the Buick Century (Mr. Shay) "complained that he was being followed and was very upset." The ATF agents then explained to the Boston detective who they were.

Appearing before the grand jury on 16 February was Mary Alice Flanagan, mother of Kristen Flanagan, the daughter of Thomas L. Shay. On the 20th appeared David Shilalis, man friend of Mrs. Nancy Shay. Friends and relatives of those who testified knew that the investigation was getting serious, for prosecutors do not usually seek an indictment unless they believe they can persuade a grand jury to issue one, based on the existing evidence. Before an indictment, prosecutors face two possible outcomes of a crime: they indict someone or they don't. Afterwards, there are two additional sub-options: they indicted the correct person or they didn't. If the indicted person isn't the correct person, a trial will usually determine that person is not guilty, but on occasion, a jury will confirm the mistakes of the grand jury and the prosecutor and convict an innocent person. That's the worst possible result of an incorrect indictment. It's a good prosecutor's nightmare.

On 19 February, Special Agent Jeff Kerr and Thomas D'Ambrosio interviewed Todd Leach, the nephew of Donna Shea. Leach told the agents that he was sent into a Radio Shack store to purchase about $150 worth of parts, mostly wire, for the 1986 Quincy device. Also, he said that helped Alfred Trenkler build the 1986 device by taking a magnet out of a discarded loudspeaker. Leach was eleven years old at the time. To others, Todd Leach had indicated an interest in obtaining the $65,000 reward so he could help his uncle, John Shea, husband of Donna Leach Shea, who was in jail.

On 21 February 1992, an undated letter from Tom Shay to Randy Stoller was faxed to ATF Agent Vic Palaza from the Fall River, Mass. Police Department. How and why the Fall River Police Dept. had the letter is not known, but Randy Stoller may have lived in Fall River. Perhaps Randy received the letter and arranged with Vic Palaza to have it faxed from a police station near his home or the Attleboro store, which turned out to be Fall River. The text of the short letter, is in a cartoon-like balloon, "*Dear Randy, Hello. I just wanted to tell you that I am very sorry about what happened to you. I have lost every friend that I ever had, because of my actions and this incident. I'm sorry. This letter to you is Hope* [sic] *of my Heart that your friendship will return to you. I'm going back to Texas. I will write to you. Soon. Ok. Friends forever, even if I wasn't the best, (more ------ worst) I will write. Your Friend, Tom. P.S. You will hopefully get your first check soon for $100.*"

In February, Donna Shea stopped by the ARCOMM office at 82 Broad Street, and brought a friend, James Harding, whom Donna recommended to Alfred for employment. One reason for the visit and the referral appears to have been the $65,000 reward, but Alfred did not know that, nor did he know that they were recording the conversation. On 20 February 1992, Harding was scheduled to appear before the grand jury and to bring with him any tape recordings which he and Donna Shea might have made relating to the case. Harding hesitated, and his grand jury appearance was rescheduled for 5 March. He finally gave the U.S. Attorney's office his recordings after being arrested for his non-cooperation. He then tried to work with the Government as an undercover agent. Harding and

Donna Shea had previously visited Alfred at his office and, while recording him, tried to steer his conversation toward incriminating statements.

Also visiting the ARCOMM offices from time to time were ATF Agents Jeff Kerr and/or Thomas D'Ambrosio. At times, they seemed to view the investigation as a cat-and-mouse game and on a few occasions they stayed in the office after Judy Fredette left for the day. They even took a few phone messages from ARCOMM clients and tauntingly left them for Alfred. Those messages have been discarded.

On 19 February 1992, Jeff Kerr and Thomas D'Ambrosio interviewed John Coyle, a friend of Alfred Trenkler who had been referred to them by Donna Shea. He repeated the allegation that "he was subjected to Trenkler's electronic monitoring of a sexual encounter which he (Coyle) had within the confines of his room. He stated that Trenkler had placed a bugging device inside his (Coyle's) stereo, providing Trenkler and friends the ability to ease [sic, eavesdrop] drop."

Once again, the government seems to have misinterpreted or misreported actions by Alfred Trenkler. Wrote Alfred in 2007, "The government loved to take harmless pranks and raise them to have serious implications. In 1980 I was housesitting on Canton Ave. in Milton with Donna Leach, she had not married John Shea yet, and Jack Coyle. Jack had this habit of listening to whacked out old show tunes. As a prank I attached an FM transmitter to his record player so that when he played his show tunes they could be heard on any FM radio in the house, a 100 foot range at most. We all had a laugh about it, including Jack Coyle, no harm done. In fact, he kept the turntable and might actually still use it." The house was on a lot one house away from Alfred's parents' home and was owned by a family friend who was a grandson of U.S. Supreme Court Justice Lewis Powell.

In another letter, Alfred wrote, "He [Coyle] was not too concerned [about the transmitter]. He kept using his record player and never even asked me to remove the transmitter. Needless to say we remained friends up through 1992."

It was good that Coyle had kept it, because the ATF investigators took it, presumably for analysis, where they could have easily determined that the FM transmitter took electronic wire signals which were traveling to the stereo speaker and transmitted them also as FM radio signals. The FM transmitter had no ability to transmit human-audible sounds, and it was not a bugging device. The transmitter was only turned 'on' when the stereo was on, so if it had been intended to pick up audible human sounds, it would have been a poorly conceived project as the sound of the music would have drowned out any sounds of voices.

In the last week of February, the ATF interviewed employees at the 197 Mass. Ave. Radio Shack store. Dwayne Armbrister remembered handling the 18 October 1991 sale to "S A H Y." Coincidentally, perhaps, the store manager, George Nightingale knew Tom Shay because his roommate, Edward Carrion, had a relationship with Shay and Shay had been in their apartment many times. The third interviewed employee knew nothing relevant. These three sterile reports belied the excitement ATF must have felt to get to that store for those interviews. In November, ATF's Cindy Wallace picked a Radio Shack 275-602 toggle switch as the switch likely used in the Roslindale Bomb. ATF then searched Radio Shack's sales records for the past year and found several sales in Boston, including the sale on 18 October 1991 at the 197 Mass. Ave store to "S A H Y." Significantly, thought the ATF investigators, the store was across the street from the ARCOMM worksite at the Christian Science Church. They searched phone records for people names Sahy, but found none in operation. Still, the name, Sahy, was not totally unusual. In 2007, there were nine listed phone numbers for "SAHY" in the U.S., and one of those was, coincidentally, for the house across the street of a former residence of the author. In 2007, there were 774,000 Google entries for "SAHY," beginning with the Hungarian town by that name.

On 25 February, ATF Special Agent interviewed Edward Carrion, who said he was "openly gay" and had an extended, but off and on relationship with Tom Shay, beginning in the summer of 1988. His name was not in Tom Shay's 1991 address book. "Mr. Carrion also said that he gave Shay (Jr.) rides to Milton; a single family, older house but well kept, three or four times in 1989 and two or three times at later dates. Mr. Carrion said that Shay's (Jr) friend/lover lived there. Mr. Carrion could not remember the address. Mr. Carrion said that Shay (Jr.) would call him from the 'block' for rides. Mr. Carrion thought that Shay's (Jr) friend/lover name was Dave, Bill or maybe Al...

Mr. Carrion when shown a photo spread said 'I got a gut feeling' and selected the photo of Alfred Trenkler as the friend/lover of Shay (Jr) who lived in Milton. Mr. Carrion agreed to try to locate the house in Milton that he drove Shay (Jr) to."

On 27 February, Dennis Leahy was joined by ATF Supervisor Victor Palaza and they drove Edward Carrion to Milton and he directed them to Whitelawn Ave. There, Carrion walked the length of the short avenue and identified 7 Whitelawn as the home to which he took Tom Shay several times.

"Carrion said that on these occasions, Shay Jr. told him he was going to visit his lover, who was an older man who lived in Milton. Carrion described this man as being in his early 30's, with a mustache, bulky build, not very tall...

Carrion said that the last time he saw Shay Jr., with the individual he (Carrion) had previously identified from a photograph as 'Al', was at the end of 1989 and the beginning of 1990. He said he saw them together approximately five or six times, maybe more or maybe less, in the area known as 'the block'. Carrion described 'the block' as the area around the Greyhound Bus Terminal. Carrion said that he never gave 'Al' a ride home because 'Al' usually had a car. Carrion recalled that Shay Jr. had a strong hatred for his father which was probably caused by a sense of abandonment and physical abuse."

There are at least three problems with the connection of Carrion's statements to Alfred W. Trenkler.

1. He experimented with growing a mustache in the 1970's, but not since then. The person seen by Ed Carrion with a mustache was not Alfred Trenkler.

2. He did not cruise "the Block" for any reason.

3. For most of 1988-1990, when he lived in Hull, he did not have a car at all. In the Summer of 1988, his Jeep Wagoneer died, and he didn't purchase another car until purchasing his 1978 Toyota Celica in September 1990. In the interim period he was given rides by others - which explains part of his reciprocal willingness to give rides to Tom Shay in the summer of 1991. Not only did this mean that he

wasn't at "The Block" with a car, but he also was not often at his parents' home in Milton either.

On 3 March 1992 ATF Special Agents Jeff Kerr and Sandra LcCourse interviewed former Radio Shack salesperson Allan Kingsbury, who was the same age as Tom Shay. Said LaCourse's report,

"When Allan Kingsbury was shown a Radio Shack receipt dated 10/18/91 [See copy in Appendix D] and bearing the name SAHY JYT and address of 5100, he laughed and smiled... because the customer gave Dwayne, the salesman, a hard time about giving his address. Upon his review of the items listed on the receipt, he stated that he remembered finding the boxes for the customer because Dwayne didn't know where they were. When asked if he could remember anything else about the sale, he stated that he remembered that the customer was hesitant about receiving his sales receipt. He stated that the customer looked as if he wasn't sure if he wanted his receipt. He stated that to the best of his recollection, the customer did take his receipt. He stated that during the sales transaction, he was standing to Dwayne's left.

When asked to recollect the description of the customer, Allan Kingsbury stated that he thought the guy was shorter than Dwayne (who is approximately 6' 2"). He stated that he thought the customer was of medium height, and surmised that he was around 27 years of age. He stated that he thought he may have been a Middle Eastern man."

When shown a photo array, he couldn't identify a person he thought was the 18 October customer. He did, however, identify a photo of Alfred Trenkler, who had been a customer at other times. The day after that 3 March interview,

"Allan Kingsbury informed S/A LaCourse that he recalled that the customer who made the purchase on October 18, 1991, was with someone at the time of the sale. He stated that he remembered that when Dwayne had asked the customer for his address, the customer had turned around to the man standing behind him and had asked '5100 what?' He recalled that the other man may have said a popular street such as Huntington Ave... On March 11, 1992, S/A LaCourse showed Allan Kingsbury Radio Shack receipts, dated 10/18/91, which were of sales approximately one hour before and one hour after the sale to SAHY JYT, which was at 2:36 p.m. Mr. Kingsbury remembered one of the receipts which was the sale of a watch to a customer at 2:38 p.m."

Allan Kingsbury was not called by the prosecution or the defense to testify at Shay's or Trenkler's trial. Perhaps the prosecution was deterred by the apparent overeagerness of Kingsbury to please them and help them solve the Roslindale Bomb case. He had told the grand jury that he had asked the 18 October 1991 Middle Eastern purchasers if they were going to use the items to build a bomb. As the six items were more likely to be useful for a school science project than to build a bomb, the claimed forensic insight would have seemed far-fetched. At his second grand jury appearance, he changed his recollection, after talking with Special Agent Jeff Kerr and fellow salesperson Dwayne Armbrister, of who purchased the items on the 18th. It's not known to the author why the defense did not call Kingsbury, but it may have been because Tom Shay had voluntarily, but falsely, admitted making the 18 October purchase, thus it would have been pointless to present a witness whose recollection was confused.

No one ever asked Alfred Trenkler about his purchases at the 197 Mass. Ave. Radio Shack store. It wasn't mentioned in any ATF reports, not at hearings before Judge Zobel, and was, therefore, another costly reminder of the several decisions not to have Alfred Trenkler testify. He wrote in 2007, "*I had been at the 197 Mass. Ave. Radio Shack 2 times in the Fall of 1991. Once in September to buy a battery for a Nikon camera ARCOMM had purchased to document the work at Christian Science Monitor. Radio Shack did not carry the needed battery and sent me next door to the film processor that did have the needed battery.*

I went to that Radio Shack again in October 1991 to purchase an adaptor plug for my car stereo equalizer so that I could plug a portable CD player into it. Jim Guy, the manager, was just closing up when John Cates and I went to that Radio Shack. Jim let us make the purchase and then we left."

In his report of his 10 March 1992 conversation with James Keough, Boston Police Detective Francis Armstrong wrote that Keough had said that members of the Shay family were divided about whether Tom Shay could have had a role in the bombing, and that it was likely he was in San Francisco from which he had called and mailed a postcard. Keough said that Mrs. Nancy Shay had disconnected her phone because she believed it had been wiretapped.

Meanwhile, from South Carolina Tom Shay had contacted his attorney, William McPhee, on 4 March and indicated that he wished to come home. McPhee then contacted the Suffolk County District Attorney's office to make arrangements, and also contacted AUSA Paul Kelly, who said that there were no Federal warrants yet, and Tom was not a "target."

Also on 10 March Boston Police detectives Brendan Craven and Francis Armstrong interviewed John Doering, the owner of the "Rolling Wrench" garage in South Boston. Beginning in February 1989, he had rented space to Thomas L. Shay and to his brother Arthur Shay for their respective auto body and repair shops. Before the morning of the 28 October 1991 explosion, Doering had not seen Mr. Thomas Shay for several weeks, but on that morning Shay came to ask Doering "if he had any idea what a wooden device with magnets and wires on it could be. John told Sr. [Thomas L. Shay] that they don't use wood on cars and to John this object sounded like a bomb. Sr. just laughed this off. When Sr. arrived at the shop at approximately 10:00 a.m. he was driving the black Buick, not a gray Mazda as Sr. has stated... John then advised Sr. to call the police. A call was made to a Mercury Lincoln dealer from the garage to reconfirm what John already knew. Brendan then asked John if he knew anything about magnets. John looked at a shelf [and] then stated that the only magnets he knew about were transmission magnets. This is similar to the statement Donna Shea made in her grand jury record that Todd Leach had used transmission magnets in the 1986 bombing.... Arthur Shay was also in the garage at the time of this interview and was interviewed directly afterwards." The interview with Arthur Shay is not available. He was known to have had more military experience than his brother and to be a better woodworker.

On 12 March, AUSA Paul Kelly returned to Judge Harrington with another request for a 30-day order for electronic surveillance, this time to capture Alfred's voicemails in addition to resuming the capturing of alpha-numeric messages. In support of the application, Special Agent Jeff Kerr wrote a 41 page "2d Affidavit," which repeated most of the first Affidavit, and also included his view of the two-fold motive for the 1991 Roslindale Bomb, which was for a share of the money that Mr. Thomas L. Shay would be receiving from his civil lawsuit, and in support of that goal, "...with or without Shay Sr.'s prior knowledge, the October, 1991 bomb was designed to frame Shay Sr.'s former landlords and thus to enhance Shay Sr.'s prospects for successfully resolving his lawsuit." That is, as Tom Shay's defense pointed out at his trial in 1993, Mr. Shay could gain leverage if it appeared that Jeffrey Berry and Louis Giammarco had planted a bomb, whether detonated or not, underneath Mr. Shay's car.

Such a motive could apply to Mr. Thomas A. Shay's participation in the bomb building and planting, too. In fact, the motive would be stronger for Mr. Thomas L. Shay because if he could win a $400,000 judgment or settlement, his share would be $266,000 after deducting the lawyer's 33% contingency fee. Obviously, the father would not need to share the award with the several children, as Thomas A. Shay would have to do, if he wasn't already completely disinherited as some members of the family thought had been done. However, the act of disinheriting requires a will and Mr. Shay has stated that he did not have one. Judge Harrington issued the order authorizing the expanded 30-day electronic surveillance on the same day.

The next day, Paul Kelly and Frank Libby jointly requested an order for a 60 day extension of the previously-acquired court orders for "pen registers" on the phones of John Cates, ARCOMM, and Thomas L. Shay's and Mary Flanagan's separate numbers at 39 Eastbourne Street. A pen register records the phone numbers of calls made to and from the designated phones and is installed at telephone company facilities. The order was granted by U.S. Magistrate Marianne Bowler and ordered sealed during the pending investigation.

Alfred Trenkler continued to try to make a living, after the demise of ARCOMM under the pressure of the Roslindale Bomb investigation and resulting swirl of suspicion and duplicity. Under the corporate name of ATNS - Advanced Telecommunications Network Systems, and operating out of the former ARCOMM office on Broad Street in Weymouth, Alfred Trenkler sent two proposals on 18 March 1992 to Ed Alvera of WFXT for installing 3.8 and 5.0 meter receiver-only dishes and for 7 meter receiver antenna for a total proposed billing of almost $26,000.

On 19 March, the grand jury heard from Thomas L. Shay and separately from his attorney in the Dedham Service Center case, Alan Pransky. Also appearing was John Coyle III, the former housemate of Alfred Trenkler, whose stereo had been wired as a prank by Alfred to broadcast Coyle's music to other radios in the house shared with John and Donna Shea. Jack Wallace was also there to testify and while he and John Coyle were talking outside the grand jury room, ATF Special Agent Jeff Kerr appeared and took John Coyle away with him for a "cup of coffee." There should be a rule prohibiting investigators from talking with grand jury witnesses in the courthouse or anywhere on the day of the witness's testimony.

On 20 March Mr. Thomas L. Shay called AUSA Paul Kelly, who, together with Special Agent Thomas D'Ambrosio, returned the call. Paul Kelly understood a basic rule for investigation-related conversations, which was to have a backup witness, or a recorder, and also to write followup reports. Mr. Shay sought to clarify his grand jury testimony of the previous day. He said that at Tom's request he had driven him to Russ Bonanno's in North Dartmouth after Tom's 13 September deposition in the civil suit against the Dedham Service Center and on the way Tom had told him, the father, that Mr. Shay's lawyer had said that winning the lawsuit might bring a lot of money.

Also on 20 March, ATF Special Agent Jeff Kerr went to the "U-Do-It-Electronics" store in Needham and showed several employees photographs. Several employees recognized Alfred Trenkler, as he had been a long time customer. Two employees recognized Tom Shay, but were not sure whether it was from their work at the store or other activities.

On 23 March, Frank Libby sent Judge Harrington the first 10-day report of the second electronic surveillance order: 50 alpha-numeric messages and 39 voicemail messages. He wrote, "**The results of this initial interception period have been somewhat disappointing as we have yet to uncover any message to the Target Pager Device providing any significant investigative lead or otherwise proving to be of evidentiary value.... most of the messages intercepted apparently had to do with legitimate business involving Alfred Trenkler...**" There were two exceptions to that summary. One message was from John Cates who called to ask for a ride from the Braintree MBTA station and the other was from Donna Shea requesting money allegedly owed to her. Trenkler felt that Shea was somehow seeking to obtain the reward money, or somehow otherwise to turn Trenkler's difficulties to her advantage.

The two subsequent 10-day reports, on 1 and 13 April failed to turn up any investigative leads, and the 30-day electronic surveillance order was allowed to lapse and Frank Libby said he would not seek another.

Tom Shay was in San Francisco using the name of "James Keough" and trying to earn a living as a beggar and a masseur. He had one of the accoutrements of any business which was an apparent waiver of liability form, which read, "*JAMES KEOUGH MASSAGE SERVICES, San Francisco, CA 415-719-6908. I _____ (client)[8] do hereby acknowledge that I have explained all back problems and consent to massage to be given by James Keough Massage Services (JKMS) and relieve JKMS of any and all liabilities....*" Tom Shay was not dumb, even if he was "*whaky*," to use a term used later by Judge Zobel.

In San Francisco, he befriended an author and comic strip writer, Fred Burke, and had several conversations with him. On 20 March, a Federal Warrant for Shay's arrest was obtained from U.S. Magistrate Joyce Alexander for "*unlawful flight to avoid prosecution.*" The next day, Special Agents Kerr and Leahy, and Boston detectives Brendan Craven and Francis Armstrong flew to San Francisco to find Tom Shay, and, assisted by San Francisco police, they went to the "Tenderloin" area of the city.

A local bartender, Scotty Schuenke, recognized a photo of Tom Shay early in the morning of 24 March, known locally as "James Keough," a male prostitute and masseur, and led the team to him at about 3:00 a.m. Schuenke approached

Shay/Keough and told him that a man with him, who was Special Agent Jeff Kerr, wanted to take Shay to his hotel room with him. This was a white lie. Shay climbed into the back of Kerr's car and told Schuenke that he had just returned from Reno where he had lost about $30,000 in the slot machines, but had just won $280. There was another white lie, about Kerr's alleged confusion about how to get back to his hotel, so the car was stopped and the three emerged. Kerr then put Shay under arrest, and was asked to get back into the unmarked car. When Shay refused, Jeff Kerr handcuffed him and asked Schuenke to call the San Francisco police for assistance, which arrived shortly, and Shay was taken to the San Francisco City Jail and later held on $5 million bond bail.

Shay was interviewed at 4:00 a.m. by Special Agent Dennis Leahy and Boston Police detective Brendan Craven. The ATF report by Dennis Leahy said, in part,

"... Shay also said that he met Trenkler 2 years ago, slept with him once and went to a party with him once and had been to his house once and that Trenkler's house was located in Quincy... Shay also said that he had been to Al's (Trenkler) work site once and watched him work, and that he thought it was in Cambridge. Shay, when asked if he knew that there was a Radio Shack across the street from where Al Trenkler worked said, 'so what there's one on Boylston Street too.' "

At 6:00 a.m. Shay asked if it was ok if he slept, and he did. Shay's account of his relationship to Alfred Trenkler differs from Trenkler's in five respects:
1) They met in June 1991 which was nine months previous rather than two years,
2) Trenkler did take him to his Quincy Apt for about 4 hours early one morning before taking him to a home on Richmond Street in Dorchester,
3) They had never been to a party together,
4) They had never "slept together," and
5) Trenkler had never taken Shay to any of his work sites.

On 25 March, Special Agent Jeff Kerr and Detective Brendan Craven went to Reno, Nevada to investigate Shay's activities there and Agent Leahy and Detective Armstrong located Fred Burke and seized Shay's belongings there.

Shortly thereafter, Tom Shay called Fred Burke from the San Francisco jail, and dictated to him the press release below:

25 March 1992
FOR IMMEDIATE RELEASE
TO: San Francisco News Editors
FROM: Thomas A. Shay, 20 years old
        case # 1363174
        San Francisco County Jail
I, Thomas A. Shay, the son of Thomas L. Shay, of 39 East Warren [sic] Street, Roslindale, Massachusetts am being held at the San Francisco County Jail at bail of over $5 million cash for a crime I did not commit. My story: On October 28, 1990 [sic], a phone call was made to the Back Bay Station, an Orange Line station in Boston, and a bomb threat was made. At that time I had just entered the station. I was arrested and let go five hours later, having not been charged with the bomb threat they were talking to me about.
On October 29, [sic] 1991, my father, Thomas L. Shay, drove up his driveway and felt a scrape under his car. Once parked, he went in back of his car to see what the

scrape was. He found a wrapped box of some kind and threw it to the side, thinking it was just a piece of trash. In the morning, he went to throw the package away, and he looked at it carefully. Deciding that it was wrapped in this certain way for a reason, he decided to call the police. When they did not arrive within the half hour, he borrowed a neighbor's car, drove it to the Boston police station in Roslindale, and asked officer Jeremiah Hurley and officer Francis X. Foley of the bomb squad to join him in going back to his house and looking at a package that he was suspicious about. On the way, he explained to the officers that he had moved the package three times between 8:00 p.m. on the 29th and 10:00 a.m. on the 30th.[sic]

Once the officers got there, they directed my father into the house so that they could go down and look at the package. A third officer arrived at the scene and was directed into the house by one of the officers. The third officer and my father were inside, when they heard an explosion outside the house. Hurley and Foley were going to touch the device and it blew up in their faces. The two officers were not wearing protective gear. That night, the Alcohol, Tobacco and Firearms division, the Boston Police Department, the bomb squad, the Federal Bureau of Investigation, and the Central Intelligence Agency came. Forty Federal investigators came from Washington, D.C. because they discovered that the bomb was so technically advanced that they wanted to investigate further. They went through the grass around the house with magnifying glasses.

I had heard what happened and called a press conference to clear my father's name of involvement with putting a bomb under his car. I told the newspeople that my family wanted to clear my father's name, that he had no involvement in any gambling or drugs, and that either a sicko put the bomb under the car or someone put it there at random. Certain things were printed in the newspaper about me - about my being gay, about my being on a local television show to talk about being gay. The federal investigators took my Boston address book and called up all my friends; parents and told them that their son or daughter might be gay. Two or three of my friends got kicked out of their houses because of this.

At this time, my father had a lawsuit with Deadham [sic] Service Center at 106 Washington Street in Deadham [sic] Massachusetts. I was also involved in the case at the Deadham [sic] Service Center as a witness to another explosion that had happened in which one of the workers threw a quarter stick of dynamite into a fifty gallon drum of thinner. The explosion made my father lose his hearing.

I was told to leave the city by Boston officials because my name is the same name as my father's. I left the city as I was told and went to a friend's house for the weekend. At the end of the weekend I came back and found that some other things had happened. Officer Hurley was dead. I went to the Boston Homicide division to talk to the officers and was grilled for over fifty minutes by the officers, who said that I had something to do with it. Then I was let go and went home, where I was arrested for the bomb threat of 1990. I did six months in the county jail and was let go on probation.

When the probation was over, I decided I didn't want to be in the city anymore and travelled [sic] to San Francisco about two months ago. I was trying to start a new life, beginning my own massage business and getting my life together. I had written a friend a postcard and forty federal investigators went sent to look for me. On the

23rd of this month I was arrested by two federal investigators and assaulted by one during questioning.

When I got to the San Francisco County Jail, I was told that I had a choice to either waive my rights and return to Boston or resist going back. Once I resisted, Governor Wells [sic, William Weld was the governor of Massachusetts at the time.] of Massachusetts was given ninety days to submit a warrant to Pete Wilson [governor of California] to extradite me back to Boston. The Federal officers told me that one of my friends, Al Trenkler of Boston, who builds satellites, was a suspect in building the bomb. I feel this is not true, and I know this is not true. They're only doing this because I made a big stink back in Boston and told the news that the Boston Police didn't know what they were doing because they weren't wearing protective gear to look at the device.

The truth of it is that they can't find the person who built the device and put it under my father's car, so they're trying to mess with me. Please help me from being extradited from San Francisco to Boston, because when I was in Boston I was treated unlawfully and beaten up. I am innocent and I am being held here against my will. The Federal investigators are refusing to give me a lie detector or polygraph test. As I sit here in this jail, I get depressed more and more each day. If there are any good lawyers out there or anybody that that you think can help me, please come visit. Positive ID is required to get in to the jail. I am here at the San Francisco County Jail under the name of Thomas A. Shay, case #1363174.

Dictated by telephone to Fred Burke, (415) 864-2978.

Back in Boston, Tom Shay's attorney said to the _Boston Globe_ that his client had been subpoenaed to appear before the grand jury, but that he was not a "target" of the inquiry. Said William McPhee, "... _I don't believe he will be indicted for the bombing._" However the _Boston Herald_ article about Shay's San Francisco arrest said that "_Shay has emerged as a suspect in the blast and is believed to have had at least one accomplice, according to sources._"

In a followup _Boston Herald_ article, McPhee said that Tom Shay had told the police all he knew in interviews the previous fall. When the reporter asked McPhee if Tom Shay would cooperate further with the investigation, presumably including grand jury testimony, Atty. McPhee replied, "_Currently, since they're taking such an interest in him, as a subject or target... it wouldn't make sense for him to cooperate unless we got assurances they weren't going to prosecute him._" The related article in the Quincy _Patriot Ledger_ said, "_But until he_ [McPhee] _can determine whether authorities think Shay is responsible for the bomb blast, McPhee has advised his client not to speak with officials. If he is a target in the probe, McPhee said Shay may refuse to cooperate and invoke his Fifth Amendment right not to incriminate himself. 'He will do what is in his best interests,' McPhee said._"

Again, the pursuit of truth became secondary to the ability to procedurally block it out of concern that something offered during such cooperating would come back to hurt. Alfred Trenkler's efforts to cooperate had that result as they were either misinterpreted or misunderstood.

On 26 March Special Agent Dennis Leahy and Boston Detective Francis Armstrong interviewed Fred Burke. Leahy's report described Burke's brief acquaintance with Tom Shay, but did not mention the previous day's press release. Back in Boston on the same day, Randy Stoller and Edward Carrion testified before the grand jury. A year later, in a 17 March letter to Nancy Gertner, Terry Segal wrote that "*my information is that much of the grand jury time was spent exploring the gay issue...*"

The press release was sent to the Boston newspapers and for the first time, Alfred Trenkler was publicly named as a person of interest. Before the investigators told Tom Shay that they had taken the names from his address book, and that Alfred Trenkler had detonated the M21 Hoffman simulator in 1986, Tom Shay hadn't said a word to anyone about Alfred Trenkler being involved. Even in the press release, Tom Shay said about Alfred Trenkler, "*The Federal officers told me that one of my friends, Al Trenkler of Boston, who builds satellites, was a suspect in building the bomb. I feel this is not true, and I know this is not true.*"

However, if Alfred Trenkler was involved, despite Tom Shay's lack of knowledge about such involvement, then Tom would no longer be part of the story, so he gradually spun himself and Alfred Trenkler into it. Unfortunately, his web was so complex and so tight that the jury believed he must have been involved, and Alfred Trenkler, too.

For the *Boston Herald*, for its story on 28 March, "*SUSPECT: FEDS THINK BUDDY BUILT DEATH BOMB,*" Tom Shay was interviewed by phone from the San Francisco Jail. He maintained his position regarding his role, "*I had nothing to do with the bombing in Roslindale,*" and "*I don't go out and try to kill people.*" However, the confidence that his acquaintance Al Trenkler had nothing to do with it now became a softer statement, "*I couldn't tell if he did or he didn't because I don't know.*" Regarding his relationship with Alfred Trenkler, he began with a minimization of the truth, "*I met Trenkler twice,*" he said, which is four fewer than the number of times Alfred Trenkler recalls (4 rides in June and 1 in July and 1 accidental encounter in August). Then Shay said, "*I've known him a couple of years and I've gone out with him twice.*" The article briefly described the dismissed charges against Trenkler arising from the 1986 Quincy incident.

Perhaps because his father wouldn't talk with Tom after the bombing, and because he was now talking with the police more than he was talking with Tom, Tom was turned, or was turning, against his father, too. He said to the *Boston Herald* reporter, Shelley Murphy, "*The hell with my father because he thinks I actually went out and tried to kill him, that's what the police told me. The hell with him. I'm looking out for my own ass now.*"

In his phone call with Ms. Murphy, which he initiated, Tom Shay "*claimed investigators offered him a deal in exchange for his cooperation. He claimed they told him he'd only have to serve 10 years in prison if he cooperated against the person who built the bomb and that killed Hurley. But Shay claimed he rejected the alleged offer because, 'I did not do the crime and I will not admit to something I didn't do.'*" To that claim, AUSA Paul Kelly, "*branded Shay's claims about a deal 'absolutely outrageous. There have been no deals or propositions offered to anybody in connection with this investigation.'*" Kelly's outrage seems a bit exaggerated, as he did try thereafter several times to make such a deal with Tom Shay.

Shay told Ms. Murphy that he had offered to take a lie detector test and he self-infected the "Princess Diana Blame Disease" when he "*insisted police began targeting him because 'I made a big stink back in Boston and told the news that the Boston Police didn't know what they were doing because they weren't wearing protective gear to look at the device.*' " It's one thing to fend for one's innocence, but it's another to spur anger among the police, as such a statement was sure to do. Tom Shay rarely calibrated the expected reactions to what he said.

The headline of John Ellement's 1 April 1992 *Boston Globe* story, "*QUINCY MAN MADE BOMB, SHAY SAYS,*" was worse than the story. The article did not name Alfred Trenkler, although Shay gave Trenkler's name to John Ellement, who wrote that he was not able to reach the unnamed man nor his attorney for comment. Element wrote, "*In the interview, Shay identified the man by name describing him as a 'friend of mine for a couple of years . . . He builds satellites and he's the only high-tech guy in my phone book.'* "

The *Herald*'s Shelley Murphy said that Alfred Trenkler, by name, could not be reached for comment, and the *Globe*'s Ellement said the same thing, without naming Trenkler. Unfortunately, this probably meant that Alfred Trenkler was taking his new lawyer's advice not to talk to the press - which made it look like he had something to hide. Instead, he would have been far better off if he had at least said what he said to television reporter Charles Austin the following December, "*I am an innocent man. I had nothing to do with this case.*" Even better would have been a short statement along the lines of:

1. I barely know Tom Shay, having met him in June 1991, with the extent of my acquaintance being that I gave him five rides in my car to his requested destinations.
2. I haven't seen Tom Shay since August 1991.
3. I've never met Tom Shay's father and don't know where he lives and have never been there.
4. I know nothing more about Tom Shay's family relationships other than he spent much of his childhood in state-sponsored institutions.
5. I was involved in a prank gone too far in Quincy in 1986 when I detonated an Army noise simulator as a favor for a friend. It was a stupid thing to do, and, fortunately, it caused no damage to a person nor to the truck. The charges were dismissed the next year at the Quincy District Court.

In short, Alfred Trenkler needed a "Tylenol Public Relations Strategy," so named after Johnson & Johnson's successful efforts to rebound from a number of contaminated Tylenol containers in 1982. One difficulty with not making a public statement was that Alfred Trenkler was stuck with the ATF's versions of his non-public statements to them. Thus, by the time of his trial the ATF could claim that his statements to them were inconsistent and therefore not worthy of belief. If Alfred had made more public statements, assuming they were consistent, the ATF could not have pinned that label of inconsistency on him. It was especially harmful because Trenkler chose not to testify at his trial, where he could have clarified any of those alleged inconsistencies.

Since his scheduled grand jury testimony in February, James Harding had sought to negotiate with the U.S. Attorney's office about the tape recordings he and Donna Shea made in November/December 1991. On 1 April 1992, AUSA Frank Libby wrote a "memorandum to File" summarizing, even before hearing the tape, Harding's statements about the four recorded conversations with Alfred Trenkler.

The first was in an alley just outside the ARCOMM office in November where Donna Shea, Harding and Alfred Trenkler discussed the 1986 Quincy incident. The second was at Donna Shea's home where Harding and Shea tried to get Trenkler to admit a role in the 1991 Roslindale Bombing, with Harding saying, "Cut the shit, Al, what really happened?" Harding told Libby that he advised Trenkler to "cut a deal, but wait until you get indicted." The third recording, at an unknown location, was not noted further by Libby. The fourth was on Boylston St. in Boston while Alfred was waiting to pick up John Cates at work. There was discussion of Tom Shay and his assumed flight to San Francisco, and unsubstantiated allegations that Mr. Thomas L. Shay was somehow "Mob connected," and that the Dedham Service Center was a front for illegal drug dealing. Libby had either not yet heard the untranscribed tapes, or he chose not to comment on them.

Like several of Alfred Trenkler's friends, Harding and Shea seemed to be convinced of Trenkler's role in the Roslindale Bombing because of their awe of his electronics abilities. The lure of the reward money apparently led them to attempt to be self-appointed undercover agents.

In court on 1 April 1992, Paul Kelly sought a secret court order to install a beeper on Alfred Trenkler's 1978 Toyota Celica because there was "probable cause to believe that Alfred Trenkler uses and will continue to use the subject vehicle as a means to travel to various locations and meet with unidentified co-conspirators, or to take other actions to conceal his involvement in the above-described offenses" i.e. building and placing the Roslindale Bomb. The application was supported by a four-page Affidavit by ATF Special Agent Thomas D'Ambrosio who summarized the reasons for probable cause. Interestingly, he was more cautious about Alfred Trenkler's relationship to Tom Shay, saying that the two were acquainted and that Tom Shay "may have had a sexual relationship with" Trenkler. Once the idea had been planted, and in the absence of strong denials by Alfred Trenkler, the false story of their sexual relationship grew. U.S. Magistrate Robert Collins approved the 30-day order. The beeper allowed investigators to constantly track the whereabouts of Trenkler's car.

Also on 1 April, Boston officers Tom Pratt and Kevin Pumphret escorted Tom Shay back to Boston by plane. At the airport, they were met by members of ATF and the press to whom Shay spoke, "*I have come back to Boston to deal with my problems...I want to start off by saying, I am not guilty of any crimes that took place in the dealing with the Roslindale Bomb blast that killed Officer Jeremiah Hurley and injured Officer Francis X. Foley. When I gave my first press conference I was looking out for my family. Now I am looking out for myself. I will take a lie detector, polygraph, anything, to prove I had nothing to do with the bombing. The only thing I'm guilty of is trying to protect my family. Right after it happened, I thought . . . [trails off], A lot of things went through my mind...I've already had a hard life... My life is pretty screwed up...*" Reported Pratt about the trip into Boston, "Shay seemed very excited in the wagon, he was happy about all of the media that came and met him. He told the officers that it wasn't one of his better interviews."

The *Boston Globe*'s 2 April story by John Ellement about Shay's return was headlined, "*SHAY DENIES ROLE IN FATAL BOMBING*" said, "*Shay's allusion to not having any ties to anyone suspected of involvement was an apparent reference to a Quincy man Shay implicated earlier this week.*" However, Tom Shay did not implicate Trenkler, at least not yet. In fact, in his written press release from the San Francisco Jail, he said he didn't believe Trenkler had any role.

That same day, 2 April, there was a bail hearing in Boston Municipal court before judge Timothy Gailey, and bail was set at $100,000, according to ATF Special Agent Dennis Leahy. Tom Shay was represented by Attorney William McPhee.

In Shelley Murphy's 3 April _Boston Herald_ article, "*BOMB SUSPECT'S MOM SAYS 'HE'S SCAPEGOAT,'* " Mrs. Nancy Shay stated, "*'They're saying Tommy didn't like his father, he had a motive to do this and he knows sickos because he's gay,' said Nancy Shay, 47 of Quincy. 'They're trying to make a case.'* " Her comments seemed remarkably prescient and accurate. The article also named Alfred Trenkler again, and cited his role in the 1986 Quincy incident.

Tom Shay was sent to the Suffolk County Jail on Nashua Street in Boston where he wrote to Randy Stoller. "*Hello Randy, How are you doing! I hope that business is doing well for you. I'm back in Boston. I guess you know that by now. I was on the news, for a couple of days when I got back. I have a phone number of a cute boy in S.F. for you.....His name is Fred Burke... Please come visit me. I'm at the Nashua Street Jail...* "

On Sunday, 5 April, another inmate, Mark Means, wrote a "*To Whomever It May Concern*" note to the guards that he had an argument with Tom Shay and that Shay said he would retaliate against him. Soon, he saw Tom Shay on the telephone making a call and later standing by the phone which was ringing. When Shay did not answer it, Means picked it up, and it was the telephone operator stating that a bomb threat had been made from that phone and that the police would be coming. Later, Tom Shay was moved to the psychiatric ward of the jail.

On Monday, 6 April 1992, Shay wrote a note to his jailers, in general, "*To the Officer IN Charge I want to use a telephone to call Frank Armstrong of the Boston Homicide div. to tell him the whereabouts of the man who built the bomb that killed Officer Jeremiah Hurley on Oct. 28, 1991. Now, PLEASE !!! If not... If you don't submit this letter to your proper and higher rank, just leave your names on this paper and #'s, and Return this Please. If you Don't you will find your names as part of a Hate crime involving the Investigators or the ATF, Boston Homicide, FBI, Local and State and Federal. Investigation of violating civil liberties and Rights of a telephone in an Investigation of the Bombing. PS (!?)*"

The two Boston newspapers published the story on Tuesday, 7 April. The _Boston Herald_'s L. Kim Tan, wrote in the story, "*JAILED SUSPECT EYED IN NEW BOMB THREAT*," that a 20 year-old woman in Brighton had received a call on Sunday that there was a bomb in her apartment. The woman had no known connection to Tom Shay and the police thought the collect call (but unaccepted) went to her through Shay's dialing of random numbers.

In the _Boston Globe_'s 7 April article, "*POLICE SAY THREAT PHONED FROM JAIL*," the Suffolk County Jail spokesperson, Gerard Lydon, said the Boston police were investigating the call which occurred when Tom Shay was logged in as using a pay phone at the jail.

On 8 April Detective Fogerty wrote the following "Note to File, *On Wednesday, April 8, 1992 Detective Fogerty received a telephone call from Thomas Shay, Junior. Shay asked to speak with Detective Armstrong and was informed that Detective Armstrong was not in the office. Shay stated that Detective Armstrong was supposed to be in Court with him today.*

Shay asked me to tell for (?) Detective Armstrong to have Detective Armstrong come visit him in the jail tomorrow, April 9, 1992. The call was received at 4:15 p.m."

On 9 April, Radio Shack employee Dwayne Armbrister appeared before the grand jury, as did David Millette and Patricia O'Donoughue, friends of Alfred Trenkler.

On 13 April, Detective Brendan Craven served a grand jury subpoena on Thomas Thomson, "a member of the gay community," and a friend of Alfred Trenkler. Thomson told Craven that Trenkler sometimes set off M-80 firecrackers in the Fenway Gardens area and Thomson wasn't happy with it. Craven's report contrasts with Alfred's work with Thomson on radio support for the "Neighborhood Watch" program. Alfred wrote in 2007 of the one incident that Thomson referenced, "*I believe it was 1986 or 87 when John and Donna Shea had brought Bob Craig and I out to eat at the Sun Tuey Chinese restaurant on Cambridge Street in Boston. We left and Donna wanted to get some laughs at the Victory Gardens* [an area of privately maintained garden plots in Back Bay]. *John and Donna typically go to their vacation campground in Ossipee, New Hampshire owned by the Knight family. On the way back to Weymouth, Mass. they would usually stop at the fireworks store and make their purchases. Evidently, they had recently been to New Hampshire because soon after arriving* [at the Victory Gardens area] *John pulled out either a cherry bomb or an M-80 and set it off to scare a crowd of people. After a few of these were set off my friend Tom Thomson came by, upset at all the noise. He wanted me to get John to stop, a request I made, but John being John, stop means do some more. This was a one-time occurrence on one night and out of my control. Contrary to the implications, I was not 'into' fireworks; fun to look at. but that's pretty much* [all] *of my participation."*

On 15 April, A. John Pappalardo became the new U.S. Attorney for Massachusetts, replacing Wayne Budd, who had served since 1989. The change made no known difference to the ongoing investigation of the Roslindale Bombing.

END NOTES

1. William Paley, *The Principles of Moral and Political Philosophy.*
2. Also called BATF, as in Bureau of Alcohol, Tobacco and Firearms. From its inception in the Revenue Dept in 1920 until absorbed into the Dept. of Homeland Security in 2003, the ATF was part of the U.S. Treasury. For an ATF history, see *Very Special Agents - The Inside Story of America's Most Controversial Law Enforcement Agency–The Bureau of Alcohol, Tobacco, and Firearms*, by James Moore, University of Illinois Press, 2001.
3. Thomas Waskom would testify at the trials that there were likely no "sticks of dynamite" in the bomb, but rather an amount of ammonia dynamite wrapped in a page of a magazine and tape. The two or three blasting caps or detonators were likely placed inside the block of dynamite.
4. It's believed that no reward money was ever paid to an applicant. Two phone calls placed to the Boston Police Department about the specific "Roslindale Bomb" reward resulted in promises for a returned call, but none came.
5. Philip H. Suter, was the son of Philip Suter, who married Josephine Johnson Barnum, the mother of Josephine Barnum Trenkler Wallace. Thus Philip H. Suter was the stepbrother of Josephine Wallace, and the stepuncle of Alfred Trenkler. The highlight of Mr. Suter's civic career was to organize, as the Chair of the Concord, Mass. Board of Selectmen, the town's U.S. bicentennial celebration in 1976, where he introduced President Gerald Ford. He graduated from Milton Academy and Harvard Law School, and was a partner for 40 years at the Boston law firm of Sullivan and Worcester.

6. The version given to the jury in the Thomas A. Shay trial was, "He said, 'What are you crazy after what had happened.' " (TS 11-146) At the Alfred Trenkler trial, Evans said almost the same words, "...he said to me, 'what are you crazy after what happened.' " (TT 8-118) Both statements under oath at trials differ from Agent D'Ambrosio's affidavit, especially from the phrase, "after what I tried to do to him."

7. In a June 2007 letter to the author, Alfred Trenkler wrote, "Contrary to Dennis Leahy of the ATF, I did not say I thought the son hated the father. I said the son told me the father was embarrassed to have the son around because of his son's recent "coming out" appearance on Tom Bergeron's "People are Talking" program in 1990.

8. The copy viewed for this book seems to have been collected by someone with a sense of humor because the names, "Paul Kelly & Frank Libby" are typed on the "Client" line.

CHAPTER 3: U.S. ATTORNEY, GRAND JURY AND PRE-INDICTMENT (17 APRIL 1992 TO 15 DECEMBER 1992)

> *"Unless a man feels he has a good enough memory, he should never venture to lie."* Montaigne[1]

"... at approximately 4:15 p.m. Alfred Trenkler was arrested, without incident, on Bolyston Street in Boston by ATF agents and the Boston Police, Trenkler was arrested on an outstanding Rhode Island warrant for larceny over $1000....and held at the Boston Police Area D4 lockup...." So wrote Special Agent Sandra LaCourse in her report of Alfred Trenkler's arrest on 17 April. What she didn't report was that it was on a Friday afternoon before a Massachusetts long weekend, due to the Patriots' Day holiday, which made a longer stay in jail more likely.

Alfred Trenkler wrote of that same arrest,

"On 17 April 1992, Friday, I was on Boylston Street, Boston on the way to pick up my roommate, John Cates at the Fleet Bank where he worked. At the stoplight just before the Fleet Bank I was surrounded by ATF agents and Boston Police. I was transported to Area D in the South End of Boston. In the Booking Room I asked what I was being arrested for but was not told. ATF Special Agent Dennis Leahy said, 'You know what this is about?' I said, 'No, I'm waiting for you to tell me.' Leahy then said, 'I hope you've got your life together, you're about to spend the rest of your life in prison.' I said, 'What happened to 'We don't convict innocent people?' ' Leahy just laughed and said, 'Al, if you feel like talking to me just tell one of these cops. I'll be around all weekend.'

When I finally got to call my attorney, Terry Segal, he told me that I had been arrested because of some bounced check from 1988 or 1989 to a steel company in Rhode Island which turned out to have been a banking error.

I was kept in a cell at the Area D lockup. My jacket was taken. My shoes were taken and there was no mattress, only a metal bed. The back door was left open to make it nice and cold. I was fed a cold McDonald's cheeseburger that night, [and] for breakfast, lunch and dinner on Saturday and breakfast on Sunday.

For company, Saturday they planted a middle aged man posing as a drunk in my cell. A one man cell, although there were plenty of empty cells. The man asked why I was locked up. I told him because of a bounced check. He asked what else and I said that's all. He kept asking what else they had on me and that he could not believe I was locked up for a bounced check. He went on to say I could talk to him because he was some drunk that no one listens to. I told him to go to sleep and that I didn't feel like talking. Thank the stars I had taken transcendental meditation. I meditated on and off the rest of the time there.

I had been denied bail because the Feds lied to the state judge and said I had multiple arrest warrants and was a flight risk. My attorney found a judge that discovered the fabrication and allowed my bail on Sunday.

Normally, Alfred would have been released on bond or cash bail on Friday afternoon, but the prosecution claimed, according to Alfred, that Alfred had multiple charges pending and that he was a flight risk, which forced Alfred's lawyers to work harder.

He learned Transcendental Meditation at the Hingham, Mass. center in the mid-1970's with his friend, Kurt Ochs. Then, it was a one to three month course. The author learned TM in the mid-1970's too, but that was just a coincidence.

The Saturday 18 April newspapers covered the arrest, but relied upon unnamed sources for their stories and neither reporter was able to obtain a comment or statement from Alfred Trenkler or his lawyer. The _Globe_'s story, "*POLICE HOLD SUSPECT IN FATAL BOMBING*," by John Ellement, continued his restrained unwillingness to name the "*Milton man*" who was jailed. It was Alfred Trenkler, who, according to the Saturday story as written on Friday, "*was expected to remain in custody over the weekend.*" The story reviewed the status of the case, including Tom Shay's expected commitment to Bridgewater State Hospital for a mental health evaluation. His lawyer, "*William C. McPhee also said his client, Thomas A. Shay, has been found to have a history of 'slight mental retardation.' McPhee further said Shay had an extra Y chromosome, one more than normal.... McPhee said Shay has ignored his orders not to speak with reporters or investigators regarding the homicide case and apparently lacks an understanding of the serious legal problems he faces... McPhee noted that his client has a 13-year history of psychological difficulties and that he has spent most of his adult life in some form of institutional care.*" Interviewed by Ellement, Tom Shay said that he had called AUSA Paul Kelly earlier in the week.

The _Boston Herald_'s 18 April 1992 article by Shelley Murphy, "*MAN IN BOMB PROBE ARRESTED FOR LARCENY,*" again directly named Alfred Trenkler as the new suspect in the Roslindale Bomb case, and as the man arrested on Friday by Boston Detective Brendan Craven, with ATF Special Agents present. Murphy then wrote that Tom Shay, in an apparent defense of Trenkler, "*accused investigators of targeting Trenkler because his name was in Shay's address book and he's mechanically inclined.*" The article continued, "*This week, the younger Shay told the Herald that he had a 'gut feeling' his father planted the bomb in a bid to make it appear the owners of a Dedham service station were trying to kill him. The elder Shay is suing the men for $400,000. 'I had nothing to do with it.' said the younger Shay. 'My father says it was me and I say it was my father.' The elder Shay declined to comment on his son's charges but his lawyer, Alan J. Pransky said, 'It is totally crazy that the father would do this to himself. This happens to be false allegations from the son. This is the third time he has announced he solved the crime.'*"

Alfred's high profile arrest was unusual, as it is rare that a person owing money to a Rhode Island corporation would be arrested and jailed in another state by a metropolitan city's police. Of course, even though a city policeman made the arrest, it was the Bureau of Alcohol, Tobacco and Firearms that was driving the case. A Suffolk County Assistant District Attorney essentially represented the State of Rhode Island in the Boston Municipal Court, as the case morphed into a fugitive-from-justice case.

What was the intended message of this extraordinary effort by ATF? One possibility was to entice Alfred Trenkler into admitting his role in the Roslindale

Bomb to another inmate, hence the placement of the purported drunk in Alfred's call. Even then, with only one day of jail time in his life, Alfred Trenkler sensed the purpose of his unusual cellmate.

The background of the Rhode Island civil case was that 2 1/2 years previously, in September 1988, Alfred's former company, AWT Associates, paid Rusco Steel of Warwick, Rhode Island $1,349.38 for steel used to build a tower for a micro-wave antenna. However the check was returned due to insufficient funds due to a mistake by Alfred's bank. Rusco Steel attemped to resolve the matter with a certified letter to Trenkler sent to his parents' home in Milton, but the letter was not accepted. The company pursued the claim in the Rhode Island courts but failed to collect. Alfred Trenkler was unaware of those efforts. Somehow the claim came to the attention of the ATF and the Rhode Island Attorney General. All for $1,349.38. It cost more than that to arrest, jail and bail Alfred Trenkler.

Also in ATF Special Agent Sandra LaCourse's report on 17 April was a summary of Tom Shay's appearance in Boston Municipal Court with his attorney, Bill McPhee. One charge was for the alleged phoned bomb threat to the Back Bay MBTA station in November 1990. The second charge was for a threat allegedly made from the Suffolk County Jail to a Brighton woman on 5 April 1992. There was also the pending charge for "streetwalking" in 1990. Judge Anthony Sullivan scheduled a competency hearing for 22 April, and a probable cause hearing for 27 April. Shay remained in jail as his mother could not make the $10,000 cash bail. In practical terms, that means exactly that - $10,000 in cash to the court or $100,000 through a bail bondsman. The bail was likely high because of the pending Federal investigation and because of Shay's previous flight to California.

On Sunday, 18 April 1992, Tom Shay wrote to William McPhee. According to a summary prepared later, Shay wrote, "...*please don't use mental illness as a defense, I am as sane as you are, use that in 13 years of being in schools & institutions, I have never done anything violent, I didn't do this or get a bomb from someone else. It is time for you and I to have a press conference, you have put it off for five weeks, I have lost every friend I had. Set up a news conference on national TV, New York Times, every press agency in New England, Hard Copy, Current Affair, 20/20, 60 minutes. My family thinks I won't be indicted because I was with friends or them from Thursday night until Monday morning [24-28 October 1991]. Had no knowledge bomb going to be there.*"

On Tuesday, 20 April, AUSA Paul Kelly wrote a letter to William McPhee, to advise that his client, Tom Shay, had called Kelly on 10 April and 15 April. Kelly cautioned Shay about any such call without his lawyer, and Shay was alleged to have asked Kelly not to tell Shay's lawyer that Shay had called. Shay said that he was unhappy with McPhee because Shay claimed McPhee wasn't accepting his calls. Not coincidentally, at the end of Kelly's letter he asked McPhee to advise Tom Shay that Kelly would no longer be taking his calls. There were no self-incriminating statements made during the short call, Kelly said. However, "During the first call, he read me a short letter (which he had apparently written to me) in which he claimed his father was responsible for the Roslindale Bombing that killed Officer Hurley. During his second call he read me a letter which he has written to his father, blaming him for the bombing." (Frank Libby said in a pre-trial hearing on 29 September 1993 that the purported letter to Paul Kelly was never received). (TSH 4-6)

Kelly said that he had advised Shay not to call him again.

The letter to Shay's father is below:

Dear Dad:

I am so depressed. I really dont know where I should start. I loved you dad. Before you could say that I could do something as horrible as you said that you thought I did. I am a boy that has had problems all his life, and now you tell the police that you think I did this to you. You are a fucking asshole. You were never a great father, not one I would give a trophy to. But of all the senseless things you could say about me. I have already been put through 13 years of bullshit. This is the last letter or anything you will ever have from me. ever. I want to let you know that either way it goes, you will lose. I am going on the Federal witness protection plan. All of your South End buddies I have all written to. The list of [names omitted], *are just a couple of the 60 names on the list and of pictures including yourself. For illegal tax avation* [sic, evasion], *gambling, bar running, drug smuggling, bribery and exstortion. The Feds are tapping your phone, all of your fiance's phones. Video tapping your house. The Waltham Tavern.[2] The Franklin Cafe. Both gambling houses in the South End. The one in J.P.* [Jamaica Plain], *Castle Island 5 in Southie* [South Boston], *2 in the North End. Your friends will do one of 3 things to you. The Feds expect it. Kill you. Mark you as a rat, or make your life very fucking hard.*

I dont care what they do to you. I stuck up for you in the beginning. I put my neck out for you. But now I'm looking out for #1 me, and I have come clean. They know about your German Lugar [sic, Luger, a well-known German pistol]. *Give that up and exspect a $5,000.00 fine. They know about all of the stuff you have. In the voltall* [sic] *Station in Milton. all the shotguns that are unlicensed. Don't try to get rid of them. Give them up. I have taken 5 lie detector tests and pasted* [sic, passed] *all of them. I hate to say it, but, well good luck Pops. The word from the Peters side of the family is Jeanie, Amy, Paula, Nancy, myself and Mother don't want to ever have anything to do with you ever again. As I write my last words I shed a tear. Your son Tom Peters. 'xoed'*

PS. The Feds know about everything. They know that when your life gets hard that you will have a press conference and start to tell the truth and say that you know the guys that did this or you did or and I did not. ByBy Pops."

The letter can be interpreted as supporting Tom Shay's guilt or innocence, but it's hard to believe that a person who knew about the bomb, and who conspired to have it built and placed, could have written such a letter with such indignation, because his own father thought he might have tried to kill him. Why not interpret the letter as Tom Shay apparently intended it? In legal terms, why not in the "*light most favorable to the defendant.*" There's Thomas A. Shay, who lived away from home for most of his youth, finally getting closer to his natural father, as sometimes happens when wayward boys emerge from adolescence and testosterone poisoning. And what happens? His father is the target of a bomb and then publicly states that he believes that his son may have tried to kill him? That straw appears to have broken Tom Shay's weak psychological back.

On Thursday, 22 April Alfred Trenkler appeared in Boston Municipal Court on the Rhode Island charge and was ordered to pay Rusco Steel. The next day a certified check for the owed amount was hand delivered to the Office of the Rhode Island Attorney General by Alfred and his stepfather, Jack Wallace. The same day, the Rhode Island Attorney General's office asked a Rhode Island court to dismiss the "*above entitled matter under Rule 48 (a) Rules of Criminal Procedure*" because Trenkler had made "*full restitution*" and [the] *president of the Rusco Steel Company was "extremely satisfied with receiving his money.*"

While the Roslindale Bomb case was not related to the Rhode Island case, Trenkler's attorney, Terry Segal, did comment strongly outside the courtroom, according to Shelley Murphy of the _Boston Herald_, in her 23 April article, "*My client maintains he is completely innocent in that matter, which was a terrible tragedy.*"[3] Alfred Trenkler was asked directly by a reporter if Tom Shay was his friend and Trenkler said "*No,*" and declined to make further comments, as he was advised by Terry Segal. Alfred's recollection in 2007 was that this was only the second time that reporters had directly asked him a question.

John Ellement's 23 April story in the _Boston Globe_ captured the key phrase of Terry Segal's statement, as quoted above, as "*perfectly innocent,*" as compared to Shelley Murphy's capturing of "*completely innocent,*" and that is the source of the title of this book. Beyond his statement, Segal declined to answer further questions about Trenkler's relationship to Tom Shay. In the article, unnamed sources said that the bomb "*was either remotely detonated, triggered inadvertently by the officers, or detonated by random radio or microwaves that afternoon.*" Thus, there would never be a charge that Trenkler or anyone deliberately detonated the bomb when the Bomb Squad offers were inspecting it with the deliberate intent of killing or harming them.

At the competency hearing on 22 April, despite the 1989 finding of competence by the doctor at Bridgewater State Hospital, Atty. McPhee argued that Shay was not competent to stand trial for the two bomb threat charges. A court psychologist stated that Shay was competent, and the probable cause hearing remained scheduled for the following Monday, 27 April.

On 23 April, appearing before the grand jury were James Harding, Nancy Shay, mother of Tom Shay, and Andrew Robinson, a friend of Alfred Trenkler. Robinson had helped Trenkler and his roommate in the early 1980's paint their house and was a social friend, too. Robinson and his parents moved to Florida in the mid-1980's and Alfred kept in touch with him. In 1990, Alfred traveled to Florida for a vacation and interviewed for a job there, and it was from that interview that Alfred learned about the Christian Science antenna project back in Boston. Robinson did not testify at Alfred's trial.

On 27 April Paul Kelly wrote a "Memorandum to File" with subject: "Shay Jr. Telephone Calls to Shelley Murphy of Boston Herald.

On Thursday, April 23rd, Shay Jr. called Shelley Murphy and asked her two questions:

1. 'What would happen if Trenkler says I did it and the Feds believe him?'

2. 'What would happen if the Feds think Trenkler built the bomb, but they also think that I'm involved?'

According to Shelley, Shay Jr. was nervous, somewhat emotional and unsure of himself when asking these questions. Shay Jr. is usually more manipulative and self-assured when talking with Shelley.

On Friday, April 24th, Shay Jr. again called Shelley Murphy and told her that he had received a written communication from Trenkler (via a third-party) in which Trenkler allegedly states that he is very upset by the investigation, and that he will 'be there' for Shay Jr. Shay Jr. then asked Shelley if she would print a public apology from him to Trenkler (for his having included Trenkler's name in his press release). In his written apology Shay Jr. apparently claims he was 'set-up' by Detective Frank Armstrong who told him (Shay Jr.) that Trenkler had 'fingered him'. Shay Jr. goes on to state that he had met Trenkler only twice, both times in 1991: once at the Ramrod Lounge (in May) and once at Copley Place (in Sept/Oct.) At the end of the letter, Shay Jr. writes 'p.s. - Dad, I know you had some involvement in the bombing, so give it up.' Shelley reports that Shay Jr. was much more protective of Trenkler during this call than at any time previously, and that he repeatedly said that Trenkler was a 'good guy'.

For what it's worth, from her many conversations with Shay Jr., Shelley believes (1) that he's definitely involved and (2) that there is 'something there' with Trenkler."

In this era of sensitivity of press-government relations, after the I. Lewis Libby trial and conviction, it's interesting to see how the press can affect a criminal prosecution. Regarding the content, Alfred Trenkler has never written any letter to Tom Shay, and thus never sent any letter to him when he was in jail. Shelley Murphy never talked with Alfred Trenkler for his side of any story she wrote about him, which contrasts with her apparently close contacts with Paul Kelly. It's likely that she attempted to reach Trenkler, but was advised by Terry Segal not to do so. There is a practical reason for that disparity, too, as Shelley Murphy would need Paul Kelly as a source for her reporting long after the Alfred Trenkler case was gone.

Also on 27 April, William McPhee wrote to Tom Shay to urge him not to call Paul Kelly nor the media; and told him that he would withdraw as his counsel if he didn't take his advice. It was like telling the moth to stay away from the candle.

As for the places that Tom Shay and Alfred Trenkler had met, it's encouraging that Shay said it was only two times, but one of them was definitely not the Ramrod Club. The fifth ride that Alfred Trenkler gave to Tom Shay was from the Copley Place area to John Cates' bank - a distance of a few hundred yards, and driving that distance did not give much time for a relationship.

The letter to Mr. Thomas L. Shay that Kelly's memo referenced was never received, and the previously mentioned "*Dear Dad*" letter did not have such a quote. It made sense that Shay was protective of Alfred Trenkler, because as far as Shay knew, Alfred Trenkler had nothing to do with the Roslindale Bombing. Shay probably felt badly that Alfred Trenkler's acquaintance with him, which involved only a few car rides, had led to so much trouble for Trenkler through no fault of his own. Of course, as Trenkler was a "target" and represented by a lawyer, he couldn't just pen a letter and tell Shay that he wasn't involved, or visit him at the jail either. For several reasons Alfred Trenkler sought to keep his distance from Tom Shay.

Tom Shay's request to Shelley Murphy for help in publishing a public apology to Alfred Trenkler is instructive. As with his accusation of Ralph Pace at the 31 October 1991 press conference, he sought the press's help in getting a communication to someone when a simple letter or phone call would have sufficed; but a letter or phone call would not give him the much-desired publicity.

On 28 April, ATF Special Agents Thomas D'Ambrosio and Jeff Kerr, case agent for the Roslindale Bomb investigation, interviewed Randy Stoller, who had already been interviewed by the Boston Police on 3 November 1991 at the Boston Police Homicide unit. Stoller told the agents about his counselor-like, ride-providing relationship that he had with Tom Shay. He also corroborated Alfred Trenkler's statements that one of the five rides he gave to Tom Shay was to Stoller's store in Attleboro. Said the report, "He stated that on one occasion Shay received a ride to his store (Saltzman) from an individual he described as a white male, approximately 5'7", balding and dressed in work clothes. He stated that the man drove a beat up light colored car. The man stated that he climbed radio towers. Stoller believes that the man may of [sic, have] said that he owned his own business." The described person was surely Alfred Trenkler, but unfortunately, Stoller was not asked to estimate the date of that encounter, which was in June of 1991. Jeff Kerr also recorded a final statement about the man who gave Tom Shay a ride that day, "Stoller stated that he got the impression from the meeting that Shay and this man had a physical relationship." We don't know if Stoller said that in response to a leading question or from what observations he received that impression. Was, for example, Shay touching Trenkler in some way? Was Trenkler touching him back, which was highly unlikely? Inexplicably, the report was written on 8 December 1992, more than seven months after the interview.

Sometime after that interview, Tom Shay wrote Randy Stoller a suicide note. *"Dear Randy: I'm sorry I ever lied to you. I'm sorry I ever hurt you. I loved you like a father, a brother, a friend. I'm sorry that you had gone through what you did. I never meant to hurt you. I just never knew how to treat any one. By now you have gotten the newspaper I have committ [sic] suicide. Because I realized how I have treated people all my life. I had no involvement in the Bomb. Honestly. I killed myself because I realized I'm only a bother to society. Not any more. I was running on fumes of love. I lost everyone. Randy, please come to my funeral as friend. OK! Don't be mad. Just go to my funeral ok? One last wish that is all. Don't say you can't cancel your plans. I don't know what else to say except Good Bye. Love you always, as a Brothers. X O X O X O X O X O X O .. O's are Kisses, X's are Loves."*

Also on 28 April 1992 ATF agents in Los Angeles interviewed the retired "Ice Capades" clown, Freddie M. Trenkler about his son, Alfred. Mr. Trenkler was identified by the ATF as "Alfred Trenkler, Sr." even though he was not known by that name, and even though his son, Alfred W. Trenkler was not "Jr." Mr. Trenkler said that he knew of his son's interest in electronics and that when he last talked with Alfred on Christmas Day, 1991, there was no indication that anything was amiss.

On 30 April James Quinlan testified before the grand jury. He was a friend of Alfred Trenkler's and Donna Shea's in the early 1980's. There was no contact with him in the 1990's and Quinlan was not called to testify at Alfred's trial.

In the Suffolk County Jail in Boston, a guard wrote a report on 1 May 1992 about Thomas Shay. Dennis Morelli wrote, "...*I heard several inmates talking about all the violence on TV in LA. One inmate said, "They should drop a bomb on L.A. At that time Inmate Thomas Shay said, 'I specialize in driveways, not towns.'*" Regardless of whether Tom Shay was involved in the Roslindale Bomb, he should be given some credit for a sense of humor. At least Ronald Reagan might have thought so, when remembering his 1984 comment on live radio, "*The bombing starts in five minutes.*" Even though the guard apparently thought it worth preserving, as a type of admission; the prosecutors, for all their zeal and belief in the guilt of Tom Shay and Alfred Trenkler did not pursue this report. It could easily have become a "*He said, he said,*" problem. Tom Shay wrote his own version of his confrontation with Dennis Morelli and said he was sending it to Shelley Murphy at the *Boston Herald* and to Sheriff Robert Rufo, and to his attorney, William McPhee.

The grand jury was busy and by 4 May had heard testimony from 50 witnesses, according to AUSA Paul Kelly's letter of that day to William McPhee. Many of the witnesses, said Kelly, incriminated Tom Shay in the Roslindale Bombing. Kelly was writing McPhee to seek Tom Shay's cooperation in order to convict a confederate who must have assisted Shay in his alleged plot to kill his father. Wrote Kelly, "We believe we know the identities of the responsible parties, but quite frankly, securing a conviction against them would be a tall order at this point.

I would hope that Mr. Shay does not want to 'take the fall' alone....

Here's the deal... Mr. Shay essentially has two (2) options at this point: (1) he can sit tight, and eventually get indicted for the murder of Officer Jeremiah Hurley alone or (if further evidence develops) with others; or (2) through you, he can step forward now and offer me a truthful and accurate proffer concerning his role and the role of others. If he sits tight, and later is indicted and convicted, we will, at a minimum, seek a non-parollable life sentence at FCI-Leavenworth. If, on the other hand, he agrees to a truthful proffer, I offer the following (so long as his information is truthful, complete and subject to corroboration):
  A. Exposure to a federal prison term of no more than 10-20
      years (depending upon the value of his information);
  B. Consideration as to the location (and prison level)
      where the sentence will be served;
  C. Assistance with any and all pending charges.

This is a serious proposal, and (to the extent possible) should be considered very seriously by Mr. Shay. This offer is open to Mr. Shay only until Friday, May 15. Time is of the essence. If you and he are interested, I will schedule an initial proffer session with ATF Special Agent Jeff Kerr and me only....

For the sake of justice, I hope to hear from you. Good luck with your client."

It was an interesting expression for Paul Kelly to use, "For the sake of justice."

Apparently unconnected to the proffer proposal, Tom Shay wrote, on May 6, two letters to Governor William Weld, who was a former the U.S. Attorney for Massachusetts from 1981 through November 1986. The two letters, (see Appendix D) began with a drawing of the world, and the description, "*Somewhat clean, 30, Homeless, Lots of drugs and cars. No work. 10,000 Die a day. It we don't save it* [the world] *in ten years.... World War 2. Nothing & nobody left. P.S. Please write me back. I am the man that is the suspect in the Roslindale Bomb blast. I'm Thomas Shay, Jr. I am innocent. I had no involvement whatsoever. I am putting my time to worthwhile causes while I'm in jail. I don't know who did it, but when they find the real man...."*

The second letter showed a diagram with a title, *"Our World Someday"* and contents of boxes: *"No more drugs - No more guns - No more violence - No more Polution - No more Homeless! - No more Racism"* and *"More More More More - Love Peace - Truthfullness - Jobs - I am proud to be an American!! - Thomas A. Shay - Low Cost Housing - Clean Air & Water - Free Medical Care - Food - No more War! - No more Biggotry - No more Diseases - No more lying & Cover Ups."*

Thomas A. Shay was surely not going to be remembered as a typical Federal defendant nor bomber. These letters were not introduced at his trial for any purpose. The defense was unable or unwilling to show directly how unstable Tom Shay could be. The best way would have been to put him on the witness stand and then show him those letters and ask for an explanation. The defense team was divided on this tactical question, but decided against exposing Tom Shay. Maybe the defense just didn't want to humiliate Tom, but was humiliation better than almost 16 years in prison? If the jurors could have seen more of Tom Shay, there would have been less chance of a conviction.

Also on 6 May, William McPhee forwarded on to Tom Shay, by messenger, copies of materials sent to him by Paul Kelly, including a redacted copy of the 18 October 1991 Radio Shack receipt.

Meanwhile, Federal agents continued to pursue Alfred Trenkler. On 8 May 1992, Alfred visited his former employer, ATEL and its president, Sharpless Jones, to inquire about more business. The next day, Sharpless called Alfred and asked him not to do any more business with ATEL because after Alfred left the ATEL office the previous day two policemen came in and asked Jones what was Trenkler was doing there. Jones did not want to jeopardize his business with government customers by any asssociation with Alfred Trenkler.

On 11 May 1992 Tom wrote to Attorney McPhee that *"I have not been to a Radio Shack store since 1989 in Revere when I purchased a foghorn with Ralph Pace,"* and that the "SAHY" receipt was a *"setup."* He also stated that he had never been to Alfred Trenkler's home in Milton. It's unlikely that he purchased a foghorn at a Radio Shack in Revere, either, because Radio Shack does not sell foghorns.

About this time, Alfred was told by his and John Cates' landlord that the local mail carrier had been told to write down the return addresses of all mail sent to Cates or Trenkler. Later, it was noticed that mail sent to Alfred to his parents' address was being opened and resealed. Alfred did not use the Quincy apartment as a mail address.

On 15 May, Richard Bender testified before the grand jury. He was the part owner of Greenview Landscaping in Hull for which Alfred Trenkler worked sometimes in the 1980's. Also, Greenview shared the same building as AWT Associates, the company run by Alfred Trenkler and Richard Brown. There were personal and business relationships among the partners and employees of both companies; until they all soured and Greenview Landscaping moved. Bender was another grand jury witness who was not asked to testify at Alfred Trenkler's trial.

From time to time in this case, an event occurs which may or may not be related to the larger issue of who built the Roslindale Bomb. On 18 May 1992, Alfred Trenkler reported to the Quincy Police that his car had been vandalized, and that some tools and car radio parts had been stolen. ATF Special Agent Jeff Kerr thought the incident sufficiently relevant to capture it in a 10 June 1992 report.

Also on the 18th of May, Terry Segal wrote Paul Kelly to ask for fair treatment for Alfred Trenkler if an indictment should be issued against him. Given the rough treatment, including public arrest and 17-19 April weekend jail time, given to Trenkler for the the Rhode Island debt of $1,349.39, it seemed to be a fair request. It was a short letter:

Dear Paul:

I represent Alfred Trenkler.

If Mr. Trenkler is indicted, given the extensive and often inappropriate pre-trial publicity already in connection with this matter, I specifically request that Mr. Trenkler be permitted to voluntarily surrender.

If Mr. Trenkler is indicted, please call me and I will produce him.

Needless to say, an indictment and bail hearing will receive extensive coverage, which, given the pre-trial publicity, could form the basis for change of venue. Arresting Mr. Trenkler and dragging him into the courthouse and F.B.I. in handcuffs will only make it more difficult for him to get a fair trial in this District."

This was the first indication of Segal's concern about the slanted pre-trial publicity, but he never did request a change in venue nor ever object to the biased publicity. Alfred recalled in 2007 that Segal was advised that the judges outside of Boston might be less receptive to Alfred's defense. Perhaps most importantly, Segal didn't change his public relations strategy which was to say very little, or nothing, and to prevent Alfred Trenkler from saying anything to the media.

If Paul Kelly responded, it's not an available document. With actions speaking louder than words, the important response came later in the year, on 16 December, with guns drawn on Morrissey Boulevard, a main highway between Quincy and Boston.

On 20 May 1992 William McPhee wrote in a "memo to file" that Paul Kelly had told him that the ATF "*can prove through forensic testing that the dynamite was wrapped in a magazine that was at some point in Tom's possession and sent to Tom.*" Tom Shay wrote back to McPhee that he couldn't understand such a claim because he wasn't involved with the Roslindale Bomb in any way. Perhaps McPhee simply misunderstood Paul Kelly's representation or Paul Kelly misunderstood what the ATF was telling him, or perhaps Kelly was blowing smoke at McPhee in the hope of igniting a fire; but there was no ability to tie the fragment of *MuscleMag International* back to Tom Shay, nor to anyone else.

On 21 May, William McPhee wrote to Tom Shay about his press conference request. "*It doesn't appear I can make you understand that the media is not your friend, they will not publish what you want, ie, a request that your friends who left you because of questioning and harassment by the FBI come back and speak to you, and it is clear they have their own agenda in reporting this story... I am trying to impress upon you the fruitlessness in you[r] going half-cocked and keeping the Boston media entertained."*

On 28 May 1992 Thomas D'Ambrosio and Jeff Kerr interviewed Leslie Arsenault, a friend of Tom Shay's older sister, Nancy. To help her friend, Leslie offered to go visit Tom, as Nancy was unable to do so because of her criminal record. Arsenault visited Tom Shay on 19 May and Shay asked her to help encourage others to visit him as he was lonely. Jeff Kerr's report closed with, "Arsenault stated that for the majority of her visit, Thomas Shay read from material which he had prepared prior to her visit. She stated that he wanted her to keep the writings so that she would be able to gain a better understanding of the person that he was." The report noted that five documents were given to the agents, but they were not part of the report. Unfortunately, they were not available for the author of this book, nor were they mentioned at Tom Shay's trial. One letter to Leslie has been found and it's presented in its entirety:

"Dear Leslie, After you left I cried so much. I can't make it in life anymore. Take care of Nancy, ok. By the time you receive this letter I should already be decieced [deceased]. *That is the way I have planned it to go down. I really like you. But it is just too late for me. I would take 20 of my best friends and all of my family to keep me alive now. Thank you for visiting me. Don't be mad at me. Just say a couple of prayers for me, ok. Love Tommy Shay. PS. Write a nice ulegy* [eulogy] *ok. and don't be sad and cry. Be Happy I am Free From depression."*

Also on the 28th, the Atlantic Street, Quincy landlord of John Cates and Alfred Trenkler, Michael Green, testified at the grand jury. He was not called to testify at the Alfred Trenkler trial.

On 4 June 1992, Tom Shay was in the U.S. Marshal's lockup in the Federal Building to give a sample of his handwriting. His attorney, William McPhee, could not attend due to a required court appearance in Dedham that arose that morning and he gave Paul Kelly and ATF agents Tom D'Ambrosio and Jeff Kerr permission to obtain the handwriting sample without him. He talked directly by phone with his client, Tom Shay, too. It was predictable that Shay would talk a lot without his attorney present, and that's what he did. A four-page report, in the format of an undated memorandum, entitled, "*STATEMENTS MADE BY THOMAS A. SHAY IN JUNE 1992*," was prepared, probably by Paul Kelly. ATF reports are usually on special ATF report forms. This was the first time that Paul Kelly had met Tom Shay. The first four pages were about a meeting on 4 June, and the last two pages were about a meeting with Tom Shay on 11 June. Below are relevant excerpts of the memo regarding the 4 June meeting.

"...AUSA Kelly then asked Shay Jr. what his attorney had told him, which Shay Jr. said 'he said it was okay to talk to you guys.' AUSA Kelly then asked the agents to begin the process of taking the handwriting samples. Shay Jr. protested and said he'd do the handwriting later and that he wanted to 'talk first.' Shay Jr. then began freely carrying on a conversation with both agents. He was reminded of the seriousness of the matter and told that it may not be in his best interests to talk with us. Shay Jr. stated that he was innocent of any involvement in the bombing and wanted to talk.

Shay Jr. challenged the agents to show him what evidence they had that connected him to the bombing. Shay Jr. stated that he was a 'good detective.' At that point Agent D'Ambrosio showed Shay Jr. an enlarged copy of the Radio

Shack receipt of the 10-18-91 transaction. He was asked what, if anything, he saw on the slip that was significant. Shay Jr. stated 'the components,' and 'the fact that the store is near Christian Science.' Agent D'Ambrosio then pointed out three (3) additional factors: (1) the name ('Sahy'), (2) the telephone number ('3780') and the date (10-18-91 ... ten days prior to the bombing). At that point Shay Jr. became visibly upset, he stood up and said 'wait a minute, wait a minute ... I've seen that receipt before.' When asked where, Shay Jr. responded 'in the back of Al Trenkler's car on the floor.' Shay Jr. then stated that the slip he saw was the same, but was pink in color and smaller that the copy which had been shown to him.

At this point AUSA Kelly asked Shay Jr. if it was he who purchased the items listed on the receipt. Shay Jr. gave a half smile, but said nothing. AUSA Kelly asked Shay Jr. to describe the interior or the Radio Shack store, which he did accurately. AUSA Kelly then told Shay Jr. that the clerk remembered him and said 'damn, your [sic] tall' when Shay Jr. went to pay for the items. Shay remembered this comment by the clerk, and recalled that he then said to the clerk 'you know what they say about tall guys with big feet!'

Shay Jr. then stated that Trenkler had magnets in the back of his car along with the pink receipt. He described the magnets as being about the size of a quarter. He also described the box they came in. He said that he was playing with the magnets while inside Trenkler's car which upset Trenkler. At Agent Kerr's request, Shay Jr. drew a diagram of the magnets and the box.

Shay Jr. then began speaking about his close friend Randy Stoller and insisted we not contact him or bother him.

At this point, at AUSA's Kelly direction, handwriting exemplars were taken. This process took 30-45 minutes. Shortly thereafter the U.S. Marshal's began calling for Shay Jr. to return. Shay Jr. insisted that he stay longer and talk some more, saying he had some things to tell us about Trenkler.

Over the course of the last 60-90 minutes, part of which occurred in AUSA Kelly's office and part in the U.S. Marshal's offices upstairs, Shay Jr. talked about the following:

1. Shay Jr. admitted that his earlier statements about knowing Trenkler only a year, and meeting him on only two occasions, were false. He told us that he had known Trenkler for 2-3 years and had seen him on several occasions, especially in September and October, 1991.

2. Shay Jr. described Trenkler as a good listener. He said Trenkler gave him money occasionally and rides in his car. He stated that he had sexual relations with Trenkler.

3. AUSA Kelly asked Shay Jr. about his comments to the media on October 29, 1991 (as reported in the Boston Herald on 10-30-91) that this father was incapable of building a 'remote control' bomb. When asked how he knew it was remote control at this point -- before the experts even knew this fact -- Shay Jr. said it was just 'a guess.'

4. Shay Jr. said that Trenkler had a workshop that he had visited once which was located next to a tower in either Marshfield or in the Norwood/Walpole area. He described the workshop as being inside a small brown or tan stucco building

that stood atop a cement base next to a 50 foot electrical tower. Shay Jr. said that this stucco building had a window in it, and that on one occasion when he looked through the window into the building he saw electrical parts and tools.

5. Shay Jr. made various other comments and remarks about Trenkler, his family, his sexual orientation and other subjects. Other than as outlined above, at no time did Shay Jr. admit direct involvement in the circumstances leading up to the Roslindale Bombing."

Jeff Kerr's 24 June report on the same 4 June meeting said about the Shay-Trenkler relationship, "Shay additionally stated that he and Alfred Trenkler had associated quite frequently. Shay estimated that the two were together approximately seven (7) times with each time lasting an extended period. He stated that the two had been together often and that on two occasions Trenkler had taken him to his (Trenkler's) work sites.

Shay stated that it was possible that somebody like Al Trenkler may have listened to his (Shay's) complaints about his father. He stated that this person, possibly Al Trenkler may of [sic, have] set about to build a bomb to hurt his (Shay's) father thinking he was doing a favor. Shay stated that this was and is not an end which he desired and that if the aforementioned scenario occurred, it occurred independent of him (Shay)."

This was one way that Tom Shay's webs of stories were spun, by testing the strength of the strand by saying to someone that an event was possible. If the strand held, then the "possible" event might later become an actual event, and a new "possible" event might be spun further from that.

Of the authors of the two reports of that 4 June meeting, Paul Kelly appeared to be the one more willing to believe Shay. Jeff Kerr noted the tentativeness of part of what Shay said.

There were many problems with what Tom Shay had told Kelly and Kerr, as Paul Kelly later realized and memorialized in several "Memos to File." One such problem was Shay's claim that he had seen a pink copy of the 18 October 1991 Radio Shack receipt in Alfred Trenkler's car. The problem was that the "customer copy" of all Radio Shack receipts are yellow, not pink.

In the second part of Paul Kelly's apparent "memorandum to file" Kelly memorialized a followup meeting with Tom Shay which occurred on 11 June in the offices of the U.S. Attorney. He wrote,

"Following the handwriting session on June 4, Shay Jr. contacted AUSA Kelly and Agent Kerr by telephone and requested to speak with the agents at the U.S. Attorney's Office on June 11. Shay Jr. stated that Attorney McPhee no longer represented him.

On June 11, at his request, Shay Jr. was brought to the U.S. Attorney's Office. His counsel was notified and confirmed that he was 'off the case.' Shay Jr. was carefully informed of his rights by Agent D'Ambrosio. He then signed a written waiver of his fifth and sixth amendment rights.

For the next few hours, Agents D'Ambrosio and Kerr interviewed Shay Jr., during which time he denied that he was involved in the bombing and stated .he felt that Bill Bayonne [sic] and Phil Smith of the South End were responsible. Shay Jr. claimed his father owed these guys money from gambling debts.

While some of the session was spent with Shay, Jr. acting foolish and appearing not to fully appreciate the seriousness of the interview, at most times, he was responsive and cooperative. Shay Jr. had with him several pages of handwritten notes which he read from, but refused to show the AUSA or agents. His notes were broken into the following topics, each of which he spent time talking about:

1. Places he's been with Trenkler
2. People who have seen Trenkler and he together
3. Al Trenkler and money
4. Topics of conversation between he and Trenkler
    a. sex
    b. cute boys
    c. family
    d. electronics
    e. Trenkler's work
5. How he feels about Trenkler
6. The last time he talked with Trenkler
7. His whereabouts the weekend prior to the bombing
8. Random thoughts
9. Things he wants the government to do for him.

Shay Jr. repeatedly asked if we could arrange to hypnotize him. When asked why, he said that he had heard that hypnosis allows certain repressed memories to come out, and that a person cannot lie when under hypnosis. Shay Jr. was told that we would look into this and discuss it further when he had a new attorney to represent him."

On the cover of the European paperback edition of her book, *Vanishing Acts*[4], Jodi Picoult wrote, "*It takes two people to make a lie work. The person who tells it and the one who believes it.*" So much did Paul Kelly, Thomas D'Ambrosio and Jeff Kerr want to solve the Roslindale Bomb case that they were willing believers of Shay's lies. Even when parts of Shay's stories were proved to be false, the investigators held fast to their belief that the remaining statements were true and were willing to take a bad case to trial on that slender basis.

Tom Shay's claim in June 1992 to ATF Agents Thomas D'Ambrosio and Jeff Kerr that "Bill Bayonne and Phil Smith" should be suspects in the case was significant because Mr. Thomas L. Shay would give, or already did give, his 1986 Buick to William Baiona or Phil Smith, as is described later.

In 2007, Tom Shay read these pages and it's tempting to believe his statement that he had told Thomas D'Ambrosio that he had seen the Radio Shack "*before*" in his father's car and not Alfred Trenkler's. Also, he now stated that Alfred "*Trenkler never gave me money. We never had sex. None of the statement made by the ATF & Kelly are trued on page 106* (this page as it existed in his copy of the manuscript] *I never said any of those things. I never said my father sexually abused me. That's a lie.*" One problem with D'Ambrosio's recollection that Shay noticed that the 18 October 1991date of the Radio Shack Receipt was ten days before the bombing, D'Ambrosio didn't record what would have been Shay's more likely response that it was his mother's birthday.

An unexpected development came on 8 June when police searched two Hyde Park apartments for bombs and bomb parts after a dispute between two roommates. Said John Ellement's 10 June 1992 story in the *Boston Globe*, "*Officials also said yesterday that six 'wired devices' removed from the apartment of Dennis E. Owen by the Bomb Squad on Monday were dummies - devices that appeared to be bombs, but had no explosive materials attached to them.*"

A connection to the Roslindale Bomb case was made, according to the 10 June 1992 *Boston Herald* article by Andrea Estes, "*MAN PLEADS INNOCENT TO TOSSING ACID AT FRIEND.*" The connection was that Owen's rommate, and purported victim, Derrick Massey, "*told police that Owen was building a bomb and that he'd warned two police officers 'I'll make a bomb better than the one (I made) that killed Hurley.'*" The possibility of a link to the Roslindale Bomb case was sufficiently large to bring AUSA's Paul Kelly and Frank Libby to the estranged men's apartment during the investigation. ATF investigators also assisted in the case.

The roommate's quote was printed slightly differently in John Ellement's *Boston Globe* article, "*HYDE PARK MAN IS SAID TO BE PROBED IN BOMB DEATH.*" Stated the article,

"*A roommate of Owen's, according to a source, also quoted Owen as saying, 'I'll make a bomb better than the one I did for Shay.' Authorities are investigating whether Owen was referring to Thomas L. Shay or Shay's son, Thomas A. Shay, or whether the reference was to some other person.*

The roommate also told police that Owen had photographs of one of the Shays in his apartment, but officials would neither confirm nor deny that they had found any such materials in Owen's apartment, which they searched into the evening." The article said that Tom Shay had no known relationship to Dennis Owen, and no photographs or other documents were found which would show such association.

This story was the third occasion that Alfred Trenkler recalled in 2007 that he had been contacted by the media during the Roslindale Bomb case. When it appeared that the link between the Dennis Owen and the Roslindale Bomb case might be significant a reporter called Alfred Trenkler at his apartment in Quincy for his comments. Alfred remembers the question, "*How does it feel to be off the hook, now that the probable bomb maker has been found?*" Alfred responded that he was very pleased because now everyone would know what he had been saying from the beginning which was that he was innocent and not involved in the Roslindale Bomb in any way. He said that he was looking forward to life becoming more normal again. Those comments were never published, as the Owen-Roslindale Bomb connection seemed to fade away. Alfred remembered in 2007 that he had understood that Dennis Owen worked as a chemist in a construction company.

There were no other calls from the media as they had received the message from Terry Segal that there should be no contacts. To Alfred, Terry said that he should stay away from the press because the press was obviously talking with Paul Kelly and other "*unnamed sources.*" This strategy of abandoning the media campaign in the face of the prosecution's own media campaign was a disastrous strategy. Alfred did not dispute the advice as he had recently had a difficult experience with the media after his friend, John Shea's, arrest. Alfred had been interviewed by "A Current Affair" and then was asked some questions "*off-the-record.*" Unfortunately, the reporter broke the promise of confidentiality and the "*off-the-record*" comments were broadcast, which lead to another relapse in the friendship between Alfred and John Shea's wife, Donna.

The Terry Segal advice regarding the media paralleled the decision not to have Alfred testify at any hearings, or at his trial and parallels the experience of the two recent presidential candidates from Massachusetts, Mike Dukakis and John Kerry, who didn't respond quickly enough to the efforts by the other side to paint a picture of them. In the absence of Alfred's story, the other side's story prevailed, and prevailed, and prevailed. In the case of these early stages of the campaign for Alfred Trenkler, it was the "*unnamed sources*" whose characterization of him was the one which stuck.

The next day's article, on 11 June 1992, by John Ellement on the incident, "*SEARCHES SHOW NO LINK TO BOMB DEATH OF OFFICER*," quoted Paul Kelly as saying "*there doesn't appear to be any association between the Shay investigation and the matters that unfolded...*[the past two days]" Thus, the incident seemed to be another instance of the "Lindbergh Baby 200" syndrome where about 200 people claimed some involvement in the kidnapping and murder of Charles and Anne Lindbergh's baby son in 1932. The Roslindale Bomb case in Boston was one of the most sensational crimes in Boston in the 1990's, and association with it was valuable to some, including Tom Shay. On the other hand maybe there was a connection between Dennis Owen and Tom or Thomas L. Shay, and the police did not ask the right questions.

On 12 June, William McPhee[5] withdrew as Tom Shay's attorney, shortly after learning that Tom Shay had met with Paul Kelly without him. In another employment change, Alfred Trenkler hired James Harding as a commissioned sales representative for ATNS. Harding showed a strong interest in the Roslindale Bomb case and often engaged Alfred in related conversations, and had several bizarre ideas. By Alfred's account years later to Mark Brodie, "*Harding then plays another game. He tells me that if I were to draw a diagram of the Roslindale Bomb, he would go and get all the necessary parts, put them together just like the Roslindale Bomb and go blow up Shay Sr's car to 'prove' that someone else was after Shay Sr. thus proving my innocence. I tell Harding that he is crazy, that I had no idea how the bomb was put together because I had nothing to do with it in the first place and why would I want to be involved in something that I had nothing to do with in the first place.*

Harding offered me cash and the keys to a house on Cape Cod to 'get away' for a while, the media had said that an indictment was just days away. I told him I was not going to run, that I knew of my innocence.

Harding even discussed firing my attorney Terry Segal so that Harding could set me up with an official to make a deal against Shay Jr. I told Harding that there would be no deals because I was innocent."

On 18 June 1992 Jeffrey Berry, part owner of Dedham Service Center through the corporation Berr-Giam, testified before the grand jury, with a promise of immunity from prosecution. The Service Center was where Thomas L. Shay rented work space for auto body shop and where an M-80 firecracker was tossed into a trash can in October 1987. That incident led to the lawsuit by Mr. Thomas L. Shay against Ber-Giam, the optimistic resolution of which the prosecution claimed motivated Tom Shay to try to kill his father. Berry and his partner, Louis

Giammarco, were suspects in the Roslindale Bomb case, but Berry testified without claiming his Fifth Amendment rights against self-incrimination.

As another reminder of the political importance of the Roslindale Bomb case, the Massachusetts Legislature passed Chapter 78 of the Acts and Resolves of 1992, which directed the Boston Retirement Board to retire Officer Francis X. Foley on disability, with a remainder interest to his wife, Claire. The declared disability was "totally and permanently."

On 9 July 1992[6] Tom Shay wrote an unsigned letter or a diary-like note. *"I pray that someday people will believe me in what I am about to say and to see my life and life the way I believe and see it. That love, no matter what its form or how it comes wrapped, is worth the price no matter how high. Between the choice of money or love, I'll take love, for the sake of my family and friends, love does not come easy. ... I would give my life for love, never for money, for money is material and could leave any day. For love is eternal, nobody could buy or take it away. For I will always hold the memories of my dad and I at the shop or at a field playing catch. For there is my mother who made my favorite meals and comforted me on sad days when I had tears. For I will cherrish [sic] them Both in my heart, no matter what. Then there are my sisters that gave me special times, one on one together the memories will last forever, and then there are my friends and acquaintances that I had lost, but there are good memories that I will never forget. I want to say I'm sorry to everyone, I have made myself a suspect because I said things that were lies, I made myself a suspect because I did not care. The devil's spirit was inside me and made me not care, for yesterday God took his thrown [sic, throne?] inside of me and gave me the love I need. I say God will prevail, Glory to the old might[y] God our king, Glory to God in the Highest, for he gave us all life. I am not looking for sympathy nor a prayer. God will take good care of me I'm sure either way."*

On 16 July, Anastasiose Vasiliadis, an acquaintance and potential business associate of Alfred Trenkler, testified before the grand jury. He had talked with Alfred after the bombing. He was not subsequently called to testify at Alfred Trenkler's trial.

Also in July, Alfred Trenkler hand painted his Toyota a flat black. As he put it later, *"I had business meetings to attend - appearance means everything."* Even though the police knew Alfred Trenkler's location and his work place and a lot about his friends and family by this time, the rumor still emerged that he painted his car black to somehow evade detection by the police.

On 29 July, Tom Shay's request for a hypnosis session was granted and he was taken from the Suffolk County Jail to the ATF office. There he met with his new public defender attorney, Jefferson Boone, and also his former attorney, William McPhee, for an hour and a half. The two-hour hypnosis session, conducted by Dr. Malcolm Rogers, began at 8:00 p.m. and was videotaped and was "live monitored," presumably through one-way glass windows, by the two attorneys, AUSA Paul Kelly, and ATF Special Agents Thomas D'Ambrosio, John Gibson, Jeff Kerr and Dennis Leahy. After Shay was taken back to his cell, Jeff Kerr reported that Dr. Rogers told the investigators, but not Jefferson Boone, that he thought that Shay had "feigned hypnosis and had simply reiterated events as he had previously done during interviews with AUSA. Paul Kelly and ATF Agents Thomas D'Ambrosio and Jeff Kerr.

On 30 July 1992 Shay made a collect telephone call during business hours to Special Agent Jeff Kerr. Kerr accepted the charges and informed Shay that Agent D'Ambrosio would be listening in to Shay's questions. Shay acknowledged that this was acceptable.

Shay asked Kerr what was going on with the hypnosis results? Kerr and D'Ambrosio informed Shay that it was the general feeling of all observing parties, excluding Shay's attorney, Jefferson Boone, that Shay had not been hypnotized and that he had faked being in a hypnotic state through two hours of interviewing.

Shay stated that he had a sore neck the entire session and that when Dr. Rogers told him that his (Shay's) eyes were getting heavy that he had to make them feel heavy. Agent Kerr stated to Shay that he felt that Shay had faked the entire session and asked Shay why he did not just tell Dr. Rogers that he wasn't being hypnotized. Shay responded saying that he was afraid to say anything because he thought that everybody would be mad at him.

Shay further stated that Dr. Rogers failed to ask him the right questions. He stated that he wanted to be hypnotized again and that he would pay for the session.

Shay was informed by Agents D'Ambrosio and Kerr that ATF would not be excepting [sic] his collect calls and that it was theirs and other observers collective opinion that he (Shay) was obviously not going to make a genuine effort during any hypnosis session. Shay was informed that since he apparently did not wish to cooperate, all contact between Shay and law enforcement officials attached to the Roslindale Bombing investigation would be terminated."

However, because those same law enforcement officials wanted so much to solve the case, they went back to Shay later, and again. Paul Kelly went on vacation for two weeks and upon his return he tried again for a hypnosis session for Tom Shay and wrote to Jefferson Boone on 18 August,
"Dear Jeff:

... Please inform Tom that we were not surprised or angered by what transpired at the first session. While we would have preferred him to have acknowledged that he was never in a hypnotic state, Dr. Rogers tells me that an occurrence such as this is not necessarily uncommon.

As I now understand it, a person must want to be hypnotized in order to achieve a successful and productive hypnotic trance. If Tom wishes to try again, I will be happy to accommodate him, so long as the session is scheduled to occur within the next two weeks (on or before August 31, 1992)."

A second hypnosis session never occurred.

On 13 August 1992 Tom Shay, still in the Suffolk County Jail, called at least three media sources to announce a press conference at 7 p.m. However, as was reported in the *Boston Globe* article on the 14th, "*SHERIFF NIXES SHAY NEWS CONFERENCE*," permission to conduct such an event was denied.

"*Thomas A. Shay attempted to hold a press conference last night at the Nashua Street Jail to answer what his lawyer calls 'trumped-up charges' of making bomb* threats, but was denied permission by jail authorities. Shay, 20, called at least three local media outlets yesterday to say he would meet with reporters at 7 p.m., but Gerard Lydon, a spokesman for Sherriff Robert C. Rufo, said he [Shay] had not requested permission for the event. 'And quite frankly, if he had requested permission, we would have denied it. We don't allow inmates to hold press conferences. If we did, we'd have press conferences here 24 hours a day.' "

At some point in the complex prosecutions that eventually go to trial, the future defendant is advised that s/he is a "target" of the prosecution, and not merely a person being interviewed to ascertain facts in a case. The U.S. Attorney's office notified Alfred Trenkler in a 4 September 1992 letter that he was such a "target" as he was suspected of building the Roslindale Bomb. Shelley Murphy wrote, in her _Boston Herald_ story on 16 September, "*QUINCY MAN EYED IN BOMBING*," that Trenkler could not be reached for comment and that Terry Segal said, "*I really can't comment on that case,*" and that the prosecutors would not comment on the record. The article revealed that "*the younger Shay told the Herald he recently underwent hypnosis in an effort to help investigators and convince them he was being truthful.*" That raises again the question of how conscious Tom Shay was of his lies. Shay had been in the Suffolk County jail since March and was scheduled for a suppression hearing Friday, 18 September in his 1990 MBTA bomb threat case.

The article recounted the 1986 Quincy incident and stated, "*The charges were continued without a finding after Trenkler cooperated with authorities in an unrelated case involving drugs, sources said.*" Once again unnamed sources were used to publicize incorrect statements, as Alfred Trenkler never cooperated with any police about any drug charges. He had never been interviewed about drug charges, never testified, never been charged and never made any deal. The "unnamed sources" were surely law enforcement people, and one intentional or unintentional effect was to make it appear that the 1986 incident was a very serious matter that could have been dismissed only if the police had used it to their advantage to solve a more serious crime. It wasn't true, and no one on Alfred's defense team said anything about the allegation, which continued to appear later in Ranalli's articles. Once again, Trenkler was failed by his lawyers in two ways, first by telling him not to talk with the press, and second by failing to conduct any kind of a reasonable public relations campaign themselves. They relied upon the U.S. Attorney's office to define the public's image of Alfred Trenkler.

On 10 September 1992 Mr. Thomas L. Shay's lawyer, F. Jay Flynn, wrote to Jefferson Boone to advise of the plan to request a Writ of Habeas Corpus to bring Tom Shay from jail to the trial of his father's civil suit against Jeffrey Berry, Louis Giammarco and Ber-Giam. The trial never occurred, and the case was settled.

On 16 September the Department of Justice in Washington approved Paul Kelly's and Frank Libby's request to hypnotize Randy Stoller. It's not known by the author what truth the prosecutors were seeking with this plan, but a videotape of the hypnosis session was provided to Nancy Gertner on 18 June 1993, just before Tom Shay's trial. Stoller was one of the very few people who could confirm the correct date and time of one of the actual times that Alfred Trenkler was in the company of Tom Shay, as Alfred gave Shay a ride to Stoller's place of work in June 1991.

The _Globe_ article by John Ellement came a day later, on 17 September, "*MILTON MAN IS TARGET OF PROBE.*" To Ellement, Segal said, "*I am not going to comment.*"

He could see that one or more people in the investigation and/or prosecution teams was/were leaking or giving information to the media as "*sources*," but Segal apparently felt that saying anything would not help his client, or violate the lawyer's Rules of Professional Conduct or both. Rule 3.6 on "Trial Publicity" states that

"A lawyer who is participating or has participated in the investigation or litigation of a matter shall not make an extrajudicial statement that a reasonable person would expect to be disseminated by means of public communication if the lawyer knows or reasonably should know that it will have a substantial likelihood of materially prejudicing an adjudicative proceeding in the matter...." However,

... a lawyer may make a statement that a reasonable lawyer would believe is required to protect a client from the substantial undue prejudicial effect of recent publicity not initiated by the lawyer or the lawyer's client. A statement made pursuant to this paragraph shall be limited to such information as is necessary to mitigate the recent adverse publicity."

In other words, a lawyer who is careful about his/her standing within the legal profession will want to say very little publicly about any pending investigation or trial, even though the other side is leaking information to the media. Thus, the rules of the legal game, and not a concern for public availability of the truth, govern what can be said. It's rare that a lawyer is formally disciplined for violating such a rule, as one's reputation within the guild is a powerful governing tool.

Interestingly, such rules do not bind a client, and s/he can say whatever s/he wants, but when that happens, then the lawyers lose control of the game and the information about the game.

John Ellement's 17 September *Boston Globe* article stated that he had interviewed Tom Shay the previous day and that Shay said he was informed on 16 April that he was a target of the U.S. Attorney's and grand jury investigation, and that he now was represented by a new lawyer, Jefferson Boone. Also, "*the younger Shay detailed the amount of time he spent with Trenkler... Shay said that if one added up the total number of hours he had spent with Trenkler it would probably 'equal a week.'* "

Continued the article, " *'If Al Trenkler did this, he did this on his own,' Shay said. 'I didn't know him as a guy who used explosives. I didn't know him as a guy who would hurt people. I knew him as a guy who was mellow, who was not a drinker, who was not a drug user. He cheered me up sometimes when I met him.'* " It's tempting in this book to do exactly what Paul Kelly and Frank Libby did - believe the statements they liked and fail to acknowledge that many of the other statements were lies. This phenomenon is called here the Selective Truth Temptation (STT).

Tom Shay's estimate of his total number of hours with Alfred Trenkler "equaling a week" can be improved upon. Below is the time estimate for the six times Alfred Trenkler met Tom Shay in the summer of 1991

1. Ride to Quincy (20 min.), few hours sleep (3), then ride to Dorchester (15 min) Total: 3 hours, 35 minutes.
2. Ride from Boston to Attleboro. Total: 1 hour.
3. Ride from Boylston Street to mother's home in Quincy. Total: 20 minutes.
4. Ride from Park Square to Nahant and back to mother's home in Quincy. 1 hour;

dozing on couch, 2 hr. Total: 3.0 hr.

5. Ride from Hynes Center, Boylston St. to Fleet Bank, Boylston St. Total: 10 minutes.

6. See at White Hen in Boston. Total: 15 minutes.

Total: three hours twenty minutes of conversational time, plus four hours of non-sexual, separate catnaps, for a total of eight hours twenty minutes.

The _Boston Herald_ ran a story on 17 September by Jack Meyers, "_CASHIER IDS BOMB SUSPECT MAN DENIES BUYING PARTS FOR EXPLOSIVE_," which also revealed details of grand jury testimony by the unnamed cashier. Meyers wrote that Alan Pransky, Mr. Thomas L. Shay's lawyer, had testified about his conversation with Tom Shay about what would happen to his father's lawsuit if his father were to die. Pransky would not comment on his testimony, but did state that the Shay vs. Berr-Giam lawsuit had been settled the previous week for an undisclosed dollar amount.

Another named source in the story was, predictably, Tom Shay, who interviewed with Jack Meyers by telephone from the Suffolk County Jail. Shay was reported to have said, "_I never bought one thing in that Radio Shack. I'd take a lie detector test (to prove it)._" About his father's lawsuit, Tom Shay "_said he asked Pransky numerous questions about the lawsuit three years ago, but couldn't remember asking what would happen if his father died._" Said Shay, "_I could have asked that question because I had a hyper day that day learning my father was suing someone for half a million, but it didn't mean I was planning on killing him," Shay said._

The suit was settled out of court this week, but lawyers refused to disclose the settlement.

'My father's been good to me all my life,' the younger Shay said. 'He never laid one hand on me, although he did a good job of beating on my mother and I watched it.'

Also on 17 September, ATF Special Agents Thomas D'Ambrosio and Jeff Kerr went to 39 Eastbourne Street to re-interview Thomas L. Shay. As reported by Jeff Kerr, he told the investigators "he had read the newspaper articles relating to his son, Thomas A. Shay, and that he was not disturbed by the references to his alleged abuse of his former wife. Mr. Shay said that he was not surprised that his son would make those statements to the press.

Mr. Shay was advised that his son may be released from jail the following day. Mr. Shay stated that he 'knows what Tom looks like.' "

The report stated that Mr. Shay reaffirmed his earlier statements about the bomb, and that he didn't realize what it was, until it exploded.

The 18 September _Boston Globe_ carried an article by John Ellement and Matthew Brelis, "_PLEA BARGAIN IS CONSIDERED IN BOMBING CASE._" The agreement struck by Jefferson Boone and Suffolk County District Attorney Ralph Martin was for Tom Shay to plead "_sufficient facts to support a guilty finding_," for the 1990 MBTA bomb threat, but that he was not guilty - one of many legal sleights-of-hand to avoid calling a spade a spade. However, Superior Court Judge Julian Houston would not accept the agreement. The case then was to go to Judge Robert Banks to consider Jefferson Boone's motion to suppress evidence, but Judge Banks was in another case, and not available. Finally, knowing that Federal charges were imminent, the Suffolk County district attorney asked Judge Elbert Tuttle to dismiss the state charges against Tom Shay for the MBTA bomb threat. Aware of the State-

Federal interplay, Judge Tuttle said to the lawyers, *"You two are doing a little dance in this courtroom and I am not going to participate in this dance,"* according to Doris Wong's article in the *Boston Globe* the following day, the 19th, *"THREAT CASE DISMISSED, BOMBING SUSPECT REARRESTED."*

The Ellement and Brelis article went beyond the MBTA bomb threat story to summarize the status of the Roslindale Bomb case and said that *"The younger Shay is suspected by investigators of persuading Alfred W. Trenkler, 36, of Milton to build the device for him."* Again using unnamed sources, the article said, *"Investigators can place them* [Shay and Trenkler]*, including several occasions on which Shay stayed at Trenkler's apartment, the sources said."* The article revealed the existence of the 18 October 1991 Radio Shack receipt, *"Sources also said investigators have found an Oct. 18, 1991, receipt from a Radio Shack store made out to a person with the last name of 'Sahy.' Among the items listed on the receipt is a toggle switch of the same model that killed Hurley, sources said. Shay once sought to disguise his identity by changing his last name to Ashay.*

Moreover, a clerk at the store has testified before the federal grand jury that 'Sahy' was more than 6 feet tall as is Shay and was able to pick Shay's picture out of a photo array. A source familiar with the grand jury testimony said the clerk also claimed 'Sahy' had a scar on his lower lip."

Despite the apparent leaking of secret grand jury testimony by the U.S. Attorney's office, the ATF or by Boston police, there was no response from Alfred Trenkler nor Tom Shay nor their attorneys about the claim of the length of the Trenkler-Shay relationship. Except for Tom Shay's denial, there was no response about the Radio Shack receipt. The "scar on his lower lip" claim was never mentioned at Tom Shay's trial, because the claimed identification of Shay by cashier Dwayne Armbrister was ruled inadmissible as it was achieved through an impermissibly suggestive process. Also, his fellow salesperson, Allan Kingsbury, had stated that the purchaser was a "**Middle Eastern man**," according to ATF Agent Sandra LaCourse's report.

Shelley Murphy of the *Herald* also predicted the Federal charges in her 18 September article, *"SUSPECT IN OFFICER'S BOMB DEATH MAY BE JAILED ON FEDERAL CHARGE."* Her article also captured the coming drama on that day, *"The suspect in a Roslindale Bomb blast that killed a Boston police officer expects to be a free man today after pleading guilty to an unrelated charge that's kept him in jail for six months.*

Thomas A. Shay, 20, of Quincy, has scheduled a press conference this morning outside Suffolk Superior Court to celebrate his freedom, according to his lawyer, Jefferson Boone.

But Shay may be in for a rude awakening. Sources said he'll probably be scooped up immediately by federal officials on new charges...Sources said authorities fear Shay may flee since he's a prime suspect in the Oct. 28 blast....

Although the younger Shay admitted he had a troubled childhood - including 13 years in state schools and institutions - he said, 'My father has never done anything in his life to make me want to kill him.' "

As the newspapers' unnamed sources had predicted, Tom Shay was arrested on Federal charges one-half hour after the MBTA bomb threat charges were resolved at the State Superior Court. This was the closest Shay would be to freedom until his eventual release from Federal prison ten years later on 30 August 2002. The Federal charges of communicating a bomb threat from the Suffolk County Jail to the woman in Brighton were contained in the 24 September indictment from a Federal grand jury. They were supported by the 18 September 1992 Affidavit from ATF Special Agent Thomas D'Ambrosio, who relied upon the statements of Shay's fellow inmate, Mark Means, referenced in the affidavit as "W-1." The arrest was made by ATF Special Agent Dennis Leahy and Boston Homicide detectives Brendan Craven and Francis Armstrong. Clearly, they were more interested in the Roslindale Bomb investigation than in the minor telephoned bomb threat, and Tom Shay was kept in custody. He was arraigned by Magistrate Robert Collings on 25 September and trial was scheduled for Monday, 23 November 1992.

Dennis Leahy's 30 September report of the 18 September 1992 activities continued, "While in the holding area Shay said 'I'm not the guy who bowled [sic, built] it, I'm not the guy who got the dynamite, I'm not the guy who placed it, I'm not violent.' Shay also said that they [sic] guy who identified him as being at Radio Shack had committed perjury as he knew Shay from the 'block.' Shay also said that he knew 'G's' roommate and the 'G' worked at Radio Shack." "G" is assumed to be George Nightingale, roommate of Edward Carrion.

Shelley Murphy's and David Weber's 19 September _Boston Herald_ story was about Shay's plea-bargain negotiations and was headlined, "*A MAN SUSPECTED OF ORCHESTRATING A BOMBING THAT KILLED A POLICEMAN SEEKS DEAL.*" Wrote Murphy and Weber, "*A man suspected of orchestrating a bombing that killed a Boston police officer last October was offered a deal of 20 years in prison in exchange for his cooperation against accomplices, a lawyer claimed yesterday.*

The deal offered earlier this summer to Thomas A. Shay, 20, by federal prosecutors was rejected because Shay insists he wasn't involved in the bombing, said his lawyer, Jeffrey Boone."

Jefferson Boone seemed to believe that it was important to work with the media and ensure that your side of the story is aired. The jury pool has to come from somewhere.

That was about the same time that AUSA Paul Kelly said it was "*outrageous*" to suggest that the U.S. Attorney's office would consider a plea bargain in this case of the death of a police officer.

On 25 September, the _Boston Herald_ carried Shelley Murphy's story, "*POLICE TO STUDY SUSPECTED BOMB-BUILDER'S HANDWRITING,*" which reported that Alfred Trenkler had voluntarily gone to the U.S. Attorney's office and given a handwriting sample, "*to be compared with various receipts and documents*" according to the article. Interestingly, no item of handwritten evidence was introduced at either Shay's or Trenkler's trial to link either man to the Roslindale Bomb. It must follow that the investigators had what they believed to be relevant papers with incriminating handwriting and that the handwriting did not match Shay's nor Trenkler's. It's not known what those papers with handwriting were, nor why they weren't used by the defense to show their clients' non-involvement. Surely, if Shay's and Trenkler's handwriting did match that on the relevant papers, the match would have been used at a trial, so why not the reverse? When asked about Trenkler's visit to the U.S. Attorney's office, Terry Segal said, "*I have no comment on the case other than to say my client is innocent and was not involved in this tragedy."*

Jeremiah Hurley was not forgotten. On 1 October at a ceremony at the State House, he was awarded posthumously the George L. Hanna Medal of Honor for bravery in the line of duty. His surviving partner, Francis X. Foley was also honored with the same award.

Tom Shay wrote an undated letter to his mother, perhaps in the Fall of 1992. Excerpts from the letter are below.

"Dear Mother, Hello from Jail, I love you. Mom I am very depressed, I am innocent, and I am scared. The cops & Feds kind of made me say things that weren't true, put things in my head and I said things that were false just to make the cops happy. I am now in trouble for life now, maybe jail for life or... If possible, I hope if I am convicted, and anyone can be convicted on a conspiracy charge, I will ask for [the] death penalty. I want you to know that I love you for 3 things....

...do me this last favor, for you, for me, for God The man who gave us all life. do something with your life, don't start Monday, start Today. Clean the house thorough...."

About this time he wrote a letter (See Appendix D) to "Tom" or "Roy," with copies to the Boston media. *"I am very depressed and I want you to tell the world why. I am depressed because I am not a murderer, I am not a violent person. I [do not] use weapons or violence and never have, never will. I am depressed because every day I see young men like myself being violent, killing one another for money or respect. Who gives anyone the right to take away a life that God gave to a human being. It's sad, young black and white boys, teenagers and adults killing friends over girlfriends, killing over respect and money.... I spent 13 years from age 5-18 in DSS and every time there was a fight, I tried to stop it and after felt bad that someone would want to hurt anyone for something so foolish. It's not just violence, it's death at a young age that depresses me, or throwing your life away over violence. When Ryan White died I was so sad I cried for days.... Please respond within 24 hours....I do wish that this letter means something and could help someone, as I would love to be a part of saving young lives of our future."* [Ryan White died on 8 April 1990 at the age of 18 from AIDS contracted during blood transfusions necessitated by his hemophilia. He was forced to leave his middle school due to anti-Aids discrimination, and later became a hero and spokesperson for people with AIDS.]

Paul Kelly tried again in October to obtain relevant information from Tom Shay in return for a light sentence, considering that a police officer had died. Kelly wrote to Jefferson Boone on 6 October 1992 with his latest offer,

"Dear Jeff :

This letter will confirm our telephone conversation of yesterday. It is my understanding that your client, Thomas A. Shay, has now expressed a willingness to speak with federal agents investigating the death of Boston Police Officer Jerry Hurley.

You explained to me that Mr. Shay, while possessing information which is relevant to our investigation, denies any criminal intent or direct knowledge of the activities leading up to officer Hurleyfs tragic death. You further explained that Mr. Shay recognizes that he may bear some responsibility as an accessory after the fact or for obstruction of justice, and that he desires an outcome of no more than three (3) years incarceration in a minimum security setting or hospital environment.

As I explained, the U.S. Attorney must approve all plea agreements. This office is unable to propose any final plea offers until after it has conducted a full proffer session with a defendant or subject and (1) is satisfied that the person is being truthful and candid, and (2) fully understands what role, if any, the person played in the alleged offense. If, after talking with Mr. Shay, we are satisfied that he has been entirely truthful and cooperative with us, and that his role is as you described, I believe that we will be able to arrange an outcome in or about the range desired by Mr. Shay. If, however, his role was greater and more involved than that described, we obviously will need to have further discussions with you concerning available sentencing options. Moreover, I have informed you, based on my ongoing discussions with representatives of the Suffolk County District Attorney's Office and the Boston Police Department, that in the event that federal charges are brought against him, there will be no state prosecution of Mr. Shay arising out of the facts or circumstances surrounding the death of Officer Hurley. A truthful proffer session is the required and essential starting point.

The terms under which the contemplated proffer will be received are as follows: No statements made or information provided by Mr. Shay will be used directly against him, except for purposes of cross-examination and impeachment should he be a witness in any proceeding and offer testimony or evidence materially different from any statements made or information provided during the proffer, or in a prosecution based on false statements made or false information provided during the proffer.

The foregoing reflects the present agreement between the government and Mr. Shay. It is understood that the government incurs no additional obligation as a result of the proffer; specifically, the government is not hereby agreeing that the defendant will not be prosecuted.

If you and your client agree that this letter accurately describes the agreement between your client and the government with regard to your client's proffer, please confirm this by signing in the appropriate spaces below.
Very truly yours,
Paul Kelly"

The letter was countersigned and returned by Jefferson Boone and Tom Shay as Paul Kelly had requested, in order to show agreement with the proposed terms.

On 7 October 1992, ATF Special Agents Jeff Kerr and John Paolillo interviewed Nancy Shay at the Quincy home of her daughter, Amy Lenar. Also present, surprisingly, were Thomas A. Shay, and Deputy U.S. Marshall Roger Bryant, who was guarding Shay. From Jeff Kerr's report,

"Mrs. Shay stated that one early morning, prior to October 28, 1991, an exact date she could not remember, she returned home to her apartment at approximately 2:00 AM. She stated that when she entered the apartment she observed an unknown male sleeping on the couch in her living room and her son Thomas A. Shay sleeping on the floor in the same room.

Mrs. Shay stated that she was angry at her son Thomas for bringing home a boyfriend to her house for an overnight stay. She stated that she awoke her son and asked him who the individual on the couch was. She stated that her son told her, that the man was a friend of his and that the man was very nice. Mrs. Shay stated that she became enraged and ordered her son to 'Get that fucking guy out of my apartment now.'...

Mrs. Shay stated that she observed her son Thomas and a man she described as short and balding. She stated that the man turned to her son and said that they should leave because his (Thomas') mother was very angry.

Mrs. Shay stated that they left the house and that her son didn't return until late the following day.

Mrs. Shay stated that she knows the man in her apartment on the aforementioned night was Alfred Trenkler. She stated that she knows this man for two reasons. One reason is that she clearly remembered the man's description and that when she observed Trenkler's photograph in the newspaper she immediately knew he (Trenkler) was the man in her apartment with her son. She stated that the second reason, was her son Thomas' confirmation of the same on a day sometime after the bombing incident on October 28, 1991."

Of no known consequence was the non-report of anything Tom Shay may have said during the interview. It wasn't like him to remain silent under such circumstances. Also, it apparently wasn't yet clear to the ATF agents how important was the length of Tom Shay's acquaintance with Alfred Trenkler. Thus, the report does not indicate any attempt to help Mrs. Shay be more specific about the date of her early morning return.

Mrs. Nancy Shay later changed her mind about her identification of Alfred Trenkler as the person in her apartment in those early hours one morning. She told members of Nancy Gertner's legal team a year later on 25 June 1993 that the man she was in her living room was "*very slender,*" which she saw clearly, as the man was undressed from the waist up. Also, she believed that the incident in her home occurred in late winter 1990-91, approximately in March, because she recalled her son Tom saying, "*You can't throw him out; it is cold and snowing.*" Mrs. Shay's changed identification of Alfred Trenkler was not clarified at her son's trial, but it would surprise the prosecution at the trial of Alfred Trenkler.

On 9 October, ATF Special Agents Edmond Gronin and Sandra LaCourse went to the "Glad Day Bookstore" on Boylston Street in Boston. The store was known for its specialization in books favored by gay men. Thomas A. Shay was known by several staff people to have come to the store, but no one recognized a photograph, in a photo array, of Alfred Trenkler. This was, at least, one occasion where eye-witness non-identification seemed to accord with reality, as Alfred Trenkler maintains that he has never been in that store.

On 13 October, Paul Kelly wrote a "Memorandum to File" about a call he received from Mr. Thomas L. Shay that day, "to say the following:

1. He vigorously denies ever sexually abusing Tommy. He called Tommy's accusation 'an out-and-out lie,'

2. His daughter Paula recently told him that she had been raped as a child by their Uncle Stan (now deceased), as had her sister Amy. Paula also said that she

had been sexually abused by a neighbor in Hyde Park. Mr. Shay claimed no previous knowledge of these events.

3. Mr. Shay believes that his ex-wife, Nancy Shay, is a 'liar' and is not telling us the truth about Tommy's involvement in the bombing. He also said that Tommy, and his daughters Paula and Amy have difficulty telling the truth.

4. Tommy worked at Bradlee's in the Dedham Mall back in 1988-89 for a short period of time. There is a Radio Shack store directly across from Bradlee's.

5. Mr. Shay reiterated what Tommy said to him when he went to visit Tommy at the jail back in early November, 1991: 'Dad, where did you go Saturday night?' Nancy Shay also later made the statement to Mr. Shay, 'I should have stayed with Tommy Saturday night.'

On 13 October, Nancy Shay, sister of Tom Shay, called the ATF to advise, according to Agent John Paolillo's report, that

"Approximately a week ago Ms. Shay received a phone call from her mother. She indicated that her mother was in an intoxicated condition at the time of the call. Her mother advised that Al Trenkler told Tommy Shay (date unknown) that he (Trenkler) had been sexually abused as a child. Trenkler then asked Tommy if he had ever been sexually abused. Ms. Shay stated that Tommy answered that question 'yes' just to satisfy Trenkler. Also, Ms. Shay's mother stated that prior to the bombing, Trenkler told Tommy that he had a surprise for him. Immediately subsequent to the bombing, Trenkler allegedly asked Tommy how he liked the surprise. Ms. Shay was unable to give either when or where the above conversations took place. This was the only significant information she recalled receiving from her mother related to the bombing. Ms. Shay said she would contact ATF if anything further relating to this matter should arise."

Obviously, Tom's mother had talked with her son, and she strongly hoped that he was not involved; so any theory that laid blame elsewhere was favored. The problem with the story was that no part relating to Alfred Trenkler was true. That is, Trenkler never told Shay, nor anyone, that he had been abused as a child; he never asked Tom Shay if he was abused; he never said he had a surprise for Tom Shay; and he never communicated with Tom Shay again after accidentally running into him in August in Boston, with John Cates as a witness. Tom Shay made up everything that he had said to his mother about Alfred Trenkler and which was passed on to the ATF.

Despite the reported failure of plea-bargain negotiations with Tom Shay, Paul Kelly continued to hope that Tom Shay was part of the solution to the Roslindale Bomb case. Kelly wrote the following as a record of his conversations with Tom Shay:

"Memorandum to File
Subject: Proffer by Tom Shay, Jr.
Date: October 14, 1992
To: File
From: Paul V. Kelly

Tom Shay Jr. gave a proffer to SA Jeff Kerr, SA Tom D'Ambrosio and me on October 6, with a follow-up on October 9.

The most notable things he had to say were as follows:

1. He was sexually abused by his father as a young child, between 20-30 times.
2. He has known Al Trenkler for 2-3 years and had a sexual relationship with him as recently as the 6-8 week period prior to the bombing (10/28/91).
3. He was living outside of Massachusetts and returned sometime in August, 1991 to give a deposition in his father's pending lawsuit.
4. He met Trenkler at the Club (Boylston St.) shortly after his return to the area.
5. Two weeks later, Trenkler invited him out on a friend's boat to go scuba diving for the day. During this boat trip, Trenkler, Shay and another unidentified white male (mid-30's, dark hair mustache, 200-220 lbs., tattoos on upper body, named 'John' or 'Jo Jo') tossed 3 grenades into the ocean somewhere off Provincetown. The grenades were beige in color and resembled World War II German grenades.
6. He saw Trenkler again a week later in the Fenway area. Trenkler gave him a ride home to Quincy.
7. At some point during the meetings described above (most likely during the boat trip), Shay and Trenkler talked about several personal matters, including their families, their sexuality etc. Trenkler told Shay that he had been sexually abused by his natural father as a young child.
8. Shay, in turn, told Trenkler that he too had sexually abused by his father as a child.
9. He further told Trenkler that he believed his dad had some form of cancer and that if his father were dead he would 'get $500,000.' (Shay later tried to clarify this statement by saying he told Trenkler that if his father died he'd 'be rich' -- meaning, according to him, from his father's inheritance, which included a coin collection.
10. Trenkler told Shay that he was going to build him a 'surprise,' but did not elaborate on what he meant by that. Shay claims that Trenkler knew that he (Shay) had a birthday approaching.
11. In or around October 18, Shay and Trenkler spent a great deal of time together over 2-3 days. Shay recalls one day in which he accompanied Trenkler to the Christian Science Building, to Radio Shack, and then to a tower that Trenkler had done some work on which was located either in Norwood, or in the Marshfield area.
12. During this 2-3 day time, Shay brought to his mother's apartment and intended to have him stay the night. At or about 3:00 a.m. Ms. Shay returned home, got very angry, and tossed Trenkler and her son out of the house. (Ms. Shay confirmed this during an interview by ATF on October 8, 1992). After leaving the house in Quincy, Shay claims that he and Trenkler went to Manchester, MA. and stayed with a friend of Shay's.
13. Shay admits that it was he who made the purchase at Radio Shack on October 18 involving the receipt for 'Sahy.' Trenkler sent him into the store with a handwritten list of items to buy and a $50 bill. Shay paid for the items with a $20 bill, after learning that the store would not accept the $50 bill. Shay claims he believed the items were needed by Trenkler to repair an antenna, and that they did not relate to the 'surprise' that Trenkler was building.

14. Following the Radio Shack purchase, they drove to the alleged tower. During the ride, Shay observed (and handled) several small magnets that were located in Trenkler's car. The magnets were round, the size of a quarter, and 'looked like they went to a Tyco set.'

15. In and around October 18, he and Trenkler also shopped for electronics equipment and other materials at other stores, including You-Do-It Electronics and B-J's Wholesalers.

16. Approximately one week after the trip to Radio Shack, Shay beeped Trenkler to go out for a ride. Trenkler picked him up and told him they were taking a ride to the Quincy Quarries.

17. Upon arrival, Trenkler took a large black plastic trash bag (actually 3 bags inside one another) filled with various items and tossed in one of the quarries. Trenkler told Shay that the items in the bag were 'part of the surprise .... only you and I will know about it.... and the cops will never find it.' Shay observed several items in the bag, including wire, tape, electrical components, a surgical gloves. Trenkler placed the remaining unused Hefty bags and container inside the bag along with a large cinder block, and then knotted the bag and tied some kind of heavy fishing line around it. Shay then punched holes in the bag with his finger to release any air and make it easier to sink. Trenkler threw it out the first time, but it got stuck on a ledge not far under the water. Shay pulled it up (the line cut threw [sic] the gloves he was wearing), and threw it out again. This time it dropped very, very deep. Trenkler then cut the line.

18. Shay believes Trenkler saw this as an opportunity to take revenge against Shay's father, and his own (for the sexual molestation).

19. Trenkler told Shay that he had obtained dynamite and blasting caps from a guy in New Hampshire who blows up granite.

20. The day after the explosion (October 28), Trenkler came to see Shay at his mother's apartment in Quincy. He asked Shay 'how'd you like the surprise?' Trenkler explained that he meant the explosion. He further stated 'I almost made you rich.' Shay claims he got very upset and told Trenkler never to tell anyone about that . . . 'I'll never tell anybody if you never tell anybody.'

21. Shay has been over to Trenkler's apartment between 3 and 9 times, and stayed overnight 3-4 times over the 2-3 years he has known him.

22. Trenkler owned a remote control car which Shay saw at Trenkler's apartment. It was a black dune buggy with yellow tires. (Shay drew us a diagram of the control unit).

23. Trenkler came to visit Shay a second time in December, 1991 following Shay's release from jail on the state warrant. This visit occurred on same day that Jimmy Keough cut his wrists. Shay told Trenkler that he was leaving town. Trenkler tried to convince Shay not to leave the area because it "would look bad" and because 'they'll find you.' Trenkler said he was staying around; he then gave Shay some money.

24. Trenkler told Shay about the 1986 bomb. He also told him that he beat the charge by offering the police some information on a drug investigation.
cc: AUSA Frank Libby"

This proffer is full of errors and lies. It's unfortunate that the rigidities of the legal system didn't encourage Paul Kelly to simply contact Alfred Trenkler's attorney and ask for a response to these allegations. If he had, and if Terry Segal had replied with Alfred's responses, they would have appeared as are presented below to every one of the numbered points, which related to Alfred Trenkler. Paul Kelly later realized, (see his 15 January memorandum to file, below), that a lot of what Tom Shay said was wrong, but he continued to want to believe that there was enough truth in his statements to convict Alfred Trenkler, and maybe Tom Shay, too. Paul Kelly was suffering from the Selective Truth Temptation (STT). What percentage of lies would it have taken to persuade the prosecutors to **avoid** any Shay statements? 50% lies? 60% 70%? In the world of love or business, all it often takes is one significant lie to destroy a relationship. In the world of criminal law, it seems to take much more.

Below are 24 comments which parallel Paul Kelly's 24 proffer points.

1. Before the media coverage of the Shay family, Alfred Trenkler had no knowledge of any allegations of abuse of Tom Shay in his home.
2. Tom Shay met Alfred Trenkler in June, 1991. They were together for five requested rides to Tom Shay-requested destinations. Their last meeting was in August, 1991. There was never a sexual relationship between the two.
3. Before the media coverage of the Shay family, Alfred Trenkler had no knowledge of Tom Shay's travels.
4. Tom Shay and Alfred Trenkler have never been to any "club" together.
5. Tom Shay and Alfred Trenkler have never been on a boat together and Alfred Trenkler has never seen a hand grenade and certainly never tossed any into the ocean.
6. One of the five rides Alfred Trenkler did give Tom Shay was from Boston to Tom's mother's in Quincy. The first of the five rides, in June 1991 was first to Alfred Trenkler's apartment in Quincy, and then a few hours later to Richmond Street in Dorchester, which is less than one-mile from the Milton line.
7. Tom Shay and Alfred Trenkler did not discuss their families and their sexuality, and Trenkler never said he was abused by anyone. First, there was no truth to the allegation, and second, even if he had been abused, he would not discuss them with a 19-year old mere acquaintance.
8. Tom Shay never told Alfred Trenkler that he had been abused as a child.
9. Tom Shay said nothing to Alfred Trenkler about his father dying of cancer nor about any expected "riches" nor supposed future inheritance for Tom Shay. Given Alfred's exposure to the wealth of others, such a topic would not have made an impression anyway.
10. Alfred Trenkler never told Tom Shay that he had any surprise for him.
11. Alfred Trenkler had not seen Tom Shay since a chance encounter in August. Thus, there was no 2-3 day time spent together. Never.
12. One of the five rides Alfred Trenkler gave to Tom Shay was late one June night, and it was to Nahant and then to Tom's mother's in Quincy, where Alfred fell asleep on a couch. When Tom's sister, Paula, saw Alfred there, Alfred left. It was not Mrs. Shay, as she has stated under oath that she had never seen Alfred Trenkler before. Again, the last ride Alfred Trenkler gave to Tom Shay was in July, 1991.

13. Alfred Trenkler had no role in the 18 October Radio Shack Purchase, nor did he ever give Tom Shay $50.00 or $20.00 to purchase anything, anywhere.
14. Alfred Trenkler had no role in the purchase, and he and Tom Shay did not go anywhere after any such non-purchase; and there were no loose magnets in Trenkler's car.
15. Alfred Trenkler and Tom Shay never went shopping together for anything, anywhere.
16. Alfred Trenkler has never been to the Quincy quarries with Tom Shay, and had not seen Tom Shay since a chance encounter in August, 1991.
17. Alfred Trenkler was never at the Quincy quarries with Tom Shay, and the entire "disposal" scenario was a complete fabrication.
18. Alfred Trenkler never discussed with Tom Shay, Shay's claim of molestation by his father, and Trenkler was not angered by what he didn't know. As Alfred Trenkler knew almost nothing about Mr. Thomas L. Shay, and had never met him, and as he had never been abused by anyone, revenge against Mr. Shay was an impossible motivation.
19. Alfred Trenkler has never purchased dynamite nor blasting caps from anyone in any state, and thus never has told anyone, including Tom Shay, that he had.
20. Alfred Trenkler did not go see Tom Shay after 28 October, and had not seen him since the chance encounter in August 1991. There was only one contact between them since August 1991 and that was a speaking/listening, non-visual contact from different cells in the Federal lockup facility in Boston on 25 June 1993. The six previous contacts were accidental, at least from Trenkler's perspective, and the 1993 voice contact between cells was not his idea either.
21. Tom Shay was at Alfred Trenkler's apartment, shared with John Cates, only once, in early June 1991 from approximately 3:00 a.m. to 6:00 a.m., It was raining, and there was nowhere else to leave Tom Shay after offering to give him a ride to his father's home and subsequently being told that he couldn't go to that home. Alfred had purchased his Toyoat Celica in September 1990 and moved to that apartment in October of 1990.
22. There was no remote control car in Alfred Trenkler's apartment in 1991. Alfred Trenkler has never owned a remote control toy car. Not one. The remote control car used in the 1986 device was purchased by Donna Shea when she and Alfred went to the Quincy Ave., Quincy Radio Shack, but it was her money, and Alfred didn't own it. After that purchase, she had Alfred take it with him, so as not to interest her children in a toy what was about to be cannibalized. Alfred and his roommate, Bob Craig and Bill Miller played with it for a few evenings before its remote control pieces were incorporated into the M21 Hoffman simulator.
23. Alfred Trenkler did not visit Shay at his house after his release from jail in December 1991. The last time Alfred Trenkler saw Tom Shay was an accidental meeting in August 1991. All previous contacts between Alfred Trenkler and Tom Shay were accidental as well, at least from Alfred Trenkler's perspective.
24. Alfred Trenkler never discussed the 1986 Quincy M21 Hoffman incident with Tom Shay. He felt it was a stupid prank that went too far. He regretted it even before the detonation, and he rarely mentioned it to anyone. He had never mentioned it to his roommate and much trusted friend, John Cates, until the police knocked on their door on 5 November 1991. There was no cooperation

with the police about any drug investigation in 1986. The 1986 case was dismissed by the Norfolk County District Attorney in 1987, after a one year continuance without a finding or informal probation. Alfred had accepted responsibility for his role. The press reports of the dismissal of the case came from unnamed sources, probably close to the police, ATF or prosecutors, and had the effect of making the 1986 device seem more important than it was.

Also, it would have been useful for Paul Kelly to forward to Terry Segal a copy of Tom Shay's handwritten notes which were prepared for the proffer session and kept by the prosecutors. (See Appendix D.) The rekeyed contents are listed below, with the prosecutors' descriptive notes in **Verdana**, Shay's handwritten notes in *Italic*, and with comments in Bookman Old Style CAPS afterwards.

"Handwritten Notes by Shay Jr. To Help Corroborate His Story (10-15-92)"

Page 1. "Stores that he and Trenkler shopped at together."

"1. Radio Shack, Boston, 2. Radio Shack Braintree, 3. NHD Roslindale, 4. Grossmans, Quincy, 5. Do-It-Yourself-Electronics [Needham], 6. ACE is the Place Hardware [Brockton], 7 Bradlees, Dedham Mall, 8. Hobby Town, Dedham Mall. (Also Radio Shack Dedham Mall), 9. Somerville Lumber, 10. BJ's Wholesale Club. Cape Cod, 11.True Value Hardware, P-town [Provincetown], 12. Sears, Dedham Mall, 13 ADAP Auto Parts, Dorchester. I paid for all purchases."

ALFRED TRENKLER NEVER SHOPPED WITH TOM SHAY AT ANY STORE AT ANY TIME, INCLUDING THOSE LISTED HERE.

Page 2. "Location of 2 towers" *"Towers [illegible] Beeper comp, Building Boge [sic] 5, Cherry pickers, airport, Fence5X5 5X5"*

ALFRED TRENKLER NEVER TOOK TOM SHAY TO ANY WORK SITE HE HAD EVER WORKED ON, INCLUDING ANY COMMUNICATIONS TOWERS.

Page 3. "Trip to Vermont with Trenkler" *"Going to meet friends and pick up some goodies; 5-6 hours ride till Cindy Mitchell STOP; 5 min till she arrived; Cindy's parents' names are Connie and Gary; Corvet [sic] 1986 red; Woke up at Border; Woke up 2d time at Toll area 1-2 hours later. Showed ID; 1-2 hours later arrived at camp; Down 24C Main Highway to 2 Lane main rd, to 2 lane dirt road to 1 lane dirt road, 30 men with rifles; Lots of trucks with green plates; JoJo was surrounded by skin heads and others; JoJo greeted us; Green Screen Tents 30-40; Trash cans burning; Cartridge and casing and other goods; Lots of Army & Navy surplus and good; Hand signals with every guard."*

ALFRED TRENKLER NEVER WENT TO VERMONT OR ANY OTHER STATE WITH TOM SHAY. THIS ENTIRE TRIP WAS FICTITIOUS, AS PAUL KELLY LATER NOTED.

Page 4. "Magnets he saw in Trenkler's car." *"Quarter size; 1/2 ounce weight; 50-60 per box; Blue Box; Special; Metalic [sic] color when the sun hits it; 3 Quarter with [sic] of magnets shown to me. [And a drawing of an apparent box for magnets with a space for "special buy" and "Ace is the Place", $7.99. Come to ( )"*

ALFRED TRENKLER HAS NEVER PURCHASED A BOX OF MAGNETS AND HAS NEVER HAD ANY MAGNETS IN HIS CAR AS SEPARATE IDENTIFIABLE ITEMS.

Page 5. "Description of guy in S.F. That Shay talked to" *"Problems, kid I knew from P-town. Tall kid from Alaska. Dark hair, wire glasses Brown eyes 170-180. Huskey. Went to school in P-town. Friend of Joel at Realistate [sic] comp. in P-town. Worked the Tenderloin district. Next to QT's. I told him what I though happened with Al and why I changed my name and age and why I was in SF. CA."*

THERE IS NO APPARENT SUBSTANTIVE RELATIONSHIP TO THE CASE, EXCEPT THE NAME "AL."

Page 6. "People who saw Shay and Trenkler together Sept - Oct 1991." "Nancy Shay, Sr., Quincy, 2. Nancy Shay, Jr., Softball, 3. Randy's Store, Store, White Hen Pantry man, Aly, 5. Chuck from Greyhound, Dan O'Neil at AA meeting, Tocresdsi [sic], 7. Glad Day Bookstore, Clay Perry, 8. David Shilalas at Falls, 9. Rich Brown at Als House., 10 Robert Zampella at ObSessions, Boston, 12, Friend at Manchester By the Sea, 13. Jo Jo John, 14. Cindy Mitchell, 15 Al's landlord, 16. Girl at campus Mass Bay that worked at Coat Rack, Chris in ...... 18. Brown student body at P.B.I. River Road[?], 19. My friend at Copley Security, 20. Dennis Theven [sic] at Buddies, 21 Kent 141 Micky [sic].

ALFRED TRENKLER WAS NOT SEEN BY ANY OF THE ABOVE PEOPLE WITH TOM SHAY IN THE MONTHS SEPTEMBER OR OCTOBER BECAUSE THEY WERE NOT TOGETHER. THE LAST TIME ALFRED TRENKLER SAW TOM SHAY WAS IN THE COMPANY OF JOHN CATES IN AUGUST AT THE BOYLSTON STREET, "WHITE HEN PANTRY." FURTHER, THE FOLLOWING CAN BE NOTED REGARDING THE LIST OF PEOPLE ABOVE.

1. ALFRED TRENKLER HAD NEVER SEEN NANCY SHAY, TOM SHAY'S MOTHER UNTIL ALFRED'S TRIAL WHERE SHE SAID SHE HAD NEVER SEEN HIM BEFORE,

2. ALFRED TRENKLER HAS NEVER SEEN NANCY SHAY, TOM SHAY'S SISTER BEFORE. ALFRED TRENKLER NEVER WENT TO A SOFTBALL GAME WITH TOM SHAY.

3. ALFRED DID TAKE TOM SHAY TO RANDY STOLLER'S STORE IN ATTLEBORO IN EARLY JUNE 1991.

4. A "WHITE HEN PANTRY" MAN WAS PRESENT IN EARLY JUNE 1991 WHEN ALFRED TRENKLER GAVE TOM SHAY A RIDE. ALSO, A "WHITE HEN PANTRY" MAN MAY HAVE OBSERVED THE CHANCE MEETING IN AUGUST 1991, IN THE COMPANY OF JOHN CATES.

5. ALFRED TRENKLER HAS NO KNOWLEDGE OF "CHUCK" AT GREYHOUND, AND DID NOT ENTER THE GREYHOUND STATION IN 1991.

6. ALFRED TRENKLER WAS NEVER IN AA (ALCOHOLICS ANONYMOUS) AND DOES NOT KNOW DON O'NEIL.

7. ALFRED TRENKLER HAS NEVER BEEN TO THE "GLAD DAY BOOK STORE." WHEN THE ATF VISITED THE STORE ON 9 OCTOBER 1992 AND NONE OF THE THREE EMPLOYEES, INCLUDING THE OWNER, RECOGNIZED A PHOTO OF ALFRED TRENKLER. CLAY PERRY WAS NOT ONE OF THE THREE.

8. ALFRED TRENKLER DOES NOT KNOW DAVID SHILALIS, BUT DID LEARN FROM THE INVESTIGATION AND TRIALS THAT HE WAS THE MALE FRIEND OF TOM SHAY'S MOTHER.

9. RICH BROWN SAW TOM SHAY THAT MORNING EARLY IN JUNE WHEN HE AND ALFRED TRENKLER DROVE TOM SHAY TO A HOME ON RICHMOND STREET IN DORCHESTER. SHAY HAD SLEPT A FEW HOURS AT TRENKLER'S APARTMENT, AFTER HAVING NOWHERE TO GO ON A RAINY NIGHT.

10. ALFRED TRENKLER HAS NEVER BEEN TO "OBSESSIONS" AND DOES NOT KNOW ROBERT ZAMPELL.

11. ALFRED TRENKLER DOES NOT KNOW JIM BERK AT BACK BAY FENS.

12. ALFRED TRENKLER HAS NO KNOWLEDGE OF A FRIEND IN MANCHESTER BY THE SEA WHOM HE MIGHT HAVE SEEN IN 1991.

13. ALFRED TRENKLER DOES NOT KNOW A "JO JO JOHN."

14. ALFRED TRENKLER DOES NOT KNOW A "CINDY MITCHELL."

15. TO ALFRED'S KNOWLEDGE, NEITHER OF HIS LANDLORDS, MIKE OR GEORGE GREEN HAS EVER SEEN OR MET TOM SHAY.

16. ALFRED TRENKLER DID NOT GO TO THE CAMPUS OF MASS BAY COMMUNITY COLLEGE IN 1991.

17-20. ALFRED TRENKLER DOES NOT RECOGNIZE ANY NAME OR PLACE IN THE REMAINING THREE ON THE LIST.

Page 8 "Boat Trip with Trenkler" "*Boat Trip; White Engine; parking area 100 feet from dock; surf and boat sales shop #3 across street; car silver with trunk; concushion* [sic] *grenades, mesh bog blue yellow air tanks, black diving gear; Booie* [sic, buoy] *Dark Green with # and Bell; Coast Guard near Dock area; Joel and old whitey sae me and JoJo and Al; Capt John Restaurant paid cash; JoJo had tattoo air bowne* [sic, airborne?] *vic....., with sideway bird; JoJos weight 180-220 muscle, short stock, late 30's, balding....; Tattoes web names of firls hkk.W5.666; Walked up Main St.; Won't Scooter living Al had trouble y.... in the water; When back in Weymouth I carried equipment to cement and JoJo brought it to his car, JoJo's. Me and Al left first.*"

ALFRED TRENKLER HAS NEVER BEEN ON A BOAT WITH TOM SHAY.

Page 9. "Remote Control Vehicle at Trenkler's Apt" "*Like dune buggy; cleat type wheels; 1 pound weight; shocks like monster truck; Black remote; yellow siding; possibly belonged to people upstairs; silver spokes; tin antenna on car.*" [then drawings of remote and car.]

ALFRED TRENKLER NEVER HAD A REMOTE CONTROL VEHICLE, WHETHER OWNED BY HIM OR ANYONE ELSE, IN HIS APARTMENT AT 133 ATLANTIC AVE. THE ONLY REMOTE CONTROL VEHICLE HE EVER HAD IN A DWELLING WAS IN 1986 WHEN HE HAD THE TYCO UNIT DURING THE LAST WEEK OF AUGUST 1986, BEFORE IT WAS CANNIBALIZED FOR THE 1986 M21 HOFFMAN DEVICE.

Given the difficulties the U.S. Attorney's office was having with a proffer from Tom Shay and with his various versions of the truth, Terry Segal stated to Alfred Trenkler that he didn't believe that he [Trenkler] would ever be indicted. Such confidence was misplaced.

On 17 October 1992 Karen Marinella of Channel 56, WVLI-TV, interviewed Thomas A. Shay in the Plymouth County Jail.[7] Portions of the interview were broadcast on that channel and portions were shown later to the juries in the trials of Thomas A. Shay and Alfred Trenkler. Defense lawyers in each case labored to minimize the amount of the tape which was entered, but it may have been better for each jury to see the entire tape and see the full extent of Tom Shay's web of lies. The difficulty was that it was impossible to cross-examine a videotape and Tom Shay chose not to testify.

Below are presented in *italic* are the statements in the interview by Thomas A. Shay as they pertain to Alfred Trenkler or which are known to be false. Karen Marinella's questions or comments are in ***bold italic***. Presented beneath Shay's statements are the author's comments in CAPS. [A copy of most of the interview, with comments, is contained in Appendix E.]

PAGE 2 of the transcript of the interview. (The opening statement of Thomas A. Shay). *"I never asked Al Trenkler to - to do any type of physical harm by use of explosive or otherwise. He did this on his own without my knowledge, and I don't really know why."*

ALFRED TRENKLER HAD NOTHING TO DO WITH THE 1991 BOMB. SHAY'S STATEMENT TO KAREN MARINELLA CONTRADICTS HIS 25 MARCH 1992 *"PRESS RELEASE"* FROM A SAN FRANCISCO JAIL, WHICH SAID, *"THE FEDERAL OFFICERS TOLD ME THAT ONE OF MY FRIENDS, AL TRENKLER OF BOSTON, WHO BUILDS SATELLITES, WAS A SUSPECT IN BUILDING THE BOMB. I FEEL THIS IS NOT TRUE, AND I KNOW THIS IS NOT TRUE."*

"I did make purchases of electronic goods at a number of stores for Trenkler, but my knowledge of what I was buying was for Trenkler's work".

ALFRED TRENKLER NEVER REQUESTED THOMAS A. SHAY TO MAKE ANY PURCHASES OF ANYTHING, ANYWHERE, IN ANY STORE. NO WITNESSES EVER STATED THAT THEY SAW THOMAS A. SHAY AND ALFRED TRENKLER IN ANY STORE TOGETHER. ALFRED CUSTOMARILY PAID FOR HIS PURCHASES WITH A COMPANY CHECK. THERE WERE NO RETAIL STORES FOR ALFRED TRENKLER'S WORK OF INSTALLING MICROWAVE ANTENNAS ON BUILDINGS OR TOWERS. EITHER TRENKLER'S CUSTOMERS HAD THE REQUIRED EQUIPMENT OR ALFRED TRENKLER ACQUIRED IT FROM OUT-OF-STATE SUPPLIERS. THUS, THERE WAS NO CHANCE THAT TOM SHAY PURCHASED ANYTHING IN ANY STORE FOR ALFRED TRENKLER'S WORK. TOM SHAY ACKNOWLEDGED IN A 2007 LETTER THAT HE NEVER MADE ANY PURCHASES WITH ALFRED TRENKLER.

"After the explosion, I knew who built it because he said in September, early October of 1991, that he was building me a surprise. I really didn't know what it was. I thought it was [a] remote control car."

ALFRED TRENKLER NEVER TOLD THOMAS A. SHAY THAT HE WAS BUILDING HIM A SURPRISE. SHAY MADE THE SAME CLAIM TO ASSISTANT U.S. ATTORNEY PAUL KELLY, BUT KELLY LATER WROTE IN HIS 10 NOVEMBER 1992 "MEMO TO FILE,... 4. The whole story about Trenkler building him some unknown 'surprise' was a hoax."

ALFRED TRENKLER NEVER BUILT ANYTHING FOR THOMAS A. SHAY AND NEVER GAVE HIM ANYTHING, EXCEPT FIVE RIDES IN HIS CAR IN JUNE AND JULY 1991. THE SIXTH AND LAST TIME ALFRED TRENKLER SAW THOMAS A. SHAY, AS OF 17 OCTOBER 1992, WAS A CHANCE ENCOUNTER IN BOSTON IN AUGUST 1991.

PAGE 3. *"In October, I saw some electrical equipment in a bag, and he said it was part of my surprise. We dumped this bag in a 300 depth [sic] of water. He said the cops would never find the stuff, and I didn't know what that meant."*

ALFRED TRENKLER NEVER SAID TO THOMAS A. SHAY THAT ANY ELECTRICAL EQUIPMENT HE OWNED WAS TO BE PART OF ANY SURPRISE FOR SHAY. ALFRED TRENKLER NEVER DUMPED ANYTHING WITH THOMAS A. SHAY ANYWHERE AND NEVER SAID ANYTHING ABOUT POLICE NOT FINDING ANYTHING.

AS OF THE DATE OF THE INTERVIEW, ALFRED TRENKLER HADN'T SEEN THOMAS A. SHAY SINCE A CHANCE ENCOUNTER IN BOSTON IN AUGUST, 1991.

IN OCTOBER, ALFRED WAS WORKING 6-7 DAYS A WEEK ON THE CHANNEL 68, CHRISTIAN SCIENCE AND VIDEOCOM MICROWAVE SYSTEMS PROJECTS AS WELL AS REMODELING HIS BROAD STREET WEYMOUTH OFFICE.

"The ATF incited [sic] *a 100-man diving task force to find the package."*

LOCAL AND ATF INVESTIGATORS SPENT CONSIDERABLE TIME LOOKING FOR EVIDENCE IN LOCATIONS IDENTIFIED BY THOMAS A. SHAY, BUT FOUND NOTHING. THESE WILD-GOOSE-CHASE SEARCHES MAY HAVE INCLUDED USING DIVERS AND UNDERWATER ROBOTS IN THE QUINCY QUARRIES FOR SEVERAL DAYS. ASSISTANT U.S. ATTORNEY PAUL KELLY, WROTE IN HIS 10 NOVEMBER 1992 "Memo to File...5. He never accompanied Trenkler to the Quincy quarry, or participated with him in disposing of evidence."

"By order of the federal government and the federal authorities I cannot disclose the whereabouts of the package."

THIS STATEMENT IS ABSURD ON ITS FACE.

PAGE 4. *"I met Al Trenkler in 1989, possibly early 1990, at a bar, and I got a ride home to Quincy from him, and he was a student at Wentworth Tech. He was into electronics. I - I'm into building things and that's how I kind of got to know him, basically, an acquaintance like a very good friend."*

ALFRED TRENKLER FIRST MET THOMAS A. SHAY AT A WHITE HEN CONVENIENCE STORE IN BACK BAY, BOSTON, IN JUNE OF 1991 WHEN SHAY ASKED FOR A RIDE HOME. ALFRED TRENKLER GRADUATED FROM WENTWORTH INSTITUTE IN 1977, 14 YEARS EARLIER. IN 1989, ALFRED TRENKLER WAS LIVING AND WORKING IN HULL, MASS. WITH NO CAR. HE DID NOT OWN A CAR AGAIN UNTIL SEPTEMBER OF 1990.

PAGES 5-6. *"Let me say Al Trenkler and I shared that I was abused as a child under the Department of Social Services care sexually, and so wasn't he by his father, and I think because of this, he thinks that my father put me in the Department of Social Services and then he went beserk out of his mind and possibly went out and built this surprise for me to make me maybe happy, you know, but-"*

FROM THEIR VERY LIMITED CONVERSATIONS DURING FIVE RIDES IN JUNE/JULY 1991, ALL AT SHAY'S REQUEST, AND ONE CHANCE ENCOUNTER IN AUGUST, 1991, THOMAS A. SHAY TOLD ALFRED TRENKLER EXTREMELY LITTLE ABOUT HIS BACKGROUND, BUT ENOUGH FOR TRENKLER TO SEE THAT SHAY WAS A TROUBLED YOUNG MAN. ALFRED TRENKLER EXPRESSED NO REACTION TO SHAY'S FEW STATEMENTS ABOUT HIS LIFE.

ALFRED TRENKLER WAS NOT ABUSED BY HIS FATHER, NOR BY HIS STEPFATHER, AND HAS NEVER STATED NOR IMPLIED OTHERWISE TO ANYONE, ANYWHERE, AT ANY TIME.

REGARDING THE *"SURPRISE"*, SEE THE STATEMENT ABOVE, AND THE ENTIRE MEMO BELOW, BY ASSISTANT U.S. ATTORNEY PAUL KELLY IN HIS 10 NOVEMBER 1992 "MEMO TO FILE" THAT THIS CLAIM BY SHAY OF A "SURPRISE" WAS A HOAX.

PAGE 6. *"You see, he's an acquaintance. I would talk to him once a month, maybe twice a - twice a month. You know, it wasn't like I was with him twenty-four seven."*

INDEED IT WASN'T. ALFRED TRENKLER MET THOMAS A. SHAY IN JUNE OF 1991 AND GAVE HIM FIVE CAR RIDES TO SHAY'S REQUESTED DESTINATIONS IN JUNE AND JULY, AND SAW HIM AGAIN IN AUGUST, ONCE, IN A CHANCE

MEETING. ALFRED TRENKLER NEVER CALLED THOMAS A. SHAY AND NEVER TALKED WITH HIM ON THE PHONE, EXCEPT ONCE TO CALL HIM TO TELL HIM TO STOP CALLING. THAT'S SIX FACE-TO-FACE ENCOUNTERS AND ONE TELEPHONE CALL OVER THE PERIOD OF JUNE-JULY-AUGUST, 1991.

PAGE 6 *"Three years."* [in response to the question by Karen Marinella, ***"But your relationship or your friendship or your acquaintance went over a period of two years?"***]

"THREE YEARS" IS FALSE, AS THE PERIOD WAS THREE MONTHS.

PAGE 6 *"We, you know, went out and did things. Went bowling and the movies and stuff like that."*

ALFRED TRENKLER NEVER "DID" ANYTHING WITH THOMAS A. SHAY EXCEPT FIVE RIDES, A CHANCE ENCOUNTER, TOGETHER WITH JOHN CATES, AND A TELEPHONE CALL TO STOP SHAY FROM MAKING CALLS TO HIM. ALFRED TRENKLER AND THOMAS A. SHAY NEVER WENT BOWLING TOGETHER AND NEVER SAW A SINGLE MOVIE TOGETHER. THE LAST TIME ALFRED TRENKLER WENT BOWLING WAS IN THE 1980'S.

PAGE 6-7 *"Friends. Well, ac- he was an acquaintance. I have friends that I spend twenty-four/seven with and I have friends that I talk to every now and then."* [Marinella, ***"And he was one of those - somebody you'd see now and then."***] *"Right"*

SEE ABOVE. NONE OF THOMAS A. SHAY'S FRIENDS, WHO WERE INTERVIEWED BY ATF AND BOSTON INVESTIGATORS, KNEW ALFRED TRENKLER, OR WHO HE WAS OR OF HIS ACQUAINTANCE WITH TOM SHAY.

PAGE 7 *"We have the same feelings. We have - he was abused and I was abused, and we relate."*

ALFRED TRENKLER WAS NEVER ABUSED BY ANYONE, AT ANY TIME.

PAGE 7 *"We cried together"*

ALFRED TRENKLER AND THOMAS A. SHAY DID NOT CRY TOGETHER.

PAGE 8 *"He was angry that it - that it had happened to me and maybe that was my father's fault or my mother's fault because it was in those schools."*

ALFRED TRENKLER WAS NEVER ANGRY ABOUT ANY PART OF THOMAS A. SHAY'S PAST LIFE. THOMAS A. SHAY NEVER TOLD HIM ABOUT ANY SUCH SCHOOLS. ALFRED TRENKLER WAS ANGERED, HOWEVER, BY THOMAS A. SHAY'S LYING TO HIM AND HIS REQUEST FOR TRENKLER'S BUSINESS CARD UNDER FALSE PRETENSES AND BY HIS ANNOYING PHONE MESSAGES. AS THOMAS A. SHAY TOLD ALFRED TRENKLER NOTHING ABOUT HIS UPBRINGING, EXCEPT FROM WHAT MIGHT BE INFERRED ON THAT FIRST REQUEST RIDE "HOME" WHEN SHAY REMEMBERED THAT HIS FATHER REALLY DIDN'T WANT HIM "HOME". ALFRED TRENKLER FELT NO ANGER TOWARD SHAY'S FATHER NOR TOWARD HIS MOTHER.

PAGE 8 *"So he builds a bomb, tries to kill my father and thinks that I'm going to be happy over it, maybe even thinks that I'm going to collect a half million dollars because my father's in a lawsuit with some people."*

ALFRED TRENKLER NEVER EVEN KNEW THE NAME OF THOMAS A. SHAY'S FATHER, NOR WHERE HE LIVED. THOMAS A. SHAY NEVER TOLD ALFRED TRENKLER ABOUT HIS FATHER'S LAWSUIT AGAINST THE DEDHAM SERVICE CENTER. ALFRED TRENKLER NEVER HURT ANYONE IN HIS LIFE. IN FACT, HE

HAD SERVED AS A VOLUNTEER IN RESCUING PEOPLE. IN THE FALL OF 1991, ALFRED TRENKLER WAS IN THE MIDDLE OF A LARGE BUSINESS CONTRACT WITH THE CHRISTIAN SCIENCE SOCIETY AND WAS REMODELING HIS WEYMOUTH OFFICE.

PAGE 9 *"I was helping* [by the claimed purchase at Radio Shack] *to purchase stuff for his work to build antennas or lights or whatever."*

ALFRED TRENKLER NEVER REQUESTED THOMAS A. SHAY TO MAKE ANY PURCHASES OF ANYTHING, ANYWHERE, IN ANY STORE, FOR ANY PURPOSE.

ALFRED TRENKLER INSTALLED MICROWAVE ANTENNA EQUIPMENT PROVIDED BY HIS CUSTOMERS. RADIO SHACK WAS NOT A SUPPLIER OF SUCH MICROWAVE EQUIPMENT.

PAGE 9 *"Because I like to handle money and he's got, you know mega hundred dollar bills... but Al had me go in there and purchased these things. He said, go across the street. He gave me a list. I went in there. I got the stuff. Al came in behind me, and he knew that I like to purchase, you know, I like to be the guy with the money and, you know, go out to a restaurant whatever, and buy the stuff."*

ALFRED TRENKLER NEVER HAD A HUNDRED DOLLAR BILL AT ANY TIME IN THE PRESENCE OF THOMAS A. SHAY. ALFRED TRENKLER NEVER REQUESTED THOMAS A. SHAY TO MAKE ANY PURCHASES OF ANYTHING, ANYWHERE, IN ANY STORE, FOR ANY PURPOSE. ALFRED TRENKLER ALWAYS PAID FOR HIS WORK-RELATED PURCHASES FROM A JOINT BUSINESS CHECKING ACCOUNT. ALFRED TRENKLER NEVER GAVE THOMAS A. SHAY A LIST FOR ANYTHING TO BUY. ALFRED TRENKLER NEVER WENT INTO ANY STORE WITH THOMAS A. SHAY, EITHER BEFORE OR AFTER.

THOMAS A. SHAY WAS NEVER AT ANY OF ALFRED TRENKLER'S WORK SITES.

PAGE 10 *[Marinella: "**But you went with him on a trip where explosives were purchased?**"] "But not the explosives that were in the bomb."*

ALFRED TRENKLER HAS NEVER PURCHASED EXPLOSIVES, AND NEVER WENT ON SUCH A TRIP WITH THOMAS A. SHAY. THE ONLY TIME THE TWO TRAVELED TOGETHER WERE IN FIVE CAR RIDES TO DESTINATIONS REQUESTED BY THOMAS A. SHAY, E.G. HOME, RANDY STOLLER'S WORKPLACE IN ATTLEBORO, TO HIS MOTHER'S CONDO IN QUINCY, A NON-PARTY AND THEN TO HIS MOTHER'S HOME IN QUINCY AND DOWN BOYLSTON STREET TO FLEET BANK IN BOSTON.

ASSISTANT U.S. ATTORNEY PAUL KELLY WROTE IN HIS 10 NOVEMBER 1992 "Memo to File...8. There was no trip to Vermont and Canada with Trenkler to obtain munitions from some 'Soldier of Fortune' camp."

PAGE 11 *[Marinella: "**what was he saying to you that this was going to be used for?**"] "For antennas, for towers, that something was broken in Norwood or the tower that he works at in Hingham."*

ALFRED TRENKLER HAD NO CUSTOMERS IN NORWOOD AND NOTHING WAS "BROKEN" THERE, AND CERTAINLY NOTHING THAT THOMAS A. SHAY COULD HELP FIX WITH A SMALL RETAIL PURCHASE. ALFRED TRENKLER NEVER WORKED ON ANY PROJECT, WHETHER A TOWER OR OTHERWISE, IN HINGHAM. DESPITE ATF'S EFFORTS, THOMAS A. SHAY WAS NEVER ABLE TO TAKE THE ATF INVESTIGATORS TO ANY ALLEGED TOWER WHERE HE WENT WITH ALFRED TRENKLER, BECAUSE NONE EXISTED.

PAGES 11-12 *[Marinella: "**And this was over what? a three month period of time or so?**" "Yeah. I must have gone to, I'd say between 25 and 50 stores with him and purchased all kinds of stuff, but everything - there's only two things that I purchased that were inside the explosive device that killed Officer Hurley and -"*
*[Marinella: "**What were those two things?**"]*
"The toggle switch and the AA battery holder."

ALFRED TRENKLER NEVER WENT TO A SINGLE STORE WITH THOMAS A. SHAY TO BUY ANYTHING. NOT ONE. NO WITNESS HAS EVER CLAIMED OTHERWISE. THOMAS A. SHAY WAS WRONG ABOUT THE BATTERY HOLDER AND TOGGLE SWITCH. THE AA BATTERY HOLDER IN THE ROSLINDALE BOMB WAS NOT A RADIO SHACK PRODUCT, AS IT CAME FROM THE FUTABA REMOTE CONTROL RECEIVER. FURTHER, THERE WAS NO EVIDENCE THAT THE SPECIFIC TOGGLE SWITCH ON THE 18 OCTOBER 1991 RECEIPT WAS IN THE ROSLINDALE BOMB. THERE WAS ONLY EVIDENCE THAT IT WAS OF THE SAME MODEL.

PAGE 12 *"I mean, actually, the only weird part about it* [the purchases] *was all the money that I got back from - in the receipts, I got to keep the receipts.... Trying to find them at my house right now, and I got to keep the money, you know. If I paid with a 50, and it was $5 worth of stuff, I got to keep the $45. "*

NO SUCH RECEIPTS WERE FOUND BY THOMAS A. SHAY AS NONE EVER EXISTED AS HE NEVER MADE THE CLAIMED PURCHASES WITH ALFRED TRENKLER. THERE WAS NEVER A $50 PURCHASE, NOR A PURCHASE FOR ANY OTHER AMOUNT, AND THOMAS A. SHAY NEVER KEPT THE CHANGE FOR ANY SUCH NON-PURCHASE WITH ALFRED TRENKLER. THE GOVERNMENT NEVER PRODUCED ANY RECEIPTS THAT THOMAS A. SHAY SPOKE ABOUT FOR A SIMPLE REASON: THERE WERE NONE.

PAGE 13 *"I thought it was kind of weird that he was letting me keep all the money after I spent those fifties and hundreds."*

THERE WERE NO PURCHASES, NO FIFTIES AND NO HUNDREDS. NEVER. NONE. ALFRED TRENKLER PAID FOR HIS COMPANY EQUIPMENT PURCHASES WITH COMPANY CHECKS, DRAWN ON A SHAWMUT BANK ACCOUNT IN QUINCY, MASS.

PAGE 13 *[Marinella: "**-did you think...he was building**?"*
"- a surprise. I started to think, you know, what has he - I thought he was building me a remote control car because I had loved-"
*[Marinella: '**Mm-hmm-**"] "- to play, you know, cars and trucks similar to the stuff and, you know, then he said, I'm - we're going to go and dump this stuff, I'm going to go out, you know, and go dump this stuff under 300 depth of water. I'm thinking - he says, you know, the police are never going to find it, and I said to myself, what does he mean by this. The police? What's the police have to do with my surprise?"*

ALFRED TRENKLER NEVER GAVE ANYTHING TO THOMAS A. SHAY EXCEPT FIVE CAR RIDES TO REQUESTED DESTINATIONS, AND ONE OF HIS BUSINESS CARDS.

THERE WAS NEVER A "SURPRISE". ASSISTANT U.S. ATTORNEY PAUL KELLY LATER WROTE IN HIS 10 NOVEMBER 1992 "Memo to File... 4. The whole story about Trenkler building him some unknown 'surprise' was a hoax."

THERE WAS NEVER ANY DISCUSSION ABOUT DUMPING ANYTHING IN WATER, WHETHER IT BE 3 FEET OF WATER, 20 FEET OR 300 FEET. THERE WAS NEVER ANY MENTION OF HIDING ANYTHING FROM THE POLICE.

PAGE 14 *[Marinella: "**Did you ask?**"] "I did ask what the police had to do with my surprise, and he just said, you know, mumbled something. I don't know."*

THOMAS A. SHAY NEVER ASKED ALFRED TRENKLER ABOUT THE PURPOSE FOR THE PURCHASES, BECAUSE THERE WERE NO PURCHASES AND HE NEVER ASKED ABOUT A "*SURPRISE*" AND HE NEVER ASKED ALFRED TRENKLER ABOUT THE RELATIONSHIP OF THE POLICE TO THE "*SURPRISE*". THERE WAS NO "*SURPRISE*" AND THERE WAS NO PREDICTABLE INTEREST BY THE POLICE IN ANY SUCH NON-SURPRISE.

PAGE 14 *"Yeah. I didn't know anything about actual bombs. Never mind the stuff we talked about, but actual bombs being made like the 1986 bomb what was found in the Quincy Fish Company truck, I never knew anything about that until the 28th."*

ALFRED TRENKLER DISCUSSED NOTHING OF HIS PERSONAL LIFE WITH THOMAS A. SHAY AND DID NOT INCLUDE ANY MENTION OF ALFRED'S ROLE WITH THE 1986 M-21 HOFFMAN ARTILLERY SIMULATOR PLACED AND DETONATED ON THE REAR SIDE OF A TRUCK IN QUINCY.

THUS, SHAY'S DENIAL OF KNOWLEDGE OF THE 1986 INCIDENT, BEFORE 28 OCTOBER 1991, IS SURELY TRUE. THOMAS A. SHAY LEARNED ABOUT THAT 1986 INCIDENT FROM THE BOSTON POLICE OR FROM THE ATF AGENTS WHEN HE WAS QUESTIONED BY THEM OR FROM THE MANY NEWSPAPER ARTICLES.

PAGE 15 *"Alfred Trenkler's lawyer w__ go make - Terry Segal went to make a deal with Paul Kelly. Paul Kelly would neither give me the deal, a person that is not violent, that h__ no."*

ALFRED TRENKLER'S ATTORNEY WAS TERRY SEGAL, BUT HE NEVER SOUGHT TO MAKE ANY KIND OF A DEAL WITH ASSISTANT U.S. ATTORNEY PAUL KELLY, BECAUSE ALFRED TRENKLER WAS COMPLETELY INNOCENT OF ANY INVOLVEMENT. HE HAD NO INFORMATION TO OFFER THE GOVERNMENT. IN FACT, ONLY THOMAS A. SHAY WAS OFFERED ANY DEAL BY THE U.S. ATTORNEY'S OFFICE, AND THAT WAS WITH THE GOAL OF SNARING ALFRED TRENKLER.

PAGE 16 *"... and he [Paul Kelly] knows that Al Trenkler is the dangerous one..."* ALFRED TRENKLER HAS ALWAYS BEEN, AND CONTINUES TO BE, A NON-VIOLENT PERSON.

PAGE 16 *"... Al Trenkler told the police only me and Tom Shay know, he said, we're the only people that know. He went to Paul Kelly and said, I want to make a deal... I believe that Al Trenkler, if he gives himself up, will say Tom Shay had no involvement because I had no actual involvement, no knowledge, until after it exploded."*

ALFRED TRENKLER SAID NOTHING LIKE THAT TO THE BOSTON POLICE NOR TO THE ATF AGENTS NOR TO THE ASST. U.S. ATTORNEY, AND NOTHING LIKE THAT WAS EVER RECORDED IN ANY OF THE VOLUMINOUS REPORTS OF THIS CASE. IT MAY BE THAT SHAY IS REFERRING TO DENNIS LEAHY'S CLAIM THAT ALFRED SAID, "*IF WE DID IT, THEN ONLY WE KNOW ABOUT IT. HOW WILL YOU EVER FIND OUT AND IF NEITHER ONE OF US TALKED?*" (TT 11-73) HOWEVER WHAT ALFRED TRENKLER ACTUALLY SAID WAS, "*IF NEITHER ONE OF US DID ANYTHING WHY WOULD ONE SAY THE OTHER DID ANYTHING?*"

ALFRED TRENKLER HAS NEVER SPOKEN TO PAUL KELLY AT ANY TIME NOR ABOUT ANY DEAL. THE ONLY ONE OFFERED A DEAL BY PAUL KELLY WAS THOMAS A. SHAY, BUT SHAY WAS DEEMED UNTRUTHFUL. TO THIS DAY, ALFRED TRENKLER HAS NEVER SPOKEN WITH PAUL KELLY. PERHAPS IT SHOULD BE A REQUIREMENT THAT EVERY PROSECUTOR MEET THE PEOPLE THEY ARE PROSECUTING BEFORE THEY GET INTO THE BULL RING OF A TRIAL.

PAGE 17-18 *"I was not sure that Al Trenkler did it or not. There is still a piece missing in the case. Al Trenkler doesn't know it....There's a - still a piece missing and the puzzle can't be solved until we get that piece. How did my father know it was a bomb?"*

ALFRED TRENKLER DEFINITELY DOES NOT KNOW WHO BUILT THE BOMB AND DIDN'T KNOW ANYTHING ABOUT IT UNTIL HE READ A NEWSPAPER ACCOUNT IN HIS CHIROPRACTOR'S OFFICE ON WEDNESDAY AFTERNOON ON 30 OCTOBER. THOMAS L. SHAY HAD PREDICTED TO A PSYCHOLOGIST THE PLACEMENT OF A BOMB UNDERNEATH HIS CAR PRIOR TO THE INCIDENT.

PAGE 19 *[Marinella: "**You haven't - when was the last time you heard from Al Trenkler?"]***

"1991, before - well, I got a - I got a note through a guard at the Nashua Street jail in Boston, but I can't prove that."
*[Marinella: "**Saying?"]***
"From Al Trenkler saying he wanted to talk to me. Said don't tell them anything, you know, don't say anything about your purchases. That's exactly what it said."

AS OF 17 OCTOBER 1992, THE DATE OF THIS INTERVIEW, ALFRED TRENKLER HAD NOT TALKED WITH THOMAS A. SHAY SINCE AUGUST, 1991. ALFRED TRENKLER HAS NEVER WRITTEN A NOTE TO TOM SHAY, AND WROTE NO NOTES TO TOM SHAY IN JAIL AND NO SUCH NOTE HAS BEEN FOUND. THE GOVERNMENT AND SHAY'S AND TRENKLER'S ATTORNEYS HAVE COPIES OF SEVERAL LETTERS TO AND FROM THOMAS A. SHAY AT SEVERAL JAILS. NONE WAS TO OR FROM ALFRED TRENKLER. THOMAS A. SHAY CANNOT PROVE THAT HE RECEIVED SUCH A LETTER, BECAUSE NONE WAS EVER WRITTEN.

PAGE 20 *[Marinella: "**Okay. In the course of your relationship with Mr. Al Trenkler, you never sat down and talked about how you could get revenge on your father or -"]***
"Nope, Nope, nope."

ALFRED TRENKER AND THOMAS A. SHAY NEVER SAT DOWN TO TALK ABOUT ANYTHING OF SUCH A NATURE.

PAGE 22 *"I never said that I disliked my father or anything like that to Al Trenkler. I said that it's my father's responsibility of why I was in those schools."*
*[Marinella: "**Mm-hmm.**"]*
"Al Trenkler took it as, gees, this guy's a real asshole. You know?"

EXCEPT FOR THOMAS A. SHAY TELLING ALFRED TRENKLER THAT HE COULD NOT BE DRIVEN TO HIS FATHER'S HOME, AFTER ALL, ON THAT FIRST REQUESTED RIDE "HOME", THOMAS A. SHAY SAID NOTHING TO ALFRED TRENKLER ABOUT HIS FATHER, NOR ABOUT HIS YEARS IN INSTITUTIONS FOR CHILDREN AND ADOLESCENTS.

IN FACT, THOMAS A. SHAY HAD ALFRED TRENKLER DRIVE HIM TO A HOUSE ON RICHMOND STREET IN DORCHESTER CLAIMING THIS WAS HIS FATHER'S

HOUSE, BUT THAT WAS ANOTHER LIE. HIS MOTHER LIVED ON RICHMOND STREET IN THE LATE 1980'S.

PAGE 23 *"I'm telling you, we share that same thing... Al Trenkler was abused by other people... He couldn't get back at his father so he decides to get back at my father.... That's how Paul Kelly sees it. That's how the Feds see it. That's how I see it."*

ALFRED TRENKLER HAD NOTHING IN COMMON WITH THOMAS A. SHAY, AND THAT CERTAINLY DID NOT INCLUDE ANY MEASURE OF ANY KIND OF ABUSE AS DEFINED BY THOMAS A. SHAY.

PAGE 25 *[Marinella:* **"I have to ask these questions, Tom. I mean, I mean, I - how many things have - have we talked about the past few months that perhaps haven't happened yet or perhaps the truth was stretched a little bit? I mean, you've told me from day one you knew nothing about this from day one, and now this is a complete turnaround so I have to ask you why I should believe this now. I have to. Tell me."]**

THERE WAS NO GOOD REASON, AND THE INTERVIEW SHOULD NOT HAVE BEEN SHOWN ON TELEVISION WITHOUT ANY COMMENTS OR FACT CHECKING. IT SHOULD NOT HAVE BEEN SHOWN TO EITHER THE SHAY AND TRENKLER TRIAL JURIES IN THE ABSENCE OF ANY ABILITY TO CROSS-EXAMINE TOM SHAY OR OTHERWISE VERIFY THE ALLEGATIONS HE MADE.

PAGE 30-31 *[Marinella:* **"Again, I'm just asking because so many things that you and I have talked about in the past few months, A, haven't happened, or, B, the truth - ... has been stretched."]**

UNFORTUNATELY, NO ONE EVER FOLLOWED UP ON THE INTERVIEW WITH ANY KIND OF "FACT CHECKING" WORK. KAREN MARINELLA WAS CORRECTLY SKEPTICAL, BUT CHANNEL 56 SHOULD NOT HAVE BROADCAST THE INTERVIEW WITH OUT FACT CHECKING.

PAGE 31 *"I never saw Al Trenkler build the bomb so he might not have, but little pieces add up. I purchased the Radio Shack stuff for Al Trenkler. Then the stuff's found in the bomb that killed the cop. Al Trenkler's the one that had the stuff so Al Trenkler must have built it, the one that has something of building a bomb. He's in electronics and, also, like a fingerprint, the bomb that he built in '86 is exactly - there's only two different things about it was what I was told by the Feds, what - what was in the bomb. It was like a fingerprint in '86 to the '91."*

THOMAS A. SHAY PURCHASED NOTHING FOR ALFRED TRENKLER AND IT'S DOUBTFUL, EVEN THOUGH CLAIMED BY THE GOVERNMENT, THAT THERE WERE ANY RADIO SHACK PARTS IN THE 1991 BOMB. THERE WAS NEVER ANY OFFER OF PROOF THAT ANY OF THE ITEMS ALLEGEDLY PURCHASED BY THOMAS A. SHAY AT THE 197 MASS. AVE RADIO SHACK STORE WAS ACTUALLY FOUND TO BE PART OF THE BOMB. NO EVIDENCE WHATSOEVER.

PAGE 32 *"... I have investigative techniques. In my mind I can put things together. Once Terry Segal - my lawyer Jefferson Boone told me that Terry Segal was trying to make a deal with this, I thought to myself, shit. You know? Why should he be making the deal? I had nothing to do with this. My story doesn't corroborate. I, but if I had - if there were two of me, if I was twins, I'd bet my other half, his life or my life, I should say, that Al Trenkler's going to come in and say Tom Shay didn't have anything to do with this, this is the story."*

ALFRED TRENKLER'S LAWYER, TERRY SEGAL, DID NOT TRY TO NEGOTIATE A PLEA WITH THE U.S. ATTORNEY'S OFFICE. JEFFERSON BOONE NEVER SAID SO, TO ANYONE.

AN INNOCENT MAN SHOULD NOT HAVE TO PLEAD GUILTY TO A CRIME HE DID NOT COMMIT. AS FAR AS ALFRED TRENKLER KNOWS, THOMAS A. SHAY HAD NO ROLE IN THE BUILDING OR PLACEMENT OF THE ROSLINDALE BOMB EITHER.

PAGE 33 *"He's* [Trenkler] *the dangerous one... He's the one that built it."*
ALFRED TRENKLER HAD ABSOLUTELY NO ROLE IN THE BUILDING AND PLACEMENT OF THE ROSLINDALE BOMB.

PAGE 34 *"... Every time I was in Paul Kelly's office, the U.S. Attorney's office, I always said Al Trenkler had done it, had done this on his own. I've always stuck to that story, and I always will stick to that story."*
THOMAS A. SHAY HAD NO EVIDENCE OF ALFRED TRENKLER'S ROLE IN THE BUILDING AND PLACEMENT OF THE ROSLINDALE BOMB BECAUSE THERE IS NONE TO BE FOUND. THOMAS A. SHAY ALSO TOLD ASST. U.S. ATTORNEY PAUL KELLY THAT HIS FATHER, THOMAS L. SHAY, BUILT THE ROSLINDALE BOMB FOR THE INSURANCE MONEY AND IN ANOTHER VARIATION, THAT THOMAS L. SHAY'S BROTHER, ARTHUR SHAY, BUILT IT.

PAGE 35 *"... Also, I have a book coming out.... My lawyer has already hired a - a ghost writer. There's going to be a book. There's already going to be a book. There are already two people on it, one guy from the Parkway Transcript, and another person writing a book but I already forgot."*
NO BOOK BY THOMAS A. SHAY HAS EVER BEEN WRITTEN OR PUBLISHED.

PAGE 36 *"... The inmates in here call me rat, but I'm not going to let Al Trenkler go out and make a deal with somebody for something and then say something about me that I didn't do. Why - why shouldn't I go out and get the better deal?"*
ALFRED TRENKLER DID NOT MAKE ANY DEAL WITH THE U.S. ATTORNEY'S OFFICE AND NEVER OFFERED TO MAKE SUCH A PLEA BARGAIN DEAL. IT'S A COMMON PRACTICE IN POLICE INVESTIGATIONS TO TELL A SUSPECT THAT ANOTHER SUSPECT IS NEGOTIATING A PLEA BARGAIN, AS WAS APPARENTLY DONE IN THIS CASE.

PAGE 37 *"... they want to close this case. They want to just indict me and indict Trenkler and get it over with, but they want Trenkler, in a way more than they want me."*
JUDGING BY THE DISPARITY IN THE SENTENCES GIVEN BY JUDGE ZOBEL TO THOMAS A. SHAY AND ALFRED TRENKLER, THOMAS A. SHAY'S ASSESSMENT OF THIS ASPECT OF THE CASE SEEMS CORRECT.

PAGE 39 *"... my fingerprints aren't on that bomb, but there could be a half a fingerprint on that bomb that could be Al Trenkler's."*
ALFRED TRENKLER HAD NO INVOLVEMENT IN THE MAKING OF THE BOMB, AND HIS FINGERPRINTS ARE NOT ON ANY OF THE FRAGMENTS.

THE ATF AND BOSTON POLICE INVESTIGATORS DID RECOVER FINGERPRINTS FROM THOMAS L. SHAY'S CAR AS WELL, BUT NO INFORMATION HAS BEEN RELEASED ABOUT THE OWNERS OF THOSE PRINTS; AND ALFRED TRENKLER HAS BEEN DENIED ACCESS TO THEM.

After the television broadcast of portions of the Marinella interview, there was no attempt by Alfred Trenkler's lawyers to untangle the web of lies of Tom Shay. There was no request for an interview with Alfred Trenkler, as it was the lawyers' view that the truth was for the courts to determine, but trials are inefficient and ineffective engines of truth. Karen Marinella was and is a respected TV journalist and she would have given Alfred Trenkler a fair interview if she had been asked. Without a response, the public and more importantly, the investigators and AUSA's, believed that some or all of her interview with Tom Shay was true; and such belief was dangerous. The Selective Truth Temptation can be strong.

On 3 November, Detectives Francis Armstrong and Brendan Craven of the Boston Police Dept interviewed Larry Plant who was with Tom Shay in the Orientation Unit of the Plymouth County House of Correction on 13 October. Armstrong's report stated,

"Plant then asked Shay if he did in fact do it. Shay responded that he and his partner did. That his partner Al Trenkler had stated that he had a surprise for Shay. Shay later learned that Trenkler had a bomb which was intended to kill Shay Sr., so that Shay Jr. and Trenkler could split Jr.'s share of a $500,000 life insurance.

Shay went on to say that he was abused by his father. Along with members of the clergy, counselors and psychiatrists during his childhood. Plant told Shay that he did not want to hear what his father did to him.

Shay stated that Trenkler built the bomb with magnets, but that they fell off. Shay told Plant that Hurley's radio triggered the explosion. Shay stated that Trenkler had rigged the bomb so that Sr.'s car radio would trigger the device. Plant stated that Shay laughed about the fact that Hurley was killed....

Shay stated [to Plant] that he got the explosives at a National Guard barracks on the North Shore. Shay told Plant that he had explosives training in the US Army.

Plant stated that he felt that Jr. was telling lies when he began to giggle.

Plant stated that Shay Jr. said he would get even with his old man for what he had done to him. Jr. stated that when he wraps up his three years that the feds have promised him he will do [in] his old man.

Shay did not discuss who planted the bomb. However, he stated that, 'We ran after we left it there.' Plant understood 'we' to the mean Trenkler and Shay. Shay stated that when his father saw the bomb in the driveway he knew Jr. had planted it.

Shay states that he contacts Trenkler through one of his sisters. Plant was told by Shay that Trenkler is in California. Trenkler is afraid that Shay will rat him out. Plant had one conversation for 2 hours with Jr. on the 13th of October and approx. 6 more during the next 3 days.

Shay would say that he is not protecting Trenkler, then his mood would shift and he said, 'I can't let them (Feds) get to Trenkler, because then they'll know everything.'

Shay stated that he was working with the Feds and that he was taking time out in the ocean to show them where pieces of the bomb materials were thrown by him and Trenkler.

Shay stated that he had tried to kill his father in the past, but he could never overpower the elder Shay. Shay stated that he had been trying to kill his father since he had been released from the Baird Center in Plymouth.

Plant stated that Shay is not well liked by the prison population at Plymouth... no one can trust his erratic behavior.

Plant states that Shay takes pleasure in the fact that he is going to get away with this crime. Shay stated, 'I'm gonna do my three years and I also busted those cops.' Craven and I both asked what Plant meant by, 'busted.' Plant stated that it was prison jargon for getting over on or pulling a scam on someone."

Assuming that Plant's recollection is accurate, there are several problems with Shay's statements, as they relate to Alfred Trenkler.

1. There was no "surprise" from Alfred Trenkler for Tom Shay.

2. There was no $500,000 insurance policy for the life of Tom's father. There was a lawsuit, and the defendant corporation had insurance with a limit of $400,000, but there were six children and stepchildren of Thomas L. Shay. Assuming that the law suit were totally successful, which even Tom Shay understood to be unlikely, it wasn't clear that Tom Shay would inherit anything. One of his sisters had stated that she understood that Tom had been disinherited; but Tom may not have known that. If he was eligible to inherit a share it might have been between $10-25,000, which would mean, perhaps $5-12,500 for Alfred Trenkler. Was $5-12,500, with a potential payout perhaps years away, enough to encourage an acquaintance to murder someone? Alfred Trenkler was then working on a contract with the Christian Science Church that was netting more than that amount, and there were prospects for far more. Also, Alfred Trenkler cared less about money, and what it could buy, than most people.

3. Alfred Trenkler has never had any contact with any of Tom Shay's sisters, except that Paula saw Alfred Trenkler at her mother's apartment very briefly in June 1991.

4. Alfred Trenkler has been to California, once, in 1980, when he flew to Los Angeles with a New Hampshire friend, David King, for the sole purpose of driving David's car back to Gilsum, New Hampshire. It was an opportunity for Alfred to drive across the country. David had worked as a bit actor in Hollywood.

5. Alfred Trenkler never went on a boat with Tom Shay for any reason, let alone to dump unused parts from a construction project to build a small bomb. Such debris could have easily fit inside a paper grocery bag; and one would not need to go out into the ocean to dispose of the contents which might fill a grocery bag or two.

6. Alfred's total of 3.1 hours of conversational time with Tom Shay, was less than half of the total length of Larry Plant's 8 hours of conversations with Tom Shay.

On 9 November, Paul Kelly tried yet again to secure a plea agreement with Tom Shay. He wrote to Francis O'Rourke, Shay's new attorney along with Jefferson Boone, with an offer to consider a proffer of information by Tom Shay. The first paragraph states,

"This letter will confirm that the U.S. Attorney for the District of Massachusetts (the 'U.S. Attorney') will consider an accurate, truthful and complete proffer from your client, Thomas A. Shay, in connection with an ongoing investigation being conducted by this office. Given our recent experience with Shay being untruthful with us, please stress to him the importance of this requirement of truth and candor. Unless we are satisfied that he has been completely truthful, there will be no plea discussions with him following the proffer stage."

As with one earlier letters, this letter was co-signed by Tom Shay and his attorney, Francis O'Rourke. It illustrates what H.L. Mencken called a definition of re-marriage, "*the triumph of hope over experience.*" Given the content of his "Memo to file" he would write the following day, Kelly's reference to Shay being "untruthful with us" was a major understatement.

On 10 November, Paul Kelly wrote the extraordinary "Memorandum to File" which recognized the lies previously told to him by Tom Shay. Unfortunately, Kelly continued to believe that some of Shay's statements could still be relied upon to convict Alfred Trenkler. He continued to suffer from the Selective Truth Temptation [STT].

"Memorandum
Subject: Retraction by Thomas Shay, Jr.
Date: November 10, 1992
To: File
From: Paul V. Kelly

Yesterday I was summoned to the U.S. Marshal's lock-up by Attorney Frank O'Rourke to speak with his client, Tom Shay. I was joined by SA Jeff Kerr of ATF. My last contact with Shay was less than one week ago (in the lock-up with SA Jeff Kerr) when I advised Shay (1) we had been unable to corroborate any aspects of his 'story', (2) we had received recent information from various sources indicating his involvement in the bombing, and (3) I expected to indict him for murder.

Shay stated that out of fear of being charged and spending the rest of his life in prison, he had lied to me and the agents in several significant respects. Those aspects of his 'story' which he admitted were untrue are as follows:

1. He was not sexually abused by his father
2. He never went on a scuba diving trip with Trenkler
3. He fabricated the story about 'Jo-Jo'; there is no such person
4. The whole story about Trenkler building him some unknown 'surprise' was a hoax
5. He never accompanied Trenkler to the Quincy quarry, or participated with him in disposing of evidence
6. Trenkler never came to his house following the bombing on 10-28-91; he has not had face-to-face contact with Trenkler since before the bombing
7. He never saw a remote control car at Trenkler's apt.
8. There was no trip to Vermont and Canada with Trenkler to obtain munitions from some 'soldier of Fortune' camp
9. He and Trenkler never shopped together at the Dedham Mall
10. The tower he had told us about was not located in the Kingston/Marshfield area.

Shay then told us a new 'story' which he claimed was truthful -- obviously we have a high degree of skepticism. His new story may be summarized as follows:

1. He has known Trenkler for 2-3 years and was involved with him during the 6-8 week period prior to the bombing.
2. He told Trenkler that his father had sexually abused him (even though it wasn't true).
3. Trenkler told him that he had been sexually abused by his natural father
4. He told Trenkler about his dad's anticipated recovery of several hundred thousand dollars from a pending lawsuit.
5. Sometime in September, 1991, Shay, Trenkler and Rich Brown went on a boat trip on a small boat that Brown rented.
6. He and Trenkler have been to Provincetown together.
7. He asked Trenkler to build him a remote-controlled pick-up truck containing a bomb with magnets on it. Shay claims that he planned to go to a parking lot and get his 'jollies' by attempting to blow-up an unoccupied car. (This is not a credible explanation.)
8. He and Trenkler did visit Radio Shack on Massachusetts Ave. on 10-18-91.
9. He and Trenkler purchased a remote control unit from a hobby store (name unknown) at the Braintree Mall (South Shore Plaza) sometime in September, 1991. He recalls the price was approximately $300.
10. He and Trenkler visited other stores together (need more information).
11. Trenkler told him he obtained his dynamite from a guy in New Hampshire (name unknown).
12. He accompanied Trenkler on a ride to New Hampshire sometime in September - October, 1991. They visited a guy in the North Conway area who was somehow affiliated with or employed at a rock quarry.
13. Trenkler does know someone in New Hampshire who drives a red car named Cindy Mitchell. [sic]
14. Trenkler did come over to Shay's apartment sometime in early October, 1991 and was tossed-out by Ms. Shay.
15. He has stayed over [at] Trenkler's apartment and has had a sexual relationship with him.
16. Following the bombing, maybe the next day, Trenkler called him at his mother's house. During the call Trenkler told Shay not to worry because he had taken the remnants of the bomb and tossed them into the quarry in Quincy known as 'Niggers Heaven' where a boy recently drown. [sic]
17. He saw Trenkler building the device inside a shack adjacent to an electrical tower somewhere in Weymouth. He recalls seeing the magnets, and described the remote control unit.

Finally, Shay told us that he had received a threatening telephone call last Friday. Another inmate handed him the telephone, whereupon a deep male voice said, in effect, '...if you say anything more about Trenkler, we'll have your throat slit (for a carton of cigarettes).' Shay refused to identify the inmate who handed him the phone." [A copy of the memorandum to file, with Alfred Trenkler's annotations, is included in Appendix E.]

Again, Assistant U.S. Attorney Paul Kelly would have significantly helped his own understanding of the case if he had communicated these 17 new claims to Alfred Trenkler's attorneys. Then his "high degree of skepticism" would have been validated and he might have questioned whether he was pursuing the right people. However, he was part of the adversarial justice system, and each side is usually very careful about what it tells the other. If one side shows his or her hand too soon, he or she might lose the game, regardless of the fate of the truth. The following May, Paul Kelly did send similar information to Nancy Gertner, but there is no record of her response and no copy of any forwarding of the letter to Trenkler's attorneys and no indication that Paul Kelly received any feedback from Terry Segal.

To the extent that any of the 17 statements incriminated Alfred Trenkler in the Roslindale Bombing, they were as false as the 24 recorded by Paul Kelly on 13 October 1991. Each is noted below.

1. ALFRED TRENKLER KNEW TOM SHAY DURING THE SUMMER OF 1991 AND HIS LAST FACE-TO-FACE CONTACT WAS IN AUGUST 1991. ALFRED TRENKLER ONLY CALLED TOM SHAY ONCE, FOR THE PURPOSE OF TELLING HIM TO STOP CALLING HIM.

2. TOM SHAY DID NOT TELL ALFRED TRENKLER OF ANY ALLEGED SEXUAL ABUSE BY MR. THOMAS L. SHAY.

3. ALFRED TRENKLER NEVER TOLD TOM SHAY ABOUT ANY ABUSE BY HIS NATURAL FATHER, ALFRED (FREDDIE) TRENKLER, AND THERE WAS NONE.

4. ALFRED TRENKLER FIRST LEARNED ABOUT MR. THOMAS L. SHAY'S LAWSUIT FROM A NEWSPAPER ACCOUNT OR FROM A BOSTON POLICE OR ATF INVESTIGATOR; BUT NOT FROM TOM SHAY.

5. ALFRED TRENKLER NEVER WENT ON A BOAT TRIP WITH TOM SHAY, AND NEVER WITH RICH BROWN EITHER AND WITH EVEN GREATER CERTAINTY, NEVER WITH BOTH OF THEM TOGETHER.

6. ALFRED TRENKLER AND TOM SHAY NEVER WENT TO PROVINCETOWN TOGETHER. THE LONGEST OF TOM SHAY'S REQUESTED RIDES WAS TO RANDY STOLLER'S STORE IN ATTLEBORO, NEAR THE RHODE ISLAND BORDER.

7. TOM SHAY NEVER ASKED ALFRED TRENKLER TO BUILD ANYTHING FOR HIM, INCLUDING ANY KIND OF A REMOTE CONTROL DEVICE.

8. TOM SHAY AND ALFRED TRENKLER NEVER VISITED ANY RADIO SHACK STORE TOGETHER.

9. TOM SHAY AND ALFRED TRENKLER NEVER PURCHASED ANYTHING TOGETHER AND NEVER ANY REMOTE CONTROL DEVICE. ALFRED TRENKLER HAD NEVER TAKEN SHAY TO THE BRAINTREE MALL OR ANY OTHER SOUTH SHORE SHOPPING AREA. THE FUTABA RECEIVER IN THE ROSLINDALE BOMB WAS AN OLDER MODEL WHICH HADN'T BEEN PURCHASED RECENTLY BY ANYONE.

10. TOM SHAY AND ALFRED TRENKLER NEVER VISITED ANY STORES TOGETHER. ALFRED TRENKLER FIRST MET SHAY OUTSIDE A "WHITE HEN PANTRY" STORE IN BOSTON, BUT THAT WAS AFTER TRENKLER'S PURCHASE OF CIGARETTES OR OTHER ITEMS.

11. ALFRED TRENKLER HAS NEVER PURCHASED DYNAMITE ANYWHERE, AND NEVER DISCUSSED THE POSSIBLE PURCHASE OF DYNAMITE WITH TOM SHAY OR ANYONE ELSE.

12. ALFRED TRENKLER AND TOM SHAY NEVER TRAVELED TO NEW HAMPSHIRE TOGETHER, NOR TO VISIT ANY FRIEND WHO WORKED IN A ROCK QUARRY.

13. ALFRED TRENKLER NEVER KNEW A PERSON NAMED CINDY MITCHELL, NOR DOES HE RECALL KNOWING ANYONE FROM NEW HAMPSHIRE WITH A RED CAR.

14. ALFRED TRENKLER NEVER VISITED TOM SHAY'S MOTHER'S APARTMENT IN OCTOBER 1991. HE WAS THERE BRIEFLY ONE NIGHT IN JUNE 1991 WHEN HE DOZED ON A COUCH; AND LEFT AFTER TOM SHAY'S SISTER, PAULA, OBJECTED TO SHAY'S PRESENCE. ALFRED RECALLS THAT THE SISTER WAS POLITE TO HIM.

15. TOM SHAY WAS IN ALFRED TRENKLER'S APARTMENT, SHARED WITH JOHN CATES, ONCE IN JUNE BETWEEN ABOUT 3:00 A.M. AND 6:00 A.M. BEFORE BEING TAKEN TO RICHMOND ST. IN DORCHESTER. HE SLEPT ON THE COUCH, AND THERE WAS NO SEXUAL RELATIONSHIP BETWEEN THEM.

16. THERE HAD BEEN NO CONTACT BETWEEN ALFRED TRENKLER AND TOM SHAY AFTER THE 28 OCTOBER 1991 EXPLOSION. IN FACT, THERE HAD BEEN NO CONTACT SINCE AUGUST. AFTER ALFRED TRENKLER READ ABOUT THE EXPLOSION ON 30 OCTOBER, AND SHARED THE COMMENT WITH JOHN CATES THAT THE WHOLE STORY WAS A CRAZY AS TOM SHAY; ALFRED DID NOT CONTACT TOM SHAY EVEN TO EXPRESS CONCERN OR FOLLOW HIS CURIOSITY. IT WAS A CRAZY AND TRAGIC EVENT WHICH RELATED TO SOMEONE ALFRED TRENKLER HAD BECOME ACQUAINTED WITH THE SUMMER OF 1991 AND WAS GENERALLY TRYING TO AVOID. THE ROSLINDALE BOMB INCIDENT ONLY REINFORCED THE AVERSION.

17. TOM SHAY NEVER SAW ALFRED TRENKLER BUILD ANYTHING.

Finally, the implication that Alfred Trenkler was responsible for an alleged threatening call made to the Plymouth County Jail is entirely unfounded. The terms, "ridiculous" and "ludicrous," also fit.

AUSA Paul Kelly's findings led to the inevitable failure of the plea-bargain discussions, as Kelly's 12 November letter to Francis O'Rourke and Jefferson Boone confirmed. Kelly wrote, "I am writing at this time to formally advise you [of] what I have been saying for the past several weeks. To date, ATF has been unable to corroborate any aspects of the proffer provided to us by your client, Thomas A. Shay. It seems that the only independent evidence tending to confirm Shay's story is that which federal investigators had uncovered prior to Shay's recent proffer.

Given the foregoing, absent new evidence being brought to my attention that substantially corroborates significant aspects of Shay's proffer, I am unable to conclude that he has been 'entirely truthful and cooperative' concerning the offense under investigation or his role therein."

Sometime during Francis O'Rourke's brief representation, Tom Shay wrote an undated letter to Randy Stoller. *"Dear Randy, How has life been treating you, Good I hope! Its been a while since we have seen each other. I would like to see you, the Feds said they could get you up to see me and I told them I know that you would come on your own and that you had enough problems. I miss you Randy a lot. I hate to ask you to do this, But it's for a good reason. You are going to be asked to go to*

Federal Court at my trial. If you don't go on your own, my lawyer will subpoena you to court to testify. You might come one day or 10 days. It's up to how my lawyer works in your testimony. No matter what occurs I want you to write me a letter, with what your whole January & February schedule is going to be like. Tell me what's been going on & stuff and like my lawyer says, the more cooperation we get, the better. It is for you and us. My lawyer's #'s are listed below. If you have the need to call, do so, except [sic, accept] my calls, write to me and visit me soon. I will write or call when you respond. Don't worry about the press. Your name will remain in code on the stand. No pictures, or TV, Press will be near or around you. Sincerely, Thomas Shay." Curiously, although Tom Shay seemed to be able to call people and receive calls and to write people and receive visits, he never called Alfred Trenkler after 28 October, nor wrote to him nor asked for a visit from him. As with many other aspect of this story, the prosecution would interpret the absence of contact one way, and Alfred Trenkler another. Alfred Trenkler never sought to contact Tom Shay either, though his lawyers should have.

On 19 November, Mrs. Nancy Shay returned to testify before the grand jury, resuming her testimony which began the previous April.

On Monday, 30 November 1992, Tom Shay called the _Boston Globe_ from the Plymouth County House of Correction, which resulted in Tuesday's story, "_BOMBING SUSPECT AWAITING CHARGES._" Shay said that he would be indicted during the week of 14 December, and the reporters Matthew Brelis and John Ellement wrote that their unnamed "_sources confirmed Shay's account yesterday, saying that officials are prepared to indict Shay, 20, of Quincy and his one-time associate Alfred W. Trenkler, 36, of Milton, on five counts._" The article said that AUSA Paul Kelly had no comment and neither did Jefferson Boone.

The article said, "_Trenkler and Shay became associated in the spring or early summer of 1989, and investigators say they can place them together on many occasions, including several times when Shay stayed at Trenkler's apartment._" Also, while noting that both "_Shay and Trenkler have denied any involvement in the death of Hurley,_" the article said that Shay had once said, " '_If Al Trenkler did this, he did it on his own._' " No correction was requested by Alfred Trenkler nor his attorney, but advising reporters of corrective information would not have violated the rules against trying one's case in public. It would show a concern for the truth.

Shay's prediction of indictment and the date were quite accurate, so perhaps prosecutors who read the article were heartened to see that Tom Shay could actually reveal truth, and they were in a good position to corroborate that one about the upcoming indictment. Still, they would have been wiser and more humane if they had stuck to a variation of Ronald Reagan's view of arms agreements, "_mistrust and verify._"[8]

On 2 December, the _Boston Herald_ carried the story of Tom Shay's failed plea bargain negotiations, "_REPORT: BOMB SUSPECT'S DEAL WITH FEDS FELL APART._" Relying on a call from Tom Shay and unnamed government sources, reporter Jack Meyers wrote that "_the negotiations for a cooperation agreement ended after the suspect, Thomas A. Shay, 21, was found to be deceiving federal and state investigators, according to sources familiar with the case._"

The article continued, "S_hay, the son of Thomas L. Shay, who called Boston Police when an unusual device dropped from his car at his Eastbourne Street home, has_ *told the Herald he tried to strike a deal with the U.S. attorneys handling the case, but the talks ended when he was found to be lying about aspects of the case.*

Shay approached authorities in early October about cooperating and provided investigators with extensive statements, some of which implicated Trenkler, whom federal prosecutors have notified is a 'target' in the case, sources said.

Agents from the federal Bureau of Alcohol, Tobacco and Firearms and Boston Police homicide detectives investigated Shay's statements but were 'unable to corroborate large portions of his story' said one source.

The investigators found Shay 'minimized' his own role in the bombing, which killed Boston Police bomb squad officer Jeremiah J. Hurley Jr. and badly injured his partner Francis X. Foley, sources said.

Prosecutors had sought Shay's cooperation in gathering evidence against the bomb's builder, believing at the time they needed Shay to get a conviction, sources said.

However, according to sources, prosecutors now are preparing to indict both men even without Shay's cooperation. An indictment could be sought before the grand jury within the next three weeks, they said.

One of Shay's lawyers, Jefferson Boone, said he had no way of knowing what the grand jury and prosecutors are planning to do. When asked about Shay's efforts to strike a deal, Boone refused to comment.

Trenkler was charged with unlawful possession of an explosive in 1986 for allegedly building a bomb triggered under a fish company truck in Quincy. That bomb was nearly identical to the one that killed Hurley, sources have told the Herald."

The reaction from Alfred Trenkler and his attorneys was not noted, but they could have informed Jack Meyers and the *Boston Herald* that the device using an M21 Hoffman artillery noise simulator was not *"nearly identical"* to a device with the equivalent of 2-3 sticks of dynamite. As First Circuit Court of Appeals Chief Judge, Juan Torruella wrote later in dissent, *"Equating the two devices is like equating a BB gun with a high caliber rifle."* If a response through the media by the Trenkler legal team was feared to violate the ethical prohibitions on arguing one's case in the media, the lawyers could have protested to a Federal Magistrate the continued leaking of details of the case.

The work of the grand jury continued. On 3 December, the grand jurors heard from Lawrence Plant, the fellow inmate of Tom Shay, and inmate informer, at Plymouth County House of Correction. At the future trials of Tom Shay and Alfred Trenkler, he would be one of several to describe conversations with Shay which purportedly show Shay's involvement with the Roslindale Bomb. Also at the grand jury, separately, were Mr. Thomas L. Shay's neighbors, Eleanor McKernan and James McKernan. A week later, on 10 December, Donna Shea returned for a second round of testimony, following up on her first appearance on 13 February.

On 15 December, Attorney O'Rourke called AUSA Paul Kelly to ask him to come meet with his client, Thomas A. Shay. Below is Paul Kelly's recollection of the interview, as written three weeks later on 5 January 1993.
"Memorandum
Subject: Meeting with Tom Shay, Jr.
Date: January 5, 1993
To: File

From: Paul V. Kelly, Assistant U.S. Attorney

On Tuesday afternoon, December 15, 1992, I was working in my office when I received a telephone call at approximately 3:00 p.m. from Attorney Frank O'Rourke requesting that I come up to the U.S. Marshal's lock-up to speak with his client, Tom Shay ('Shay Jr.'). Knowing that I was about to indict Shay Jr. the following day (which I did not disclose), I declined to go upstairs. About twenty (20) minutes later Attorney O'Rourke called again to tell me that Shay Jr. was insisting to speak with me and that it might be worth [my] while to come to the lockup. I agreed to go upstairs for a few minutes.

Upon my arrival at the U.S. Marshal's office I spoke with Attorney O'Rourke who asked whether any discussion with Shay Jr. could be covered by our earlier written proffer agreement. I agreed. Upon entering the cell area I observed Shay Jr., who appeared to me to be in a somber and serious mood. His manner, demeanor and comments to me reflected fear and apprehension. Throughout the approximately thirty (30) minutes that I spent with Shay Jr. (with O'Rourke present the entire time), he was logical and very lucid, without the mood swings exhibited during some of my previous visits with him.

Shay Jr. asked me 'If I tell you the entire truth and agree to cooperate and testify, how much time am I looking at?' I explained to him that would be up to the judge, but that 'I would expect a sentence of around twenty (20) years.' With that, Shay Jr. proclaimed 'I can't do twenty (20) years; I can't be in prison until I'm 40.' I then told him that while such a sentence sounded harsh, it was certainly preferable to a non-parolable life sentence (which appears to be mandated by the federal sentencing guidelines).

Shay Jr. later asked me, 'What's your theory?' When I asked what he meant, he said, 'What's your theory about why we did it?' I told him that I would not discuss the government's evidence or its theory with him. Shay Jr. then stated, 'Well, if your theory is that we did it for the insurance money, your [sic] right. Trenkler was promised one-half of my share, which would have been at least $100,000.' Shay Jr. continued, 'it made no difference to me that it was my father, I still haven't even thought about that that much. In fact, if someone came to me right now and offered me that kind of money to kill my father, I'd do it again.' I then asked Attorney O'Rourke if I could ask Shay Jr. some questions. He said, 'that's up to him, he's the one who wanted to speak with you.' Shay Jr. said it was okay to ask him a few questions.

I asked, 'Where'd you get the dynamite and blasting caps?' He responded. 'That was all Trenkler, I had nothing to do with that.' He proclaimed not to know how or where Trenkler had obtained the explosives.

I asked, 'Where was the bomb built?' Shay Jr. said 'in a shed adjacent to a radio tower somewhere in the Quincy or South Shore area.' He insisted that he has been truthful about this point all along.

I asked, 'Where and when was the bomb attached to his father's car?' He said, 'A couple of days before the explosion while the Buick was parked in the vicinity of the Waltham Tavern in the South End of Boston.' Shay Jr. said that Trenkler attached the device, not him, and that he never got out of the car. He mentioned that he saw the bomb when Trenkler had it inside the trunk of his car (his description of the same was pretty accurate), and that he thought Trenkler stuck it on the gas tank or muffler (although he wasn't really sure).

At this point, I had a meeting to attend downstairs and had to leave. Rather than leave Shay Jr. feeling as if he'd been double-crossed, I told him very bluntly that he would be indicted very soon (although I did not say that it would happen the next day, since I did not want to read my comments in the morning papers). He asked what the charges would be. Attorney O'Rourke interjected and reminded Shay Jr. that they had already talked about that. Shay Jr. asked me whether we would seek the death penalty? I told him that issue had not been decided, although I though it was unlikely. Finally, I told Shay Jr. that if and when an indictment was returned, that would not mean that he and I would not be able to talk further. On the contrary, I told him that, after speaking with his attorneys, he may well want to speak to me again -- so long as he was prepared to be completely candid and truthful.

The foregoing is prepared from memory nearly three (3) weeks after the fact. It is not intended to be a verbatim recital, but I believe it captures the essence of what was discussed."

This interview occurred 13 days after the _Herald_ reported the termination of plea-bargain negotiations due to Tom Shay's unreliable lies. In fact, the lying was becoming a reliable practice, but Paul Kelly still suffered from the Selective Truth Temptation, and wanted to believe that Shay could tell him enough selected bits truth to persuade the jury of Trenkler's guilt.

The only new allegations were Tom Shay's statements about how Alfred Trenkler placed the bomb underneath Mr. Thomas L. Shay's car on Saturday evening, 26 October, and how the bomb was in the trunk of Trenkler's car. As noted before, Alfred Trenkler had not seen Tom Shay since a chance encounter in August 1991, and there was never a bomb in the trunk of Trenkler's car. If there had been, the carpet sample taken by the ATF in the early morning of 6 November 1991 would have contained detectable traces of dynamite. None was found.

Below is Alfred Trenkler's response to the Quincy/South Shore shed lies, "_First, there are a limited number of towers in Quincy. The only two that I can think of would be at the Quincy quarries, one being cellular, one which has a stucco building next to it and both tower and shed are surrounded with a fence. This site I do not or [have] ever had access to, or ever been in. The second would be the MCI tower also at the Quincy quarries. Both tower and shed also surrounded with a fence and also which I do not or [have] ever had access to, or ever been in. As for anywhere else in the South Shore, I have never been in any sheds next to radio towers nor ever had any access to them nor have I ever been in any. As for sheds near 50 foot electrical towers in the Weymouth area, I am not aware of any in existence._"

On 2 December, 1992 James Harding was wired by the ATF with a radio transmitter and attended a meeting with Alfred Trenkler at the ARCOMM offices as "CI #97, a Confidential Informant for ATF. Outside the building with radio reception equipment were ATF Special Agents Jeff Kerr and Thomas D'Ambrosio and Boston Detective Brendan Craven. As Harding emerged from the building he recorded his satisfaction on the tape, "_Well, that's one less gay guy for the St. Paddy's Day_ *parade next year."* However, his optimism was misplaced as Alfred Trenkler said nothing to him that was incriminating. Later, Kerr and D'Ambrosio met with Harding to give him further instructions, but the meeting did not go well. On 12 December, ATF Special Agent Jeff Kerr decided to terminate the relationship with James Harding, because "CI #97's method of operation conflicted with ATF's investigative philosophy and were not acceptable to the agents... and as a result authority for the CI to use electronic monitoring was rescinded."

The Harding effort was only one of the failed hi-tech efforts. During 1992, the orders for electronic surveillance of the phones and pagers of Alfred Trenkler, John Cates, Thomas L. Shay and Mary Flanagan were extended for a total of three 60 day periods, with no incriminating results. The most recent orders were signed by U.S. Magistrate Marianne Bowler on 13 May and expired on 13 July. With that activity dried up, the only remaining orders dealt with the delicate question of when the Government would be required to notify people who were the objects of the wiretapping, and also those whose calls had been intercepted. On 21 April 1992, AUSA Frank Libby asked for a 90 day postponement on the notification requirements, as some of the electronic surveillance was being extended. Supporting that request was a three-page affidavit by ATF Special Agent Jeff Kerr which said that notifying the subjects of the electronic surveillance would "undoubtedly jeopardize this ongoing investigation." Additional 90-day extensions of this postponed obligation to notify were granted in July and in October.

Thus, by 15 December, several aspects of the investigation into the Roslindale Bomb were not going well. The informant, James Harding, produced nothing of value and his continued use would jeopardize the rest of the case. The electronic and physical monitoring of Alfred Trenkler produced nothing incriminating. None of the physical items seized during the several searches of Alfred's locations produced anything with any connection to the Roslindale Bomb. The $65,000 reward had not produced any useful leads.

However, the prosecutors moved forward despite the difficulties with the case. While some prosecutors are careful to proceed only when they are convinced themselves of guilt beyond a reasonable doubt of suspects, others feel that it is sufficient to build enough of a case so that the burden of the final decision can be shifted to the shoulders of twelve jurors. We'll likely never know the exact standard applied by Assistant U.S. Attorneys Paul Kelly and Frank Libby, but whatever it was, they decided to press forward with the next step: indictment. Actually, it was not a difficult step as there is considerable truth to the adage that "a good prosecutor could indict a ham sandwich."[9]

In Cambridge in mid-December, Alfred Trenkler and his ATNS team were installing a satellite dish at Massachusetts Institute of Technology. In describing his initial ARCOMM work for MIT, Alfred Trenkler shows his business sense and integrity. *"When I first met with Randy* [Winchester, Communications person at MIT] *he had no idea what kind of work I could do. I had sent him a company profile in Sep of '91 and he had told me that he had a lot of work planned that he would have to subcontract out. The first job he had for me was concerning an old* [satellite] *dish that had been installed by an inexperienced person, and Randy assumed that the whole dish had to be replaced and wanted a price to replace the dish and get a new receiver system. I gave him the price to replace* *everything (around $8,000.00) but when I came to the site, I showed him that all that was needed was a $50.00 dollar part and about $550.00 worth of labor to replace it. It was at this point in time that Randy was telling me abut the cable system that he wanted a bid on in the near future as well as other possible projects..."*

Alfred's work with Randy Winchester and MIT was weathering the corporate change to ATNS and the hovering cloud of accusations regarding the Roslindale Bomb. Randy Winchester had work for Alfred and Alfred was good at it. One of the first MIT projects for ATNS was a 16 January 1992 repair project and the December 1992 satellite installation contract was worth $10,000. Also in December 1992, Grant Crane asked Alfred to install 50 Motorola mobile radios in its vehicle fleet at its Readville branch. This proposed contract included an annual service contract which would gross $80,000. This career path was promising for Alfred Trenkler right through 15 December 1992.

END NOTES
----

1. Montaigne, in *Essays*.
2 The Waltham Tavern, at the corner of Waltham Street and Shawmut Ave. in Boston's South End, lost its liquor license in January 2006 after a Federal sting operation which found extensive drug dealing. The Licensing Board determined that both of the two listed owners of the tavern were deceased. One of them was Josephine Baiona, the wife of "reputed mobster Philip 'Sonny' Baiona, a convicted bookmaker who, a week after the tavern was shut down, pleaded guilty to selling cocaine and OcyCodone in 2002." (*Boston Globe*, "Say Goodbye, or Good Riddance, to old pub," 15 September 2007.
3. Shelley Murphy wrote that the key phrase was "completely innocent," as compared to John Ellement's recording of "perfectly innocent." Either the reporters heard the same sentence differently or Terry Segal said it differently when talking to each reporter separately.
4 Jodi Picoult, *Vanishing Acts*, Washington Square Press and Atria Books, 2005. The quote also appears on page 82 of another edition.
5. William McPhee was later disbarred in 2001 for mishandling clients' funds and cases.
6. The date of the handwritten letter appears to be Jul 9 91 or 94, but Tom Shay refers to himself as a 'suspect,' so it's guessed that he wrote this in 1992. The note is sufficiently thoughtful that it may have been written on 9 July 1993 when he was in court being tried; but the handwriting does not look like a "3".
7. The Plymouth County House of Correction, was to play a significant part in the story of the Alfred Trenkler case. Located in Plymouth, the home of the original Pilgrims, the jail's most important moment in the late 20th Century was the escape in 1985 of Charles Taylor who later became a Liberian guerrilla leader. Taylor had been arrested by U.S. Marshals for immigration violations and, like many Boston Federal detainees, including Tom Shay and Alfred Trenkler, was sent to Plymouth. After his escape and return to Liberia, he became the disputed leader of Liberia during a multi-faceted civil war; and is now awaiting trial in The Hague for crimes against humanity.
8. The original 8 March 1983 statement by President Reagan was, "Trust, but verify."
9. Another variation was from former Chief Judge of the New York State Court of Appeals, before he was himself indicted by a grand jury, "Even a modestly competent district attorney can get a grand jury to indict a ham sandwich."

> *"O, what a tangled web we weave,*
> *When first we practise to deceive!"*
> Sir Walter Scott[1]

The next step of the investigation and adjudication of the Roslindale Bomb was the five count indictment, issued by the grand jury on Wednesday, 16 December 1992. It was superseded by the substantially similar three count indictment below on 24 June 1993, upon which the trials of Thomas A. Shay and Alfred Trenkler were conducted.

SUPERSEDING INDICTMENT
COUNT ONE: (18 U.S.C. S371 - Conspiracy)
The Grand Jury charges that:
In or about September and October, 1991, at Boston, Quincy and elsewhere in the District of Massachusetts, THOMAS A. SHAY and ALFRED W. TRENKLER, defendants herein, did knowingly and willfully combine, conspire and agree with one another to commit certain offenses against the United States, to wit:
(1) receipt of explosives in interstate commerce with the knowledge and intent that the same would be used to kill, injure and intimidate another individual and damage and destroy real and personal property, including an automobile, in violation of Title 18, United States Code, Section 844(d), and
(2) attempted malicious destruction, by means of fire and explosive, of an automobile used in and affecting interstate commerce, in violation of Title 18, United States Code, Section 844 (i) .

Manner And Means Of Conspiracv
1. It was part of the conspiracy that the conspirators discussed and agreed to kill Thomas L. Shay (DOB: 7-5-44) of Roslindale, Massachusetts.
2. It was further part of the conspiracy the conspirators assisted one another in acquiring explosives and other materials to be used in the construction of a remote-controlled explosive device.
3. It was further part of the conspiracy that one or more of the conspirators affixed the explosive device to the undercarriage of an automobile owned and operated by Thomas L. Shay, to wit: a 1986 Buick. The device later exploded, killing Boston Police Bomb Squad Officer Jeremiah Hurley and seriously injuring his partner, Boston Police Bomb Squad Officer Francis Foley.

Overt Acts
4. In furtherance of the conspiracy and to effect the objects thereof, the following overt acts, among others, were committed by the conspirators.
(a) In or about September, 1991, SHAY solicited the assistance of TRENKLER in a plan to kill his father, Thomas L. Shay.
(b) In or about September, 1991, TRENKLER, who had a background in electronics, agreed to construct a remote controlled explosive device, knowing the same would be used by SHAY in an attempt to kill his father.

(c) On or about October 18, 1991, SHAY purchased and acquired electrical components needed for the construction and testing of the explosive device.

(d) In or about October, 1991, TRENKLER built a remote controlled explosive device consisting of dynamite, blasting caps and other materials.

(e) On or about October 27, 1991, the conspirators surreptitiously affixed the explosive device to an automobile owned and operated by SHAY's father, Thomas L. Shay.

All in violation of Title 18, United States Code, Section 371.

COUNT TWO: (18 U.S.C. S844(d) - Receipt Of explosive Materials; 18 U.S.C. 52 - Aiding And Abetting)

The Grand Jury further charges that: In or about October, 1991, in the District of Massachusetts, THOMAS A. SHAY and ALFRED W. TRENKLER, defendants herein, did receive in interstate commerce certain explosive materials, including dynamite and detonators, with knowledge and intent that said explosive materials would be used to kill, injure and intimidate Thomas L. Shay, and cause damage and destruction to his real and personal property, including a 1986 Buick automobile. The above-described unlawful conduct directly and proximately caused the death of Jeremiah Hurley and serious personal injury to Francis Foley, both public safety officers who were performing their official duties.

All in violation of Title 18, United States Code, Section 844(d), and Title 18, United States Code, Section 2.

COUNT THREE: (18 U.S.C. §844(i) - Attempted Malicious Destruction Of Property By Means Of Explosive; 18 U.S.C. S2 - Aiding And Abetting)

The Grand Jury further charges that: On or about October 28, 1991, at Boston in the District of Massachusetts, THOMAS A. SHAY and ALFRED W. TRENKLER, defendants herein, knowingly attempted to maliciously damage and destroy, by means of fire and explosive, a 1986 Buick automobile which was owned by Thomas L. Shay and used in interstate commerce and in activities affecting interstate commerce. The above-described unlawful conduct directly and proximately caused the death of Jeremiah Hurley and serious personal injury to Francis Foley, both public safety officers who were performing their official duties.

All in violation of Title 18, United States Code, Section 844(i), and Title 18, United States Code, Section 2.

That same day, Wednesday, 16 December, at 1:15 p.m. Alfred Trenkler was arrested at gunpoint by approximately 10 officers at a stoplight on Morrissey Boulevard, across from the defunct Neponset Drive-In movie lot. The ATF officers were in plainclothes and the uniformed Boston Police were in unmarked cars. Alfred was driving with two employees, Brian O'Leary and Richard Marshall, to his bank to deposit an MIT check to ARCOMM for $10,000. They had come from their work installing a satellite microwave link antenna at MIT. O'Leary was one of Alfred's most trusted friends and employees, and he was the carpenter of the group. Whenever, ARCOMM or ATNS needed woodwork done, such as for staging or platform, Brian O'Leary would do it. Alfred had no woodworking tools, beyond a hammer and handsaw.

As Alfred was entering the courthouse where he was arraigned, he was asked by TV newsman Charles Austin, *"Do you have anything to say?"* Alfred Trenkler responded firmly, *"I am an innocent man. I had nothing to do with this case."*

Alfred Trenkler was taken to the Plymouth County House of Correction, one of the regional facilities used by the Federal Government for housing its detainees.

On Thursday, 17 December the daily newspapers covered the indictment and arrest, and the law enforcement press conference. Jack Meyers' _Boston Herald_ article, *"FEDS INDICT QUINCY MEN IN FATAL BOMBING,"* said that U.S. Attorney A. John Pappalardo announced the indictment and several other law enforcement officials were present. The Boston ATF manager, Terence McArdle, said that more than 20,000 man hours had been invested in the investigation, including over 500 interviews. Boston Police Commissioner Mickey Roach and Suffolk County District Attorney Ralph Martin praised the investigation. The article stated that AUSA's Paul Kelly and Frank Libby *"plan to introduce evidence that Shay's motive was twofold: to collect $200,000 or more in insurance money for a pending lawsuit involving his father, while simultaneously getting revenge for his father's abuse and neglect, according to an informed source. 'He (the younger Shay) was in line to receive a couple hundred thousand dollars in insurance money from a pending lawsuit,' said the source."* One wonders how informed the *"source"* was or how deliberate was the exaggeration about the value of Mr. Thomas A. Shay's lawsuit or whether Meyers knew that Tom Shay, the son, was so uninterested in getting money from that lawsuit that he declined to participate as a plaintiff despite his own real injuries to his hearing from the October 1987 blast.

Regarding Trenkler, the article said, *"Dressed in blue jeans, work boots and a striped button-up shirt, Trenkler made an initial appearance in court yesterday and shook his head while Magistrate Judge Marianne B. Bowler read the charges against him."* Terry Segal was quoted, *"At trial when all the evidence is presented, it will become clear Al Trenkler was not involved in the tragic events in this case."* Not quoted was Segal's instructions to Alfred Trenkler, *"Don't talk with anyone."*

Tom Shay's arraignment was scheduled for the 17th, to which he would be brought from the Essex County House of Correction in Middleton where he was in Federal custody for the Brighton false bomb threat.

Matthew Brelis's article in the _Boston Globe_, *"2 HELD IN BLAST FATAL TO OFFICER"* noted that the retired and injured Francis X. Foley was present at the announcement of the indictment. The article said that A. John Pappalardo stated that two of the five counts of the indictment carried a possible punishment of death, but that prosecutors had not yet made the decision on whether to seek that penalty. Terry Segal was quoted, *"Alfred Trenkler is innocent of all charges."*

On Thursday the 17th, William David Lindholm was brought to the Boston U.S. Attorney's office from a Northampton, Mass. Federal jail facility for an interview allegedly unrelated to the case of U.S. v. Trenkler. Ostensibly, the meeting was to give information to the U.S. Attorney's office and to a federal grand jury[2] about his former drug smuggling associates, thereby setting in motion a coincidental, or not-so-coincidental, chain of events. He had been sentenced in December 1990 to 97 months in prison for marijuana distribution and income tax evasion and had been most recently serving his sentence at a prison in Texas.

Two days previously, on 15 December, Lindholm dropped his appeal of his 1990 conviction. Perhaps he already had an agreement with the Government about reducing his sentence in return for the drug-related testimony, or in return for his expected availability to testify against Whitey Bulger. It seems unlikely that it was in return for his upcoming efforts with Alfred Trenkler because the chances of success would have seemed low. However, maybe Lindholm calculated that his appeal chances were also low and that this was the way to prove his intention to help the government.

His interview on the 17th ended about 3:00-4:00. While in the lockup in the Federal building, he met Tom Shay, from whom little was heard. Lindholm then missed his 3:30-4:00 van, whether by design or by accident, to the Essex County jail in Middleton, Mass., and was taken to the Plymouth County House of Correction, in the late evening. Tom Shay didn't miss the bus to Middleton. Was it merely a mistake that Lindholm missed the van to Middleton? Was the schedule of that van so rigid that it couldn't wait for a prisoner who was surely on the list for the return trip? A prison van isn't like a municipal bus which picks up people at a bus stop. The driver knows who is scheduled to be in the van and who isn't.

At Plymouth, Lindholm was placed in the same holding/orientation area as Alfred Trenkler, who had come there the previous day. Of the group that came with Alfred, he was the only one remaining in the Orientation Unit. Was it an accident that he was left behind so he could meet David Lindholm? A related question was why was Lindholm not sent back to Boston the next morning, so he could catch the afternoon van back north to Middleton? Alfred was in that morning van to Boston for his bail hearing. One clue to the answer is the apparently extensive effort by the investigators and prosecutors to find or place inmate informants with Alfred Trenkler, and to persuade his previous friends and acquaintances, such as Michael Coady, to testify against him. Former Plymouth County House of Correction inmates David Magarry and Paul Shaw were willing to testify later about their observations of such law enforcement efforts to entice jailhouse snitching. If there was activity observed to achieve an informant among several "X" inmates and "Y" inmate steps forward as an informant, isn't it likely that that investigators were working with "Y" too? Two other inmates at Plymouth were a father and a son from the Lowell area and they would recall that Alfred was with them during that "Lindholm weekend," and that Lindholm was never alone with Alfred, and that Alfred ate his meals with them.

Lindholm was sick according to Alfred Trenkler, perhaps with the flu, and spent much of the weekend on a bed, near the public telephone. At some point, Lindholm and Trenkler met and discovered their mutual Milton background and they talked, but Alfred was cautious about jailhouse informers. He had been advised by Terry Segal to beware of informers, and he already had the experience the previous Patriots' Day weekend April with a cellmate who claimed to be a public drunk, and was placed in Alfred's cell, even though there were several other empty cells on the floor. That man seemed to want Alfred to talk and confess, just like the James Harding tried to do. Alfred Trenkler had been in jail only for a total of two days in Plymouth and 3 days the previous April in Boston, but he was learning about the system. Alfred was also suspicious because Lindholm had claimed that he had lived on Whitelawn Avenue, a very short street of about 22 homes, and that his mother had rented an apartment in the "Dunn" family's home at 25 Whitelawn in the 1960's. Trenkler had no recollection of Lindholm ever living on that street., and Margaret Dunn and her two adult sons, Paul and James, lived only four houses away on his side of the street. Later, she would rent a room in her house, but Alfred and his family knew all the other tenants in that apartment in the 1960's and David Lindholm and his mother were not among them. If Lindholm had not lived on Whitelawn, that left the question of how Lindholm had obtained the name of the Dunn's, and why he thought he needed additional "bonding" assistance. One would have thought that the common Milton background would have been enough.

Nonetheless, Trenkler shared with Lindholm what little could be safely shared, he thought, such as his Mass. Safety Squad experience, and Lindholm later spun that together with newspaper reports into a believable web for investigators. Surprisingly, they didn't talk about golf, which Lindholm played for Milton High School's team for three years, and which was a favorite of Alfred's stepfather and brother. Nor did they talk about wrestling, at Lindholm was on the Milton varsity team and Alfred wrestled at Park School. Their conversations were too short for such leisurely meanderings.

David Lindholm saw, at some point, the opportunity to give information to the government that would be more valuable to the government and to him, than any of the drug-related information he had communicated the previous Thursday. It would be his claim that Trenkler confessed to him. When he left the unit at Plymouth, he said to Alfred, "*Good luck, Trenkler.*" After he left the Plymouth County House of Correction on Monday, 21 December, he contacted law enforcement officials to tell them the story of Alfred Trenkler's alleged admissions, and he was quickly put in touch with ATF and the U.S. Attorney's office. The coincidence of Lindholm's placement was yet another bizarre twist in this case. One question for Alfred Trenkler was how David Lindholm knew about the Dunn residence and about how Mrs. Dunn rented a room out from time to time, always to a single man or woman. Was that information fed to Lindholm by the Federal investigators or others? Alfred Trenkler didn't tell him.

On the morning of the 18th, the <u>Boston Herald</u> carried Jack Meyers' story of Shay's arraignment, "*SHAY PLEADS INNOCENT IN FATAL BOMBING.*" Wrote Meyers, "*In an interview after his hearing Shay accused authorities of trying to sabotage his defense by getting rid of the court-appointed lawyers he has had during the yearlong probe that led to his indictment.... He also accused authorities of concocting the bomb threat case* [from the Suffolk County Jail to Brighton] *against him, saying he is not stupid enough to place a collect call bomb threat using his own name.*"

Matthew Brelis' story in the 18 December 1992 <u>Boston Globe</u>, "*SUSPECT IN FATAL BOMB BLAST ARRAIGNED,*" cited an unnamed source as saying "*that the younger Shay and Trenkler met about three years ago* [making that 1989 when Shay was 16] *when both were frequenting gay bars in Boston. Despite vastly different backgrounds, the two became friendly.*" The article did not explain how, in a state with a 21-year old age requirement for drinking in bars, that the 16-year old Shay would have been allowed to enter, nor did it attempt to verify the information with Alfred Trenkler. An interview with Alfred Trenkler would have revealed that Alfred didn't drink alcohol and did not go to bars and he owned no car in 1989-

1990 when he was living in Hull. Brelis summarized the different backgrounds of Shay and Trenkler and included the quote from Alfred Trenkler's 1975 Thayer Academy yearbook about "*having a good time.*" [See Chapter 1]. Brelis wrote that "*Law enforcement sources said Trenkler was shocked when police, who had been following him all morning, arrested him.*" The Wednesday afternoon arrest occurred "*minutes after a federal grand jury returned the five-count indictment....*" No one has ever explained why Terry Segal's request to Paul Kelly for a civil voluntary arrest was not sufficient for the ATF and Boston police. In the absence of an explanation, it can be assumed that the investigators wanted a public, humiliating, and newsworthy arrest.

Later on 18 December, after a two-day postponement at the request of the U.S. Attorney's office, there was a detention, or bail, hearing and arraignment in Federal Court before U.S. Magistrate Marianne Bowler. Was the postponement requested to give David Lindholm more time to talk with Alfred Trenkler? The purpose of the hearing was to determine if Alfred Trenkler should be jailed until his trial or released on bail, and the purpose of bail would be to ensure his presence at trial. Neither bail nor pre-trial detention are intended as punishment, but solely as methods of ensuring attendance at trial. Nonethleless, the path to punishment with pre-trial incarceration is often paved with good intentions.

Another consideration at such hearings is to ensure that an indicted person will not commit crimes while awaiting trial. The hearing began with Alfred Trenkler not being allowed to change into a civilian suit. He was in the same clothes he was wearing two days previously when arrested, minus his socks which the ATF agents had taken, without explanation. At the Plymouth County House of Correction, he was not allowed to shave nor to have any new socks.

The only government witness was Jeff Kerr who testified about Alfred Trenkler's living arrangements over the past three years. Through the questions of Assistant U.S. Attorney Paul Kelly, Agent Kerr stated that the living arrangements were spartan, with no telephone at his ATEL apartment and no regular bed at 133 Atlantic Avenue, where John Cates paid the rent. Kerr stated that Alfred Trenkler had a Federal tax lien for $4,900, and he explained the problem with the unpaid amount to Rusco Steel of Rhode Island. Alfred Trenkler had allegedly not filed his Federal income taxes for the years 1987, 1988 and 1990 and for the years 1989 and 1991, his reported income was $4,193 and $6,399, respectively.

The defense had little time to prepare, but Alfred Trenkler did file his tax forms in 1987 and 1988. However, his company had no profits, so there were no earnings. In 1989 he worked part-time at ATEL and earned $4,303, and in 1990 he had earned $22,221 working for ATEL and paid $1,377 in taxes. Before the indictment, Alfred Trenkler was working with the IRS to pay a $2,600 balance, but there was no $4,900 tax lien on him.

Kerr testified that he was at Trenkler's arraignment on Wednesday, 16 December and said that Trenkler had said to Magistrate Bowler that the Pretrial Services Report was accurate, including the statement that he had "*no history of substance abuse.*" (Transcript, 12/18 p.12) Kerr then summarized his interviews with Trenkler's roommate, John Cates, and former roommates Robert Craig and John Coyle who recalled their use of cocaine and marijuana with Alfred Trenkler. Kerr said that he had interviewed Patricia O'Donoghue, 23 years old, who said that

Alfred Trenkler had sold her and other students drugs when she was aged 15 and in high school.

Agent Kerr had asked Alfred Trenkler in February 1992 about his drug use and "*He said that he was a previous user of cocaine, that he was trying to clean up his act.*" (T 12/18 p.15) Kerr was asked about Alfred's criminal record and he began by describing the April 1992 arrest as a "*fugitive from justice*" on the Rhode Island check case. (T 12/18 p.16) That problem had begun in 1989, with the bouncing of a $1,349.38 check to Rusco Steel, and for failing to attend his arraignment.

In such hearings, the rules against hearsay evidence are less stringent than in full criminal trials. In summary, the government's position was that Alfred Trenkler was a person who should be jailed prior to trial.

On cross-examination by Terry Segal, Special Agent Jeff Kerr agreed that Alfred Trenkler's work was reliable and well-received by customers. His business relationship with one customer, Videocom of Dedham, Mass., was 6-7 years old. Kerr confirmed that the investigation of the Roslindale Bomb had, so far, taken 20,000 person hours, including 500 interviews. Twenty thousand man hours is the equivalent of 10 person years. Segal established that there had been extensive publicity about the case and Alfred Trenkler showed no inclination to flee the state. Segal introduced several newspaper articles into evidence to show that Alfred likely knew of the impending indictment. In fact, Alfred Trenkler had significant work projects to complete and was staying put.

Then there was an early illustration of how legal procedures trumped the truth. As one of the criteria for determining whether to hold a person in pretrial confinement is the seriousness of the crime and the defendant's connection to it, Terry Segal asked Agent Kerr, "*What is the evidence that ties my client, Mr. Trenkler to this particular unfortunate tragedy?*" (T 12/18 41) AUSA Paul Kelly objected on the grounds that Mr. Segal was embarking on a "*fishing expedition*" for details of the government's case, and that Kelley had not covered that issue in the direct examination so it was out-of-bounds for cross-examination. Magistrate Bowler sustained the objection. Segal tried asking the question in a different way, but with the same result.

Terry Segal then said that he could recall Agent Kerr as his witness and ask these questions on direct examination, but was trying to save time. Paul Kelly argued that he was not arguing that detention was required by the seriousness of the crime, and he was content to have the Magistrate consider the grand jury's indictment as the indication of the relationship of Alfred Trenkler to the crime. He said, "*But in terms of the weight of the evidence, which is obviously what Mr. Segal is going after, I believe that's improper, and free discovery is what he's looking for.*" (T 12/18 43) The legal game forbade "free discovery" as the discovery of facts and truth was permitted only upon certain requests at the right time. Learning those facts and truth too soon would violate the sense of fairness in the legal jousting that constitutes a trial.

On redirect, Paul Kelly returned to the issue of the risk of flight, i.e. that Alfred Trenkler would flee the state. Agent Kerr said that he had interviewed Alfred's friends, Patricia O'Donoghue and Andy Robinson, from whom he learned that because "*the investigation was applying more heat on Trenkler, that he stated he was considering moving to Florida.*" (T 12/18 52)

Terry Segal cross-examined and established that Alfred Trenkler had only one conversation about Florida with Robinson, who lived in Florida, and that O'Donoghue's knowledge came only from Robinson. Also, the conversation with Robinson was before 9 April 1992, and thus before all the publicity in the newspaper linking Alfred Trenkler to Tom Shay and the 28 October 1991 Roslindale Bomb. It wasn't stated how the ATF found Andy Robinson, but the link to him likely came from the approved electronic surveillance of Trenkler's phones.

Terry Segal did not mention his own role in the Florida relocation option which was that he had supported the idea when Alfred mentioned it, as a way to get away from the adverse publicity.

Alfred's mother, Josephine Wallace, described Alfred's education and work, and noted, "...*he was never a 9-to-5 person. He wanted his own business.*" (T 12/18/92 p. 60) She affirmed that the family home had a value of approximately $325-340,000 and was owned without a mortgage; and she was willing to offer it, and risk it, as security to ensure Alfred's presence at trial. Alfred's stepfather, Jack Wallace, also testified, and said that he and Josephine Wallace put up the $1,000 bail for Alfred in April, and they also provided the funds to pay Rusco Steel; and had secured the legal services of Terry Segal. He described Easter dinner at the family home with Alfred and was permitted to say, due to the lesser hearsay rules of such a hearing, that Alfred said that one of the ATF Agents had said to him, "*Get used to this, Alfred, because you are going to be here for the rest of* [your] *life.*" (T - 74)

The tone of the prosecution's questions must have seemed ominous to Segal and Trenkler. Paul Kelly asked Jack Wallace about the difficulty in securing Alfred's release over Easter weekend in April, "*And is it fair to say he* [Terry Segal] *finally found a friend of his who happened to be a judge who agreed to deal with the matter* [of bail]?" Terry Segal objected, but the attack by Kelly was unnecessary and hypocritical, too. That is, it was the Government that decided to arrest Alfred Trenkler on a minor charge on Good Friday afternoon on 17 April 1992 and to seek to have him remain in jail over an Easter and Patriots' Day weekend. Having chosen to time the arrest to maximize the inconvenience to Alfred Trenkler and his family, it did not seem fair to complain that Trenkler's attorney used an available emergency judge procedure for matters arising during weekends.

Other defense witnesses were Brian O'Leary, a friend and employee, and through whom Segal established that Alfred's use of drugs was minor and did not impair his ability to work. Also testifying were ARCOMM customer Frank Cavallo, vice-president and general manager of Videocom of Dedham. Questioned by defense lawyer Scott Lopez, Cavallo vouched for the professional work done by Alfred Trenkler. Richard Marshall, another friend, did the same, as did Randell (Randy) Winchester of MIT. Harrison Williams was a Milton neighbor and a fellow member of the Milton-Hoosic Club and he testified about Alfred's work as the sound and lighting person for the benefit plays produced at the Club.

Next was Dr. James Melby, another family friend of the Wallaces and Alfred and Allen Stikeleather, both of whom spoke well of Alfred's generosity in giving his electronics expertise to the Milton Hoosic Club's productions. A letter from retired Mass. Superior Court Judge George Hurd was submitted and accepted into evidence. Judge Hurd said, "*It's inconceivable to me that Alfred will not appear at trial and other court appearances.... His roots go deep in the community of Milton and Quincy. He's far too intelligent not to realize what problems he would encounter were he to absent himself."* (T 12/18/92 136)

David Wallace, Alfred's brother, testified about Alfred's training and work with the Massachusetts Safety Squad, a voluntary service organization. First Aid training was required to participate, and members had a special decal on their automobiles. Recalled, Jack Wallace described how two I.R.S. employees came to the Wallace family home seeking Alfred on the Monday after Easter, 19 April, which was a state holiday due to Patriots' Day. Afterwards, Alfred went to the Quincy IRS office and worked out an agreement with the manager of that office.

Alfred Trenkler did not testify. If he had, he could have explained in more detail the nature of his work and current projects requiring his presence. Also, he could have explained the solution to the claimed tax problem which included the fact that the IRS had lost his 1983 tax returns and Alfred had given them his copy in order to assist them. Also, Alfred would have testified about his longstanding belief in non-violence. He could have testified directly about the statement that Jack Wallace had testified Alfred had said an ATF Agent said. Alfred Trenkler has written that Dennis Leahy said to him at his 17 April 1992 weekend jailing, *"Well, Al, I've been at this for many years and I'm telling you that your life is soon to be over, mark my words."*

Also, Alfred could have explained the how the idea of temporarily relocating to Florida arose. In September 1990, during his ATEL vacation in Florida where he stayed with his childhood friend, Andy Robinson, he had been offered a job doing work similar to what he was doing in Massachusetts. He declined that offer. In 1992, when the investigation and publicity began focusing on him, Terry Segal suggested, after learning about the 1990 trip and job offer, that it might be a good idea to temporarily move to Florida to escape the inevitably bad publicity. This was another indication of his approach to public relations for criminal defendants, which was to avoid rather than proactively pursuing the media. Alfred called Andy Robinson about the idea, hence the ATF's knowledge of the option; but Alfred decided against it because work with his new company, ATNS was going well.

Assistant U.S. Attorney Paul Kelly argued for detention, i.e. no bail, for three reasons:

1. the crimes for which Trenkler was indicted involved violence, as defined in the Bail Reform Act;
2. the crimes were punishable by death or life imprisonment; and
3. the risk that Alfred Trenkler would flee.

Kelly said, *"...the government believes that there is clear and convincing evidence that this defendant does present a danger to the community and there are* [sic] *no combination of conditions which will reasonably assure the safety of the community."* (T -124) Kelly described the Roslindale Bomb crime and said that *"those who are alleged to have participated in heinous offenses of the nature charged in this case, are essentially domestic terrorists, in my estimation, who clearly present a profound danger to the City of Boston..."*

Paul Kelly argued that Trenkler had stated in a "Pretrial Services report" that he was not an abuser of drugs, but ATF Agent Kerr had testified that Trenkler had used illegal drugs and even sold them to children. Trenkler had sworn that the report was true. He felt that "use" was not the same as "abuse."

Terry Segal argued that Alfred Trenkler was not a flight risk and the proof of that was his non-flight during the entire year of 1992 when it was becoming clear that the Federal Government was pursuing him. In early December, the Boston newspapers were predicting an indictment, and still there was no flight. During this time James Harding, a.k.a. CI #97, was making his illegal tape recordings and one of them contained his own offer to assist Alfred in "hiding out" for a while, by offering him the keys to a cottage in Plymouth. Alfred said he would not do that because that's what guilty people do, and besides, he had work to do for his customers.

Magistrate Bowler expressed concerns about three charges of court default against Trenkler that she saw on his record, but Scott Lopez argued that the three cases involved minor offenses such as speeding and attaching an incorrect license plate to a vehicle were all dismissed. Not found guilty nor innocent, but dismissed, and therefore there was no default. The defaults arose because Alfred Trenkler's driver's license continued to have his address as 7 Whitelawn Avenue, Milton, and he would only get legal notices when he returned to his parents' home from time to time.

Terry Segal requested that bail be set and the Alfred Trenkler be permitted to live at his parents' home, perhaps even with a radio-transmitter ankle bracelet. His parents worked within minutes of the home and could return frequently to ensure his presence. At home, Alfred Trenkler would be able to assist in his own defense and go to Segal's office and also work and maintain his income and work for his employees. The hearing was adjourned while Magistrate Bowler considered the issue of bail or detention for Alfred Trenkler who remained in custody of the U.S Marshal Service pending a decision.

Jack Meyers captured the contrast well in his 19 December _Boston Herald_ article, "_2D SUSPECT ARRAIGNED IN ROSLINDALE BOMB BLAST_," when he wrote, "_Prosecutors and defense lawyers painted vastly different portraits of Alfred W. Trenkler...._" If Trenkler had testified perhaps the gap would have been narrowed for the media as well as for Magistrate Judge Bowler. Predictably, and even before 9/11, Meyers grabbed the dramatic label affixed to Shay and Trenkler by the prosecutors, "_domestic terrorists_," and "_noted Trenkler had been a transient with a drug problem since leaving his family's Milton home a decade ago._" It was a bleak image of a man who had employed several people over the past year, and who had lived in only three places in the past five years with only two roommates, and who had never been arrested or even questioned by the police about drug use.

In a reversal of the roles of the two Boston daily newspapers, the headline for Matthew Brelis' 19 December article in the _Globe_ was more dramatic, "_US URGES: HOLD BOMB SUSPECT, PROSECUTOR LABELS MAN A 'TERRORIST'_" Even though he did not interview Alfred Trenkler, Matthew Brelis tried to capture a bit of his feelings, "_Trenkler displayed little outward concern at the three-hour hearing, even though he faces life in prison or the death penalty if convicted on all counts._

When his mother, testifying about his background in electronics and the type of work he has done for various communications companies, said, 'I don't understand any of his work; I just know it involves satellites,' Trenkler laughed softly to himself."

An interview with Jack Meyers and Matthew Brelis and testimony under oath would have been a far better way to present Alfred Trenkler to the public than the strategy of silence.

In the _Boston Sunday Globe_ of 20 December 1992, John Ellement and Matt Brelis summarized the case so far, "_IN BOMBING CASE, 3-YEAR PROBE TOOK 14 MONTHS._" First, they described the dramatic arrest of Trenkler, who was driving two of his employees to a bank in his 1978 Toyota Celica - now black after Trenkler repainted it himself in the summer of 1992. " _'It was like a movie,' said Brian O'Leary, one of the two passengers in Trenkler's car. 'There were all of these guys with their_ [guns] _out, pointing at us.'_ " Explaining the headline, Ellement and Brelis wrote, "_...the agents and detectives compressed what amounts to nearly three years of investigative work into 14 months..._" Perhaps they were referring to the 20,000 man hours, which is 10 man years. They quoted Alfred's mother who said on the day of the detention hearing, " _'We know he didn't do it,'_ she said, _'He had nothing whatsoever to do with this.'_ "

Ellement and Brelis addressed Shay's statements, "_... Shay has acknowledged knowing Trenkler - Shay was in fact the first to publicly link Trenkler to the case. Shay said that the two met at the Back Bay train station._" The reporters did not clarify that Shay only mentioned Trenkler, for the first time in almost five months after the Roslindale Bomb explosion, when the ATF Special Agent Dennis Leahy and Boston Detective Brendan Craven told him in March 1992 in the San Francisco Jail that Trenkler was now a suspect after finding his name in Shay's address book. As with all other stories about the Shay-Trenkler relationship, they had it wrong, in that Tom Shay did not meet Alfred Trenkler in the Back Bay train station. They met in June 1991 at the "White Hen Pantry" convenience store in the Fenway area, and they had never gone to the train station together.

As Magistrate Bowler considered her decision on bail, Judge Edward Harrington, a former U.S. Attorney for Massachusetts, issued an order on 22 December 1992 for AUSA's Paul Kelly and Frank Libby to send form letters to those people and organizations whose phone calls had been intercepted during the 1992 electronic surveillance of phones and pagers of Alfred Trenkler, John Cates, Thomas L. Shay and Mary Flanagan. After giving the background of the court orders, the letter to those whose calls had been intercepted said simply, "**During the period of authorized interception, one or more electronic or wire communications from you to the above described voicemail function was intercepted.**"

Also on the 22nd, the U.S. District Court appointed prominent defense attorney, Nancy Gertner, to represent Tom Shay, instead of Francis O'Rourke whom Jefferson Boone had requested. The _Globe_, and not the _Herald_, covered the story, "_COURT APPOINTS GERTNER TO REPRESENT SHAY._" Gertner graduated from Yale Law School in 1971, two years ahead of Hillary Rodham and Bill Clinton. Her first major criminal case was the 1975 defense of Susan Saxe who was involved in a politically-motivated bank robbery where a Boston policeman, Walter Schroeder, was killed. At that trial, Gertner used the risky tactic of resting her case without calling any witnesses or Susan Saxe, and preventing the prosecution from presenting more of its case through cross-examination of defense witnesses. The jury was deadlocked and a mistrial was declared. Saxe later pled guilty and was sentenced to seven years in prison for her role as a driver in the robbery. Thus,

Nancy Gertner was familiar with the trial tactics of not having a defendant testify, and having a short defense.

On 23 December, Paul Kelly sent a letter to Nancy Gertner and Terry Segal promising to send soon the requested discovery materials. Also, as was required, he wrote, "The government has provided promises, rewards or inducements (as described below) to the following witnesses:" and he listed, Christopher Henry, Mark Means, Robert Evans, Donna Shea, Jim Harding, Jennifer Powers, Jeffrey Berry, Thomas Shay. Paul Kelly stated that Jeff Berry "was granted immunity pursuant to a court order on June 17, 1992, and thereafter testified before the grand jury." Regarding Donna Shea, he wrote, "Prior to her second appearance before the grand jury, she asked us about any help we might be able to provide with her husband's case (John Shea).... we advised her that it was unlikely that her husband would derive any benefit from her testifying before the grand jury." The letter did not mention her other assistance to the ATF agents. With respect to James Harding, this was the first time Alfred Trenkler was advised that his employee was assisting the prosecutors. Wrote Kelly, "A supplemental letter more fully describing Harding's actions will be supplied to counsel."

On Christmas Eve, Magistrate Bowler issued her 32-page decision which denied bail. Most of the decision was a review of the indictment and the testimony at the 18 December detention hearing. She concluded, "*The government argues that the defendant is a 'domestic terrorist' and presents a profound danger to the community. This court agrees for the reasons set below.*"

She noted that most of the character witnesses knew little of Alfred's lifestyle during the last ten years. She cited one witness's testimony of marijuana use on the job as showing Alfred's "*reckless disregard for the safety of his defendant's co-workers as well as others in the area who could be injured as the result of professional judgment altered by the use of controlled substances.*" Not presented as evidence was a videotape made in 1986 by Donna Shea of Alfred and his work crew at a Cumberland, Rhode Island work site AFTER WORK passing a marijuana joint around to workers John Shea, Bob Craig and Brian O'Leary. It's believed that Donna Shea gave that videotape to the ATF.

Magistrate Bowler addressed Terry Segal's proposal for an electronic bracelet but ruled it "*totally out of the question. It is conceivable that with the defendant's skill he could easily defeat the monitoring system.*" There was no evidence before her on the risk of such defeat of an electronic bracelet. Perhaps, like Alfred's friends from childhood, adolescence and adulthood, Magistrate Bowler was intimidated by Alfred's high-tech abilities and was fearful that he could do almost anything related to electronics.

Regarding the risk of flight she questioned whether Alfred Trenkler really lived with John Cates at 133 Atlantic Street and seemed to accept Special Agent Jeff Kerr's testimony that there was not a bed at that apartment. Such reasoning ignored the fact that Jeff Kerr obtained a search warrant for that address 11 months earlier because it was Alfred Trenkler's residence and Trenkler was there at the time of the search and he was still there at the time of his arrest and he had to have slept somewhere in the apartment. The Pretrial Services report writer had apparently called John Cates' number and Cates allegedly advised that Alfred Trenkler did not live there. Perhaps Cates was annoyed at the government's unfair intrusion into his and Alfred's lives, or he was making a strictly accurate observation that Alfred was then living not with him because he was in jail at the time of the December 1992 call; but his denial and attitude was held against Alfred. Magistrate Bowler is another example of how Alfred Trenkler's own testimony may have helped him persuade the judge. She concluded that only continued detention could ensure Alfred Trenkler's presence at his trial.

On Christmas Day, Andrea Estes wrote the *Herald*'s story, "*JUDGE DENIES BAIL TO QUINCY MAN TIED TO FATAL BOMBING.*" Matthew Brelis wrote the *Globe*'s article, "*JUDGE DENIES BAIL FOR QUINCY MAN TIED TO FATAL BOMBING.*"

On 29 December, Alfred's attorneys filed a 30-page "*Motion to Revoke Magistrate Judge's December 24, 1992 Detention Order and Request for Oral Argument,*" and had to request the court's permission to exceed the court's 20 page limit on such motions. Scott Lopez made the same arguments as made to Magistrate Judge Bowler, but was again handicapped by the lack of Trenkler's testimony. Alfred would have directly denied any claim, submitted through Jeff Kerr's permitted hearsay, that Alfred had ever sold drugs to children. In his Motion, Lopez was limited to say that the testimony about such sales did not say that they were recent sales, which was not a strong argument. Alfred could have testified directly about his interest in employment in Florida, not as an escape, but a real job opportunity. He could have explained his perception of Governor William Weld's proposal for a state death penalty for people who kill policemen through explosives, instead of having such perceptions be introduced by hearsay testimony of his brother, David. He could have explained his lifestyle and that he really DID live at 133 Atlantic Street. As for drug use, former President Bill Clinton and President George W. Bush have both used illegal drugs.

Finally, it must be easier for a judge to deny relief to an inanimate defendant than to a live, talking, engaging witness on the stand who has explanations for allegations made by prosecutors and their witnesses. Would having an innocent defendant testify guarantee success? No, it would not, but what alternatives should have been used to avoid the ultimate result, the pre-trial jailing and conviction of an innocent man? Pursuit of the truth by a defendant's own testimony is one way to avoid that slippery slope. The percentage of convictions for those incarcerated prior to trial is high.

In support of Alfred Trenkler's Motion to Revoke the Magistrate Judge's detention order, Terry Segal composed an affidavit for himself. He affirmed that Alfred Trenkler DID live at 133 Atlantic Ave., Quincy. Also, he had talked with David Sawyer of the Federal Pretrial Services unit who knew of no case where a defendant using an electronic ankle bracelet had electronically defeated the system. A few, however, had simply fled with the bracelet remaining affixed to the ankle.

On 5 January AUSA's Paul Kelly and Frank Libby sent letters to Nancy Gertner and Terry Segal to advise them that the U.S. Attorney, A. John Pappalardo, had decided not to seek the death penalty for either defendant, but would be seeking "a mandatory term of life imprisonment for each defendant."

On 30 December 1992 AUSA Paul Kelly wrote to Terry Segal about James Harding "to more fully describe the interaction between James Harding and the government during the course of this investigation.... it is highly unlikely that the government will call Mr. Harding as a witness against your client at the trial of this matter. Obviously, a final decision on this issue will be made at a later point, closer to the trial date.

The government first learned of James Harding on or about February 13, 1992 when Donna Shea disclosed to us that she and Harding had a three-way conversation with Al Trenkler sometime within the previous two months, and that Harding had recorded the conversation by means of a concealed recorder."

Kelly then described in detail the efforts to obtain a copy of the micro-cassette, which culminated with Harding's Federal arrest in the lobby of the Federal building in Boston. Kelly said, "Following Harding's arrest, a search of the lobby area of the federal courthouse resulted in the discovery of a microcassette of the above-described three-way conversation (a copy of which is being produced to you)....

The government had little or no contact with Harding between late April and early October, 1992. There may have been isolated telephone calls to one of the investigators, but nothing of substance.

Beginning in or about mid-October, 1992, Harding began making periodic telephone calls (every week or so) to SA Jeff Kerr, BPD Detective Brendan Craven or AUSA Kelly to pass along unsolicited pieces of information concerning Trenkler and his activities. There was no formal relationship between the government and Harding during this time....

On or about December 2, 1992, Harding produced to investigators three (3) microcassettes containing unsupervised (and undated) recorded conversations between himself and Trenkler. He informed the government of his desire to have a further conversation with Trenkler that evening.... the USAO [US Attorney's Office] authorized the ATF's use of Harding as a CI [Confidential Informant]. ... Harding subsequently recorded a conversation between himself and Trenkler that evening.

On December 9, 1992, ATF agents had further contact with Harding... it became apparent to investigators that Harding was not fully amenable to supervision and instruction.

On December 12, 1992, ATF terminated Harding as a CI....

Harding's activities, and the recordings which he made of various conversations with Trenkler, played no role in the government's decision to seek an indictment in this case."

As Paul Kelly knew, it was against state law to record someone without his or her consent. Thus, Alfred Trenkler could have sued James Harding and could also have urged the Norfolk County District Attorney or the Massachusetts Attorney General to pursue criminal charges against James Harding for the recordings he made prior to his being deputized as CI #97. Such legal efforts would have exposed the underside of the government's case, the use of infomers. There were other individuals who were equally untrustworthy, but with whom the U.S. Attorney's office continued to work, and even presented a few of them as prosecution witnesses at Alfred Trenkler's trial.

It may have been that Terry Segal viewed such efforts as a waste of time and money, but he might have used the Harding tapes to his advantage. Among the undecipherable noise on the tapes were Alfred Trenkler's denials of any involvement in the Roslindale Bomb. It should have been useful with the argument that if a trusted employee, at least until his undercover work was exposed, could not persuade Alfred Trenkler to admit any involvement in the bomb, how likely was it that Alfred would freely discuss his alleged involvement with someone whom he knew less well, such as a fellow prisoner? The challenge was to get such exculpatory statements into evidence as an exception to the hearsay rule; but it could not be done. If Trenkler's statements have been incriminating, then they could have been admitted by the prosecution as a "statement against penal interest," one of the exceptions to the hearsay rule. That's the way the system works: a hearsay statement of innocence is inadmissible, but a hearsay statement of guilt is admissible. Perhaps that application of the rule exists to increase the pressure on defendants to testify, despite the constitutional right not to do so.

On 11 January 1993 the U.S. Attorney's office filed a "Memorandum in Opposition" to Trenkler's "*Motion to Revoke the Detention Order.*" That Memorandum was accompanied by a three-paragraph Affidavit by AUSA Paul Kelly who sought to defeat the defense argument that Alfred Trenkler had expected an indictment and had not fled. Kelly first cited a phone call by the discredited James Harding to Boston Detective Brendan Craven with the information that Alfred Trenkler did not expect to be indicted for weeks, if not months, which was exactly what Paul Kelly had told Trenkler's lawyer, Terry Segal. Then Paul Kelly stated, "According to the arresting officers, including Special Agent Jeff Kerr and Detective Craven, Trenkler appeared completely stunned and surprised when he was apprehended pursuant to the federal arrest warrant on December 16, 1992." As Brian O'Leary say to a reporter, "*It was like a movie...*"

What Alfred was surprised about was the traffic-stopping aggressiveness of the arrest, with guns drawn, despite his lawyer's request for a civilized voluntary arrest. There was never any evidence or suspicion that Alfred Trenkler was armed or dangerous. The timing was not a surprise and Alfred was not planning to make a last minute escape before the indictment.

In a two-page order on 13 January, Judge Rya Zobel upheld Magistrate Judge Bowler's detention order, concluding, "*In light of the extraordinary seriousness of the offenses charged, the possibility of life imprisonment without parole, defendant's itinerant lifestyle, and his past inattention to court orders, the detention order is hereby adopted by this court.*" Said the <u>Boston Globe</u> on the 15th, "*BOMB SUSPECT TO BE DETAINED.*" By referring to Alfred Trenkler's "*itinerant lifestyle,*" Judge Zobel seemed to be punishing Trenkler for his failure to adopt most middle class values by purchasing his own home or getting married and having children. He had lived with two roommates over the previous eight years, (Bob Craig 1984-88, John Cates 1990-92), with an intermediate period where he lived alone in a unit above ATEL. In Washington, Congressmen have lived in their offices from time to time without stigma.

The unspoken message of Magistrate Judge Bowler and of Judge Rya Zobel was that they thought there was a good likelihood of a jury finding Alfred Trenkler guilty. That's the hidden message of the "*extraordinary seriousness of the offenses charged*" phrase. If the charges seemed to be more of a stretch to the judges, then detention would have been less likely.

Also on 13 January, ATF special agents Thomas D'Ambrosio and Jeff Kerr interviewed William David Lindholm in the U.S. Attorney's office in Boston, with

AUSA Paul Kelly and Lindholm's attorney, Roger Cox in attendance. Jeff Kerr wrote the report.

He related how Lindholm was sent to Plymouth on Thursday evening, 17 December and how met Alfred Trenkler in the Orientation Unit in the early morning hours of Friday, the 18th. By Friday evening there were only four men in the unit, including Lindholm and Alfred Trenkler. On Saturday morning, Lindholm and Trenkler had breakfast together and Lindholm told Trenkler about his living in Milton and even for a year in the "Dunn" home on Whitelawn Ave., the same street where Alfred Trenkler lived. Lindholm told Trenkler that his father attended Thayer Academy and Milton Academy, after Trenkler said that he had attended both schools.

The two discussed lawyers, and Kerr wrote that "Lindholm stated that he told Trenkler that his decision on which attorney would represent him would be the biggest decision of his life from this point on....He stated that Trenkler professed his innocence. He stated that he instructed Trenkler to be very active in his own defense and to not soley rely on his attorney." The advice was prophetic and sound, but unfortunately, David Lindholm's subsequent actions destroyed any chance of appreciation from Alfred.

Jeff Kerr reported that Lindholm said "as he continued to get to know Trenkler, it occurred to him that Trenkler was gay. He stated that he came to this conclusion based on a few insights. He stated that Trenkler had an attraction for young boys. He stated that Trenkler told him that he met Shay at a bus station and that he knows that bus terminals are often hang outs for older gay males looking to meet young gay males. He stated that Trenkler told him of joining a group called the Park Drive Crime Watch Group..." Once again, the ATF was quite willing to record statements about the sexual preferences of individuals, without asking them directly. In the report, Jeff Kerr was not required to provide other evidence of the "young boys" allegation which was outrageous and false. Alfred Trenkler did not meet Tom Shay at a bus station. Also, Alfred Trenkler did not merely join a Park Drive Crime Watch Group. He and Tom Tompson created the "Fenway Community Watch."

In every story, there is humor and this report contained some, too. Rearding Tom Shay, Kerr reported that Lindholm "stated that he told Trenkler that he had been in lock up with Shay for a few hours on December 17, 1992 and that if his observations were correct, Shay couldn't put the batteries in a flashlight. He stated that Trenkler told him that he was correct in his assessment of Shay."

The report was not all about the Roslindale Bomb. Kerr reported, "He stated Trenkler told him about a cousin who works for Fidelity Investments in Boston, Massachusetts and how this individual was going to refer him, Trenkler, to a high tech company for work." It must be noted that Alfred Trenkler didn't trust William David Linholm enough to tell him the name of that cousin. Lindholm didn't have a name to tell Kerr, and at trial Lindholm confirmed that Alfred Trenkler didn't give him a name. (TT 13-16)

Kerr wrote that "Lindholm stated that [on] Sunday evening, December 20, 1992, Trenkler said to him, 'Even if I built the bomb, I didn't put it on the car.' Lindholm stated that Trenkler then paused and said, 'I built the bomb, but I didn't place it on the car, I don't deserve to die or spend the rest of my life in prison.' " Alfred Trenkler wrote in 2007, "*Lindholm took 'poetic license' to the extreme. He mentioned my biggest problem would be the '86 incident and how it would be used as a 'prior act' to get me convicted for '91 and face the death penalty. I said to him, 'so I built the '86 device; it was a harmless prank, I don't deserve to die or spend the rest of my life in prison for some firecracker incident.' *"

As if that was not enough to cause the interviewing officers to increase their desire to convict Alfred Trenkler, Lindholm pushed the "Princess Diana Blame Disease" button. Wrote Kerr, "He stated that the reason he is speaking to the government is because when Trenkler talked about the officers involved in this tragedy, he seemed almost to ridicule them, saying that they should of [sic, have] had bomb suits on and that the officers were negligent. He stated that Trenkler told him that it was the officers failure to suit up in armor that caused their injuries, not the strength of the destructive device. He stated that Trenkler showed no remorse for the officers."

Of this allegation, Alfred Trenkler wrote in 2007, "*By coincidence Larry Plant was at Plymouth in the Orientation Unit with Tom Shay; Plant was sick; Plant and Shay spoke in hushed voices; and Shay allegedly said it was the officers' fault. It was if Plant and Lindholm had the same scriptwiter.*"

Thus, we have Alfred Trenkler in jail who is discrete enough not to share a name of a cousin with an important role at Fidelity Investments who is then sharing with this man he barely knew something which could put get him a death sentence or life in prison? A smart man would not make such a mistake and William David Lindholm "stated that Trenkler was very smart." However, when something is said into the ears of a person who wants to believe, e.g. ATF agents and AUSA's, it sometimes doesn't matter if it makes sense.

Whatever his geographical and procedural route, and however much pre-meditated and by whom, Lindholm's arrival at Plymouth, was for him, a potential informer's jackpot, just as the ATF investigators thought they had hit the jackpot with Lindholm. He was just like the inmates who had met Tom Shay and heard him talking, too much-according to the inmate code- about his alleged role in a high stakes crime. There were several such inmates: Robert Evans, James Gannett, Daniel Fitzgerald, Mark Means, Kevin Norris, Larry Plant, and Christopher Henry.

It's not known which, if any, of the snitches against Tom Shay had been planted to listen to his stories, but each of them knew an opportunity when it arose. They took what they heard and embellished it to make it more attractive to investigators, and Lindholm was much smarter and more articulate than the others.

Also, William David Lindholm was luckier than the other jailhouse informants, for he found himself in proximity to the man believed to be the **mastermind** of the conspiracy. It's tempting to wonder whether ATF and/or the U.S. Attorney's office knew in advance about Lindholm's Milton background and, at some point, seized upon the chance that a jailhouse admission might be possible. Certainly, law enforcement officials have placed informants in the same cells as other suspects in the past in many, many other cases, and as Alfred believes happened with the purported drunk in his cell over the weekend of 17 April 1992. Sometimes the informants are real police officers, but using other inmates is safer, despite their credibility problems.

In any case, concluding from the coincidence of Lindholm's Plymouth placement that he was intentionally planted may be the same, and incorrect, logical leap which the prosecution made when it saw the coincidence of Alfred Trenkler's name in Tom Shay's address book together with the report of the 1986 device. Coincidence does not establish a causal relationship, and certainly does not establish such a relationship beyond a reasonable doubt. As Sigmund Freud is reputed to have said, "Sometimes a cigar is just a cigar."

On 4 January Judge Rya Zobel approved Assistant U.S. Attorney Robert Ullmann's Motion to Dismiss the charge against Tom Shay for the telephoned bomb threat to the woman in Brighton in April 1992. The short Motion stated, "*As grounds therefor, the government states that dismissal of this matter is in the interests of justice.*" As telephoning a bomb threat is a serious felony that could have brought several years of prison to Tom Shay, it's not known to the author why the charge was dismissed. Did the U.S. Attorney's office no longer believe in its M-1 informer, Mark Means? Whatever the merits of the original charge, the telephone bomb threat charge was no longer needed as a way to secure Thomas A. Shay in pre-trial confinement, as the December indictment for the Roslindale Bomb provided sufficient cause for that pre-trial jailing.

On 14 January 1993 the ATF Laboratory reported no connection between wires and bolt cutters and other tools and equipment taken from Alfred Trenkler and the Roslindale Bomb. On the 15th, Thomas Waskom, an ATF Explosives Enforcement Officer later to testify at evidentiary hearings and both Roslindale Bomb trials, gave a summary report about the Roslindale Bomb: "DEVICE DESIGN AND CONSTRUCTION

The materials evaluated in this investigation are consistent with an improvised explosive weapon that had functioned. The device was constructed using a quantity of ammonia dynamite, two electric blasting caps and a fuzing and firing system. The fuzing system was a 'FUTABA' remote control set and the firing system was a toggle switch, 9 volt batteries, and the two blasting caps connected together by electrical conductor. This entire assemblage was concealed in a plywood box. In addition, magnets were glued to the outside of the plywood box."

Basic interviews continued in the ATF investigation, and on 21 January 1993, Thomas D'Ambrosio and Jeff Kerr met with Judy Fredette, the part-time secretary for ARCOMM. She stopped work for the company in January 1992 because she wasn't getting paid and the company was failing. Rich Brown had taken the checkbook with him and stopped making any payments to anyone and started selling off company equipment "*out the back door,*" to use Alfred's phrase. She said that Alfred Trenkler had visited her about five times since the demise of ARCOMM and that he had mentioned Tom Shay only once and "only to say that he and Shay were together on one occasion." Special Agent D'Ambrosio wrote, "She said that ARCOMM did not use timecards to keep track of hours worked by the employees." This is perhaps a good example of how inaccurate ATF reports can be, because ARCOMM did use timecards. In the collection of defense documents were several time cards for Judy Fredette herself, and some for Nurdan Cagdus. They are posted on Alfred's website.

On 16 January 1993 began a trail of hope and frustration when Alfred was in a van to the Federal Courthouse in Boston from the Plymouth County House of Correction, which is about a one-hour ride. In the van was Edwin L. Gaeta, who had been indicted on 16 December 1992 for drug smuggling and sales of machine guns, and he told Alfred that he had useful information about the Roslindale Bomb. It seemed promising to Alfred as Gaeta said that the targeted Roslindale street was a cul-de-sac as was Eastbourne Street, and that there was a retired policeman (compared to the actual retired fireman) on the street, and that there was an underlying dispute which involved a lawsuit, as indeed there was, by Mr. Thomas L. Shay. The conversation went no further. Was this another person who had read some details of a famous crime in the newspaper and who saw a way to gain personal advantage? Or was this someone who, following some code of ethical behavior, saw an injustice and wanted to help?

On 25 January Jeff Kerr interviewed Kevin Troy Norris, another former fellow inmate of Tom Shay, at the Suffolk County House of Correction at the time of the 5 April 1992 false bomb threat to a Brighton woman. Now an inmate in Cedar Junction State Prison in Walpole, Mass., Norris said that Shay asked him to protect him from other inmates, including Mark Means, who identified Shay as making the bomb threat. For such protection Norris was paid $20.00 a week in cash by Shay, which he received periodically from his attorney, Bill McPhee. Norris began demanding more money. "Norris stated Shay told him he, Shay, had placed the bomb under his father's car, attaching it to the vehicle's gas tank. He stated Shay said when he placed and made the bomb he was very careful and wore gloves. Norris stated when he asked Shay why he would do this, Shay told him that it was because of what his, Shay's father had done to him and his sisters. Norris stated Shay claimed his, Shay's father had sexually abused and physically battered him and his sisters. Norris stated Shay told him that as a result of these abuses, he, Shay had spent a number of years in Psychiatric Homes.

Norris stated he asked how he built the bomb. He stated Shay said he and another guy, whom he did not identify, purchased components of the bomb at a Radio Shack. Shay stated that the other individual helped pay for the components. Norris stated Shay never explained how to make a bomb despite his being asked this question. He stated that Shay said if people gave him lighters or if he had a microwave he could build a bomb and that because of this knowledge people should not mess with him.

Norris stated Shay said the officers had no case against him. Norris stated Shay bragged about being a cop killer. He said the cops investigating the case were stupid because they had believed his father was involved."

Kevin Norris was not called to be a witness at Tom Shay's trial.

On 26 January, Magistrate Judge Marianne Bowler issued a "*Final Status Report*" of the case at that point, and stated that the case against both Shay and Trenkler was scheduled for trial on 22 February, only a month away.

On 6 February 1993 Alfred Trenkler turned 37 years old. His businesses were gone and he was in jail under spartan conditions. Still, irrepressibly confident of his innocence, and not yet aware that his short-lived acquaintance with William David Lindholm would become almost as dangerous as his acquaintance with Thomas A. Shay, he worked with his lawyers to prepare for the trial. He accepted the views of his high-priced lawyers that the way to defeat the indictment was in the courts run by lawyers according to rules and statutes developed by lawyers. He was persuaded that nothing outside the courtroom should matter, and thus he kept his public silence.

At 37 years of age, he could still emerge from jail and resume his high-tech career, and probably not be as openly conversational with short-term friends.

Then followed a series of discovery motions by Terry Segal to learn as much as possible about the Government's case. There were two Motions for Discovery of Exculpatory Material, and another for a Bill of Particulars. While the two defendants were still indicted together and planned by the Government to stand trial together, motions were being filed separately by the two sets of lawyers representing Tom Shay and Alfred Trenkler.

Then came the U.S. Attorney's 28 January 1993 Motion to compel Channel 56 to furnish a copy of its 45 minute 17 October 1992 interview of Thomas A. Shay by Karen Marinella. Channel 56 resisted on First Amendment grounds.

On 12 February 1993 Terry Segal, Alfred Trenkler's attorney, filed a motion to separate the trials of Thomas A. Shay and Alfred Trenkler on the grounds that Shay's frequent public statements would unfairly prejudice the case against Alfred Trenkler. On 16 March, Paul Kelly and Frank Libby, Assistant U.S. Attorneys, filed a motion in support of such severance, citing a U.S. Supreme Court case often cited by Judge Rya Zobel at Shay's trial, <u>Bruton v. U.S</u>[3]

Further, they noted that that Shay's separate trial had already been scheduled by the judge for 28 June 1993. For unpublicized reasons, the prosecutors made the choice to try Shay first. They surely presumed that it would be the easier conviction and it would help assure the conviction of the second.

Also on 12 February, Terry Segal filed several motions to suppress, or make inadmissible at trial, evidence seized during previous "consent" searches of 5-6 November 1991 and the Search Warrant searches of 31 January. The grounds for the motions were that **"there were deliberate and material misrepresentations of fact in the affidavit upon which the Magistrate-Judge relied in issuing the** [search] **warrant."** For the "consent" searches on 5-6 November, there was the obvious question of whether there was actual, and legally permissible consent. The Motions included affidavits from Alfred Trenkler, John Cates, and Alfred's former lawyer, Martin Cosgrove. While such motions are almost automatic for criminal defense lawyers, they established the perception that Alfred Trenkler had something to hide. During those searches he said otherwise. The defense was perhaps being extra careful, but there was nothing seized that showed any connection to the Roslindale Bomb.

The motions to suppress included three motions to suppress statements allegedly made by Alfred Trenkler to investigators on 5 November 1991, and 31 January and 4 and 5 February 1992. Trying to suppress the Government's claims for Alfred's statements was a different matter from the suppression of evidence seized, because of the "He said, he said" problem. If Alfred's statements could be suppressed by any means, then there would be no need to refute them at trial. This was to be a key problem for the defense as it decided at some point that Alfred Trenkler would not be testifying in his own defense, and would leave others to recall what he said and when.

In support of the Motion, Alfred Trenkler completed a seven page, 45 paragraph affidavit presenting his view of the 5/5 November consent searches, the 31 January search warrant searches and the 4 February visit to the ATF office. Portions of the affidavit are presented here:

"21. At some point Leahy sat at my desk [at ARCOMM] and asked me about the 1986 incident.

22. He asked me to draw a diagram of what I had built in 1986, which I did. To my knowledge, this diagram was thereafter destroyed.

23. Leahy then asked me whether, based on my knowledge of electrical engineering, I could draw a diagram of the bomb that went off in Roslindale. I said, 'No.' Leahy then asked what I knew about dynamite and blasting caps and I said, 'Absolutely nothing.' Leahy then said, 'Oh well. Just asking.' At no time did I draw a diagram of the bomb that exploded in Roslindale, as has been alleged.

39. It is not true that I ever said to Agent Leahy or anyone else [at the search of my parent's garage] that I was willing to talk to them even though my lawyer said not to. I was not willing to talk to them, did not want to talk to them, and did not wish to have anything to do with them. At the same time, I believed that I was required to stay there and observe them as they continued their search.

40. On February 4, 1992 I arrived at the Tip O'Neill Federal Building ATF office to pick up the business records which were taken from my briefcase during the search of 133 Atlantic Avenue on January 31,1992. Picking up my records was the sole purpose of my visit.

41. It was my understanding that the ATF agents involved in the search had agreed to provide me with a copy of these records and had made arrangements for me to pick them up at 11:OO a.m.

42. When I arrived I informed Leahy, who met me at the door, that I was there for my records. Leahy said, 'We'll have your records for your shortly,' Leahy then escorted me to a conference room and sat me down, at which point Agent LaCourse entered the room.

43. Leahy then began to ask me questions about my relationship with Tom Shay, Jr. At no time was any mention of my attorney made as has been alleged in Leahy's investigatory report.

44. During Leahy's questioning, I asked him again for my records, specifically, the records for the jobs I was working on at that time. Leahy responded, 'The copies are taking a little longer than I expected.' I asked Leahy for my records a third time and received in effect the same response.

45. After waiting for copies of all my records for approximately two hours, I was given copies of only my business phone book which consisted of 30 pages. I did not receive a copy of any other business records, particularly the records I needed for the jobs I was working on at that time."

On 16 February ATF Special Agent Thomas D'Ambrosio and Boston Detective Brendan Craven interviewed William Miller in Braintree. Miller had worked for Alfred on two microwave antenna construction jobs, including the work for Marcus Communications in Vernon, Connecticut in August 1991 and the MIT project in December 1992 at the time of Alfred Trenkler's arrest. Reported Thomas D'Ambrosio, "Miller stated that on one occasion, Trenkler mentioned Thomas Shay, stating that he really didn't know Shay and had seen him once or twice."

On 17 February, the prosecutors asked to delay the trial until 17 May, and the defense responded a week later that it had a schedule conflict; but these dates would later become moot.

On 19 February Boston Police Officer Thomas Rose was killed at a police station when a man grabbed Rose's gun during a struggle and shot him. The *Boston Globe* reported the story the next day, and also published another story, without a byline, *"BOSTON OFFICER WAS FOURTH KILLED SINCE 1988."* Jeremiah Hurley was the third, and Boston would not soon forget him.

On 23 February, Special Agent Jeff Kerr interviewed James Gannett and Daniel Fitzgerald at the Essex County Jail in Middleton, Mass., where the inmates had met Tom Shay. Gannett said that Shay had several envelopes of newspaper clippings about him and the Roslindale Bomb and Gannett read them. Gannett "...stated that Shay claimed that the bomb was detonated by a walkie talkie. He stated that Shay said, a friend of his named Alfred Trenkler built the bomb. He stated Shay told him that he wanted to kill his father for ten million dollars.

Gannett stated Shay told him the explosive used in the bomb was two sticks of dynamite and some plastic explosive. He stated Shay claimed Trenkler worked around and with electronics and that this vocation made it much easier for him, Trenkler to build the bomb.

Gannett stated Shay told him that he observed the explosion at his father's residence. He stated Shay told him the cop who was killed as a result of the blast, picked up the bomb and put it in his lap as he examined it just prior to detonation."

Special Agent Kerr reported that Fitzgerald was not present at the above discussion, but that he had met Shay and that Shay had sent him a number of letters, which he gave to Jeff Kerr, and which are unavailable. Gannett was not called to testify at Shay's upcoming trial.

On 28 February 1993, ATF agents led the first assault by ATF and other law enforcement agencies on the Waco, Texas compound of David Koresh, causing the death of four ATF agents and six members of Koresh's group. Reinforcements were requested from around the country and 16 agents from Boston, including Special Agent Jeff Kerr went to Waco to assist. Most of Boston's agents returned on 21 April, after the deaths of 85 people, including 17 children, in the compound's fire two days previously. The embarrassing disaster was later said to have motivated the ATF to achieve success with the convictions of Tom Shay and Alfred Trenkler. Tom Shay said that Paul Kelly affirmed that motivation by ATF and Alfred Trenkler said that his U.S. Marshal escorts had said the same thing and that "*Washington is calling the shots.*"

On 2 March, Tom Shay's attorneys filed several motions. One was to suppress 12 incriminating statements Shay had made to police on 29 and 31 October 1991 and during the March/April arrest in California and return, and later to psychiatrists. Another was to suppress any statements to the grand jury by his mother which may have arisen from a statement Tom Shay made to ATF agents or AUSA's in her presence during plea-bargain negotiations. The others were in the nature of discovery, e.g. the "*Motion... for Disclosure of Bad Acts, 'Specific Conduct' and Criminal Convictions, if Any,*" and the "*Motion for Exculpatory Evidence.*"

On 8 March, the prosecutors responded briefly but vigorously to Terry Segal's Motions to Suppress evidence and statements.   AUSA's Paul Kelly and Frank Libby both signed the Opposition which said, in part, "The foregoing motions are based upon affidavits (of Trenkler and his roommate, John Cates) which are replete with knowing or reckless falsehoods and perjurious statements. The motions are not supported by any memoranda of reasons or legal authority. The motions merely contain unexplained conclusory legal allegations."

Attached to the Opposition was an affidavit by ATF Special Agent Victor Palaza which said that Alfred Trenkler and John Cates were cooperative and friendly on 5-6 November 1991 and freely gave their consent to search 133 Atlantic Street, and Alfred Trenkler was often "chatty" and often said that he had "nothing to hide." His visit to the ATF offices on 4 February, wrote Palaza, was entirely voluntary and lasted so long, the ATF agents had to ask him to leave.

The trial of the indictment for the Roslindale Bomb case was severed into two trials by an order by Judge Zobel on 8 March. She said later in the Trenkler trial that she wanted one trial, but because the prosecutors and defense both asked for separate trials she reluctantly agreed.

If there had been a joint trial of Alfred Trenkler and Tom Shay, they would have been in close proximity on the first day of the trial for longer than their entire previous acquaintance; and the trial would likely have lasted more than a month.

END NOTES

---

1 *Marmion*, by Sir Walter Scott.

2. On 19 July 1994, AUSA Paul Kelly stated in an Affidavit that David Lindholm was returned to Massachusetts to testify before a grand jury.

3. "In United States v. Bruton, 391 U.S. 123 (1968), a co-defendant admitted to a postal inspector that he and the defendant committed a robbery. The postal inspector testified that the defendants committed a robbery. The co-defendant did not testify. Although limiting instructions were given to disregard the confession as against the defendant, the defendant argued that his Sixth Amendment rights under the Confrontation Clause were violated. The Supreme Court held that because of the substantial risk that the jury, despite instructions to the contrary, looked to the incriminating extrajudicial statements in determining the defendant's guilt, admission of the co-defendant's confession in a joint trial violated the defendant's right of cross-examination secured by the Confrontation Clause. 391 U.S. at 136-37. (as cited in U.S. v. Pickard and Adderson, District Ct of Kansas, 29 July 2003, at http://www.freepickard.org/motionsbycourt/0040104-360.html)

Chapter 5: Pretrial for Thomas A. Shay and Alfred Trenkler - 9 March 1993 to 27 June 1993

> *"Our system of criminal justice is best*
> *described as a search for the truth."*[1]
> Janet Reno, Attorney General of the United States, 1993-2001

With her 8 March 1993 order severing the Roslindale Bomb trial into two trials, Judge Rya Zobel ordered that the trial of Tom Shay begin on 17 May and of Alfred Trenkler in early August. In their request for severance, the prosecutors reasoned that Shay should go first because he had been incarcerated for a longer period of time than Alfred Trenkler, but Shay's initial incarceration was for an entirely different offense, and both men essentially were incarcerated on the same day, 16 December, for the Roslindale Bomb case. The U.S. Attorney's office recommended a trial date for Alfred Trenkler of the first or second week in September. While the two sets of lawyers were therefore on their own in some respects, they continued to work together, but not enough to agree on a common defense strategy and alternate theories of the crime. Nancy Gertner pointed primarily to Mr. Thomas L. Shay and sometimes to Alfred Trenkler as the primary villains. At the subsequent trial of Alfred Trenkler, Terry Segal pointed to the already-convicted Tom Shay as the man responsible for the Roslindale Bomb.

On 17 March Terry Segal filed a motion for a speedy trial for Alfred Trenkler by June 1, or in the alternative for his release on bail from pre-trial detention if the prosecutors were not ready to proceed on that June date.

Also on 17 March there was a hearing on the 28 January motion by the U.S. Attorney's office to compel Channel 56, WLVI-TV, to produce a copy of the 17 October 1992 Karen Marinella interview with Tom Shay. They wanted the entire 45 minute interview, as only portions had been broadcast publicly. The _Boston Herald_'s Shelley Murphy reported the story on the 18th, "*FEDS SEEK BOMB SUSPECT'S TV INTERVIEW.*" She wrote, "*Attorney Mark Tully, who represents WLVI-TV, argued that the prosecution's goal of building a case doesn't outweigh Channel 56's First Amendment interests against becoming a research tool of government.*" Again using unnamed sources, she reported, "*Shay was cooperating with the government against Trenkler at the time of his interview with Channel 56, but he was indicted after investigators were unable to corroborate his story and suspected he minimized his role in the blast, sources said.*" Unfortunately, the government misunderstood Shay by 180 degrees with the idea that Shay was **minimizing his role**. What he was really doing with all his public statements and his negotiations with the government was publicly **inserting himself into a role** in the Roslindale Bombing, while avoiding criminal responsibility. His only real connection was that the Roslindale Bomb seemed to target his father. The prosecutors needed a conviction, and the admissions by Tom Shay looked like other admissions by other guilty defendants in the past, but the other defendants were not like Tom Shay. In fact, the admissions were too good to be true.

Matthew Brelis wrote the 18 March story for the _Boston Globe_, "*COURT TO RULE ON CH. 56 RELEASE OF SHAY TAPE.*" Given the extensive leaking by "*unnamed sources*" of facts and the legal steps in the case, it was ironic that AUSA Frank Libby was reported to have argued that Channel 56 should have no problem with breaking the confidentiality of sources, as "*no unnamed sources are included....*" The article's last paragraph read, "*Law enforcement sources have said they believe Trenkler built the bomb at Shay's request and that Shay wanted to kill his father because of his unhappy childhood and because he believed he would inherit up to $400,000 that his father stood to gain in a civil suit.*" The "sources" seemed to have forgotten that Mr. Thomas L. Shay was living with the mother of his fourth child, and there were two other stepdaughters, too; and he might have even disinherited Tom Shay after the 1988 theft of money and jewelry from 39 Eastbourne.

At the same hearing, Judge Zobel announced that she had rescheduled Alfred Trenkler's trial for the first week of August, and Shay's trial had already been scheduled for 28 June.

In response to the article's summary of what "*law enforcement sources have said*," Alfred Trenkler and his lawyer should have been able, consistent with lawyers' ethical standards on media relations, to issue a countering statement. It might have stated, "Alfred Trenkler did not build a bomb for Tom Shay, and if Tom Shay had made any such request for assistance to kill his father, Alfred Trenkler would have quickly dismissed the idea as another Tom Shay fantasy thread. If Tom Shay had persisted with such a request, Alfred Trenkler would have reported him to the police." No such statement was issued as the courtroom was considered to be the proper forum for resolving legal disputes. No formal complaint was made to the court about the prosecution's leaks to the press either.

On 19 March, the ATF laboratory in Washington concluded that Tom Shay's handwriting matched that of documents of the "James Keough Massage" service and that Alfred Trenkler's handwriting matched some, but not all of the sampled ARCOMM checks. Given that Tom Shay was not disputing his massage work in San Francisco and that the check signing roles of the partners in ARCOMM were not relevant to the Roslindale Bomb investigation, the report accomplished nothing. If its conclusion was exactly the opposite, it would also have made no difference.

On 20 March, Shelley Murphy of the *Boston Herald* wrote the page 5, page-wide story, "*POLICE ACCUSED OF COERCION - BOMB SUSPECT CLAIMS SEARCH ILLEGAL.*" The story was based on Alfred Trenkler's 12 February Motions to suppress and his 17 February Affidavit in support of those motions. The article said "*Trenkler alleges that Boston Police Detective Peter O'Malley 'was visibly hostile and threatening toward me. He used foul language and at times I thought he was going to hit me.'*" Murphy noted that Detective O'Malley had recently received a four day suspension arising from his allegedly intimidating witnesses during the Carol DiMaiti Stuart murder investigation. AUSA Paul Kelly "*accused Trenkler of 'trying to bootstrap himself and take unfair advantage of Detective O'Malley's recent problems arising from the Stuart investigation without factual support to back up his allegations.'*" Kelly said, "*The government is prepared to demonstrate that the allegations concerning Detective O'Malley's conduct are either false or grossly exaggerated.*" O'Malley had been removed from the Roslindale Bomb case in 1992, but not because of the allegations in the Stuart case, but likely because he thought that the focus on Tom Shay and Alfred Trenkler was taking the investigation in the wrong direction. He had been focusing on Mr. Thomas L. Shay and the 1987 firecracker/barrel explosion at the Dedham Service Center.

The article addressed Trenkler's claim that when he was placed in the back seat of a car on the night of 5 November 1991 at 133 Atlantic Street, he sat next to a duffel bag of ammunition, guns and other weapons. Wrote Murphy, *"ATF Special Agent-in-Charge Terence J. McArdle said it was 'absolutely ridiculous' to suggest a suspect would be left in a car with an arsenal. We don't keep guns in the back seat of cars in duffle* [sic] *bags.' said McArdle,' "* but Alfred Trenkler had said they were sport bags, not duffel bags. When Alfred Trenkler told an ATF Special Agent about the bag with the guns, the agent promptly moved them to the car's trunk. The guns were probably used at the Boston Police target range on Long Island, just four miles away. There was no statement in the article from Alfred Trenkler nor Terry Segal, and the article closed by stating that a hearing was scheduled on the Motion for 3 May.

On 22 March 1993, Paul Kelly memorialized his call to Terry Segal the previous week with the startling news "that I have a credible witness who is prepared to testify to various admissions by your client, including the fact that Trenkler said it was he who built the bomb which exploded in Roslindale on October 28, 1991. The government has made no promises, rewards or inducements to this witness."

When Alfred heard of this claim, it was apparent by the "no promises" clause that the "credible witness" was an inmate or someone in trouble with law somewhere, but Trenkler had little idea of who it might be. That is, among the people he talked with at the Boston Police jail in Boston in April, and the Federal lockup in the Federal building in Boston in December and at the Plymouth County House of Correction beginning in December, he couldn't remember having a distinctively longer conversation with one person more than others. He narrowed the list down to a few people, and William David Lindholm was one of them, but Alfred made no admissions of anything to him or anybody. Sometime thereafter, it became known in Trenkler's unit at the Plymouth facility from newspaper accounts that the prosecution was planning on using an inmate informer to testify that Alfred Trenkler had admitted his role in the Roslindale Bomb case. After the news hit the unit, there were a lot of conversations about who the informant could be, among those still in the unit. One inmate called Terry Segal's office to offer to help counter the expected testimony of others in the unit, whomever they might be. Another inmate recalled seeing AUSA Paul Kelly meeting with a fellow inmate at Plymouth and that set of speculation that Kelly's meetingmate was the source. Fortunately no one was physically confronted about the rumors, and no one was hurt or killed, as sometimes happens when jailhouse informants are exposed.

Terry Segal had hired or retained one of the best explosives experts in the country, Denny Kline. In his initial preliminary report, he identified several problems with the ATF's evidence. The most significant arose when he disassembled a Radio Shack #275-602 and found that its contacts were different from those retrieved in the bomb debris. He concluded in that preliminary report to Terry Segal that either his purchase of a #275-602 was of a more recent vintage than that used in the Roslindale Bomb, or that Cynthia Wallace was mistaken in her identification of the toggle switch. This was the equivalent of finding another man's DNA underneath the fingernails of a female strangling victim. [See the applicable pages of the report in Appendix E.] On 17 March 1993, Segal wrote to Nancy Gertner about several investigatory matters, thus showing that they were working together, and he wrote about the switch, "*Denny Kline, the retired F.B.I. bomb expert I hired, will send a letter which I will send to you. Interestingly, he told me today he purchased a toggle switch which Shay is alleged to have purchased on October 18th, and the switch does not match the remnants of the toggle switch ATF has as part of the physical evidence in this case.*" Terry Segal never told Alfred Trenkler of this discovery, and Alfred did not learn of it until many years after his trial, when his stepfather, Jack Wallace, and his half-brother, David Wallace, found the correspondence and photos of the contacts in the legal files of Nancy Gertner's former law firm, Dyer and Collura. It's not known why the photos of the contacts were in Gertner's case files and not in Segal's. If Denny Kline's analysis was correct, the photographs of the switch contacts were the exculpatory equivalent of an alternate suspect's DNA found at a murder scene. However, that opinion must have changed, because his preliminary view that the Radio Shack toggle switch contacts were different from those found amidst the Roslindale Bomb debris was not in his final report, and the issue was apparently dropped.

On 2 April, Judge Zobel denied the U.S. Attorney's motion for the Channel 56 videotape. Judge Zobel said the motion was premature because it was not yet certain that the government would need the tape. She stated that there might not be a trial at all if Shay pled guilty or if he were declared incompetent to stand trial. It would only be admissible, Judge Zobel reasoned, if Tom Shay did testify and the tape could be used to impeach his testimony. Later, she changed that view. On 8 April, the Boston papers covered this media-sensitive aspect of the Roslindale Bomb case. The *Boston Herald* had a short notice in the "*Regional*" section on page 34, "*JUDGE KO'S PLEA FOR CH. 56.*" Actually, Judge Zobel KO'd the prosecution's motion to compel. The *Boston Globe*'s article, "*BID IS DENIED ON TAPE OF SUSPECT*," had no byline and noted that the denial was temporary and the Motion could be renewed if it became clear that Shay would stand trial.

On 5 April ATF Special Agents Victor Palaza and Dennis Leahy interviewed Michael Coady, who had been referred to them by Donna Shea. Dennis Leahy reported in full:

"Mr. Coady states as follows:

Mr. Coady said that he was about 15 years old (1985) when he met Al Trenkler and that Trenkler supplied him with drugs and after several months sexually molested him. Mr. Coady said that he was not gay and that being sexually molested 'fucked my life up.' Mr. Coady said that he dropped out of high school and basically was a street person for a time. Mr. Coady said that he knew Trenkler from about 1985 through 1987. Mr. Coady said that Trenkler was a drug dealer who also used drugs, and that Trenkler was dealing and using about 1 ounce of cocaine a week.

Mr. Coady said that Trenkler was extremely manipulative and had a sexual obsession with younger males. Mr. Coady said that Trenkler stole money for drugs from his grandmother[2] who was very wealthy and at one time married to P.T. Barnum. Mr. Coady said that Trenkler was an 'electronics whiz' and that he went with Trenkler to a telephone pole, near Wilmington Ford, where Trenkler did some electronics work. Mr. Coady expressed strong distaste for Trenkler and feels strongly that by Mr. Trenkler sexually molesting him it has caused great mental anguish to him. Mr. Coady also said that Trenkler liked multiple sexual partners at the same time and that Trenkler used to frequent the Blue Hills, looking for male sexual partners.

Mr. Coady said that Trenkler was from Milton, attended Thayer Academy and correctly described defendant Trenkler to the undersigned."

This report regarding Michael Coady is perhaps the most extreme example of the contrast between the ATF's perception or understanding of an event or person, and Alfred Trenkler's. Alfred never, for example, worked on telephone poles and he had no clients in Wilmington. Also, the content of the report contrasts with Coady's subsequent testimony at Trenkler's trial, when, for example, it was stated that he was 28 years old in 1993 and thus 20 years old in 1985 and not 15 as was stated in the ATF report. The ATF agents would not have known that Alfred Trenkler was often in the Blue Hills area because he did volunteer work for the "Friends of Blue Hills" and worked at the WGBH radio tower site in the Blue Hills reservation for the Catholic Archdiocese of Boston. As he went often to his parents' house, the road through the Blue Hills Reservation is the best route to the South Shore Plaza shopping area. Also, he went dirt bike riding and 4-wheel driving in the Blue Hills.

Below are Alfred Trenker's contemporary notes prepared for his attorney, Terry Segal, regarding Mike Coady.

"1) Met in 1983 in March at a parking lot in the Blue Hills in Braintree MA, an area people from Milton typically drove through to get to the South Shore Plaza, and needed a ride home because his bicycle had conveniently broken down (later he told me this was his way of meeting people) This meeting was witnessed by a Danny Curran of Weymouth who had met Coady a year before I did and warned me that this kid was an opportunist and dishonest. Curran had pulled me over to warn me, since Coady had pulled the same broken bike routine on him. I met Curran in 1984, and he told me that Coady stole his wallet and spent the cash and tried to use the credit cards.

2) As for sexual conduct I did not molest him as reflected in the ATF report.... Months after I had met him, I brought him to a party in Duxbury.

3) Coady was not a street person. He lived with his parents in Braintree at 77 West Street.

4) His brother, Bill Coady, had met me some time in 1984 and was a friend who also warned me of his brother Mike's exploits. Bill could verify that Mike knew exactly what he was doing before he met me.

5) As for Mike Coady's age, he was born 5-21-65 which made him 18 in May 1983. In the ATF report he says he was 15 in 1985, but he turned 20 on 21 May of that year.

6) Coady says he dropped out of high school. If he did it was not because of me, unless he was kept back a year or two and decided to drop out of high school.

7) As for who supplied the drugs, it was Mike Coady that had all the connections. Also, if I was selling drugs to him or supplying drugs to him why would I be writing checks to him. It was he that was selling marijuana and coke.

8) As to selling drugs, this never happened. Besides Mike's brother and one of Mike's friends, I did not know any of Mike's friends. As for friends of mine, Mike met Donna [Shea] on a few occasions, and met some of my friends at a party in Duxbury.

9) As for stealing money from my grandmother, this is total bullshit and is totally undocumented. Also, any money I spent on drugs with him came from my checking account.

10) After 1984 I did not associate with Coady and had moved into a house with a Copeland Draper and his girlfriend Kim until December of 1985, at which time I moved into a house with Bob Craig. Bob Craig will testify that Mike Coady would come by our house and apartment and try to see me but I would avoid him. Brian O'Leary, during 1985, had chased him away from my house in Milton (Woodward Court) because we caught Coady breaking into my Jeep and attempting to steal equipment and hold it for ransom. Between 85 and 89 Coady would find my address through an employee of the phone company and would show up at my various addresses but I would avoid him. In 1988 Bob Craig and I moved to Hull. On 31 October 86 I had Michael Coady's license ran on the LEAP's computer system which generated the information that he was born on 21 May 1965. Also I had called the phone company to complain that Coady was obtaining my address through an employee of the phone company, since my phone number was unlisted, and I was told later that this individual, in the phone company had admitted to giving my address to Coady and had been fired."

In 2007, Alfred wrote again about Michael Coady.

"...When I originally met 'Mike' Coady in 1983, he had shown me 'his' license with his photo but the name on his license said 'William Coady' of 77 West Street in Braintree. Coady had introduced himself as 'Bill' Coady, and was, from the license, 22 years old. I was 27 at the time. This information would be available at the Registry of Motor Vehicles, but Terry [Segal] did not deem it important.

From time to time I bought pot from Mike Coady ('Bill'), whose sister, according to Mike, sold the stuff. I slipped and inadvertently revealed where I hid my checkbook in my Jeep. I had a soft top thus my doors did not lock. Evidently, Coady took some checks from the back of my checkbook and cashed them at various places, usually between 10 to 50 dollars at a time, enough not to really notice, until I had a call from the Braintree Savings Bank informing me of a check cashed by one 'Mike' Coady of 77 West Street, Braintree. I poured [sic] over my account and noticed checks with a signature that was close to mine but obviously not my signature if scrutinized. The checks were made out to people I did not know and places I did not do business with. This was a bit confusing. I called the Coady residence to meet with 'Bill' Coady in order to confront him about the stolen check(s). I say confusing because the person I met was not 'Bill' Coady that I had met but in fact the real Bill Coady (Mike's brother). It turned out that Mike Coady had obtained an ID in Bill's name by

*going to the Registry claiming to have lost his license using Bill Coady's birth
certificate to obtain a duplicate license, allowing Mike to purchase liquor and go
to bars and nightclubs.*

*It was at this point I cut Mike 'Bill' Coady off in mid-1984 and I moved in with
Kip Draper and his girlfriend Kim, his future wife. (I had met Coady in late 1983.
In 1983, Coady was 18, and I spent much of the year recovering at my parents'
from hepatitis.*

*In 1984 I met Bob Craig through a friend of mine, Brian O'Leary, and Craig
and I would end up renting a house in Quincy and starting AWT Associastes.
Coady found my address at Kip and Kim's and was witnessed by Brian O'Leary
stealing a milk crate from my Jeep with various off-road equipment in it. Brian
ran over to Coady's car and removed the keys in order to force Coady to give
back the milk crate. However, Coady was driving one of those cars that would
operate with the key removed and he sped away only to return to give back my
milk crate in exchange for his keys.*

*In 1985-6 Coady found where Craig and I were living on Randlett Street in
Quincy. The house was sold in July of '95 so we moved to 35 Union Street in
Quincy. Within a short amount of time Coady showed up again. Both Craig and I
threatened Coady to stop stalking us as well as asking him how he keeps finding
us. Of course, he never said."*

The challenge of untangling the truth regarding Alfred Trenkler's relationship to
Michael Coady would come at Alfred's trial - and the trial would fail the challenge.

On 7 April 1993, and apparently concentrating on claims regarding Alfred
Trenkler's sexual life and alleged gay relationships, ATF Agents Victor Palaza and
Dennis Leahy interviewed Paul Nutting. Dennis Leahy's report stated briefly:

"Mr. Nutting said that he knew Al Trenkler and Tom Shay (the younger) and
had seen them together in the Blue Hills area several times probably in the
1989/1990 time frame. Mr. Nutting said that the Blue Hills area was a known
gay hangout for free sex. Mr. Nutting said that he thought that Al always drove,
usually in a blue pickup truck and that sometimes they would separate in the
Blue Hills and sometimes they would stay together. Mr. Nutting said that he
remembered Tom Shay also being in the Provincetown area and that Shay would
sometimes wear an 'ACT UP' T-shirt.

Mr. Nutting said that he knew Al since the early 1980's and Shay since about
1989. Mr. Nutting said that he may also have seen them at several gay parties
which were held in private homes. Mr. Nutting said that he lived in Milton,
Massachusetts at the time. Mr. Nutting said that Tom Shay had a bad
reputation and was widely known in the gay community."

Alfred Trenkler's contemporary response stated, in part, *"1) I must see a picture
of Paul Nutting - I don't ever remember this person... 5) I never owned a pickup truck - blue or otherwise... 8) I have never been to the Blue Hills with Tom
Shay. I have never been to a 'gay' party in Milton. I lived in Milton in 1980 and
1983-5. From 1986 to 1992 I lived in Quincy and Hull."* In 2007, Trenkler noted
as well that he did not own a car between 1988 and September of 1990 and he
lived in Hull during that time, approximately 20 miles from Blue Hill.

Again, the trial should have been the place to sort out the truth of the ATF report of Paul Nutting's knowledge about Alfred Trenkler, and the correct date of the initial acquaintance of Trenkler and Tom Shay; but it was not to be.

Also on 9 April, ATF Agent Victor Palaza went to 39 Eastbourne Street and "Mr. Shay produced a used wood paint stirrer that was located in his garage. Mr. Shay stated that the stirrer was in his garage on October 28, 1991....The stirrer was retained as evidence." This was more than seventeen months after the explosion, and Palaza appeared to accept Mr. Shay's representations about the stirrer. The request for the stirrer originated with Alfred Trenkler who saw an open can of flat black metal primer paint with a stirrer inside in a police photograph of Thomas L. Shay's backyard. He brought that to the attention of Terry Segal who passed the information on to AUSA Paul Kelley who then passed it to the ATF which then asked Mr. Shay for the wood stirrer. It's not known if the can of paint in the photograph was ever requested or seized, but the request should not have awaited the observations by a defendant of items in a police photograph of a crime scene.

On 12 April, in an indication of the extent to which Richard Brown was cooperating with the ATF, Brown telephoned Special Agent Dennis Leahy, who summarized the conversation in a report:

"Mr. Brown said that Jimmy Karolides [private investigator for Terry Segal] 'keeps bugging me' and my grandfather and that he won't stop calling. Mr. Brown asked that I or the prosecutor call Karolides and tell him to stop the telephone calls. Mr. Brown said that he did not want to speak with Karolides as the 'guy is guilty as sin' referring to Al Trenkler. Mr. Brown was instructed that it was his decision to speak with Mr. Karolides or not to speak with him.

Mr. Brown again telephonically, in a second call, said that he had just spoken to Karolides for about 20 minutes and the [sic] Karolides said to him that the government was lying and that Al Trenkler was at ARCOMM painting the day of the bombing. Mr. Brown said Karolides was hostile to him and said that Brown would receive a subpoena for his business records if he did not cooperate with Karolides. Mr. Brown said that he does not remember Al Trenkler painting at ARCOMM the day of the bombing. Mr. Brown again requested that ATF or the U.S. Attorney's office contact Karolides to stop bothering his grandfather and he."

Jim Karolides' long career in law enforcement included 10 years as a policeman and 20 years as an ATF agent, with most of those years spent in Boston. Thus, he knew well the investigators on the other side of this Roslindale Bomb case. He recalled in 2007[3] that his former colleagues in ATF "*hated me*" for his work on behalf of Alfred Trenkler.

On 13 and 14 April, there were hearings on Nancy Gertner's Motions to suppress several Tom Shay statements and the identification of Tom Shay by Dwayne Armbrister, the Radio Shack salesperson. The hearing was made simpler by the prosecution's agreement that it would not use any statements which arose during, or as a product of, Tom Shay's negotiations for a plea-bargain, or "proffer agreement."

The first witness on 13 April was Dennis Leahy who said that he first visited the Radio Shack store at 197 Mass. Ave on Wednesday, 11 December 1991 when trying to find the source of the Radio Shack toggle switch found in the Roslindale Bomb. When he returned on 20 February 1992, he talked with 25 year old Dwayne Armbrister who was the salesperson identified on the 18 October receipt, and he had no initial recollection of that transaction nor of the person who purchased the listed items. In one photo array was Alfred Trenkler, and Armbrister thought he recognized him. Agent Leahy later showed Armbrister different individual photos of Tom Shay, and he recognized him, too.

The next government witness was ATF Special Agent Sandra LaCourse who accompanied Agent Leahy to the Radio Shack store on 20 and 24 February. She returned again on 3 March with a new photo array, which included Richard Brown's photo, and Armbrister did not recognize him. Agent LaCourse also interviewed Allan Kingsbury, who formerly worked for Radio Shack, but later worked elsewhere. He remembered the 18 October transaction and recalled the purchaser as a Middle Eastern man about 27 years of age with a darker complexion. Kingsbury also identified Alfred Trenkler as someone who had visited the store at some point but couldn't state that he was there on the 18th. On redirect examination, Ms. LaCourse acknowledged that Allan Kingsbury later changed his mind about the 18 October identification and said he was thinking about someone else who came in during the winter months, wearing heavier clothing.

The 14 April *Boston Herald* article by David Weber was headlined, "*LAWYERS MOVE TO BLOCK ID OF BOMB SUSPECT,*" and Matthew Brelis wrote the *Boston Globe*'s article, "*ID OF BOMB SUSPECT 'FLAWED,'* says attorney." Each article summarized the day's testimony, with Brelis quoting Nancy Gertner afterwards, " *'It is a flawed identification,' she said.*"

On the 14th at 2:00 p.m. the suppression hearing resumed with the testimony of Dwayne Armbrister, but not before a bench conference. AUSA Paul Kelly wanted to attempt an in-court identification of Tom Shay by Mr. Armbrister but Nancy Gertner objected as everyone in the room was wearing a suit, and Shay, when he arrived minutes later, would not be. Also, Shay wouldn't look like he was a lawyer, either. Few lawyers practicing before the Federal Court are younger than 24 years old, and on that day, as Nancy Gertner said, Shay would have been the "*only person in this courtroom under thirty.*" (TSSH 2-10 (Transcript Shay Suppression Hearing, Day 2, page 3)) Also, noted Gertner, ATF agents had already shown Armbrister a photograph of Shay and other photos had been in the newspapers several times. An in-court identification would be "*terribly unfair,*" she said. (TSSH 2-3]. Gertner reported that Attorney Jefferson Boone had seen Armbrister and Shay in the hall at the same time the previous day - but AUSA Paul Kelly said that was impossible.

On direct examination by Paul Kelly, Dwayne Armbrister said he remembered the 18 October 1991 transaction and described it as an easy, 15 minute transaction. He described the customer as "*pretty tall, slender, black hair, white, and he had a scar on his lip.*" (TSSH 2-19) The reference to the lip scar was not an isolated oddity. Before the grand jury, Armbrister had referred to the lip scar twice. Also, said Armbrister at the hearing, he had no facial hair and "*... his eyes were like sort* *of stupid looking, weird."* (TSSH 2-20] And he was taller than Armbrister's 6'2", so that made the customer *"about six-five, six-six."* (TSSH 2-21) Armbrister said he worked on commission, and the SAHY sale was small, so he rushed through it, hence the typing mistakes, and the customer was acting irritated with being asked for personal information. When SAHY left the store, Armbrister said he told his fellow employee that the customer *"was a jerk"*, because of the hard time he had given Armbrister in the information gathering process. (TSSH 2-28)

Armbrister said he was distracted by the death of his grandfather during the first ATF interview, when he had failed to recognize a photo of Tom Shay. On 8 April, the day before he testified before the grand jury, ATF agent Jeff Kerr gave him a ride to the courthouse for an interview with Kerr and Paul Kelly, the AUSA who was examining him.

Under cross-examination, Armbrister acknowledged that Allan Kingsbury was a good friend of his, as well as being a former Radio Shack employee and that after Kingsbury testified to the grand jury, he and Armbrister talked about that testimony. Armbrister testified again on the 14th to modify his earlier testimony.

Next, Paul Kelly examined ATF Special Agent Jeff Kerr, because of his 8 April 1992 interview of Dwayne Armbrister. The hearing adjourned, to be resumed on May 7, hopefully with Allan Kingsbury, who had not yet been located in order to be served with a subpoena for the suppression hearing.

Afterwards, Nancy Gertner asked Judge Zobel for help with the conditions of Tom Shay's custody at the Essex County Jail in Middleton. Gertner said, *"Mr. Shay reports that he doesn't get legal papers; that he has not been given an opportunity to shower or to shave. He describes that he's been assaulted, has stitches, he's been threatened, he's been in 23-hour lockup for the past 36 days, refused leave of phone use; that he has lost over 50 pounds because he hasn't been fed right, refused hygiene goods. And that he would like to be transferred..."* to one of the other jails that handles Federal prisoners. (TSSH 2-98) Judge Zobel said there was not much she could do, but suggested that Nancy Gertner could look into options, such as the Hillsborough County, New Hampshire Jail.

On 15 April, Shelley Murphy wrote the *Boston Herald*'s story about the hearing, *"STORE CLERK SAYS BOMB DEFENDANT BOUGHT PARTS."* While she noted that Armbrister had described a scar on Shay's lip, and that Dennis Leahy had said that there was a scar in an ATF photograph of Tom Shay, Ms. Murphy did not note that Tom Shay had no such scar. Usually, newspaper reporters do not write the headlines, so they are not responsible for their content. For this story, one can see how the headline exaggerated the day's testimony. Dwayne Armbrister recognized Tom Shay, after suggestive visits by ATF, as the purchaser of the six items from Radio Shack on 18 October 1991. One of those six items, a toggle switch, was claimed by ATF to be the same model as the one used in the Roslindale Bomb. The message for readers of the *Boston Herald*? Case solved. There was no story in the *Boston Globe* about the identification issue.

On 17 April, Matthew Brelis of the *Globe* scooped the issue of an insanity defense for Tom Shay in, *"DEFENDANT IN BLAST THAT KILLED OFFICER TO USE INSANITY DEFENSE."* The day before, Nancy Gertner had filed a *"Motion... to file Notice of Insanity defense and intention to introduce expert testimony."* The message to the public, and to investigative officers, potential witnesses and members of the victims' families, was that Tom Shay committed the crimes, but he was too mentally ill to know that what he was doing was wrong. Nancy Gertner could not be reached by the reporter for comment, and Paul Kelly had no comment.

On 22 April, prosecutors Paul Kelly and Frank Libby filed a Motion to require Tom Shay to submit to a mental health examination by a Government psychiatrist. They made the motion after, they wrote, talking with Nancy Gertner at the 14 April suppression hearing when she advised that a defense-retained psychiatrist had examined Tom Shay and had concluded that "*grounds existed for raising at trial the defense of insanity bearing on the issue of guilt.*"

On 24 April Terry Segal filed a Motion to distribute a juror questionnaire because it seemed likely that the prosecution would introduce irrelevant allegations that Alfred Trenkler was gay and because of the high sensitivity for the death of a policeman. Attached to the Motion was a proposed 12 question survey. Question 8 asked, "*Do you believe that homosexual relations between consenting adults is: a) Morally Wrong, Yes or No OR b) Should be illegal. Yes or No.*" This question might have been asked of the investigators and prosecutors in the Roslindale Bomb case.

A few questions were about family or friends working for law enforcement, and whether a law enforcement person or a defendant is more believable.

Question 11 was a sign of defense strategy, "*If a defendant in a criminal trial does not testify during his/her trial, would that cause you to believe that this is evidence of the defendant's guilt? Yes __ No __ Explain*".

In response, the prosecutors argued on 24 May against such a questionnaire, stating that Segal had offered no compelling reason for the unusual procedure. The prosecutors said that "The government prefers to adhere to the more routine, and generally effective approach of conducting the juror voir dire in open court. Rather than burden prospective jurors (with completing a questionnaire) the Clerk's Office (with mailing and processing the questionnaires), and counsel (with formulating questions and developing neutral and appropriate wording), it is the government's view that the voir dire of prospective jurors should be handled in the ordinary manner -- with due regard to any sensitive issues, such as sexual orientation."

Terry Segal responded that the compelling reasons for the questionnaire is that they would save court time, and "*encourage a more candid and honest assessment by jurors of the issues raised, particularly the issue of homosexuality...and that the use of a questionnaire will make more effective the use by prosecutors and defense counsel of peremptory challenges to jurors.*" Concluded Segal, "*Finally, and most importantly, use of the proposed supplemental questionnaire will assist the Court in empaneling a fair and impartial jury and thus ensure that Mr. Trenkler will receive a fair trial.* "

On 1 May, the <u>Boston Globe</u>, but not the <u>Boston Herald</u>, covered the story of the government-paid fees of the Tom Shay defense team. Matthew Brelis wrote the story, "*DEFENSE LAWYER TO GET $200 AN HOUR IN BOMBING CASE.*" that Nancy Gertner was being paid $200 per hour by the Federal court, and Jefferson Boone, $85, and Amy Baron-Evans, $50. The standard rates in U.S. District Court were $60/hour for in-court work and $40 for out-of-court work. The reason for the higher fee in Shay's case was that it was crime punishable by death, although the prosecutors had said they would not pursue the death penalty.

The fee controversy led on 7 May to a second article by Matthew Brelis, "*Gertner defends her $200-an-hour fee.*" Gertner noted that "*The amount spent by the government for the representation of Thomas A. Shay pales before the amount spent by the government for the prosecution of this matter or, we assume, the amount spent by the co-defendant for privately retained counsel.*" In the last article on the subject, Matthew Brelis wrote in the <u>Globe</u> on 18 May, "*ATTORNEY'S FEE EXCEEDS GUILDELINE, US SAYS,*" that the prosecution opposed the increase in Nancy Gertner's fee and noted that the prosecutors had found no fees approved elsewhere in the country higher than $125 an hour. Treading lightly on the fact that Gertner was known to be a finalist for nomination for a U.S. District judgeship, the prosecutors' motion said, "...Thomas Shay is clearly very fortunate to have counsel of the caliber of Attorney Gertner defending him... Ms. Gertner should indeed be compensated at the highest allowable rate..." but argued that the applicable statutes did not permit such a high rate. The issue remained unresolved until 20 January 1994 when Judge Zobel ordered that Shay's lawyers be paid according to the applicable statute, 18 USC 3006(d)(1).

On 8 May 1993, the *Patriot Ledger*, based in Quincy, Mass., ran a national story from the Cox News Service about the Bureau of Alcohol, Tobacco and Firearms, "*ATF AGENTS: COWBOY MENTALITY CAUSES NEEDLESS DEATHS.*" Written by Teresa Talerico and Suzanne Gamboa, the article originated from the 1992 failed initial raid at the Davidian compound in Waco, Texas. There was no reference to the local work of the ATF, even though both defendants in Roslindale Bomb case lived in Quincy, and several members of the local office served in Waco after that initial raid. The article focused on sex harassment cases in the organization and quoted Baltimore Special Agent Sandra Hernandez, "*They're cowboys... It's like, 'Boom, boom, we go in and get the job done.*" The first black agent to manage a local office, Roy Hendrix said, "*There never has been a black, Hispanic or woman in a policy making position in the bureau.*" The article did not say how many gay employees were in the ATF in 1991, and how many were in the Boston ATF office. People who were acquainted with Tom Shay were painted by ATF with a broad gay brush.

On 11 May 1993 AUSA Paul Kelly sent a summary of the Shay-Trenkler contacts to Nancy Gertner. The content is presented here, in regular Verdana font, along with Alfred Trenkler's 2006 comments (in **bold italic Verdana** here for contrast and emphasis [A copy of the letter, with Alfred Trenkler's annotations, is included in Appendix E.]

"Dear Nancy:

This letter is in response to your request for further detail concerning the topics discussed by your client on June 11, 1992 with ATF Agents Jeff Kerr and Tom D'Ambrosio. By topic area, I can report the following:

1 . <u>Places He's Been with Trenkler</u>   ***[Alfred Trenkler comments]***
  a. True Value Hardware, Roslindale_____**Never been there**
  b. Norwood Tower, Route I _____**Don't know of any**
  c. Bird Sanctuary, Cambridge_____**Been there - never with Shay, Jr.**
  d. Back Bay T-Station_____**Have not taken the T**

e. The Fens, near Ramrod Bar _____ *since the '70's.*
Met Shay, Jr. at store
next to Herbie's (a.k.a
Ramrod Bar.)

f. Quincy Home of Shay Jr _____*Drove him to Falls*
condo complex 1 time

g. Friend's House in Manchester, MA _____ *Never been there*

h. Glad Day Bookstore _____ *Never been there*
(See ATF interview with
John Mitzl, store mgr.)

i. Ed Carrion's Apartment _____ *Never been there*

j. "The Block", near Greyhound Bus Station _ *Never been there*

k. Bathroom at Copley Place _____ *Never been there*

l. Campus Lounge, Cambridge _____ *Never been there*

m. Blue Hills _____ *Never with Shay, Jr.*

n. River Road, Providence, R.J. _____ *Never been there*

o. Dedham Mall _____ *Never with Shay, Jr.*

p. 1270 Club _____ *Never with Shay, Jr./*
not since 1970's

q. Obsessions Bar _____ *Never been there*

r. Tower and shed on South Shore _____ *Never to tower with*
shed on South Shore

s. Nadia's, South End _____ *Never been there*

t. J.C. Hillary's Restaurant _____ *Never been there*

2. People Who Have Seen Trenkler and He Together

a. Nancy Shay (Mother) _____*Nancy Shay testified never*
saw me before.

b. Ed Carrion _____ *Never met the man.*

c. John Cates _____*Once @ White Hen/Once*
when picking up Cates
at work.

d. Rich Brown _____ *Once at Cates Apt. when*
gave Jr. ride to Dorchester.

e. Workers at Ramrod Bar _____*a.k.a. Herbies - next door to*
White Hen - possible

f. Trenkler's landlord _____ *John Cates' landlord? Mike*
Green - not to my knowledge

g. Friends at Blue Hills _____ *Never with Shay, Jr./Went*
with Cates to walk dog.

h. Mickey (?) _____ *Don't know anyone named*
Mickey.

i. Dan O'Neil, aka Kevin Daniels_____ *Don't know person by either*
name

j. Trenkler's friends _____ *Other than Cates & Brown,*
none of my friends.

3 . Al Trenkler and Money
   a. Trenkler paid for goods purchased with a credit card
      (in someone else's name)_____ **Never.**
   b. Trenkler gave him $10.00 or $20.00 occasionally___ **Never.**
   c. Trenkler bought a bird for Ed Carrion's friend _____ **Never.**

4. Topics of Conversation Between He and Trenkler
   a. Sex _____ **No.**
   b. Cute Boys _____ **No.**
   c. Family _____ **No.**
   d. Electronics _____ **No.**
   e. Trenkler's Work _____ **Talked about TV/Radio/Two Way.**

5. How He Feels About Trenkler
   a. Friend
   b. Good Listener
   c. Smart
   d. Hard Worker
   e. Very Good with Electronics

6. The Last Time He Talked with Trenkler
   a. Day after bombing (10/29/91) by telephone _ **NO. Only time I called was to tell him to stop calling voicemail in August of 91. Last time I talked with him was in August, together with John Cates.**

7. His Whereabouts the Weekend Prior to the Bombing
   Thursday Night - With Gary Starkey in Quincy
   Friday - Applied for a job in Quincy; met Starkey at a movie theater at 7:00
      P.M.; got paid $50.00 to have sex with a guy by the racquetball club in
      Braintree (late evening); spent several hours at Store 24 with Steve
      and Scott; went home at.... (later page(s) not immediately available)

Paul Kelly sent a copy of that letter on 13 May, along with other materials to Terry Segal. It isn't known when or whether Alfred's feedback was given back to Tom Shay's legal team, for if it had, Nancy Gertner would have been more clear about the Shay-Trenkler relationship at Tom's trial.

Unfortunately, due to the rules of the lawyers' game, Trenkler's feedback did not get back to Paul Kelly, either, for that was the imperfect role of the trial: to present the facts to the jury. This was another lost opportunity for the truth, for if Paul Kelly had seen Trenkler's responses, he would probably have recalled his own two "Memos to file" about the lies that Tom Shay had told him. Then he might have questioned whether it would be appropriate or even ethical to try to present any evidence at either Shay's or Trenkler's trial which included statements by Tom

Shay about the case. He might also have questioned his own assumptions and beliefs about the Shay-Trenkler relatiionship, which was minimal.

On 12 May the Shay suppression hearing heard testimony from Tom Shay, and the newspapers took note. Headlined Matthew Brelis's article in the _Globe_, "*SUSPECT IN FATAL BOMBING TESTIFIES*." The issue for his testimony was whether his statements on the evening of the 31 October 1991 press conference were voluntary, even though he wasn't formally arrested until he asked to leave the South Boston Homicide Unit offices. Said Shay, "*When I walked into the bus station the news people were in front of me and the exits were manned by police... I knew I had warrants out and I thought they would arrest me.*" Judge Zobel asked Shay how he knew they were policemen, and asked if they were in uniform; and Shay responded, "*No, But I know cops... They were suspicious and in suits and I had seen three or four Ford LTD's outside and I know them to be unmarked police cars.*" Asked Paul Kelly about the end of his interview at the police station, "*You got up to leave because you thought you could leave?*" Shay responded, "*No, I was testing them. I knew I would be arrested.*"

Ralph Ranalli wrote the _Boston Herald_'s article, "*BOMB SUSPECT SAYS HE WASN'T READ HIS RIGHTS.*"

On the day of those articles, 13 May, Judge Zobel turned to the Trenkler side of the case, and began what was agreed to be four two-hour days of hearings to consider Terry Segal's 12 February "Motions to Suppress" evidence seized, and statements of Alfred Trenkler. Segal's partner, Matthew Feinberg, represented Trenkler.

For the government, Paul Kelly affirmed that the there was no plan to use any of the items seized during the 5/6 November and the 31 January 1992 searches as evidence, so suppression of seized evidence was a moot question. In the absence of seized items, the prosecutors intended to use statements that an unattached loud speaker was observed in the Cates/Trenkler apartment. The importance of the loudspeaker is unclear, as it was observed by the investigators on the night of 5/6 November and it was still in the same place on the night of 31 January 1992. Also, Paul Kelly stated that Alfred Trenkler allegedly drew two diagrams for the agents at the ARCOMM location. The first was of the 1986 device and the second was a hypothetical diagram of what the 1991 bomb might have looked like. The prosecutors planned to introduce statements allegedly made by Alfred Trenkler to ATF agents. The questions were: Were the searches consensual? and Were the statements voluntary?

Under direct examination by AUSA Frank Libby, ATF Special Agent Thomas D'Ambrosio described the 5/6 November searches. At 133 Atlantic Street in four or five vehicles were four investigators from ATF (D'Ambrosio, Sandra LaCourse, Dennis Leahy and Supervising Agent Victor Palaza) and seven from the Boston Police Department (Detective Barnicle, William Fogerty, Dennis Harris, Bill Mahoney, John McCarthy, Timothy Murray, and Peter O'Malley,) and one from the Quincy Police Dept. (Thomas Tierney) for a total of twelve. All were in plainclothes and all wore holstered, but non-visible, handguns.

Agent D'Ambrosio was with the smaller team that also went later with Trenkler to his ARCOMM office. Regarding the requested search of his parents' garage, D'Ambrosio testified that in response to Alfred Trenkler's concern about waking his parents and having to explain the presence of Agents Leahy and himself, the agents recommended that Alfred "*could make up whatever story he wanted. He could tell his parents whatever he wanted to as to who we were. He could tell them we were coworkers.*" (TSH 1-59, Transcript Suppression Hearing, Day 1, page 59] Thus, ATF agreed to white lies.

D'Ambrosio described the short search at the garage and then skipped to the end of the night with the return drive to Alfred Trenkler's disabled car and to a store where Alfred went inside and purchased cigarettes and then to his home where Alfred agreed with Peter O'Malley to take a lie detector test. Then Paul Kelly presented a diagram of the 1991 device that he had asked Agent D'Ambrosio to draw on that very day of the hearing to recreate the diagram that D'Ambrosio and Leahy allegedly asked Alfred Trenkler to draw on the night of the search, but which was not taken as evidence or otherwise preserved. The diagram showed two sticks of dynamite with a single wire to each stick, but the actual bomb contained two or three detonators and had no "sticks" of dynamite. Rather, as was presented at the trials, there were 2-3 pounds of ammonia dynamite "slurry" wrapped in tape and a page of a magazine.

Then Agent Thomas D'Ambrosio described the search of the ARCOMM offices on 31 January, and then his short participation with Agent Leahy and Alfred Trenkler in the ATF conference room on 4 February 1992. He said to Trenkler that his representations of his relationship to Tom Shay had been inconsistent thus far, and Trenkler said "*that he had, in fact, known Tom longer than he said he knew him. In fact, he remembered first meeting him in June of 1991, and that was a significant time, because his roommate was away on vacation at the time.*" (TSH 1-70) The charge of giving inconsistent stories to investigators can be a hard one to shake once alleged, but there was never a claim by Alfred Trenkler that he had met Tom Shay any LATER than June 1991. A major problem in the case was that the investigators were claiming that Tom Shay met Alfred Trenkler years, not months, earlier.

About the 1986 Quincy device, D'Ambrosio said that Trenkler said, "*you know, I was involved in that. And, really, it was just a firecracker, I think was the term he used. It would never hurt anybody, and he was not the type of person that would hurt anybody, and that he had nothing to do with the incident in Roslindale.*" (TSH 1-70)

During cross-examination by Matthew Feinberg, D'Ambrosio acknowledged that he drew his recreations of the alleged two 5/6 November 1991 diagrams on 13 May 1993,.the day of the hearing, which came 18 months after the 31 January 1992 search. Also, he clarified that the smaller group which went in one car to the parents' garage in Milton was composed of Boston Detectives O'Malley and McCarthy in the front seats and Special Agents Leahy and D'Ambrosio in the back seat - with Alfred Trenkler in between them, with his explicit consent after D'Ambrosio's question to him, "*You have the shortest legs. Do you mind sitting in the middle?*" (TSH 2-23) No ATF "Search Consent" forms were used during the evening.

Day 1 of the suppression hearing ended with Feinberg still cross-examining D'Ambrosio and Judge Rya Zobel had indicated several times that she was not pleased with the slow, painstaking pace of the hearing. Day 2 was scheduled to begin at 2:15 p.m. on the 14th and go for three hours. Judge Zobel sought Matthew Feinberg's assurance that further cross-examination of Agent D'Ambrosio would focus only on the 4 February 1992 events and not on the previous two searches. Feinberg replied, "*I don't want to commit myself totally at this moment,*" and the judge replied, "*Well, I'm committing you.*"

Only one newspaper covered the 13 May hearing. Ralph Ranalli wrote the article in the *Boston Herald*, "*AGENT SAYS SUSPECT OK'S SEARCH.*" Ranalli introduced a new term into the media coverage, when he wrote, "Prosecutors charge that Trenkler, an engineer, **masterminded** the bombing." [emphasis added] The image of Alfred Trenkler was forming in the public mind, and it was neither good nor accurate, nor challenged by Trenkler's legal team.

For Day 2, on 14 May, Terry Segal and Matthew Feinberg were present on behalf of Alfred Trenkler, and Feinberg continued cross-examination of ATF Special Agent Thomas D'Ambrosio. It became clear that the 5/6 November search team was under the leadership of the Boston Police Dept, and the 31 January searches were ATF-directed searches; and the judge was not pleased with the reexamination of matters previously covered.

On recross-examination, Matthew Feinberg established that Dennis Leahy's 17 January 1992 report of the 5/6 November 1991 searches was the first ATF or Boston Police mention of the two diagrams allegedly drawn by Alfred Trenkler on 5/6 November.

AUSA Paul Kelly then examined ATF Special Agent Dennis Leahy. When Alfred Trenkler answered the door on 5 November 1991 and saw the police "*He asked if we were here about a previous call he had made to the police about someone taking pictures or being in a car,*" and Agent Leahy replied that he had said "*No.*" (TSH 2-36/7)

Agent Leahy spoke of seeing the unattached electronic speaker, which was turned so he could see a doughnut-shaped magnet in the back.

Regarding the search at the Wallace's, one light moment was that Alfred Trenkler wanted to make a phone call, because his own was dead, so he asked Agent Leahy if he could use his ATF portable phone, and permission was granted.

Regarding the pickup of copies of materials on 4 February, Agent Leahy said the materials were ready when Alfred Trenkler arrived at 11:00 a.m., but later acknowledged that not all of Trenkler's documents had been copied. During the approximately two hour visit, Alfred Trenkler left the agents for several minutes to go outside the office for a cigarette.

Paul Kelly established that Agent Leahy had read Alfred Trenkler's "Affidavit in Support of the Motion to Suppress" and on three separate issues was asked, "Is that consistent with your recollection of the events, sir?" and Dennis Leahy responded, "*No it's not.*" (TSH 2-82) Matthew Feinberg had said early in the hearing that "*...perhaps Mr. Trenkler*" would testify and now the prosecution was challenging him to do so.

Matthew Feinberg cross-examined and Judge Zobel's impatience occasionally reappeared. She asked, "*I still don't understand what it has to do with this,*" and after hearing Mr. Feinberg's response, she asked, "*So?*" (TSH 2-92) She was not humorless, however, and at one point described a meeting of the large group of officers before the 5 November search as a "*convention in the parking lot*". (TSH 2-

32)

On the van trip back to Plymouth on 14 May, Alfred Trenkler was joined again by Edwin Gaeta. He repeated his statement of January that he had information which would be useful to Trenkler, and he added that he would be interested in meeting with Alfred's attorneys at the House of Correction in the evening of the following Thursday, 20 May.

On day 3 of the hearing, Monday, 17 May, Matthew Feinberg resumed his recross-examination of Dennis Leahy, who said that several days after the alleged drawing of the diagram of a hypothetical Roslindale Bomb by Alfred Trenkler at D'Ambrosio's and Leahy's request, he talked to the Assistant U.S. attorneys about the diagram and also called Richard Brown at the ARCOMM office and discussed it with him.

Mr. Feinberg established that Dennis Leahy never intended to make available to Trenkler copies of all the documents taken from Alfred Trenkler's briefcase on 31 January. He only made copies of a list of addresses. (TSH 3-28) He denied telling Alfred Trenkler that copies of other materials would be made if he waited at the ATF office for them, thus making Trenkler's continued presence there entirely Trenkler's own idea. Regardless of whether he said or didn't say that the documents would be copied and ready, the idea that he could seize business documents, (and the briefcase arguably was not within the scope of the search warrant at all), and not return copies as soon as possible is unfair to an accused but still innocent person.

Quincy Detective Thomas Tierney was the next prosecution witness. His testimony was necessary because Mr. Feinberg would not agree to a stipulation with Paul Kelly as to what the investigating officers were doing on the afternoon and early evening of 5 November. It was an issue because the defense argued that the officers intentionally chose to knock on Trenkler's and Cates' door late at night in order to intimidate them and make them feel more vulnerable. Kelly offered the explanation that the officers didn't know where Trenkler lived and went to his parents' house and then followed Richard Brown's Lincoln Continenal for two hours after he left work. They thought that Alfred Trenkler was in the car with Brown. Feinberg wouldn't accept that explanation so, Quincy Detective Thomas Tierney, who already knew Alfred Trenkler, was called to testify.

Explaining how he knew Alfred Trenkler, Tierney said, "*I was involved in a case back in 1986 with Mr. Trenkler.... Possession of an infernal machine, a fish truck was blown up in West Quincy.*" (TSH3-41) Tierney's Quincy Police computer had Trenkler's current address because of Alfred's call to report suspicious activity about a week or two previous and noted in Chapter 2.

Detective Tierney explained how he and others worked on the afternoon and evening of 5 November to find Alfred Trenkler and then described how he knocked on a door at 133 Atlantic Street, and it was the door to the home of Mike Green, the landlord of John Cates. Tierney said that Green said, "*I know why you're here, because of the bombing over in Roslindale where the police officer was killed....He said, well, I've seen that Shay kid here numerous times.*" The police then left, in order to assemble the search team. Also, Tierney described how the police found Alfred Trenkler's disabled car in a parking lot on Mechanics Street where Nurdan Cagdus lived, before they knocked on Cates's and Trenkler's door at about 11:00

p.m.

Matthew Feinberg did not challenge Tierney's characterization of the 1986 incident, "*fish truck blown up*," nor did he inquire further about the statement that Tierney had "*seen that Shay kid here numerous times.*" Mike Green later told Alfred Trenkler that Tom Shay had been to his house, upstairs, many times to visit with his housemates, which had nothing to do with Alfred nor John Cates. Also, most of those visits were before Alfred moved to Cates' apartment in September, 1990. However, Tierney's statement, without clarification, fit into the police's continued belief that Tom Shay had been to Cates and Trenkler's apartment "*numerous times,*" thus making Trenkler's claim of a brief and recent (July-July) acquaintance less believable.

Detective Tierney was excused and Judge Zobel asked the lawyers if they could figure out some way that John Cates' testimony could be heard as he had been requested to come to court on the 1st, 2d and this 3rd day of the hearing, in order to be available when necessary. He had been waiting outside the courtroom, as he was not permitted to hear the testimony of others.

The next witness was ATF Special Agent Jeff Kerr who was examined by Paul Kelly. Agent Kerr noted that three or four unmarked cars were following Richard Brown's silver Lincoln Continental on the afternoon of Tuesday, 5 November, but they lost it in traffic. Agent Kerr then returned to the Homicide office of the Boston Police Dept. and did not participate in the searches that night.

He was, however, involved in the search of 133 Atlantic Street on 31 January 1992 and he disputed Alfred Trenkler's statement in his Affidavit that he brought his briefcase with him when he returned to the apartment after taking John Cates to work. Kerr said the briefcase was in the apartment when he was searching it, and thus was properly subject to the terms of the search warrant. This was one of the few occasions when the investigators' version of events was directly contrary to Alfred's. In this example, either Alfred had it in his hands when he returned to the apartment, or it was already in the apartment.

John Cates was the next witness called by the Government, and was examined by Frank Libby. Cates said that he had moved to Jamaica Plain about two months before the hearing, and thus about the 17th of March 1993. Libby asked if his relationship with Alfred Trenkler was an "*intimate relationship*" and to her credit, Judge Zobel asked, "*What difference does that make?*" and then added, "*It's irrelevant.*" (TSH 3-110)

Instead of joining the judge in objecting to the question due to the irrelevance of sexual preference to the issue of the validity of the search, Matthew Feinberg inexplicably said that he would stipulate that Trenkler's relationship to Cates was "*intimate,*" to use a delicately vague word. However, they didn't have a sexual relationship because Cates was seriously ill with hepatitis B, which would lead to his death in 2005. It was a lost opportunity to challenge a substantial anchor of the government's case which was Alfred Trenkler's allegedly aggressive homosexuality. It did not need to be part of the Government's prosecution, and even if it did, certainly not to the extent that it was drilled by the Assistant U.S. Attorneys. The defense should have denied its relevance and the prosecution should have stayed away from such private conduct.

On the issue of the consent to the search, Cates testified that he said to the police, "*If you don't have a search warrant, you can't search the apartment.*" (TSH 3-123) After he was asked to go outside, and when sitting in the back seat of a police car, he repeated his refusal to permit a search.

During his direct testimony through questioning by Matthew Feinberg, the hearing was stopped around 5:00 p.m. by Judge Zobel. When discussing how much more time would be needed, Paul Kelly estimated he would need approximately two more hours as he anticipated the need to counter Alfred Trenkler's testimony, saying, "*My understanding is that Mr. Trenkler will testify.*" (TSH 3-130) The last day of the hearing was scheduled for 14 June, but because of the difficulty of scheduling it didn't occur until 1 September, after the Shay trial and guilty verdict.

Rule 12.1(a) of the *Federal Rules for Criminal Procedure* provides that the prosecution may demand before trial an explanation, or alibi, for the defendant's actions during a period covered by the indictment. Pursuant to the rule, Paul Kelly and Frank Libby requested on 27 May Alfred Trenkler's alibi for 18 October, because "Evidence will likely be offered at trial that defendant Trenkler was in the immediate vicinity of this [Radio Shack] store while defendant Shay was inside." Curiously, the prosecution did not make a similar request for the 24 or 36 hour period prior to the 28 October 1991 explosion, during which time someone must have placed the bomb underneath Mr. Thomas Shay's Buick, according to the Government's theory.

On 20 May Terry Segal and Matt Feinberg drove to the Plymouth County House of Correction not to visit with their client, Alfred Trenkler, but to talk with Edwin Gaeta from 7:30 to 9:00 p.m. Gaeta told them that a friend of his, whom he could not name for fear for the friend's and his own safety, had been offered $10,000 to kill Thomas L. Shay. His friend did not want to shoot Mr. Shay, so he built a remote controlled bomb. At some point in the discussion, according to Alfred's recollection in 2007, Gaeta stated that he understood that the dynamite was removed from its standard cylinder brown paper because it was old and was leaking. This was not a detail about the bomb that was known to many. However, his friend backed out of the plot and Edwin Gaeta was offered the job of placing the bomb at 39 Eastbourne. Gaeta was not a bad choice for the work, because he made little secret of his work in the U.S. Army where he was part of a secret commando group and he claimed to have personally killed 40 people. He was about 6' 1", approximately 50 years old and, according to Matt Feinberg, "*highly intelligent and physically powerful.*" He said he had written a book about his exploits, called *Abracadabra* and submitted it unsuccessfully to five publishers. He said he had been a "*very successful corporate executive who got drunk at a bar and went out and committed a series of burglaries,*" according to Terry Segal's account. Gaeta rejected the proposed murder-for-hire idea, but thinks that someone else may have accepted. Gaeta shared this information with Feinberg and Segal, because, according to Segal, "*he felt sorry for Trenkler because he was innocent.*" However, he would not reveal the name of his friend, to whom he owned a debt of gratitude; unless the friend received a guarantee of immunity from the Government. Segal wrote, "*We indicated we had no power to promise immunity, but hoped he would reveal the name to clear an innocent man, our client. We also indicated that if his information solved the crime he would have a shot at the $65,000 reward.*"

This was high-stakes negotiation, and it came just a few months before Alfred's trial. Feinberg and Segal said they would talk with Gaeta's lawyer, the well-known Paul Markham, and see what they could do. Unfortunately, they did not have the power to offer immunity, and it was unlikely that the U.S. Attorney would do so either as that office was already locked into its theory of the case, that Shay and Trenkler were the builders and co-conspirators.

Was it a coincidence that $5,000 may have been the contract price for placing the bomb, and that Mr. Thomas L. Shay had given, with the U.S. Attorney Office's permission, his 1986 Buick worth $5,000, to the bartender at the Waltham Tavern in Boston? Mr. Shay testified under oath that he gave his car to Philip Smith because his friend didn't have a car and needed it. (TT 6-138) This was within three months of the Roslindale explosion and during the period when Mr. Thomas L. Shay was still considered as a suspect. It was before the defense team had a chance to have its expert examine the car.

On 28 May 1993, Nancy Gertner filed a "*Memorandum in Support of the Motion to Suppress* [the] *Identification*" by Radio Shack sales person Dwayne Armbrister of Tom Shay as the person who purchased items from his store on 18 October. Using testimony from the 13-14 April hearings, she argued that at the first visit of the ATF agents to Mr. Armbrister in February, he did not recognize a photograph of Tom Shay in a photo array, but after several more ATF visits, and by the time of his April 1992 grand jury testimony, he remembered Shay as being the 18 October 1991 purchaser of the six items on the receipt. He also said at the hearing on the Motion that he remembered that Tom Shay had a scar on his upper lip. However, Tom Shay did not have such a scar and the only indication of a scar came from the poor photograph he was shown by ATF.

Also on 28 May, Nancy Gertner filed a "*Memorandum in Opposition to Government's Motion in limine to Admit Evidence of 1986 Bombing.*" She argued that the 1986 and 1991 devices were so "*distinctly dissimilar... that it shows two different people built the two devices, so that it is not probative of Trenkler's identity as the person who built the 1991 bomb.*" Also, the 1986 incident occurred long before Tom Shay met Alfred Trenkler and that "*the government's proposed use of the 1986 device against Shay Jr. is... an attempt to convict him of 'guilt by association.' *" Introducing any of Alfred Trenkler's statements about the 1986 device would be unfair to Tom Shay, because "*Trenkler will not be testifying in Shay Jr.'s trial,... and admission of those statements would violate Shay Jr.'s Sixth Amendment right to cross examine witnesses against him.*" In passing, Gertner had announced a significant aspect of her trial strategy, which was not to ask Alfred Trenkler to testify.

On 7 June, Terry Segal replied to the Government request for alibi information that Alfred Trenkler was at the ARCOMM office at 2:30 p.m. on 18 October and that he would offer at trial the testimony of Richard Brown, Nurdan Cagdus and David Flaherty to establish the truth of that statement. In a subsequent response, Segal added the name of Mark Ramboli, an accountant providing services to ARCOMM. Also, pursuant to Rule 12.1(b) Terry Segal asked for the names of witnesses the government planned to call to establish that Alfred Trenkler was in the vicinity of 197 Mass. Ave at that time and day. The two prosecutors responded to the request on 10 June with the names of six potential witnesses: Dwayne

Armbrister, Richard Brown, John Cates, David Flaherty, James Harding and Thomas A. Shay. Curiously, both sides expected that two witnesses, Richard Brown and David Flaherty, to establish that Alfred Trenkler was simultaneously in two locations 15.9 miles away.

On 11 June, attorneys for both defendants filed a joint motion to dismiss Counts II or III and IV or V of the original indictment on the grounds that they were "multiplicitous." The redundancy was due to repeating allegations that defendants' actions caused the death of Jeremiah Hurley (II and IV) and injuries to Francis Foley (III and V). On 17 June, Paul Kelly and Frank Libby jointly signed a letter in response which accepted the defendants' view of the indictment, and said that the U.S. Attorney's office would seek a superseding indictment, which was later issued on 24 June. Counts II and III were merged into a new Count II, and III and IV merged into the new Count III.

On 12 June, Matthew Brelis of the _Boston Globe_ wrote of the prosecution's claim that an ATF database report showed that the 1986 Quincy device and the 1991 Roslindale Bomb were made by the same person. Headlined, "_DEFENDANT IN OFFICER'S DEATH IS SAID LINKED TO EARLIER BOMB_," the article stated "_A computer analysis of more than 14,000 bombs planted nationwide between 1979 and 1991 found only one bomb that was nearly identical to the bomb that killed a Boston Police officer in 1991, according to court documents._

The matching bomb was planted in Quincy in 1986 and built by Alfred Trenkler..."

The prosecutors' memorandum argued that they should be able to present the computer analysis at Tom Shay's trial in two weeks, in order "_to prove at trial that one of the conspirators, either Shay or Trenkler, had the knowledge, skill, ability and experience to build an explosive device._"

Nancy Gertner could not be reached for comment, and Terry Segal stated that he will file a "_detailed response that refutes many points._" However, that filing received virtually no media coverage, and Alfred Trenkler lost another opportunity to present truth in the case.

On 15 June, Judge Zobel announced her decisions on several Motions which granted some relief to Shay. She suppressed Dwayne Armbrister's identification from photographs of Tom Shay, and suppressed statements made by Tom Shay to AUSA Paul Kelly on 4 and 11 June 1992. However, the subsequent use of portions of the Karen Marinella interview dissolved some of the value to the defense of the suppression of Arbrister's identification, as Shay discussed the Radio Shack purchase. [Since the 14 April hearing, there had been a third and fourth day hearings on 11 and 12 May, but the transcripts were not readily available. The newspapers' coverage of the 12 May hearing, and Tom Shay's testimony, is summarized above.]

On 17 June, Matthew Brelis wrote for the _Boston Globe_, "_RULING BY JUDGE LIMITS BOMB PROSECUTION._" Brelis wrote the ruling was a "_major blow_" and quoted an unnamed source, " '_This case is a circumstantial case and any time you start taking away evidence it weakens the case,_' _said a law enforcement source familiar with the investigation._ '_Armbrister's identification was important to us._' " The same source said "_her ruling could also hamper efforts to prosecute Trenkler, because the case against him is even more circumstantial..._" The article did explain that Armbrister could not initially identify Shay, and quoted Shay's lawyer, Amy

Baron-Evans as saying, "*We are gratified by the decision and think it is the right one.*" The AUSA's could not be reached for comment. To Ralph Ranalli of the *Herald* who wrote the story, "*JUDGE BARS STORE CLERK'S ID OF BOMB SUSPECT,*" Baron-Evans said, "*The fact that it has been suppressed will have a substantial impact on the trial.*"

On 18 June, Alfred Trenkler's lawyers filed a 20 page Affidavit from explosives expert, Denny Kline, about the prosecution's claim that the 1986 Quincy device and the 1991 Roslindale device had the same "signature" and thus were built by the same person. The Affidavit was in support of Alfred Trenkler's Motion to exclude evidence of the 1986 device because it was irrelevant to the 1991 Roslindale Bomb case. Kline concluded that "*In summary, in my opinion, even though the devices have some common similarities such as the use of a remote radio control system, a toggle switch, and the use of magnets, these generic similarities provide little, if any, assistance in determining a common scheme or plan with respect to both devices, or more importantly, the identity or signature of the maker of the '91 device.*" On 25 June, the Government responded with an Affidavit from its explosives expert, Albert Gleason, who concluded that the two devices were likely made by the same person.

Also on 18 June the prosecutors sent a list to Nancy Gertner of 43 potential government witnesses, including Tom Shay and Alfred Trenkler. Of that list, 17 would testify. Not included on the list were 14 people who did eventually testify, including most of the ATF and Boston Police witnesses. For both sides of the trial it was like presenting a staged play and not knowing until a few minutes before the curtain call who was going to play which roles.

On 19 June, the *Boston Herald* strongly criticized the suppression of the Armbrister identification with an editorial, "*TILTING JUSTICE'S SCALES,*" which stated in full:

"*U.S. District Court Judge Rya Zobel seems hell-bent on keeping Thomas A. Shay Jr. from spending the rest of his life behind bars. Shay is the sterling fellow federal officials believe attached a bomb to the underside of his father's car 20 months ago.*

The bomb, which exploded, killed a Boston police officer, Jeremiah Hurley, and permanently disabled and maimed Officer Francis Foley.

Zobel has already bent over backwards for Shay, allowing him not one, not two, but three court-appointed attorneys. Defendants unable to retain counsel are generally assigned one court appointed lawyer at the standard rate of $60 per hour for in-court time and $40 for out-of-court time.

Shay's gaggle of defenders - one of whom costs $200 per hour for all court time - duns the state a grand total of $335 an hour. Zobel's coddling of Shay is not just unusual; it's costly.

Federal attorneys have filed a motion challenging Shay's right to three lawyers at taxpayer expense. But Zobel has yet to rule on that.

Instead, this week she further undermined the government's case by ruling inadmissible the testimony of Dwayne Armbrister, a Radio Shack clerk, who has said that 10 days before the explosion he sold Shay components found in the bomb. Because of Zobel's ruling, a jury will not hear Armbrister testify that on Oct. 18, 1991, a customer walked into the Radio Shack store across the street from the

Christian Science Monitor at 2:30 p.m. and bought a toggle switch, an AA battery holder, and a small lamp capable of testing circuitry.

A jury will not hear Armbrister read the name on the receipt this customer signed: 'Sahy' - potentially 'Shay' with the two middle letters transposed. Or hear him repeat the last four digits of the customer's phone number - Shay's father's phone number, again with two digits transposed.

A jury will not hear Armbrister explain why he didn't immediately identify Shay when shown his picture by authorities; but how, when he did make the identification, he was positive the man he waited on was Shay.

Zobel's exclusion of evidence that a jury should have the right to hear, and her special treatment of Thomas Shay, are not justice.

A courtroom is supposed to be an even playing field. Zobel's courtroom seems rather dangerously tilted."

Perhaps if the <u>*Boston Herald*</u> had waited until the 29 June release of the entire opinion, it might not have been so hostile. That 8 page published opinion carefully analyzed the background for Shay's statements on 29 and 31 October and Judge Zobel permitted those statements to be introduced later at Shay's trial. Even though she said that she did not believe Shay's testimony that he felt he was under arrest after the Trailways Bus station press conference, she did believe other parts of his testimony, which assisted the next two rulings in her opinion.

Judge Zobel ruled that Shay's statements to prosecutors on 4 and 11 June must be suppressed because they were made without the presence of his attorney and the prosecutors knew he was represented by counsel, William McPhee, at the time. Even though Tom Shay said that he had "fired" McPhee, Judge Zobel said that the prosecutors should have waited for Shay to acquire a new attorney before listening to his statements.

Regarding Dwayne Armbrister's identification of Tom Shay as the 18 October customer, she agreed that it was an identification achieved by the overly suggestive work of the ATF. Also, a fellow employee, Allan Kingsbury, remembered a man of a significantly different description making the 18 October Radio Shack purchase.

On 19 June 1993, Tom Shay's legal team interviewed his sister, Nancy, who said that almost every day for a few months before the explosion, Tom came to see her at work at "Everything Yogurt," at South Station. She said that he never once mentioned Trenkler's name. She doesn't recall ever seeing Trenkler, though the ATF told her Tom said he had brought him to one of her softball games. She said that Tom would have mentioned Trenkler if he had any relationship with him and would definitely have not been able to keep himself from mentioning Trenkler if he'd been planning a bombing with him.

She didn't see him on the 28th, but Tom came to see her at work, as usual, on the day after the explosion, 29 October. Nancy Shay reported that during that visit, Tom Shay appeared surprised by the bombing, and he was worked up about it, and she knew right away he was going to draw attention to himself over this. She said, *"Keep your mouth shut."* She knew he'd be the one to say something stupid just to get the attention from it. She never thought he had anything to do with it, but knew he'd use it to get attention. Then he called the papers and TV stations, told them one crazy story after another, just to keep them coming back. Her view was that he talked to the media because he was so lonely and didn't want to be forgotten. Nancy Shay said that her father, Thomas L. Shay, thought that his son tried to kill him because the police convinced him, and even believed that another member of the Shay family was part of the conspiracy.

After the several Motions and hours of hearings on those Motions, the only bit of evidence which was suppressed was the out-of-court identification of Tom Shay by the Radio Shack clerk, Dwayne Armbrister as the person who made the 18 October 1991 purchase. Were the suppression hearings worth doing, one might ask? A defense lawyer might say yes, because information was learned during the hearing about the prosecution's case and will make easier the preparation for trial. However, these hearings with several witnesses who were required to return to testify at the trials, took valuable judicial and prosecutor time. With 20/20 hindsight it now appears that at least some of Judge Zobel's often-stated push to shorten the trial may have come from the length of time already spent on the case.

On 23 June, Terry Segal asked the Court by Motion, to order the prosecution to *"present a proffer of proof on the co-conspirator declarations and conspiracy evidence it intends to offer at trial."* In the supporting Memorandum, Segal argued that such a proffer was *"particularly appropriate in this case where 1) the defendants' trials have been severed, 2) there is no direct evidence that either defendant was a member of the conspiracy charged, and 3) the government is required to prove by a preponderance of the evidence that a conspiracy existed..."*

The only time Alfred Trenkler ever saw Tom Shay, after their last accidental meeting in the Fenway area in August 1991, was in the Federal Building lockup on 25 June 1993. Below are the contemporaneous notes for his lawyer by Alfred Trenkler of his verbal, non-line-of-sight, interaction with Tom Shay. Both defendants were there for their respective hearings on pre-trial issues.

"At Federal Building Lockup 25 June 93
1) Jr. said he never told Carrion where I lived in Milton - He (Jr.) never knew, had never been there (Jr.), Carrion never brought him (Jr.) there; Shay admits I never told him (Jr.) I even lived in Milton.
2) Jr. said that Carrion did give Jr. rides to Belvedior [Belvoir] *Rd in Milton and Richmond St. in Dorchester.*
3) Jr. Says Feds told him (Jr.) that Al offered Gaetor [Edwin Gaeta] *$10K to kill Jr. and the Feds were holding Gaetor* [sic].
4) Jr. told me he made up the story about the Quincy quarries just to toy with the Feds. He said he purposely lied to 'screw' with them.
5) Jr. said he knows I did not do this, he said the Feds and Frank Armstrong put my name into Jr.'s head.
6) Jr. says that he thought the guys from S. Boston did this and mentioned about how the father was followed around by someone - we have this BPD report.
7) Jr. said that his father was making mistakes in his statements - he is looking guilty - a Jr. quote.
8) Jr.'s sisters told him (Jr.) that he (Jr.) was screwing up Sr.'s lawsuit.
9) Jr. then started to brag to the other people in the lock up about the media attention he has received and that he (Jr.) was famous.

10) Jr. said the Feds took him to the Quincy quarries and they were met by Navy Seals to look for plastic bag of items in Shay's story.

11) Jr. said that Critchner's [Scott Critcher] *brother Shawn Dunlap was out to nail Jr. for the $65K.*

12) Jr. said he heard police suspected me after the police dug up my name through the '86 incident and the police quizzed him about the '86 incident and about my name.

13) Jr. said he met Todd Leach at Scott Critchner's [sic] *Quincy party.*

14) Says Carrion is out to get Jr. for the $65K.

15) Jr. said he knows that if the bomb killed his father the lawsuite [sic] *would not go through and no one would get any money (You and I read otherwise + Alan Pransky in GG* [grand jury] *states if Sr. died the money would go to the heirs.)*

16) Told me the lawsuite [sic] *was settled for $30K.*

17) Says the inmates that are testifying against him are lying, they want the $65K and get out of jail free card and that he (Jr.) never told them (inmates) anything that I am reading about.

18) Told me the last time he saw my car was in town on Boylston St when he put a bunch of invitations to some nightclub on the windshield of my Toyota in July of '91 (this was on the 1200 block of Boylston Street - both John and I remember the papers on my windshield but until 25 June 93 I never knew who put them there.)

19) Did not mention Radio Shack but said that all of those people, Ed Carrion, George Nightingale, Dwayne Armbrister, and Allan Kingsbury all knew each other and all know Tom Shay, Jr. from the Ramrod Bar and from George Nightingale's apartment.

20) Shay again started to brag about the media coverage he was receiving when some other prisoner told Jr. to shut up.

21) Jr. said he had all the files I have and wanted to know who Donna Shea was - I would not answer. Wanted to know if I knew Ed Carrion. I said I never met him. Then he asked if I was sure, that he was a big guy and could not miss him. I again said I had no idea and that I was tired and trying to sleep.

Shay kept on rambling away - it is no surprise as to why inmates have information about Shay, he was quoting things out of the discovery materials and openly talking about it with the other inmates in the Federal lock up.

Another inmate told me (from Middleton) that Jr. was a real idiot and that he (Jr.) was talking about his (Jr.'s) case in detail and would tell anyone anything about the case.

Shay then started again, he said he was accumulating lighters and was going to stick them in the microwave and blow it up.

Finally the attorneys came for Jr.

NOTE: Nancy must tell Tom Shay to shut his mouth!!"

On 26 June, with the opening day of the Tom Shay trial only one day away, the <u>Boston Herald</u> reported the filing of the 24 June Motion by Nancy Gertner to have two trials for Tom Shay: one for determination of whether he was involved or not, and the second, if he were found by a jury to have committed the acts, to determine whether his mental condition made him criminally responsible. In "*SUSPECT IN FATAL BLAST SEEKING 2 FED TRIALS*," Ralph Ranalli quoted Nancy Gertner, "*This is a very circumstantial case, the government has admitted that,*" Gertner said yesterday. "*But the implication of an insanity defense is an admission of guilt. It would be enormously confusing for the jury to hear the two together.*"

The article continued, "*In one of several other motions filed Thursday, Gertner also asked for a delay of the trial on grounds of 'extraordinarily prejudicial pre-trial publicity' because of a* Boston Herald *editorial which ran last Saturday. The editorial criticized Zobel's ruling that the testimony of a Radio Shack employee who said Shay bought several electrical components was inadmissible at trial.*

Gertner also asked Zobel to suppress the admission of Shay's address book as evidence, and to block any evidence that Shay fled to San Francisco in 1992. The motion argues that Shay was fleeing a default warrant from a 1990 charge of phoning a bomb threat, not from the bombing that killed Hurley."

The next day, the trial of 21-year old Tom Shay was to begin.

END NOTES

1. "Message from the Attorney General," in Convicted by Juries, Exonerated by Science: Case Studies in the Use of DNA Evidence to Establish Innocence After Trial, by Edward Connors, Thomas Lundregan, Neal Miller and Tom McEwen, U.S. Dept. of Justice, 1996.
2. Alfred's maternal grandmother, Josephine Johnson Barnum Suter of Milton, died on 27 July 1986 at the age of 91. She was never married to Phineas T. Barnum, but her first husband was descended from his brother, William Barnum. Alfred's paternal grandmother Trenkler lived in Austria.
3. Jim Karolides has retired and produces jazz with several others, and has recorded several CD's. See www.styleisbackinstyle.com.

Chapter 6: Trial of Thomas A. Shay - 28 June 1993 to 27 July 1993

*"As polo is the sport of kings,
trials are the games of lawyers."*[1]

The trial of <u>United States of America vs. Thomas Shay, Jr.</u> (Cr. No. 92-10369-Z) began inauspiciously on 28 June 1993 without his correct name, but that was changed to Thomas A. Shay in the transcript for the second day of trial. During the trial, the participants continued to call the father and son "Shay, Sr." and "Shay, Jr." Here, as elsewhere in this book, the father is called Mr. Shay or Thomas L. Shay and the son is called Thomas A. Shay or Tom Shay.

With the presentation below of each day of the trial is a one-line list of all the trial days with the "X's" marking trial days to date, and "O's" marking future trial days.

```
28 29 30 1 2    6 7 8 9    12 13 14 15 16    19 20 21 22 23    26 27
X  O  O  O O    O O O O    O  O  O  O  O     O  O  O  O  O     O  O
```
Day 1: Monday 28 June

The first two days of trial were taken with preliminary matters, including arguments on several pre-trial motions. The defense Motion was to postpone the case because of publicity elsewhere in the country about bombs, and that Motion was denied. Another Motion was the prosecution's Motion to use the Channel 56 Karen Marinella interview videotape and the request was taken under advisement.

Next day's headlines: none

```
28 29 30 1 2    6 7 8 9    12 13 14 15 16    19 20 21 22 23    26 27
X  X  O  O O    O O O O    O  O  O  O  O     O  O  O  O  O     O  O
```
Day 2: Tuesday, 29 June

Showing the connection between the two cases, the name of Alfred Trenkler was mentioned 122 times by the Government, Shay defense team and the judge on the second day of Tom Shay's trial. No one was there to refute or clarify the statements about Alfred Trenkler, and thus Judge Rya Zobel's image of him was sure to suffer further. The judge and the prosecutors were the only people who participated in both trials, as there was a new jury and new defendant and defense team in the second.

A trial is an inexorable and highly scripted process that often loses sight of its fundamental purpose: to do **justice** by exposing **truth**, and those terms were rarely used in the Roslindale Bomb trials as the gears of grinding acceptable evidence toward the jury overwhelmed other matters. One preliminary matter in Tom Shay's trial was whether the Government could introduce evidence of the M21 Hoffman Artillery Simulator that Alfred Trenkler detonated in 1986 in Quincy. The problem for Shay's primary defense attorney, Nancy Gertner, was that if any such evidence was introduced, she would not have the ability to cross-examine, apparently assuming that co-defendant Trenkler would not be testifying.

The law on the trials and evidence for alleged co-conspirators is complicated and designed, like all the other legal rules, to balance the constitutional rights of the defendant against the rights of the government. The idea of Alfred Trenkler testifying at Tom Shay's trial was never discussed between Alfred and his lawyer, Terry Segal. Wrote Alfred, "*There was no discussion whatsoever about my testifying at Shay Jr.'s trial by any parties. I would have, if asked.*" Given all the effort to separate the trials, it might have seemed inconsistent for Terry Segal to propose to Nancy Gertner that Alfred Trenkler testify at Tom Shay's trial, but it would have been helpful to Tom Shay **and** to Alfred Trenkler. For one thing, it would have been harder for Nancy Gertner to blame Alfred Trenkler for doing most of the work in the conspiracy if he was there to tell the jury that he knew nothing about it. His appearance wouldn't guarantee jury belief, but it's far easier to believe that an invisible, out-of-sight person is a wrongdoer than a person who appears in front of you face-to-face.

Paul Kelly was very concerned about a possible ruling that the evidence about the 1986 device would not be admitted and if "*... an acquittal results, a horrible injustice will follow, in my judgment.*" (TS 2-72) Shortly thereafter, Nancy Gertner described an opposite injustice when she said, "*There is a substantial risk here that an innocent person is going to be convicted exactly on the same facts that Mr. Kelly is talking about.*" (TS 2-95) At this hearing, Judge Zobel announced she would delay her ruling on the Government's Motion to introduce evidence of the 1986 device. On Day 16 of the trial she ruled that such evidence could not be admitted.

A key issue for both trials would be how to understand or respond to the statements made by Tom Shay after 28 October 1991. Said Gertner, "*To the extent that we are explaining these statements* [by Tom Shay] *as the statements of somebody who would basically admit to the World Trade Center bombing if that would give him press, that -- it seems to me that bears on all the issues in the case.*" (TS 2-7]

The hearing turned to the defense's June Motion to "bifurcate" the trial and separate it into two sections: first to determine if Shay had done anything criminal, and, second, if so, whether he was insane at the time, i.e. mentally responsible. The judge asked, "*Is it certain the defendant will have an insanity defense?*" to which Ms. Gertner replied, "*Yes.*" (TS 2-14) Unfortunately, the problem with announcing a plan for an insanity defense is that a lawyer is almost conceding that his or her client actually did something wrong.

One of the major themes of the trial was Shay's gender preference, although it's hard to see what difference the Bomb Maker's gender preference made to Officers Hurley and Foley. Nancy Gertner advised the Court that Thomas A. Shay denied that he was a homosexual, but was "*bisexual.*" (TS 2-14) Subsequences references to his preferences ignored the distinction. Others might say that Tom Shay was asexual due to his having an extra chromosome.

A 12-person jury was empaneled along with four alternates after ensuring that none knew either of the defendants, or any of the major witnesses. They were asked their views about homosexuality and whether they could reach a fair verdict, regardless of those views. Some had concerns about upcoming vacations, and work. They were told that the usual juror work day was during mornings so some jurors could work during the afternoon. The jurors were permitted to take notes.

Next day's headlines:

Boston Herald: "*JUDGE DELAYS RULING ON FED CLAIM OF BOMB SUSPECT'S TIE TO 2ND CASE*" by Ralph Ranalli. This was the evidence which prosecutors sought to present in Shay's trial of Alfred Trenkler's involvement in the 1986 Quincy incident.

28 29 30 1 2	6 7 8 9	12 13 14 15 16	19 20 21 22 23	26 27
X X X O O	O O O O	O O O O O	O O O O O	O O

Day 3: Wednesday, 30 June

On Day 3, all trial participants went to 39 Eastbourne Street for a "site view." Back in the courtroom, there was another discussion of the anticipated "insanity defense" problem and prosecutor Paul Kelly summed up the defense's position, "*As I understand it, the defense is not going to press a full-blown insanity claim; however, it intends to present testimony of an expert psychiatrist who will in fact say that you can't believe anything that Tom Shay says for whatever reason.*" (TS 3-44) He objected strongly to such expert testimony, despite his own findings expressed in his "*memorandums to file*" on 14 October and 10 November 1992 that most of what Thomas A. Shay told him was untrue. He only believed what he wanted to believe as he suffered from STT (Selective Truth Temptation).

Next day's headlines:

Boston Globe: "JURY EMPANELED IN BOMBING CASE"

Boston Herald 1: "JURY TOURS SITE WHERE BOMB KILLED HUB COP" by Ralph Ranalli This article also reported that Judge Zobel had ordered WVLI-TV to provide to the prosecutors a copy of the 17 October 1992 Karen Marinella interview with Tom Shay.

Boston Herald 2: "FEDS TARGET NEW EVIDENCE IN FATAL BOMB TRIAL" AND "JURY TOURS SITE WHERE BOMB KILLED HUB COP - PANEL STUDIES ROSLINDALE PROPERTY BEFORE OPENING ARGUMENTS IN TRIAL" by Ralph Ranalli This article noted that the jury had seven women and five men. In light of the Marinella interview where Tom Shay said that he had purchased two items that were used in the Roslindale Bomb, prosecutors asked Judge Zobel to reconsider her motion to suppress the Armbrister identification. Also, the article reported that she denied the motion to delay the trial due to excessive publicity.

Patriot Ledger: "JURY IN SHAY TRIAL VISITS BOMB SITE" no byline

28 29 30 1 2	6 7 8 9	12 13 14 15 16	19 20 21 22 23	26 27
X X X X O	O O O O	O O O O O	O O O O O	O O

Day 4: Thursday, 1 July

On Day 4 Judge Zobel welcomed the jury and instructed them about their coming role, including the details about schedule and coffee breaks. She told them they were permitted to take notes, but only during the testimony by witnesses. Jurors were told that they could not take notes during the opening statements. One has to wonder about the reasons for that prohibition, as it would be helpful to jurors to remember the claims of both sides, as compared to what they would actually deliver during the trial. Notebooks were to stay in the courtroom throughout the trial until their prospective use for jury deliberations at the end of the trial.

Paul Kelly began his opening statement for the United States Government with a description of the 28 October 1991 explosion of the Roslindale Bomb, "*the ultimate* weapon of terror." (TS 4-5] Although the trial arose from a three-count indictment, Kelly stated that Alfred Trenkler and Tom Shay were "*charged with four criminal charges... they are charged with conspiracy...receiving explosive materials... attempted malicious destruction of property by means of explosives as well as what is known as aiding and abetting one another.*" He didn't say that the charges involved murder or manslaughter, although he did say at the end of his statement that the actions of Tom Shay resulted "*in the tragic death of Officer Jeremiah Hurley and the maiming of his partner Francis Foley.*" He described the events leading up to the explosion and then summarized the expected testimony of witnesses about Tom Shay's statements and actions. Paul Kelly stated that the evidence would show that Tom Shay "*had an acquaintance with this Mr. Trenkler dating back at least to 1989 and that the two may have had an intimate relationship.*" [TS 4-15]

He directly addressed the question of why the case was in Federal Court, saying that it was because the detonators were manufactured outside Massachusetts and because Mr. Shay's Buick was often used as a loaner by customers who took it out of state, "*and that's why the federal Government has an interest.*" [TT 4-18] While he explained why the Federal Court had jurisdiction, the jurors may still have wondered why the Federal prosecutors were pursuing this case, which was because they had the investigative resources to make the case against Tom Shay and Alfred Trenkler. The Boston Police, without the aid of national databases and laboratories, were focusing on Mr. Thomas L. Shay as the prime suspect, and also the Dedham Service Center defendants.

Paul Kelly said that the jury would likely see the videotape of the Trailways bus terminal press conference, with Tom Shay's effort to blame Ralph Pace of Stoughton; and they would hear portions of the Karen Marinella interview.

Nancy Gertner gave the opening statement for Thomas A. Shay's defense, and she reminded the jury of the presumption of innocence, "*The judge said to you during your collection that Tom Shay is innocent. He is innocent now. He is innocent throughout this case. And he is innocent unless, unless, the Government can prove that he's guilty beyond a reasonable doubt.*" (TS 4-25)

Gertner said it was the government's role to present its case, and her role would be to question that case. Specifically, she told the jury that she would ask questions about Mr. Thomas L. Shay's motives and role. She told the jury that they would hear that Mr. Shay "*told his psychologist, the psychologist that he went to see on this subject of this lawsuit* [the civil lawsuit against the Dedham Service Center], *that he told his psychologist, September of 1991, a month before this incident, the testimony will be that he told the psychologist that he feared being blown up in his car. He feared being blown up in his car. And others will testify that in fact he was afraid to start his car for fear* [of an explosion], *that this was a month before.*" [TS 4-31]

The first witness in the Government's case was Boston Police Officer Denise Corbett, who was known as Denise Kraft at the time of the explosion and prior to her marriage. She was one of the first police officers on the scene and one of the only people to see the pre-explosion bomb, which she described as "*...the black box, approximately 3 inches thick and 12 inches long, 5 inches wide about.... it had a bunch of little circular magnets on top of it and two, two big round circular objects on the center*" and it appeared to be made of wood. (TS 4-53, 63)

Corbett said that Thomas L. Shay had told her that "*he picked the device up and threw it against his house. And then later on he got to thinking that it was a bomb and he didn't want any children to play with it, so he brought it back and put it back on the driveway.*' [TS 4-52] Later, he put it between his van and his older GTO Pontiac. Corbett's testimony that Shay said that he threw the device against his house closely paralleled the 29 October Boston Police Dept interview of Mr. Thomas L. Shay by Detectives Fogerty, O'Malley, and Thomas who reported that "*He threw it aside on the side of the house.*"

Corbett was at the scene when the deadly bomb exploded and used her radio to call for help.[2] At the close of his direct examination, AUSA Paul Kelly showed Officer Corbett what he called a "*mock device*" [TS 4-64] which was a model of the Roslindale Bomb as created by the ATF. It was entered as Government Exhibit No. 4. [A 2007 drawing of the Roslindale Bomb, based on reported descriptions, is in Appendix D.]

Then the court took a recess. One issue that had to be addressed was the visible emotional effect on the members of the Foley and Hurley families during Officer Corbett's testimony. A few had to leave the courtroom. AUSA Paul Kelly told the court he would talk to the families about the need to avoid such disruptions. Also, Judge Zobel ordered that the seat area reservation signs in the court, "Police" and "family" be removed as a trial in her court was not a church wedding or a funeral and there were no reservations for anyone.[3] Also, she might have said that it was wrong for court officers to intentionally place the family directly in front of the jury.

Nancy Gertner cross-examined and established that it was obvious to Officer Corbett that the box was made of wood, but there were no questions about the condition of the box, particularly whether there was any evidence of damage due to either being scraped off the bottom of Mr. Shay's car, or from Mr. Shay's throwing the box to the ground. There was no redirect examination, and hence no recross-examination.

The last Boston Policeman to testify was Sergeant Thomas Creavin, was also early at the scene at 39 Eastbourne. He remembered that Jeremiah Hurley, "*had his knife and was scratching the side of the box with his knife. He made a remark that there were no seams on this box. He said it looks like some piece of machinery that was made in a factory. I can't find any openings on this box.*" (TS 4-93) Sergeant Creavin did not state that Officer Hurley had noticed any damage to the pillbox "bottom" of the bomb or other part. If the bomb had fallen from Mr. Shay's car after colliding with the concrete surface of the driveway, there should have been some fracturing or collapsing of the fragile box. Instead, Officer Hurley stated it was so cleanly made as to appear factory made.

Sergeant Creavin was not asked about the subsequent Boston Police lab tests, such as for fingerprints. The jury did not hear that of all the 17 fingerprints found on Mr. Shay's car, none was traced to Tom Shay, and none to Alfred Trenkler, either. In fact, the police have never released the results of their fingerprint analyses and never stated whether they identified any of the owners of those fingerprints. One reason for concern about this situation is that four years later, the Boston Police Fingerprint Lab incorrectly identified a fingerprint in a case involving a shooting of a policeman and Stephen Cowans was wrongly convicted and spent six years in prison until exonerated in 2004. Subsequently, the Fingerprint Lab was reorganized.

The last to testify on Day 4 was Special Agent[4] Daniel Boeh of the U.S. Bureau of Alcohol, Firearms and Tobacco, who was the leader of ATF's Northeast Region National Response Team. There are four such teams, with approximately 20 members each, in the country. Boeh described how the team members assembled at 39 Eastbourne Street and began collecting every piece of the exploded bomb they could find.

Day 4 of the trial adjourned at 12:50 p.m. Throughout the trial, each trial day's proceedings were scheduled for a half-day and would adjourn usually within ten minutes, plus or minus, of 1:00 p.m.

Next day's headlines:

Boston Globe: "OFFICER TELLS OF ROSLINDALE BOMB SCENE AT SHAY TRIAL, RELATES VICTIMS' PLEA by Matthew Brelis. He reported that Officer Hurley's family was so affected by the testimony of the bomb scene that they "*ran from the courtroom.*"

Boston Herald: "DYING COP'S FINAL PLEA: TELL FAMILY I LOVE THEM" by Ralph Ranalli

Patriot Ledger: "WITNESSES DESCRIBE HORROR OF FATAL BLAST" by Stephen Walsh, this article noted that Denise Corbett "*wiped tears from her eyes as she described the bomb scene...*"

28	29	30	1	2		6	7	8	9		12	13	14	15	16		19	20	21	22	23		26	27
X	X	X	X	X		O	O	O	O		O	O	O	O	O		O	O	O	O	O		O	O

Day 5: Friday, 2 July

ATF Special Agent Daniel Boeh resumed his testimony on Day 5, still with direct examination by Frank Libby. The short cross-examination by Nancy Gertner showed there was no dispute about the extent of the ATF site examination.

ATF Special Agent Chris Porreca described how he found white residue on the outside wall of the home next door at 35 Eastbourne Street, which was the home of Ruth Leary, the owner of the Mazda that Thomas L. Shay was to begin repairing on the 28th. The residue was confirmed to be from the ammonia dynamite explosive. Also found in that wall was a piece of one of the two detonators or blasting caps, with a telltale red and yellow wire.

James McKernan lived across the street at 36 Eastbourne and was a recently retired Boston Fire Dept. fireman. He said that he had lived in the neighborhood for 31 years, but he didn't know what business Thomas L. Shay was in, nor for how long he had lived there. He didn't know Thomas A. Shay.

Mr. McKernan took a regular walk several days a week and began his walk on 28 October at approximately 20 minutes after 11:00. He noticed an unfamiliar compact car parked on the Street and when he exchanged glances with the driver, the car "*took off around the corner.*" (TS 5-54) Mr. McKernan was asked the color of the car and remembered it as a "*grayish blue.*" (TS 4-55) He was careful about the observation and memorized the license plate number and its setup as being a three alpha and three numeric numbered plate - like nearly all Massachusetts registered cars.

However, he forgot the number later during the commotion after the explosion. This was one of the special moments in the entire case where a slight change of events might have made all the difference.[5] If James McKernan had remembered that number and if the driver of the car had some role in the bombing, a tragic injustice might have been avoided, for the driver definitely was not Alfred W. Trenkler and not Tom Shay.

He finished his walk at 12:00 noon and was inside his house with his wife, Eleanor, and son Thomas, and his sister-in-law Evelyn Pirello and her son, Robert, when the explosion occurred.

On cross-examination Nancy Gertner asked Mr. McKernan if he had a cell phone, on the theory that a cell phone could have set off the bomb, accidentally or intentionally. Paul Kelly objected for "*relevance*" and explained, "*I still think that's not relevant. It is not relevant how the bomb is detonated.*" (TS 5-79) He went on to say that the Government would soon be presenting an expert witness who was going to explain how the bomb was detonated. Sometimes, lawyers make objections to evidence in a case more out of habit than out of concern for bringing forth the truth.

There were many bench conferences out of earshot of the jury where the lawyers and the judge would exchange views on how a particular witness or question should be handled. Sometimes, poignant observations were made. In a conference after McKernan's testimony, Judge Zobel summarized one of the defense's theories about who built the bomb: Thomas L. Shay. Said the judge, "*It is the defendant's theory because if the defendant, as I understand the defendant's theory, it is that Shay, Sr., was the author of the device, and that - - or at least he knew it was there, or that he had something to do with it, and that he did not -- that he was careful not to have anything happen while he was around it, so that he may have disarmed it for a period of time. I mean at least I think that's the theory.*" Responded Nancy Gertner, "*Yes*". (TS 5-79) Tom Shay did not participate in these bench conferences, although he had the right to do so. If he had participated, he might have conveyed to the judge a better sense of who he was, especially since he was not going to testify. It would have been another occasion in a trial where an action might be permitted for one purpose, but which can achieve another as well.

On direct examination Stephen Adams of the Austin Powder Company described how its "Austin Rock Star" detonators are manufactured in Austria and are distributed throughout the U.S. His regional office, based in New Hampshire, sells annually about 600,000 detonators, or blasting caps, at a retail cost of about $3.00 each. The location of his work in New Hampshire helped the Government make its case that by somehow "*receiving*" explosive materials in interstate commerce, Shay and Trenkler were violating Federal law. There was no evidence that either Shay or Trenkler had acquired detonators or dynamite from Austin Powder or from any other company.

Cynthia Wallace was a forensic chemist of the ATF and a member of its Northeast Regional Response Team and had just written a chapter in a 1993 book about the analysis of explosives.[6] She was the trial's first "*expert*" witness after presenting her qualifications to the court, whose opinions are entitled to greater respect by a jury. She identified from a fragment of a sticker on a remnant piece the fusing mechanism as being manufactured by Futaba[7] which specializes in remote control devices. (TS 5-102) Other remnants of the bomb were admitted into evidence and included fragments or pieces of

- 12 button magnets,
- pages 24-25 of the July 1991 issue of Robert Kennedy's *MuscleMag International*,[8]
- four Duracell AA brand batteries,
- five 9-volt Duracell batteries
- a plastic Futaba brand battery holder,
- two contacts which were identified as coming from a Radio Shack toggle switch, Model number 275-602,
- a large ring or donut shaped magnet, a ceramic type magnet (*"We could determine that the outer diameter of this was ...a little bit bigger* [than] *three and half inches."*) (TS 5-116),
- three different types of tape: black electrician's tape, silver duct tape and white-backed plastic tape, and
- two Austin Rock Star detonators.

Ms. Wallace established that a type of Superglue or "*Crazy Glue*" was used to join the wood to wood and magnets to the wood.

Also admitted were "exemplars" which are newly purchased examples of the items from which the bomb fragments came, such as the Futaba Servo (Gov't Exhibit 15), a Futaba brand receiver unit with a white wire protruding (Gov't Exhibit 16), a Futaba brand battery holder with two AA 1.5 volt Duracell batteries in it, and a Duracell 9-volt battery in its original packaging (Gov't Exhibit 17G).

The most important exemplar may have been the Radio Shack toggle switch, model #275-602, which was entered as Government Exhibit 36B. Cynthia Wallace described the photograph she had of the toggle switch contacts recovered from the bomb site. She said, "*...I took photographs of -- in this case, this is on quarter-inch graph paper. I took a photograph as a contact as we received them, of the blast damage. It had soldered one strand of wire coming off of them. When I made this photograph, this is how the contacts looked, they have been straightened out,* [and I] *compared them to the exemplar. You can see in the exemplar, it is not taken apart -- ok.*" [TS 5-121] Thus, the jury was not able to compare the contacts from the Model #275-602 switch to those recovered from the bomb. It was a vitally important comparison, and Cindy Wallace was the only person to have made that comparison directly.

At the end of Day 5, Paul Kelly announced to the jurors that "*Oh, Ms. Lesperance reminds me that you should go upstairs and on the way pick up your checks.*" (TS 5-124) However innocuous, such communications from the Assistant U.S. Attorney gave the impression that the jury, like the grand jury, worked for the prosecution and not for the court. On the other hand, such a distinction fails when one realizes that it was the United States Government that prosecuted Thomas A. Shay and Alfred W. Trenkler and it was paying these temporary jurors their minimal daily wage.

The trial adjourned at 1:00 p.m.

Next day's headlines:

Boston Globe: "*SUSPICIOUS CAR SEEN NEAR BOMB*" no byline

Boston Herald: "*FED EXPLOSIVES EXPERT DISSECTS MAKEUP OF BOMB THAT KILLED COP*" by Ralph Ranalli

Patriot Ledger: *"NEIGHBOR TELLS OF SEEING CAR DRIVING AROUND*
BEFORE BLAST" by Patriot Ledger staff

28 29 30 1 2	6 7 8 9	12 13 14 15 16	19 20 21 22 23	26 27
X X X XX	X O O O	O O O O O	O O O O O	O O

Day 6: Tuesday, 6 July

Paul Kelly continued with his direct examination of Cynthia Wallace. She
explained how she identified the sources of the fragments, the most important of
which were the contacts, identified as coming from a Radio Shack, single pole
single throw (SPST) toggle switch, Model 275-602. This model is still available, 14
years later, at Radio Shack, but for $2.69, or more than twice the 1991 price of
$1.29. There were no identifiable markings, " *...so I began looking through our
exemplar collection of all different types of switches...and the only exemplar that had
contacts like this were the Radio Shack toggle switch I described. This information
was then supported later when I found that the adhesive, impressions in the
adhesive where I could see the nut mark and the thread marks from the thing
sticking up on top of the toggle switch.*"

Paul Kelly then asked,

Q. "*Each of those three items: The thread marks, nut marks, the contact points,
match only one toggle switch in your exemplar library.*"

A. "*Yes*". (TS 6-11)

Matching a part to the whole is only as good as the comprehensiveness of the
collection and the knowledge of ATF employees of the entire marketplace of
switches. There was no indication of the size of the ATF exemplar collection. Also,
it was not noted that the dimensions of the threads and nuts may be governed by
industry standards for such switches.

The cross-examination of Cynthia Wallace was conducted by Nancy Gertner, who
did not challenge Ms. Wallace's lack of expertise in this area, as she was identified
and qualified as a chemist. Her identification of the glue and the dynamite was
well within that area of expertise, but identification of metal parts of an electric
switch was not. By this time Ms. Gertner would have received the letter sent to her
by forensic consultant, Peter DeForest., on 4 July, with "*possible cross-examination
questions,*" such as, "*Isn't the basic circuit design of this bomb really quite simple?*"
However, perhaps pressed by the tight trial schedule, she was not able to fully
utilize his ideas.

Nancy Gertner quickly established that the button magnets AND the donut
magnet could have come from, quoting Gertner, "*an inclinometer, used in an
autobody shop and may be ordered through a catalog...*" (TS 6-28) That possible
source was mentioned in one of Cynthia Wallace's earlier reports on the case. ATF
acquired such an inclinometer, used for wheel alignments for older model cars, and
Wallace determined that the magnets were similar to those found in the bomb. (TS
6-31). Gertner was seeking to show the jury the likelihood of other suspects. Of
those likely to have access to autobody equipment would be Thomas L. Shay, his
brother, Arthur Shay, and the Rolling Wrench garage, and the employees and
owners of the Dedham Service Center. On the other hand, Tom Shay and Alfred
Trenkler had no such access to an unused inclinometer.

Bringing out more details of the bomb, Gertner established that the box was made of 1/4 inch plywood, and she restated Cynthia Wallace's opinion *"that the switch fragments we recovered are from the Radio Shack switch no 275-602."* (TS 6-59) There was no defense challenge to the identification of the toggle switch, despite its pivotal role in the case. If the toggle switch was not from Radio Shack, then the 18 October 1991 Radio Shack receipt would be meaningless and relegated to the correct role of being just another unrelated coincidence. Perhaps there really was a "Jyt Sahy" with a phone number with 3780 as the last four digits. "Jytandra" is a common Indian name and there were many students in the Boston area from India, and many of them were studying electrical engineering.

Trying to establish the time period during which the bomb could have been placed under the 1986 Buick, Nancy Gertner asked Cynthia Wallace about the length of time that the AA batteries in the fusing circuit could maintain their strength, but Wallace did not know if relevant tests had been done; and deferred to others.

Asked about possible pieces of human hair, Wallace stated that clothing fibers had been found attached to the white, plastic-backed, tape, but the fibers appeared to be so ordinary as to make further testing unnecessary; so none was done.

Assistant U.S. Attorney Frank Libby conducted the direct examination of the next prosecution witness, Thomas Waskom. He was an ATF explosives expert and he described the physical structure of the bomb, saying *"The recovered materials of the explosive section consisted of four different things, actually. It had the explosive itself, the actual physical explosive* [ammonia dynamite]*. Around it was wrapped a page out of a magazine, a muscle magazine. We know that was in direct contact with the explosive material, because of the fragments, the portions, residue of the explosive that was left on the magazine on the paper. Stuck to that was gray duct tape. Some people call it hundred-mile-an-hour tape, some people call it duct tape, but it was approximately two inches wide. The paper page had a wrapping of that. Over the top of that, according to examination, was* [sic] *six layers of black electrician's tape. We know the material looked very similar to this."* (TS 6-133)

Noteworthy in this description was that the explosive was stated to be in a solid mass, rather than in "stick" form.

Inside the wooden box was a smaller box or compartment which contained the Servo motor and the switch to trigger the firing circuit. He explained the electronic circuitry of the bomb, with a fusing circuit which powered the switch and the firing circuit which triggered the blasting caps. He noted that the five 9-volt batteries in the firing circuit were wired together in series so as to deliver a 45 volt charge to the blasting caps. This was puzzling as the bomb's detonators required only a 1.5 volt charge for detonation. (TS 6-122) The Bomb Maker was apparently smart, but not an expert in basic electrical work, and not overconfident that he had enough power for detonation. As so often happened in the trial of Tom Shay because there was no one defending Alfred Trenkler, the jury was not reminded that an electrical engineer would simply not have built the Roslindale Bomb with such a dramatically unnecessary excess of voltage. The prosecution's case on this point was as if it was arguing that a professional chef was the likely maker of a cake with thirty times the recommended level of vegetable oil, or a automobile tire installer was the person who intentionally pumped thirty times the recommended air pressure into a tire.

Importantly, Thomas Waskom stated that the Futaba radio receiver in the bomb needed to be, or was designed to be, in a line-of-sight connection with the transmitter. Such line-of-sight radio contact could be as long as a mile, but it could not be interrupted by buildings. Thus, the Bomb Maker could have designed the bomb to be detonated by someone parked on Eastbourne Street at the time of the presence of Thomas L. Shay' in his car. Mr. McKernan's committing to writing of that six character license plate might have made all the difference. On the other hand, the Bomb Maker might have intended to follow Mr. Shay and detonate the bomb at some location away from the home. Or the Bomb Maker may have intended that the bomb was never to be detonated at all, but merely to look as if that was the plan.

Then Waskom gave a demonstration of how a person would detonate the bomb using the remote control with two light bulbs being presented as the unexploded bomb, noting that "*In order for the operator to get something like this to function, he would be some ways away, both for his own protection and the fact that it's a crime, and he doesn't want to get cause* [sic[*caught and that.* [sic]. *He would have it in this position, ready position, he raises the antenna slightly - - if you watch the board - - what I'm going to do is push this lever which will send a signal to that receiver which sends the signal to the Servo motor, turns the arm and throws the switch. 3, 2, 1, fire.*" (TS 6-131). It was dramatic theatre, as the light bulbs shone, but there was no evidence about how the bomb was actually detonated on 28 October.

The bomb was made, Waskom continued, of ammonia dynamite which "*normally when it comes from the factory in stick form, it is like a long cylinder. It's approximately as large as a broom handle. It's an inch and a quarter across the diameter of the stick. The stick is typically eight inches long and crimped on each end.*" (TS 6-134) If the Bomb Maker began his work with sticks of dynamite, he had been careful to remove the brown paper, and especially with the printed sections bearing the name of the manufacturer; as no trace of any of the brown paper was found on Eastbourne Street. Then the sticks would have been massaged into one solid mass and the detonators inserted. Alternatively, the explosive could have been homemade, such as the explosive made by Timothy McVeigh in Oklahoma City in 1995 and been made to look very much like dynamite.

The day's session recessed at 1:02, with a repetition of the judge's oft-stated reminder "*not to talk about the case or read or watch any accounts in the media about it...*" (TS 6-137)

Next day's headlines:
Boston Globe: "*EXPLOSIVES EXPERT TESTIFIES VS. SHAY*" no byline
Patriot Ledger: "*EXPERT RECREATES BOMB THAT KILLED OFFICER*" by
Stephen Walsh This article captured the drama which transcripts miss, beginning, "*With a flick of a switch, a federal explosives expert set off a simulated bomb yesterday during the federal trial of Thomas A Shay, 21, of Quincy.*

With a hiss, two small lightbulbs substituted for blasting caps briefly, bouncing light off the family of a police officer who was killed by the original bomb in a Roslindale driveway in 1991.

'Three, two, one, fire,' Alcohol, Tobacco and Firearms Agent Thomas Waskom yelled from the last row of the audience gallery, where he held a white plastic

remote control box...."

"Prosecutors... set up a simulated version of the bomb for the jury...about 8 feet in front of the jury and abut 15 feet from Hurley's family members, who were seated in the front row of the audience gallery."

28 29 30 1 2	6 7 8 9	12 13 14 15 16	19 20 21 22 23	26 27
X X X XX	XX O O	O O O O O	O O O O O	O O

Day 7: Wednesday, 7 July

Frank Libby's resumed his direct examination of Thomas Waskom who described the small crater in the earthen gap between the paved dual tracked driveway at 39 Eastbourne. He said, "*... The crater itself was two to three inches deep. It was approximately four inches across, and eight to ten inches in length.*" (TS 7-4) Waskom estimated that the bomb weighed between 6 and 6 1/5 pounds. A full stick of dynamite weighs about 1/2 pound.

Through cross-examination by Nancy Gertner, Thomas Waskom indicated he was familiar with a publishing house called Paladin Press which publishes, among other books, books about how to make bombs, or Improvised Explosive Devices (IED's)[9]. Advertisements for Paladin Press were found in the back pages of *MuscleMag International* magazine.

Returning to a theme of an earlier question to Cynthia Wallace, Nancy Gertner asked Thomas Waskom if there had been a test to see how long the four AA batteries in the Futaba battery holder could last as power was being drained to keep the receiver inside the small compartment ON, to receive the planned signal from the transmitter. Waskom said no such tests had been done. Perhaps significantly, the defense did not request that such tests be done. It may have been a better tactic, to plant seeds of doubt in the jury's mind about the possible time period during which the bomb could have been planted underneath Thomas L. Shay's Buick, but failing to methodically answer that question failed the trial's function as an engine of truth. More would be learned at the Trenkler trial.

Waskom had previously described a "*slide switch*" from the Futaba mechanism that was very likely in the bomb, and which functioned as a safety switch in the fusing circuit, but no one who observed the actual pre-explosion bomb, reported seeing such a switch. Waskom did not believe that there was a safety switch in the explosives circuit. Safety switches are used in IED's and other bombs to provide some measure of safety to the maker of a bomb so that it does not explode prematurely. Such switches could be turned ON until the bomb is placed in the planned location of the intended explosion.

One of the points Nancy Gertner sought to explore was that if Thomas L. Shay had built the bomb or known who built it, he could have turned off the slide switch or safety switch during the period the bomb was underneath his car, and during the time he placed the bomb next to his house, up to the point when he placed it between his Pontiac GTO and his van. Then, the slide switch could have been turned ON, whereupon the bomb was armed and potentially deadly to anyone who touched it. In fact, Waskom could not explain why the bomb did not explode earlier. Perhaps Jeremiah Hurley's body had acted as an antenna and made the Futaba receiver more sensitive to other radio or electromagnetic signals, in addition to those of the intended transmitter? If so, then why didn't the bomb explode when Thomas L. Shay had it in his hands, unless the slide switch was turned OFF.

Waskom was not asked how a stray signal could have set off the bomb in a residential area when the same bomb was not detonated the previous day when Mr. Thomas L. Shay was driving his car through Metropolitan Boston which is a very active radio frequency area, with millions of watts of radio frequency energy spanning frequencies between 35 Megahertz and 23 Gigahertz.

Then again, it may have been that there was never a plan by the Bomb Maker for a transmitter to be used at all, leaving the purpose of the bomb only to be a feint to make people think that there was a realistic threat of an explosion. Nancy Gertner's argument was that such a feint would give legs to Mr. Shay's lagging lawsuit. If that was the goal, then it was exceeded.

Nancy Gertner noted in a question that Officer Francis Foley, who would testify later in the trial, had indicated in a report that he had seen the Servo motor moving and at that point he and Jeremiah Hurley knew that the explosion was imminent. If he had seen such a movement, and there is no reason to doubt otherwise, then how was it that the insides of at least one part of the bomb was exposed? Did a piece come off during the handling of the bomb by Thomas L. Shay?

Describing the Bomb Maker, Waskom said, "*I would say the person that built this device was very painstaking. In my construction of the device, the device was glued together, quarter inch pieces much* [sic] *plywood, glued together and also nailed with two penny nails. I had a tremendous problem trying to get two penny nails into a one quarter inch of plywood without it splitting open. The person was very careful about how he did it and what he did.*" (TS 7-28) One wonders if he tried drilling a small diameter pilot hole which most woodworkers know is the way to avoid splitting wood when using nails. The box was spray-painted black, too, in order to hide it. The paint had not been tested to see if it was of a type of spray paint that is commonly used on automobiles or general home use.

Waskom noted that the bomb was specifically designed to be triggered by a remote control process and not by a timer or by a device, such as security alert lights or horns, that are sensitive to motion. If the Bomb Maker intended that he bomb actually explode while Thomas L. Shay was in the car, the operator of the transmitter would have to be nearby to see him in the car. Of course, if the Bomb Maker wanted to escape detection, he would more likely have placed himself on the route to Kristen's school or Shay's favorite coffee shop and then pressed the transmitter button. The problem with that scenario is the short life span of the batteries as was noted at the trial. The Bomb Maker had only a limited number of hours between the placing of the bomb underneath the Buick and the detonation. After that, the bomb would be dead.

Referred by Nancy Gertner to U.S. Military standard manuals on the design of Improvised Explosive Devices, Waskom agreed that it was Standard Operating procedure to design a bomb with two detonators, in case one failed. The military manuals prescribe putting the two detonators in two different circuits, but the Bomb Maker put them in the same firing circuit, thinking perhaps, that two was always better than one.

This seventh day of the trial saw the most important witnesses, so far. Thomas Waskom, whose understanding of the workings of the bomb was the most detailed, was followed to the stand by Thomas L. Shay, father of Thomas (Tom) A. Shay. Originally the prime suspect, Mr. Shay was transformed into a witness for the prosecution, and not also classified as a "hostile" witness. Thus, he appeared to have testified against his only son in the belief that Thomas A. Shay tried to kill him or he was trying to shift suspicion away from himself. It was a major blow to Tom Shay's case. It's unclear when or how Mr. Thomas Shay began to believe the prosecution's case or even that his son was involved. Perhaps it was when he learned that the defense would seek to blame him for the bomb. There was likely a double effect on the jury of Mr. Shay's testimony, and both were against Tom Shay. First, the father knew the son well and apparently believed his son wanted to kill him and apparently believed he had reason to do so, despite the seemingly good times they had had together that fall. Second, it showed a level of animosity of the father toward the son, that jurors could assume was reciprocated by the son toward the father.

Paul Kelly examined Mr. Shay, who explained that he had stopped working full-time as an autobody repair person in 1989 and was depending upon Social Security Disability payments for his income. The disability arose from the 1987 explosion at the Dedham Service Center, but he had continued working for two years after that. When he closed the business, Shay Auto Body, at the Dedham Service Center, he sent a card to his customers, and the card contained his home phone number at 39 Eastbourne, 327-7380.

He had purchased the 1986 Buick new in 1986 and was now using it as a loaner in his part-time business in autobody repair. He also worked part-time at the Rolling Wrench garage in South Boston, where his brother, Arthur, worked, and he also owned a blue 1984 Oldsmobile "Cutlass".

During the week of 21-25 October, Mr. Shay had worked on the car owned by Louis and Roslyn Rotman and they had used the Buick during the week. On Friday, 25 October, he had returned to the Rotmans their car and retrieved his own. On Saturday evening he drove the Buick to the South End to watch his friends play whist and double parked on the public street. From there, he drove to the Golden Gates Chinese Restaurant and picked up food to take home where he arrived about 9:30 p.m. The Buick was at his house from then until Sunday morning when he left on errands at 8:30 in the morning. He went to Malden, apparently with a bomb now attached to his car, to give some auto repair advice to a person referred by a friend. Mr. Shay testified that he wasn't sure if the "M" town was Malden or Medford. On the way to Malden, he stopped at "McDonalds" or "Burger King" on Boylston Street in the Fenway section of Boston to use a restroom. Coincidentally, this was near the "White Hen Pantry" store on Boylston Street where Alfred Trenkler met Tom Shay for the first time, in June that same year. After Malden, he went to Chelsea Naval Hospital to visit an uncle, William Hayes, the husband of his Aunt Alice, in the Soldiers' Home. Then he went to South Boston to a donut shop for coffee and two donuts, and later to his Aunt Alice's in Dorchester. He returned to 39 Eastbourne Street at about 11:30 a.m., after driving approximately 40 miles on city streets. When driving into his driveway, he heard a grinding sound underneath the car, but didn't know what it was, and didn't see anything during a cursory inspection.

At 1:00 his woman friend, Mary Flanagan, and their daughter, Kristen, went out in Mary's car. At that time, Thomas L. Shay moved the Buick out to the street and the same sound occurred, and he saw the shiny black box with 12 round objects on one side. He didn't know what it was and dropped it on the grass near a trash barrel and went inside to watch a football game. Thinking and wondering what the box could really be, he came back outside and moved the black box to a spot on the driveway just in front of his Pontiac GTO. [See the drawing in Appendix D.]

On the morning of Monday, 28 October, he was scheduled to work on the 1990 Mazda sedan of a neighbor, Ruth Leary. The car had been picked up over the weekend in Leary's absence, and he used it on Monday morning to take Kristen to school. Then he drove to the Rolling Wrench garage and talked with his brother and John Doering. Doering later recalled that Thomas L. Shay was driving the Buick at that time. Shay told the jury and Paul Kelly that he also made inquiries about the possible nature of the black box, and then he went to the neighborhood's closest police station. He may have gone home first and changed cars and then driven the Mazda to the police station; but he told at least one person that he walked to the police station. At the police station, he explained what he knew about the mysterious box, and was advised to go home, not to touch the object; and to wait for the police to arrive. He was almost apologetic about bothering the police about such a matter, but was advised to take it seriously and that it was "*better to be safe than sorry.*" He drove home, or was driven home by the police, and waited.

The police arrived shortly thereafter and Mr. Shay explained the circumstances again and went inside his house. Then the explosion occurred. Mr. Shay gathered some towels and brought them outside to assist in staunching the bleeding of both officers.

The investigation began immediately after the two wounded officers were taken to the hospital and Shay was asked for the names of people who didn't like him, and he responded, "*Well, I gave them the name* [sic] *of some people, you know, that could be construed as, maybe, enemies.*" (TS 7-99) Those names weren't revealed in court, and they don't even appear in the police reports. It was obvious that the names of Jeffery Berry and Louis Giammarco were on the list, due to the civil lawsuit, but others were not. It is assumed here that the name of his son, Thomas A. Shay was not one of the names. Also, the name of Alfred Trenkler was certainly not included either, as Mr. Shay had never met Alfred Trenkler, nor ever heard the name, except perhaps at the "Ice Capades" many years earlier.

Assistant U.S. Attorney Paul Kelly then went back through some of the background of Mr. Shay's relationship to his son who had moved into the 39 Eastbourne St. home with his father and Mary Flanagan in late 1987 or 1988. However, an "*incident*" occurred which caused the father to kick the son out of the house and forbid him from returning. Calling this episode an "*incident*" was the result of a bench conference with the judge. What Thomas A. Shay actually did, at the age of 16, was steal coins and jewelry worth about $6,000 from his father and Mary Flanagan on 20 June 1988, and then flee to Florida and live as good a life as he could. The jewelry had been inherited by Mary Flanagan from her mother, in whose house Mary and Kristen Flanagan and Thomas L. Shay lived.

Abiding the rules of evidence it was agreed among the judge and lawyers that the jury would not be told what actually happened, in the belief that such knowledge would prejudice them against Thomas A. Shay. Given the subsequent guilty verdict, it seems likely that the jury may have thought that the incident was far worse the theft of money and valuables. Did they think that Thomas A. Shay had assaulted a member of the family? Did they think that he may have threatened the lives of anyone, including the father? We'll never know, unless members of the jury come forward with information about their deliberations.[10]

On 14 September 1991, the day after Thomas A. Shay's deposition for the father's civil case, Mr. Shay drove his son back to Russ Bonanno's in North Dartmouth. Later in the month Mr. Shay took his son to a card party in the South End, where some loud noises occurred in the neighborhood. Being a curious young man, and eager to be where the action is, Thomas A. Shay, the son, left the card playing and rushed outside to see what was happening, while the father was strongly urging him to stay inside, as it might be dangerous. This was another illustration of Mr. Shay's fears of harm. So upset was Mr. Shay with his son's irresponsibility, in his view, that Mr. Shay drove Thomas A. Shay home to the Quincy home of his former wife, and Thomas A. Shay's mother, Nancy Peters Shay.

On 12 October, Mr. Shay and a group of friends were planning to go to the dog racing track in Seabrook, New Hampshire and Mr. Shay asked his son to come along. Later, they went to the Franklin Cafe, a tavern in Boston. So taken with this renewal of a father-son relationship, Thomas A. Shay, the son, wrote a note to his father and gave it to him. Mr. Shay testified that he read a few words of it and then put into the ashtray of his car.

Paul Kelly had a copy of that letter and asked Thomas L. Shay to read it, "*Dad, thanks for a real fun time. I hope that we can do this more often. It's like old times, being here with the guys and you. I will go over a friend's house tonight and go home tomorrow. I can walk from here. dad thanks, apostrophe, for being my dad again, apostrophe, I will call about David's car tomorrow and will see you Thursday around ... I will see you Thursday or Wednesday, see you, love Tommy.*"

Startlingly, this was the first time that Mr. Shay had read the entire letter. It had been recovered from the ash tray in Mr. Shay's car by William Fogerty of the Boston Police on 1 November 1991.

Thomas L. Shay was asked by Paul Kelly about his relationship to his son after the bombing, and Mr. Shay said that he had visited his son at the Norfolk County House of Correction in Dedham on the Friday or Saturday after the explosion. Paul Kelly asked Mr. Shay if Thomas A. Shay had caused him any discomfort and he replied, "*Well, after we had a conversation Tommy said to me, I only want to know one thing, Dad, and I said, 'What's that Tommy?' He said, 'Where did you go Saturday night?'*" Shortly thereafter, the visit ended without a response nor a question by Mr. Shay as to why Thomas A. Shay asked that question. Mr. Thomas L. Shay was not a highly verbal person, but he did report that question to the police investigators who were waiting for his report on the visit with Tom Shay. (TS 7-134/35)

Asked about Thomas A. Shay's 18 June 1990 appearance on the Tom Bergeron TV show, "*People are Talking,*" Mr. Shay said that he watched it, and when his son announced that he was gay; he was not much surprised. Nancy Shay also appeared on the program, about gay teenagers, and stated that one of her daughters was also gay. Mr. Shay never talked with his son about that TV show nor about Thomas A. Shay's sexual preference. Plainly, it was not something that Mr. Shay preferred to talk about. The jury was shown a one-minute segment of the program, Government Exhibit 26, ostensibly to reveal something about the relationship about Mr. Shay to his son, but it was plainly an effort to disparage the defendant, Thomas A. Shay, before the jury. This was an example of those instances in this trial where statements are shown to the jury and the jury is instructed to ignore what is said, but to pay attention to the demeanor of the speaker or to the relationships observed. The prosecutors can be presumed to having wanted to show the defendant publicly stating he was gay. The trial adjourned at 12:59 p.m. right after the showing of the videotape. Nothing could be said by the attorneys about the videotape. It was like a witness who could take the stand and make a statement but not be questioned. The jury would not know more about how Tom Shay viewed that event, because he would not be testifying.

Next day's headlines:

Boston Globe: "*FATHER TESTIFIES AGAINST MAN ACCUSED IN BLAST THAT KILLED OFFICER*" by Matthew Brelis The article reported that Thomas L. Shay "*stumbled*" as he read Tom's handwritten letter to him, for the first time.

Boston Herald: "*SENIOR SHAY FACES ACCUSED SON IN COURT*" by Ralph Ranalli. He reported that Mr. Thomas L. Shay's testimony was the first time he had seen his son, Tom, in more than a year.

Patriot Ledger: "*EXPERT SAYS OFFICER KNEW BOMB WAS ABOUT TO EXPLODE*" by Stephen Walsh He wrote, "*In a tragic twist, the bomb officers themselves may have made the blast possible by touching the bomb, essentially serving as a boost to the receiver, 'the way you do when you touch a television antenna,' Waskom said.*"

28 29 30 1 2	6 7 8 9	12 13 14 15 16	19 20 21 22 23	26 27
X X X X X	X X X O	O O O O O	O O O O O	O O

Day 8: Thursday, 8 July

The eighth day of the trial began on 8 July 1993, and with a caution by Judge Zobel, after some disruptive emotion shown by members of the victims' families the previous day. With a trial about such a horrible death of one policeman and the maiming of another, strong emotions were certain to appear. Said the judge, "*I have enormous empathy for you, I understand why you're here, but let me tell you that at the moment my primary concern is in having a trial that is run with full integrity. It is not possible to have a trial that, that is -- well what's the word I'm looking for -- an honest trial and a fair trial if members among the spectators indicate in any way to the jury that there is some kind of serious emotional involvement by them. It affects the jury. There have been three incidents in the course of this trial, and I simply request that you not do this again. If there is any danger whatsoever that you may feel some emotional outburst repress it. Do not put your hands to your face, do not in any way show your concern about this, and your emotional involvement in this, because it will affect the trial. It will imperil the trial and we may just have to do it all over again. So, if there is any danger whatsoever that you will feel affected by the testimony in the case, I ask you, please, not to leave en masse, but leave before it happens and not to come here and affect the trial and the fairness of the trial in any respect whatsoever.*" (TS 8-2) One reason why the behavior of the family members was important was that they consistently occupied what appeared to be reserved seats in the front row on the right hand side of the courtroom, immediately adjacent to the jury.

Then there was a bench conference to consider the question of whether Mr. Shay should be advised of his Fifth Amendment rights under the U.S. Constitution. Nancy Gertner brought the problem to the judge's attention as she felt that she would soon be asking Mr. Shay about his past actions which Gertner believed may border on criminal conduct. Ms. Gertner told the judge and the Assistant U.S. Attorneys, "*All I can tell you is that I have been in touch with the lawyers who represented the defendants* [in the civil case against the Dedham Service Center], *and the lawyers who represented the defendants feel so strongly about this man's profile that they called the police the day after the bombing to suggest to them areas of investigation. So, in my discussions with them, and they did more research. .....The other side of the coin, this man is not particularly intelligent.....*" (TS 8-21) On the other hand Paul Kelly was concerned that if the jury heard the judge advising Mr. Shay of his rights, the jury might think of him as a criminal. The judge then did have a discussion with Mr. Shay about his rights against self-incrimination, and he said understood them.

Then came probably the most difficult cross-examination of the trial as Nancy Gertner sought to persuade the jury that Thomas L. Shay had some role in the building and placement of the bomb. Also, she tried to paint him to the jury as a poor communicator and poor husband and father. Unfortunately, the effect may have been to engender sympathy for him, for he was perhaps similar in background and personality to several members of the jury.

Ms. Gertner began her questioning of Mr. Shay's activities during the weekend before the bombing beginning on Friday, 25 October. That afternoon, he picked up Kristen at school in the '86 Buick and parked it on Eastbourne Street upon his return.

That evening, Thomas L. Shay, and Mary and Kristen Flanagan went in Mary's Lincoln Town Car to the Ringling Brothers Barnum and Bailey Circus at the old Boston Garden. If they or the ATF investigators knew that Alfred William Trenkler was descended through his mother from Phineas T. Barnum's brother, William, they might have thought the coincidence helped their case, just as many other coincidences seem to have done. No one knew at the trial knew, so the connection was not attempted. Also, it would have been totally irrelevant as were several of the other coincidences.

For most of Saturday, the Buick remained parked on Eastbourne Street, but Mr. Shay drove it to his club in the South End early Saturday evening. There, it was double parked on the street from about 7:00 p.m. to about 8:30 p.m. From there he drove to the Golden Temple Chinese restaurant on Beacon Street in Brookline and arrived home around 9:30. He parked the Buick on Eastbourne and it stayed there until his errands on Sunday morning which began around 8:30.

Nancy Gertner pressed Mr. Shay about what he did with the box after its discovery. Why did he, for example, finally place it in the driveway where it was closer to where Kristen might be playing? Why did he seemingly casually drop the box, or throw it as was earlier reported, to the ground next to the house? His response was that he simply didn't know what it was and didn't yet fear nor expect that it was a bomb. Although he discovered the device when backing up the Buick, and saw it in the driveway thereafter, he didn't know whether it might have come from Mary's car or his. He thought so little of the box that he didn't tell Mary about it, but he was having a "*tiff*" with her since Saturday (TS 7-91) and he wasn't talking with her about anything.

She didn't ask Mr. Shay for more details about his driving in metropolitan Boston for several hours on Sunday 27 October 1991 with a wooden-boxed bomb underneath his car, and how he managed to drive over the road bump at McDonalds or Burger King without damaging or dislodging the bomb. She didn't ask further about Mr. Shay's description about how he heard the bomb scrape against the concrete driveway twice and then how it was pulled off by the contact with that concrete. If the bomb scraped against the grass center strip, then it would have made far less noise. She didn't ask about the condition of the box as he found it. Was it damaged? She might have asked how, if it didn't fall off or wasn't damaged during several miles of urban roads, was it that the bomb was scraped off the bottom of Mr. Shay's car without visibly damaging the fragile plywood-nail-superglue wooden box?

On Monday morning the 28th, he drove to the Rolling Wrench Garage where his brother, Arthur, and the garage's owner, John Doering, worked and he talked with them about the mystery box. Arthur and John suggested that Shay go to the police as it sounded like a bomb to them. Nancy Gertner didn't explore further how it was that Mr. Shay could have suspected for so long that someone was going to plant a bomb under his car or otherwise harm him, and then when a mysterious box appeared from underneath the car, it took a brother and business associate to convince him that it looked enough like a bomb to be reported to the police. Mr. Thomas Shay had already shown that he was not shy about reporting incidents to the police, as he had done earlier in the year about the car following him and in 1989 about the body shop debris dumped at his driveway.

Mr. Shay also drove to the Chapman Lock dealer who had installed Z-lock systems in several of his cars and the cars of his customers. There, he talked with Roy Kaplan who said that the Z-lock work didn't involve placing anything like the small black box underneath any car. Then he went to the Area E police station.

Nancy Gertner asked Shay what he might have had in his hands when he emerged from his car at home, and Shay said that it might have been a cardboard box with some spare hand tools. She was probing to see whether Shay actually had the bomb in his car, but hadn't told anyone; and maybe hadn't yet flipped the slide switch, either. However, as not every detail of the case could be ferociously pursued, no one ever asked Mr. Shay to deliver the claimed cardboard box to the investigators. Tom Shay had told Jefferson Boone that he had never seen his father with a cardboard tool box.

At the time of the explosion, he was outside the house talking with Officer Denise Kraft (later Corbett).

Shay was asked about who might want to hurt him, and was reminded of the 23 October 1989 incident, shortly after he left the Dedham Service Center, when a pile of assorted auto body parts was dumped on his driveway, apparently at the direction of Louis Giammarco, of the Dedham Service Center. Shay had gone to the West Roxbury District Court at that time to get a restraining order against such actions. Despite that level of apparent animosity, it wasn't clear from Shay's testimony that he had included Jeff Berry and Louis Giammarco on his oral "*enemies*" list given on request to a Boston Police officer on the 28th.

Gertner focused on Shay's fears of death and retaliation, which he denied until being confronted with his previous statements. She quoted Shay's statement in his first deposition in 1991 in the Ber-Giam civil case where he said, "*I remember that day sitting on a car van seat reading a newspaper. I can remember my son, I can remember my brother. I can remember us almost being killed because of some stupid premeditated violent act.*" (TS 8-106) He said that he came to that view later, but at the time of the 30 October 1987 explosion as a "*stupid prank*". (TS 8-109)

She asked Shay about his treatment with the neurologist, Dr. Biber, "*In December of 1990, did you tell Dr. Biber that you worried constantly that the people who were responsible for the explosion were trying to kill you?*" Mr. Shay responded, "*That could be.*" (TS 8-110) She continued, "*Do you remember telling Dr. Biber that you were afraid to start your car lest it explode in December of 1990; do you remember telling Dr. Biber that?*" Mr. Shay responded, "*No.*" (TS 8-111) As Mr. Shay said he did not remember making such statements, Ms. Gertner asked him to read aloud Dr. Biber's notes written after a 17 September 1990 visit, "*he has become hypervigilant and he's afraid to start his car lest it explode.*" (TS 8-112) Thomas L. Shay's memory was not refreshed, and he did not remember making such statements.

Mr. Shay also was asked about his weekly visits to a psychiatrist, Dr. Chengalis, for his PTSD (Post Traumatic Stress Disorder) in 1990-1991, with this exchange:

Q "*You told him that you feared that the two men who played the joke on your would hurt you?*"

A "*Yes.*"

Q "*You feared your house, right, something would happen to your house, right?*"

A "*No*"

Q "*... you were frightened that people were out to harm you is that right?*"

A "*Yes.*" (TS 8-113)

She did not ask Mr. Shay about a diagram that he had allegedly drawn for his psychiatrist, or that the psychiatrist had drawn based on Shay's description, showing a bomb underneath his car seat. She didn't pursue the 50+ of times that Mr. Shay had been thought to have expressed fear to his psychiatrist about being physically harmed.

Gertner asked Mr. Shay if he had ever heard of *International Muscle Magazine*, which was actually *MuscleMag International*, but he answered "*No*", and it's unlikely that correcting her error would have made a difference in his answer. Again, she was seeking to show the jury that Thomas L. Shay likely had a role in the building and placement of the Roslindale Bomb.

Gertner asked about Shay's many lawsuits, most of which were settled by payments to him. However, her taunting of Thomas L. Shay may have produced sympathy rather than disgust. She began the exchange with:

Q "*In fact, you have sued people a number of times for accidents which you had, right?*"

A "*Yes.*"

Q "*In fact, sir, is it fair to say that you bring a lawsuit about once every five years.*"
A "*There's no timetable.*"
Q "*Just whenever you need the money?*" (TS 8-127)

The settlements from these lawsuits included:
$ 2,000 from the MBTA for injury to a finger in an escalator. 1970's.
$ 5,000 from a car accident. 1970's.
$ 4,000 from a broken finger caused by a fall at a Merit gas station. 1970's.
$100,000 from a car accident. 1981-82.
$ 22,000 from a car accident. 1986.
$ 3,800 from injury at Disney World during visit with Mary and Kristen in
         October 1990. (Asked Gertner, "*Did you sue Mickey Mouse?*" and "*Yes.*"
         was the matter-of-fact answer.) (TS 8-131)

Nancy Gertner continued to try to show that Thomas L. Shay needed money in 1991, as his only income was a monthly Social Security Disability payment of $600, plus part-time auto body work. She established that his income in 1986 was about $80,000 and in 1987 $81,000.[11] Then came the explosion in 1987 and his cessation of work in 1989, and the initiation of the lawsuit against the Dedham Service Center, which was covered by a $400,000 insurance policy.

However, the lawsuit was not going well because the defendants' were deposing Thomas L. Shay's doctors and they were questioning his injuries. She asked Shay about a 28 June 1991 report from his neurologist, Dr. David Cohen, "*that essentially said that you had no damage.*" (TS 8-142) Paul Kelly objected to the question because it didn't permit cross-examination of the doctor. As Mr. Shay said he didn't see the report, Gertner couldn't question him further on that subject. Again, the rules of evidence prevented the jury from seeing facts that could have been perhaps an important indication of Mr. Shay's character and his possible motivation for setting up an apparent bomb threat against his life. There was no mention of summoning Dr. Cohen to testify.

Then Nancy Gertner asked Thomas L. Shay about an April 1991 report from a psychiatrist, Dr. Robert Weiner, and Shay claimed not to recall who Dr. Weiner was. Shay said he also did not recall an April 1991 report from an eye doctor, James Patton.

Mr. Shay said that he did not know that his former psychiatrist, Dr. Chengalis, had been deposed on 23 October 1991, just five days before the bomb explosion, and that he didn't know that James Patton was scheduled to be deposed on the day of the explosion.

Despite considerable evidence that Thomas L. Shay's lawsuit was in trouble, and, indeed, Shay may even have feared that his SSI's monthly payments may have been jeopardized by the allegations of non-disability, Nancy Gertner was not able to show that Shay was much concerned. Therefore, it was hard to persuade the jury that he could been motivated to take such an extreme measure as plant a bomb or something that looked like a real bomb. She then changed the line of her questioning.

After Tom Shay's theft of his father's coins and Mary Flanagan's jewelry in June, 1988, known only as an "*incident*" to the jury, Mr. Shay said that he had seen his son, the defendant, only a few times. One was after the son's deposition in Mr. Shay's civil suit in September 1991. Also, he saw him at the club in the South End with the loud noises in September 1991, and later in September when he gave Thomas A. Shay money for a dentist appointment, and then there was the trip to the Seabrook Race Track in October 1991. The explosion and suspicion fueled by the investigation destroyed the already fragile relationship. Before the trial, the last time Mr. Shay saw his son was more than a year earlier.

Nancy Gertner's efforts painted Shay as an unemotional, though sometimes angry and abusive, man who didn't care about his son until recently when his son could help him in the civil suit against the Dedham Service Center. However, proving that characterization of Thomas L. Shay didn't seem to show that the son was any less interested in trying to kill him. The jury could have concluded from this line of testimony that the defendant had good reason to hate his father.

On another subject, Mr. Shay agreed that his son had not previously shown interest in joining the civil suit against Jeffery Berry and Louis Giammarco either as a co-plaintiff because of his own injuries from the 1987 explosion or as a child suffering from the loss of companionship from his father. The point of this line of questioning was to cast doubt on one of the two charged motives for killing Mr. Shay: to obtain a share of the hoped-for, but hardly expected, $400,000 return from the lawsuit. That is, if Thomas A. Shay was that interested in the money, he would have joined the lawsuit. If his initial disinterest was overcome by a subsequent interest in money, he still could have joined the lawsuit at any time, just as the original 1989 complaint had been amended in April 1991 to add Kristen Flanagan as a plaintiff for loss of consortium. Gertner established that Mr. Shay did not have a will, but it wasn't established whether his family knew or didn't know whether he had a will. One rumor in the family was that Mr. Shay had disinherited Tom Shay, and if Tom Shay had heard that speculation, his motivation to kill for a share in an inheritance would have been reduced to zero. Even if Tom Shay thought his father had a will, he knew that his father had not provided adequate child support to his children after his separation from Nancy Shay, and as Tom Shay had stolen several thousands of dollars in valuables, it's doubtful that Tom could have conceived that his legacy would have been more than a token amount. Such long term calculations were not typical of Thomas A. Shay, who did not usually plan far ahead.

Ms. Gertner did not explore the true value of the Dedham Service Center case which had been settled out-of-court the previous September for an amount that was kept confidential until the upcoming trial of Alfred Trenkler. As the jury had heard the value of the upper limit of the Dedham Service Center's insurance policy of $400,000, and as each juror had probably calculated roughly what Tom Shay might have expected to inherit, it would have been helpful for the jury to know that the settlement was for the relatively small amount of $27,000. Gertner's client, Tom Shay, knew about the settlement, and it was publicized in a September 1992 *Boston Herald* article, but perhaps she didn't know. Perhaps she did know, and intended to present that information to the jury through questions to Mr. Shay, the right moment passed and the testimony moved to other subjects.

Finally, Nancy Gertner asked about the police search at 39 Eastbourne Street and his written consent, but Shay couldn't remember the form and couldn't remember being advised of his rights to object to such a search without a search warrant. The form was witnessed by his former attorney in the Dedham Service Center lawsuit, Alan Pransky, and by Boston Detective Lt. Edward O'Malley. Shay was asked if it was a lie that he had been advised of his rights, and he had a Perry Mason moment when he responded, *"I'm not saying that's a lie. I never lied about anything."* (TS 8-162) Surely the jury was sympathetic, even though the question did not ask whether he was lying, but whether it was a lie that others had lied.

Nancy Gertner returned to Mr. Shay's earlier direct testimony about the one visit by Mr. Thomas Shay to his son, a year previously, when Mr. Shay had reported to the police that his son had asked him, *"Where did you go Saturday night?"* [TS 7-135] What Mr. Shay did not report to the police, nor reveal in his answers to Mr. Kelly's direct examination was that Tom had denied to his father his involvement in the Roslindale Bomb in this exchange with Nancy Gertner:

Q: *"You also didn't tell them that he also said, 'Dad, I had nothing to do with this.' "*
A: *"I'm not to clear on this."*
Q: *"Didn't he say to you, 'I had nothing to do with this?' "*
A: *"Yes."* [TS 8-166].

Paul Kelly asked a few questions on redirect and established that the first time Mr. Shay talked with his son after the 1991 explosion was on the night of Thursday/Friday, 31 October/1 November 1991.

Mr. Shay never did demur to a question with a claim of his Fifth Amendment constitutional right to remain silent or not answer a question.

On recross examination, Nancy Gertner continued to try to paint Thomas L. Shay as an angry emotionless man. As noted earlier, even if she had been successful, wouldn't that have made it more likely the possibility that his son would dislike or even hate him, but enough to try to kill him? That seemed too far a stretch. Also, the defense questioning seemed to show that Mr. Shay was not very smart or clever, thus reducing the chance a juror could see him as a conniving enough to plant a bomb to make it look like someone was trying to kill him.

Soon after his testimony, Mrs. Nancy Shay wrote to her son, Tom, *"Don't let it get to you about* [what] *your Father said. He never was a very good Father. Believe me, you're too good to be his son anyways."* The family struggle had moved to U.S. District Court.

The trial adjourned at 1:05 p.m.

Next day's headlines:

Boston Globe: *"DEFENSE SHIFTS BOMB TRIAL FOCUS TO SHAY'S FATHER"* by Matthew Brelis

Boston Herald: *"DEFENSE GRILLS DAD OF BOMB SUSPECT"* by Ralph Ranalli

Patriot Ledger: *"FATHER TESTIFIES HE HELPED POLICE INVESTIGATE HIS SON"* by Stephen Walsh. *"Thomas L. Shay, 49, said he visited his only son at the Nashua Street jail in Boston last year at the request of police and later gave them the details of his visit."* The article said there were 75 people in the audience during Mr. Thomas L. Shay's testimony under Nancy Gertner's cross-examination.

28 29 30 1 2	6 7 8 9	12 13 14 15 16	19 20 21 22 23	26 27
X X X XX	XXXX	O O O O O	O O O O O	O O

Day 9: Friday, 9 July

As usually happened in this case, the trial day began with a bench conference, and on this day it was about the course of the investigation. Nancy Gertner had been trying to show that the investigation focused too soon on Thomas A. Shay and Alfred Trenkler, and not enough on other possible suspects, including Thomas L. Shay. Frank Libby told the judge and Ms. Gertner that two events in the first few days of November changed the investigation: finding the name of Alfred Trenkler in Thomas A. Shay's address book, and the receipt of a report from the Quincy police about Alfred Trenkler's role with the 1986 M21 Hoffman Artillery Simulator in Quincy. Libby claimed that Trenkler had, at first, denied knowing Thomas A. Shay, though he didn't say to whom that denial was given, and there was no reference to a report. Alfred Trenkler never denied that he knew Tom Shay. Such a denial seems unlikely since Trenkler knew that Tom Shay had his business card and had called him several times; and Trenkler likely knew that Tom kept an address book. Second, Kelly stated that the Shay-Trenkler relationship went back two years.

Testimony resumed with the direct examination of Christopher Guy Shapley, an automotive expert, who testified about how the bomb was attached by magnets to the Buick and how it could have stayed attached during travels throughout Boston, but then could have been detached in Mr. Shay's driveway. He testified that the two large magnets were strong enough to keep a device weighing 18-20 pounds attached to the underside of the car. As the Roslindale Bomb was estimated to weigh about 6 to 6.5 pounds, Mr. Shapley concluded that there was ample magnetic force to keep the bomb attached to the car during Mr. Shay's travels in Boston on Sunday 27 October. However, Shapley also concluded that the magnetic force was not so strong as to cause the fragile box to fracture, break or collapse when coming into contact with the ground or driveway. He said that the bomb must have slid along the bottom of the car until some gaps appeared in the car's metal surface, causing a weakening of the magnetic force and the dislodging of the bomb - all without damaging the bomb's thin plywood box. He said it was a close call, and if the bomb had been just one inch thinner, it would not have come in contact with the ground at all. [TS 9-38]

Nancy Gertner established that if the bomb had been just a little thicker, it would have been crushed or severely damaged. Thus, there was a very narrow window of chance for the bomb to have both survived the driveway and fallen off. If it had not fallen off, it would have remained attached underneath Mr. Shay's car through the time at which the batteries would die.

Ms. Gertner questioned his techniques and his use of photographs rather than an actual examination of Mr. Shay's car. His analysis of the scrapes underneath Mr. Shay's car was based upon a comparison of the scrapes he photographed with his own camera in 1992 compared to the scrapes seen in the photographs taken by the Boston Police immediately after the bomb explosion. Where there were scrapes on both photographs, he was able to draw inferences from them, but as he had no photographs of the underside of the Buick before 28 October, he could not be sure about the sources of the scrapes. Nancy Gertner asked the crucial question, "*How could it be that this box would have fallen off the car, leaving the metal fragments without any - without crushing the box? And your analysis was that it had slid on and then slid off, and that's how this occurred; is that fair to say?"* [TS 9-47] He replied affirmatively.

Then she asked Mr. Shapley if he had seen the Boston Police videotape of their *"unsuccessful attempt"* (TX 8-54) to recreate the scraping of the bomb against the driveway and its drop from the car. He had, and Judge Zobel initially said that he could not comment on the video, *"but until the videos come into evidence, their description is not properly before the jury. So the jury will disregard the description."* [TS 9-55] Moments later, however, he did discuss the contents of the tape and there was no indication that the jury had seen it, or that the jurors would ever see it. Mr. Shapley could not explain why the police were not able to achieve either the scraping or the drop, and presumably the scrapes, too, except with a mockup device that was much thicker than the actual bomb. Jefferson Boone reported in an internal defense memo that the photographs or video he had seen of the re-enactment showed the thick box being crushed by the weight of the car. If the police had achieved scraping and movement of the bomb along the bottom of the car, the resulting scrapes would have destroyed the validity of the photographs used by Mr. Shapley. He said that the box used by the police in the videotaping was thicker than the actual bomb, but that it didn't have the mini-box sticking out underneath.

Mr. Shapley said that he have been told that there were fragments of each type of magnet, alnico/small and sintered/large, that had broken off and were found still adhering to the underside body of the car. [TS 9-68] The report of the fragments found still attached to the car was not entered into evidence. [Also, it's not been available to the author.]

Then Ms.Gertner focused on the breaking of a few of the magnets before the explosion and the apparent presence of magnet fragments imbedded in Mr. Shay's car. The question was, *"there was nevertheless enough force so that this sliding literally ripped away some pieces of metal fragments into the undercarriage of the car?"* He answered affirmatively, and then she asked the followup question, *"And how can it be then that there's enough force to have ripped away portions of the magnets and not do damage to the box?"* [TS 9-71] Also, she noted that the superglue gave way for some magnets as well. He responded with a scientific explanation of how it could happen.

However, even if Shapley was correct that the bomb was, in fact, attached underneath Mr. Shay's Buick, and even if it became detached while he drove into, or backed into, his driveway, there still remained the question of whether Mr. Shay had actually driven throughout Boston on Sunday with the bomb attached underneath his car.

The defense did not attempt to present the videotape of the attempted recreation of the Buick driving into and out of the 39 Eastbourne Street driveway with an object magnetically attached underneath. Such a showing would have cast doubt that the history of the bomb prior to noon on 28 October 1991 occurred as Mr. Thomas L. Shay said, and if any part of his story could be shown to be false, then all of it was subject to doubt and questioning. There was no testimony about a mark left in the driveway caused by the scraping of the bomb, with sufficient force to detach it from the bottom of the Buick. Jefferson Boone recalled that the turf in the driveway was dug up. There was no testimony about any scrapes or damage to the bomb before it exploded. The jury was then left to ask how there could have been sufficient magnetic force to keep a black box weighing slightly more than six pounds attached to the underside of a car traveling through Boston's streets, but that same force was later not large enough to cause any damage to the box when it was pulled from the car by its contact with the driveway.

Next to testify was William Bridgeforth of the Boston Police Dept. who transported Thomas A. Shay from the Area E police building in West Roxbury to the Homicide Department in South Boston in the early morning of Tuesday, 29 October. At that time, Bridgeforth said that Shay "... *told me he had heard about the officer who had got killed. And that he was sorry about it and wished he could turn back the hands of time and make it not have to have happened.*" (TS 9-88) As a claimed admission by a defendant, and thus an exception to the hearsay rule, the statement was not challenged by the defense, but there can be an interpretation of Shay's statement that is not an admission at all. That is, anyone could have said it, just as we are all sorry that 9/11 happened and that we all wish we could turn back the hands of time to 9/10. Wishing to turn back the hands of time does not require responsibility for the regretted event, such as a crime or a hurricane.

The hearsay rule prohibits a witness from testifying about what another person said if the purpose is to present that other person's statement for its content. That is, the statement, "*Tom Shay told me he graduated from high school,*" would not be admissible if offered for the purpose of proving that Tom Shay graduated from high school. Tom Shay, however, could take the stand himself and make such a statement, even though it's false. He could so testify, because the trial process provides for truth-testing through cross-examination. For a hearsay statement, there no such opportunity for cross-examination.

There are several exceptions to the hearsay rule because statements made under certain conditions are deemed to be inherently believeable. In Shay's trial, there were two exceptions which were used most often by the prosecution: statements against penal interest and admissions and statements showing a state-of-mind. Regarding penal interest, the reasoning for the exception is common sense belief that no one would knowingly make a statement which might subject him or her to criminal penalties, so the statement must be true. However, as will be painfully apparent in the personality of Tom Shay, he made untruthful statements regardless of their effect on himself or on others. Getting attention was the primary goal.

The basis for the second widely-use exception, state-of-mind, is that emotions don't lie as much as words. Thus, regarding the statement above, that Tom Shay wished time could be turned backward, purportedly showed his remorseful state-of-mind about the Roslindale Bomb.

In some cases, such as this case involving Thomas A. Shay who made statements on the most slender bases of reality, the exceptions should not apply as there was little that could support the truth of his statements. The only statements of Tom Shay that should have been admitted as exceptions to the hearsay rule should have been those which were verified or corroborated by other evidence. In the hypothetical, a high school diploma would be required - and it didn't exist at the time of trial. He earned his GED while in prison in 2002 at the age of 30.

Thus, it's the view of this book that none of the statements made by Tom Shay which showed any involvement in the Roslindale Bomb should have been admitted, as they were not sufficiently verified or corroborated by other sources.

Bridgeforth also testified, "*He told me he was an EMT* [Emergency Medical Technician], *He showed me an EMT ID and badge, and he told me that his mother owned, like, five condos in the condos he lived in.*" (TS 9-92) Neither statement was true, but Bridgeforth did not inquire further. After Thomas A. Shay's interview with the homicide detectives, Bridgeforth took Shay to his mother's home in Quincy around 3:30-4:30 a.m. Alfred Trenkler was not the only person to give Tom Shay a ride in 1991.

Next to testify was Boston Police Officer Miller Thomas, who was one of the two detectives who interviewed Thomas A. Shay in the early morning of Tuesday, 29 October 1991. Detective Thomas said that Tom Shay said that "*maybe things would have been different if I hadn't been to those* [boys] *schools, something to that effect.*" (TS 9-126) This statement was also admitted as an admissions exception to the hearsay rule even though the statement could easily have been interpreted in a way that was not an admission. If, for example, Tom Shay had not gone to those schools and foster homes, he might have been living at home at the time of the 28 October explosion and might have prevented it.

Tom Shay related to Officer Bridgeforth how he had been thumbing through a copy of *Fortune* magazine in an attorney's office with Alan Pransky earlier in the fall, and Shay said that he saw an advertisement for a $250,000 Lamborghini and said to Pransky, "*How much money will my father get for this* [lawsuit]*?*" and Pransky said "*Lots.*". Then Tom Shay said, when pointing to a photo of the Lamborghini, "*...Will I be, will my father be able to afford something like this?*" and Pransky allegedly replied, "*Absolutely*". (TS 9-129/30) Then Miller Thomas described Tom Shay's demeanor, "*He pushed back on the chair, pushing back raising the front part of the chair, put his hands behind his head and gave a very wide grin and smiled.*" (TS 9-130) For those few boys who anticipate that their father may be able to buy a Lamborghini, sitting back and smiling would be a very normal reaction. However, if your father has the misfortune to be the target, or apparent target, of a bomb, sitting back and smiling arguably can mean something else. The prosecution argued that it meant that Shay was involved in the making and placing of the Roslindale Bomb.

Later, Detective Thomas said that Thomas L. Shay had indicated to him that "*Mary Flanagan had barred Shay, Sr.'s son, Shay, Jr. from ever coming to that residence...*" (TS 9-135) This was because of the 1988 "*incident*" at 39 Eastbourne Street.

Late in the day, Nancy Gertner began her cross-examination. Detective Thomas said Thomas L. Shay said that when he first picked up the black box, he said it was about the same size as a "*Russell Stover*"[12] chocolate candy box.

The trial adjourned at 1:01 p.m., until the following Monday, 12 July.

Next day's headlines:
Boston Globe: "*DETECTIVE'S TESTIMONY SUPPORTS THEORY IN BOMBING CASE*" by Matthew Brelis
Boston Herald: "*SUSPECT SAID TO KNOW BOMB WORKINGS*" by Ralph Ranalli
Patriot Ledger: "*JUDGE ASKED TO LINK BLASTS*" by Stephen Walsh. The

article described the prosecutors' renewed Motion to introduce evidence at Shay's trial of Afred Trenkler's role in the 1986 Quincy incident, despite there being absolutely no evidence that Tom Shay knew about it.

28 29 30 1 2	6 7 8 9	12 13 14 15 16	19 20 21 22 23	26 27
X X X X	X X X X	X O O O O	O O O O O	O O

Day 10: Monday, 12 July

Still being cross-examined by Nancy Gertner, Miller Thomas said that Boston police investigators had driven with Thomas L. Shay over his entire Sunday route to Malden, Chelsea, South Boston, Dorchester, etc.

Shifting to Thomas A. Shay, Miller Thomas said the police had investigated the claim that he was an EMT and found it to be false. The prosecution objected to this line of questioning and a bench conference resulted, with the judge asking where the questioning was going:

"Gertner: *'It's a two-fold purpose, one to show he's* [TA Shay] *simply not all there, and the other to show he's simply not there and these statements are not reliable. In other words, the same measure by which the Court determines voluntariness: Does he know what he's doing and is it to be relied on, is exactly what the jury is going to have to decide.'*
Mr. Libby: *'I don't know what 'all there' means. Either we have an insanity defense in this case or we don't. It seems to me counsel wants to have her cake and eat it too. She wants to get this notion that somehow her client is suffering from some psychological deficit. She doesn't want to plead it as a defense and raise it in the normal course, but we can have expert testimony. She simply wants to walk that motion across the jury. It's perfectly improper to do that.'* " (TS 10-22)

The problem for the lawyers and judge was that the insanity defense is used to avoid responsibility for a criminal act, but Nancy Gertner was trying to show her client's mental instability as an explanation for why he claimed a role in a criminal act, when, in fact, he had no such role. It was an unusual problem that no one in the courtroom was fully prepared for.

Continued Gertner, "... *Here we talk about preexisting mental condition, adequacy* [sic], *documented by existing records, which reflect on his desire for attention, his inability to even to give a fair medical history to be trusted -- in the earlier records, now not* [sic]. *And we will offer that testimony... That's an affirmative defense."* (TS 10-25) The court concluded the conference, *"Well, you may inquire as to whether they learned of his background and hospital, boys' schools, and so on. You may inquire as to the witness's perception as to demeanor and appearance. You may not inquire of the witness's perception of mental state....."* (TS 10-26)

Nancy Gertner continued to question Miller Thomas and determined that Thomas A. Shay had lied when he said that he and his family went to South Carolina to buy firecrackers and when he said that he worked with his father in the auto body business in 1987 when the Dedham Service Center explosion occurred.

Gertner then asked Miller Thomas about the 31 October Thomas A. Shay press conference at the Trailways bus terminal, and the prosecution objected successfully, which led to a bench conference. Then Judge Zobel felt it necessary to explain a bit of the trial process to the jury, *"Let me explain to the jury, when counsel are called the witness to the stand, and inquires about a series of subjects then on cross-examination, counsel may only inquire about those subjects. So that if Mr. Libby had asked about topics 1 through 10, Miss Gertner may ask only about 1 through 10 on cross-examination. If she asks only about 1 through 5 on cross-examination, then next round Mr. Libby is limit[ed] to 1 through 5 and can't again be ask[ing] about 6 through 10. We're always trying to narrow the scope, not expand it. And he's correct that this witness did not testify about anything having to do with October 31. Therefore, she's now going beyond the scope of the preceding examination and therefore the objection is sustained."* (TS 10-38)

Note that the judge said that the goal is to keep narrowing the scope of questioning in order to save time and move the trial forward. She didn't state the goal of seeking the truth through cross-examination. Judge Zobel worked hard to move the case forward. At one point she pleaded with both lawyers, *"Why are we reviewing this excruciating detail of all this stuff?"* (TS 10-20) Trials are expensive and need to be managed, but wrongful convictions are expensive, too, in many ways, so the constant effort to limit the scope of this trial was penny wise and pound foolish.

Boston Police detective Dennis Harris testified next. He was assigned to go to Thomas A. Shay's announced press conference and record it with a video camera at the Trailways bus terminal downtown on Thursday, 31 October. That task was passed to Detective Timothy Murray, but Harris did drive Thomas A. Shay to the Homicide Unit in South Boston for another voluntary interview. The detectives were in civilian clothes.

During Detective Harris's examination, the prosecution played a 40-50 minute videotape of the press conference, as recorded by the police. The playing of this tape was a major problem for the defense lawyers, as they had no chance to cross-examine anything said on the tape, unless they decided to put their client on the stand and show him to be the liar that Ralph Pace was said to have said he was to a reporter in the video. How else was the jury to know that there was no $30,000 loan to Tom Shay, and that none of his sisters was training to become a policeman and that the Boston police neither told him to leave town, nor left any messages, via Tom's mother, to return. The tape never should have been shown to the jury as it was replete with falsehoods, many of which the prosecution knew to be false. [See the excerpts of the video in Chapter 2, Early Investigation.]

Harris stated that, at the interview in South Boston, Thomas A. Shay said that he thought his father felt that he, the son, had something to do with the bombing. After the interview with other detectives, he was arrested on a previous warrant and Detective Murray drove Tom Shay to the "Identification Section" in the South End for fingerprinting and photographs. At that location, Detective Timothy Murray played a little trick on Thomas A. Shay by telling him that his father had called and said to tell Thomas A. Shay that he loved him. The goal of the trick was not explained. Afterwards Tom Shay was driven back to the Homicide Unit in South Boston.

On cross-examination Harris agreed that Thomas A. Shay cried at that point. There was no such call from Thomas L. Shay at that time. Perhaps it was a prank gone too far.

The next witness was Detective William Fogerty who was one of the detectives who interviewed Thomas A. Shay the night of 31 October in South Boston. Shay told them he had first heard about the explosion on the 10 p.m. television news and he had hitchhiked to 39 Eastbourne and was advised there to go to the police station for more information. During this interview, Tom Shay was told his father was coming to the station to visit Tom, just to see, according to Detective Fogerty, his reaction. Fogerty testified that Tom Shay said that his father would hit him if he came to the station. After the interview, Shay was arrested on an outstanding warrant for a probation violation. It was then that his belongings were searched and his address book found. The pages of the address book were photocopied and the book was returned to Shay's backpack. Repeating what Detective Harris had related, Detective Fogerty said that Tom Shay was taken to the "Identification Unit' and when he returned, he was in a room where he could see a remote control car in the next room. Then Tom Shay drew a diagram of a remote control bomb, which is shown in Appendix D.

There was a bench conference and Judge Zobel changed gears and asked the defense, "*Yes. When can I have the law you want me to look at pertaining to this psychiatric business?*" The defense replied "*soon,*" or by the next day, and the judge said, "*Among other things, the prosecution would like to have a ruling on that as well. Part of their case will depend on it....*" (TS 10-88)

Cross-examination by Nancy Gertner continued,

Q "*And Mr. Shay said, he did not drink or do drugs and he wanted to take a polygraph; is that right?*'

A "*Yes Ma'am.*"

Q "*He said all the information he knew was from his sister on* [or] *television.*"

A "*That's correct.*"'

Q "*He said that he had driven his father's car four times in the last four years, do you recall that?*"

A "*Yes, Ma'am*"

Q "*Did you determine afterwards that was a lie?*"

A "*Yes Ma'am.*"

Q "*He said sometime ago he built an aircraft carrier in a hobby shop, do you recall that?*'

A "*Yes Ma'am.*"

Q "*Did you ever determine whether that was true?*"

A "*No ma'am I did not.*"

Q "*He said he used to make model submarines and sink them by throwing M80's at them?*"

A "*Yes, ma'am.*"

Q "*Do you recall whether that occurred and make a determination whether that was true?*"

A "*No ma'am.*"

Q "*Mr. Shay also indicated to you that Ralph Pace of 23 Jefferson Street, Stoughton was somehow involved; is that right?....*"

A "*Yes, Ma'am, he did.*"

Q "*Did you ever investigate Mr. Pace?*"

A "*Yes Ma'am.*"

Q "*Did anything that Mr. Shay said about Pace turn out to be true?*"

A "*I don't believe so, but he did know Mr. Pace....*"

Q *"Did you determine that Shay, Jr. had borrowed a car from Pace?"*
A *"Yes, Ma'am."*
Q *"And owed him money?"*
A *"That I'm not sure of."*
Q *"That Pace wanted to adopt Shay when Shay was 16 or 17."*
A *"That was not true...."*
Q *"And he also said he had a beeper from Metromedia."*
A *"Yes, ma'am."*
Q *"Did you ever determine whether that was true?"*
A *"Yes, ma'am."*
Q *"And was that true?"*
A *"No. Ma'am."* (TS 10-113/116)

Thus, Nancy Gertner was able to show the jury that many of Tom Shay's statements at the Trailways press conference were not true, without actually asking the witness for Shay's actual statement which would have been inadmissible hearsay. The statements had already been seen and heard by the jury in the Trailways press conference videotape, which was admitted as a state-of-mind exception fo the hearsay rule.

Ms. Gertner then established that on the night Shay was arrested, 31 October/1 November, the first call he was permitted to make was to Byron Pitts, a Channel 5 TV reporter, instead of a family member or lawyer. Tom Shay's penchant for publicity had a higher priority than his or Alfred Trenkler's freedom.

Later, he did talk with his father for about five minutes and he was permitted to call Russ Bonanno. Detective Fogerty testified that Tom Shay said *"that he loved his father."* (TS 10-96) In response to a question, Tom Shay said he was not the kind of person who would hurt someone in order to get attention.

On redirect, Frank Libby established that some of what Tom Shay said in the press conference about Ralph Pace was true: he was an accountant, he lived in Stoughton and he had sought to assist Tom Shay by becoming his foster parent. Again, about Tom Shay's statement, the prosecution sought to persuade the jury that even though Tom Shay's statements had layers of truth and untruth, like the layers of nesting dolls, his lies about the Roslindale Bomb contained a core layer of truth that he was involved. However, it was, in the example, a doll deeper inside that contained truths from which Shay spun his stories. In this instance the kernel truth was that the bomb exploded at his father's home. Everyone knew that. It was the jury's job to determine at which larger size, the doll began to be untruthful.

Day 10 ended at 1:00 p.m.

Next day's headlines:

Boston Globe: "OFFICER TESTIFIED ON PROBE OF BOMBING" by Matthew Brelis
   He wrote that Nancy *"Gertner is expected to call a psychiatrist who will testify that the younger Shay made statements to get publicity and did not care whether they were truthful."*

Boston Herald: "JURY SEES BOMB SUSPECT'S PRESS CONFERENCE TAPE" by
   Ralph Ranalli

28 29 30 1 2	6 7 8 9	12 13 14 15 16	19 20 21 22 23	26 27
X X X XX	XXXX	X X O O O	O O O O O	O O

Day 11: Tuesday, 13 July

The almost daily bench conference began about the issue of Thomas A. Shay's behavior and what evidence could be introduced about his lying. Judge Zobel said, "*Going backwards, I do believe it's too late* [for the defense] *to raise any* [defense of] *diminished capacity. No notice was given and I don't think, I mean, I do believe it would be unfair to the Government at this late date suddenly to change horses again. As to that, I don't think the defendant can do it.*" (TS 11-2) The script had to be followed, even if it meant that the jury would be deprived of information which might be useful for its deliberations.

On the familiar concern with moving the trial along, she said, "*We have increased the number of side bar conferences exponentially in the last couple of days. I'm going to decrease it again.*" (TS 11-19)

Then on the issue of admitting evidence of Shay's lies, Judge Zobel said to Nancy Gertner, "*Why, can you be selective: Sometimes he says things that aren't true, that are wild; sometimes he says wild things that are true. Why, if I allow you to put in his comments, his wild comments that are not true, should they* [the Government] *not be allowed to put in his wild comments that turn out to be true.*"

To which Ms. Gertner replied, "*Because, just as the Government didn't object to questioning about wild occupational things that don't implicate prior bad acts. In other words, I am selective about, precisely for this reason, showing that these don't implicate prior bad acts. This is not an incident in which he was the perpetrator. This is* [an] *incident he claimed to be a witness, and it was completely fanciful. If I were to ask about instances where he represented he was the perpetrator--*"

Judge Zobel responded, "*The problem is that he is somewhat indiscriminant when lying or not lying. And if you put in only the instances when he lied, I don't know why the Government shouldn't be able to put in only the instances when he didn't lie, in order to paint a more event picture.*"

Mr. Libby. "*Precisely.*" (TS 11-20/21)

The problem for the court was that the entire criminal system is based on the concept that the government investigates, prosecutes, and convicts people who almost always deny they have done what they are accused of doing. Sometimes people readily admit what they've done, or are induced to admit it with a plea bargain offer, and they plead guilty. The system doesn't have a pigeon hole for the person who spins story after story about his participation, or that of others, in a crime, most of the details of which are wrong and then fights the actual criminal charges when they come.

We understand people who inflate their resumes or otherwise lie to make themselves appear better in someone's eyes. When the lies are stripped away, there is usually some bit of truth. At other times, as with claims of achievement such as reaching the North or South Pole, one begins to get skeptical as claimed detail after claimed detail is proved false. If most of the story is false, is there a kernel of truth, and if so, which kernel?

In John Mark Karr's case there were kernels of truth in the story that he killed JonBenet Ramsey as he had known the Ramsey's and even been in their house on a previous occasion; and he wanted to get out of his Thailand jail. However, it now appears that the entire story of his role in the murder was false, not because his several tellings were inconsistent with each other; but because the one consistent story contained certain falsehoods, such as being in Colorado when his family could prove that he was home with them a thousand miles away. It's not known why Karr wanted to be the post-hoc killer of Jon-Benet Ramsey, but publicity seemed to have something to do with it. It certainly was for Tom Shay, who wrote in an 8 August 2007 letter, "*Like a seal basking in the sun, the TV cameras and news flashbulbs were my chance to be famous, or infamous. It was the wrong type of attention and yet I didn't care. I would have said I had killed Jimmy Hoffa or knew where he was buried just to be on TV.*"

In other famous cases, people have voluntarily confessed to crimes they could not have committed. Best known among such instances were the reportedly 200 people who stepped forward and claimed to have had a role in the kidnapping and murder of the baby son of Charles and Ann Morrow Lindbergh.[13] In 1993, however, the concept of false confession and voluntary false confession[14] was not as widely known as it is today with our more certain knowledge that people have confessed to crimes which DNA has said, with certainty, that they did not commit.

In the case of Thomas Arthur Shay, the prosecution knew of the multiple lies, but they needed to solve a horrible crime and some of the pieces of Thomas A. Shay's stories fit in with THEIR hoped-for truth. They convinced a grand jury of their truth extract and the indictment was issued. They had succumbed to the Selective Truth Temptation (STT).

Another now-familiar "factitious disorder" is "Munchausen Syndrome by Proxy" where people will "*deliberately mislead others into thinking they (or their children) have serious medical or psychological problems, often resulting in extraordinary numbers of medication trials, diagnostic tests, hospitalizations and even surgery... that they know aren't really needed....*"[15]

The use of the concept of "*voluntary false confession*" rather than, or in addition to, "*pseudologia fantastica*" would have helped Tom Shay because the term, "*voluntary false confession*" focuses only on the lies that the defense sought to eliminate - the incriminating ones. The problem with "*pseudologia fantastica*", by itself, was that it applied to ALL lies, and it didn't require that EVERYTHING be a lie. Thus, the U.S. Attorney's office could pick and choose and label as truthful what it wished.

Resuming with witnesses on Day 11 of the trial, the Government called Edward Carrion, a 38-year old computer network designer.   He told the court that he met Tom Shay in the spring of 1988 in the "*Block*" area of Boston "*where young men gather to be picked up by older* [gay] *men.*" (TS 11-57] Nancy Gertner could have objected to the admission of his comments about the "*Block*" as prejudicial. It's not relevant what type of neighborhood was the first meeting place for Carrion and Tom Shay. Perhaps Nancy Gertner was resigned to the constant pressure by the Federal Government to make Tom Shay's sexuality or gender preference a part of the record, that she saved her quiver of objections for what she felt were more important issues. Still, Carrion could have met Tom Shay, and Tom Shay could have met Alfred Trenkler at a ball game, a beach, an historical society meeting or anywhere. The Government did not need to drag in his sexuality.

Ed Carrion said he was a friend of Tom Shay for three years before the relationship stopped one night in October 1991, when Shay woke Carrion and his roommate up. Shay posed as a police officer and demanded that someone let him in. Carrion didn't and Tom Shay stalked away. (TS 11-58,74) According to Edward Carrion, that incident occurred "on about" [TS 11-74] 18 October. Carrion's identification of the 18th, and he correctly stated that it was a Friday, was significant because that was the day of the Radio Shack purchase by "Sahy." The defense team had stated earlier in the case stated that there was no alibi for Tom Shay for his actions on the 18th as he did not know of his activities on that day. However, as the prosecution had now stated that the disruption at Carrion's apartment was on the 18th, perhaps Tom Shay could have been asked to recall that evening and work backwards in his mind to 2:36 p.m., and earlier, on that day. As it was his mother's birthday, and as parents often know quite clearly what their children did for them on their birthdays, determining Tom Shay's activities on that day should have been easier. It's not known whether that was done. Perhaps the incident at Carrion's apartment, was not on the 18th at all.

Even if not exactly correct, the date was significant in another way. Shay's comedic visit to Carrion's apartment marked the final end of their relationship, which had ended months before. The date is important because Edward Carrion's name was not in Shay's address book when copied by the police on the night of 31 October 1991. It was another indication that Tom Shay did not meet Alfred Trenker before the summer of 1991. If Tom Shay had been using that address book much earlier than that summer, Carrion's name would have been in it.

Carrion was asked by Paul Kelly if he had ever observed Tom Shay "*in possession of any body building magazines*," and Carrion responded affirmatively, but didn't remember any titles. (TS 11-75)

The most important part of Ed Carrion's testimony regarded Tom Shay's relationship to Alfred Trenkler. Carrion said that he had taken Tom Shay to the address of 7 Whitelawn Avenue in Milton three or four times in the summer of 1989. (TS 11-62) That was Alfred's childhood home, and the home of his parents,[16] but Carrion acknowledged that he had never met anyone at that home, which he recognized from a photo. Carrion did, however, testify that he had seen Alfred Trenkler at that home and described him as an "*older man, in his late twenties, early 30s. Balding on top. Somewhat heavy set. Shorter. Best described him as monk-like looking.......*" (TS 11-62) Carrion identified Alfred Trenkler from a set of photos shown to him at the trial. He was asked by Paul Kelly if he had seen Tom Shay in the company of Alfred Trenkler at any other times, and Carrion said, "*Yes*", approximately 2-3 times in the vicinity of the "*Block*," in the 1989 to 1991 time period. (TS 11-64) There was no one there to defend Alfred Trenkler, but that testimony was incorrect.

Edward Carrion concluded his direct testimony for the prosecution by stating that Tom Shay was interested in electronics and remote control objects. Carrion had recommended that he purchase supplies at Radio Shack, as that was where he shopped.

Surely not coincidentally, Edward Carrion's roommate and friend, George Nightingale, worked at the 197 Massachusetts Avenue Radio Shack store in Boston.

During cross-examination by Nancy Gertner, Carrion said that he had once worked as a police officer and that he had told Dennis Leahy and Richard Palazzo [Victor Palaza?] of the ATF that he would be willing to audiotape conversations with

Tom Shay if they wished. Carrion saw Tom Shay about 8-9 times in 1991. He denied that the offer of a reward of any influence in his relationship to the ATF and police and stated that he only learned about the existence of the reward *"approximately ten days ago was I informed of a reward in this matter, and it was in a conversation with Mr. Nightingale, after one of your associates has* [sic] *called Mr. Nightingale and asked him that specific question, if I ever knew of a reward..."* (TS 11-98)

Carrion said that he never remembered Alfred Trenkler's full name, and was not even sure of his first name, thinking it was *"Bill, Dave or Al..."* (TS 11-98)

Nancy Gertner returned to the theme of Tom Shay the story-teller, and spinmeister and had this exchange with Edward Carrion:

Q *"He said that he reported in the fall of '91 that his father was terminally ill; is that right?"*

A *"That is what he told me?"*

Q *"That his father had leukemia or cancer or something?"*

A *"Yes."*

Q *"In fact, it's fair to say that his story about his father changed several times in the very same retelling; isn't that right?"*

A *"That's exactly what I said."*

Q *"And in fact, he would do that frequently; is that right?"*

A *"Yes."*

Q *"He would start to say something with great honesty or seeming honesty, and by the end of the paragraph change the story, right?"*

A *"That's Tom."* (TS 11-106/7)

As the length of the acquaintance between Tom Shay and Alfred Trenkler was an important aspect of the case, more could have been done to throw doubt onto Carrion's testimony and identifications.

The next witness was Thomas A. Shay's first defense witness and she was directly examined by Nancy Gertner. Evelyn Pirello appeared out of order, as she had personal plans to be out-of-state when the defense's case was to begin. She was the sister of the across-the-street neighbor of Thomas L. Shay, Eleanor McKernan, wife of James McKernan. On 28 October 1991, she was in her sister's home and saw Thomas L. Shay get out of his car with a box-like object in his right hand. *"To my fast look. it just looked like sort of a tool box, you know, like a foot long and kind of - - well, it could be, not a tool box, it was something dark in his hand, you know. I'd say it was about a foot long."* (TS 11-115) She had a clear recollection of Mr. Shay because she believed he had cut her off when she entered Eastbourne Street and she *"snarled a little bit"* at him, but her son, Robert, urged her not to *"say anything."* (TS 11-114)

Robert Pirello testified next and he had a more clear recollection of Mr. Shay and what he was carrying and had this exchange with Nancy Gertner:

A *"I saw a tool box in his left hand, I believe it was, and another box in his right-hand."*

Q *"What was the box you saw in his right-hand?"*

A *"Similar to a metal box, a metal box, similar to a ratchet set.... probably six inches wide, maybe one inch deep by about maybe ten inch, 8 or ten inches long."*

Q *"And it was a consistent color, right?"*

A "*Yes.*"

Q "*And he had a green tool box in one hand and then this object in the other hand?*"

A "*Yes.*" (TS 11-124)

After the testimony of the Pirellos for the defense, including their cross-examinations by Paul Kelly, the prosecution resumed its case with Robert Evans, the first of the inmate informants, or jailhouse snitches, as they are commonly called, to testify for the Government in the cases against Thomas A. Shay and Alfred W. Trenkler.

Robert Evans, was serving a sentence for breaking and entering to finance his drug habit, and was in the Quincy District Court basement lockup on 1 November 1991 when he heard the name of Thomas Shay called out. He recognized the name from reading about the Roslindale Bombing in the newspapers, so he engaged Tom Shay in off-and-on conversations. After a day's discussion with Tom Shay, and mostly listening to him, Robert Evans wrote a letter to his wife, Diane, which he read to the Court,

"*Diane, call Boston police, don't let no one know about this. Tell them I was in a holding cell with Thomas Shay at Quincy District Court and he told me all about y [sic] killing that cop. One A, he told me about the guy who made the bomb; two, and asked me how much time he would get for murder; three, told me about the effects of a high explosive; four, if he could get on bail, he'd screw. Down at the bottom, it says, I want a complete pardon of all my cases as a personal recognizance on my bail right now, and I'll testify in court.*" (TS 11-149)

Nancy Gertner cross-examined him and established that he, as with other inmate informants to come, had mixed motivations for coming forward. Everyone knows how the system works. No one likes a rat or informer, but everyone knows that the way to get a reduction in one's sentence is to help the government convict someone.

Day 11 of the trial adjourned at 12:59 p.m.

Next day's headlines:

Boston Globe: "WITNESS LINKS TWO IN FATAL BOMB CASE" by Matthew Brelis

Boston Herald: "FORMER FRIEND OF BOMB SUSPECT SAYS HE SPOKE OF RESENTING DAD" by Ralph Ranalli The '*former friend*' was Ed Carrion.

28 29 30 1 2	6 7 8 9	12 13 14 15 16	19 20 21 22 23	26 27
X X X XX	X X X X	X X X O O	O O O O O	O O

Day 12: Wednesday, 14 July

Cross-examination of Robert Evans continued on Day 12. Nancy Gertner established that Tom Shay said to him that his mother lived in a $125,000 condo, which was another probable, but not obvious lie. Also, Gertner showed that Robert Evans made the story sound more appealing to the police, and she showed several inconsistencies between what Evans said to the grand jury and what he said at the trial. Most seriously, she showed how opportunistic Evans was and how important it was for him to do what the police wanted.

Tom Shay's friend, Russell Bonanno of South Dartmouth, Mass., was the next to testify for the Government. He testified that Shay called him on the afternoon of Tuesday, 29 October, and asked if he could come to stay for a while. He arrived between 9-11 that night. He left for Boston on Thursday evening, 31 October, around 6 p.m. when Russ gave him a ride to the New Bedford bus station.

Bonanno's next contact from Tom Shay was a call from the South Boston Homicide section of the Boston Police Department. After Shay finished talking, a policeman came on the line and told Bonanno that if he could help, he should call the police, which Russ did the next day. The result of that call was that ATF Special Agent Jeff Kerr gave Bonanno a telephone recording device which could be turned on when a call came in from Tom Shay.

During cross-examination Bonanno stated that during all his discussions with Tom Shay as a counselor and friend, Shay had never mentioned the name of Alfred Trenkler to him, but he did talk about other people. For example, Tom Shay described to Bonanno how he owed money to Ralph Pace. An obvious time for such a reference to Alfred Trenkler would have been the few weeks in September 1991 when Tom Shay stayed with Bonanno until he asked Shay to leave on Sunday, 22 September due to a dispute about the presence of Shay's two kittens, which violated the dormitory rules.

Bonanno's next contact with Tom Shay was on Saturday, 28 September when Tom Shay called him. Bonanno was in Boston at the time, so he picked up Shay at his mother's in Quincy and drove him to South Dartmouth. They talked a lot, and a few hours later Bonanno drove him back to Quincy. The final contact before the 28 October bomb explosion was on 14 October when Tom came to the St. Lukes Hospital in New Bedford to visit Bonanno who was there after an emergency room visit.

The next time he heard from Tom, after his return to Boston on the evening of 31 October via bus to his Trailways bus terminal press conference, was a letter received sometime before 9 February 1992, when he called Russ Bonanno, and which call was recorded. Bonanno read the letter to the Court:

"Dear Russ, Hello Russ. This letter is very important. I am in jail right now. I am scared and depressed. The police think I built the bomb or had something to do with it. We both know that I don't know -- we both know that I don't know. That black tape I got at your house, they're going to try to use it against me in court. My attorney's going to need you to bring you and that tape down to the office. His name is William McPhee, 21 McGrath Highway, 3205 Quincy, Massachusetts, 0269, 617-471-9307. He's a real nice guy. Call him and explain our relationship as friends, how we met, what you do for work, when I came over to your house, and when that black tape came into my hands. That black tape is a big part of this case. It's probably the only lead the police have. Get it to my lawyer and you'll save me. Okay.
P.S. You're the only friend I've got on this case, don't let me down. Write me a nice, long letter to pass my time here in jail. I need to hear from a friend like you. Right [sic] *to my house and my mother will bring it on my next visit, okay?"* (TS 12-112)

After his release from jail, Tom Shay fled to California. He did call Russ Bonanno from San Francisco on 9 February 1992 and the tape of that call was played to the jury, but no transcription was made. The *Boston Globe* article about Bonanno's testimony reported that Shay said on the tape, *"The cops still think I did it,"* which was alleged to be Shay's motivation for fleeing the state. Also, he said, *"I'm broke and hungry and I'm in some old man's hotel room and I'm on the road and I only have one set of clothes.... I've learned to trust people and then I can't give too much trust because I have warrants out for me... I'll never be on 'America's Most Wanted.' But you're a cop, too, you know. So it's like you're my friend, but you're a cop. So, I mean, you're going to rat me out if I give you the address, huh?"* In the Spring of 2007 Tom Shay's fantasy about being on "America's Most Wanted" almost came true.

At the end of her cross-examination, Gertner established that Tom Shay never admitted any role in the bombing to Russ Bonanno. That's significant because it appeared that Bonanno was the closest person to Tom Shay's soul and mind. There was less need or no need to brag to him or otherwise spin lies.

The next witness on Day 12 was another jailhouse informer, Christopher Henry. He too was in the Quincy District Court lockup and he, too, heard Tom Shay brag that he had been arrested because of the Roslindale Bomb. On cross-examination, Nancy Gertner established that Assistant U.S. Attorney Frank Libby, who did the direct examination of Henry, had written a letter to the Norfolk County District Attorney's office describing Henry's cooperation with the U.S. Attorney's office in the Roslindale Bomb case. Henry did not get as much relief for his cooperation as he had hoped.

After his testimony, the jury was excused and there was a short bench conference where Nancy Gertner expressed her frustration that ATF Special Agent Jeff Kerr seemed to be spiriting witnesses away from the courtroom before Gertner could talk with them, as he had done with John Coyle before his grand jury testimony a year earlier. Paul Kelly took responsibility in this one instance, saying, *"This morning at the break, I turned to Agent Kerr and said [to] take Mr. Bonanno and give him a soft drink and cup of coffee, I rewound the tape and he followed my directions. His intention, I'm sure, was not to try to block access [to Ms. Gertner]."* (TS 12-149) Another problem with the exchange was that the prosecutors were buying a soft drink or coffee for a prosecution witness. It's not the same as finding a job for a witness, or a ski vacation, but it's a favor nonetheless, and should have been avoided.

The court adjourned at 12:55.

<u>Next day's headlines</u>:

<u>Boston Globe</u>: *"TAPED CALL TO FRIEND IS PLAYED IN SHAY ROSLINDALE BOMBING TRIAL"* by Matthew Brelis In addition to the quoted segments of the tape given above, Brelis also wrote that Tom Shay had *"telephoned Russell Bonanno to ask him to send a gold chain that Shay had given him."*

28 29 30 1 2	6 7 8 9	12 13 14 15 16	19 20 21 22 23	26 27
X X X X X	X X X X	X X X X O	O O O O O	O O

Day 13: Thursday, 15 July

Prior to taking witness testimony, Paul Kelly advised the Court (the Judge and Nancy Gertner) that he intended to call two "hostile" witnesses, John Cates and Nancy Shay, and asked the Judge's permission to question each by using leading questions - not otherwise permitted. Gertner had no objections, and permission was given. Aside from its plain meaning, the term "hostile" has a special significance in trials, as the sponsoring lawyer may impeach the credibility of his/her own witness on direct examination, instead of waiting for cross-examination - the subjects of which are restricted by the scope of the direct examination. Said Kelly, "*Just so the Court knows, both witnesses are not only hostile to the Government but clearly associated with the adverse party.*" (TS 13-2)

John Cates, the roommate and friend of Alfred Trenkler, was called to the stand as a "hostile" witness for the government. He testified that he first met Tom Shay at the Blue Hills reservation in 1988 or 1989 and Shay remained only an acquaintance and the relationship did not grow any deeper. In fact, Cates intentionally avoided him. Paul Kelly showed Cates a photo of Alfred Trenkler and repeated the description given by Ed Carrion, that Alfred Trenkler "*looks like a monk, doesn't he?*" (TS 13-7) Nancy Gertner objected, and Judge Zobel agreed that the rhetorical question was inappropriate - but the jury heard it, none the less.

Paul Kelly asked more about Alfred Trenkler, "*He's experienced in remote control?*" John Cates answered "*Yes,*" (TS 13-7) but he need not have. He knew little about electronics was not an expert in such matters, but Nancy Gertner did not object; and didn't see it as a major problem for her client even though it painted a more sinister portrait for the jury of Alfred Trenkler. A more acceptable question might have been, "*Have you ever seen Alfred Trenkler operating a device using remote control operations?*" Cates could have answered that question on the basis of his own personal observations, and not his appraisal of Trenkler's skills, and the answer would have been "No."

On cross-examination, Nancy Gertner brought up the nature of his relationship with Alfred Trenkler, which was a "*pretty much exclusive*" relationship, and that it began in October 1990. (TS 13-15) Gertner also asked about sex, "*And you were intimate as well, rice* [right]?" and Cates responded "*Yes*" (TS 13-15) When two unmarried heterosexuals are living in the same small apartment, and if one is a defendant, do lawyers in an interstate bombing homicide case ask them if they are intimate? It was an unnecessary and irrelevant question and was asked by Trenkler's co-defendant's lawyer.

John Cates described the time that he had discussed Tom Shay with Alfred Trenkler. It was during the summer of 1991 and they were driving on Boylston Street and came upon Tom Shay and they talked about him. Cates told Trenkler that Tom Shay was a person to avoid as he "*just seemed kind of whacky.*" (TS 13-21/22) Cates testified that he and Alfred Trenkler saw Shay again later and gave him a ride from the 1200 block on Boylston Street to the Copley Plaza area, about 400 yards. Cates didn't note that that ride was the fifth and last which Alfred Trenkler ever provided to Tom Shay. Also, he was not asked whether that was the first time that he had ever discussed Tom Shay with Alfred Trenkler. The answer would have been that it was the first time, and that answer would have been helpful to show the minimal level and duration of the Tom Shay acquaintance with Alfred Trenkler. Nancy Gertner had a lot of issues to juggle, but showing the true brevity of the Shay-Trenkler acquaintance should have been a priority. It's rare for friends to agree to try to kill the parents of their friends, but it's even more rare for a mere acquaintance to do so.

John Cates described how Alfred had his calls come to a pager, so incoming calls would not tie up Cates' home phone.

During Paul Kelly's redirect examination, Cates described how he and Alfred had discussed how Alfred had brought Tom Shay to Cates' apartment in June, while Cates was on vacation in Europe. That was the night of Alfred's first acquaintance with Tom Shay when he allowed Shay to sleep a few hours before taking him to Richmond Street, Dorchester, the next morning. Kelly tried to make it show that Alfred Trenkler was somehow hiding this information from Cates. Kelly didn't ask Cates, however, how he first learned about the Roslindale Bomb, which was when he and Alfred Trenkler were at an appointment with the chiropractor they both were seeing. It was Wednesday afternoon, 30 October and they shared a communication between them which was that the Roslindale Bomb story was about as crazy as Tom Shay; and that was before the 31 October news conference. As Kelly didn't ask about that event on direct, Nancy Gertner was not able to ask about it on cross-examination. Her recourse was to bring John Cates back to testify as a witness for the defense, which she did later in the trial on 15 July.

The next witness was Larry Plant, another jailhouse informer. Said Judge Zobel, "*So this is another witness who is going to tell us about Shay's statements?*" Paul Kelly responded, "*It is, your Honor.*" (TS 13-54) He might have reassured her a little by noting that Daniel Goldrick, the initial such informant, was not scheduled to testify and neither were several others who had offered to testify about what Tom Shay had told them. Larry Plant was at the Plymouth County House of Corrections in mid-October 1992, for obtaining legal drugs with false prescriptions, when he encountered Tom Shay, the walking talking "get-out-of-jail-free" card.

Testified Plant, "*He told me that, he told me that they did it. He told me how they did it and why they did it.*" (TS 13-58) Plant said that Shay said he had friend who said to him, "*Well, I got a "surprise for you*". One wonders what Paul Kelly was thinking of his moral or legal obligations as he heard this testimony. Seven months earlier he had written his 10 November 1992 "*Memorandum to File*" after hearing this same "surprise" story from Tom Shay, "*4. The whole story about Trenkler building him some unknown 'surprise' was a hoax.*" In any case, he said nothing to the judge or to the defense or to the jury about his own conclusion regarding this fanciful "*surprise*", which was that it was a hoax.

If the prosecutors had not already known that the "*surprise*" was a hoax, then it would have fit the frequently seen pattern where criminals minimize their own roles in a crime. They weren't prepared for someone like Tom Shay who exaggerated his role in a crime enough, from zero to something, to make him seem important and newsworthy, but he hoped, not enough to get him convicted. He miscalculated, not only for his own freedom, but also for Alfred Trenkler.

Plant said that Tom Shay had told him that he and Trenkler had built the bomb together and described its radio control and components; and said the primary motives were the share of the $500,000 prospective inheritance and getting even with his father. Asked Kelly, "*Did he make any statements concerning where they had obtained any components or explosive material?*" and Plant answered, "*Only that they had gotten, I think the explosive, from the National Guard Armory in the North Shore.*" (TS 13-63) Again, did Paul Kelly think back to his own 10 November Memorandum "*To: File*" where he wrote, "8. There was no trip to Vermont and Canada with Trenkler to obtain munitions from some 'soldier of Fortune' camp?" Stealing from a 'soldier of fortune' camp is a lesser problem for Shay than stealing from a National Guard Armory, so Paul Kelly may have thought that exposing the lie of the 'soldier of fortune' camp makes a theft at a National Guard armory more likely, again using the assumption that criminals usually minimize their roles in crimes. Again, Kelly was suffering from the Selective Truth Temptation and he was hoping, hoping that Tom Shay was telling the truth. However, people who give voluntary false confessions or admissions should not go to prison because a prosecutor hopes that amidst all the statements made by a defendant that there a few that are truthful and that **those** statements are the incriminating statements. People who knew Tom Shay, drew the opposite conclusion, perhaps, that he had no idea of where the dynamite came from.

Paul Kelly asked Larry Plant, "*What if anything did Mr. Shay say about where they had discarded any of the leftover materials?*" and Plant answered "*This was, this was where he went into [a] great deal. He had said they taken it out into the ocean and dumped it at sea, three miles out into the ocean. And that as long as he could recover the parts of the bomb, that he had a deal with the Government, that he would get a three-year prison sentence and that would be all, he would be able to beat the case as long as they didn't find out.... as long as they didn't find Trenkler.*" (TS 16-63) Again one can ask, and what would Judge Zobel and the jury have thought if they had had Paul Kelly's 10 November memo in front of them as Paul Kelly asked these questions. About disposal, Kelly wrote, "5. He never accompanied Trenkler to the Quincy quarry, or participated with him in disposing of evidence." Also, Paul Kelly knew exactly what kind of a deal he offered to Tom Shay in return for his information and cooperation, and it wasn't what Larry Plant testified that Tom Shay described.

A trial attorney is prohibited by ethical rules from intentionally presenting testimony which is s/he knows to be false. However, Larry Plant was likely giving substantially truthful testimony; but what he said that Shay told him was false and Paul Kelly knew it. Judge Zobel knew about the 10 November 1992 Kelly memo, because it was a point of contention when Terry Segal sought to compel Paul Kelly to testify as a witness in the U.S. v. Trenkler case. However, even if Judge Zobel knew about Paul Kelly's candid memos to his file about Tom Shay's lies, the jury had no idea that some of what the prosecutor was presenting was known by the prosecutor to be false.

To pre-empt anticipated questions from Nancy Gertner, Kelly asked Larry Plant why he had come forward with this testimony and he said he had friends who were police officers and he had tried to imagine what it was like to be the Hurley family and live with the death of a policeman; and trying to do what is right, etc, etc. It must have been hard in that courtroom to keep a straight face during that testimony.

Nancy Gertner picked up on a last statement by Plant about "*as long as they didn't find Trenkler*" and asked if Shay said that Trenkler had fled or was in hiding. Responded Plant, "*I don't recall. I think if, and I could be wrong, that he did say he [Trenkler] was hiding in California.*" (TS 13-69) Nancy Gertner responded, "*Right,*" but said nothing else, so the jury likely thought that Shay's co-defendant had fled to California, just as did Tom Shay. However, it was not true that Alfred Trenkler had fled to California, and the prosecutors knew that, but there was no one defending Alfred Trenkler,

Gertner drilled deeper into Shay's claim of constructing the bomb, as stated to Larry Plant:

Q "*Right. And then he said that he built the bomb with Trenkler, he and Trenkler together, right?"*

A "*He said he helped him.*"

Q "*He helped him. And then he said that he brought it to where his father was, right?*"

A "*Yes.*"

Q "*And put it on the car, right?*"

A "*Yes, ma'am.*"

Q "*And that the car -- that the gas tank was triggered by a radio frequency as soon as you turn the car on, right?*"

A "*That the bomb was triggered, yes.*"

Q "*Right. So that when his father came out and turned on the car, the radio would go, the bomb would go off, right?*"

A "Could you repeat that?"

Q "*As soon as his father turned the radio on, the bomb would go off; is that right?*"

A "Yes." (TS 13-79)

This line of testimony reminds me of a teen-age prank I'd heard about in the 1960's, where a practical joker and driver of a VW would ask a gas station attendant, in the "full-service" days, if s/he could check the water coolant. Sometimes, the attendant would return and say that it was "*OK.*" The problem, and joke, was that a VW was air-cooled and had no water coolant.

The 1991 Roslindale Bomb was not triggered by turning on a radio receiver. It was apparently built to be triggered by some kind of electromagnetic transmitter, the signal of which was received by the Futaba mechanism in the bomb, but the jury was not reminded how the bomb was detonated and thus was not led to understand that what Plant was saying that Tom Shay said was false.

Gertner continued with the questions about the prosecution's claimed motive for the case: getting money and getting even.

Q "*And he said that the reason that Trenkler did this was because there was a life insurance policy; is that right?*"

A "*Yes, ma'am.*"

Q '*And that his father had taken out a life insurance policy on himself, on his father?*"

A "*Right.*"

Q "*And that Tommy would get the money if the father dies, did he say that to you?*"

A "*I don't -- all I remember him saying words that, that Trenkler would could* [sic] *have his share. What he* [sic] *motive was to get even with his dad.*"

Q "*Right. He was saying to you that Trenkler would have Tom Shay, Jr.'s share of his father's life insurance policy; is that right?*

A "*Yes, ma'am.*" (TS 13-79)

The life insurance policy was allegedly for $500,000 and Plant said Tom Shay told him nothing about the Dedham Service Center incident or lawsuit. What was the jury to think about all this smoke? Was it entirely made up out of whole cloth, or was there something to it? If there was there something, was there something beyond a reasonable doubt?

Plant agreed with Nancy Gertner that it was unusual and dangerous for prisoners to brag to other prisoners about their crimes, but Tom Shay wanted to talk. Asked Gertner, "*And he was bragging about the crimes that he did, right?*" Plant responded, "*He was bragging about being able to acquire a tank or an F 16 fighter jet or any amount of arms that anybody would want, and he would get listeners for it, and he liked that.*" (TS 13-83) There was no need to pursue this line of questioning or to question whether Plant heard it wrong as it was patently absurd.

To Plant, Tom Shay was excitable and excited. Plant testified,

A "*... He seemed -- the only things that seemed to excite him was making a deal with the Federal authorities....*"

Q "*But how did you know that it was the federal authorities?*"

A "*Because he said he would come back from the phone, and he would say I'm going out on the boat tomorrow....*"

Q "*But he told you every day he was going out with the federal authorities in a boat looking for the bomb fragments in the ocean, right?*"

A "*Right, he didn't say every day. For a couple of days, that's what he would come back saying he was going to be doing the next day.*"

Q "*Okay. Once they found these bombing fragments, he would say get a three-year deal?*"

A "*Yes.*"

It was unknown to the jury whether ATF agents and others took Tom Shay out on a boat to look in Massachusetts Bay for the dumped remnants of the bombmaking work, but such a search did not occur. However, it was reported subsequently in the 29 July 1993 *Boston Globe* that ATF agents and local police did search for several days the Quincy quarries with divers and a small submersible robot from the Woods Hole Oceanographic Institute, but there was no mention of those trips in available ATF reports or prosecutor memos. There has never been any disclosure of the cost of these searches which probably totaled tens of thousands of dollars. In any case, nothing was found relating to the Roslindale Bomb, as the dumping stories were more Tom Shay lies. If the jury had known how willing the investigators were to believe Tom Shay's stories and how wrong those stories were, the jurors might have been more skeptical about such stories.

Gertner continued,

Q "*Did he tell you anything about Trenkler?*"

A "*Just that he knew how to build a bomb.*"

Q "*He told you that Trenkler was the person who knew all about C 4 explosives, right?*"

A "*He just said C 4. I think that had to do, if I remember correctly, that had to do with how he stole it or bought it or whatever. He said he's the one that knew how to get the C 4 or got the C 4.*" (TS 13-85)

There was no evidence of any C 4, a powerful plastic explosive used by the military and terrorists, in the Roslindale Bomb. However, because of the way that evidence is presented to a jury, no one could just tell the jury immediately the truth about the absence of any C 4. Nancy Gertner would have to wait for the ATF explosives expert, or her own, to convey that information to the jury. By that time the point of noting the weakness of Larry Plant's testimony would be lost.

Plant was the last jailhouse informant to testify. There were several others who had testified before the grand jury, but it can be assumed that the others had credibility and cross-examination problems for the prosecutors. One tactic suggested by an 11 March 1993 letter from Jefferson Boone to Nancy Gertner would have been for the defense to call all such "admission" witnesses in order to show the jury that Shay told so many varieties of such admissions than none could be believed. As the hearsay rule barred them from presenting non-incriminating statements which were false, they could just bring as many as possible of the incriminating statements. The risk, however, was that the jury would still believe the core of each admission, i.e. that he was involved.

Richard Brown, business partner to Alfred Trenkler, was the government's next witness. He was questioned by Frank Libby, and he wasn't hostile to the Government. When he stated his age of 27, Judge Zobel commented that "*He's almost elderly,*" which brought laughter. The term "elderly" had been a running joke in the trial, as Alfred Trenkler's parents were called "elderly", so there was a question of the beginning age for that status.

Richard Brown first met Alfred Trenkler in 1986 at a party and he worked with Alfred in AWT Associates (Alfred's initials) from 1987-88 and with the company that they formed together in 1991, ARCOMM. Brown said that ARCOMM was transformed from a success to a failure in October, 1991, but was not asked why, which is curious because the company had just completed most of the work in the large Christian Science Monitor microwave antenna project.

Again the prosecution appeared to think that Alfred's sexuality was important in the trial of Thomas A. Shay. Asked, Frank Libby,

Q "*... did you become familiar with Mr. Trenkler's sexual orientation?*"
A "*Yes.*"
Q "*What was his sexual orientation?*"
A "*Well, I found out some years* [after] *meeting him for the first time that he was gay.*"
Q "*Was that any matter of some controversy between the two of you, the fact that he was gay?*"
A "*It didn't matter to me. I mean it was a business relationship...*"

There was no objection to the question, even though it was irrelevant to the case against Thomas A. Shay. Judge Zobel said nothing either. It was to Brown's credit that Alfred Trenkler's sexual preferences didn't matter to him, and he still didn't fully understand Alfred's preferences. As no one was defending Alfred Trenkler at this trial, no one focused on an important point, which was that Trenkler's friend and business partner simply didn't know Trenkler's sexual preferences for several years after they met and had been doing business together, which means that it wasn't something immediately obvious with Alfred, whatever his sexuality. It wasn't a part of his life that he flaunted in front of others. Most of his friends in his teen-age years didn't know his sexual preferences either.

Frank Libby asked Brown when he first saw Alfred Trenkler and the defendant, Thomas A. Shay, together and he said it was at the beginning and end of a weekend in 1990 when Alfred lived in South Boston where he worked and lived at his employer's offices, ATEL. Brown said that he gave Tom Shay a ride in his Lincoln Continental to a T station on the Sunday of that particular weekend, making that the second time.

The third time he saw him was when he came to Alfred Trenkler's apartment, shared with John Cates, to go with Alfred to a business meeting. [That was Alfred's first acquaintance with Tom Shay, in June 1991, and both Richard Brown and Alfred took Tom Shay to a home on Richmond Street, Dorchester, at Shay's request.]

On cross-examination by Nancy Gertner, Brown acknowledged that Alfred Trenkler had accused him of writing checks for personal use without Alfred's authorization. She reminded Brown that he was uncertain in his earlier interviews and grand jury testimony of the identity of the person with Alfred Trenker over that weekend at ATEL in 1990. It might have been, for example, Chris Punis, a friend and later employee of Alfred's. This was an important point, for if the person he saw with Alfred on that weekend in 1990 was not Tom Shay, then the first time he saw Tom Shay with Alfred Trenkler was that morning in June 1991 when Alfred had given Tom Shay his first of five rides. That would leave only three people who claimed to have seen the two of them together before June 1991: Tom Shay himself, though not consistently, Edward Carrion, Paul Nutting and the next witness.

Nancy Shay, mother of Thomas A. Shay was called as a "hostile" prosecution witness. Trying to show the motive for Tom Shay's attempt to kill his father, Frank Libby asked about the abusive family history, and Nancy Shay said that as a child Tom Shay had seen his father abuse her.

Regarding her former husband's lawsuit against the Dedham Service Center, Nancy Shay said that her son, Tom, expected to get nothing from that lawsuit. She defended her former husband and his desire to be a better father. Sometimes, she testified, he would "*sneak*" a visit to Tom, so that Mary Flanagan would not know. (TS 13-154)

She moved to her current condo in Quincy in November 1990, and was in a rented apartment before that, and at her own home on Belvoir Road in Milton for 12 years before that. Frank Libby asked Nancy Shay if she had ever met Alfred Trenkler and she said, "*No,*" whereupon Libby reminded her of her grand jury testimony that Trenkler may have been one of "*Two people who lived in Milton, two men*" who came to her Belvoir Road home and went away with her son, Tom Shay. (TS 13-158) In 2007, Tom Shay identified those two men as Ralph Pace and Randy Stoller. Nancy Shay was reminded of her grand jury testimony where she answered "*Uh-huh*" to the question, "*At about the same time he* [Tom Shay] *told you this fellow that came to pick me up was Al Trenkler?*" (TS 13-159)

Confronted with an apparent inconsistency between Nancy Shay's trial testimony and her grand jury testimony, Judge Zobel addressed the jury on its role, "*Let me explain to you, members of the jury, one of the judgments that you will have to make in the course of your deliberations on your verdict is whether you believe what each and every one of the witnesses has told you, the extent to which you believe what the witnesses have told you. In other words, you have to make a judgment as to the believability of every single witness and then decide what you will give credence to, and what not. One of the things that you may take into account in judging whether you believe a person, is whether the person has given inconsistent answers in the course of the testimony whether the person has given answers here that may be different from answers that the person gave, that the witness gave on an earlier occasion. When the lawyers ask the witness or confront the witness with what they perceive to be or think is, or say it is an inconsistent earlier statement, the first thing you have to decide is whether it is, in fact, inconsistent. And then if you determine that the witness said one thing here and the witness said something else there or earlier, then you have to decide does that affect your judgment of the believability of the person and how much. So No. 1, is what the witness said earlier really different from what the witness is saying here, and if so how does it affect your judgment of the believability of that person?"* (TS 13-160/61)

This distinction was not necessary at Alfred Trenkler's trial because Nancy Shay, when seeing Alfred Trenkler in the flesh stated that she had never seen him before.

Nancy Shay's testimony was then suspended until Day 14. Judge Zobel now asked the lawyers for drafts of requested jury instructions, so she could prepare, but also so she could understand where the two parties were taking the case and with what evidence.

The court adjourned at 1:07 p.m.

<u>Next day's headlines</u>:

<u>Boston Herald</u>: *"EX-CELLMATE: SHAY TOLD OF BOMBING - RECOUNTS JAILHOUSE TALK"* by Ralph Ranalli. He wrote, *"A key part of Gertner's defense is that Shay made his self-incriminating statements due to a mental illness."*

28 29 30 1 2	6 7 8 9	12 13 14 15 16	19 20 21 22 23	26 27
X X X X X	X X X X	X X X X X	O O O O O	O O

Day 14: Friday, 16 July

The day began with the sharing of the news that Nancy Gertner had been nominated by Senator Edward Kennedy to be a U.S. District Court judge. At the predictable pre-testimony bench conference, the conferees discussed how or whether to deal with the nomination *vis. a vis.* the jury. Thus, the prosecution was now battling with a future judge of their cases and Judge Zobel was now dealing with a future peer.

Nancy Shay resumed her testimony and she answered *"Yes"* to the question of whether Tom Shay had said *"that he had seen Al Trenkler and met Al Trenkler in some clubs around town, is that true?"* (TS 14-13) She also said that in 1991, she had come home around 2-3 in the morning and found an unknown man asleep on the couch in her apartment. She said she was angry and the man rushed out the door. She said that Tom Shay told her later that the man was Alfred Trenkler. Frank Libby asked her whether that encounter was *"within a month of October 28th, 1991, true?"* and Ms. Shay answered, *"I just know it was cold weather... I don't know if it was...."* (TS 14-19)

Nancy Shay stated that Tom Shay left Massachusetts in January 1992 because he was afraid of having to go to jail because he had missed a probation appointment. What the lawyers and judge agreed not to tell the jury was that Tom Shay had missed that appointment because his sister's boyfriend, James Keough, had tried to commit suicide that morning and the appointment was secondary to other considerations. Although that may have been upsetting to jurors and may have taken precious trial time to clarify, it still would have been helpful to Tom Shay's case if the jury had known more about why he didn't meet with his probation officer.

Under cross-examination, Nancy Shay stated that Tom had never shared the name of Al Trenkler with her until after his November-December 1991 jail time. She said, "*Tommy told me in Nashua Street jail that* [it] *was Al on the couch.*" (TS 14-26) It was obvious hearsay with a statement from a very unreliable person, Tom Shay. However, there was no objection as the prosecution was probably pleased to hear evidence about the Trenkler-Shay relationship. Later, Nancy Gertner asked Nancy Shay, "*It is fair to say that he not only mentioned the name Trenkler, but he also mentioned other names, right?*" (TS 14-50) Unfortunately, Ms. Shay was not able to answer, as Frank Libby objected. With that question, Nancy Gertner was seeking to open the issue that Thomas L. Shay owed money to possible enemies from gambling debts, but Nancy Shay was not permitted to answer because of the hearsay rule. There was no indication by Nancy Shay that Tom Shay thought at the time that Alfred Trenkler had any role in the 28 October bombing. There was no other reported mention by Tom Shay of the name of Alfred Trenkler until the Federal and Boston agents visited with Tom Shay at the San Francisco jail in March 1992. It was then that they told Shay of their finding Trenkler's name in his address book after copying it on the night of 31 October after the Trailways press conference, and of Trenkler's role in the 1986 Quincy Hoffman Artillery Simulator incident.

Two more Tom Shay lies evaporated when Nancy Shay said that she had never been in a position to buy and sell condos, and that her family never went to South Carolina and purchased firecrackers.

On the crucial day of 28 October 1991, Nancy Shay said that she went to her job in a jewelry store in Boston and that Tom Shay was asleep at her home at that time. She did not know about the bomb at 39 Eastbourne until Tom and Paula and David Shilalis, Nancy's manfriend, picked her up at the T station after work. Nancy Shay said that Tom was "*all upset. He was worried about something happening to his father, and said he was going, you know, to see if he could see his father.*" (TS 14-44)

Nancy Gertner asked Nancy Shay, ""*Did Tom, in the conversations that you had with Tommy, in the fall of 1991 and afterwards, did he ever tell you who he thought might have done this to his father?*" whereupon Frank Libby objected on the grounds of "*relevance.*" (TS 14-48) Nancy Gertner, soon to be a Federal judge said, "*These are statements from the defendant about the event,*" and Judge Zobel responded, in sustaining the objection, "*Well I know, but they are being offered by the defendant and not by the government.*" and Gertner was now cross-examining, not directly examining. For a jury to hear the truth, it would have to be according to the prescribed rules, or not at all. Too often the result was: not at all.

Judge Zobel continued, "*.... I believe whatever the rights the Government may have to offer statements by the defendant, the defendant doesn't have the same right to offer his own statements.*" (TS-14-49) That is, he doesn't unless he chooses to testify, and be subject to cross-examination.

Later, frustrated with the course of the cross-examination, Judge Zobel said at a bench conference, "*This woman, frankly, it doesn't seem to me, to be capable of remembering specific conversations enough to tell us it happened to her on this occasion, it happened on another occasion. And it's all incredibly vague, which is of course the other problem with it. It is impossible to cross-examine her.*" (TS 14-51)

Nancy Gertner continued, "*The Government's case will fall entirely on the basis of these statements, and so they will say the October 31st version was wrong; what he said in Channel 56 was right. And what I'm trying to show is prior consistent statements that hang together as one version, rather than another. I don't think that fits into the categories of self-serving admissions.*" (TS 14-52)   Judge Zobel restated it, "*What she's offering it for really, as I understand it, is the point that this guy was talking sometimes over here and sometimes over there.*" (TS 14-53)

Frank Libby said that if the defense wants to get such statements, she can "*call her client...*" to the witness stand, a type of dare to Nancy Gertner.

Judge Zobel responded to a Frank Libby question, "*The relevance of it is to show that the defendant was making statements about tanks one day and about boats the other day and about airplanes another day, that he was making statements about doing it one day--.*" Frank Libby asked, "*That's relevant to what issue?*" and Judge Zobel explained, "*It is relevant to her argument and to her defense that this guy, this guy's statements can't be trusted.*" (TS 14-53) and later, "*No as I understand the defense, it is that you cannot give face value to the inculpatory statements because there are so many others, and you've got to look at them all, and then you can see that the inculpatory statements simply can't be credited, not that he says he didn't do it, simply the statements that said I did do it are simply not worthy of belief because there is so much out there that's to the contrary.*" (TS 14-54)

It was such a long bench conference, that Judge Zobel felt compelled to explain to the jury, "*Members of the Jury, understand that we operate under rules that sometimes get very complicated, and they become particularly complicated when we try to fit a specific question into a set of very general rules, and we're now arguing about the application of a general rule to the specific facts here.* (TS 14-57)

However, that was not the end of it, as Nancy Gertner tried to bring to the jury statements by Tom Shay that were untrue or questionable, which can only be done by an approved exception to the hearsay rule; so the lying had to be viewed as conduct rather than speech. At the next bench conference, Judge Zobel stated, "*... As I understand the defense, it is not that the jury should believe the statements that say 'I didn't do it,' but, rather that the jury should look at the whole course of conduct and, therefore, pay attention to none of it because this guy is obviously nuts.*" (TS 15-58)

Frank Libby responded, "*That's precisely the point, your Honor, she wants to make use of an insanity defense without pleading it in argument,*" and Judge Zobel replied, "*No.*"

Frank Libby continued, "*Absolutely, that's the very argument here: You can't trust what he says --*" (TS 14-58) as he had a hard time fitting this part of the puzzle. Frank Libby knew very well how untrustworthy Tom Shay was, but he didn't want the jury to see. He just wanted the jury to hear the inculpatory statements, even if both he and Paul Kelly already knew that most of them were false.

Judge Zobel said, "*No insanity in the sense of not understanding right from wrong, but whackiness, in the sense, that this guy, not understanding what's good for him, and therefore talking all over the lot, to the press, to the marshals, to the prisoners.*" (TS 14-58/9)

Frustrated, Frank Libby countered, "*It is an insanity defense.*" and Judge Zobel returned, "*It is not.*" (TS 14-59)

Returning to the testimony of the witness, Nancy Shay, Nancy Gertner asked her if Tom Shay ever read or possessed muscle or body-building magazines such as *International Muscle Magazine*, again misnamed, and Nancy Shay said "*No.*"

Unfortunately, Mrs. Shay was not asked by the defense what she knew about Tom's activities on 18 October, the day of the Radio Shack purchase. Mrs. Shay did testify about her knowledge of the dental appointment on 16 or 17 October, for which Mr. Thomas L. Shay gave Tom some money. Her birthday was on the 18th and she would have likely recalled many events on that day, including when she saw or talked with her five children. In 2007, she recalled that her son Tom had purchased two kittens in the North Attleboro area for his mother for her birthday on that day. However, Russ Bonanno had already testified that he ejected Tom Shay from his apartment on Sunday 22 September because of the presence of the two kittens, thus making unlikely their purchase on 18 October. Still, if such a purchase, or other known activities on his mother's birthday, could have been presented to the jury, Tom would have had a good alibi, but there was no defense effort to describe to the jury what Tom Shay was doing on the 18th, particularly at 2:36 p.m. None of her other children were called to testify about what they knew of Tom's whereabouts on their mother's birthday on 18 October 1991.

Then the case turned dramatically away from what Thomas A. Shay said to anyone and back to the Roslindale Bomb investigation as presented by Special ATF Agent, Dennis Leahy. Examined by Paul Kelly, Leahy said that there were no remote control toys found at the house of Thomas L. Shay. Shay was the initial primary suspect, along with 8-10 others, until the course of the investigation changed with the information about Trenkler's 1986 M21 Hoffman Artillery Simulator and the discovery of Trenkler's name in Tom Shay's address book.

Leahy described how he located the Radio Shack receipt #098973 from the Radio Shack store at 197 Mass. Ave. in Boston. He and the ATF were looking for sales of Radio Shack toggle switches, No. 275-602. They had a long list from Radio Shack's corporate offices, and narrowed the search from there. They found 2-4 possibilities but focused on the receipt entered into evidence as Government Exhibit 33 because of the date of 18 October 1991 and the apparent last name of the purchaser, "SAHY" with first name or initials, "JYT". Leahy noted the initials DRA of the apparent salesperson, who turned out to be Dwayne Armbrister. Copies of the receipt were given to the jury, and then the testimony about the receipt stopped, even though that receipt was the only physical piece of evidence in the trial which threatened to link Thomas A. Shay to the bombing.

The receipt listed six items purchased, including the #275-602 toggle switch. The others were a battery holder for 4 AA batteries, a small lamp, small lamp holder and two small plastic "*project*" boxes. There was no attempt by Nancy Gertner to challenge the authenticity of the receipt and admission into evidence. Was it genuine? Were those items really purchased by a real person named "JYT *SAH?.*" The typeface on the receipt of the name and associated information (5100, 1C[or 10]:3780, BOSTON 02115) were different from the typeface used for the rest of the document. Was there an effort by the defense to examine the store's receipts immediately before and immediately after the claimed purchase at 2:36 p.m. on 18 October? Did they look like that? In any case it was admitted. Then came a shift to a statement by Alfred Trenkler to Leahy.

A long bench conference began as Paul Kelly sought to have Dennis Leahy testify about what Alfred Trenkler told him during the search of the garage at 7 Whitelawn Ave., during which a role of duct tape was seized. The problem with such testimony was that, again, Alfred Trenkler was not present in the courtroom, and there was no one there to challenge Leahy's testimony. However, because another policeman, William Fogerty, heard the statement, Judge Zobel decided to permit Leahy to testify about it. Leahy's role during that part the search at 7 Whitelawn was as the team leader, but at the other two searched sites that day he acted as chauffeur for a Dr. Hobbs who was carrying a mechanical *"explosives sniffer"* with which he searched for chemical traces of explosives. None was found at any location or in any vehicle.

During the bench conference, Nancy Gertner made an interesting statement about the status of the alleged Trenkler-Tom Shay relationship, "...*the state of the evidence so far is that Trenkler and Shay may have hung around together. Given the Government's due, they may have hung around together once or twice in October, and that was it. And that's all that will ever be.*" (TS 14-100) She was almost completely wrong. In fact, the two men did not hang around together, and the last time that Alfred Trenker actually saw Thomas A. Shay was in August, and in the company of John Cates. Again, the jury did not hear Trenkler's side of the story, and no one was there to defend him. It must have been very frustrating for the members of Alfred Trenkler's family who attended Shay's trial to hear the incorrect evidence about Alfred being presented without challenge.

The judge ruled that the prosecution could ask about Trenkler's statement. Duly asked by Paul Kelly, Dennis Leahy said that Trenkler *"made statements concerning blasting caps in great detail, how blasting caps have a shunt on them, how they have two electrical wires that come out of the blasting cap that connect as antenna, and he also said that dynamite can, through heat, cause to explode dynamite that is located next to other dynamite.*" (TS 14-125/6) Leahy thought it unusual that Trenkler would know what a shunt was, but that was more of an indication of Leahy's ignorance about Trenkler than Trenkler's expertise with bombs. Electrical engineers know what shunts are, and know that wire can act as an antenna. Also, their basic knowledge of materials, and from hearing from time to time of serial explosions in fireworks factories, would lead them to understand that exploding dynamite would probably cause other dynamite to explode.

Nancy Gertner began her cross-examination by noting that the search for remote control devices at Thomas L. Shay's home at 39 Eastbourne was not reflected in any reports, and Leahy said that was because it was a consent search, where searchers can look for anything and everything and are not limited to what they have specified in a search warrant. The questioning ended with a bench conference to discuss the admissibility of portions of the Channel 56 videotape interview of Thomas A. Shay by Karen Marinella.

The court adjourned at 1:02 p.m.

Next day's headlines:

Boston Globe 1: "SHAY TRIAL HEARS ATF EXPERT" by Paul Langner

Boston Globe 2: "COLLEAGUES SAY GERTNER'S COMMITMENT SHOULD SERVE HER WELL ON FEDERAL BENCH" by Matthew Brelis

Boston Herald: "SUSPECTED BOMBER'S MOM LINKS SON TO 2ND SUSPECT" by

Ralph Ranalli He wrote, "*The mother of accused 1991 bombing suspect Thomas Shay said yesterday she kicked a man off her couch who turned out to be Alfred Trenkler of Quincy, her son's co-conspirator...*" [At the upcoming trial of Alfred Trenkler, when she would see Trenkler face-to-face, she said she had never seen him before. Thus, she was in the unfortunate position of mistakenly having testified in a way at Tom's trial that helped to incriminate him.]

28 29 30 1 2	6 7 8 9	12 13 14 15 16	19 20 21 22 23	26 27
X X X X X	X X X X	X X X X X	X O O O O	O O

Day 15: Monday, 19 July

The cross-examination of Dennis Leahy continued and he stated that the Radio Shack toggle switch No. 275-602 was made by a Taiwanese company, Shin Chin, but that ATF had difficulty communicating with that company. Leahy thought that that company was the exclusive supplier of that switch. However, Nancy Gertner did not explore aspects of the receipt which required explanations. What were the other five items on the receipt? Were there samples, exemplars, of those other items available for the jury to see? What are the other five items normally used for? What might a customer be building when purchasing all six at once?

In his redirect examination Paul Kelly asked if "*To the best of your knowledge, sir, based on this investigation, was there anybody in the State of Massachusetts having the last name, S A H Y?*" and Leahy responded, "*Not that I'm aware of.*" (TS 15-24) The ATF had checked with the phone company and there was one listing for "*Sahy,*" but the phone company said it was a misprint, and the correct spelling was "*Fahy*" Neither Kelly nor Nancy Gertner asked any of a number of followup questions about how many "*Fahy*" telephone entries were in Massachusetts. In 2007, there were 80 such listings and 18 began with the initial J.

Under cross-examination Dennis Leahy agreed that sometimes rock needed to be removed from sites of when installing the foundations for large antennas. Thus, Alfred Trenkler had reason to know something about such blasting, but he has said recently that he never had to have any blasting done on any of his antenna sites. If previously undiscovered rock was found during preparation for construction of a tower, it would have been the owner's responsibility to remove the rock.

Regarding the Radio Shack receipt, Nancy Gertner established what Paul Kelly had not, which was the presence of a four digit number on the receipt with the out-of-order four digits, 3780, of Thomas L. Shay's phone number, 327-7380. However, those four digits appeared in a place on the receipt for an I.D. number, not a telephone number. Radio Shack sales people have always tried to maintain the company's database for customers by asking for full phone numbers, a practice which has caused concern among some customers for their privacy.

The next witness for the prosecution was Dwayne Armbrister, a salesperson for Radio Shack at the 197 Mass. Ave. store. He testified remembering a customer coming in on 18 October with a list, on 1/4 of a sheet of paper, of items to purchase. Armbrister processed the sale and remembered being flustered by the impatience of the customer, so he input the customer's name on the wrong line on the receipt, and misspelled it, too. Nancy Gertner requested a mistrial on the issue of Armbrister's claimed identification of the 6 foot 3 1/2 inch Tom Shay, which identification had previously been shielded from the jury; but the motion was denied. Judge Zobel noted that the defense apparently conceded that Shay had been in that Radio Shack store a few times in the Fall of 1991, but would not concede that Armbrister's claimed identification of Shay as being the man who made the 18 October 1991 purchase was Shay. (TS 15-39) Also, unrelated to the 18 October 1991 receipt, Armbrister appeared to identify Alfred Trenkler or Thomas A. Shay from a photo array, Government Exhibit 34, as a customer who had come to that store 2-3 times in the fall of 1991. (TS 15-49) However, it was never clearly stated by Dwayne Armbrister who the person was at Photo No. 2 in the array. Previously, Special Agent Dennis Leahy almost said who the person was whom Armbrister identified, but he was interrupted by an objection and the issue was apparently dropped. (TS 14-95)

Paul Kelly tried to exclude the other ways that Armbrister might have been already familiar with Tom Shay and asked "*Mr. Armbrister, are you gay, sir? Pardon the personal nature of the question, but are you gay?*" (TS 15-55) As shown elsewhere, Paul Kelly seemed to be assuming that all gay men in Boston knew each other, and that they had certain common characteristics, that were relevant to the case at hand. However, no one asked if Armbrister might have seen Shay in the company of another employee of the store, George Nightingale, whose roommate, Ed Carrion, was a friend of Tom Shay's.

Paul Kelly and Frank Libby asked the same question of most of Shay's acquaintances, but not Russ Bonanno, perhaps because he provided material assistance to the prosecution by taping a Shay phone call. No one who was asked the question answered "*No*" and no heterosexuals were asked that question and no heterosexuals were asked if they were heterosexual.

From Seattle to testify came Frederick M. Burke, who lived in San Francisco when Tom Shay was there from January through March, 1992. Burke described how he first met Tom Shay, who had introduced himself as James Keough, "*... I was walking down Castro Street and got to a section of the street where panhandlers often sit, and there was a young man with a large poster board sign with black lettering on it, about 20 lines worth of lettering. And the sign said that his boyfriend had been killed by gay bashers in Boston, that he had gone on television and had talked about it, and in fact, led to him being ostracized by his family, that he had been kicked out of the military for being gay, and that he was in San Francisco to start over...*" (TS 15-59)

Burke took an interest in "*Keough*" and allowed him to store his personal belongings at his apartment, and they had several conversations. Shay used the name of his sister's boyfriend, James Keough, because Shay had taken Keough's I.D. from Quincy. The name of Trenkler had come up in those conversations and Burke asked Shay if he thought that Trenkler had anything to do with the Roslindale Bomb. Burke testified, "*He said, 'I don't know,' very sadly, very resolutely, very quietly.*" (TS 15-67) Burke had a sense that Shay was afraid of Alfred Trenkler, saying, "*I got the impression that he was fearful of this Al Trenkler person.*" (TS 15-67) The statement was admitted not for its truth, which would have violated the hearsay rule, but as an example of Shay's state-of-mind or conduct. Admitted, however, it was. One problem, not caught by the defense, was that the timing of that conversation was wrong. Tom Shay had never mentioned Alfred Trenkler's possible role in the Roslindale Bomb to anyone until the police told him of **their** connecting the two men to the Roslindale Bomb during the interviews in the San Francisco jail. The statements that Burke recalled probably came during his phone calls with Shay after the police interviews.

Nancy Gertner sought to explore with Burke Tom Shay's claim to him that he had appeared on the "Oprah Winfrey" TV show. Paul Kelly objected because of the hearsay rule and the court sustained the objection, saying, "*Mr. Kelly is right. The fact that he talks about Oprah Winfrey without evidence that* [it] *is untrue, you can't make the argument.*" Gertner protested that, "*It isn't offered for the truth,*" and that it was offered for the same reason as Shay's previously admitted statements to Larry Plant about being able to acquire tanks and planes. The difference for Judge Zobel was that "*It's relevant that he said it, unless it is obviously not true, Oprah Winfrey, unless we have evidence that he was or wasn't on Oprah Winfrey.... That's so obvious. I mean, that one the jury can deduce on its own* [that Shay's purchasing] *tanks and fighter planes* [would be absurd]. *Oprah Winfrey is a different story. Lots of people are on Oprah Winfrey.*" (TS 15-79] Because Nancy Gertner was not able at that time to provide proof that Tom Shay was never on the "Oprah Winfrey" show, such as with a witness from the program, she was not able to tell the jury about yet another fanciful story by Thomas A. Shay. Discovering the truth in a criminal trial is a time-defined process. If facts were not available during the approximately 60 hours of trial, then the facts would not be known to the jury, and the jurors were going to make their decision without waiting for additional facts.

Gertner continued with the line of questioning to Fred Burke.
Q "*Sometimes he would say one thing and sometimes another?*"
A "*Yes.*"
Q "*Sometimes in the same sentence, he would contradict himself?*"
A "*In the same half-hour.*"
Q "*Same half-hour. And it's fair to say that that was about everything?*"
A "*Everything.*"
Q "*Details of his life, his identity, everything?*"
A "*Everything.*" (TS 15-87)

For example, Burke said that Shay told him that his father did not have any gambling debts, and then about two days later that he did.

After Shay was arrested, he called Fred Burke and asked him to distribute a press release. Burke didn't want to come to the police station, so he had Shay dictate it to him and then he faxed it to various media outlets. The press release was admitted as Defendant's Exhibit 10 for identification only, which meant that Nancy Gertner could not fully explore its contents with Burke as it, too, would violate the hearsay rule. While it might be used later for appellate or other purposes, the jury was not permitted to see it. The release read,

"*25 March 1992*
FOR IMMEDIATE RELEASE
TO: San Francisco News Editors
FROM: Thomas A. Shay, 20 years old
        case #1363174
        San Francisco County Jail

I, Thomas A. Shay, the son of Thomas L. Shay, of 39 East Warren [sic] Street, Roslindale, Massachusetts am being held at the San Francisco County Jail at bail of over $5 million cash for a crime I did not commit. My story: On October 28, 1990 [sic], a phone call was made to the Back Bay Station, an Orange Line station in Boston, and a bomb threat was made. At that time I had just entered the station. I was arrested and let go five hours later, having not been charged with the bomb threat they were talking to me about.

On October 29, [sic] 1991, my father, Thomas L. Shay, drove up his driveway and felt a scrape under his car. Once parked, he went in back of his car to see what the scrape was. He found a wrapped box of some kind and threw it to the side, thinking it was just a piece of trash. In the morning, he went to throw the package away, and he looked at it carefully. Deciding that it was wrapped in this certain way for a reason, he decided to call the police. When they did not arrive within the half hour, he borrowed a neighbor's car, drove it to the Boston police station in Roslindale, and asked officer Jeremiah Hurley and officer Francis X. Foley of the bomb squad to join him in going back to his house and looking at a package that he was suspicious about. On the way, he explained to the officers that he had moved the package three times between 8:00 p.m. on the 29th [sic] and 10:00 a.m. on the 30th [sic].

Once the officers got there, they directed my father into the house so that they could go down and look at the package. A third officer arrived at the scene and was directed into the house by one of the officers. The third officer and my father were inside, when they heard an explosion outside the house. Hurley and Foley were going to touch the device and it blew up in their faces. The two officers were not wearing protective gear. That night, the Alcohol, Tobacco and Firearms division, the Boston Police Department, the bomb squad, the Federal Bureau of Investigation, and the Central Intelligence Agency came. Forty Federal investigators came from Washington, D.C. because they discovered that the bomb was so technically advanced that they wanted to investigate further. They went through the grass around the house with magnifying glasses.

I had heard what happened and called a press conference to clear my father's name of involvement with putting a bomb under his car. I told the newspeople that my family wanted to clear my father's name, that he had no involvement in any gambling or drugs, and that either a sicko put the bomb under the car or someone put it there at random. Certain things were printed in the newspaper about me - about my being gay, about my being on a local television show to talk about being gay. The federal investigators took my Boston address book and called up all my friends; parents and told them that their son or daughter might be gay. Two or three of my friends got kicked out of their houses because of this.

At this time, my father had a lawsuit with Deadham [sic] Service Center at 106 Washington Street in Deadham [sic] Massachusetts. I was also involved in the case at the Deadham [sic] Service Center as a witness to another explosion that had happened in which one of the workers threw a quarter stick of dynamite into a fifty gallon drum of thinner. The explosion made my father lose his hearing.

I was told to leave the city by Boston officials because my name is the same name as my father's. I left the city as I was told and went to a friend's house for the weekend. At the end of the weekend I came back and found that some other things had happened. Officer Hurley was dead. I went to the Boston Homicide division to *talk to the officers and was grilled for over fifty minutes by the officers, who said that I had something to do with it. Then I was let go and went home, where I was arrested for the bomb threat of 1990. I did six months in the county jail and was let go on probation.*

When the probation was over, I decided I didn't want to be in the city anymore and travelled [sic] to San Francisco about two months ago. I was trying to start a new life, beginning my own massage business and getting my life together. I had written a friend a postcard and forty federal investigators were sent to look for me. On the 23rd of this month I was arrested by two federal investigators and assaulted by one during questioning.

When I got to the San Francisco County Jail, I was told that I had a choice to either waive my rights and return to Boston or resist going back. Once I resisted, Governor Wells [sic, William Weld was the governor of Massachusetts at the time.] of Massachusetts was given ninety days to submit a warrant to Pete Wilson [governor of California] to extradite me back to Boston. The Federal officers told me that one of my friends, Al Trenkler of Boston, who builds satellites, was a suspect in building the bomb. I feel this is not true, and I know this is not true. They're only doing this because I made a big stink back in Boston and told the news that the Boston Police didn't know what they were doing because they weren't wearing protective gear to look at the device.

The truth of it is that they can't find the person who built the device and put it under my father's car, so they're trying to mess with me. Please help me from being extradited from San Francisco to Boston, because when I was in Boston I was treated unlawfully and beaten up. I am innocent and I am being held here against my will. The Federal investigators are refusing to give me a lie detector or polygraph test. As I sit here in this jail, I get depressed more and more each day. If there are any good lawyers out there or anybody that that you think can help me, please come visit. Positive ID is required to get in to the jail. I am here at the San Francisco County Jail under the name of Thomas A. Shay, case #1363174.

Dictated by telephone to Fred Burke, (415) 864-2978."

Nancy Gertner asked Fred Burke, "*You asked him if he had anything to do with the bombing, and he said no?*" and Burke said, "*Yes.*" Then she asked about Shay's fears,

Q "*At one point he told you, too, that he was afraid someone was going to kill him in the prison?*"
A "*Yes.*"
Q "*And he said it was some kind of Mafia thing?*"
A "*Yes.*" (TS 15-90/91) No one at the trial compared that fear to Burke's earlier recollection that Tom Shay seemed fearful of Al Trenkler.

Burke said that he had about 6-7 phone conversations with Tom Shay and Shay seemed to imply in one, the conversation dictating the press release, that Alfred Trenkler was involved in the Roslindale Bomb, even though the press release said othewise. "*In the second conversation, when I asked him outright: was Mr. Trenkler involved in the bombing, Al Trenkler? He said: 'I don't know.'*" (TS 15-93)

Special Agent Jeff Kerr was next for the prosecution and his testimony was brief. Like Dennis Leahy, he explained that the investigation shifted focus after the first few days, but that they implemented a mail cover on several people, in addition to Trenkler, such as Thomas L. Shay, Mary Flanagan and Louis Giammarco.

With a *"mail cover,"* law enforcement agencies ask the post office to record the origins of mail sent to designated individuals, which can be done without a search warrant. Also, there were electronic devices placed on various phones. On cross examination, Nancy Gertner continued to try to show that the investigation focused too soon on Alfred Trenkler and Thomas A. Shay, and missed the more likely suspects. While the investigation did change its focus because of Tom Shay's address book and the 1986 incident in Quincy, Shay's statements and flight must have seemed to confirm the wisdom of that change. What the defense team needed to do was present evidence pointing to the involvement of others.

The next prosecution witness was Thomas L. Shay's attorney in the civil suit against the Dedham Service Center, until September 1991, Alan Pransky of Needham, Mass. He withdrew in September because he believed that he had become a witness to the perceived lies by one of the defendants, Jeffery Berry. Withdrawal was required by a provision of the ethics rules which govern lawyers. The new lawyer, Jay Flynn, agreed to split with Pransky the contingency fee for any sum which might be awarded to Mr. Thomas L. Shay from the Dedham Service Center case.

Alan Pransky first met Thomas A. Shay, the son, in March 1990 and met him again only when driving him to the 13 September 1991 deposition. Under direct examination by Frank Libby, Pransky said that Shay asked him who would *"own the lawsuit"* if his father were killed and Pransky said that it would continue, and the proceeds, if any, would go to his father's estate. They discussed the possible value of the suit as $300,000 which would be shared by his heirs by will or by his family and children if there was no will. (TS 15-125)

Even though no longer the attorney for the civil suit, Pransky continued to act as Thomas L. Shay's lawyer in other matters, and he came to 39 Eastbourne Street on the day of the bombing to assist Mr. Shay and the investigation in any way he could. As it appeared to him that the Dedham Service Center lawsuit might be relevant, he brought his files on the case with him to show to the police.

The next visit to the Shay-Flanagan home was requested by Mr. Shay on the night of 31 October, and Pransky arrived around midnight. There were three detectives at the home and then there was a phone call from Thomas A. Shay for about three minutes. Pransky testified that Mr. Shay *"...said that he loved his son, that he would stand by him, and that he wanted his son to do what was right."* (TS 15-136) Pransky left the house about 2:30 a.m., and then went to the Boston Police Station, where he told the police about his conversation on 13 September with Thomas A. Shay about his father's civil lawsuit,

As the trial had moved quickly through the last several witnesses, Nancy Gertner was not prepared to cross-examine as she had left her relevant files at the office, so it was agreed that the cross-examination of Alan Pransky would begin the next day, on Day 16.

A major question of evidence was whether to admit evidence of the 1986 explosion by Alfred Trenkler in Quincy of a military Hoffman Artillery Simulator, and statistical evidence and expert testimony about the similarity between that device and the 1991 Roslindale Bomb. The court held a *voir dire* inquiry with

Steven Scheid who operated the ATF computerized database called the "*Explosive Incident System*" or EXIS. The total size of the database was not given, but about 4,000 incidents were added every year.

Scheid explained his queries to the EXIS database, with the first being the time period from 1 January 1979 to 31 December 1991, which produced 40,867 incidents. Of those, he asked the computer for "*bombings or attempted bombings*" and the number dropped to 14,252,

Next for "*target: cars and trucks*" - 2,504,

Next for "*under vehicle*" - 428,

Next for "*remote control*" - 19, and finally

Next for "*magnets*" - 7. (TS 15-143)

One of the seven was the 1991 Roslindale Bomb and another was Trenkler's 1986 Hoffman Artillery Simulator. The other five were known as "North Ridge," "Campbell," "Philadelphia," "Coral Gables" and "New York City."

Cross-examined by Amy Baron-Evans of the defense team,[17] Scheid acknowledged that the 1986 device was not entered into the EXIS database until after the 1991 Roslindale Bomb, and it was entered by those who already knew they were searching for similarities - and wanted to find them among the two Massachusetts explosions. Hence the data was suspected of being biased toward similarity. Amy Baron-Evans also established that the absence of the Quincy explosion from the EXIS database meant that there were a lot of other local events which were also not entered into the system. She noted that if Scheid had asked the EXIS database for those explosions caused by dynamite, the Quincy device would not have appeared. Similarly, if "Futaba" or "superglue" or "Tyco" had been asked, the 1991 Roslindale and the 1986 Quincy devices would not have appeared together in the same report.

Thus, the jury heard that a computer had decided that the bombs were similar, but only because of the way queries had been put to the computer. Alfred Trenkler believes in 2007 that this use and the use in his own trial, were the only times that the EXIS database had been used in any trial, before or since, to show similarity between bombing incidents in order to show "signature".

Next to testify was Thomas Waskom, who had testified earlier about the 1991 Roslindale Bomb. He stated that on the basis of reports he had read, the 1986 Hoffman Artillery simulator had a built-in detonator, and thus no blasting caps, and inside was an ounce and a half of photo flash powder, a high explosive. An ATF manual describes flash powder as a "Class B" fireworks. Flash powder was also used by photographers for instant light before the advent of flashbulbs and their electronic successors.

The 1986 device had two 6-volt size "J" Duracell batteries and both devices used AA batteries. Waskom said that a toggle switch was used in both devices, but that the switch in the Quincy device was a safety switch and in the Roslindale Bomb it was a firing switch. He said that a light bulb was used in the 1986 device, from a statement by Alfred Trenkler and that a light bulb could have been used for a test of the 1991 Roslindale Bomb, but that it wasn't built into it.

Thomas Waskom concluded, "...*it is my opinion that the same person built both devices.*" (TS 15-194)

Cross-examined by Nancy Gertner, Waskom conceded that there was no plywood in the 1986 device and no superglue either and the use of the duct tape was different; and that the use of the toggle switches were different. He agreed that in 1986 there was one larger magnet and in 1991 approximately 14 of smaller size. Finally, he agreed that the configuration of the 1991 device was all explained in the "*how to*" IED Manual by the United States government, and already entered into evidence as Exhibit 47. (TS 15-201)

The defense then called its own witness, Donald Hansen, who noted that the 1986 device was haphazard compared to the sophistication of the 1991 bomb. For example, there was little soldering in 1986 and a lot in 1991. Hansen concluded there were not enough similarities to conclude that they had the same signature, i.e. that they were not made by the same person.

The court adjourned at 1:00 p.m.

Next day's headlines:

Boston Globe: "WITNESS SAYS SHAY QUERIED HIM ON WILL, PROCEEDS OF LAWSUIT" by Sean P. Murphy

Boston Herald: "KEY RULING EXPECTED IN HUB BOMB CASE" by Ralph Ranalli

The New Yorker: "A CASE NOT CLOSED" by Seymour Hersh [published on 1 November 1993, but relating to the signature question in the Shay Trial.] This article compares the inadequate government intelligence about the Mideast to the attempt by the U.S. Attorney in the "Roslindale Bomb" case to show that the 1986 M-21 Artillery Simulator and the "Roslindale Bomb" had the same "signature" and thus were made by the same person. Hersh was skeptical about both claims.

"....*This happened on July 19th, when the signature issue was the focus of a hearing held, with the jury excluded, in the United States District Court trial, in Boston, of Thomas A. Shay, who was accused of conspiring in 1991 to plant a car bomb in an attempt to kill his father; a Boston policeman had been killed while attempting to defuse the device. Shay's co-defendant, Alfred W. Trenkler, had been charged with unlawful possession of an explosive connected with a bombing in 1986. A federal bomb expert from the Treasury Department's Bureau of Alcohol, Tobacco and Firearms testified that he had been able to match the signature of the bomb that Shay was alleged to have planted to the 1986 bomb that Trenkler was alleged to have built. A second A.T.F. witness claimed that a computer analysis of more than fourteen thousand bomb incidents had further established the link between the 1986 and 1991 devices. The defense witness for Shay was Donald Hansen, the former San Francisco bomb-squad officer, and he repeatedly made the point that the A.T.F. forensic experts had emphasized only the similarities between the two devices, ignoring the many differences. Hansen told the court that there were only generic similarities between the two bombs—that his examination found 'no particular method of twisting wires or no real distinct technique employed.'*

In a bench ruling the next morning, Judge Rya W. Zobel said that the government could not put forward any testimony in an attempt to link the 1986 and 1991 bombings. The two devices were similar, 'without question, but I am not persuaded that they are identical,' Judge Zobel concluded. 'That

is, I do not think, and find, that it is not so unusual and distinctive as to be like a signature.'

When I spoke with Nancy Gertner, Shay's attorney, this summer, she recalled that before the judge's ruling there had repeatedly been newspaper stories citing federal officials as saying 'that these were signature bombs.' She added, 'It's very, very frightening that foreign policy is being made on this.' "

28 29 30 1 2	6 7 8 9	12 13 14 15 16	19 20 21 22 23	26 27
X X X X X	X X X X	X X X X X	X X O O O	O O

Day 16: Tuesday, 20 July

Judge Zobel began the day with two rulings, beginning with the 1986 device, where she had to balance the claimed relevance of the 1986 device to the anticipated unfair prejudice to Thomas A. Shay if were introduced. She found that the 1986 was relevant, but as it would be highly and unfairly prejudicial; she forbade evidence of the 1986 device, and hence the EXIS information, as well, to be used as evidence.

Then, as if to balance the decisions for the day, against and for the Government, she ruled against the defense's motion to bring an expert witness, Dr. Robert Phillips, to testify about Shay's lying. Nancy Gertner had presented Dr. Phillips' diagnosis which he communicated to her in a 19 July 1993 letter in which he said that he had personally interviewed Tom Shay on two occasions in April and May for a total of 11 hours and that he had reviewed a total of 62 separate documents including psychological interviews of Shay and his family members.

Dr. Phillips stated that it was his opinion that:

"1. Thomas A. Shay Jr., is a young adult of low average to subaverage intellectual functioning who possesses concurrent deficits in adaptive functioning that render him less effective in meeting the standards expected for his age range in such areas a social skills and responsibilities, daily living skills, personal independence and self-sufficiency.

2. Further, it is my professional medical opinion that Thomas A. Shay, Jr., has identifiable deficits in intellectual functioning consistent with those individuals who are diagnosed as having a learning disability.

3. Supportive clinical evidence exists that Mr. Shay exhibits certain personality traits that are inflexible and maladaptive and cause significant functional impairment and subjective distress that appear to rise to a level of a diagnosable personality disorder. The manifestation of Mr. Shay's personality disorder historically is recognizable in early childhood and has continued to manifest itself throughout his adolescence and early adult life.

4. Additionally, it is my professional medical opinion, within a reasonable degree of medical certainty, that Mr. Thomas A. Shay, Jr., has in the past, and episodically at present continues to suffer from generalized symptoms of anxiety and depression that appear to be situational in nature and attributable more so to his inherent maladaptive ability to cope with such circumstance as a result of his personality organization rather than the inherent nature of the circumstance itself.

Psychodynamic Formulation:

It is my professional medical judgment, based on the aforementioned clinical findings, Thomas A. Shay Jr. is a dysfunctional individual whose dysfunction is in large part attributable to a longstanding underlying personality disorder which has contributed substantively to his psychic dysphoria and feelings of personal inadequacy. Mr. Shay's longstanding behavioral and emotional problems beginning in early childhood and continuing at present are pervasive and contributory to his developmental maladjustment which has caused him both unfortunate emotional and sociological sequelae.

I am also of the opinion within a reasonable degree of medical certainty, that Mr. Shay harbors several unresolved conflicts central to the issues of his ineffective parenting by mother and father and protracted institutionalization as a young child and adolescent. Because of his personality organization, Mr. Shay is incapable of moving forward in an effective fashion that would integrate his inner feelings with the reality of his external world. The failure to successfully integrate such process and come away with the satisfaction of having either succeeded or minimally putting forth one's best effort is one of the fundamental building blocks of an integrally solid self-esteem. Mr. Shay is clearly at a deficit in this area of personality structure in large measure because of his inherent characterological organization, the traits which are unique to his personality, and the maladaptive behavioral patterns through which these egodystonic experinces are grounded.

A significant symptom of all of the above is an uncontrollable urge to spin out webs of lies which are ordinarily self-aggrandizing and serve to place him in the center of attention. Put otherwise, coping for Mr. Shay, given his personality structure, entails seeking attention, tailoring his words to the audience, creating fantasies in which he is the central figure and through which he attempts to enlist his audience -- this is known as <u>pseudologia fantastica</u>. <u>See</u> attached bibliography. Mr. Shay's stories are an attempt to draw others into his fantasy world in order to meet the interpersonal needs which were not met during his childhood.

Finally, it should be noted that Mr. Shay has a genetic chromosomal disorder, seminiferous tubular dysgenesis, resulting in his having 47 rather than 46 chromosomes. Persons who suffer from this genetic abnormality are known to be at risk of exhibiting various degrees of mental deficiencies. Talkativeness with little substance to the content of speech is an outstanding behavioral trait of those individuals who suffer from this genetic disease. Clearly, this medical condition only further exacerbates if not etiologically explains the character pathology we see in this individual.

Diagnoses:

 Axis I - *Identity Disorder*
    Rule out Bipolar Disorder: not otherwise specified.
 Axis II - *Personality disorder not otherwise specified with dependent,*
    narcissistic, immature and self-defeating features.
    Factitious Disorder - Pseudologia fantastica.
    Rule out Borderline personality disorder.
 Axis III - *Klinefelter's syndrome (seminiferous tubular dysgenesis.)*
 Axis IV - *Psychosocial stressors: extreme family discord, history of parental*
    abuse and neglect, severe characterologic dysfunction.
 Axis V - *Global Current Assessment of Functioning - significantly impaired*
    due to life circumstances and diagnoses described herein.

<u>*Conclusion:*</u>

At present, I am of the opinion, within a reasonable degree of medical certainty, that the nature and scope of Mr. Thomas A. Shay Jr.'s symptoms of mental distress, the effect on Mr. Shay of his mental distress, and the factors substantially contributing to his mental distress are the result of outstanding characterologic emotional dysfunction, the etiology of which is causally related to Mr. Shay's developmental history, inherent psychopathology, and medical condition. A central symptom of Mr. Shay's underlying condition is the uncontrollable urge to spin out webs of lies in an attempt to draw others into his fantasy world and place him in the center of attention."

Judge Zobel denied the motion to present Dr. Phillips as an expert witness and said, *"With respect to the psychiatric expert offered by the defendant, as I understand that, it is offered to show that the defendant has an uncontrollable need to draw attention to himself and will say anything to satisfy his need, and in particular, it is offered to explain away his inculpatory statement. Under [Rule] 702 expert evidence is admissible to assist the jury to understand evidence or to determine a fact in issue. The record in this case is replete with the defendant's contradictory statements, indeed, his fantastic ones about tanks and bombers, and other things. Under these circumstances, the jury does not need expert evidence on the issue of the defendant's credibility. And there is, with respect to this evidence, the additional danger that the expert will go beyond the brief references to -- I think it's called -- pseudologia fantastica in the areas that are in fact inadmissible such as diminished capacity, personality, deficit, and so on. The quintessential question is whether the jury will believe what the defendant says, and on that question, given this record, the jury does not need any additional expert evidence or any expert evidence. Accordingly, I will rule out the defendant's proffer on that issue, and your objection is noted as is the government's* [to the judge's exclusion of evidence regarding the 1986 device]." (TS 16-4)

Then the jury returned and Nancy Gertner resumed the cross-examination of Alan Pransky. Generally, she established that the defendants in Thomas L. Shay's lawsuit were claiming that Shay was faking his injuries, and the pace of the defendants' evidentiary discovery was quickening in the fall of 1991.

After a long bench conference to consider whether Pransky would be required to testify about his fee arrangement with Thomas L. Shay, or whether it was confidential through attorney-client privilege, he was required to testify. The fee was a contingency agreement, for 33 1/3%. Gertner tried to show that Pransky thus had a financial interest in the case and the more it looked like Jeffery Berry and Louis Giammarco of the Dedham Service Center were responsible for the 1991 Roslindale Bomb, the more likely he would get his fee. She argued, through questions, that that was the reason why Pransky didn't tell the police quickly about his allegedly incriminating 13 September conversation with Thomas A. Shay, about the implications of his father's death to the distribution of money from the civil lawsuit. By Gertner's theory, Pransky had waited until three days after the explosion to tell the police about the conversation because that would shift suspicion away from Berry and toward Tom Shay. Alan Pransky disagreed that the eventual allocation of responsibility for the 1991 bomb would have had any such effect.

Then the jury was shown selected excerpts of the October 1992 Channel 56 interview by Karen Marinella of Thomas A. Shay. The excerpts were not transcribed within the court record, but Paul Kelly did tell the jury, in his opening statement of one section of the interview beginning with a statement by Tom Shay, "*I must have gone to between 25 and 50 stores with him and purchased all kinds of stuff. There's only two things that I purchased that were inside that explosive device that killed Officer Hurley.*"

Marinella: "*What were those two things?*"

Shay: "*The toggle switch and the double A battery holder. The Radio Shack clerk on Mass. Ave recognized me, and I don't know why he recognized me, but Al had me go in there and purchase these things. He said, Go across the street, he gave me a list. I went in there and bought the stuff.*" [TS 4-20]

There were no comments or arguments by the lawyers before or after the showing of the tape. Thus, the jury was left to understand that what Thomas A. Shay said on the tape was true - unless it had been contradicted by other evidence in the trial. The jury did not know, therefore, that most of what he said about Alfred W. Trenkler was false. Tom Shay had not gone to a single store, not one, with Alfred Trenkler. The jury did not know that Paul Kelly, among others, knew that several statements were false because they were about Tom Shay's conversations with him. Also, Paul Kelly knew that many other statements were false, such as the allegation about the "*surprise*" from Trenkler to Shay. He knew that there was no evidence that the items purchased by "S A H Y" were actually in the Roslindale Bomb.

The last scheduled prosecution witness was Francis X. Foley, father of four children and the wounded partner of the deceased bomb squad officer, Jeremiah Hurley, of whom he spoke warmly and movingly. Foley described the bomb "*... it looked like it was a black box, and what I thought was electrical tape, rolls of electrical tape around the --on top of the box, and it appeared just like a solid piece of wood, actually and with electrical tape on it.*" (TS 16-83). Foley moved the object out from underneath the GTO. He said that he and Hurley were not too concerned about the object, still not knowing what it was, because Thomas L. Shay had told them that he had found it the previous day and that he had moved it a couple of times.

When he moved it, "*.. I knew at that point it wasn't electrical tape because of the weight. It was kind of heavy and lopsided. There was a box or something connected to the underside.... and it had been spray painted.*" (TS 16-84)

Foley testified that he left the object with Hurley and turned to take the other people down to the sidewalk to talk with them. It was about five minutes. Looked at the divot in the grass where the box had fallen off the car. Shay was upset and excited. Then Foley went back to Hurley to ask about next steps.

Foley said, "*Gerry said something to the point that it had a switch -- and at that time I knelt down approximately four feet away and I was putting on my glasses and I thought I observed was a Servo. I said, Gerry, is that a Servo.*"

Paul Kelly then asked, "*What happened then?*"

Responded Francis X. Foley, "*As I said it, I saw the arm moving... Yes, I saw it move and there was a detonation.*" (TS 16-88) He could see the Servo through a small crack in the box.

Foley then described the devastation of the blast and his and Jeremiah Hurley's injuries.

Nancy Gertner did not cross-examine and the trial adjourned at 12:30 p.m.

Officer Foley's testimony at the end of the prosecution's case was a dramatic stunt, and Judge Zobel should have prohibited such timing, if she had known about it in advance. Nancy Gertner didn't object to the timing, so maybe such theatrics are part of the legal game.

What Francis Foley said about the bomb would have been useful at the beginning of the trial, especially the testimony about seeing the Servo move. By the end of the trial, the jury had already been told at least once how the device worked. Also, he could have been asked by the defense about the condition of the box. How was it damaged, if at all? And was that damage due to the scraping from the underside of Mr. Thomas L. Shay's car and against Mr. Shay's driveway? Officer Foley had said that he had seen the Servo through a crack on the box, but was that a crack built into the device or was it the result of the collision with the driveway's concrete or from being tossed to the ground by Mr. Thomas L. Shay? Did Mr. Foley agree that there were two wires sticking out of the box as Mr. Shay had told Officers Corbett and Maloney?

Instead, Foley's testimony was offered for the sole reason of playing to the emotions of the members of the jury. If his testimony had been useful for facts about the case, he would have testified before the grand jury, but he did not. Because of Foley's knowledge of what happened on 28 October 1991, Jefferson Boone had predicted before the trial that Foley would be the prosecution's first witness.

Nancy Gertner understood that there was nothing new in his testimony and that a cross-examination might be interpreted as a blame-the-victim tactic; so she asked nothing. Francis Foley might as well have taken the stand and said to the jury, "*Please convict the defendant for the sake of Jerry Hurley and Frank Foley. We agree with our brothers in uniform that Tom Shay is partly responsible for this deadly bomb.*"

The trial adjourned at 1:00 p.m.

Next day's headlines:

Boston Globe: "OFFICER AT BOMBING TRIAL TELLS OF PARTNER'S DEATH" by
   Sean P. Murphy

Boston Herald 1: "SURVIVOR TESTIFIES IN SHAY TRIAL" from the Associated Press

Boston Herald 2: "SUSPECT FINGERS FRIEND IN VIDEOTAPE - CLAIMS BOMB WAS
   'SURPRISE' " by Ralph Ranalli He reported, "*After the trial broke for the day,
   however, Shay's attorney continued to insist that none of Shay's statements
   are trustworthy. She also continued to pursue her allegations that it was
   Shay's father, Thomas Sr., who built and planted the bomb.*"

Patriot Ledger: "INJURED OFFICER TESTIFIES AT SHAY TRIAL" by Nelson
   Wang, Associated Press (same article as in *Boston Herald*)

28 29 30 1 2	6 7 8 9	12 13 14 15 16	19 20 21 22 23	26 27
X X X X	X X X X	X X X X X	X X X O O	O O

Day 17: Wednesday, 21 July

This was the day the defense began its case, but, as usual, there were some preliminary matters. The Channel 56 tape was admitted into evidence as Government Exhibit 46 and the prosecution and defense joined in a stipulation about what was reported in the newspapers about the 1991 Roslindale Bomb. The gain for the defense was that it showed that some of the statements by Tom Shay about the bomb could have been based not on his own knowledge as the Roslindale Bomber, but as a reader of the Boston newspapers - and read them he did. His mother and Russ Bonanno had previously testified that Tom Shay kept whatever clippings and TV news videos he could about the Roslindale Bomb. The stipulations were read to the jury:

"Facts: One, the indictment in this case was returned by a Federal grand jury on December 16, 1992.

Two, on or about Wednesday, October 30th, 1991, the <u>Boston Herald</u> reported that Thomas Shay, Jr. had stated on the previous day, October 29th, 1991, that the Boston Police had 'drilled [sic] him for 90 minutes and during this interview had asked if his father could build a remote control,' the paper further reported quoting Shay, Jr., that Shay, Jr. responded to the police 'no, definitely, he doesn't have the technique to do it.' The paper further reported that during this interview, according to Shay, Jr., 'Investigators told him the bomb was made of C 4, a classic [sic, plastic] explosive.'

No. 3. On October 30, 1991, the <u>Boston Globe</u> reported that Thomas Shay, Jr. told reporters that 'police were trying to determine whether Shay, Sr. was capable of constructing an explosive device himself.' On October 31st, 1991, the <u>Boston Herald</u> reported that investigators at the scene now believed that the detonation was triggered by a 'remote control mechanism.' So agreed and stipulated." (TS 17-17)

The prosecution's actual final witness was Boston Police Detective Frank Armstrong, who appeared in court with the sole purpose of bringing into evidence a personal effects bag which he said was Thomas L. Shay's bag, which he had recently retrieved, in July 1993, from Mr. Shay's home, i.e. during the trial. The bag was allegedly used by Mr. Thomas L. Shay in 1991. As Frank Armstrong had been present in the courtroom during the trial, it was irregular to leave a courtroom and retrieve an item for the same trial. Nancy Gertner objected on a chain-of-custody issue. That is, as the trial was almost two years after the explosion, how could anyone know that this was the same bag which may have been in Mr. Shay's hands when he exited Ruth Leary's Mazda upon returning from the police station on 28 October 1991? Other questions might have been asked about the contents of the bag and why Mr. Shay would need them when he was living at home and not staying overnight anywhere else.

There were no questions about whether Detective Armstrong had attempted to retrieve the cardboard toolbox that Thomas L. Shay had claimed he also was carrying upon his return from the police station.

Judge Zobel allowed the exhibit as she wanted the trial to move along, but she did take the time to explain to the jury one of the problems with this witness's testimony, *"Members of the jury you will recall -- did I explain to you about sequestered witnesses, perhaps I did not -- in most trials, I ask witnesses who are going to testify to wait outside, not to be in the courtroom while other witnesses testify. And the reason is that when a person hears somebody else talking about the events about which that person is then going to tell us later on, it tends to change or affect, in some way, what it is that they're going to tell us, the person is going to tell us. So in order to keep the memory and the recall of the witnesses pure, if you will, we ask them to wait outside so they shouldn't hear what other people say, and thus perhaps they have their recall affected in some way. This witness apparently was in the courtroom, when other witnesses testified. And I think that we're going to meet this issue again with some witnesses coming later on so we will deal with [it] at this moment by cross-examining the witness about what the witness may have heard."* (TS 17-21/2)

The prosecution's case had ended. Of the 43 prospective government witnesses that AUSA's Paul Kelly and Frank Libby had advised Nancy Gertner could testify, more than half, or 26, did not testify for the prosecution. They included: John Doering, Mary Flanagan, Louis Giammarco, Michael Greene, Dan Goldrick, James Keough, Allan Kingsbury, Todd Leach (because the 1986 device was not permitted to be considered by the jury), Mark Means, Eleanor McKernan, Kevin Norris, Paul Nutting, Ralph Pace, James Quinlan, Paula Shay, Donna Shea (because the 1986 device was not permitted to be considered by the jury), and Randy Stoller. The jury did not know about the left-out 17, or they might have wondered what truth these witnesses could have added to the trial that would have helped the jury make the best possible decision.

Also before the testimony of the first defense witness, Nancy Gertner made a motion for acquittal of Thomas A. Shay for lack of Federal jurisdiction. Judge Zobel denied the motion because there had been testimony that the 1986 Buick had been taken by Thomas L. Shay's auto body repair customers out of state and because the Austin detonators came from New Hampshire.

Judge Zobel said, *"This case raises pure credibility issues."* (TS 17-25)

Josephine Wallace, mother of Alfred Trenkler, was the first defense witness and she testified that Alfred never stayed overnight at the family home in the summer and fall of 1991. He worked in the garage from time to time and came over for a family dinner, but never overnight. On the question of whether Alfred's natural father had abused him, as Tom Shay had alleged in statements already admitted into the trial, Mrs. Wallace said, *"He was an ice skater. He was actually the lead comedian in the Ice Capades, and a very gentle person,*[and] *would never abuse anyone."*(TS 17-32)

The next witness for the defense was John Cates, who had previously testified as a "hostile" witness as required by the prosecution. Now being directly examined by Nancy Gertner, Cates described his and Alfred Trenkler's activities over the weekend of 25-27 October 1991. This was an interesting twist for the trial of one alleged co-conspirator, as Shay's defense found it necessary and useful to try to account for the activities of the non-present co-defendant, Alfred Trenkler, as well as the activities of Tom Shay. Cates said they were home on Friday evening and he went to work on Saturday. Alfred usually picked him up after work. On Saturday night he and Alfred went to dinner at the Dorchester home of a friend, David Millette. They were asked to go to a Halloween party, but didn't go. They were home around 2 a.m. Sunday morning and slept until about 10:30-11:00. Then, as it was Cates' only weekly day off, they did chores such as laundry and shopping.

They spent Sunday evening together, and Alfred Trenkler drove Cates to work on Monday morning the 28th and picked him up at 4:30.

Gertner did not ask when he and Alfred Trenkler learned about the Roslindale Bomb at the home of Tom Shay's father, just as Paul Kelly did not ask that question during his direct examination of the "hostile" witness, John Cates. If she had, Cates would have said, as noted earlier, but the point is important, that he and Alfred had been in a car accident the previous summer and that they were both going to weekly chiropractor appointments on Wednesday afternoons. At their appointment on Wednesday, 30 October they together saw a *Boston Globe* article and commented that the bombing story was about as crazy as was Tom Shay.

Next, Cates was asked about the police search of his apartment on the evening of 5 and 6 November 1991. He heard banging on the door and then six officers came into his small one-room apartment. Cates testified, *"The search wasn't exactly consensual."* (TS 17-51). He described the 31 January search which occurred during the day. His landlord called him at work to tell him about it.

Paul Kelly cross-examined and he was truly hostile as he began, *"Mr. Cates, you are very hostile towards the Unites States of America, are you not, sir, yes or no?"* and Cates answered, *"No not towards the United States of America, at all."* (TS 17-54) The judge should have stopped this personal and irrelevant attack even without an objection by the defense, which didn't come. Later, John Cates acknowledged that he would, if necessary, lie for his friend, Alfred Trenkler, but would not do so under oath.

Roy Kaplan of the "Sound Security" store in West Roxbury testified that he installed Z-locks in cars belonging to Thomas L. Shay and his customers. Z-locks are crime prevention devices which prevent cars from unauthorized use or starting. He testified that Mr. Shay asked about the black wooden box he had found, and Kaplan told Mr. Shay on 28 October 1991 at approximately 11:30 a.m. that no part of the Z-locks is installed underneath the body of a car. Kaplan said that he had to say that twice to Mr. Shay, who *"seemed strange or weird, something strange about him, I don't know if that was that one time or if that's just the way he is, because I don't really know him too well."* [TS 17-80] Frank Libby did not cross-examine.

Scott Critcher worked at the "Store 24" in Quincy from 4:00 p.m. to midnight and testified that he met Thomas A. Shay on the afternoon of Friday 25 October 1991 for the first time. Shay stayed at the store until the end of Critcher's shift and then they walked to Quincy Square and talked and exchanged addresses and went separate ways. Critcher saw him the next evening at Critcher's home where he was hosting a Halloween party, and he estimated that Shay stayed until about midnight. On Sunday evening, 27 October, Tom Shay hung around Critcher's "Store 24" until midnight and they walked to Critcher's home together, and then Shay left.

The next time Scott Critcher saw Tom Shay was on 2 January 1992 when Shay spent the night with him. The next day, they both went to Nancy Shay's condo before Scott went to his job at 6 p.m. The next night, 4/5 January, at 2:00 a.m., Tom Shay called Critcher and then Tom, his mother and David Shilalis all came over to Critcher's and stayed the rest of the night. On the 5th, they went back to Nancy Shay's condo. Scott Critcher hadn't seen Thomas A. Shay since then.

Critcher testified that Tom Shay had told him that he was afraid of going back to jail, which testimony was allowed into evidence as it was for a state-of-mind exception to the hearsay rule. Interestingly, Critcher said that Tom Shay did not mention the Roslindale Bomb during their three days of contact.

Perhaps Paul Kelly felt he was losing his case as he showed increasing hostility to witnesses. To Critcher he said, "*So your memory has a two-hour Kentucky windage[18] factor on it?*" (TS 17-97) Nancy Gertner objected and Judge Zobel agreed it was improper.

Greg Calver was also a cashier, or Customer Services Representative, at "Store 24" in Quincy. On the night of 26-27 October, Saturday, Thomas A. Shay was there beginning at midnight, for about two hours, until 2 a.m. Shay talked with Calver about the party he had been to at Scott Critcher's.

Gary Starkey of Quincy met Tom Shay in Quincy Square in mid-October. They talked for an hour and half and Shay went to Starkey's with him for the night, and left the next day at noon. Starkey saw him again at Scott Critcher's party, on Saturday the 26th from about 11:30 to 12:30 a.m. Sunday. Once again, the Assistant U.S. Attorneys seemed inappropriately interested in the sexual preferences of witnesses, as when Frank Libby asked Gary Starkey on cross-examination, "*And you are, would you please tell us, pardon the private nature of the question, you're openly gay, are you not?*" (TS 17-108) None of the victims of this harassment from the prosecutors objected to the questions and the defense and judge said nothing either.

After Starkey's testimony, Nancy Gertner moved to have the jury sequestered during its deliberations, but Judge Zobel was reluctant to do that because the Federal building was not air-conditioned over the weekend, and apparently she did not believe it was in her power to order that such cooling be maintained. Gertner was concerned about the publicity about the case in the media, which the jury was likely to see or hear. As an example of such news articles not wanted to be seen by the jury, the <u>Boston Herald</u> ran a story about how the judge excluded testimony about the 1986 device; but any reader, including a wayward jury member, could have read it.

Judge Zobel told the jury that the end of testimony would come the next day, Thursday, and then there would be closing arguments and her charge to the jury on Friday. She had not yet decided on sequestration. One jury member was a hairdresser and was concerned that if she couldn't work over the weekend she might lose her job. Trials are human affairs and sometimes the mundane crowds out the pure.

The trial adjourned at 12:10 p.m.

Next day's headlines:

<u>Boston Globe</u>: "STATE RESTS ITS CASE" *by Sean P. Murphy* Excerpts from the article:

"*after presenting evidence that Shay admitted involvement in the 1991 bomb blast... Shay's own admissions during a 32 minute television interview, and a receipt from a Radio Shack store indicating he may have purchased some of the bomb's components 10 days before its detonation, were among the strongest pieces of evidence presented by the prosecution...Gertner has attempted to show that Shay was mentally unstable and willing to say virtually anything to news*

reporters so long as he got the attention he craved. Judge Rya Zobel denied Gertner's request to call a psychiatrist as a witness to testify about Shay's mental condition."
Boston Herald: *"FRIENDS SAY BOMB SUSPECTS BUSY WHEN EXPLOSIVE SET"* by Ralph Ranalli

28 29 30 1 2	6 7 8 9	12 13 14 15 16	19 20 21 22 23	26 27
X X X X X	X X X X	X X X X X	X X X X O	O O

Day 18: Thursday, 22 July

The day began with a long bench conference about the expected testimony of the next witness, Tom Shay's former attorney, William McPhee. The primary question was whether Tom Shay learned about the existence of the Radio Shack receipt from William McPhee or whether he knew about the claim of his purchase of bomb parts at Radio Shack because he actually was the purchaser. McPhee represented Tom Shay from November 1991 until June 1992, and he had received a copy of the 18 October 1991 Radio Shack receipt from Paul Kelly during their plea bargaining negotiations in early May, 1992. McPhee had sent it and the other materials, to his client, Tom Shay, by courier, but was not there physically when he opened the package. Once the outline of McPhee's expected testimony was established, the jury was returned and he began trial testimony.

He described the mailing of the Radio Shack receipt to Shay and said that he had talked with Tom Shay several times thereafter and he was confident that he discussed the receipt with him; which therefore should confirm that Shay had actually received the document and understood what it was. Because of the hearsay rule, McPhee was not permitted to relate to the jury that Tom Shay had explicitly told him that he had not seen that receipt before receiving it from McPhee. Again, if Tom Shay had told McPhee that he HAD seen the receipt before, McPhee could have related Shay's statement verbatim to the jury because it would have been a "statement against penal interest" exception to the hearsay rule. However, because his true statement to McPhee was NOT incriminating, McPhee could not pass it on to the jury.

David Shilalis, the man friend of Nancy Shay, the mother of Tom Shay, was the last defense witness. On Saturday, 26 October, Shilalis and Paula Shay and Tom Shay were at Nancy Shay's condo all day Saturday, and he gave Thomas A. Shay a ride to the Halloween party at Scott Critcher's that night. Then Shilalis and Nancy Shay went to Richard and Amy Lenar's and stayed overnight. Amy was Nancy's daughter. Shilalis and Nancy Shay came back to her condo on Sunday and Tom Shay was there on the couch.

The unemployed David Shilalis said he watched TV on Monday, 28 October, and that Tom Shay was with him all day. They were watching the 6 p.m. news, with Paula Shay, too, when the news report came on the TV about the explosion at 39 Eastbourne and Shilalis testified that Thomas A. Shay was as shocked as everyone else. Then, they went to the MBTA Station to pick up Nancy Shay, who was returning from work.

Under cross-examination by Paul Kelly, Shilalis said that he had moved in with Nancy when she lived in Milton on Belvoir Road. Then they moved to Richmond Street in Dorchester, and then to Falls Boulevard in Quincy.

Under redirect examination Shilalis was asked if he would lie for Thomas A. Shay and he said "*No*," without bothering to make the distinction John Cates had made about lying and lying under oath. There was no re-cross-examination and that was the quiet end of the trial testimony.

David Shilalis's testimony brought Thomas A. Shay's defense to a very low key end compared to the dramatic end of the prosecution's case with the painful testimony of the wounded Francis X. Foley. A more effective end for the defense would have been for Tom Shay to take the stand and testify at length and be cross-examined.

During any criminal trial, a defense lawyer needs to make several important legal strategy decisions, and one of the most important is whether to recommend, or allow, if the defense counsel is a more forceful person, his or her client to testify. When a defendant does make that choice, s/he waives any right during the testimony, especially under cross-examination, to refuse to answer a question on the grounds of self-incrimination. Often, a lawyer recommends that a client not testify because the unsavory information the jury will learn about the defendant will make it more likely for jurors to convict than not.
At least that's the choice for a typical client with a criminal record.

What to do with a client who everyone knows spins stories and seems helplessly awash in lies? What could possibly go wrong for Thomas A. Shay on the stand? That depended on what he was planning to do, and whether he had the mental capacity to follow through with that plan. If he indicated to his attorney that he was prepared to acknowledge his previous lies and explain why he said what he said in every instance; taking the stand would have made sense. The jurors would, of course have asked themselves if he is now telling the truth and the quick prophylactic answer to a pre-emptive posing of the question would be, "*Well, I'm now under oath.*" Everyone lies to some extent when not under oath, so the distinction can make sense.

On the other hand, in the discussion that he surely had with his attorneys, Nancy Gertner and Jefferson Boone, Tom Shay may have not agreed to unravel the mess he'd created for himself, and Alfred Trenkler, and all the law enforcement people and members of the victims' families, who were determined to find the Bomb Maker and accomplices, if any. Even if he did show that awareness in a discussion, how could she be sure of what he would say on the stand? However, if under cross-examination, or even direct examination, Tom Shay was shown to be an exaggerating liar on almost *every* verifiable aspect of his stories; would there be a good chance that jury would see that he could not have had a role in the making of the bomb? Or would the jurors have thought that where there was so much smoke, there must be fire? Enough to cause an explosive verdict?

Between Jefferson Boone and Nancy Gertner, there was disagreement on this vital issue. Boone was mildly supportive of Tom Shay's testimony, but Nancy Gertner was strongly against it, so there would be no testimony.

Tom Shay did testify in his own behalf at a hearing on 12 May 1993 when he sought to suppress statements he had made to the police after the Trailways bus terminal press conference. He said that the police took him involuntarily. Perhaps one attempt at testimony under oath was enough for Gertner, but there was no explicit statement to that effect.

Nancy Gertner might have put Tom Shay on the stand as a "hostile" witness, if that is possible for a defense witness to do with her own client. The primary objective of such testimony would be to discredit the previous apparent admissions, so she would be impeaching the credibility of her own client and that's usually not permitted. The assumption of the court system is that defense lawyers argue that their clients are telling the truth, not lies, unless the client is insane, and Tom Shay was not insane.

The parties agreed to a stipulation which was read to the jury, that James McKernan was unable to identify Alfred Trenkler's car in a photo array of cars shown to him. This saved the court time by avoiding the necessity of having Mr. McKernan return to testify.

The prosecution presented no rebuttal evidence, but there was very little presented by the defense to rebut.

With the jury excused, the lawyers and judge had a "Charge conference" to discuss the upcoming judge's charge to the jury. Judge Zobel decided not to sequester the jury.

The trial adjourned at 11:30 a.m.

Next day's headlines:

Boston Globe: *"LAWYER: SHAY WAS TOLD OF BOMB-CASE EVIDENCE"* by Sean P. Murphy

The article stated that *"McPhee's testimony* [that he gave Tom Shay a copy of the Radio Shack receipt long before the Marinella interview] *may provide an opening for Nancy Gertner, Shay's attorney, to argue that Shay's admissions on Channel 56 were Shay's reckless attempts to explain away the evidence he knew the government was planning to use against him."*

Boston Herald: *"CLOSING ARGUMENTS DUE IN BOMBING TRIAL"* by Ralph Ranalli

"Shay, 21, is charged with conspiring with an alleged lover, Alfred Trenkler, 37, of Quincy, to plant a radio-controlled car bomb underneath his father's car.... The most compelling piece of evidence was a videotape, in which Shay told WLVI-TV/Channel 56 that Trenkler built the bomb for him as a 'surprise' and admitted to buying some of the parts." No unnamed sources told Ralph Ranalli that the U.S. Attorney's office understood that the "surprise" angle was a hoax. Unfortunately, no one from Alfred Trenkler's side told Ralph Ranalli that Tom Shay was never a "lover" of Tom Shay, either.

28 29 30 1 2	6 7 8 9	12 13 14 15 16	19 20 21 22 23	26 27
X X X X	X X X X	X X X X X	X X X X X	O O

Day 19: Friday, 23 July

Paul Kelly began his closing argument by passing to the jury copies of Jeremiah Hurley's death certificate. Neither the document nor the fact of Jeremiah Hurley's death was in dispute during the trial and there was nothing to clarify or explain. He just passed it out for dramatic effect, and the stunt should not have been permitted. It added no facts for the jury to consider. Kelly summarized the construction of the Roslindale Bomb: *"two to three sticks of rewrapped dynamite, placed inside a carefully constructed wooden box, with a double circuitry, appropriate power sources, remote control to send a signal to a receiver, to move the arm on which you heard was called a Servo motor and a Servo arm so that once the signal is sent, it throws the arm which, of course, then flips the toggle switch and causes the detonation of the bomb. The arm and the toggle switch, as you can see, are married together inside the actual device.*" (TS 19-6) In fact, the power sources were NOT "appropriate", but no one objected. It's not appropriate to use 45 volts of power when a mere 1.5 volts will perform the desired task.

Kelly replayed part of the Ch 56 videotape. He said that Armbrister had identified Alfred Trenkler as going into that 197 Mass Ave. Radio Shack store two or three times in the fall of 1991. However, it's not clear that it was ever stated to the jury that the person Armbrister recognized as being the person in Photo No. 2 in the six photo array was actually Alfred Trenkler or even Tom Shay.

Kelly asked rhetorically, "*So what have we learned about an* [sic] *Al Trenkler during the course of this trial?*" Kelly stated that Trenkler owned duct tape which Kelly claimed that the chemist, Cynthia Wallace, had said was "*consistent*" with the tape used in the Roslindale Bomb. (TS 19-12) Surely there were jury members who understood how duct tape has become a mainstay for home and car repair work, and that it was present in a lot of American homes.

Paul Kelly said that Alfred had a rather difficult financial situation in 1991, but the only evidence of that was from Richard Brown, who was alleged by Alfred Trenkler to have misappropriated funds from the company. On the contrary, the jury heard that ARCOMM was completing a major project for the Christian Science Church.

Kelly reminded the jury that Alfred Trenkler owned a small Toyota and, despite the stipulation that Mr. McKernan could not identify it from a photo array of cars, he still tried to link that car to McKernan's observation that there was a compact car on Eastbourne Street on the morning of the 28th.

Continued Kelly, "*...you learned that the defendant was somewhat fearful of this man Trenkler, according to witness Fred Burke, and, indeed, that he believed that he was dangerous.*" (TS 19-13) However, the jury was also told that Shay was afraid that the Mafia would murder him in prison. Neither fear was real. The allegation by Fred Burke was one of many that begged for explanation by Tom Shay on the witness stand.

Kelly reminded the jury of the claimed 2-3 year length of the relationship between Alfred Trenkler and Tom Shay, and of Ed Carrion's driving Shay to Whitelawn Avenue "*on five or six occasions.*" (TS 19-14) [Tom Shay states in his "Testimony" in Appendix B, that Carrion took him to Shay's mother's home on Belvoir Road, but never to Whitelawn Ave., and never to the home of Trenkler's parents.]

He noted Nancy Shay's identification of the short man picking up her son at Belvoir Road and her seeing a short man in a couch at her house in 1991, who Tom Shay later told her was Trenkler; and from Richard Brown who said that he had seen them together in 1990 at ATEL.

Paul Kelly claimed a personal and financial motive for Tom Shay to want to kill his father, Thomas L. Shay. The missed dental appointment, for which the father had provided the son money, was 16 or 17 October and on the 18th was the Radio Shack purchase and that same evening was Shay's visit to Carrion's apartment, ending with the angry sending away of Tom Shay.

Kelly reminded the jury of the lure of the large possible lawsuit settlement and possible inheritance for Tom Shay. Despite the end-of-trial stipulation about the appearance of indications of remote control in the bomb, Kelly noted that Tom Shay was telling the press that the police asked him if his father could build a remote control device, and then said that the ATF team didn't determine it was a remote control device until later.

Near the end he replayed portions of the videotape of the Karin Marinella interview and later an audio tape of a portion.

Paul Kelly concluded, "*I ask you on behalf of the United States of America, on behalf of the memory of Jeremiah Hurley to return a verdict of guilty on each of the three counts against the defendant. I thank you.*" (TS 19-31)

Nancy Gertner began her closing statement by noting that the defendant's case was only a day and a half because the defendant didn't need to say very much due to the weakness of the prosecution's case. However, using 20-20 hindsight she was wrong about that. We don't know why her case was so short. She could have called witnesses to discuss Tom Shay's institutional upbringing, and more about how he loved his father. There was some testimony about Tom Shay's troubled childhood, but not enough. Perhaps the prosecution would have objected successfully; but it was worth a try. There could have been testimony about how all his teeth were removed at age five due to periodontal disease. She could have had one or more of Tom Shay's sisters testify. She could have returned Russ Bonanno to the witness stand to describe what happened when Tom Shay acquired, and was caring for two kittens. Family members and others could have testified about Tom Shay's uncaring attitude about money. In this respect, he was like Alfred Trenkler. The jury had to be shown that, for all his faults, Thomas A. Shay was not a person who could be involved with the building and placing of a deadly bomb.

Gertner could have introduced more witnesses, including Alfred Trenkler, to better establish when the acquaintance between Alfred Trenkler and Tom Shay actually began, assuming that she really knew about, or believed, Trenkler's claim that it began only in June 1991 and ended in August. Alfred Trenkler said in 2007 that he talked with Nancy Gertner only once, in a three-way phone call from the Plymouth County House of Correction in 1993, with Terry Segal. Alfred told her then that he had met Tom Shay in June 1991 and his relationship was merely a short acquaintance, with five rides in Alfred's car and one chance meeting in the Back Bay.

Gertner urged the jury to follow the requirements of reasonable doubt and pay no attention to lifestyle. She called the case a big puzzle - or two puzzles, "*... you'll have to ask yourself whether these ramblings are guilt beyond a reasonable doubt, and then I'm going to ask you to step back from the puzzle pieces, all together, and say from what you know of this rambling defendant, who can't keep his mouth shut, who says anything to anyone, whether* [he] *escapable* [is capable] *of an elaborate conspiracy that requires secrecy, planning and discretion, right.*" (TS 19-36)

She argued that the reason Thomas L. Shay could throw the box around is that he knew that the slide switch was off, and then turned it on later, and that Thomas L. Shay's behavior doesn't make sense for a lot of reasons.

Gertner corrected Paul Kelly on his claim that the duct tape matched tape found in Alfred Trenkler's garage. "*They never matched,*" she said (TS 19-48)

About her client, "*Everyone who talks about him talks about how he lusts for attention, how much he needs it, how much he wants, it, how much he is drawn to it.*

So slowly -- Mr. Kelly is quite right. -- He talks about it all the time, and his talk lands him as a suspect, and they look at this address book and the investigation takes a curve...." (TS 19-49)

Questioning the claimed financial motive for Tom Shay to kill his father, she asked rhetorically why didn't he become a party to the suit? Why did he skip the early depositions? At this point, she could have noted the extreme unlikelihood of Alfred Trenkler being motivated by the possible money IF Mr. Thomas L. Shay's lawsuit was won and IF Tom Shay inherited any of it. Also, it would have been a good time to remind the jury that the lawsuit had been settled for $27,000, but she couldn't do that because that fact hadn't been presented as evidence in the trial.

Nancy Gertner stated that contrary to the picture of Tom Shay's hating his father, things were getting much better - and the father was courting the son.

Then she shifts to talk about Alfred Trenkler, "*I am not going to quibble with Carrion. Trenkler is very important to the Government's case, because they recognize that Tommy can't build this bomb himself. They recognize that. He doesn't have the capacity. God knows he doesn't have the capacity. So they believe that it was his relationship with Trenkler that in fact provided the means, remember motive, opportunity, means. His relationship with Trenkler, even if Carrion is right, that they met in '88, '89, that they drove him six or seven times to White Lawn Avenue, if that relationship from what we know of Tom Shay's relationship enough to support this conspiracy, right? Forgive me, this is a man who has had lots of boyfriends. The evidence is he stays with Bonanno for two weeks and he's gone. He stays with Critcher a couple of days and he's gone. Is anything you know about the Trenkler relationship enough to say that Trenkler would say to him, 'Hey, Tommy, I'm going to kill for you?' Does that make any sense, even if he went to him seven times? Let's look at this for a moment. Everyone in their case, Shay, Sr., the lawyer, agrees that Tommy was not around in the summer of 1991. Everyone agrees that he didn't come back until September of '91 for this lawsuit. And then he's living with Bonanno, not Trenkler. Everyone agrees that in October he was staying with his mother. To be sure, he knew A1 Trenkler. To be sure, he was in the book. But is there anything that you're hearing about this that suggests that this relationship can support the weight of this bomb.*

The Government would say that Tom, that you should believe Tommy's statement that Trenkler and he talked to each other about their abuse and that they -- Trenkler wanted this line [sic] *and Channel 56 talked about what Trenkler wanted to do what Tommy's father had done to him. Do you have any reason to believe that? Do you have any reason to believe that about Trenkler's family?*" (TS 19-54/55)

Then Nancy Gertner presented a fundamental problem for the jurors, "*How can you pick and choose?*" Shay's truthful statements from his untruthful statements. (TS 19-61) "*Maybe Mr. Kelly is right, maybe you can pick and choose, you know, let's take the most consistent story that evolved. That's the portrait that should come out. Can you say that beyond a reasonable doubt when you've heard all the rest.*" (TAS 19-62) "*The Government can't edit one piece, and say to you this is really what it's about. You have to take that piece and look at the whole.*" (TS 19-66)

Gertner said that Shay was acting more like an amateur investigator. He was trying to solve the crime. Trying to figure out who tried to intimidate or kill his father or make it look like that. And he gave all his ideas about the crime to everyone.

She concluded that the jury should find Thomas A. Shay "*not guilty beyond a reasonable doubt*," [TS 19-68] but that may have been confusing because it's not the standard to apply. As noted earlier, a jury should find a defendant Not Guilty even when jurors believe that s/he probably did what was accused. A Not Guilty verdict would be required in that case because "probably" is not as strong as "beyond a reasonable doubt." She continued, "*And you will have done an extraordinary service, because then maybe the ATF and the Boston police and the U.S. Attorney's office can go out and find the real person who did this.*" (TS 19-68)

When she said that "*everyone agrees that Tommy was not around in the summer of 1991,*" she was simply wrong. It's unclear to what degree Nancy Gertner really understood the level of the Trenkler-Shay acquaintance, but it was extremely important that the jury understand the brevity and timing of that relationship. Not only was it only for five rides in June and July, and one chance meeting in August, but this all occurred more than two months before the explosion. If Nancy Gertner did not understand, then the jury could not be expected to understand either. The indictment alleged that the conspiracy was hatched in September and October, but if there was no contact between the alleged conspirators, apart from Shay's unanswered phone calls, then how could a conspiracy be found to exist at all, let alone beyond a reasonable doubt? There was only one witness, Mrs. Nancy Shay, who described seeing Trenkler and Tom Shay together in October, and she was vague about the time. Also, as would be seen during the upcoming Trenkler trial, she was uncertain about whether she saw Alfred Trenkler at all. In fact, she didn't, and she testified at that trial that she never had seen Alfred Trenkler before his trial which was to begin in a few months, on 25 October.

Prophetically, Nancy Gertner urged the jury to make the right decision. "*There's no other moment that's comparable. You can't say to me a week from now, two weeks from now, I'm sorry, I made a mistake. You see, that would be too late.*" (TS 19-69) Perhaps, however, even as late as 2007, members of the Tom Shay jury can come forward with the questions they wanted to ask even back in 1993, as well as the questions raised in this book.

Frank Libby delivered the prosecutor's rebuttal which took more than his allotted ten minutes. He began by asking the jury to dispel the "*ridiculous notion*" (TS 19-71) that Mr. Thomas L. Shay had any role in making the bomb and later to ignore the idea that Alan Pransky had any motives other than helping law enforcement. Interestingly, just as Nancy Gertner asked the jury to ignore the lifestyles of Tom Shay and his friends, Frank Libby asked the jury to ignore their views about Thomas L. Shay as a father.

Frank Libby urged the jurors to listen to the audio tape of Tom Shay's phone call to Russ Bonanno where he said that "*the cops think I did it.*" (TS 19-78) On its face, that statement doesn't shouldn't carry much weight as the police believe that everyone they arrest for a serious crime is guilty from day one.

Libby concluded, "*We're confident, ladies and gentlemen, that when you view the evidence in its totality, you will understand, having sat through this evidence, that we built this bomb* [sic, perhaps a typo or Freudian slip] *for you from the evidence, that you understand the significance now, today, sitting here after all of this evidence as to what this particular toggle switch means, how it ties this defendant into this case, and we would ask you to return a verdict of guilty on each of the three counts in the indictment."* (TS 19-78)

Then the judge called a short recess. When the jury returned, she delivered her charge to the jury, where she explained to the jurors their task ahead and the law and how to apply it to the facts they determine. As with the rest of the trial, there was a mixture of principled justice and administrative detail. An example of the latter was her request, *"Although we have transcripts of this trial, I ask you please not to ask me to let you have a transcript. Decide the case based on your memory of the evidence and on the basis of your notes.... So I ask you, please, not to ask me because, then, I would have to say no, and I don't like to do that."* (TS 19-92) This was one of the most clear occasions when administrative efficiency in the trial trumped the search for the truth. Why shouldn't the jury have had access to all the transcripts?

Every juror in a criminal trial wonders what the defendant is really like and whether s/he will actually hear and see the defendant on the witness stand. On the strong recommendation of his lawyers, Thomas A. Shay chose not to testify and Judge Zobel explained to the jury its proper response. *"The defendant does not have to take the stand, he does not have to explain anything, and you may draw no inference whatsoever from the fact that the defendant in this case chose not to take the stand."* (TS 19-92) However, there is never any guarantee that the jury would not make such inferences. The only clue to Thomas A. Shay's behavior in the trial was a comment made by Judge Zobel to Nancy Gertner during a bench conference. The judge interrupted the focus of the discussion and said, *"Excuse me, one second. Is your client acting up while all of you are here? Does he need a babysitter at counsel table."* Nancy Gertner replied, *"No, he's all right,"* but we must wonder what Tom Shay was doing, and what the jury thought, not only of that incident, but of his demeanor throughout the trial. Body language must have been interpreted by the jurors in some way, as Tom Shay was a restless young man. (TS 14-95/6)

Judge Zobel explained the oft-heard term about reasonable doubt. *"Proof beyond a reasonable doubt is not proof beyond all possible doubt, nor is it proof to a mathematical certainty. Proof beyond a reasonable doubt is proof that leaves you firmly convinced that the defendant is guilty..... It is doubt in the mind of a reasonable juror who is earnestly seeking the truth. It is doubt based on reason and common sense..... It is not sufficient for the Government in a criminal case to establish a probability, even a strong one, that the defendant is guilty. And the defendant certainly may not be convicted on the basis of suspicion or conjecture."* (TS 19-93)

She explained each count of the indictment, and what actions came within the criminal prohibition. She cautioned, *"But the law imposes that responsibility for the acts of another only if the defendant knowingly and willfully associates himself with the venture. It is not enough to show that he was present or even that he knew what was going on. The Government has to prove he knowingly became a participant to some degree. It doesn't have to prove that he was the prime mover. But if you find that the defendant knowingly and willfully participated in the building and placing of this bomb in some way, if he participated in some way, he may be found to be responsible for the acts of any coventurer; that is, a person cannot insulate himself from criminal responsibility by having other people do his dirty work. Knowingly and voluntarily simply means, knowingly simply means something voluntarily with knowledge, as opposed to doing something by mistake or by accident or even by negligence. Willfully means to do something purposely, with the intent to disobey the law, with the intent to violate the law, with a bad purpose of violating the law."* (TS 19-96)

How important was the question of "why"? She explained, *"There has been reference, in the course of this trial, to the defendant's motive. Motive is different from intent. Intent refers to the state-of-mind with which one does an act. Motive is what prompts a person to act, that is, the reason for doing an act. The Government doesn't have to prove any motive, although the evidence as to a defendant's motive may shed light on his intent, which the Government does have to prove. So, you may consider the evidence as to motive as it intends to shed light on his intent."* (TS 19-97)

She returned to explain the counts of the indictment, but notably began with Counts 2 and 3, and then Count 1, because 1 said that defendant *"knowingly and willfully"* (TS 19-105) conspired to do 2 and 3. That was one hint to the jury about the required consistency of verdict. Unspoken was the idea that if Thomas A. Shay wasn't guilty of Counts 2 or 3, he was unlikely to be guilty of Count 1 either.

Judge Zobel explained the constitutional law issue of interstate commerce and that it was enough for jurisdiction in the case that the jury conclude that at least one element of the bomb had been moved from one state to another, and not necessarily by this defendant.

She finished her charge and then listened to lawyers' objections or requests for further clarification, out of earshot of jury, and then added that intent in Count 1 is not just to violate the law, but intent *"to do it with the intention to achieve the object of the conspiracy, which is the other two offenses."* (TS 19-112)

In a final mixture of principle and details she sent them off, *"Members of the jury, the case is now in your hands, and I charge you to commence your deliberations. We will send up the exhibits as soon as we have gone through them. Please take your notebooks with you."* (TS 19-113)

After she excused the four alternates with appreciation for their work, she said *"Ms. Gertner wants me to tell you that you* [the remaining 12 jurors] *are not going to be here tomorrow,"* (TS 19-114) and reminded them that they would be deliberating in the afternoon, this being Friday, but that they would not be working over the weekend. Was that an indication to the jury that the defense counsel was apprehensive that her case was so weak that the jury would rush to find Tom Shay guilty so they could quit their deliberations in order to avoid working over a hot weekend?

The jury retired at 12:40 for its deliberations.

Then the defendant, lawyers, judge and spectators had to wait for communications from the jury, if any. The first message came ironically, *"Is there a remote control available to use on the video player?" They were told that one was not available, and that "you'll have to jump up and down and push the buttons, but the exercise is good for you."* (TS 19-116)

Implementing the jury's request that it be released at 4:00, the court adjourned at 3:59.

Next day's headlines:
Boston Globe: *"DELIBERATIONS BEGIN IN ROSLINDALE BOMBING CASE"* by Sean P. Murphy
Boston Herald: *"FATE OF ACCUSED BOMBER LIES IN HANDS OF FED JURY"* by Ralph Ranalli

Sunday's headlines:
Boston Globe: *"JURY MULLS BOMB CASE AS ATTORNEYS READY FOR 2ND TRIAL"* by Ralph Ranalli *"Prosecutors charge that Shay and Trenkler were friends and lovers and that they conspired..."* Alfred Trenkler was a reluctant acquaintance of Tom Shay, and by the end of August, even more reluctant. He was never a friend and certainly not a lover of Tom Shay.

Sunday, 25 July. Not a trial day, but Nancy Gertner talked with Tom Shay on the phone, and he wrote a note to her afterwards and presumably gave it to her on the next day at trial.

"Dear Nancy, It is Sunday and just got off the phone with you. I am sorry that I said whatever and no Good Bye. Just a click. I am innocent and feel that I will get a conviction for a number of reasons, #1 Because I say things that are not true, to get attention. #2 Because the jurors are most probable Homophobic. #3 Because a police officer is deceased. #4 Because I have a hung jury that just wants to get this trial over with . (#5 Because my sisters would rather see me in jail than see my father in jail, after all he gave them life, money! I gave them nothing except a pain in the rump and I am used to jail, 7 years in mental hospitals, 7 years in foster homes and boys schools. 2 years in jails. No, Tom won't mind spending his life in Jail.) Nancy G., I would mind. I am sick of this case, sick to my stomach that a cop died, all my life I have basically worshipped police officials, G.O.A.L. Gay Officers Association League. Scott Stanley, Ed Carrion, Jim Burk, James Pasqualley, Russ Bonanno, Robert Zampell. My address book had less the [sic] 30 people in it, 1/5 of them were or had once been a cop. I loved cops and still do. I know that is one thing I will never lie about, that and my being innocent, although I sometime will lie for attention. And I would never hurt my dad. I love him and always will no matter what. I just wish he loved me too! I am and have always gotton [sic] what I wanted or needed. The non-violent way. When I came back to New York I had $600.00. When I came back from S.F. I had $550.00. In my life I have taken money but never in a B.and E. Breaking entry (from someone I did not know.) I never in my life hit anyone, I always used words, or talked it out. and let's get something straight, my Dad never mollested [sic] me, nor did he put me in D.S.S. D.S.S. took me out of my home, and the people child care workers and Priest and nun are the ones who sexually and physically and mentally abused me. They said let us, let me, do this, do that and you can go home to your father, and I did it because that's what I wanted is to be with my father. Well Nancy my life is in your hands. Do what you think is best. Sincerly [sic], Tom Shay P.O. The picture of my father and me we're [sic] we are happy togeather [sic], I am sure there are about 5 happy pictures for every 1/2 bad time me and my dad had togeather [sic], and it's the good times we have shared not the bad ones that I remember."

28 29 30 1 2   6 7 8 9   12 13 14 15 16   19 20 21 22 23   26 27
X X X XX   XXXX   X X X X X   X X X XX   X O

Day 20: Monday, 26 July

The day began with the information that a remote control for the TV in the jury room was available. With all the discussion about this request, it must have been a surprise to at least a few people that no one audibly made the connection to that key element in the trial: the remotely controlled bomb. How many members of the jury realized that a TV remote control could have triggered the Roslindale Bomb? That question may not have affected the question of Shay's guilt, but it would have brought the issue right into the jury room.

The jury asked for copies of the indictment and for a transcript of the judge's instructions, despite her admonition about asking for transcripts. Nonetheless, she okayed both requests.

The jury's significant question was about Alfred Trenkler: *"Could you review the indictment as to how Alfred Trenkler is a codefendant. We are not considering Al Trenkler here?"* (TS 20-2)

Judge Zobel tried to explain to the jury how to deal with the issue that bedeviled the trial from the initial indictment, how to try separately two members of a conspiracy. She responded to the question, *"The indictment, as you see, has charged two people, Mr. Shay and Mr. Trenkler, with three separate offenses... The Government, having charged both, will ultimately have to prove both guilty of these offenses. But before you now is only Mr. Shay. So that although you have evidence that the Government says, suggests, that Mr. Shay and Mr. Trenkler did this, only Mr. Shay is before you. And you will have to review all of the evidence, including that which appears to implicate Mr. Trenkler, in deciding whether Mr. Shay and Mr. Trenkler, first, agreed to commit these offenses and, second, participated with each other in committing these offenses. And I am not sure how else I can explain this to you. Mr. Trenkler is not on trial before you now, only Mr. Shay is. But because they are charged with agreeing with each other and because they are charged with participating with each other, you have evidence of the conduct and statements of both.*
Does that answer the question?
Not really?
No?" (TS 20-8/9) Apparently, she saw heads shaking sideways.

Then Nancy Gertner asked for a bench conference and the lawyers and judge discussed how to better clarify the question of how the jury could consider the evidence against Alfred Trenkler. After the discussion, Judge Zobel tried again to explain to the jury.

"Counsel suggested that although it is only Mr. Shay who is now on trial, in practical effect, you really have to decide whether Mr. Shay and Mr. Trenkler did the things that the Government has said they did and whether the Government has proven that they did it beyond a reasonable doubt. Because only two people are charged. So really, you have to decide whether those two did what they did [sic, what they were charged with doing], *even though only one of them is now on trial before you."* (TS 20-13)

Thus, even though not at the defendant's table, Alfred Trenkler was on trial, too, and even though the evidence the jury heard against Trenkler was unchallenged and much of it was inaccurate, the jury was still instructed to consider whether "*those two did what they did.*"

Next day's headlines:
Boston Globe: "*JURY STILL STUDYING ROSLINDALE BOMB CASE*" no byline

28 29 30 1 2	6 7 8 9	12 13 14 15 16	19 20 21 22 23	26 27
X X X XX	XXXX	X X X X X	X X X X X	X X

Day 21: Tuesday, 27 July

This was to be the last day of deliberations. The jury asked for an audio tape player, and it was supplied. The request probably meant that the jury listened to the tape of Tom Shay's call to Russ Bonanno before he left Massachusetts in January 1992 or from a call made from California. The transcript did not contain the contents of the tape but Frank Libby referred to the contents in his closing statement. He said that Thomas A. Shay had said, "*The cops think I did it.*" From the verdict, it appears that the jury took Tom Shay's statement as somehow being an admission, but it was just an observation, and a correct observation at that. The police believe that everyone they recommend for prosecution is guilty. Three hours later, the jury returned at 12:26 with a mixed verdict. After 13 hours of deliberations, over three days, the 12 jurors found Thomas A. Shay guilty on Count 1, not guilty on Count 2 and guilty on Count 3. The jury was then thanked and excused.

Nancy Gertner's immediate reaction was surprise. She said, "*This verdict, I want an opportunity to think about it somewhat. This verdict is very perplexing, your Honor, given the evidence.... Counts 2 and 3 were not distinguishable factually; yet, they found not guilty on Count 2 and guilty on Count 3.*" (TS 21-6)

On the issue in Count 2 of the receipt through interstate commerce of explosive materials, the jury heard no testimony linking Tom Shay to explosives, so the only possible connection would be through the invisible Alfred Trenkler. The jury didn't know that there was no chemical trace found of dynamite in Trenkler's car or in his residence or at his place of work. The jury didn't know that Trenkler had voluntarily consented to the cutting and seizure of a piece of carpet from his Toyota. Tom Shay had told AUSA Paul Kelly in 1992 that he and Trenkler had, using Trenkler's car, disposed of the waste materials from bomb making, and that they had, again using Trenkler's car, planted the bomb underneath Thomas L. Shay's car on Friday, 25 October. Not only were these more lies from Tom Shay, there was simply no physical evidence to back them up; and Paul Kelly and Frank Libby knew that they were untrue.

The trial of Thomas A. Shay was a puzzle within the larger bomb puzzle. Judge Rya Zobel saw part of her role was to keep the wheels of justice, or injustice in this case, rolling smoothly and on time. She also had a sense of humor and was the second most prolific source of the laughter during the trial. First in that regard was Nancy Gertner who provoked laughter, as recorded by transcripts, seven times. One witness, Evelyn Pirello, provoked laughter twice. The ever-serious, single-minded true believer prosecutors incited not one laugh, leading one to ask whether more perspective on the human condition would have helped these two men as they struggled with the Tom Shay puzzle.

It is argued here the investigation and trial of Thomas A. Shay resulted in a wrongful conviction. The rules of evidence seemed to be more successful in shielding the truth rather than revealing it. What went wrong? The appeal process for Thomas A. Shay began shortly, but the larger question of why any long, professionally managed and argued trial should result in a wrongful conviction under our system of justice remains a major question for our society and is beyond the scope of this book. How can innocent people be convicted beyond a reasonable doubt? That it happens is a national scandal.

The trial of Alfred W. Trenkler was next, and it raised the same questions.

Next day's headlines:

Boston Globe 1: *"SHAY GUILTY IN FATAL '91 BLAST"* by Matthew Brelis The article said that Francis Foley praised the verdict and said that Jerry Hurley would have been pleased and commented prophetically, *"I just hope it gives his family some peace."* Unfortunately, it would not.

Continued the article, *"The verdict was the result of painstaking police work,' Boston Police Commissioner William Bratton and Terence McArdle, special agent in charge of the Boston ATF office said at a press conference yesterday.*

Law enforcement sources said the verdict is a huge morale boost for the US Attorney's office and will help improve relations between federal law enforcement and Boston police....

That receipt, coupled with Shay's admission in a WLVI-TV (Ch. 56) interview...presented strong circumstantial evidence....

Throughout the trial Shay frequently smiled at spectators. Yesterday, he appeared stunned by the verdict. He sat slumped over in his chair and stared ahead....

His mother, Nancy Shay, said her son is innocent, 'He is a very loving and giving child. I think he made the whole thing up and got himself into trouble by talking. He has a fascination with the media.' "

Boston Globe 2: *"US PROSECUTORS TURN TO SHAY CODEFENDANT"* by Matthew Brelis He wrote, " 'That videotape was very important to us,' a juror who did not want to be named said during a telephone interview yesterday. The juror also said a tape of a telephone conversation Shay made to a friend when he was in San Francisco hiding out after the bombing was important. On the tape Shay said he was in San Francisco because 'The cops still think I did it.' "

"... the juror who was interviewed said the jury did not think the elder Shay was capable of making the bomb. The juror and one other juror both said the jury thought evidence was suppressed that the jury should have been told about, but would not be more specific. 'The deliberations were very traumatic and soul-searching and we did the best job we could,' another juror said."

For the first time, it was revealed that Tom Shay's lawyers continued to negotiate for a plea bargain even during the first parts of the trial. *Said the article, "Shay tried to enter into another agreement with the government after his trial started June 28. Shay was willing to enter a so-called Alford plea in which he would acknowledge the government had enough evidence for a jury to find him guilty, but wouldn't admit his guilt, law enforcement sources said....*

Sources said Assistant US Attorneys Paul V. Kelly and Frank A. Libby - at the urging of the Boston Police Department and the Hurley and Foley families -

rejected the Alford plea."

<u>Boston Herald</u> 1: *"SHAY GUILTY IN FATAL BOMBING - LONG SENTENCE SOUGHT IN OFFICER'S DEATH"* by Ralph Ranalli. He quoted Boston Police Commissioner William Bratton as stating that Frank Libby and Paul Kelly were *"two of the finest prosecutors I've ever had the pleasure of working with."*

<u>Boston Herald</u> 2: *"SHAY'S MOM BLAMES HIS FASCINATION WITH ATTENTION"* by Ralph Ranalli The article stated, *"...his mother said outside the courtroom, 'He is fascinated with attention, he had a need for attention..' That attention was lacking in Shay's childhood, which according to testimony at trial was spent largely in foster homes and youth programs. Nancy Shay was divorced from Shay's father, and the family's life, according to one attorney close to the case, 'redefined the term dysfunctional.' "*

<u>Boston Herald</u> 3: *"OFFICER WOUNDED IN '91 BOMBING PRAISES VERDICT"* by Ralph Ranalli The article quoted Francis Foley, *" 'I'm just so grateful to (Assistant U.S. Attorneys) Paul Kelly and Frank Libby,' he said. 'Without the ATF and the prosecutors we wouldn't have been able to ever pursue the case.' "*

<u>Patriot Ledger</u>: *"SHAY CONVICTED IN FATAL EXPLOSION - QUINCY MAN FACES LIFE IN PRISON"* by Stephen Walsh He wrote, *"The six-man, six-woman jury deliberated for 13 hours and requested a videocassette recorder and television at one point to watch an interview Shay gave to a local television station....*

Assistant U.S. Attorney Paul Kelly said he was pleased by the verdict, which he said ended an investigation more thorough than any he had ever seen.

'This is a case of law enforcement coming together when a member is slain,' Kelly said."

<u>The Two Columns of Truth Presented to the Jury; It Chose One, Beyond a Reasonable Doubt.</u>

PROSECUTION'S TRUTH	TOM SHAY'S TRUTH
<u>Roslindale Bomb</u>	
-Shay purchased parts.	-No. Had no interest in such things, but he did say to Karin Marinella that he purchased parts.
-Alfred Trenkler built it	-No. Was busy at work all fall.
-Alfred Trenkler acquired explosives.	-No. Never acquired any explosives.
-Conspired for the money.	-There was no such interest in his father's lawsuit, beyond awe at the numbers.
-Fled state to escape prosecution.	-Went to California to avoid probation problem and also by habit.
<u>Alfred Trenkler</u>	
- 2-3 year relationship with Trenkler	-Acquaintance began in June 1991 and with five hitched rides in Jun/July and one accidental meeting in August.
-Relationship was sexual	-Acquaintance was not sexual

-Shay told Trenkler of hatred for father -Shay did not describe nor show such feelings.

Other reasons for conviction
-Failed to convince jury that none of his statements could be trusted.
-Tom Shay did not testify at his trial.
-Tom Shay's lifestyle and homosexuality.

END NOTES
<hr>

1. Morrison Bonpasse, 7 February 2007, in LaGrasse, France.
2. In a 5 December 2006 column, "NEW COMMISH STANDS IN SOLIDARITY AFTER HUB COP TRAGEDY," in the <u>Boston Herald</u>, Michele McPhee noted that Denise Corbett's apparent suicide by gunshot was at least indirectly caused by her continued distress at seeing the 28 October 1991 explosion. McPhee is the <u>Herald's</u> Police Bureau Chief.
3. At Alfred Trenkler's 4 April 2007 hearing, the author was asked whether he was there for the defendant's side or the Government's and was directed to the right hand side of the spectator area.
4. Later in the trial Judge Zobel asked Special Agent Dennis Leahy why the term "Special" was used. He said it was just in the job title, as he was just an "ordinary agent". (TS 14-76)
5. The phrase may remind readers of the last part of Robert Frost's, *The Road Not Taken*, "I took the one less traveled by, /And that has made all the difference." Jotting down a license number of an unusual car at an unusual place CAN make a difference. In Buffalo, NY, Joan Dorn wrote down the license number of such a car when she was jogging and the police later used that number to apprehend the killer of Dr. Slepian who provided abortion services in that city. On 8 June 2007, the FBI gave her a $25,000 check as a reward.
6. Cynthia Wallace continues to work at ATF, and in 2004 shared the writing of another article for the Annual Proceedings of the American Academy of Forensic Sciences, "Use of Principal Components Analysis in the Individualization of Smokeless Powders" at www.aafs.org/pdf/dallas04.pdf. Cynthia Wallace had no known relation to the mother and stepfather of Alfred W. Trenkler, Josephine and John D. Wallace.
7. From the home page of the Futable website comes these excerpts, "*Over a quarter of a century ago Futaba started providing the most comprehensive radio control product selection and service possible to hobbyists. Futaba systems and products were quickly accepted and acclaimed by flyers, drivers and enthusiasts alike. Futaba's combination of advanced technology, high performance and reliability and excellent service earned a well-deserved reputation as the industry's finest. Innovations like PCM 1024, high tech manufacturing techniques and high output servo design have justifiably earned Futaba leadership status amongst our competitors. But for all the engineering and computers and electronic wizardry there is a critical element we feel is just as important. To provide the R/C hobbyist with the best possible equipment to enjoy their hobby we enlist the considerable talents of many top professionals in their individual fields of endeavor. Input by our team of consultants is absolutely invaluable in the design and refinement of our systems, at http://www.futaba-rc.com/.*"
8. The publisher, Robert Kennedy is not related to the Massachusetts family of the late U.S. Attorney General and Senator, Robert F. Kennedy. *MuscleMag International* continues to be published. A view of the cover of the July 1991 issue is at http://www.shopmusclemag.com/product.asp?productid=666.
9 The same term, IED, is used to describe the lethal roadside bombs and other bombs used in Iraq against U.S. Army vehicles including tanks.
10. Members of a Federal jury are free to discuss their deliberations, but no member of the Shay jury, or the Trenkler jury has come forward with any information. Federal law does prohibit lawyers in the case from pursuing those jury members and trying to influence them in any way, but it doesn't prohibit others, including the media from making respectful inquiries.
11. The transcript at page 8-131 says "180,000" for 1987 just after stating $80,000 for 1986. It's likely that the "1" in 180,000 should have been a "$".

12. "Russell Stover" claims to be the largest manufacturer of boxed chocolates in North America. See http://www.russellstover.com/

13. "Confess Now, 'nay' later?" by John Shultz, *Kansas City Star*, 19 August 2006, at http://www.williams.edu/Psychology/Faculty/Kassin/files/Karr%20-%20KC%20Star.pdf

14. See Peter Quintieri and Kenneth Weiss, "Admissibility of False-Confession Testimony: Know Thy Standard," *Journal of American Academy of Psychiatry Law*, Vol 33, No. 4, 2005 at http://www.ncbi.nlm.nih.gov/entrez/query.fcgi?itool=abstractplus&db=pubmed&cmd=Retrieve&dopt=abstractplus&list_uids=16394232; Louise Chang, "John Mark Karr and the False Confession: Why," WEB MD, online Article 126, http://www.webmd.com/content/Article/126/116509.htm?pagenumber=3; Alexandra Perina, "The False Confession," *Psychology Today*, March/April 2003 at http://psychologytoday.com/rss/pto-20030430-000002.html

15. "Dr. Marc Feldman's Munchausen Syndrome, Malingering, Factitious Disorder, & Munchausen by Proxy Page," at http://ourworld.compuserve.com/homepages/Marc_Feldman_2/

16. Alfred refers to Jo and Jack Wallace as his "parents" even though Jack is really his stepfather. Jack became Alfred's stepfather when Alfred was very young and has stood by him as much as any father possibly could.

17. During the trial one source of irritation and light banter for Nancy Gertner, was that she faced a team of two prosecutors and sometimes she would be arguing with both of them, and the Judge would caution the prosecutors that the Government could speak with one voice. With the appearance of Amy Baron-Evans for the defense, the running joke was turned on the defense. At the end of the trial, just before the charge to the jury, Amy Baron-Evans had recommendations and Paul Kelly said, in his only attempt at humor, "*They're double-teaming us, your Honor.*" Nancy Gertner replied, "It is about time." (TS 19-111)

18. Kentucky Windage is the adjustment that a person with a rifle or shotgun makes in his/her aim for the wind. For example, if there is a strong wind from the west, and a person is aiming for an object to the North, the Kentucky Windage adjustment would be to aim the gun slightly to the left, or westward, to allow for the wind's effect on the bullet or shot. In the context of Paul Kelly's statement it means that he was accusing Scott Critcher of adjusting his memory of events by two hours, so as to give Tom Shay two more hours of alibi time.

Chapter 7: Pretrial for Alfred W. Trenkler - 28 June 1993 to 24 October 1993

"I'm on a mission to get the truth out." [1]
Former U.S. Attorney for Massachusetts A. John Pappalardo, 2005

On 19 July 1993, Scott Lopez, of the Trenkler defense team, wrote a 13 page *"Affidavit... in opposition to Government's Motion in limine to admit evidence of 1986 bombing."* The affidavit challenged the validity of the use of the ATF EXIS database to show "signature" or commonality between the 1986 device and 1991 Roslindale Bomb. The affidavit included 19 pages of sample forms and reports from the EXIS database. Excerpts follow:

A. Purpose and Capabilities of the System.

12. It is a matter of common knowledge that any database computer program is only as reliable as the information that is contained in the system and the capabilities of the system. Given the materials provided by the government during discovery, it appears that the EXIS system's purpose and capabilities are not consistent with the government's purported use of the system in this case. The EXIS system, which is described by Mr. Scheid as a "database of explosives incidents" is inherently limited by the quality and amount of information that is placed in the system's memory....

B. The Nature Or Type Of Information Stored On The System.

15. In addition, a careful examination of the information on the computer printouts from the EXIS system amply demonstrates that the nature or type of information is not "detailed forensic information." In fact, not one feature identified by the government is detailed or specific enough to provide any assistance in determining signature. For example, the category of "remote control" provides no detail as to the specific type of remote control component utilized (i.e. improvised v. manufactured; functional or non-functional or even the frequency used). Similarly, the category "toggle switch" does not identify the specific toggle switch used (i.e., model numbers, double throw v. single throw, toggle switch v. microswitch) or the manner in which it was used (firing system v. non-firing system). Clearly, the category of "duct tape" is not specific by any means and the category of "soldering wires" makes absolutely no distinction regarding whether the components as manufactured contained solder or whether the maker of the bomb utilized solder to build the device. Finally, the other three categories, namely "bombings and attempted bombings," "cars and trucks," and "circular magnet to undercarriage" are so hopelessly generic as to provide no assistance at all with respect to making a forensic comparison of one device to another.

C. Adding and Retrieving Information From EXIS System.

16. Implicit in the government's reliance upon this computer system as the basis for its expert's opinion is the assumption that the manner in which information is placed into system is reliable, accurate and complete. However, based on the information provided, it does not appear that this is the case.

17. For example, the first assumption this Court must make is that federal, state and local agencies report explosives incidents to ATF even when ATF is not involved in investigation. As indicated above, this assumption is not necessarily valid .

18. The second assumption this Court must make about the information that is placed in the computer is that the individuals reporting incidents to ATF on the forms provided have both the knowledge and experience to accurately report the information in the proper category on the ATF forms. Obviously, local departments do not have officers who possess the background and qualifications of ATF agents and FBI agents with respect to explosives incidents.

19. In addition, as the forms provided by the government during discovery indicate, the ATF forms for reporting incidents are not detailed, and require a thorough knowledge of the EXIS Computer Codes, and their significance, to assure accuracy.

20. Moreover, there does not appear to be a uniform form which all agencies utilize to report explosives incidents as indicated by the three different forms provided by the government during discovery. Compare ATF Worksheet Form, FBI Incident Report Form, and ATF Incident Report Form attached hereto as Exhibit B.

21. Notwithstanding the above issues, of even greater significance is the time at which information is placed onto the computer system. For example, the government presumably would like to have this Court believe that when the computer search of the EXIS system was conducted in this case, the 1986 incident was identified as a match. A condition precedent for this factual conclusion would be that the 1986 was already on the EXIS database. However, a careful examination of the documents provided in this case would seem to indicate otherwise.

23. Mr. Scheid [in a cited article] *also provides an example of a typical search in this article. Using the example of an electrically initiated pipe bomb placed under the seat of a vehicle, he explains that the computer would be asked to search for four fields: "electrically initiated pipe bombs," "pipe bombs," "placement under the seat of a vehicle" and "vehicles."*

24. The obvious mathematical fallibility of this system is that the greater number of "fields" the computer operator combines in his or her search determines the number of "matches" that will occur. For example, if one was to only search for the field "electrically initiated pipe bombs" ALL pipe bombs fitting this description would be retrieved. However, by combining the field of "placement under the seat of a vehicle," with electrically initiated pipe bombs" ALL electrically initiated pipe bombs which were either not placed under the seat of a vehicle or not reported as being placed under the seat of vehicle are eliminated and therefore the number of matches is reduced

25. The significance of this mathematical truth is that the number of fields queried can predetermine the number of matches retrieved. Thus, if one wanted to reduce the number of matches all one would have to do is increase the number of fields.

26. Applying this mathematical certainty to the case at hand it is obvious that by increasing the number of fields to include "bombings and attempted bombings," "remote control," "toggle switch," ,etc., the number of possible matches is reduced until only one match occurs. For this reason, the time at which the information is placed into the computer is a very important consideration in determining the accuracy and reliability of the system.

27. In this case, it appears that the 1986 incident was added to the EXIS database after the 1991 Roslindale incident....

28. In all likelihood it was not until Alfred Trenkler's beeper number was found on the person of Thomas A. Shay, Jr. that Trenkler became a suspect. Once Trenkler became a suspect, ATF agents or Boston Homicide officers learned of the 1986 incident. After the agents and officers learned of the 1986 incident the 1986 incident was added to the EXIS database. To date there is no evidence to suggest that the 1986 incident was either reported to or investigated by ATF. Thus, the 1986 incident would not have been added to the EXIS system at any earlier point in time.

29. This time line is very significant because, assuming the 1986 incident was placed onto the EXIS system after the 1991 incident, so long as the 1986 incident was described in terms similar to the 1991 incident a match would result. Additionally, so long as enough fields were combined to exclude all other explosives incidents, the only devices that would appear similar by a computer search would be the 1986 and 1991 incident. Thus, once the 1986 device and 1991 device were described in similar terms, it would appear that out of 14,000 bombings and attempted bombings only two (2) matched. Now the government desires to premise its expert's opinion on this so-called "signature" evidence. However, common sense would seem to indicate that this "evidence" should be closely scrutinized.

30. It also appears from the documents provided that changing and updating specific inaccurate information has little or no effect on the match at issue. For example, the query search done on or about December 14, 1992, indicates that toggle switch in the 1986 incident was listed as a Radio Shack toggle switch. The specific information on the December printout was "SW (Switch), RASH (Radio Shack) , Toggle, Double Throw." See EXIS Codes for abbreviations. However, the June 1, 1993 printout for the 1986 incident has the toggle switch listed as "SW, UNKN (Unknown), Toggle, Double Throw." Thus, even though the December information regarding the 1986 incident was inaccurate and had to be updated, it did not affect the search results. This is true despite the fact that the 1991 incident is listed in both search printouts as "SW, RASH, Toggle, Archer SPST" ("SPST" is an abbreviation for Single Pole, Single Throw switch). This inaccuracy and its lack of effect on the search demonstrates that: 1) inaccurate information does not necessarily affect the computer's results; and 2) differences in the more specific information about the components such as the manufacturer (Radio Shack) and the type of toggle switch (single throw v. double throw) also does not affect the outcome.

31. In fact, what is reasonable to conclude from this database is that so long as enough similar fields are placed onto the database when describing an explosives incident a computer operator can be assured of making two devices match when these fields are combined in a search. Moreover, despite all the other dissimilarities between the two devices, so long as these dissimilarities are not "queried" or searched, they will have no affect [sic] on the search. This is true even though the 1991 device is listed as a "professional job" and the 1986 has no similar appellation.

32. Thus, even though of the nine (9) devices listed in the June 1, 1993 EXIS computer printout:

1. 9 of 9 devices had magnets;
2. 9 of 9 were affixed under vehicles;
3. 8 of 9 were placed by a person;
4. 7 of 9 were remote control;
5. 7 of 9 list wire (although none can be constructed without wire) ;
6. 5 of 9 used Futaba Remote Control (not 1986 incident)
7. 4 of 9 used glue (not 1986 incident) ;
8. 4 of 9 used wood (not 1986 incident);
9. 4 of 9 used blasting caps (not 1986 incident); and
10. 3 of 9 used box enclosures (not 1986 incident) ;

because only "certain features" "determined to be common" were "queried," the desired match resulted.

33. In sum, a common sense analysis of the government's contention indicates that the purpose and capabilities of the system do not support its argument. The computer's intended purpose is to establish leads for further investigation. It is not intended or designed to be relied upon to establish a signature. Moreover, the nature or type of information stored in the system is not "detailed forensic information" as alleged, but rather non-specific, generic and non-forensic information. Furthermore, the manner in which information is placed into the system is not complete, reliable, or accurate and can be easily manipulated. Additionally, the manner in which the information is retrieved from the system is wholly dependent upon the information that is placed into and contained within the system. As a result, the value of this computer system to establish a signature is minimal at best. Thus, permitting an expert to rely upon this system as a basis for his or her opinion would not only compound the inadequacies of this system, but also would establish a dangerous precedent."

Scott Lopez didn't explain that the 1986 device wasn't placed under the Capeway Fish truck at all. According to Alfred Trenkler, it was placed on the frame on the left side of the truck just in front of the left rear tire, so as to be away from the gas tank. There was no need to hide the device as it was at night, and it was going to be detonated as soon as it was placed on the truck.

In Steve Sheid's testimony in the Shay case, the following queries were made, Incidents in database, 1 January 1979 to 31 December 1991 - 40,867.
Next for *"bombings or attempted bombings"* - 14,252,
Next for *"target: cars and trucks"* - 2,504,
Next for *"under vehicle"* - 428,
Next for *"remote control"* - 19, and finally
Next for *"magnets"* - 7. (TS 15-143)

If he had known that the 1986 device was not "under vehicle," his final queries would not have included the Roslindale Bomb AND the Quincy device in the same final grouping of 6.

Another way to look at the fallacy of the analysis used by Stephen Scheid is to suppose that there was a database with all psychotherapists' treatments in U.S. on a database and then create hypothetical questions.
Incidents in database, 1 January 1979 - 31 December 1991 - 10 million,
Next for *"males"* - 4 million,
Next for *"Irish descent"* - 40,867.
Next for *"involved in bombings or attempted bombings"* - 14,252,
Next for *"near or involving cars"* - 2,504,
Next for *"involving criminal or civil lawsuits"* - 428,
Next for *"involving injuries"* - 19,
Next for *"occurring in the last week of October"* - 7, and finally
Next for *"occurring within one-half hour of noon"* - 2. The result is a collection of two incidents in the U.S.: the 1987 incident at the Dedham Service Center and the 1991 Roslindale Bomb. Does this conclusion mean much? No, not much, and neither did Stephen Scheid's numbers from the EXIS database which purported to show similarity between the 1986 and 1991 devices.

On 22 July 1993 Terry Segal filed a "*Motion to establish new trial date and conditions of release.*" The background was that during the Shay trial, Judge Zobel indicated that the previously scheduled date of 16 August would not be possible for Trenkler's trial and therefore the U.S. Attorney's office likely would be unable to comply with the requirements of the Speedy Trial Act for persons in pre-trial confinement. Segal agreed with Paul Kelly that he would waive Alfred Trenkler's rights to a speedy trial if Kelly would agree to a pre-trial release from custody.

Segal proposed release conditions of "*home confinement at 7 Whitelawn Avenue in Milton, MA and electronic monitoring be imposed. Defendant further suggests that said electronic monitoring be fashioned to permit him to travel to counsel's office and to other significant locations escorted by counsel or counsel's employee.*" Ralph Ranalli covered the story in the 30 July <u>Boston Herald</u>, "*2D BOMB DEFENDANT MAY BE FREED.*"

In that 22 July motion, Segal requested a new trial date for December, due to other trial commitments.

Alfred Trenkler's lawyers watched closely the trial of Tom Shay, but they could not participate. After the trial of Thomas A. Shay ended with the mixed, but guilty, verdict on 27 July 1993, Alfred Trenkler and his lawyers knew it would not be easy to secure an acquittal for him. What jury considering the case of a co-conspirator could ignore the fact that another jury found the other conspirator guilty? To find the second not guilty would be to say that the first jury made a mistake.

One of the next day's stories in the <u>Boston Globe</u> was an unnecessary reminder, "*US PROSECUTORS TURN TO SHAY CODEFENDANT.*" Written by Matthew Brelis, the article referred to Trenkler as Shay's "*one-time lover and co-defendant.*" As was true for the prosecutors, the sexual preferences of the defendants were important to the media.

However, Alfred Trenkler was never the lover of Thomas A. Shay. Not once. There was no evidence of such a relationship at Shay's trial, and Mathew Brelis did not ask Alfred Trenkler. So where did that allegation come from? Unfortunately, Trenkler's attorney never did refute the allegation, whenever it appeared, and generally advised his client not to speak to the press. Lawyers are urged to fight their cases in court, but that article could have been seen by the potential jurors and should have been corrected.

Trying to play the expectations game (Happiness Equals Expectations minus Reality) played by politicians, Brelis' unnamed "*Sources said the Shay case - with Shay's incriminating statements to law enforcement, television and jailhouse cellmates - was less difficult to prove than the Trenkler case will be.*" However, the "*sources*" didn't mention that it's far easier to convict an alleged co-conspirator when the other co-conspirator has already been convicted of conspiracy and one of the alleged criminal acts.

The article quoted Jack Wallace on the Shay verdict, "*We were very disappointed, obviously,... But Alfred's case is entirely different. We are still very confident that he is absolutely innocent and had nothing to do with it.*"

The article concluded, "*Kelly said the government has yet to decide whether it will force Shay to testify against Trenkler,*" and then quoted Amy Baron-Evans, a Shay defense attorney, as saying "*They can't force him to testify, and if they do he will commit perjury, because he doesn't know anything* [about the Roslindale Bomb]."

However, perjury means to lie under oath, and she meant either the actual testimony or previous statements under oath with which such testimony might conflict. The only time that Tom Shay testified under oath was at a 12 May 1993 hearing where he tried to suppress the statements he had made. Also, he did sign at least one of his plea-bargain proffer statements. Perhaps what Baron-Evans meant is that if Tom Shay testified the way that the prosecutors expected, and admitted to the crimes; then he would be lying and would be in conflict with previous statements, whether under oath or not. However, even though it wasn't known with certainty what Tom Shay would have said, it would have been better for the causes of truth and justice for him to testify. [See Appendix B for what Tom Shay states in 2007 would have been his testimony.] Even if he had told the complete truth at his trial or at Alfred Trenkler's upcoming trial, he still could have been subject to perjury charges as those truthful statements likely conflicted with previous lies under oath.

On 29 July Matthew Brelis wrote a summary article for the _Boston Globe_, "_INITIALLY SHAY HAD IMPLICATED LOVER_" which said that before his trial, Shay "_was cooperating with the federal government and implicating his lover, who allegedly built the bomb._" As every newspaper reader knows, or thinks they know, only guilty people agree to plea bargains with prosecutors, and if Tom Shay was really guilty, then Alfred Trenkler likely was, too - so the message to Boston was clear that Trenkler was guilty. Neither the U.S. District Court nor the _Globe_'s readers were ready for the theory of "voluntary false confession." There may have been some in Boston who believed that Albert DeSalvo's confessions, later recanted, as the "Boston Strangler" were falsely made, but they were not on the radar screen in 1993.

Brelis confirmed that the prosecutors had searched the Quincy quarries, using a mini-submarine from Woods Hole. What the unnamed "_law enforcement sources_" did not say was that AUSA Attorney and others understood why the "_elaborate_ [search] _efforts were fruitless,_" which was that they were a hoax by Shay, to use Paul Kelly's label. There was no dumping by Alfred Trenkler of anything in any Quincy quarry. Brelis's unnamed sources did not confirm that the police had also taken a boat, with Tom Shay aboard, to look in Massachusetts Bay for the dumped parts as well.

Wrote Brelis, "_Boston police detectives and federal agents from the Bureau of Alcohol, Tobacco and Firearms were also unable to locate the South Shore shack next to the radio tower where Shay insisted his lover, Alfred Trenkler, an engineer built the bomb._" Again, they didn't find the shack because it didn't exist, as Shay's story was a hoax; and now the _Globe_ was using the "_lover_" label which wasn't denied by the Trenkler defense team as it should have been, and strongly, too.

The trial of Alfred Trenkler was originally scheduled for 22 February 1993 as a joint trial with Tom Shay, but the prosecutors had requested a delay until 17 May, along with the severance of the two cases. Terry Segal responded with a request for 1 June. On 22 July, Terry Segal filed a motion for a further postponement because of schedule conflicts to a date in December. As part of the request for a delay, Segal agreed to waive Trenkler's rights to a Speedy Trial in return for his being released to home confinement.

The 31 July _Boston Globe_ reported on the potential release, with the short article, "_QUINCY ENGINEER MAY BE RELEASED,_" which noted that the Speedy Trial Act would require a trial for Alfred Trenkler by 16 August, or nine months after his 16 December 1992 detention. The act requires a trial within 70 days, but there were several exceptions for tolling that period, including the time when a co-defendant was on trial.

Judge Zobel responded to the 22 July request for Trenkler's conditional release with the 2 August release of Alfred Trenkler from jail and into house arrest at the home of his parents in Milton, and he was required to wear an ankle bracelet. The bail bond was $500,000 which was covered by the appraised value of the Wallace's home, plus additional surety. Headlined the 3 August *Boston Globe*, "*BOMBING SUSPECT, FREE WAITING TRIAL.*" Alfred moved into a room in the third floor and worked hard with a computer and typewriter on his defense. The man who was labeled a "*domestic terrorist*" and who was too dangerous to release on a conditional release the previous December, and whose alleged co-conspirator was just convicted, was now deemed safe for home release for no better reason than the failure of the court and prosecutor and defense to agree on an earlier trial date. There was no acknowledgement by anyone about the reversal of the unfairly harsh December 1992 and January 1993 decisions of Magistrate Marianne Bowler and Judge Zobel to keep Alfred Trenkler in custody. Andrea Estes wrote the 3 August *Boston Herald* article, "*2D BOMB SUSPECT OUT OF JAIL,*" about the release. She reminded readers of the earlier determination by Magistrate Bowler when she agreed "*with prosecutors that he 'presents a profound danger to the community.'* Marianne Bowler had written in December, in her 32-page order, "*Based on the defendant's demonstrated expertise in the area of electronics and telecommunications, the use of an electronic bracelet is totally out of the question.*" Estes repeated the Herald's refrain, "*Prosecutors charge that Shay and Trenkler were lovers and conspired to murder Shay's father.*"

One of the restrictions of the release order was that Trenkler could come to Terry Segal's office only once a week between the hours of 10 a.m. and 4 p.m. Segal requested that the hours be expanded to 8 a.m. to 6 p.m. because some people Trenkler needed to meet with were not available during their work hours. Judge Zobel denied the motion.

If one of the reasons for the original incarceration had been the hope that a jailhouse informer could be found to testify to admissions by Trenkler, they already had achieved that goal, thus reducing the interest in continued incarceration. Also, although it apparently was not part of the decision process, Alfred Trenkler had a perfectly clean and non-violent record while in custody in Plymouth.

Judge Zobel responded to the second part of Terry Segal's 22 July Motion with a new trial date with an order on 12 August that the trial would start on Monday, 25 October and that the hearings on Trenkler's motions to suppress would resume on Thursday and Friday, 9 and 10 September, 1993. Terry Segal then filed a motion to request a further postponement until 9 November, due to a previously scheduled state murder trial.

On 18 August, Terry Segal dashed Alfred's hopes for one way out of his predicament with a one sentence letter, "*I spoke to Paul Markham, Gaeta's lawyer. He said Gaeta is not reliable, and it would be a mistake to try to compel him to testify.*" Again, Segal was very careful about the testimony from others. Even if it might be helpful, the risks of damage were perceived to be larger. We will never know what Edwin Gaeta might have said to harm Alfred's case, but we do know that his absence meant that the jury would not hear at least one of the alternative suspect theories. By the time of their verdict, the jurors had no sufficiently believable theories of alternative suspects before them. One jury had already concluded that the idea of Mr. Thomas L. Shay's possible role did not provide any reasonable doubt that Tom Shay was guilty.

There was an apparent agreement to begin the trial on 25 October, but Terry Segal filed a motion on 12 August to postpone the date to 9 November due to a conflict with a state murder trial in Superior Court on 26 October. That conflict was apparently resolved, as the Motion was denied by Judge Zobel on 16 October.

On 25 August 1993, the _Boston Globe_ published an article, "_LOCAL CELLULOID HERO BOSTON BOMB SQUAD CHIEF LENDS EXPERTISE TO FILM CREW,_" about the shooting in Boston of the MGM film "_Blown Away,_" about an explosion in Boston. The head of the Boston Bomb Squad since 1984 was Lieutenant Bob Molloy and he was assigned as a full-time technical adviser to the filming. When Molloy was first approached several months previously, he wanted no part in the production out of concern that it might jeopardize the ongoing investigation and prosecution of the Roslindale Bombing. As the fictional film has no connection to the case, he accepted the work with the filmmakers.

One of the problems with the splitting of the trials was that there were two sets of attorneys and two sets of experts and they had different theories of the roles of their clients, how the crime occurred, and how to conduct their trials. Still, there was some cooperation between the two teams, and on 31 August, Terry Segal wrote to Jefferson Boone, "_Thanks for the excellent suggestions. Please write or call with any others._"

On 2 September came the fourth day of hearings on pre-trial motions by both parties to the case. The earlier sessions were back in May where Trenkler's defense tried to show that the 5 November and 31 January searches were coercive. At the beginning, Judge Zobel tried to gauge the length of the hearing, and Paul Kelly noted that John Cates was ready to resume his testimony and as for "_Mr. Trenkler, they_ [the defense] _haven't made a final judgment on, according to Mr. Segal, on whether he will testify._" (TSH 4-2) Matthew Feinberg resumed his direct examination of John Cates. There were enough repetitive questions about Cates' legal status in the apartment and the nature of his attempt to refuse permission for a search, and technical objections to those questions that Judge Zobel said during Frank Libby's cross-examination, "_I must confess, I have some difficulty understanding the relevance of any of this, both Mr. Feinberg's and your examination. I don't know where we are going with this._" (TSH 4-31)

Later Frank Libby questioned John Cates about his claim that he was led involuntarily outside and led to sit in the backseat of a police car. After questions about whether a policeman actually had physically taken Mr. Cates by the hand, Judge Zobel commented, "_Mr Libby, I can accept the fact that nobody physically pushed him into the backseat, but that he nevertheless was placed there in the sense that he didn't decide on his own free will to go and sit down in somebody's car in the backseat. I mean, you know, he was with officers. There's no doubt about that, is there?_" (TSH 4-33/4)

Detective Timothy Murray of the Boston Police Department was then examined by Frank Libby. He testified that he had introduced himself to John Cates on the night of 5 November and extended his hand and shook hands with him and then went outside with him, voluntarily, to talk further. Detective Murray said that John Cates had voluntarily answered many questions during the conversation in the police car and that he had told Murray that he had expected the police to come, because he had received a phone call beforehand - from John Cates' friend, Eric Wilke. Also, John Cates had been shown a plastic bag of what appeared to be marijuana that had been found in the apartment, and Murray assured him that the search was not about marijuana; and Cates shrugged and said about the search, "*Sure, go ahead.*" (TSH 4-63] Cates' said in his own testimony, "*I responded that it was obvious that he had already searched, what was the point of asking me if he could search the apartment?*" (TSH 4-13)

When Alfred Trenkler left the apartment to go with officers to ARCOMM, Detective Murray quoted Trenkler as saying, "*Yes, everything is fine, I'm going to take a ride with these officers or guys, and he either said to Weymouth or to ARCOMM, and I'll be back in a little while.*" (TSH 4-64)

Frank Libby read to Detective Murray, John Cates's affidavit statement that one of the detectives said to him that he should "*use your imagination, and come up with something on* [Al], *there's a $65,000 reward, that's a lot of money.*" (TSH 4-67) Detective Murray said there was no such statement and no mention of the reward during the entire evening. As proof that there was no such statement, the Libby offered into evidence two articles from the *Boston Globe* and *Boston Herald* which announced the $50,000 reward on 12 November - a full week after the search.

Detective William Fogerty was the next witness to be examined by Frank Libby. He testified that he heard no conversation about a reward on 5 November 1991, and at the time, the reward was $50,000 and not yet increased to $65,000. Also, he was present at the 31 January 1992 search of the garage at the Wallace's and he had talked with Alfred Trenkler about his representation by a lawyer, "*He said that his lawyer had told him that he did not have to talk to the police and he was not to answer any questions. And I told him that he should be governed by his attorney's advice.*" (TSH 4-94)

The weight of Alfred Trenkler's Affidavit was discussed when Frank Libby said that when that affidavit takes issue with testimony by Special Agent Dennis Leahy and Detective William Fogerty, the affidavit "*should be ignored completely.*" Judge Zobel added, "*Unless he's subject to cross-examination.*" Then Paul Kelly added, "*Absolutely,*" and then Matthew Feinberg noted, surely with tongue-in-cheek, "*I think the two of them agree on that, your honor.*" Kelly affirmed, "*We do,*" and Judge Zobel concluded the repartee, "*I tend to agree with them on that.*" (TSH 4-101) The basic message was that unless Alfred Trenkler testified and was subject to cross-examination, his version of the challenged events wouldn't count for much, and that was a message which merited serious consideration by Alfred Trenkler and his lawyers for the entire trial.

Under cross-examination by Matthew Feinberg, Detective Fogerty said that Alfred Trenkler still wanted to talk. "*He talked about -- he was afraid that we were going to plant evidence in the garage and that we would ruin his reputation because of that. I explained to him that we weren't planting any evidence in anyone's garage or anything like that; that we were conducting an investigation and we would go where the investigation went.*" (TSH 4-111) These reputed statements, which Alfred acknowledges making, show that even though he was willing to talk with investigators, he was quite aware that law enforcement officers can pervert justice by planting evidence and distorting conversations. His natural gregariousness and interest in solving this problem won over his caution and apprehension.

While waiting for Trenkler's former attorney, Martin Cosgrove, to get to the courthouse, there were further discussion of how much longer the hearing would take, and hence the issue of Trenkler's testimony arose. Matthew Feinberg had left the door open on that possibility throughout the hearing. However, as the estimates of time-remaining seemed to include only about 20 minutes for direct and cross-examination of Mr. Cosgrove, Paul Kelly stated, "...*I just want to make sure, if I understand correctly, they are not going to be calling Mr. Trenkler as a witness?*" Replied Matt Feinberg, "*That's correct.*" Alfred Trenkler had been in the courtroom as the defendant for the entire hearing over the three days. Tom Shay had testified at his suppression hearings and had won a few points with Judge Zobel, who had not yet heard a word from Alfred Trenkler who the press was calling the "*cool,*" "*cunning,*" "*mastermind*" of the conspiracy. That impression would remain, as well as the newly formed impression of someone who will write something in an affidavit and then not wish to subject his statements to cross-examination. Preparing the affidavit without followup testimony was worse than not preparing an affidavit at all. It was his right not to testify, of course, but his lawyers' advice not to testify was a mistake as was his concurrence with that advice.

With the defense's decision, Judge Zobel reaffirmed what she had said earlier, "*If he doesn't subject himself to cross-examination as to the matters asserted in the affidavit, I will not consider the affidavit.*" (TSH 4-128)

The last witness, therefore, was Martin Cosgrove. His representation of Alfred Trenkler was informal as he never billed him for it. His primary advice was not to take a lie detector test and not to talk to the police at all. Unfortunately, Alfred did not follow that advice, and the police used his statements against him, and incorrectly. Most people think that lawyers give the advice of "*Don't talk*" because they don't want their guilty clients to slip and admit something they did. The other reason applies to Alfred Trenkler which is to prevent clients from saying something innocuous or ambiguous that the police and prosecutors will misinterpret. The next safest approach would have been to ensure that a friendly witness was nearby, or a recording device turned on, during conversations with investigators.

After the 5/6 November searches, Alfred Trenkler met with Mr. Cosgrove and the attorney then called Detective Peter O'Malley and advised him that there would be no lie detector test for Alfred Trenkler. After obtaining a new lawyer in February, 1992, that decision was never reversed, and may not have been re-examined in any way. Lie detectors have a mixed history in law enforcement, with some organizations favoring them such as ATF, and some not. In the Roslindale Bomb case, it was known that Louis Giammarco had failed a lie detector test, but it was never known why. Importantly, it did not lead to further repercussions to him. If Alfred Trenkler had taken a test and failed it, how could he have been worse off than he already was? The investigators already strongly believed that he was involved in the Roslindale Bomb. On the other hand, if he had passed it, then maybe ATF would have put some brakes on its accelerating guilt train and explore other suspects or ideas.

As the police believed that Alfred Trenkler was represented by counsel, the question of actual representation was not as important; it was rather whether the client, Alfred Trenkler, essentially waived his rights by voluntarily speaking with the investigators.

In September 1991, Martin Cosgrove represented Trenkler, John Cates and Richard Brown in their civil action arising from an automobile accident the previous summer, when they were all in Richard Brown's car. In late January 1992, he tried to help Alfred find another attorney when he had a conflict with his continued representation because he represented Richard Brown, too, and he understood that Brown had "*provided potentially adverse information*" to the Government about Trenkler. (TSH 4-156) He referred Trenkler to Tom Dwyer of Dwyer, Collura and Gertner, which, coincidentally, was the firm where Nancy Gertner was a partner, but not yet assigned to defend Tom Shay. However, Dwyer was not available, and the family was referred by others to Terry Segal of Segal and Feinberg.

After Martin Cosgrove's testimony, Judge Zobel discussed with the lawyers the issues which were involved. Surprisingly, the statements which the defense wanted to suppress were not yet known to them. They just knew there were some statements that the prosecutors planned to introduce at trial. Then there was discussion of the time required for Matthew Feinberg and the prosecutors to file written arguments after the hearings. Feinberg asked for three weeks, as he was going on vacation starting that afternoon. They agreed on two weeks for Feinberg, by 17 September and a week more for the prosecutors. After that, they would meet again at the planned start of the trial on 25 October.

Also on 2 September, Paul Kelly wrote a letter to Terry Segal to advise that he would not be using James Harding as a witness. Harding had worked briefly, and apparently unreliably, as an undercover agent for the Bureau of Alcohol Tobacco and Firearms. Wrote Kelly, "I apologize for having to send you this material from Jim Harding in continuing installments, however, this 'bizarre' character keeps delivering stuff to me. Mr. Harding is obviously a person not to be trusted <u>by anyone</u>. You have my assurance that I will not call him as a trial witness, nor will I use any tapes or other materials provided by him as part of the government's case in chief." It's not known whether Terry Segal then considered calling Harding as a "hostile" defense witness, as Harding had tried to uncover proof of Trenkler's guilt, but had found nothing. The jury was to be told that the ATF had found no physical evidence connecting Alfred Trenkler to the Roslindale Bomb, so why not tell the jury about the efforts by James Harding to trick Alfred Trenkler into making admissions? If such evidence had been introduced, it might have been easier to argue to the jury that William David Lindholm was a similar plant. If he had been using a recording device, he would have come up just as empty-handed as James Harding. However, it must be remembered that hindsight is 20/20, and Terry Segal did not anticipate losing this case with the strategies he was pursuing.

On 15 September Terry Segal filed an unusual "*Motion for authority to call Assistant. United States Attorney Paul Kelly as a defense witness*" at the Trenkler trial, because of Kelly's conversations with Tom Shay prior to his trial.

In support of this motion, defendant states:
1. During a portion of the pre-indictment period (March-June, 1992), Thomas Shay, Jr. was held at Charles Street Jail. Thomas Shay, Jr., is a co-defendant in this case, and a person whose inculpatory statements the prosecution will attempt to introduce into

evidence in this case. While at Charles Street Jail and while represented by counsel, Thomas Shay, Jr. made several collect calls to Mr. Kelly.

2. During at least two of those collect telephone calls, Mr. Shay told Mr. Kelly that Shay Sr. was responsible for the Roslindale Bombing that killed Officer Hurley.

3. Attached hereto (Exhibit A) is Mr. Kelly's April 20, 1992, letter to Shay Jr.'s then attorney, William C. McPhee, Esq., in which Mr. Kelly relates the substance of two of Shay Jr.'s collect phone calls in which Shay Jr., contrary to other statements he made to Mr. Kelly and other government investigators inculpating himself in the bombing, claims his father was responsible for the bombing. It also seems likely that during this time frame (March-June, 1992) Shay Jr. made several other collect calls to Mr. Kelly for which no written memoranda exist.

4. In early October, 1992, Shay Jr. executed a proffer agreement with Mr. Kelly in which Mr. Kelly indicated that if Shay Jr. was truthful he could expect a sentence in the range of three years.

5. On November 10, 1992, Mr. Kelly wrote a memorandum where he stated "... I advised Shay (1) we had been unable to corroborate any aspects of his 'story'... "

6. In his November 10th memorandum, Mr. Kelly, <u>inter alia</u>, stated,
Shay stated that out of fear of being charged and spending the rest of his life in prison, he had lied to me and agents in several significant respects. Those aspects of his 'story' which he admitted were untrue are as follows:...
... Shay then told us a new 'story' which he claimed was truthful - obviously we have a high degree of skepticism. His new story may be summarized as:...

7. On November 12, 1992, Mr. Kelly wrote a letter (Exhibit B) to Shay's lawyer and stated, I am writing at this time to formally advise you what I have been saying for the past several weeks. To date, ATF has been unable to corroborate any aspects of the proffer provided to us by your client, Thomas A. Shay. It seems that the only independent evidence tending to confirm Shay's story is that which federal investigators had uncovered prior to Shay's recent proffer. Given the foregoing, absent any new evidence being brought to my attention that substantially corroborates significant aspects of Shay's proffer, I am unable to conclude that he has been 'entirely truthful and cooperative' concerning the offense under investigation or his role therein.

8. On December 15, 1992, according to Mr. Kelly's memorandum of January 5, 1993, Shay Jr., in the company of his attorney, told Mr. Kelly that the bomb was attached to his father's car several days before the explosion "while the Buick was parked in the vicinity of the Waltham Tavern in the South End of Boston."

9. According to the transcript of the October 17, 1992, Channel 56 interview of Thomas Shay, Jr. by Karen Marinella, Shay said:. . .U.S. Attorney Paul V. Kelly said, it doesn't matter how much money this task force will take to find the package, it could go from $1,000 to $1,000,000, doesn't matter as long as they convict Al Trenkler...

. . . He knows that Al Trenkler is the dangerous one so he offered me, in April, 20 years and he offered me ten - five and down to three years here to go to a whitecollared prison with - out of 6,000 inmates, a federal prison, 3,500 are appellants so it's a very, you know, three years, I can do standing on my head...

. . .My father knew that was a bomb. How did he know? Nobody knows. My father denies that he ever had any threats. Paul Kelly talked to him the other day, and Paul Kelly said, 'Tom Shay, you know, did you get some threats, I don't believe you.' He said, 'I think you're a liar because I think you got threats or something in that sense...'

... From my knowledge, my father picked it up three times and threw it, but then Paul Kelly said my father changed his story. He picked it up carefully, placed it, placed it again and placed it again, and here come these officers, and they go to lift it up with a - a file. lift it up and it blows up on them.

10. Based upon the foregoing and possibly other telephone conversations between Thomas Shay Jr. and Mr. Kelly, Mr. Kelly is an important defense witness.

11. More specifically, Mr. Kelly is an important witness relating, <u>inter alia</u>, to the following matters:

a. Shay Jr.'s prior inconsistent statements made to him in at least two telephone conversations;

b. His opinions, as expressed in the November 10th memorandum (defendant requests permission to submit the entire November 10th memorandum to the Court under seal) and November 12th letter (Exhibit B) as to the credibility of Thomas Shay, Jr. See Federal Rule of Evidence 608 (a) ;

c. The fact that after executing a three-year sentence proffer agreement in October, Shay Jr. implicated Alfred Trenkler, .. and the government concluded his proffer testimony could not be corroborated.

Wherefore, defendant respectfully requests:

1. This Court permit defendant to call Paul Kelly as a witness.

2. This Court conduct an evidentiary hearing to determine the substance of any telephone conversations between Paul Kelly and Thomas Shay Jr., and determine whether Mr. Kelly made the statements attributed to him by Shay, Jr. in the Channel 56 interview.

3. This Court permit defendant to submit, under seal, the November 10th memorandum and the January 5, 1993, memorandum referred to in this motion.

4. This Court grant such other relief as is meet and just.

On 23 September 1993, Ralph Ranalli wrote about the defense Motion for the *Boston Herald* in the article, *"PROSECUTOR MAY BE CALLED TO TESTIFY IN BOMB CASE."* Ranalli wrote that *"...Paul Kelly received accolades in July for his part in winning a guilty verdict in a difficult and almost entirely circumstantial cast against Trenkler's co-defendant, Thomas A. Shay."*

The article stated, *"Kelly called Segal's motion a 'creative, aggressive' tactic yesterday. 'I don't expect it to prevail, but it's a slick move.' he said."* It's hard to miss Kelly's view of the trial as a game or sport with tactics and moves.

Recounting the contents of Kelly's 5 January 1993 "Memo to File" about the conversations with Tom Shay, Ranalli wrote, *"In the memo, Kelly said Shay told him he and Trenkler planned the bombing for insurance money and he promised Trenkler 'at least $100,000.' "* Even if Tom Shay didn't graduate from high school, the prosecutors could have done the math and they would have found that even with the unlikely possibility of a judgment to the full amount of the alleged $400,000 insurance, and even if Tom Shay were to inherit the same share as Mr. Shay's three daughters and two step-daughters, and after Mary Flanagan's share, his own share could have been far closer to $10,000 than $100,000. According to the prosecution's theory, Trenkler would have gained a portion of Tom Shay's share. If Shay were to get $20,000 and Trenkler, $10,000, that's what Alfred Trenkler could earn with one good microwave antenna installation project. It's also what he could have earned in broker commissions from his work in evaluating any single company for potential purchase by Fidelity Management Co.

The Ranalli article continued, *"Shay also said Trenkler obtained the explosives and blasting caps for the bomb and that the two built it in a shed near a radio tower on the South Shore, the memo said. Shay allegedly said Trenkler planted the bomb under his father's car outside the Warren Tavern in Boston's South End."* There was no comment from Terry Segal nor an indication that he was asked for a comment. The media now knew what the response would be, so such calls were likely not made. It surely would have been helpful, and ethically responsible to respond to the specifics of the article, such as with such a statement as, *"Alfred Trenkler never talked with Tom Shay about any bomb or about any insurance money or anything beyond directions for five rides which Trenkler gave Tom Shay in the summer of 1991. Trenkler never had any explosives, nor blasting caps nor did he ever build anything with Tom Shay anywhere. Alfred Trenkler never placed anything under Tom Shay's father's car. Finally, if Tom Shay had testified at his own trial, he would recant the self-aggrandizing statements made to Paul Kelly and told the truth."*

Paul Kelly and Frank Libby responded with a comparatively short, three page "Opposition to Defendant's Motion," which was filed on 27 September, but which was included in Ranalli's article above. They noted that every meeting attended by Paul Kelly with Tom Shay was attended by at least one other person who could testify about the discussion. The content of the two telephone calls from Tom Shay to Paul Kelly on 15 and 16 April "may be stipulated to," presumably through an agreement with the convicted Tom Shay. Second, argued the prosecutors, "Shay Jr.'s alleged 'prior inconsistent statements' are inadmissible hearsay unless Trenkler can point to an exception to the hearsay rule which otherwise controls. Third, AUSA Kelly's memorandum of November 10, 1992 is also hearsay, and is not admissible by the defense under Fed. R. Evid. 608(a) as opinion evidence concerning Shay Jr.'s character for truthfulness." Thus, even though Paul Kelly's opinion was that much of what Tom Shay said to him was false and a "hoax," no jury would ever hear his opinion. Instead, he would throw to the jury what he could legally throw, and see what stuck. Almost everything did.

On 24 September 1993 Matthew Feinberg filed his 26 page *"Memorandum of Law in support of Motions to Suppress."* He began with a statement of "I. *FACTS: On November 5, 1991, a small army of Special Agents..."* and then described the rest of that evening, and the events of 31 January 1992 and 3 and 4 February 1992. He then argued in Section II, with the following paragraph heading arguments:

"A. The Searches of November 5-6, 1991 Were Unconstitutional and
    Executed in the Absence of a Valid Consent, and

B. The Statements Made by Trenkler during the Night of November 5-6
    Were Involuntary and the Product of Custodial Interrogation, and

    1. The Defendant was in custody on the night of November 5-6, and

    2. The Defendant's statements (and drawings) of November 5-6 were
       the product of interrogation, and

    3. The Defendant's statements of November 5-6 were involuntary, and

C. The Defendant's Statements of January 31 and February 3-4, 1992,
    Were Deliberately Elicited from Him in Violation of His Sixth
    Amendment Right to Counsel.

D. The Warrants Authorizing the Searches of January 31, 1992 Are
Invalid insofar as the Affidavit in Support of the Warrant Relied
Substantially on the Fruit of Prior Warrantless, Nonconsensual
Searches.
III. Conclusion: For all the above reasons, the Defendant prays his motions to suppress
will be allowed."

The prosecutors responded on 4 October with a 38 page "Government's Memorandum in Opposition to Defendant's Motions to Suppress." The "FACTS" section covered the three disputed periods: 5/6 November 1991, 31 January 1992 and 3/4 February, 1992. It relied heavily upon testimony at the hearing by the ATF agents and Boston police and argued that Alfred Trenkler was cooperative and conversational during all three periods. Several examples of his responses to the officers requests were given, such as "Sure," and to John Cates, "We're going to my office. I'll see you later." (From the transcript at TSH 2-105 and 1-50, respectively)

Then came the argument:

"A. The Investigators' Presence In The Basement Apartment at 133 Atlantic Avenue; At ARCOMM; And At 7 Whitelawn Avenue on November 5-6, 1991 Was Pursuant to Trenkler's Valid Consent.

The prosecutors noted that "Trenkler is a college-educated man in his thirties, sophisticated enough in the world of business to lease office space and run his own electronics communications firm." When arguing that Alfred Trenkler consented to the 133 Atlantic Ave. search, the prosecutors noted, "Because Trenkler chose not to testify during these proceedings, there is nothing in the record from Trenkler supporting or contradicting this point."

The outline of the Argument continued,

"B. Trenkler's Statements to Investigators November 5-6, 1991 Were Voluntarily Made, And Were Not The Result Of A Custodial Interrogation.

C. Trenkler's Statement[s] To Investigators On January 31 And February 4, 1992 Were Knowingly And Voluntarily Made, In Clearly Non-Custodial Environments, And Are Admissible Against Him At Trial.

D. Trenkler Has Not Shown That The Government Has Illegally Obtained Fruit From A "Poisonous Tree"

III. Conclusion For the foregoing reasons, Trenkler's various Motions to Suppress should be DENIED."

The Prosecutor's facts and arguments were persuasive and thorough and confident. For Alfred Trenkler, these hearings were not a good sign. Instead of proceeding with his "*I have nothing to hide*" approach that Alfred Trenkler showed during his initial contacts with investigators, his lawyers had chosen the more frequently traveled road of denial and suppression of evidence and they looked foolish in so doing. The prosecution emerged even more confident that Alfred Trenkler was guilty and Judge Zobel still had not heard anything directly from Alfred Trenkler.

On 27 September the *Boston Globe* reported that the recent death of Police Officer John Mulligan, was the "*7TH OFFICER KILLED IN PAST 6 YEARS;*" and Jeremiah

Hurley was on the list. These articles were an almost annual and unwelcome reminder of Hurley's death. His family would never escape such unavoidable reminders, but they hoped that the upcoming trial of Alfred Trenkler would be the end of the reminders from the legal system. It was to be an unrealized hope of people who expected the system to provide real justice.

The Motion to call an Assistant U.S. Attorney as a witness was sufficiently audacious that Judge Zobel quickly scheduled a hearing on the issue for 29 September. She opened, "*I asked for this hearing because I frankly am not altogether sure what we're talking about in the motion and response. So maybe counsel can enlighten me.*" (TSH 4-2)

Terry Segal argued that if the prosecution plans to introduce hearsay exception admissions by Tom Shay of his involvement, the defense should be able to introduce evidence that Shay told Paul Kelly in two phone calls, as Segal summarized, "*My father did this.*" (TSH 4-3) This effort was an attempt to, at least in one small regard, escape the bind that Nancy Gertner was in at Shay's trial where Shay's admissions were admitted as exceptions to the hearsay role, but his statements about other theories of the crime were not. In the Trenkler trial, Segal was arguing that Kelly could testify about what Tom Shay said to him, because it's "*impeachment testimony*" which would be admissible as another exception to the hearsay rule. That is, it contradicts the truth of the other statements which were themselves exceptions to the hearsay rule.

Segal argued that a stipulation about the two phone calls "*deprives me of compulsory process. And it also puts Mr. Kelly in the advocate witness problem, where, on the one hand, he stipulates and says, Mr. Shay called me on those two times and said this, and then goes to the jury, and says: Don't believe anything Mr. Shay said to me; believe my side of the case.*"

Then Judge Zobel asked which of Shay's incriminating statements the prosecutors planned to introduce and the first mentioned were those in the Channel 56 videotape and then she correctly summarized Segal's argument, "*His point is that if statements of Shay are offered, then he wants to do, similar to, I guess, what Shay's counsel wanted to do, offer other statements to show that nothing Shay says is reliable.*" (TSH 4-5)

Frank Libby then challenged Segal's motives, "*If I may, your Honor, I'll cut right to the chase of it. This entire proceeding has virtually nothing to do with the merits of this case and everything to do with the defense team's fervent wish to knock Mr. Kelly out of this case.*" (TSH 4-5) Again, the prosecutors viewed the trial in substantial part as a game, with moves and countermoves which sometimes were more important than the forgotten rule of presenting the truth to the jury.

Judge Zobel agreed with the prosecutors on the inadmissibility of Paul Kelly's statements in his "**Memorandum to File**", and stated "*Mr. Kelly's opinion of Mr. Shay's credibility is absolutely not admissible.*" The result was that it was permissible in Federal Court in Boston for a prosecutor to present a defendant's statements to a jury, even though that prosecutor believed those statements were untrue and in general that the witness was a habitual fabricator.

That left Segal's motion requesting Kelly's testimony only with the two phone calls. Judge Zobel then said, "*So if that's all that's at issue, then the motion is denied insofar as you are seeking to disqualify Mr. Kelly or, as you put it more gently, to have him* testify. *But I will do that on condition that the government, in fact, provides the defendant with the letter and a memorandum of what was said, in a form that may be admissible in evidence."* (TSH 4-9) She said she wasn't going to disqualify a prosecutor who had worked for two years on the case for two phone calls, the substance of which could be stipulated. In general it's not a sound practice to have prosecutors personally involved in the events of a criminal case, but what would have been the harm of having Paul Kelly take the witness stand to testify under oath about two phone calls with Tom Shay? Wouldn't that step have assisted in bringing more truth to the jury? In cases where a defendant represents himself or herself, the defendant is also permitted to take the stand and testify, and also question others.

Segal pressed again that such a solution would not be enough, as Paul Kelly would be *"arguing to the jury that, ladies and gentlemen, don't believe a word of what Mr. Thomas Shay, Jr., said to me in those two telephone conversations, as listed in the stipulation; believe the rest of the government's case..."*

Judge Zobel assured Terry Segal that Paul Kelly would not be making that argument to the jury, and Frank Libby might be making the final argument in any case. Of course, that would not cure the problem of the prosecutor still trying to present a case to a jury to convince them to convict Trenkler on the basis, in part, of statements made by a person Paul Kelly knew to be untrustworthy. If not legally a problem, it doesn't seem fair.

Then the hearing continued about other discovery issues such as obtaining copies of the grand jury testimony of witnesses who didn't testify at the Shay trial, and the Government's plan to introduce evidence of the 1986 M21 Hoffman device. It was agreed that a separate hearing would be held on Friday, 22 October, the last workday before the Trenkler trial, to consider that issue.

On 27 September 1993 the prosecutors in the Alfred Trenkler case filed a 31 page "Memorandum of Law in Support of Government's Motion In Limine to Admit Evidence of 1986 Bombing." They argued in their well-documented and reasoned brief that Tom Shay had been convicted of conspiring to kill his father with a bomb and convicted of attempted malicious destruction of an automobile, and that "in order to prove the charged offenses at Trenkler's trial, the government will be required to establish that <u>one</u> of the conspirators -- Shay Jr. or Trenkler had the knowledge, skill and ability to build the 1991 Device. By virtue of its theory of the prosecution and the language of the Superseding Indictment, the government must show that Trenkler was this person."

To prove that Trenkler built both devices, the prosecutors planned to show that the devices were physically similar and designed in a similar way, as would be shown by experts and by a computer database (EXIS) analysis, and that Alfred Trenkler used others to help him acquire components of both devices. The prosecutors said their expert, Thomas Waskom, would testify that the two devices were designed and constructed by the same person.

Frank Libby and Paul Kelly argued that the 1986 incident was a "prior bad act" of a defendant which previous court cases have settled could be admitted as evidence if that earlier act shed sufficient light on the act at trial to outweigh the potentially unfair prejudice of admitting it. They argued that they must show that Trenkler was capable of building the 1991 bomb, and his admitted role in the 1986 incident shows such ability.

Among the cases cited were some that held that "prior bad acts" could be excluded from a current case only where the prior act was so "shocking" or "heinous" as to risk causing a jury to irrationally condemn the defendant for the current act because of the prior act.

It was true that the 1986 incident showed a pattern of behavior by Alfred Trenkler, but it wasn't as the government perceived. What it showed was Alfred's sense of playfulness as was seen previously with the prank with John Coyle's stereo hooked up to broadcast throughout the house he was sharing with Alfred, and Donna Leach and John Shea. It was not to broadcast Coyle's sexual activity as the ATF reported, but his strange taste in music. Playing jokes on people was part of Alfred's pattern of behavior - not building bombs.

On 8 October 1993, Tom Shay was sentenced to 188 months in prison and the public reaction was negative. *Boston Herald* Columnist Beverly Beckham's blistering column on 15 October concluded with respect to Alfred Trenkler, "*In 10 days Shay's co-conspirator Alfred Trenkler will go to trial. But why bother? Why take up the court's time? Why inconvenience other jurors? Why put the victims' families through another trial? Why spend more taxpayer dollars when the system works the way it does, when a judge, who is required by law to adhere to federal sentencing guidelines, can simply reinterpret a jury's decision, ignore premeditation and impose a far lighter sentence than a jury of '12 good men and true' directed.*"

Also on 15 October, Terry Segal filed a 41 page "*Memorandum in Opposition to Government's Motion In Limine to Admit Evidence of 1986 Bombing.*" He argued that there was insufficient evidence to show that the maker of the 1986 and 1991 devices were just one person, and only one person. He noted that the 1986 device was not intended to kill anyone, and that there is insufficient evidence to show that Alfred Trenkler was anywhere near the 197 Mass Ave. Radio Shack store on 18 October 1991. The defense expert, Denny Kline, would testify that the devices could not be concluded to have been built by the same person. Finally, he argued that the prejudicial impact of admitting the evidence of the 1986 device would outweigh probative value, and it would waste time and would confuse issues at the trial. He concluded, "*Given the government's paltry proof in this case, we submit that admission of the 1986 incident will deprive Alfred Trenkler of a fair trial, and could constitute plain error.... For the foregoing reasons, we respectfully request this Court to deny the government's motion in limine and prohibit the government from introducing in its case in chief any evidence or reference to the defendant's involvement in the 1986 incident.*"

Appoximately on 17 October, the prosecutors filed a list of 83 witnesses which the Government "*may call*" to testify at the upcoming Trenkler trial. Of that list, only 33 would actually testify.

The 18 October *Boston Herald* carried Ralph Ranalli's story about the prosecution's motion to compel Tom Shay to testify at Alfred Trenkler's trial, "*FEDS WANT CONVICTED BOMBER SHAY TO TESTIFY VS. HIS ALLEGED ACCOMPLICE.*" Ranalli wrote, "*In hearing testimony and papers filed in the case, prosecutors have said Shay has repeatedly made statements implicating Trenkler. But Shay's defense said that he is a compulsive liar, whose statements cannot be relied on as true.*" There were no comments by lawyers on either side of the Trenkler case, nor any reference to unnamed sources.

Also on 18 October Terry Segal filed a "*Motion to Suppress Statements Allegedly made to William David Lindholm on or about December 17, 18, 19, 20, 1992 and Request for Evidentiary Hearing.*" In support of the Motion, Segal noted that he had received just four days previous, on 14 October, Jeff Kerr's seven page report on his 13 January 1992 interview with William David Lindholm. (See chapter 3 of this book.) Segal continued, "*A review of this report raises a serious question as to whether the government obtained allegedly incriminating statements by knowingly circumventing Alfred Trenkler's right to have counsel present during any confrontation between him and a government agent,*" i.e. Lindholm.

Segal stated that Kerr's report does not state why Lindholm, after missing his late afternoon transportation 20 miles north to the Essex County Jail in Middleton, Mass. where he had been incarcerated, was then not only taken 41 miles south to Plymouth instead, but also left there for three days. The logical next step would have been to bring him back to his clothes and possessions in Middleton, on Friday, December 18. It was known within the Federal prison system that the U.S. Marshals do not move inmates around without orders from senior officials. The question was: who made the decision(s) to send David Lindholm to Plymouth and who made the decision(s) to keep him there.

The report did not state why Lindholm and Trenkler remained in the Orientation Unit over the weekend when all but "*six or seven*" men had been transferred to the general population.

Terry Segal concluded, "*we submit that an evidentiary hearing is necessary to determine whether Lindholm was acting as a government informant, whether Lindholm initiated a discussion of the charges Trenkler was incarcerated for, and whether the government 'deliberately elicited' alleged incriminating statements from Trenkler without the assistance of counsel as prohibited by Massiah (v. U.S. 377 U.S. 201 (1964)) and its progeny.*"[2]

What Segal did not provide was any information from Alfret Trenkler about his recollection of conversations with William David Lindholm. An affidavit would have been helpful, but only if Terry Segal would agree to let Alfred Trenkler testify at such an evidentiary hearing. Otherwise, as was stated at the 1 September suppression hearing, an affidavit of a defendant would be ignored if not supported by cross-examinable testimony. Once again, the legal maneuvering seemed like Trenkler wanted to hide statements he made, instead of denying or explaining them.

Also on 18 October, Tom Shay's attorney, Amy Baron-Evans, filed a "*Motion to Quash*" or cancel a prosecution subpoena for Tom Shay to testify at Alfred Trenkler's trial. Her role on Tom Shay's defense team increased after Nancy Gertner's nomination to become a U.S. District Court Judge. In addition to the issue of the Fifth Amendment right against self-incrimination for a person already convicted in a Federal court, but still appealing the conviction, Ms. Baron-Evans raised the issue of a prosecutor's obligation regarding the expected truthfulness of testimony. The Motion states. "*First, AUSA Kelly may not ethically offer a witness whom he has reason to believe will not tell the truth. AUSA Kelly has admitted in open court (during the sentencing proceeding), and in correspondence with counsel, that he believes many, if not most, of Mr. Shay's statements are not credible. He had made such statements in particular with respect to the proffer statements which he apparently hopes to introduce.*" Her other major concern was the potential risk for charging Tom Shay with perjury, no matter what he would say at the Trenkler trial.

Alfred Trenkler's attorneys did not file a response to the subpoena of Tom Shay. This was another lost opportunity to present the truth, or at least appear to be seeking the truth.

Another 18 October filing was the U.S. Attorney's Motion to "exclude any reference to or offering of improper evidence" by the Trenkler defense team. Specifically, the AUSA's asked that Terry Segal be ordered not to mention to the jury that the offenses for which Alfred Trenkler was charged "could have carried the penalty of death upon conviction" or life imprisonment. The apparent goal was to prevent sympathy for Trenkler, which was curious, as he eventually was sentenced to two life terms. Also, the AUSA's asked Judge Zobel "to order the defendant to disclose to the government any collateral acts or issues that he intends to use at trial to impeach the government's civilian witnesses, prior to asking such questions before the jury." This Motion showed the exquisite detail of the choreography of a criminal trial with each actor knowing in advance the lines of the rest of the cast. Judge Zobel allowed the Motion.

On 20 October Terry Segal filed a "*Motion to conduct the examination of potential jurors in a manner likely to expose juror bias.*" He stated that the "*leading and suggestive questions*" used at the Shay trial were "*unlikely to elicit candid responses from prospective jurors.*" Segal proposed the use of a questionnaire as recommended by a jury selection expert, James Bergund, whose affidavit was attached.

Also on 20 October Terry Segal filed a motion for a subpoena for U.S. Bureau of Prison records for William David Lincholm, with special concern for his whereabouts during the few weeks before his encounter with Alfred Trenkler at Plymouth County House of Correction. The U.S. Attorney's Office opposed the Motion by filing a Motion to Quash the trial subpoenas and charged "quite frankly, Trenkler appears to be engaged in a 'fishing expedition' for information." What Terry Segal was seeking was information which could explain how a Bureau of Prisons inmate in Texas, but whose hometown was Milton, could be moved to the Plymouth County House of Correction to be in the same Orientation Unit as Alfred Trenkler, with Milton roots and currently a returned resident, in his parents' home. Judge Zobel allowed the Motion to Quash on Friday, 22 October.

Friday, 22 October also saw the fifth day of suppression hearings for the Alfred Trenkler case. It was to be the longest courtroom session for the entire trial, lasting 240 transcript pages. First, Judge Zobel was concerned that Alfred Trenkler was not present. "*I want counsel to talk to me about this sort of thing before we start a hearing. He has a right to be present, and he should waive his right in open court in some manner, so that the record isn't in any way prejudiced.*" Terry Segal said that Trenkler was at home working on a project for his defense, and waived Trenkler's right to be present and Judge Zobel replied, "*I will take your oral waiver on his behalf now. I want him to sign something that says he understood he could be present and that he knowingly waives his right to be present.*" (TH 10/22 2 [transcript hearing 22 Oct, page 2]) Perhaps explained by the flurry of activity at this time, only three days before the beginning of trial, Alfred Trenkler was never advised of the problem of his absence and never was asked to sign any waiver. He learned about the problem in

2007. His role in the courtroom, as assigned to him by his lawyers so far, had been to be seen and not heard.

The first issue for the hearing was the Motion to quash the subpoenas for Tom Shay and Francis O'Rourke, one of Shay's former attorneys. Despite her nomination to become a Federal Judge, Nancy Gertner presented her arguments to quash, and began, "*And I have some concerns that this is, with all* [due] *respect, a bad faith subpoena.*" (TH 10/22 6) That is, she believed it was designed to trap Tom Shay into making perjurious statements in order to prosecute him later.

Judge Zobel asked the key question, "*What does the government expect Mr. Shay to say?*" (TH 10/22 6) AUSA Paul Kelly replied, "I would expect him to tell us that he purchased the toggle switch; that he did so at Mr. Trenkler's direction; that he has known Mr. Trenkler for some three years; that he spent a fair amount of time with Mr. Trenkler in the weeks leading up to October; that he told Mr. Trenkler about his difficult times and feelings toward his father; that he told Mr. Trenkler about some of the financial issues which the Court hear evidence and testimony about at the first trial that relates to motive. I believe that Mr. Shay will offer very probative testimony on the nature of the conspiracy between him and Mr. Trenkler and Mr. Trenkler's involvement therein." (TH 10/22 7/8)

It was a predictable prediction for Mr. Kelly, but the truth about each of those areas is almost totally opposite. One wonders whether the prosecutors really believed the charges they are making or whether it's the argument that is the challenge, and the thrill of winning with a guilty verdict. Were they "True Believers" in the Eric Hoffer sense of one who continues to believe something after the factual support for that belief has diminished? Was there any doubt in Mr. Kelly's mind? Any doubt whatsoever?   Below is what Tom Shay could be expected to say [see Appendix B], as it's the truth:

- Tom Shay did not purchase the toggle switch, but even if he
  did, it was NOT for Alfred Trenkler, whom he had not seen since
  August, 1991.
- There was not a three year relationship with Alfred Trenkler, but an acquaintance
  beginning in June 1991 which saw six face-to-face meetings for a total of
  about 8.5 hours,[3] with the last one being a perfunctory few minutes in
  August in the presence of John Cates.
- The amount of time during the ten weeks before the 28 October was
  zero minutes. That surely is less than the "fair amount of time" that
  Mr. Kelly referenced.
- Tom Shay did not tell Alfred Trenkler about his difficult relationship
  with his father, other than that he could not be taken to his father's
  home the early morning of that first requested ride because of his father's
  embarrassment arising from Tom's announcement that he was gay.
- Tom Shay did not tell Alfred Trenkler about the "financial issues" such
  as his father's civil lawsuit.

Unfortunately, Terry Segal was not able to say to Paul Kelly, "*You know, Paul, none of those statements are true. During a recess, let's talk about why I'm sure about that.*" Outside the litigation world, that's how people resolve differences of opinion. When there are differences of fact, they devise a method of finding the truth. Within the world of litigation, the truth could only be presented through straight jacketed procedures through a choreographed trial.

However, what Terry Segal could have said, as the topic of the moment was what the prospective testimony of Tom Shay could have been, "*If Tom Shay testifies as you expect, then he would been lying on every single point. Every one.*" Further, Segal could have added, and with a change in his position, "*I've changed my view on this. Alfred Trenkler now strongly supports the subpoena to Tom Shay. I hope he does testify. If he tells the lies that Mr. Kelly expects, I will cross-examine him sufficiently to show to the jury that nothing he said could be true, and certainly not to be used to convict Alfred Trenkler. On the other hand, if he testifies with the truth, i.e. that the acquaintance began in June 1991 and ended in August, and that there were no conversations about his relationship to his father, and there were none about his father's lawsuit and there were no contacts with Alfred Trenkler since August 1991, then the jury will see that Alfred Trenkler cannot be convicted on such evidence.*"

Returning to the hearing, Paul Kelly would not guarantee immunity from a perjury charge, but he did say, "*There's been this argument that this fellow is incapable of telling the truth. I don't believe that to be the case and neither do our experts. I would never ask this man questions on matters that I know he's told me something which is fanciful.*" (TH 10/22 9)

Judge Zobel and Nancy Gertner were concerned about what the prosecutors would do with Tom Shay's Trenkler-trial testimony if Shay were to prevail in his appeal of his conviction and there were a retrial. Nancy Gertner said that she would advise Shay to refuse a court order and risk further punishment for contempt, which may be another goal of the prosecution. About Tom Shay in general, she said, "*Were this a state prosecution, Mr. Shay, I feel confident, would have been found incompetent to stand trial because one of the prongs of state incompetency had to do with whether or not he could assist counsel. And he cannot. We would talk to him about issues in the case and he would talk about what he had for lunch. So the notion that he could be prepared, the notion that he could even be a competent witness, which we didn't raise in our papers, is a substantial open question. From our dealings with the man, I cannot say what the truth is or not. At all.*" (TH 10/22 11/12) She did, however, have Tom Shay testify at one of his suppression hearings on 12 May 1993, and there was no allegation that he told lies at that hearing or other claims of inappropriate courtroom conduct. Similarly, he testified at his September 1991 deposition in his father's civil case against the Dedham Service Center, and there had been no charges of perjury arising from that testimony.

Judge Zobel asked Terry Segal for his views of the Motions to quash and he said simply, "*I join with Ms. Gertner and Mr. Backman* [the attorney for Francis O'Rourke]" (TH 10/22 20) It was a lost opportunity, for if Tom Shay had actually testified as Paul Kelly had predicted, or even it not, he could be cross-examined to the point of making his statements meaningless, which would leave the Trenkler jury asking why Alfred Trenkler would want to do anything for Tom Shay other than give him rides to requested destinations.

Judge Zobel said she would think about the Motion to Quash, and Paul Kelly made a final comment, which is presented below in full.

"*With respect to the motion on Mr. Shay, a couple quick points, No. 1, Dr. Kelly has testified in this court that Mr. Shay is capable of telling the truth. 2. The items that we* would seek to adduce are items for which we have every reason to believe those items are truthful. In fact, we would offer testimony which we believe we can corroborate with other independent evidence. I certainly understand the rules on a prosecutor suborning perjury or even getting close to the line. I wouldn't do that for a minute. And no one's played hide the ball with Terry Segal. He knows exactly the myriad of fanciful things that have been said.

But a lot of defendants make self-serving statements to prosecutors when they meet them. It happens to us all the time. We have somebody tell us a story, they diminish their own responsibility and then some nuggets of truth come up, and sometimes they turn all the way around. This isn't particularly unusual.

Is the man fragile? Maybe he's fragile, whatever that means. Is he capable of telling the truth? Absolutely. Is the government acting in bad faith simply because they want to walk him into some perjury contempt charge? We couldn't care less about that. We've got a serious case ahead of us here, that's our only reason for doing this." (TH 10/22 20/21)

As Nancy Gertner had said earlier in the hearing, Paul Kelly could see 50 statements by Tom Shay and know that 25 statements were false, and then stand by the other 25 as if they were made by an entirely truthful person.

Then the Judge turned to a defense Motion to Quash the subpoena to James Karolides, the private investigator for the defense. Before agreeing to delay consideration of the Motion until Paul Kelly had had a change to review it, as he had not yet seen it, he stated why he issued the subpoena, "We served the subpoena because we had heard from a number of our witnesses about certain statements and conduct by Mr. Karolides, which we think is highly questionable in terms of suggestive remarks to a witnesses, [sic] disparaging remarks to witnesses about certain investigators or investigative tactics..." (TH 10/22 21/22]

One of the complaints against Mr. Karolides came from Richard Brown who talked by phone with Dennis Leahy on 12 April 1993. Brown asked that either Leahy or an AUSA call Karolides and ask him to stop "bugging" Richard Brown and his grandfather. In passing, Richard Brown said to Dennis Leahy that Alfred Trenkler was "guilty as sin." About a half hour after that call, Richard Brown called again and Dennis Leahy reported that Brown said that "Karolides said to him that the government was lying and that Al Trenkler was at ARCOM [sic] painting the day of the bombing. Mr. Brown said Karolides was hostile to him and said he would receive a subpoena for his business records if he did not cooperate with Karolides."

Because of the adversary nature of a U.S. criminal proceeding, it was apparently not possible for Paul Kelly to simply ask Terry Segal about the allegations regarding James Karolides, who had previously worked for the ATF for 20 years and been a private investigator for four years. Perhaps Mr. Karolides could have responded to the allegations of misconduct with a phone call or a letter, or an affidavit or voluntary testimony. Why did Terry Segal resist? Wouldn't it have been good for the defense to bring to the judge's attention some of the information that Mr. Karolides was uncovering? If such a communication back to Mr. Kelly had occurred, perhaps he would have reconsidered his perspectives on his own witnesses who made the complaints to him. Instead Terry Segal took the usual view which is that the work of private investigators is proprietary and should not be opened to view by the prosecutors.

On the other hand, if the charges against Mr. Karolides were true, and as he was a long-time former ATF employees, Mr. Kelly might have asked himself about the credibility for the ATF investigators upon whose credibility his case against Alfred Trenkler depended. Either way, it would have been helpful to get more information about the allegations, and, as has been seen, the adversary process is sometimes not the best process for gleaning truth.

Next for argument came Terry Segal's Motion to suppress any statements made by Alfred Trenkler to William David Lindholm, who arguably could be considered a government agent, and that was the question which Judge Zobel asked, "*Mr. Segal do you have any facts whatsoever to suggest that Mr. Lindholm was working as a government agent?*" (TH 10/22 23) Segal replied with the sequence of Lindholm's placements. He said, "*It's a very strange coincidence of time and place that this man can see two defendants in three days and, quote, solve the whole government's case.*" Judge Zobel then denied Terry Segal's Motion and she allowed a prosecutor Motion to quash Segal's subpoena to the U.S. Marshal's Office and the U.S. Bureau of Prisons for information about William David Lindholm's travels from prison in Texas to Springfield, Mass. to Boston, to Plymouth. What could have been the problem with furnishing that information? It might even have been available to an everyday citizen through a Freedom of Information Access (FOIA) request.

Added Paul Kelly, "*For the record, your honor, there is no cooperation arrangement with this witness.*" (TH 10/22 25) However, as everyone in the courtroom understood, Federal Rule of Criminal Procedure, Rule 35(b) provides that a defendant (inmate) may, within a year of sentencing obtain a reduced sentence if s/he "*provided substantial assistance in investigating or prosecuting another person...*" Custom is also a substantial part of law, and it is the custom for prosecutors to provide lenient treatment for inmates who help them win convictions. You don't need a handshake or a document to show that custom. Everyone knows the *modus operandi* of prosecutors and in the Shay case, the use of jailhouse informers was apparent to all. Lindholm came forward to the prosecutors less than a year after his 21 August 1991 sentencing, so he was covered by the rule.

Judge Zobel denied a prosecutor motion for a jury view at 39 Eastbourne Street, as was done at the Shay trial. She said it was not necessary, and it wasted a day of trial time. This ruling was not a good sign for Alfred Trenkler, even though it was the U.S. Attorney's office which filed the Motion for a "jury view of the crime scene." It would have been to Trenkler's advantage for the jury to see how close together the houses were on Eastbourne street and how unlikely it could have been that a person would lay in wait for Mr. Shay to get into his car at his home and watch undetected from a vantage point on Eastbourne Street. A person waiting in a parked car on a short dead end street would be either be asked if s/he needed help or directions or reported to the police.

Regarding jury selection, Judge Zobel said she would not agree to a questionnaire, and that she would review later with the lawyers the questions for the jury.

Judge Zobel denied Terry Segal's Motion to suppress the identifications of Alfred Trenkler by Edward Carrion, who was a friend of Tom Shay.

Then the hearing reached the larger issue for the day, the use as evidence of the 1986 Quincy incident. The government began the argument, and Terry Segal agreed to a stipulation that Alfred Trenkler, "*had the requisite knowledge and ability to build the '91 device."* (TH 10/22 32) That was a puzzling, unnecessary and damaging concession as Alfred Trenkler had had no known experience with dynamite nor blasting caps nor explosives in general. Also, Terry Segal stipulated that Alfred Trenkler *"made the* [1986] *device."* (TH 10/22 38) The remaining issue was whether the prosecutors would be able to use as evidence in the upcoming trial the 1986 incident to show the increased likelihood that Alfred Trenkler built the 1991 Roslindale Bomb.

The first witness was the ATF's Stephen Scheid, the operator of the EXIS database. Examined by Frank Libby, he reviewed how the submission of several queries reduced the number of similar bomb incidents in the database from 1979 onward to nine, including both the 1986 Quincy and 1991 Roslindale incidents. On cross-examination by Scott Lopez, Scheid agreed that if he had asked a different question at any point, the two incidents would not have appeared together in the responsive grouping. For example, if he asked for "Futaba" receiver, the Roslindale Bomb would appear, but the Quincy device would not. Scheid agreed that the data about the 1986 Quincy device was not entered into the EXIS system until after the 1991 Roslindale explosion.

At the completion of Stephen Scheid's testimony, Terry Segal asked for a 2 minute break, and Judge Zobel approved and also took the opportunity to announce that *"I intend during the trial to take just one break in the morning."* (TH 10/22 77) The trial of Alfred Trenkler would proceed efficiently.

The ATF's Thomas Waskom was next and he identified himself as an Explosives Enforcement Officer, or EEO for short, and an ironic note for two trials which put so much irrelevant and prejudicial emphasis on the defendants' alleged sexual preferences. He was examined by Paul Kelly and Waskom concluded *"It's my opinion, after examining all of the evidence and information that were involved in this investigation, that the person that built the 1986 explosive device and the person that built the 1991 explosive device, were the same person."* Paul Kelly asked, *"Any question in your mind about that, Mr. Waskom?"* and Mr. Waskom replied, *"No. Sir."* (TH 10/22 125) He made these claims without any drawings or schematics of the 1986 device or any photographs of debris, or any conversations with the Massachusetts explosives expert who wrote the report about the device since he had died. Thus, Waskom built his model of the 1986 device using his analysis of the 1991 device and his assumption that the same person built both devices. The effect was even worse than inputting the 1986 device information into the EXIS system AFTER the 1991 Roslindale Bomb explosion.

Terry Segal cross-examined. Because the design of the M21Hoffman had changed over the years, there were several questions about whether the explosive material came from an M-21 Hoffman which was electrically detonated or from another artillery simulator which was mechanically simulated. As Alfred Trenkler already stated to Terry Segal that he detonated it electrically with a remote control, Segal didn't need to question the type of military simulator that was used. This is another example where Alfred Trenkler had said he had nothing to hide, but where the judge could see that he was not, through his lawyer, forthcoming with information which could have been helpful. Of course, the prosecutors would charge that any information that Trenkler provided about the 1986 device would have been biased to make it appear that it was different from the 1991 device, but the offer could have been made. His testimony would have been no less credible than the ATF's inputting the 1986 incident data into the EXIS system after the 1991 explosion. Trenkler could have resolved the question of whether a light bulb was used to test the device, and how long it took him to build it - an hour and a half. There were several people at Donna Shea's at the Sunday, 31 August afternoon picnic when the 1986 device was constructed, outside and in open view. If Alfred Trenkler and the other attendees at that picnic had testified about the party-like atmosphere, the judge and jury would have been less likely to conjure up an image of a "*mastermind*" engineer cooking up a bomb in a basement somewhere. It would have shown yet another difference between the 1986 device and the 1991 Roslindale Bomb.

Several questions were asked about the model of the 1986 device that was built by the defense expert, Denny Kline, and Mr. Waskom agreed that it was a good model. Waskom said that when coming to his opinion of the same "*signature*" for both devices, he "*relied on the location where the device was placed underneath the vehicle. I relied on the materials used in the device, materials such as duct tape to contain or hold components. I relied on soldering of connections made within the device. I relied upon magnets used to hold the device in place. I relied upon information about testing of devices.*" (TH 10/22 167) At least part of his reliance was misplaced as the 1986 device was placed along the rear side of the Capeway Fish Market truck, according to Alfred Trenkler in 2007, and not underneath.

When his line of questioning with assumptions about the 1991 device bogged down and to which there was an objection by Frank Libby, Terry Segal responded that the witness had "*been asked to assume things by Mr. Libby,*" too. (TH 10/22 174)

In apparent agreement, Judge Zobel added pointedly, "*But you also told me that you would spend 30 to 35 minutes, and you have now spend* [sic] *an hour and ten minutes with this witnesses.* [sic]" (TH 10/22 174) Judge Zobel was in charge and proceeding according to the predicted schedule was important. A few minutes later, she said to Frank Libby, "*We're going do* [sic] *finish the evidence at 4 today, which is why I'm pushing.*" (TH 10/22 183)

The next witness was Denny Kline, the defense's only witness. Examined by Terry Segal, he said "*there's too many dissimilarities* [between the two devices] *to make a conclusion beyond a reasonable doubt that the same person made both bombs, it's just that simple.*" (TH 10/22 212) Under cross-examination by Frank Libby, Mr. Kline also said that he wouldn't preclude the possibility that the same person did make both of them. However, the possibility that the two devices could have been made by the same person was a far cry from Thomas Waskom's opinion that the two devices were necessarily made by the same person.

After Denny Kline's testimony around 4:00, Judge Zobel said there was no time for argument, and she could read the parties' briefs over the weekend and give a decision on the Motion first thing Monday morning, the first day of the trial. She was asked by Paul Kelly about the start time for testimony, as witnesses had to be lined up, and she acknowledged the uncertainty, saying, "*I obviously don't know how quickly we will get a jury. This is different from the last time. We've had a whole lot of publicity since then.*" (TH 10/22 235) There was no mention by Judge Zobel of the nature of that publicity, and Terry Segal said nothing about the unnamed sources who leaked information about the case to the media.

The Trial of Alfred William Trenkler was to begin at 9:00 a.m. on Monday, 25 October.

END NOTES

1. John Pappalardo, as he described his work on behalf of a Russian client. *Boston Globe Magazine*, 20 Feb 2005, page 24.
2. On 6 March 2007, the Massachusetts Supreme Judicial Court ordered a new trial for Frederick Murphy whose conviction had been secured using an informant under agreement with the U.S. Attorney's office for another case. The case, <u>Commonwealth v. Murphy</u>, 448 Mass. 452, has a thorough review of the recent cases regarding government informants. As Attorney Harvey Silverglate noted in his commentary in the <u>*Boston Phoenix*</u> about the <u>Murphy</u> case, about half of the exonerees from death row since 1977 were originally convicted using jailhouse snitch testimony. Also, the Innocence Project estimates that 15 percent of its 200+ exonerations came from convictions which relied heavily on the use of jailhouse snitches.
3. In an August 2007 letter, Tom Shay's estimate of the total time that he and Alfred Trenkler were together was 12 hours.

CHAPTER 8: TRIAL OF ALFRED W. TRENKLER - 25 October 1993 to 29 November 1993

> *"...there must be serious flaws in our*
> *administration of criminal justice,"* [1]
> Justice John Paul Stevens, 2005

25 26 27 28 29	1 2 3 4 5	8 9 10 12	15 16	22 23 24	29
X O O O O	O O O O O	O O O O	O O	O O O	O

Day 1: Monday, 25 October

The trial of Alfred Trenkler began with a muted bench conference where Judge Zobel announced her rulings on various motions. Technically occurring during Day 1 of the trial, these struggles over evidence actually began shortly after Alfred Trenkler's indictment.

[Where the recounting here of this trial overlaps that of the trial of Thomas A. Shay, repetition will be minimized. This chapter will emphasize the new information and arguments which emerged in the Alfred Trenkler trial.]

Representing the prosecution were Assistant U.S. Attorneys Paul Kelly and Frank Libby, for whom this would be the second trial with substantially the same facts. Representing Alfred Trenkler were Terry Segal, Scott Lopez and Brenda Ruel Sharton.

Even before that, the defense had filed three additional motions with the court on this opening day. One was for an order *"to preclude the government from mentioning any statements by Thomas Shay, Jr. in its opening."* Another was *"to preclude Thomas Waskom from demonstrating the manner in which the 1991 bomb was designed to explode,"* because such a demonstration implied that the bomb was detonated by an intentional remote control device at noon, 28 October 1991, but it wasn't known how the bomb was actually detonated.

A third was to *"preclude the Government from mentioning any alleged sexual relationship between Thomas Shay, Jr. and defendant in its opening."* Here, the defense struck at a core belief of the investigators and the prosecutors. The Motion said, *"defendant states that there is no evidence of any sexual relationship between defendant and Thomas Shay, Jr. other than Shay, Jr.'s unsubstantiated and uncorroborated statements that there was a sexual relationship. Thomas Shay Jr.'s statements regarding a sexual relationship are not admissible against defendant as declarations against Shay, Jr.'s penal interest or as any other recognized exception to the hearsay rule."*

Judge Zobel ruled that the evidence of the 1986 bomb could be admitted. As with the Thomas A. Shay trial, she found the evidence of the similarity of the 1986 device to the 1991 Roslindale Bomb persuasive. In so finding, she mistakenly said that both devices had *"slide switches"*, [TT 1-4] but only the 1991 device had one, and that the magnets were similar in both, but the 1986 device used a single magnet from a castaway loudspeaker. Also, she said erroneously, that both devices had *"receivers, antenna and motor that responded with a moving switch."* [TT 1-4] There were no moving parts in the 1986 device, and it was only the 1991 device that had a motor servo. With respect to the information from the ATF's EXIS system, she ruled it could be presented as evidence and she said, *"I am persuaded that the two devices are sufficiently similar to prove that the same person built them..."* (TT 1-4)

However, as the alleged maker was on trial here, as compared to the alleged co-conspirator in Shay's trial, she ruled that the possible prejudice was outweighed by its relevance. Of "*prejudice*" she drew a careful distinction, saying, "*The evidence of the 1986 bomb is without question prejudicial in the sense that it will likely harm the defendant. That is not the test, however. The question is whether it is unfairly prejudicial. It is not.*" (TT 1-4/5)

Next, she ruled on Thomas A. Shay's Motion to Quash the prosecution's effort to subpoena him to testify at Alfred Trenkler's trial. Judge Zobel said that did not believe that Shay "*can be forced to testify, even with a grant of immunity, in light of his Fifth Amendment rights.*" (TT 1-5) Paul Kelly later argued that a Federal grant of immunity would also apply to any related state court proceedings, so that Shay would not have any risk of incrimination from testimony at Trenkler's trial. Previously, he had applied for such an immunity grant, and he said strongly, that this issue "*is really central - -*" (TT 1-7) to the Government's case. The judge said she would be open to reconsideration if the issue of penal risk could be resolved, but she reminded Paul Kelly that Shay's Federal case was under appeal and that he may come back, though she didn't say it explicitly, for a retrial. In such a circumstance, and if Shay chose to testify at a retrial, a Federal grant of immunity could have been a problem. However, complexity and problems should not have eliminated the prospects for presenting truth in a trial.

Also, Judge Zobel issued a brief written opinion with her denial, as she announced at the previous Friday's hearing, of Alfred Trenkler's Motion to suppress the out-of-court photo identifications by Ed Carrion of Alfred Trenkler on 25 and 27 February 1992. She wrote that the Motion to Suppress was "*untimely,*" i.e. late. The deadline for pre-trial motions was 19 February 1993 and Trenkler filed this motion on 30 August 1993. On the merits she wrote that "*If under the totality of the circumstances, the identification is nonetheless reliable, the motion to suppress will be denied... Trenkler fails to allege a single fact in support of his claim that the Carrion identification was impermissibly suggestive. In fact, he fails even to complain about the way in which the government conducted the identification procedure. All he does is argue that because Carrion's trial testimony was a more detailed and polished version of his pretrial statements, it should be suppressed.*"

Then the judge reviewed the planned process for assembling a jury. She denied a defense motion to distribute a questionnaire, but said that the questions she planned to ask would likely include the objectives of the defense. Among her questions were numbers "*Six: Do you believe that homosexual relations between consenting adults is morally wrong.*" and "*Seven: Would your views of a witness's credibility or a defendant's guilt be influenced in any way by that person's sexual orientation?*" (TT 1-9/10) Such questions seemed appropriate to guard against prejudice, but they should not give the prosecutors a green light to routinely ask witnesses their sexual orientation, unless specifically relevant. Perhaps the parties already knew that the prosecution would seek to make sex part of Trenkler's motive, whereas in the Shay case, it did not. After asking all 80 members of the jury pool the set of questions, the *voir dire* questioning of prospective individual jurors was to be in the judge's offices, but it was open to the press and the public as if in open court.

Frank Libby then advised the court that the defense planned to have a jury selection specialist attend the *voir dire* questioning, and that the prosecution objected to that person's presence. The judge denied the objection and then welcomed the 80 person pool, "*Good morning, members of the jury, I'm Judge Zobel....*" (TT 1-14)

The Clerk addressed Alfred Trenkler with somber words: "*Would the defendant please stand? Mr. Trenkler, you are now set to the bar to be tried, and these good jurors whom I shall call are to pass between the United States and upon your trial. If you would to object to any of them, you must do so before they are sworn.*" (TT 1-14/15)

The clerk and the judge went through the same process as with the Shay trial, and the 16 person jury, including four alternates, was then empaneled, and advised to return by 10:30 the next morning.

Next day's headlines:

Boston Globe: "*JURY BEING CHOSEN FOR SECOND TRIAL ON '91 BOMBING*" by Matthew Brelis The article reported that Judge Zobel had "*denied a government motion to call Trenkler's co-defendant, Thomas A. Shay, as a witness....*

Zobel has yet to rule on the government motion to introduce evidence of Trenkler's solicitation of teen-age males, 'including his willingness to provide them with money, drugs, other material goods, and the performance of personal favors to induce . . . or maintain the relationship,' according to court documents." By quoting "court document" the article was able to avoid responsibility for determining what, if anything, was behind such charges. The short answer was nothing.

Boston Herald: "*EARLIER INCIDENT ALLOWED AS EVIDENCE AT BOMB TRIAL*" by Ralph Ranalli He wrote, "*Trenkler is alleged to be the technical mastermind of the bomb...*"

25 26 27 28 29	1 2 3 4 5	8 9 10 12	15 16	22 23 24	29
X X O O O	O O O O O	O O O O	O O	O O O	O

Day 2: Tuesday, 26 October

The jury was sworn in and Judge Zobel outlined the trial for them, including a summary of the indictment. Of substantial importance was her description of how the jury should consider the conviction of Thomas A. Shay pursuant to the same indictment. Said the judge, "*Now, I told you yesterday that Mr. Trenkler, the defendant, has been charged in this indictment in the three counts that I outlined to you. This indictment charged two defendants. It charged not only Mr. Trenkler, but also a person named Thomas Shay, Jr.* [The judge and the parties to this trial continued to follow the convention to call Thomas A. Shay, "Shay, Jr.," and Thomas L. Shay, "Shay, Sr.," even though those were not their names.] *For a number of complicated technical reasons, they were not tried together. Mr. Thomas Shay, Jr. has already been tried and he was convicted on some but not all of the counts in the indictment. I simply tell you this because I want you to be very clear that the fact that Mr. Shay was convicted on some counts has absolutely nothing to say about whether Mr. Trenkler is guilty of the charges that have been brought against him. You will need to decide whether he is guilty or not based entirely on the basis of the evidence you will hear and in no way based on the fact that Mr. Shay was convicted on evidence that, I can guarantee you, is in some respects quite different from that which you will hear.*" (TT 2-3/4)

Thus, she loaded a huge burden onto the shoulders of Alfred Trenkler. For the Shay trial, the jurors were told about an absent co-conspirator who was presumed innocent.

In this trial, the jurors were told that another jury of 12 of their peers had convicted the co-conspirator beyond a reasonable doubt on "*some but not all*" of the three counts, with "two" being the only logical possibility to deduce from the judge's statement. Terry Segal did not object.

Assistant U.S. Attorney Paul Kelly made the opening statement for the prosecution. He described the events of almost exactly two years previous at 39 Eastbourne and that Thomas A. Shay had a personal motive, i.e. that he had been abused and seen abuse in the family, and a financial motive to kill his father, i.e. his prospective share of the expected proceeds from the Dedham Service Center lawsuit. Kelly explained that the name "*SAHY JYT*" on the Radio Shack receipt, should have been "*S H A Y JR T*" as "Y" is the letter two characters away from "R" on the keyboard. It didn't seem to matter that Tom Shay never introduced himself to others as "Jr.," as that was not his name. He picked up the practice from the police after 28 October 1991 as the police had to distinguish between father and son.

Different from the Shay trial, Kelly said that "*the evidence would show that Thomas Shay, Jr. would prostitute himself to older gay males for shelter, for support, and for companionship.*" (TT 2-17) Also, the jury would hear about the 1986 Hoffman Artillery Simulator explosion in Quincy, detonated by Alfred Trenkler.

Also different was Paul Kelly's statement that when the police did their first search of John Cates' and Alfred Trenkler's apartment, Alfred Trenkler acknowledged knowing Thomas A. Shay, but stated that he had only known him for a short period of time. In the Shay trial, Frank Libby said at a bench conference, that when the police went to Cates' and Trenkler's apartment on 5 November, "*Detective Tierney* [of the Quincy Police Dept.] *recognizes Mr. Trenkler, and so forth. We establish he denies* [a] *relationship with Shay, Jr. We find out that denial is untruthful. They had had a long relationship which dates back not to 1991, but two years previously, that is our evidence.*" (TS 9-6)

Paul Kelly resumed and claimed a different denial from Trenkler which was that on 5 November Trenkler denied that Thomas A. Shay had ever been to his apartment in Quincy. Pursuing the theme of untruthfulness, Kelly said "*During this trial, the Government will present further evidence to show that Mr. Trenkler was not entirely truthful in his initial statements that evening concerning his association with Thomas Shay, Jr. and other matters.*" (TT 2-20]

Again differing from the first trial, Paul Kelly played harder with the homosexuality card and said, "*The evidence will be that Thomas Shay, Jr. and Mr. Trenkler were friends who shared a common sexual orientation and likely an intimate relationship.*" (TT 2-20)

Kelly claimed a dual motive for Alfred Trenker's participation in the conspiracy, "*First he had a personal motive. A willingness to perform this sinister act to induce and cultivate companionship and sexual relations from Thomas Shay, Jr., a younger, openly gay male; and secondarily, a financial motive, the prospect of receiving some portion of a sizable amount of money from this insurance coverage from the lawsuit that was pending against* [sic] *Thomas Shay, Jr.'s father.*" (TT 2-25)

Before his opening, Terry Segal sought a bench conference to discuss "*one comment in Mr. Kelly's opening?*" and the judge asked that they address it after Segal's opening statement. (TT 2-26) Segal began by introducing his legal team and Alfred Trenkler to the jury and said, "*This man is innocent, ladies and gentlemen. There will be no evidence that will connect him in any way with that horrible crime on October 28th, 1991 in Roslindale."* (TT 2-26/7) Instead, he continued, the evidence will show why he was accused and why it was a case of guilt by association.

Segal described the 1986 incident, *"where with a stupid prank he lit off a large firecracker."* (TT 2-27) He stressed that for all the searches conducted by the Government, there was not one piece of physical evidence which connects Alfred Trenkler to the Roslindale Bomb. Segal prepared the jury for the dubious testimony of a jail inmate who will claim that Al Trenkler, as Segal referred to him, confessed to him.

In a significant move, Terry Segal appeared to concede Thomas A. Shay's guilt and even his motives. Said Segal, *"There'll be evidence about Thomas Shay, Jr., Mr. Kelly referred to him often in this opening. It's clear that he wanted to kill his father."* (TT 2-35) Actually, it's unclear why Terry Segal said it was *"clear,"* because it made it easier for the jury to believe that Tom Shay communicated that patricidal desire to Alfred Trenkler. Not only was the testimony at Shay's trial ambiguous, but Judge Zobel specifically said at Shay's sentencing hearing on 8 October 1993, *"I am simply not persuaded by the trial evidence that he intended to kill his father."* (TS 10/8 122)

Segal addressed the purchase of the Radio Shack toggle switch and conceded that it *"matched the toggle switch that ATF meticulously recovered from the bomb debris. That's not in dispute that that toggle switch was purchased and the same number matched the bomb debris."* (TT 2-36) The identification of the toggle switch was an important forensic determination of the case. As noted in an earlier chapter, Segal's explosives expert, Denny Kline, had written a preliminary report which questioned the identification. He wrote in some detail, *'On March 15, 1993, I purchased from Radio Shack two single-pole-single-throw toggle switches, Catalogue No. 275-602. I disassembled one of the toggle switches and found that the two contact leads were two separate pieces. Therefore it can be concluded Radio Shack 275-602 toggle switch I purchased was not identical to the item BATF identified as originating form the same Radio Shack toggle switch model. This suggests that the construction of the Radio Shack Catalogue No. has changed or BATF erred in their identification. A reexamination of Submission 4 - exhibit 6 is requested to resolve this preliminary conclusion.'* However, either that reexamination didn't occur or he found sufficient similarity, and the issue was not addressed in his final report.

Despite the concession that the Roslindale Bomb contained such a #275-602, Terry Segal stated that there would be no evidence that Alfred Trenkler had any role whatsoever in the purchase of that toggle switch. Again, Segal referred to the case as being one of *"guilt by association."* He concluded by saying that he would, at the end of the trial, return to address the jury to ask them to find his innocent client not guilty.

Then Judge Zobel asked Terry Segal about his earlier request after the prosecution's opening, and he moved *"for a mistrial because of Mr. Kelly's statement in his opening, he says quoting, Shay, he wasn't the one who built it. I suggest that's a violation of the Bruton document* [Bruton v. United States, a precedent-setting case involving co-conspirators] *because in a two-person conspiracy is* [sic] *the inference from that statement is my client had to be the only one who built it. That statement could not be admitted because it's in open court."* (TT 2-39)

Judge Zobel denied the motion, without further discussion. There seemed to be a different relationship between Judge Zobel and Terry Segal from the judge's relationship with Nancy Gertner in the Shay trial. Maybe the coolness applied to the entire defense team. When Brenda Sharton was cross-examining the second witness, Judge Zobel chided her in front of the jury, "*Can we have some cross-examination that doesn't repeat the direct, please.*" (TT 2-64)

Frank Libby examined the first Government witness, Robert P. Maloney, formerly a policeman at the Area E Boston Police Station in West Roxbury when Thomas L. Shay came in about 11:45 on the morning of 28 October 1991 to report an unusual object in his driveway. Officer Maloney said he called the Bomb Squad and talked with Officer Frank Foley, and then advised Mr. Shay to go home and keep a safe distance from the object.

Through cross-examination by Brenda Sharton, Officer Maloney said that Mr. Shay had told him that the object was a metal box or "*Something like that,*" (TT 2-45) and that there were round magnets or magnets on top of it, and that there were wires which stuck out. Also Mr. Shay said that he wasn't having trouble with anyone, but that he was involved a pending civil lawsuit involving "*an automobile or automobile shop.*" (TT 2-45/6)

The next witness was Denise (Kraft) Corbett, who was examined by Paul Kelly. Denise Kraft had married Boston Policeman Mark Corbett sometime after the explosion. She was the first police officer to arrive at 39 Eastbourne on 28 October and when talking with Mr. Shay, he reminded her that when he made a report about being followed by someone in May 1991, that she had taken the report. She said that Mr. Shay had told her and Sergeant Creavin and Officers Foley and Hurley who had just arrived how he had picked up the bomb and thrown it against the house. Later, to keep it away from children, Shay said that he moved it to a spot between the cars in the driveway. However, a few of Kristen's toys were in the driveway and her future presence in the driveway was assured.

Officer Corbett described the conversations and actions just before and after the explosion, and then identified the house and the scene on photographs and drawings which were entered as Government exhibits 1-3. Then she was shown Government Exhibit #4 which was the black mockup of the bomb, as shown at the Shay trial. She was not asked about the appearance of the bomb and whether there appeared to be any damage due to the alleged scraping from the bottom of Mr. Shay's car.

During cross-examination by Brenda Sharton, Officer Corbett said that Mr. Shay had said that he thought the black box was a part of a "*Chapman lock*" (TT 2-62) Given Mr. Shay's 20 years experience in autobody work, some of which was likely with cars that had Chapman locks, such an assumption must have seemed odd to those in the courtroom with minimal understanding of how Chapman locks worked. When she went back to her cruiser to get a notebook, she assumed that Mr. Shay was accompanying her, but when she turned around, he had disappeared. She called for him, and he was inside the house. Then after the explosion, she didn't see Mr. Shay again and didn't see him providing any assistance to the police nor the wounded officers.

Under redirect examination by Paul Kelly, Officer Corbett remembered that Mr. Shay had told her that the 1987 explosion that was the subject of a civil lawsuit involved a quarter stick of dynamite.

Then the court adjourned for the day with the judge cautioning the jury to avoid any contact with any media which might be covering the case and not to read any newspapers, and to leave their notebooks at their seats. Coffee would be waiting for them in the morning, and the court would resume promptly at 9 a.m.

After the trial, Alfred's half-brother, David Wallace, wrote to Terry Segal to note that the mockup of the Roslindale Bomb did not have the two wires which Officers Corbett and Maloney (TT 2-46) had previously stated that Mr. Thomas L. Shay had stated were protruding from the box. If the wires had been present in the mockup, the jury might have wondered why Mr. Shay didn't realize quickly that the box did not belong in a car and was more likely what he feared: a bomb.

Next day's headlines:

Boston Globe: "TRIAL OPENS OF ALLEGED CREATOR OF BOMB THAT KILLED POLICEMAN" by Matthew Brelis

Boston Herald: "FEDS: BOMB SUSPECT SOUGHT SEXUAL FAVOR" by Ralph Ranalli and Sid Maher Excerpts from the article: *"Federal prosecutors yesterday charged that accused bomber Alfred Trenkler of MIlton built a bomb that killed a Boston Police officer in order to ingratiate himself with his younger homosexual lover, a convicted co-conspirator in the case.... In portraying Shay as the sole bomber; Segal's defense appears to differ greatly from that offered by Shay's attorney, Nancy Gertner, who sought to prove the bomb builder was Shay's father."*

25 26 27 28 29	1 2 3 4 5	8 9 10 12	15 16	22 23 24	29
X X X O O	O O O O O	O O O O	O O	O O O	O

Day 3, Wednesday, 27 October

Frank Libby began with the direct examination of Boston Police Officer Thomas Creavin, who was the second policeman to come to 39 Eastbourne Street. Creavin recalled that Jeremiah Hurley gently scratched the side of the box with his knife and then commented, *"This looks like a piece of machinery. There's no seems* [sic, seams] *It looks like it was made in a factory."* (TT 3-11)

During Libby's direct examination, the defense team's third member, Scott Lopez, objected to the admission of the mock up of the bomb and was summarily overruled. Later he disputed the admission of an exemplar of one of the magnets and this exchange arose and Judge Zobel asked, *"Why is it not admissible?"* Replied Scott Lopez, *"It is a chalk,"* or jury aid, such as a chart. The judge responded. *"It is something the witness says came off the device."* Frank Libby clarified that it was actually an exemplar, but the judge seemed cool to Scott Lopez.

Thomas Creavin said that Thomas L. Shay told the assembled officers upon questioning by Jeremiah Hurley and Francis Foley that he had *"observed this box as he backed his car out. He got out and picked up the box up* [sic] *and threw it over to the side of the driveway near the house."* (TT 3-14) Shay said that one of his friends said, without seeing it, that it might be a bomb, and another friend said it might be part of car's theft protection, Lo-Jack, system.

Creavin testified that Jeremiah Hurley asked Thomas L. Shay who might want to hurt him. Mr. Shay then described the [1987] explosion at the Dedham Service Center and pending lawsuit. Creavin testified, *"He said a half stick of dynamite. Somebody had put a half stick of dynamite in the barrel adjacent to the shop, and it exploded, causing a lot of damage."* (TT 3-14) Jeremiah Hurley and Francis Foley asked Mr. Shay how he knew it was a half stick of dynamite and Creavin said that Shay replied, *"I know it was a half stick of dynamite because the lawsuit was pending over that."* (TT 3-14)

Thomas Creavin said that Mr. Shay said that *"about a month prior to this he had made a report to the police that somebody had dumped a lot of machine parts in the driveway and they came from his body shop in Dedham."* and that *"...about a week prior to this, some car followed his wife, or, his girlfriend, rather, and followed her home one night."* (TT 3-14/15) Then Officer Hurley returned to the black box and the explosion occurred shortly thereafter.

On cross-examination by Scott Lopez, Officer Creavin was questioned about the quantity of dynamite Mr. Shay said was in the Dedham Service Center explosion, *"He didn't say a quarter stick of dynamite, he said a half a stick of dynamite; isn't that correct?"* Responded Creavin, *"Best I recall, yes, it was."* (TT 3-27)

Officer Creavin didn't recall Mr. Shay saying that he was familiar with dynamite, so Scott Lopez presented to the court Officer Creavin's testimony in the Shay trial where Creavin testified, *"He said, I know something about dynamite, something to that effect. I knew it was a half stick. He seemed to give answers that he knew it was a half stick of dynamite."* (TT 3-29 quoting TS 4-111) Then Judge Zobel advised the jury that one of its tasks was to assess witness credibility.

Scott Lopez continued his cross-examination, and seemed to go over what Officer Creavin had stated earlier, and said, *"Now, sir, I asked you this before,"* and Judge Zobel immediately interrupted, *"Then don't ask it again."* (TT 3-32)

Paul Kelly examined the next witness, James McKernan, and the Judge asked the defense team, *"Who will cross-examine?"* (TT 3-34) and Terry Segal said that he would. Mr. McKernan confirmed that there was an elementary school [the Wolfgang Amadeus Mozart Elementary School with 150+ students] in the neighborhood. McKernan described seeing at the beginning of his regular walk at 11:20 a compact car *"kind of bluish-gray or grayish blue... kind of a lighter shade"* on Beech Street at the intersection of Beech and Eastbourne Streets, with a direct view to 39 Eastbourne Street, on a cross-walk to the school. (TT 3-42/43) The car took off after McKernan exchanged glances with the white male driver. James McKernan said he had memorized the license plate number, but later forgot it amidst the turmoil of the explosion. He remembered that it was composed of the normal three digits and three letters, but had not been able to recall more. He even tried hypnosis.

When the explosion occurred, he and his son Tom McKernan rushed across the street to help and his son provided first aid to one of the injured officers.

Terry Segal asked about the compact car, and James McKernan said, *"It definitely wasn't white,"* and that it wasn't very old and that he didn't notice any rust marks nor any insignia's nor decals on the car, nor an antenna on the car's trunk. Segal confirmed that Mr. McKernan did not pick out a car from the photo array shown to him by the police. Further, Segal showed him a photo of Trenkler's car, with its WBCN sticker and antenna on the trunk, and two foot diameter red and white decal on the front hood, and McKernan confirmed that it was not the car he saw. Also, Mr. McKernan did not identify Alfred Trenkler from another photo array.

At the end of his cross-examination Segal reminded Mr. McKernan that he had said that the compact car he had observed was not *"old"* and then Segal asked if he thought a 1978 car would be classified as old, and McKernan replied, "*I would say it was fairly old, '78.*" (TT 3-59) Alfred Trenkler's car was a white 1978 Toyota. As Mr. Segal's efforts were directed at showing that Mr. McKernan did not see Alfred's car, he did not try to suggest that the car Mr. McKernan saw was the neighbor Ruth Leary's gray Mazda that Mr. Shay was repairing, and in which he drove to the police station.

Before Frank Libby examined the next Government witness, Daniel Boeh, Paul Kelly introduced Government exhibits 6 and 7 which were the death certificate and autopsy reports for Jeremiah Hurley.

Special ATF Agent Daniel Boeh described in considerable detail bomb investigations in general and the investigation at 39 Eastbourne Street.

There was a recess and Judge Zobel responded to one juror's question about what materials the jury would have in the deliberation room, saying, "*Nothing, except your memory and your notes. Although, we will have a transcript of most of the testimony since the reporters are preparing daily copy, I am very reluctant to give it to you, because I don't want to highlight the testimony of any one witness.*" (TT 3-86) It was a curious limitation. What's wrong with perceiving one witness's testimony as being more important that others? In the Shay trial, the testimony of Dwayne Armbrister of Radio Shack was surely more important to the issue of Shay's culpability than that of Officer Thomas Creavin who testified about the 39 Eastbourne crime scene.

Daniel Boeh said the piece of the bomb that was found furthest away from the blast was a magnet piece, stuck in a wire fence on the border between a neighbor and the elementary school. He recalled that the ATF search of the area for remnants of the bomb concluded on Thursday, 31 October, and his Northeast National Response Team held a briefing in the West Roxbury police station on Friday, 1 November.

Scott Lopez cross-examined. One of the unobserved ironic aspects of the search, was that the search team used magnets to find pieces of magnets from the bomb. Agent Boeh stated that several details about the bomb were known by the time of the briefing, but not yet the nature of the explosive material, or that the box was made of 1/4 inch plywood.

The practice of American judges is not to be involved in the questioning of witnesses, and Judge Zobel conformed to that practice. However, from to time, she engaged a witness, as in this exchange which had no bearing on the guilt or innocence of Alfred Trenkler:

THE COURT: "*Mr. Boeh, as a matter of curiosity, does a blast like this ruin windows, break windows.*"

THE WITNESS: "*It depends, your Honor. It's funny I've seen where we've had blasts real close and the windows have stayed, and other incidents where we've had blasts and windows down the street that have been knocked out.*"

THE COURT: "*And in this case?*"

THE WITNESS: "*I believe that the windows stayed intact from what I can remember. Because the blast, we only had one window on the side, and we were dealing with the sides that had no windows, we were dealing with one side. We were dealing with sides that had no windows and it was enclosed between the area that had two cars which, kind of, take some of the blast energy into the vehicles rather than letting it go out.*"

THE COURT: "*Thank you, you are excused.*"

The next witness was ATF Special Agent Christopher Porreca, who was examined by Frank Libby. He asked some general introductory questions and Judge Zobel, always concerned that the trial move forward, began this exchange:

THE COURT: "*We will finish with this witness today, right?*"

MR. LIBBY: "*I'm sorry, your Honor.*"

THE COURT: "*We will finish with this witness today?*"

MR. LIBBY: "*Without question.*" Probably with no pun intended.

THE COURT: "*I won't have to worry about the irrelevant questions, correct?*"

MR. LIBBY: "*Getting to the relevant questions.*"

THE COURT: "*Right.*" (TT 3-131)

Agent Porreca was the Evidence Technician at the scene and was responsible for logging all the collected items, and several of the remnants were entered as Government Exhibits. Judge Zobel then explained to the jury the general issue of chain-of-custody where it's important to know who has been responsible for pieces of evidence, in order to protect against tampering or degradation.

During this testimony and that of others, there seemed to be times when the lawyers would apply the philosophy, "*I object, because I can,*" rather than out of any concern that some fact or truth would be misunderstood by the jury. The resulting arguments or discussions were often distracting.

The cross-examination and redirect and recross-examinations covered no new ground except perhaps to create some doubt as to the chain-of-custody of the metal pieces, which later became known as the toggle switch contacts.

Under strong pressure from the judge, the testimony of Agent Porreca ended at 1:05 p.m.

Next day's headlines: None

25 26 27 28 29	1 2 3 4 5	8 9 10 12	15 16	22 23 24	29
X X X X O	O O O O O	O O O O	O O	O O O	O

Day 4: Thursday, 28 October

The next prosecution witness was Stephen Adams, the Regional Sales Manager of the Austin Powder Company of Kingston, New Hampshire, who was examined by Frank Libby. Adams said that the company had three competitors in the U.S. and that its detonators or blasting caps are distinctive for two reasons: the colors of their red and yellow wire pairs, and the "*delay timing sequence is stamped at the base of the aluminum shell of the detonator.*" (TT 4-9)

Brenda Sharton on cross-examination established that no one could tell how the detonators in the 1991 Roslindale Bomb were acquired or when, as they do not have individual serial numbers. Then Judge Zobel explained to the jury, as she did to the Shay jury, that Adams' testimony was primarily to establish "*interstate commerce,*" in order to permit Federal jurisdiction to try this case.

Cynthia Wallace, forensic chemist for the ATF was then examined by Paul Kelly. When it became clear that he would be questioning her as a "*fact witness*" as well as an "*expert witness*" it became necessary to qualify her has an expert, and Terry Segal told the court he had a few questions for Ms. Wallace in a *voir dire* inquiry. Then Judge Zobel explained to the jury what was happening, "*Let me explain this to the jury, the witnesses you heard heretofore are what we call fact witnesses. They told you what they did, what they saw, in the case of Mr. Adams, for example, what he knew about his product. Ms. Wallace is being offered I suspect partly as a fact witness but partly as an expert witness, that is she has some knowledge and experience in training in a particular field. And as a result of that,[she] is allowed to give you opinions that are designed to hopefully assist you in finding the facts. Opinions about things that ordinary lay persons, like us, might not know about in the field of explosives. Whenever an expert is offered, then counsel have to let you know and let me know the qualifications to give the opinions and in that case, the other side is allowed also to ask questions on qualifications before I decide initially whether the witness is allowed to testify. Now, in [sic] your job is not finish[ed], however, when I say she may testify. You, too, will have to judge her qualifications, and decide whether you are satisfied that she is qualified to give the opinions that she has given. And also, it may be -- sometimes counsel when they are dealing with an expert ask the expert to assume certain facts, and then give the opinion based on those assumptions. When that happens, I warn you, listen carefully to the assumptions that the expert is asked to make because if your determination of the facts in this case is different from the assumptions that the witness is asked to make, then the opinion the witness gives you is of absolutely no value to you."* (TT 4-19/20)

In response to Ms. Wallace's statement that she was qualified as a *"journeyman,"* Terry Segal said, hopefully with a smile on his face, *"I take it [as] a journeyman versus journeywoman."* Then Judge Zobel stated simply, *"Journeywoman"* and concluded that Wallace was qualified as an expert witness. (TT 4-21)

Cynthia Wallace described the components of the bomb which were recovered, and must have devastated the family of Jeremiah Hurley as she described the parts which were removed from his body in the operating room. She described how she did chemical analyses on the contents from underneath Thomas L. Shay's fingernails, and from his hands and clothes; but nothing matched the bomb. She said it would not have surprised her if there were some of the dynamite residue on his hands, because he had handled the bomb; but there was not.

The identification of the toggle switch was especially significant. She testified as she did at the Shay trial, *"This next photograph shows contacts that we recovered from a different switch that was also present. This photograph shows the two contacts that were recovered. First, it is two contacts from the switch that I identified these contacts to be from. What I did was, we identified that these were switch contacts, and I start going through our exemplar collection, looking at different types of switches we had. And the only one that matched these contacts was from a radio -- sorry from a Radio Shack brand toggle switch that we have an exemplar up here. It is item number eleven two -- Government's Exhibit 36-B. And also, to confirm this identification, we mentioned earlier in that small box I could identify how some of the components had been placed within the small box and showed you the one photograph that had the, the adhesive impressions left in it.... Also recovered in these glue impressions were other items that confirm my identification of the Radio Shack product number 275 602 toggle switch, because you can see that this item has an [sic] hexagonal nut on it, and that the column from the black housing up to the part of the switch, this is the toggle here, is a threaded item. And I identified in the adhesive impressions of this nut and impressions of the threads of this item which I believe were 34 threads per inch, and that was consistent from what we recovered from the inclines here, it shows these impressions from the servo."* [TT 4-

47/8] What the jury didn't know or learn was that the switch's dimensions were standard in the electric switch industry.

Paul Kelly then asked her about the comparison she did between the duct tape fragments found amidst the bomb debris and the duct tape found during a search of Alfred Trenkler's parents' garage. She said, "*And I analyzed its construction features and its composition, and found it to be the same or consistent with what I had found with the silver duct tape recovered from the device.*" (TT 4-61) She described how the tape found at the parents', (Jo and Jack Wallace, no relation to the witness) garage had been ripped lengthwise for 15 feet, with a width of 1 7/8 inches. Also, she noted that the duct tape in the bomb was also ripped lengthwise, but there was a section that was 1 9/16 inch wide. That's not as wide as 1 7/8, but it's not the same, either.

Then Paul Kelly asked her about the conclusion of the defense expert, Denny Kline, that the duct tape from the bomb could not possibly have come from the duct tape in the Wallace's garage. She disagreed. She said she disagreed with Mr. Kline's report when it said that the paint stirrer furnished to the ATF by Mr. Shay on 9 April 1993 had not been analyzed. She said "*the paint was found to be different from the paint that was on the device and* [the] *wood was different too.*" [TT 4-66] Also, and again to preempt portions of the expected cross-examination by Terry Segal, Paul Kelly asked Ms. Wallace about fingerprint analyses on the six layers of black electrician's tape sections which were part of the bomb debris. She said she did not do the fingerprint analysis.

Terry Segal cross-examined and Cynthia Wallace explained that she wrote a preliminary report while still in Boston on 1 November, which concluded that dynamite was the explosive used in the Roslindale Bomb. She explained further why her laboratory fingerprint expert didn't attempt to search for fingerprints by separating the layers of black electrical tape. However, Segal did not press hard on this absence of fingerprint analysis even though there likely were fingerprints on the tape. Before the trial, the defense team, had visited the ATF offices to examine the evidence and Denny Kline looked closely at the layers of electrical tape. Gently pulling two sections apart with tweezers, Kline observed traces of a fingerprint and he brought that observation to the attention of the ATF agents and others at the meeting. Also, he observed that there was no residue on the tape which would indicate that the tape had been dusted for fingerprints. Later, the ATF response to subsequent inquiries about the electrical tape was that the layers of tape were missing. At Alfred's trial, Cynthia Wallace was not confronted with Kline's observations, and he was not asked about them later either.

Cynthia Wallace also stated that she recommended that the investigators hire an expert with a mechanical "*sniffer*" to detect minute traces of explosives, which resulted in the retaining of Dr. John Hobbs of MIT. She and Dr. Hobbs accompanied the ATF search team during the 31 January 1992 searches of Alfred Trenkler's parents' garage, but she did not accompany Dr. Hobbs to other locations, if any. She did go to all three locations. No traces of explosives were found, nor was anything else found which could connect Alfred Trenkler to the Roslindale Bomb, except for her view of the similarity of the bomb's duct tape and the duct tape in the Wallace's garage.

Terry Segal asked about the ATF laboratory analysis done on the items taken by the ATF during the November 5/6 search of Alfred Trenkler's apartment and his office, such as wire scraps and tools. She agreed that there was nothing that could be connected to the Roslindale Bomb. Other places searched were Trenkler's car and his work location on the roof at the Christian Science Church building. Unfortunately, Mr. Segal began to refer to the ATF when questioning Ms. Wallace as "*you people*" which may have appeared hostile or condescending. (TS 4-89)

Cynthia Wallace agreed that four of the batteries found had a "*freshness code*" of July 1994. (TS 4-90) None of the batteries found at the Alfred Trenkler-searched locations had that freshness code date.

Regarding the presence or absence of soldering in the Roslindale Bomb, Segal asked, "*Ms. Wallace, isn't it true that your lab report makes no mention of solder being used in the construction of the bomb?*" and Cynthia Wallace answered, "*That's right.*" (TT 4-99) Also, she agreed that no solder was found nor taken from any of the Trenkler-related search sites. In fact, the last time that Alfred had used a soldering iron was at an ATEL project in January 1991. The work he was doing subsequently through ARCOMM with satellite antennas required crimping or bolting or plugging, but not soldering. Alfred Trenkler did not possess a soldering iron in 1991.

The glue that held the magnets to the wood and for attaching the other pieces of wood to each other was cyanocrylate, a more scientific word for the commonly used term, "superglue." Such a glue is normally intended for non-porous surfaces and it's never used by knowledgeable woodworkers to attach wood to wood.

Terry Segal continued to cross-examine Cynthia Wallace about all the analyses done on the "*submissions*", i.e. packets of objects sent to her from various search sites, which were sent to her. He asked about whether comparisons had been done among the 11 blue ballpoint pens seized from Alfred Trenkler's apartment and the blue ink that was drawn onto pieces of the bomb box for sawing alignment purposes. His questions were sometimes confusing, drawing the following request from Judge Zobel, "*Mr. Segal, the jury requests that you be clearer in whether you are asking questions in the negative or in the affirmative, because when you ask in the negative and get an affirmative answer, it's not altogether whether you're getting what it is the witness is telling us.*" (TT 4-115/6)

Segal established that of the 12 recovered button magnets, 10 were painted blue and two were painted red, and that they can be ordered by color from the manufacturer. Cynthia Wallace responded that the blue color is no longer available. Also she confirmed that at least one of the ring magnets was a "*Strontrum Ferrite ceramic ring magnet,*" and that no button magnets were found during the searches of the five Trenkler "*locations*" (TT 4-118)

Terry Segal then moved on to the tapes in the bomb (electrical, duct and white), but the tape exhibits were somehow missing, so he moved on to "*tool marks*" on the wire fragments from the bomb, but that line of questions produced nothing of use to the defense. He established that Ms. Wallace did not analyze the black spray paint in Mr. Thomas L. Shay's van in the driveway, nor the piece of plywood in his garage with the black spray paint on it.

After the jury was dismissed, Terry Segal asked the Judge to order the prosecution to provide to the defense copies of the work notes by Cynthia Wallace she used when preparing her reports. Before this request, the U.S. Magistrate had denied the request, and the prosecution was resisting, and said that the Federal Rules of Criminal Procedure didn't require such discovery. Terry Segal was especially interested in Cynthia Wallace's analysis of the type of explosive actually used. After hearing the arguments, Judge Zobel denied Terry Segal's motion. It was an example, among many, of her balancing the pursuit for truth with her perception of the need to put limits on the scope of the inquiry in the interest of time and resources. With the 20/20 hindsight of a wrongful conviction, the balance appears to have been weighed too far on the side of judicial and investigative economy. Efficiency had trumped truth. The trial adjourned at 1:07 p.m.

Next day's headlines: None

25 26 27 28 29	1 2 3 4 5	8 9 10 12	15 16	22 23 24	29
X X X X X	O O O O	O O O O	O O	O O O	O

Day 5: Friday, 29 October

Terry Segal renewed his motion for Cynthia Wallace's notes and Judge Zobel said she would consider it. He said that all he had was Wallace's conclusion that the bomb was made of ammonia dynamite, but he had no information about how Cynthia Wallace came to that conclusion. However, during this day's cross-examination, she gave a detail description of the tests and analyses she used to determine that the explosive was dynamite. (TT 5-28)

Also on this day, Terry Segal filed a "*Motion in limine to exclude all statements of Thomas Shay, Jr. at trial*," together with a 9 page Memorandum. The grounds for the motion were the principles of the <u>Bruton v. U.S.</u> case prohibiting the use of some statements by one alleged conspirator against another, and the Hearsay Rule.

Ms. Wallace returned to the witness stand and agreed that there was no match between the duct tape found in Alfred Trenkler's parents' garage and the duct tape fragments from the bomb. She also stated that she had not done a type of microscopic analysis that Mr. Segal recommended to her: calendaring.

Judge Zobel was pressing him to wind up his examination, but he took more time with complicated lengthy questions.

Unfortunately, Terry Segal went back and forth from tape to soldering and back to tape and was himself confused by the number of exhibits, and trying to bring in Denny Kline's conclusion without Denny Kline yet testifying. There were several testy exchanges with the prosecutors, which probably did not help Trenkler's case with jurors. For example, Paul Kelly was making a point during a contentious discussion and then Frank Libby apparently stood up. Judge Zobel said, "*Mr. Libby would you kindly sit down.*" and Segal added, "*They have one good prosecutor. They don't need two.*" (TT 5-30)

Segal had several good points to make: First, that none of the about-100 items taken from the five "*Alfred Trenkler locations*" (Apartment, work, parents, his car, and the Christian Science roof) had any chemical or physical connection to the bomb. Second, that Cynthia Wallace could have done more analysis on the so-called Trenkler items. Third, that she had done very little analysis of submissions from Mr. Thomas L. Shay's home or places of work. He concluded by physically and dramatically assembling the large number of items sent to Cynthia Wallace for analysis and then asked if any of them were matched to the Roslindale Bomb. The answer was, effectively, no, but the question was asked, in a contorted way, several times with objections from the prosecutors and comments by the court.

Terry Segal did not challenge the identification of the toggle switch as being the Radio Shack #275-602 and Cynthia Wallace was not asked for more details about her determination of the 1:1 comparison, and was not asked about the size of the ATF toggle switch exemplar collection. There was no other switch mentioned as being even close to a match. Terry Segal did not refer to his expert's, Denny Kline's, preliminary finding that the contacts did not come from a Radio Shack switch, as those findings were not in the final report. While the prosecution had submitted a photograph of the contacts which were found at 39 Eastbourne, no photographs of the contact pieces from the Radio Shack #275-602 switch were submitted into evidence. Thus, no one in the courtroom was able to compare for himself or herself. The conclusion that they were the same was accepted as a fact certain and set in solder.

On redirect-examination Paul Kelly established that there was, despite an earlier impression, some traces of solder in the bomb that did not come from the manufactured Futaba parts. The "*bomb builder's*" solder was on the toggle switch, which she termed the "*Radio Shack toggle switch*" and on wires connecting the 9-volt batteries. (TT 5-36)

Ms. Wallace stated that in her years of analyzing bomb pieces, she had never encountered a "*dual - primed*" bomb before, i.e. with two detonators or blasting caps.

She explained that she and another chemist decided not to analyze the ink traces in the wood fragments because the results would not mean much. Ironically, Paul Kelly established that the results would identify a class of sources, such as from a Bic pen, but would not be able to be traced to a particular pen, "*consistent, not unlike the results you reached with some of your tape.*" (TT 5-41)

On recross-examination, Cynthia Wallace again stated that there was no mention of the bomb-maker's solder in her report, but the jury heard her testify about it first-hand.

The next witness was Thomas Waskom and prior to his taking the stand, Terry Segal stated to the judge, apparently referring to his motion already submitted about blocking Waskom from doing a dramatic demonstration, "*I have a brief motion in connection with this next witness, your Honor,*" and Judge Zobel's immediate response was simply, "*Denied.*" Segal asked, "*Can I be heard on it?*" and there was discussion and then agreement that they would consider it after the recess so as not to take up the jury's time.

Frank Libby asked many biographical questions of Thomas Waskom and then sought to have him "*qualified to give expert testimony in the field of design, effect, placement, construction and reconstruction of improvised explosive devices,*" and Terry Segal asked to conduct a *voir dire* examination. (TT 5-61) Terry Segal challenged Waskom's qualifications, and his questioning became bogged down, and at one point he asked if he could ask the court reporter for a restatement of an earlier question and Judge Zobel said, simply, "*No.*" (TT 5-65) and shortly thereafter approved the Government's request to qualify Waskom as an expert in the specified areas.

The judge declared a recess and there was a bench conference about Mr. Segal's motion, which was to block the prosecution from conducting the demonstration of how the bomb exploded, as was done in the Shay trial with a light bulb. Segal argued that no one knew how the first bomb actually was detonated. There was a heated exchange, and Frank Libby continued to try to link the unidentified car at the corner of Beech and Eastbourne Streets to the explosion, but Judge Zobel observed, "*Well, there is no evidence at this point in time, is there?*" Frank Libby referred to James McKernan's testimony, and Judge Zobel repeated her point, "*That has not been in any way identified as being Mr. Trenkler or anybody associated with Mr. Trenkler."* (TT 5-68/9) Nonetheless, the prosecution was permitted to go ahead with its plan to have Thomas Waskom perform his light bulb *"explosion"* demonstration with the mockup device. Far less dramatically, the jury could have just been told that a remote control bomb is detonated in the same way someone turns on a television with a "remote." In fact, the jurors could do their own demonstration in the jury room.

Also considered at the bench conference was Terry Segal's objection to the expected testimony of Larry Plant and other jailhouse informants, and a major unknown was whether Tom Shay would testify. If he did, agreed the prosecution, there would be less need for the testimony of the jailhouse informants, assuming, as the prosecution did, that Shay's testimony would be helpful to the Government.

Returning to the witness's testimony, Thomas Waskom explained, through Frank Libby's direct examination, how the Roslindale Bomb was built. He stated that in a remote control system, the transmitter and the receiver each had a crystal for exactly the same radio frequency so as to preclude another transmitter from sending an unwanted signal. It was not known what set off the Roslindale Bomb, whether the actual intended transmitter or a stray signal from some other device.

Terry Segal cross-examined Thomas Waskom and he established that there were other ways to test a circuit, whether the firing or fusing circuit, without a light bulb. The prosecution had focused on the method using a light bulb, because one of the items purchased at the 197 Mass. Ave. Radio Shack store was a light bulb, and because it was known that Alfred Trenkler used a lightbulb to test circuits in the 1986 device. Other testing methods include volt ohmmeters and Segal sought to elicit testimony from Waskom that a trained engineer would be more likely to use a volt ohmmeter than a light bulb to test a circuit. However, the prosecution objected, because that was not an area for which Thomas Waskom was qualified as an expert, and Judge Zobel forbade the question.

Terry Segal then pointed out, using, dramatically, a light bulb he had purchased that morning, that using a small light bulb to test the 45 volt firing circuit in the Roslindale Bomb would blow the bulb out, but Waskom noted that the tester would still see a flash, indicating the circuit was working. It's not known if he would have performed that demonstration if Judge Zobel had allowed his Motion to block the prosecution from its own demonstration demonstrating the bomb detonation.

Waskom repeated the claim that the toggle switch remnant came exclusively from a #275-602 Radio Shack toggle switch saying, "Yes, the toggle switch that was in the device is consistent with the exact switch that was purchased..." [TT 5-130] Segal did not ask how Waskom came to that conclusion, or establish whether he was just repeating Cynthia Wallace's opinion. Did Thomas Waskom actually see the contacts from a disassembled Radio Shack #275-602 and make the comparison? Or did he see photographs? Waskom acknowledged that no fragments similar to any piece of the other five items purchased on 18 October 1991 were found amidst the bomb debris.

When Terry Segal asked Thomas Waskom to comment on a Paladin Press manual on how to build an IED (Improvised Explosive Device), Frank Libby objected because the manual, while marked for identification, had not yet been introduced into evidence. With that, a bench discussion was necessary, and as other matters were pending for the lawyers and judge, the jury was dismissed for the day. Judge Zobel said that Waskom and Frank Libby could look at the Paladin Press manual over the weekend, but she cautioned Terry Segal, "*But in the future, Mr. Segal please don't show the jury something until we have decided whether the jury can or cannot see it. That takes care of that.*" (TT 5-135)

Then the bench conference addressed other issues. First was the defense Motion to block the prosecution's attempt to introduce evidence of "*alleged solicitation by the defendant of teenage males.*" (TT 5-136) Judge Zobel agreed, saying "*the defendant's homosexuality is not a central issue in the case, and the evidence -- apart from the fact of not being particularly probative -- is unfairly prejudicial.*" (TT 5-135/6) One wonders why the Asst. U.S. Attorneys were seeking to introduce this evidence at all, and what evidence they thought they had. Alfred Trenkler strongly denies any such activity. Second was the prosecution's effort to introduce evidence of Alfred Trenkler's use of illicit drugs and Judge Zobel responded, "*I find that irrelevant as well, and certainly prejudicial in today's environment.*"[2] (TT 5-136).

The third issue, as summarized by Judge Zobel, was the "*alleged electronic eavesdropping on the roommate and the hot wiring of the garage door, that is, without question, relevant on the issue of the defendant's knowledge and expertise with respect to electronics in general. As I understand it, the Government's ample evidence of such knowledge that does not carry the same baggage of prejudice, and is in any event closer to the mark. There is, for example....*" (TT 5-136) However, before she ruled on the matter, and it appeared she was going to rule against the prosecution's request, Scott Lopez pointed out that the Government had already waived the request.

The reference to "*electronic eavesdropping*" was to the FM transmitter in Trenkler's housemate John Coyle's stereo which transmitted music. It was a $5.00 FM transmitter that only transmitted the music from the stereo as collected by electronic pulses and not sound signals, and it was not an eavesdropping device. Perhaps the ATF investigators had taken a good look at the old stereo which Coyle had given them, with Trenkler's FM transmitter still inside, according to Coyle, and found that it was not for eavesdropping at all. How did this Rise and Fall of an ATF Fact occur? Why did Donna Shay tell the ATF that the stereo broadcast prank was really a sick way to eavesdrop on a friend having sex? She had heard with her own ears the true result of the prank which was to broadcast Coyle's show music throughout the large house which Alfred Trenkler was sharing with his friends in the 1980's while he was housesitting a home almost adjacent to his parents'? Why did she transform it into a sinister event? Did the ATF tell her that Alfred was a proven sicko and bomber, so Donna and John Coyle, too, could reinterpret their own experiences to conform with what the police were saying? Was this a version of the Lindbergh Baby 200 syndrome? A chance to be a part of a dramatic public event and maybe collect some reward money?

The "*hotwiring of the garage door*" was in reference to Alfred's actions in 1972 when he was 16 years old. In response to the theft of items from his family's garage in Milton, Alfred had created an electrical circuit with an unused capacitor from an old television. There was no electric power service yet in the garage, so the television was located elsewhere and used to charge the capacitor, which was then hooked up to the primitive alarm system in the garage. When a person touched the handle of the garage door, s/he would discharge the capacitor and receive a mild static electricity shock. As designed, the system would not discharge when a key was used to open the door. As luck would have it, for this budding home security specialist, his stepfather, Jack

Wallace, was the first to unknowingly use or test the system. He was not pleased with the shocking success of the idea, and that was the end of the protective system. In most households across the country, the design of such a system would perhaps have been cause for hope of the development of a future electrical engineer; but in the rearview of the U.S. Attorney's office 21 years later, the system was the work of a Bomb Maker-to-be.

Returning to the motions in court, Judge Zobel reconsidered her view of the Motion to Quash the subpoena to Tom Shay to testify, as she now agreed with the prosecution that Federal immunity would also protect Shay against state prosecution. Thus, she denied the motion, and with that denial, the prosecutors suspended their motion to subpoena Francis O'Rourke, who was Tom Shay's attorney for a short time in 1992. There was another matter involving Shay's prospective testimony and Paul Kelly correctly foresaw what was coming, "... *I can envision a situation where Mr. Shay* [Tom Shay] *may nonetheless refuse to testify...*" (TT 5-137)

Just before the close for the day at 1:05 p.m. Paul Kelly left the door open for continuing to try to present evidence of Alfred Trenkler's homosexuality, saying, "*it may be that the Government may want to, as the case unfolds, ask the court* [to] *revisit that simply because it's the thrust of the Government's motivation,...*" meaning that the Government believed that sexual solicitation was a substantial motivator for Alfred W. Trenkler. (TT 5-139)

Next day's headlines: None

25 26 27 28 29	1 2 3 4 5	8 9 10 12	15 16	22 23 24	29
X X X X X	X O O O O	O O O O	O O	O O O	O

Day 6: Monday, 1 November

The day began with a bench conference about contacts between the prosecutors and the expected jailhouse informant, David Lindblom, and further consideration was delayed until the prosecutors had time to prepare a response in writing.

On this day, the prosecutors filed a "*Motion in limine to admit in evidence Shay Jr.'s statements against penal interest,*" and a supporting 46 page Memorandum. Specifically, said the motion, "*The government expects to call certain witnesses (Detective Miller Thomas; Mr. Robert Evans; Mr. Lawrence Plant; Special Agent Dennis Leahy; and Shay Jr., by means of his videotaped interview of October 17, 1992 with Channel 56) to adduce in evidence certain statements made by Shay Jr...* [as a] *'declaration against penal interest' exception to the hearsay rule, where the declarant -- Shay Jr. -- may be unavailable.*" This motion became necessary when Tom Shay announced his apparent refusal to testify at Trenkler's trial.

Another matter concerned a letter written to Dr. Philips by Paul Kelly. Ostensibly about the Shay case, the letter was viewed as having the effect, whether intended or unintended, of discouraging him from testifying in the Trenkler case. Kelly had copied Nancy Gertner and Terry Segal. Terry Segal thought it improper for the prosecution to send such a letter to a potential defense witness in a case. There was no need for the Judge to take any action as Kelly said he would not be writing another letter in any case. Unfortunately, while Dr. Phillips was a potential witness, Terry Segal did not file a Motion to have Dr. Phillips testify. With 20/20 hindsight, it's now known that Judge Zobel's likely denial of such a Motion would have been a sucessful appealable issue for Alfred Trenkler.

Continuing the cross-examination of Thomas Waskom, Terry Segal asked if the Roslindale Bomb was similar to a bomb, or IED, described in a Paladin Press IED manual and Waskom responded affirmatively. However, it was not a clear yes, as the question seemed to ask for a precise answer, so Waskom pointed out minor differences, instead of simply affirming the general similarity.

Terry Segal asked Thomas Waskom if the removal from the dynamite of its brown wrapper paper, with a manufacturer label, was a sign that the bomb maker was experienced, but Waskom didn't want to be hemmed in by the label, "*experienced,*" and Segal didn't press for some level of affirmative answer, which Waskom seemed ready to give.

As did Nancy Gertner in the Shay trial, Segal noted that a dual detonator was recommended in military manuals, but as he agreed with Waskom, in dual circuits. Segal then went further and asked if Waskom had ever seen dual detonators in single circuits, and indeed he had. "*Yes, I have seen two detonators connected to one firing line in the military, typically for training, not for, not for use.*" (TT 6-14)

Segal asked Waskom if he agreed that the Futaba servo motor system was quite simple to install into a bomb, and Waskom didn't want to use that label of '*easy*'; but said there were a few small steps to do. Then he was asked about the length of time the four AA batteries in the fusing system could last, while powering the receiver in the ON position, and Waskom said he didn't know and hadn't tested that question - just as he stated in the Thomas A. Shay trial. Segal established the point, whether intentional or not, that the presence or absence of radio signals does not affect the amount of power used by a radio received; it's either on or off. Waskom agreed that signs at construction sites that ask drivers to turn off their radios are always, "*turn off your **two-way** radios*", [emphasis added here] as such systems have transmitters, whereas regular car radios do not.

Then Terry Segal asked, "*In terms of electronics, Mr. Waskom, what do you understand the term 'shunt' to be?*" (TS 6-26) It was a strange question, because Waskom was not qualified as an expert in electronics. Surprisingly, the prosecution did not object, and Waskom answered, and went on to explain the use of the term in the world of explosives, in which he was qualified. "*A shunt is, is not normally associated with electronics. It is associated with blasting caps. A shunt on a blasting cap is a small device, in the past it has typically been like aluminum foil or a small metal ring clip, that connects the two wires coming out of the blasting cap together. It is designed to prevent static electricity from building up on one leg of the blasting cap and not on the other leg. If it builds up on one and not on the other, it has the potential of flowing through the blasting cap and could probably function. By having a shunt connected to both leg wires coming off the blasting cap, there are [sic] what would be considered same potential. There is no difference in potential, so electricity would not [go] through the cap itself.*" (TT 6-27/8)

Then Terry Segal asked a related question and Waskom said he was not "*really into electronics,*" i.e. not an expert. (TT 6-26/7) Segal asked about shunts in ohmmeters and Waskom didn't know, so the questioning turned to the construction of the bomb, "*Let me ask it this way, if you were building this device, wouldn't it have been easier to use a single relay as opposed to servo arm and toggle switch that you had to mount and glue and all that?*" (TT 6-27/8) Waskom agreed that "*It could have been done.*" but "*I don't know that I would say that it would have been easier.*" (TT 6-28) Segal asked the question again, and finally Mr. Libby objected and it was sustained. Waskom was often reluctant to be pinned down with the precise language used by Terry Segal in his questions, with the result that the point of the question was often lost.

It's unclear why Trenkler's defense attorney was urging the prosecution witness to think about how the bomb could have been made more easily except to argue that someone skilled in electronics, such as Trenkler, would not have used such an electro-mechanical device, and would have used a purely electric trigger. The more productive question would have explored why the Bomb Maker created a 45 Volt firing circuit when 1.5 volts would have been sufficient. Would an electronics engineer have done that? However, Segal did not make that point and moved back to the U.S. Military manual's recommendation for wiring the detonators. Finally, Segal asked, "*From your reconstruction of this device, sir, isn't the reel* [sic] *workmanship here, the craftsmanship relating to the building of that box?*" i.e. the woodworking? "*No.*" answered Waskom, and that was the end of cross-examination.

The point not clarified here is that the 1991 Roslindale bomb was more likely made by a woodwork expert than an electrical engineer. Even if an electrical engineer had decided to use an electromechanical design, with a mechanical toggle switch, another likely option would have been to use a miniature toggle switch as that would have required less physical force to move and would have taken less space in the bomb box.

Frank Libby, on redirect examination, asked about the How-to-do-it manuals and then returned to the question about the shelf life of batteries when a Futaba remote control receiver is turned on, asking, "*Did you see any need to perform that kind of test in these circumstances?*" and Waskom said he did not, "*Mainly because the device functioned, which tells me there was enough power there for it to operate.*" (TT 6-37) While that question and answer may have sounded like a "*Gotcha*" exchange, it really didn't answer the question. Waskom's answer was odd, as the ATF did considerable testing on the type of explosive used, even though it was known that the explosive worked. If the dynamite brown wrapper paper had been used, it would have been helpful to know when the dynamite was purchased and by whom manufactured. Similarly, with the batteries, it would have been helpful, in order to establish the time window during which the receiver would have worked; which in turn might help in understanding when the bomb was armed and when it was placed underneath Thomas L. Shay's Buick. Probably, the ATF and Boston police just didn't think of the variable of the battery shelf life for the Futaba unit. Terry Segal tried to make this point in several attempts at a question on recross-examination. The shorter the length of the shelf life time period for the four AA batteries, the more likely it would be that Mr. Shay had some prior knowledge of the contents of the bomb; and that he had armed it on Monday morning, 28 October. If Mr. Shay was the person who turned on the slide switch and armed the bomb, he probably intended to make it **look** like a real bomb, but not to have it go off. He was the next witness.

Paul Kelly then began his direct examinination of Thomas L. Shay and predicted it would take two hours. When describing himself and his family, Mr. Shay was asked about "*Thomas Shay, Jr.*" and then Mr. Shay, Thomas L. Shay, correctly stated that Tom Shay was not a "*Jr.,*" but that he understood that the Jr./Sr. nomenclature was used by the government as a shortcut for avoiding name confusion.

Mr. Shay was specific about the month of the cessation of full-time work; it was October 1989. Another specific item, whether or not relevant, was added as Mr. Shay said that he gave his 1986 Buick to a friend, Philip Smith, a friend who was described as not having any money, in the spring of 1992. This seems contrary to the common understanding that Phil Smith was the bartender of the Waltham Tavern in the South End, where Mr. Shay often went. Mr. Shay's testimony also conflicted with Paul Kelly's 11 January 1993 letter to Terry Segal where he said that Mr. Shay had transferred his car to a Mr. William Baiona of Roslindale, but didn't disclose the price or other consideration. Mr. Baiona lived one-half mile from Mr. Shay. According to Mr. Thomas L. Shay's brother, Arthur, and Tom Shay, both of whom knew both men, Baiona was the local bookie and was Smith's uncle. Also, William Baiona was likely related to the part owner of the Waltham Tavern, Josephine Baiona, the wife of the Philip "Sonny" Baiona. If the prosecutors knew of Baiona's occupation and his family connections, they should have infomed the defense lawyers, as one of the defense theories of the bombing was that Mr. Thomas L. Shay was targeted with the Roslindale Bomb because of his failure to pay his gambling debts. Terry Segal did not ask about that discrepancy about the new owner of Mr. Shay's Buick, nor about the possible relationship of Baiona and Smith and both men to Mr. Thomas L. Shay. Segal did not ask about the extent of previous gambling debts and whether there were any significant repayments during 1991. As Mr. Shay would likely have responded that the answer depended upon Segal's definition of "significant," Segal could have set the threshhold at $1,000. If Mary Flanagan had assisted Mr. Thomas Shay with any significant repayment of gambling debts in 1991, it should have been included in the answer. She had told Boston detectives George Bishop and John Messia on 28 October 1991 that Mr. Shay's gambling debts had risen to $2,300 to $2,500. Other family members believe the number was more like $25,000 until Mary Flannagan provided the money to enable Mr. Shay to repay the debt.

Organized crime in Boston had planted a bomb in 1968 underneath the car of Attorney John Fitzgerald during a dispute, when he was representing Joseph Barboza, and Fitzgerald lost one of his legs. Thus, planting a bomb was not an unknown way of communicating strong messages in Boston. Note that because that bomb was in 1968, it did not show up on the EXIS system reports that were presented at the Trenkler trial.

Paul Kelly carefully established that Mr. Shay's auto body business was involved interstate commerce, whether it be by the customers from out of state or the auto body parts made out of state or the use of the Buick as a loaner being taken out of state.

Then he turned to the weekend of 25-27 October 1991. Mr. Shay said that after going to the circus, they went to a political fund raiser in Revere, in Mary Flanagan's 1989 Lincoln Town Car.

Thomas L. Shay described his activities of that weekend, but appeared oddly tentative about the use of the 1986 Buick. When asked if he used the Buick on Saturday, 26 October, he answered, "*I don't think so, sir,*" and when asked how he traveled to his club in the South End for dinner he responded, "*I guess I drove the '86 Buick.*" (TT 6-61) After Mr. Thomas L. Shay's vague evasive responses to several questions, it's hard to see how a jury could consider this man as being the primary actor in the bomb building drama. Certainly, the jury in the earlier trial did not think so. It may have been better to focus on the "*my client didn't do it*" defense and not try to otherwise solve the puzzle.

It was established that Thomas L. Shay placed the two round objects he found with the bomb onto the bumper of his Pontiac GTO in order to determine if they were magnets. They were, so then he took them to a table on his porch. When Officers Foley and Hurley came, Mr. Shay showed them to Mr. Foley and then Foley returned them, and Mr. Shay put them on the bumper of his van.

On Monday morning, 28 October, he drove to the Rolling Wrench Garage in South Boston because he had intended to do some work there on Ruth Leary's Mazda. Kelly did not ask about Mr. Shay's conversation at the Garage with his brother, Arthur, and John Doering who advised that the device sounded like a bomb, and that was from a person who was not already paranoid about a bomb being placed in his own car. Neither Arthur Shay nor John Doering testified at either of the Roslindale Bomb trials.

Paul Kelly asked Mr. Shay what he did after the explosion, and Shay responded, "*At that point I just, I was just in shock, I didn't move - - like I said, it seemed like for the longest time...*" and later he explained further, "*I was asking for the keys, following a vehicle that was parked across the driveway because I wanted to move and get it out of the way because I knew there were people who were going to be coming for help and I wanted to do something, I just didn't know what to do. I felt like, it was so useless, somebody yelled, I guess for towels. I ran in the house. I ran upstairs and I grabbed three towels off the bed, and I came down and gave them to somebody. I don't know exactly where it was at that time, and I had moved Ms. Leary's car because I had parked her car in front of her house, and I had moved her car, went down to the next house,[to] get more room for emergency people coming.*" (TT 6-99)

Moving backwards for a few questions, Paul Kelly asked Thomas L. Shay if, when he returned from the police station that morning and exited Ruth Leary's Mazda, did he have anything in his hands, and Mr. Shay responded, "*I might have had a tool box and I also carry a black bag which I carry some personal items in.*" Asked to describe the tool box, he said, "*It could have been a cardboard box.*" (TT 6-100/01)

Then, a group of visiting students rose to leave and Paul Kelly asked the judge if "*we can suspend for a few moments. I understand that perhaps the spectators may want to file out. I'll take a few moments your Honor.*" Judge Zobel was not pleased, as she had encountered this problem of spectator disruption at the Shay trial. She brought the lawyers to the bench and said, "*Mr. Kelly, I understand this is a difficult trial. I wish you would stop trying to run the courtroom. If it's necessary to stop the trial, I will do that.*" (TT 6-102)

The questioning of Mr. Shay continued, and Paul Kelly had Government Exhibit 28 entered into evidence, which Mr. Shay said was his personal effects bag. This bag was apparently the same bag which was put into evidence, over Nancy Gertner's objection, at the end of the Shay trial.

Thomas L. Shay described how the police asked him for the shirt he was wearing on the 28th and he gave it up. Then he described to Paul Kelly the civil lawsuit against Ber-Giam and the explosion in October 1987 at the Dedham Service Center. Through Paul Kelly's leading questions, Shay said that he had told the investigating officers that the explosion was caused by a "*quarter stick of dynamite,*" but at the time he did not know what a quarter-stick of dynamite was. For the first time in the two trials, Mr. Shay then said, "*I believe my son Thomas might have mentioned it. It has some type of a powerful firework, and I believe I talked to an ATF agent and he had told me that a quarter stick of dynamite, a firework is equivalent to a quarter stick of dynamite.*" (TT 6-

105) Such testimony served to support the view that Thomas L. Shay had little familiarity with explosives and that his son, Tom, already convicted in the Roslindale Bomb case, knew more about dynamite than Mr. Shay. Neither Tom Shay nor any member of his defense team was there to respond to such a charge. It was the reverse of Alfred Trenkler's problem at the Tom Shay trial.

Mr. Shay recalled Tom Shay's deposition on 13 September 1991, but didn't know who drove his son to that deposition, even though his lawyer, Alan Pransky, testified at Tom Shay's trial that he drove him. It was when they stopped for gas that Pransky and Tom Shay had their important conversation about the value of the lawsuit and what would happen if Thomas L. Shay died. (TS 15-123) Mr. Shay's apparent nonchalance also came despite the fact that Mr. Shay had taken special care to ensure that his son did not miss this deposition, as he did on one or two previously scheduled dates, and despite the fact that he drove Tom Shay to Russ Bonanno's in North Dartmouth on the evening after the deposition.

In addition to the civil lawsuits he was asked about at the trial of his son, Mr. Shay remembered his first lawsuit which was against a lumber company where he worked, for a back injury suffered during work. The prosecution tried to show that Mr. Shay was not a frivolous litigator and asked *"Have all of these lawsuits or legal actions that you commenced been successful, Mr. Shay, have you received recovery, either by way of settlement or by way of trial?"* and Mr. Shay said, *"Yes."* Thus, the jury could infer that it was likely that he and, perhaps his son, thought the Berr-Giam case had some worth, too. (TS 6-112) However, he said that he never discussed those lawsuits with his son. Also, he appeared to have forgotten his 1984 Claim against the State's Victim Compensation Fund for $4,949.24 which was dismissed in March 1987 due to Mr. Shay's failure to respond to the Attorney General's request for more information through Interrrogatories.

Going back over the history of his relationship to his son, Mr. Shay did acknowledge that he had physically abused his former wife, Nancy Peters Shay, and that Tom Shay had witnessed such abuse; but that he had never abused his son directly. In 1987, said Mr. Shay, he sought to reacquire legal custody of Tom Shay after his approximately 13 years of institutionalized care. Tom came to live with him in Hyde Park and then they both moved into Mary Flanagan's home at 39 Eastbourne Street in Roslindale in 1988.

Then Mr. Shay recounted Tom's theft of about $300 from him at the 39 Eastbourne home, and his running away, and subsequent return home. Mr. Shay forgave him. Then the next day, Tom stole silver coins and personal jewelry belonging to Mary Flanagan, with a total value of about $10-15,000 and fled to Florida. It was this theft that Mr. Shay was permitted to describe at the Tom Shay trial only as an *"incident,"* leaving the jury to imagine what could have been the cause. After that, Tom Shay was not permitted to live again at 39 Eastbourne Street, primarily at the direction of Mary Flanagan.

In 1991, one of Mr. Shay's few contacts with his son occurred when he drove to Derry, New Hampshire to bring him back to Massachusetts, so he could attend an earlier scheduled Ber-Giam deposition. Tom Shay subsequently didn't attend that deposition and it had to be rescheduled a few times until it finally occurred on 13 September.

He described his taking Tom to the Seabrook dog racing track in October 1991 and then returning and going to the Franklin Cafe, where Tom wrote him a note. Unlike the Shay trial, the note was not in evidence and was not read to the jury. Terry Segal objected when it appeared that Mr. Shay was about to describe it, but the reasons for the objection was not clear. As Segal's strategy appeared to be that Shay did, indeed, hate his father, and that the conviction of Shay was correct; then the loving letter from Tom to his father was inconsistent with that strategy. Again, the difficulty with that strategy is that once the jury was persuaded that Tom Shay hated his father, then it was not unreasonable to believe that he told others, including Alfred Trenkler, about his feelings. Then, said Mr. Shay, Tom left the Cafe around midnight.

Cross-examination by Terry Segal began around Noon, and he asked Mr. Shay, "*Do you gamble heavily?*" (TT 6-133) Shay had already acknowledged that he liked to gamble, but he demurred on the question of degree and said it "*depends on what you mean by 'heavily.'*" Segal wanted to confront him with previous testimony where he apparently used the word "*heavily,*" but Paul Kelly objected and, in the interest of moving the case forward, Judge Zobel sustained the objection.

The next question, had a similar problem, "*Have you lost a lot of money gambling, sir?*" and Mr. Shay responded, "*No, I wouldn't say a lot of money.*" (TT 6-134) This time, Mr. Segal did read back to Mr. Shay his grand jury testimony, which Mr. Shay didn't completely recall. This type of exchange was repeated several times when Mr. Shay wouldn't recall something or when he disagreed with a word or phrase in Terry Segal's question.

Going over the fate of his Buick again, Mr. Shay said that he had transferred title in his 1986 Buick to Mr. Smith, the bartender at his club, where he had gone and double parked on Shawmut Avenue on Saturday evening, 26 October 1991. He didn't know how much the car was worth, and said that he did not owe Smith any money. At the time, the Buick was worth about $5,000, so the gift to a non-family member was substantial.

There was extensive questioning about whether Mr. Shay told the police that he "*threw*" the black box to the ground or not. In another pattern of responses, when he didn't recall making such a statement, he was asked to read police reports or grand jury testimony to that effect. Somtimes there was confusion about what to read, and then whether his memory was refreshed. Mr. Thomas L. Shay's memory was often faulty, so for his testimony, the question and answer method of presenting facts to the jury was frustrating. The jury had to decide whether his difficulties as a witness related to the possibility that he knew more about the Roslindale Bomb that he had not yet revealed.

The trial adjourned at 12:50 p.m.

Next day's headlines:

Boston Globe: "WITNESS ALLOWED IN BOMBING CASE" no byline. "*Reversing an earlier ruling, US District Judge Rya W. Zobel has said the government can call Thomas A. Shay as a witness in the trial of his bombing co-defendant Alfred W. Trenkler.*"

Boston Herald: "JUDGE RULES THAT BOMBER SHAY MUST TESTIFY" by Ralph Ranalli Said the article, "*Prosecutors allege Trenkler and Shay were lovers and built the bomb to kill Shay's father. During his trial, federal prosecutors presented evidence Shay had said Trenkler built the bomb for him as a 'gift.' But*

U.S. District Judge Rya W. Zobel ruled that in prosecuting Trenkler, Assistant U.S. Attorneys Paul V. Kelly and Frank Libby, Jr. may not present evidence that Trenkler had a 'pattern' of giving gifts to younger men he was involved with.... Defense attorney Amy Baron-Evans said yesterday that she has filed a motion asking Zobel to reverse her reversal [of the order that Tom Shay be required to testify at Trenkler's trial.]"

25 26 27 28 29	1 2 3 4 5	8 9 10 12	15 16	22 23 24	29
X X X X X	X X O O O	O O O O	O O	O O O	O

Day 7: Tuesday, 2 November

Continuing his cross-examination of Mr. Shay, Terry Segal asked whether Mr. Shay recalled telling Boston Police Officer Ahearn that he "*threw the device against the house.*" [TT 7-2] He did not recall. Mr. Shay did not recall saying the same thing to Detective McCarthy. He did not recall telling three Boston police officers that he "*was afraid of Mr. Giammarco and Mr. Berry.*" (TT 7-3] Mr. Shay didn't remember making the statement, even after his memory was refreshed by looking at the report by Detectives McCarthy, O'Malley, and Ross.

One of the defense theories about the case was that Mr. Shay's brother, Arthur Shay, was an accomplished woodworker and could have built the box for the Roslindale Bomb. Pursuing that theory, Terry Segal asked Mr. Thomas L. Shay about Defense Exhibit 80, which was a painted bookcase which Segal said was made for the newly married Thomas L. Shay and Nancy Peters Shay and which came from the home they shared before their divorce. Not described in court was the history of the bookcase after the divorce, which took it from Nancy Shay' remaining possessions to the local fire department's waiting room and then to the home of a volunteer firefighter, before it was retrieved with Mrs. Nancy Shay's assistance to become evidence in this case. What became of the bookcase after the trial is not known. If it were available, perhaps some paint could be removed to see how the saw lines were drawn. Mr. Shay said he didn't recognize it, and there was no attempt later to have Mr. Arthur Shay testify about his woodworking skills.

Mr. Thomas L. Shay was asked about the amount of the settlement of the Ber-Giam case which had occurred in September 1992. Mr. Shay declined to answer due a non-disclosure agreement, and Segal asked Judge Zobel to order him to do so. Mr. Shay said that "*Judge Zobel in the Lowell state court*" [TT 7-8] gave him the order not to disclose the amount of the settlement, and to the laughter of the knowing audience, Judge Zobel said, "*I've just overruled him.*" [TT 7-8] Her husband, Hiller Zobel, was the Massachusetts Superior Court judge.[3] So ordered, Mr. Shay stated that the amount of the settlement was $27,000. After the 33% legal fee was deducted, 10% of the remainder, or $1,800, went to Kristen and about $16,000 to Mr. Shay. Terry Segal did not ask Mr. Shay about his medical expenses from the 1987 incident and how much of the $16,000 would go to pay for those expenses. Segal didn't ask about the medical reports from the Ber-Giam insurance company's psychiatrists which indicated that Shay feared the placement of a bomb underneath one of his cars, the Buick or an Oldsmobile that he owned. Segal did not ask about a diagram which had been allegedly drawn for his psychiatrist, or by his psychiatrist, showing a car with a bomb underneath.

Terry Segal asked questions about pieces of wood and cans of black spray paint at 39 Eastbourne, but Mr. Shay either didn't remember them or explained their presence. He didn't remember the presence in his garage of a "*Grainger*" industrial supply catalog, even after seeing a police photo of his garage with a clearly visible copy. He did not recall ever ordering anything from that catalog.

Mr. Shay explained the use of his small personal effects bag, which he said he carried on the morning of 28 October, "*...I carry the black bag with me at my house, and I carry my license in that bag along with a wallet and spare set of keys and a hair brush, and I would have always taken the bag with me because that's where my license would be.*" (TT 7-31) Terry Segal asked him, apparently sarcastically, if he used his hair brush at the Rolling Wrench garage, and Mr. Shay responded, "*I can't remember that, sir. Okay,*" and Terry Segal said, "*Okay.*" (TT 7-32)

Then Segal challenged Mr. Shay on why he hadn't mentioned the black bag to any investigators sooner in the investigation than at his son's trial, and then Segal sought to challenge his memory by asking Mr. Shay to read portions of a police report. At that point, Judge Zobel intervened, "*Oh, come on, Mr. Segal, this will take forever.*" (TT 7-34) Segal then said that there were only two paragraphs, apparently missing the point that the judge, and surely the jury, did not find this line of questioning too helpful in resolving the guilt or innocence of Alfred W. Trenkler.

Terry Segal asked Mr. Shay about the re-enactment with Boston Officer William Fogerty and Alan Pransky and others of Mr. Shay's Sunday morning travels in his Buick, including the stop at "Burger King" or "McDonalds." However, Terry Segal did not attempt to present to the court a videotape produced by his private investigator, James Karolides, of cars passing over the speed bumps at "Burger King" and "McDonalds" on Boylston Street in Boston. That tape purportedly showed that it was unlikely that Mr. Shay's 1986 Buick could have passed over either of the speed bumps with the Roslindale Bomb underneath. However, the quality of the video was apparently poor.

On redirect, Paul Kelly sought to minimize the perceived level of Mr. Shay's gambling, and Shay responded that he had been to the dog track in 1991 and that he was indebted to no one in 1991 as a result of gambling. In regard to the types of spray paint, he knew the difference between flat black paint and glossy black, and that the glossy black can was likely used to touch-up a piece of molding on Mr. Rotman's car, which was the car he repaired during the two weeks prior to 28 October.

On recross, Terry Segal tried again to show Mr. Shay was a gambler and he also obtained Mr. Shay's agreement that Mr. Rotman's car was white, thus reducing the credibility of Mr. Shay's alibi that the black spray paint was used on that car.

Christopher Shapley was sworn in as an expert in automotive engineering and Scott Lopez didn't object, although he asked two questions. Through one of them, he established that this was the first case on which Dr. Shapley, as he was called at trial, had worked which involved magnets. Coincidentally, Christopher Shapley had a Pontiac 6000 which he testified had the same underbody panel as Mr. Shay's 1986 Buick, so he did some testing of the strength of magnets on his own car. He stated that the two doughnut magnets had sufficient strength to attach the bomb to the Buick, and that the button magnets really didn't add much additional magnetic strength. He theorized that the Bomb Maker used a kind of trial and error method by first attaching the button magnets, then painting the bomb box. Finding the button magnets too weak, the Bomb Maker then added the larger magnets after the painting. (TT 7-12) Shapley also presented his calculations about the likelihood of the bomb falling off the 1986 Buick in the manner described by Thomas L. Shay.

Prior to cross-examination there was a bench conference about the upcoming prosecution witnesses and exhibits, but much depended upon whether Tom Shay was going to testify and what he was going to say. The previous day, Paul Kelly had sent a long letter to the judge and Terry Segal, but it had not been seen nor read before today's court session. Frank Libby, in passing, said, *"It's clear that the defense theory here is to spread doubt amongst a variety of people as to who may be potentially culpable for this device: Senior* [Thomas L. Shay], *brother Arthur, Giammarco, Berry, what have you."* (TT 7-73)

Terry Segal was opposing the admission of any statements by police officers or by jailhouse informants of what Tom Shay said, beginning with what was expected from the next witness, Officer Miller Thomas. The discussion was suspended pending Mr. Segal's review of Paul Kelly's letter and upcoming resolution of the issue of Tom Shay's testimony.

Under cross-examination by Scott Lopez, Dr. Shapley acknowledged that he was retained in the Spring of 1992, so his calculations about the gap between the bottom of the 1986 Buick and the driveway at 39 Eastbourne were not done with Mr. Shay's actual Buick of 39 Eastbourne, as it was no longer in Mr. Shay's possession.

Scott Lopez inquired about the likelihood that the bomb could have or should have fallen off the Buick during Mr. Shay's travels on Sunday morning, 27 October, and he asked, *"Did anyone tell you where Mr. Shay went on Sunday morning, October 27th?"* (TT 7-85) Apparently exasperated by the length of the cross-examination, Judge Zobel interjected, *"It doesn't make any difference, did anyone go there? It's an irrelevant question. He said he didn't go anywhere, didn't examine the route. What difference does it make whether he knew what the route was or not."* (TT 7-85)

Redirect and recross-examination produced no new information.

What failed to be fully explained to the jury in either trial was the improbability of Mr. Shay's telling of the story of the bomb. The bomb was constructed of 1/4 inch plywood and held together by nails and superglue, but with no braces for corners. The plywood was not ordinary home construction, but a fine quality of three layers with the two outside layers being made of a hardwood and most likely oak. Such plywood is rare and was available in only a few stores in the Metropolitan Boston area, but it was old and may have come from a piece of older furniture. The fragility of the box was similar to what would happen if someone glued playing cards together with perpendicular connections to make a four cornered structure with a roof. There were essentially two boxes. One larger box, the size of a chocolates box and another smaller 1 1/4 inch thick square 2 5/8 by 2 5/8 inch box below it, when magnetically stuck to the bottom of a car. The image is like the surface of the Civil War ship, the Monitor, overturned with its square pillbox on the bottom. [See drawing in Appendix D.] The Roslindale Bomb's pillbox would have been the first to hit and ground surface such as at a "bump" in a drive-through at "McDonalds" or "Burger King" or the crest in Mr. Shay's driveway.

According to Mr. Shay, the bomb was somehow unscathed in its travels on Sunday underneath Mr. Shay's car, due to the strength of the magnetic attachment to the body and the strength of the glue attaching the magnets to the fragile wooden box. The same bomb fell off the car at 39 Eastbourne after a second sound-producing contact with the concrete driveway which was sufficiently strong to cause it to fall off. Also, the contact caused scratches on the concrete. The improbability is that the force required to dislodge the device did not apparently result in any damage to the bomb itself. No one observed that the Roslindale Bomb, and especially it's fragile "pill box," was physically damaged before Officer Hurley held it in his hands. If there was no such damage, then it's unlikely that it fell off as Mr. Shay described.

There was a recess and the bench conference resumed about upcoming witnesses and the Government's efforts to introduce the statements of what Tom Shay said to those witnesses. However, as the Court noted, the statements were admitted when Tom Shay was on trial and the statements were claimed to be admissions against penal interest by a defendant. Here, they are being offered in a trial of someone else, and with no opportunity to "*confront*", as guaranteed by the Constitution an accuser, or cross-examine him. A key problem according to Judge Zobel was Shay's lying. She said, "*The notion of the hearsay exceptions is that the testimony is inherently credible, inherently reliable, because of the circumstances in which it was given against penal interests. If you have a witness who is known to be a liar, is the confrontation clause satisfied even though it fits within a hearsay exception?*" (TT 7-91)

Then Judge Zobel read aloud extensively, about four pages, from the transcript of the sentencing stage of the Shay trial, by quoting the Government's expert, Dr. Kelly "*who was asked whether he agreed with Dr. Phillip's testimony with respect to that condition, which I think has to do with pseudologia.*
Answer[by Dr. Kelly]: 'Well, Tom Shay does make up stories, and he does love to tell tales that he is the center of, and that attracts attention to himself. He is -- he admits it in his encounter with me. He said, you know, if we were talking about mental illness, he said a crazy person would just go to the top of the building and jump off. I would go to the top of the building, summon the police and the media, and I would toy with them on the top of the building. And he goes off into this fantasy about it, and would make a bigger deal out of it, and that -- I don't have any problem with that. The term is not a diagnosis. It is the Latinization of someone who is bragger and a BS-er and a self-aggrandizing individual.'
And he then goes on and ask is asked what that has to do with his capacity to premeditate or does it have to do with his capacity to premeditate. [sic]
Answer: 'No. In fact, it can tend to indicate a pretty good capacity to do that because they have a thinking out of these tall tales, and that shows essentially the parallel ability to premeditate an action if that's what one wants to do in another instance.'
Page 32 at line 14:
Question: I will move on. 'Are you aware' -- this is on direct examination, Government's examination of its witness, 'of another situation, particularly with respect to Shay, Jr.'s records reflecting a planning forethought, particularly in June of 1989, Doctor?'
Answer: 'Well, in the psychiatric records at Bridgewater, he was sent to Bridgewater having feigned suicidal ideation in the jail to get out of the jail, and he told that to the psychiatrist at Bridgewater. He also then demonstrated to the psychiatrist how he could behave as if he had a mental illness, which he said he was planning to do if he was found guilty of the offense. So both, he feined [sic] *suicidal* [sic] *to get out of the jail and*

sent to Bridgewater to get the transfer, and also was talking about feigning mental illness if it would serve his purpose to get sent back to Bridgewater if found guilty.'

Question: Do you consider that scenario to be significant, Doctor?

Answer: 'Yes. He shows, besides his other situation, he weighs the alternative, shall I stay in Dedham or should I go to Bridgewater. If I say I am suicidal, they will have to transfer me, and he does it. That's demonstration of a capacity to premeditate.'

On page 71, at line 19, he gives an answer to a question about in which he goes all over the place and can't keep on the same subject.

'He has a very rich fantasy life. He loves to talk about himself, and his ideas, and his plans, and past exploits. He did that even as a youngster. That is not the same as a thought disorder or thought disintegration. He wants to talk about what he wants to talk about. He wants to control the social situations. The examiner or the person having an encounter with him would say he is not staying on the subject, my subject most of the time. I know of no evidence that I can recall in those records in which he has loose associations in which he has a real thought disorder. He is distractible from time to time. He wants to do what he wants to do. It's hard to focus him on things, other than what he wants to focus on, that's true now and then'

On page 85, at line 12:

'He makes up stories, in my opinion. He is a bragger. He makes up these stories in which' -- it starts before that-- no.

'He makes up these stories in which he has had fantastic economic success with grand situations. He likes to talk, and he likes to hear himself talk, he likes to brag.

So, and many of his stories are to me not credible, and many of them to other people going back to his adolescence are not credible. How long he takes to think them up, it would depend on the individual situation.'

On page 90, line 14:

Question: And is it your view that Tom Shay lies for personal motive and gain?

Answer: 'I think he does it for both.'

'And is it your testimony that you are in a position to distinguish when he is doing it under one category versus when he is doing it under another.'

Answer: 'You would have to know the specific lie to do that, and usually, a psychiatrist is not in a position to know whether what any individual is saying about situation A is, in fact, correct. Because they were not there.'

'And, in fact, his lying is such that in the Bridgewater records, did you review the fact that Dr. Nester [sic, Nestor], I believe it was, suggested that his lies are so pervasive that you can't even take a personal history from him and have any confidence that it is the truth. Did you read that?'

Answer: 'I believe I did, yes.'

Question: 'And was that in your experience as well?'

Answer: 'I took much of what he said with a grain of salt, yes.' "

After that reading, the longest statement by Judge Zobel in either trial, except for her Charges to the juries, she stated, "*This is a witness* [Tom Shay] *whose uncross-examinable statement, the government is offering. By its own evidence, this witness is absolutely and totally incredible.*" (TT 7-94/7) Yet Judge Zobel had very recently presided over Tom Shay's trial where he was found guilty, in large part due to his own statements which had been allowed into evidence.

Frank Libby persisted and said that resolving it was so important as *"It's the key to showing the conspiracy here."* (TT 7-98) Then Judge Zobel stated how the balancing of interests in an evidentiary question such as this works, *"... the more crucial the evidence, and the less reliable, the less likely it's going to come in."* (TT 7-99)

Judge Zobel straightforwardly commented on the Trailways press conference, *"Nobody in his position in his right mind would call a press conference."* (TT 7-126)

The legal system continued to struggle on what to do with Thomas A. Shay. For Shay, the decision had already been made to re-institutionalize him for another 15 years, perhaps to cure the problems created by the first 12 years of institutionalization. In this trial, the problem of Thomas A. Shay extended to the life of Alfred Trenkler. For Shay to destroy his own life with his lies was one thing, but to destroy another's was another.

Finally, Judge Zobel gave her rulings on the question of admitting Shay's statements, offered by others. The statements had been were presented to her in two "series" in Motions. Judge Zobel stated, *"All right. Here's where I am. And I'm doing this by the first series of Miller Thomas, the first item about how things would be different if I hadn't gone to the schools. I think that is evidence of a state of mind, and I don't have the same problems about reliability when we're talking about state of mind offered for the state of mind because the state of mind is what it is. And the question of reliability then is simply whether the witness is accurately recalling, and, of course, the witness is subject to cross-examination. So that statement comes in.*

The second statement is offered neither for state of mind. Nor does it fit in the exception. It does not come in.

The third issue about radio control, remote control which is part of what Mr. Segal has just alluded to, I can't rule on that, because whether this comes in or not depends entirely on the context, how the question arose, what was asked, I don't know that, or what will be asked. I don't have the transcript before me. That one I will be unable to rule on.

Series 2 which is the next bunch, question 1, that the press had killed them, I don't see what possible exception that comes in on or that it has anything to do with relevant state of mind. That is out,

The second one, I believe, is state-of-mind evidence. I would admit it on that issue.

The third statement is exculpatory, not inculpatory, and I don't see how it comes in as against penal interest when it is in fact exculpatory. That is the witness is now denying that he made an inculpatory statement, so I don't see how it could be against penal interests to deny, to make a statement that says that may be inculpatory.

Fourth, that he didn't want to see his father which clearly goes to state of mind and comes in.

The fifth one is again exculpatory. He denies that he made a statement that it was -- he denies that he made it in any kind of a deliberate way. It is not against penal interest to the extent that it is exculpatory.

And No. 6 is like No. 3 in series 1, it depends on the context as Mr. Segal pointed out, and I don't know what the context is until the witness testifies.

So that's where I am. One comes in of series 1: 1 is in, 2 is out, 3 is in. Of series 2: 1 is out, 2 is in, 3 is out, 4 is in, 5 is out and 6 depends on context." (TT 7-128/30)

A trial is a very structured and choreographed event. What the jury hears has been pre-evaluated for truthfulness. Unfortunately, in the Shay and Trenkler cases, not enough truth was presented to the jury, to outweigh the non-truth and not enough non-truth was excluded.

The problem of the "against penal interest" exception to the hearsay rule can be illustrated in another way. In his efforts to win the reward money, James Harding tried very hard to get Alfred Trenkler to admit to a role in building the Roslindale Bomb, and get it on audiotape, too. However, every time he tried, Alfred would deny any role. Harding once tried to get Alfred to draw a diagram of the 1991 Roslindale Bomb and Alfred had replied that he had no idea how the bomb was made and why would he ever get involved in such a screwy plan in the first place. Despite those many efforts, Terry Segal would not have been able to bring James Harding to testify about those conversations because they were hearsay and there was no exception to the hearsay rule for denials of participation in crimes. If Alfred had admitted any role or said anything ambiguous which might have appeared like an admission, James Harding could have testified for the prosecution and maybe even claimed some of the reward money. If the jury could have heard about James Harding's surreptitious and unsuccessful efforts, the juror would have learned about a different Alfred Trenkler, but that was not to be.

The bench conference took the rest of the morning, so it was decided not to resume the testimony from witnesses that day, but to adjourn until 9:30, Wednesday. The judge and lawyers would start at 9:00 and see what would need to be done regarding the anticipated testimony by Thomas A. Shay.

The trial adjourned at 12:50 p.m.

Next day's headlines: None

25 26 27 28 29	1 2 3 4 5	8 9 10 12	15 16	22 23 24	29
X X X X X	X X X O O	O O O O	O O	O O O	O

Day 8: Wednesday, 3 November

The day began with Judge Zobel questioning Thomas A. Shay about the prospects for his testifying in the Alfred Trenkler trial. Shay was represented by Amy Baron-Evans and Nancy Gertner whose nomination to be a Federal District Court judge was still pending before the Senate Judiciary Committee. Judge Zobel explained to Tom Shay that she had signed an immunity order, so that there could be no prosecution, in Federal or state courts, for anything he said in court in Alfred Trenkler's trial, and Tom Shay said he understood. Then came this exchange:

THE COURT: "*If you do testify, then, the only risk you run is that if you do not tell the truth and you know that you are not telling the truth, the government may charge you with perjury; do you understand that?*"

THE WITNESS: "*I understand that but on earlier dates if I lied, then it is going to veto anything if I tell the truth now, it is going to make me look like a liar anyway, so. Do you understand?*"

THE COURT: "*But that is no risk to you. The risk to you is that the government may say: Well, you were telling the truth earlier, and you're lying now; and therefore, we will charge you with perjury.*"

THE WITNESS: "*That's what I'm saying.*"

THE COURT: "*That is a risk that you run.*" (TT 8-4)

Then Shay's lawyer, Amy Baron-Evans, suggested that he still might have liability for lies given in the past under oath, or in statements given in a proffer agreement for a plea bargain. AUSA Paul Kelly insisted that there would be no such prosecution. However, if Tom Shay lied in the current proceeding, meaning probably if he said anything which contradicted his recent conviction, he could be prosecuted.

Amy Baron-Evans then noted, "... *Tom Shay would still be subject to a perjury prosecution, unless he follows the script that the government wants him to follow. He's given conflicting statements on every issue in this case. For every statement yes, there is a statement no.*" (TT 8-7)

Paul Kelly took some exception to her comments, "...*Ms. Baron-Evans makes reference to some script. There is no script, and we have not talked to Mr. Shay. We simply wish to ask questions and hear his truthful answers.*"

Then Judge Zobel summarized the risk of a perjury charge if he doesn't tell the truth today, and also that he will not have the ability to decline to answer a question on the grounds of self-incrimination. Amy Baron-Evans conferred with Tom Shay several times.

Then Judge Zobel added another important element to assist Tom Shay in his decision on whether to testify, "*I need to explain one other thing to you, and that is, now that you have been ordered to testify, that is, now that you can no longer refuse to testify, and I will, therefore, order you to testify, if you decline to testify, I will have no choice but to hold you in contempt of Court. Because once you violate a court order, that's what you are, you are in contempt of Court.*" (TT 8-8)

THE COURT: "*Mr. Shay, will you testify or not?*"

THE WITNESS: "*Your Honor, I have to refuse on advice of counsel.*" (TT 8-9)

Then Paul Kelly wanted Tom Shay to repeat that under oath, but Judge Zobel saw no reason for that and then talked further with the lawyers, trying to obtain Shay's testimony. She asked, "*Is there no way you can work this out? He's afraid of being charged with perjury.*" (TT 8-10) Later, she commented, "...*he says he would rather take the contempt than run the risk of, yet another prosecution. And he's also saying, as I understand the papers, given the government's severe dissatisfaction with the sentence he received in the main charge, he is afraid that the government will want to pile it on by using perjury.*" (TT 8-9)

The agreement that was apparently required would contain an assurance that Tom Shay would not be charged with perjury on the basis of his prior statements under oath. Despite all the news conferences and discussions with police, there were not many of those. In such an agreement, perjury could be charged, however, if his statements in Trenkler's trial could be proved intentionally false by references to other sources and documents. Such an agreement was not achieved.

The judge and the lawyers could have done a *voir dire* questioning of Tom Shay without the jury present to better evaluate what he would be expected to say to the jury. The prosecutors could have asked him all the planned questions outside the hearing of the jury, and the judge, defense and prosecutors could determine then what protection from perjury charges was needed. In short, the prosecutors didn't try hard enough to get his testimony, and the Shay and Trenkler defense teams' opposition did not help Alfred Trenkler nor advance the cause of truth.

Someday it may become more clear what the prosecutors expected Tom Shay to say, in addition to the few points mentioned by Paul Kelly earlier in the Trenkler trial. Did they think that he would say what he said to Karen Marinella, with Alfred Trenkler in the courtroom and listening? It's one thing to lie about another person when not in that person's presence; and it's another when the person is watching and listening - and on trial for his life-long liberty. Or, did they anticipate that he would say what he had said on other occasions, that Al Trenkler had nothing to do with it, as far as he, Tom Shay, knew?

It appeared that nothing could be worked out, and then there was discussion of whether the contempt would be civil contempt or criminal contempt, which would apply if there was obstruction of justice. Judge Zobel commented on how important Shay's testimony would be, "*The government is having some serious problems in the case. And to the extent he doesn't testify, the government may not have a witness to testify on these issues. That's the problem.*" (TT 8-13/14) It was extraordinary that the judge should comment that the prosecution's case was weak and that the best way it could win its case was to obtain the testimony of the person she had said earlier was "*incredible,*" or someone who should not be believed.

Then Judge Zobel addressed Tom Shay and told him she was finding him in contempt for refusing to testify and that a hearing would be held later to decide the appropriate penalty.

During these long discussions, Terry Segal was almost silent, which seemed to mean that he either did not want to see Tom Shay testify; and that was a lost opportunity. As far as Tom Shay knew from the silence of Terry Segal, his acquaintance, Alfred Trenkler, also didn't want Shay to testify. Perhaps Tom felt he should help protect "*Al,*" and not do what the prosecutors requested. It is not believed that Terry Segal interviewed Tom Shay before the trial so Segal, too, may have been concerned about exactly what Shay would say. Lawyers learn in law school that one should be careful about asking a witness a question unless you already know what the answer will be.

A basic requirement for Shay's testimony would have been for Tom Shay to tell the truth, and he could be cross-examined on what he said in open court. If he said that Alfred Trenkler was involved, then Terry Segal could have shown that everything Tom Shay said in support of such a claim was false, or unprovable. It would be easier to prove untrue if Alfred Trenkler were to testify, but that decision not to testify had been made.

If Tom Shay said that Alfred was not involved, that would be good for Alfred Trenkler. What did Terry Segal fear that Shay would say? What could have been worse than having a jury that knows that one conspirator has been convicted and refuses to testify in the trial of the other, despite being given immunity? Would a written request from Alfred Trenkler to Tom Shay have been possible? Lawyers would scoff at such a notion, but how about a letter that starts like this, "*Dear Tom, As you know, you and I had absolutely no conversations, and took no actions, and made no purchases together or had any other joint activity which had anything to do with the bomb which exploded on 28 October. Please be assured that I had nothing to do with it, separately either. My liberty is at stake and I ask that you come to testify and tell the truth about the above and about the entire and very limited extent of our relationship. Some readers of this letter may say that by stating my views, I'm leading you, which is not my intent. If you disagree with my characterization above, by all means come to court and say so; but please tell the truth. Sincerely yours, Al"* and CC the U.S. Attorney, etc. Why not? How important is seeking the truth? Is it almost as important as winning? Or more important?

Supporting the demand for Tom Shay to testify would have put Alfred Trenkler on the side of truth instead of the side of legal gamesmanship which resulted in the suppression of truth. Of course, if Terry Segal did change his mind and had joined the prosecutors in seeking Tom Shay's testimony, the request would have been stronger if he were willing to permit Alfred Trenkler to testify, too.

Wouldn't the jury have been impressed, if they had been permitted by court rules to learn about it, that the defense wanted to hear from Tom Shay, too? It's like a defendant asking for a DNA test or a lie detector test: The message is, "*Give me a chance to prove my innocence.*" As Alfred Trenkler often said to the ATF and Boston Police investigators, "*I have nothing to hide.*" This reasoning applies to the question of whether to testify in your own defense, too.

We don't know what Amy Baron-Evans or Nancy Gertner really knew about their client, Thomas A. Shay. Did they believe at the time that he was innocent? They do now, but we know more now than then. Did they believe that Alfred Trenkler was innocent? Wouldn't it have been better and more just for them to encourage their client to testify in the interest of justice? Isn't justice better served in the courtroom when people with knowledge of an event come forward with testimony? That's naive, the seasoned legal experts will say, but what would those legal experts be willing to do to reverse this wrongful conviction and avoid others in the future? Isn't it worse than naive to think that it's okay for several thousand innocent Americans to be convicted each year by a flawed legal system? As Jim Karolides reminded the author in 2007, "*it's a legal system, not a justice system.*"

We don't know what consideration Nancy Gertner and her team gave to asking Alfred Trenkler to testify at the trial of Thomas A. Shay. What could have been the harm to Shay or to Trenkler? Trenkler would have denied any participation in any bomb construction or conspiracy and he would have tightly narrowed the scope of his mere acquaintance to Thomas A. Shay. Yes, he could have been cross-examined, but what would have been the harm in that? What damaging questions could have been asked?

Also on this day, the defense filed a "*Motion in Opposition to the Government's Motion in Limine to Admit Certain Statements of Thomas Shay, Jr. Purportedly Against his Interest at Trial,*" together with a 26 page supporting Memorandum. If Afred Trenkler's defense had successfully supported Tom Shay's testimony, then they would not have needed to oppose the admission of Shay's statements, because there would have been no Motion to admit them. The courts seek to have the BEST evidence, and cross-examinable testimony is better than written statements or recollections of others' statements.

The bench conference then turned to a request by Frank Libby for reconsideration of Judge Zobel's rulings of the previous day on Shay's exception-to-hearsay statements. Judge Zobel was quite irritated with the prosecution on this, saying, "*Look, every time I make a ruling on grounds advanced by* [the] *government, then* [the] *government says: Oh, but think about it in another way. And it comes back to me with yet something else...Well it happened every time. You know, I make a ruling, and then you come with the cases and ask me to reconsider. It is unfair to do that. First of all, it make*[s] *me look like a chump; and secondly, it cause*[s] *a whole lot of extra work. Think of it all in the beginning, and let me consider it in its entirety."* (TT 8-18] Frank Libby apologized, but then he continued to argue for reconsideration.

One request that particularly galled her was the request to admit a statement that Tom Shay made about using remote control submarines as a child, for which she said, *"I mean, if the argument were simply that he had some understanding from the time that he was a child that there was such a thing as remote control devices having to do with submarines and cars, that would be one thing. But to translate that into an argument that he therefore understood the remote control device involved in this bomb and that he therefore had something to do with this bomb, it is skipping.*

The argument is skipping an essential connection which isn't there. And as against this defendant who wasn't part of this conversation, it is an impossibility.... I have told you what is in, what is out. Let us now proceed with the jury." (TT 8-34) Also, according to Tom Shay's mother, the statements about Tom Shay's having remote control submarines as a child were not true. Still the prosecutors sought to admit them anyway, regardless of their truthfulness.

Boston homicide detective Miller Thomas was the next Government witness. Examined by Frank Libby, he said he was one of the first to question Thomas L. Shay at 39 Eastbourne. After that questioning, Thomas went to the West Roxbury police station where there was a *"strategy session"* for the investigation. It was decided there that the ATF would lead the investigation of the site at 39 Eastbourne. Then he went to dinner and then to his office where he was paged to come to talk with Thomas A. Shay, who said to him and Officer O'Malley, according to Miller Thomas, *"that maybe things would have been different had he, had he not gone to boys' schools. As he did this, his head lowered and his voice trailed off."* (TT 8-62) For the prosecution, this could only have one meaning: that Tom Shay was responsible for the Roslindale Bomb. For other people, it was an ambiguous statement that could have had many meanings.

The next day, Miller Thomas returned to 39 Eastbourne and talked again with Thomas L. Shay and about his relationship with his son. Scott Lopez objected to allowing Thomas to testify on what Mr. Shay told him, but the judge allowed it for reasons she explained to the jury, *"Members of the jury, this testimony as anything else that the witness tells us Mr. Shay, Sr. told him is admissible only again for the understanding of the investigators, and for you to understand then what it is that they did as a result."* (TT 8-66) Thus, though it looked like hearsay, it was admissible testimony.

Miller Thomas then described the interview on Thursday/Friday, 31 Oct/1 Nov with Thomas A. Shay at the Homicide Dept. offices in South Boston after the Trailways Bus Station press conference, and Shay's subsequent arrest on unrelated charges.
On Sunday, 3 November, Officer Thomas and others traveled with Mr. Thomas L. Shay on a reenacted and videotaped duplicate of his trips on the previous Sunday, 27 October. One officer drove Mr. Shay's 1986 Buick and a box was taped underneath the car to recreate the presence of the actual bomb. Upon their return, they drove the Buick in and out of the driveway at 39 Eastbourne St. several times and videotaped the effort. Officer Thomas said that Mr. Shay was fully cooperative at all times, and that he was still a suspect as well.

In his short cross-examination, Scott Lopez confirmed that Miller Thomas heard Mr. Thomas L. Shay say that he *"threw"* the Roslindale Bomb against the side of the house after he found it in his driveway. Neither the prosecution nor the defense requested to play for the jury the videotape of the effort to recreate the claimed scraping of the bomb against the 39 Eastbourne driveway. The defense was the more likely moving party, as the tape showed that, for the model of the Bomb the same size as was present in the courtroom, the claimed scraping and drop-off was not recreated and thus not recorded. If the jury had seen the videotape, it might have been more willing to question Mr. Shay's version of events.

Dwayne Armbrister was next for the Government. The Radio Shack receipt for the 18 October 1991 purchase, and an enlarged view of it was admitted as Government Exhibits 33 and 33A. Under direct examination by Paul Kelly, Armbrister said he asked the customer for the last four digits of his telephone number and the customer said "*5100.*" Armbrister continued, "*So at the time I automatically punched it in. I said the last four digits to your phone number. So, he goes that's it. I go, can I have your street address, and he spelled out S A H Y, J Y T, afterwards, I said is that it? That's it. I [sic] was like the hell with it.*" (TT 8-90)

Armbrister later said that he recognized the defendant, Alfred Trenkler, who, Armbrister said, had come into the store two or three times in the Fall of 1991. Under cross-examination by Terry Segal, Armbrister agreed that he had never seen Alfred Trenkler and Thomas A. Shay in the 197 Mass. Ave Radio Shack store together.

The next Government witness was the jailhouse informant, Robert Evans, but before direct examination, there was a bench conference to consider what the Government expected Evans to say that Tom Shay said to him. Again, it was more limited than in the Shay trial because there is no hearsay of an admission or statement against penal interest against Alfred Trenkler, because the testimony was to be about Shay's statements, not Trenkler's.

During the bench conference, Paul Kelly captured a theory of the case, "*... you have effectively a totem pole motive. For example, you have the initial motive by Mr. Shay, Jr. Of course, it's the Government's theory of prosecution, and the charge in indictment, that Mr. Shay solicited and recruited Mr. Trenkler who perhaps had different motives than Mr. Shay; but Mr. Shay's motives, Mr. Shay's involvement is really critical and relevant.*" (TT 8-105/6)

Frank Libby examined Robert Evans. Several of Thomas A. Shay's statements to Robert Evans were admitted as exceptions to the hearsay rule because they were presented to show Tom Shay's state of mind rather than for the truth of the statement. Thus, Evans was permitted to state that Tom Shay asked him, "*...how much time he would receive for a murder charge in Massachusetts.*" (TT 8-116)

Robert Evans said that he had been assaulted several times in prison, and was then in a segregation unit because of fellow inmate hostility to the fact that he had testified for the government in the Shay trial in June/July.

Before the next prosecution witness, Alan Pransky, there was a bench conference and Judge Zobel, always concerned that the trial move forward expeditiously, asked why his testimony needed to go into the early parts of the investigation, "*What's the point of all that?... I understand your suggestion about the investigators' strategy. You're confusing the issue in all respects.*" (TT 8-127)

Responded Frank Libby, "*We wouldn't do it, in the first instance, unless we see ourselves having to defend ourselves on the challenge, that we weren't there doing our job, covering the bases.*" (TT 8-127) Still puzzled, Judge Zobel continued, "*Why do you have to worry about that, for heavens sake?*" (TT 8-128)

Alan Pransky testified about what he said to Tom Shay during the drive back from Shay's deposition on 13 September, about his father's lawsuit and what would happen if his father died before the lawsuit was concluded. No testimony was permitted about Tom Shay's contribution to the conversation because that would be hearsay, and there was no applicable exception in the Trenkler case to the hearsay rule as applied to Shay's statements. In Shay's own trial, the statements were admitted because Shay was the defendant.

Brenda Sharton cross-examined Alan Pransky and established that the defendants in the Dedham Service Center case were claiming that Thomas L. Shay was faking his injuries and the defendants and their insurance company were not interested in settling. Then, via a question, she explained a defense theory about who built the Roslindale Bomb, "*Now, sir, wouldn't you say that if Shay, Sr. had some proof that Berry and Giammarco were trying to hurt him again that would certainly help the lawsuit negotiation?*" Pransky answered "*No.*" Indeed, Brenda Sharton likely did not expect a different answer, but she asked the question in front of the jury, and there was no objection. (TT 8-147) She then turned to the final settlement of the case and Mr. Pransky demurred due to either attorney client privilege or the non-disclosure agreement. There was laughter again about the issue of Judge Hiller Zobel's role in the matter, prompting Judge Rya Zobel to note, "*That's what you get from connubial federalists.*" (TT 8-149/50)

At 1:00 p.m. Ms. Sharton said she had ten minutes more of cross-examination and Judge Zobel adjourned the trial, forcing Alan Pransky to come back the next morning. That would take about two to three hours out of his normal day, in order to keep the trial from going ten minutes over the scheduled 1:00 p.m. adjournment.

Next day's headlines:

Boston Globe: "*DESPITE IMMUNITY, SHAY WON'T TESTIFY IN 2D BOMBING TRIAL*" by Matthew Brelis Excerpts from the article: "*Prosecution efforts to prove Alfred W. Trenkler made the bomb that killed a Boston police officer in Roslindale two years ago were hampered yesterday when convicted codefendant Thomas A. Shay refused to testify at Trenkler's trial.... After the court hearing, several government attorneys criticized the defense attorneys for advising Shay to violate an order of the court.... Baron-Evans said she had no choice but to advise Shay not to testify because he had made many contradictory statements about the case. Because of those statements, she said, Shay could be charged with perjury by the US attorney's office if his testimony before Zobel did not conform to what the* government wanted."

Boston Herald: "*CONVICTED BOMBER REFUSES TO TESTIFY*" by Ralph Ranalli. He wrote, "*Defense attorney Amy Baron-Evans said Shay's mental problems and propensity to lie exposed him to possible perjury charges. 'If he were a sane person it would be different,' she said.*

Assistant U.S. Attorney Paul Kelly refused comment yesterday."

25 26 27 28 29	1 2 3 4 5	8 9 10 12	15 16	22 23 24	29
X X X X X	X X X X O	O O O O	O O	O O O	O

Day 9: Thursday, 4 November

A bench conference began the day with more discussion about the prosecutors' efforts to bring more of Thomas A. Shay's statements into evidence, and Judge Zobel reviewed the cases offered by the Government in support of their efforts, and noted, *"Well, I've looked at the Government's cases, and I don't think they stand for the proposition for which the Government is offering them. Let me review where I think we are."* (TT 9-2)

Judge Zobel noted that the question of what Shay statements could be admitted in the case against Alfred Trenkler would have been answered differently if the two defendants had been tried together, and added, *"However, the defendants here were tried separately because the Government agreed with defense counsel's motion for severance. Separate trials were not the choice of the Court, nor were they ordered by the court."* (TT 9-3) And later, *"What you are offering here is [sic] statements by Mr. Shay that somebody else did something. And that is precisely what Bruton doesn't allow, and it is not allowed by Richardson and Marsh. With all respect, the fatal mistake here is not to try the defendants together."* (TT 9-4)

Resuming his testimony, Alan Pransky confirmed that on 28 October when he told the police about Thomas L. Shay's civil suit, he also told them that one of the defendants in that case, Jeffery Berry, had experience with explosives, and he had a role in detonating the 1987 explosion at the Dedham Service Center. The next Sunday, Alan Pransky was with Mr. Shay and the police officers when they recreated and retraced Mr. Shay's travels on Sunday, 27 October to Medford, Chelsea, South Boston, etc.

Brenda Sharton established that Mr. Pransky waited after 28 October for several days before telling the police about his conversation with Tom Shay on 13 September, but she didn't explain to the jury, by questions to Pransky or otherwise, why she established that fact.

There was another long bench conference about the prosecutors' request to admit statements by Tom Shay which implicated both himself and Alfred Trenkler, and the judge would not permit them.

Prior to the testimony of the next witness, Larry Plant, Terry Segal noted his prior objections, so he wouldn't have to object several times, to allowing Plant to present Tom Shay's statements. Said Segal, *"The objection is basically it's not against penal interest and it's unreliable and he's [Tom Shay] a fruitcake."* (TT 9-27)

Paul Kelly examined Larry Plant and established that Plant met Tom Shay when they were both in the orientation unit at the Plymouth County House of Correction in October 1992, which Unit would later play a more prominent role in the case against Alfred Trenkler. Plant's testimony included most of what he stated at the Shay trial.

Under cross-examination by Terry Segal, Plant agreed that Tom Shay had told him that he, Shay, could acquire tanks and an F-16 fighter jet. On redirect, Plant made the distinction that Shay told him and everyone in the unit about his abilities to acquire weapons, but that his statements about the Roslindale Bomb and about the abuse he suffered at the hands of his father were in private conversations.

Paul Kelly then examined the next witness, John Cates, but he did not introduce him as a *"hostile witness"* as was done in the Shay trial. Cates described how he met Alfred Trenkler in September 1990 outside the "Ramrod Club" in Boston. They lived together from October 1990 until Trenkler's arrest in December 1992. Kelly asked Cates about his sexual orientation and Cates said he was homosexual and he had an intimate relationship with Alfred Trenkler. There was no defense objection, and no caution from Judge Zobel. Why was such a question necessary, and why was it allowed to be asked? Cates was asked several questions about Alfred Trenkler, such as his age, which normally would have been provided by public records or by Alfred himself if he were to testify.

Paul Kelly asked about Trenkler's business, too. Even though Cates knew little about it, he did say that "*It appeared to be going well.*" (TT 9-62) Kelly established that John Cates paid for the rent and utilities for the apartment he shared with Alfred Trenkler in Quincy and he sought to show that Trenkler's income was small. Several times, Kelly challenged Cates' recollection with his testimony before the grand jury on 6 February 1992 and also at the Shay trial.

Cates acknowledged that Alfred Trenkler purchased items at Radio Shack stores and U-Do-It Electronics in Needham, and that he, Cates, had accompanied him 2-3 times on such trips. One Radio Shack store was on the South Shore. Paul Kelly did not ask if Alfred Trenkler ever asked John Cates to purchase anything for him, and the cross-examination did not ask that question later, either; but it would have been useful to the jury as it evaluated the allegation that Alfred Trenkler used other people to purchase items for him.

Cates testified that a few months after 28 October, the reference date given by Paul Kelly, Alfred Trenkler spray painted his car black, to hide the rust marks. Regarding Tom Shay, Cates said that he first met him in 1988 at the Blue Hills Reservation, but had never seen him again there in the presence of Alfred Trenkler.

The court declared the morning recess for the jury, and the prosecutors resumed their efforts at a bench conference to persuade the judge to allow more Tom Shay statements, including those which might incriminate Alfred Trenkler. Exasperated, Judge Zobel said at one point, "*Cite me one case, one case in which somebody's confession was admitted against the co-defendant in the separate trial. None of the cases you've given me say that, not one.*" (TT 9-93) Frank Libby mentioned one case, Pacerella, which had been mentioned in earlier proceedings, and Judge Zobel said she would look at it, and if it supported the prosecution's position, she might reconsider. Throughout these bench conferences on Shay statements, the conversation was primarily between the prosecutors and the judge, so Terry Segal did not have to weigh in.

At this point, Judge Zobel asked about the expected length of the Trenkler case, and Paul Kelly estimated another week, until 12 November, and Terry Segal estimated that the defense would take 5-7 days to present its case. Thus, the case was likely to go beyond Thanksgiving Day, Thursday, 25 November.

John Cates resumed his testimony and said that Alfred Trenkler first met Tom Shay between June 9th and 18th of 1991, (TT 9-96) because it happened when Cates was on vacation in Europe over that period. The defense did not object to this secondhand testimony as it helped Alfred's case. Cates testified that he didn't learn about the visit until November, 1991, after it became clear that Alfred was a suspect in the Roslindale Bomb investigation.

Another way to support this dating of the first meeting of Alfred Trenkler and Tom Shay, in the absence of either Shay's or Trenkler's direct testimony would have been the testimony of Martin Alexander of Metromedia Paging Co. ARCOMM was a sub-dealer for Metromedia and Alfred was a customer, with his pager number of (617-553-0778) Mr. Alexander was prepared to testify at Alfred Trenkler's trial that Alfred was assigned that pager number only in July 1991, so that was the earliest that Tom Shay could have entered Alfred Trenkler's pager number in his address book. However, for unexplained reasons, Alexander did not testify for the defense. Alfred Trenkler believes that Alexander was intimidated by the ATF agents at the courthouse, but Terry Segal could have overcome such perceptions if he wanted Alexander to testify.

Alfred Trenkler recalls that the ATF engaged in similar badgering of two other defense witnesses, Randy Winchester of MIT and Frank Cavallo of Videocom, and that in response, Judge Zobel assigned a specific room for defense witnesses where they would not be approachable by the ATF agents.

Of the 33 names in Tom Shay's address book, 32 of them had a phone number. The only name without a number was apparently a business listing for Bill Jessup at "Copley Security" at 485 East Broadway, Room 3Q, South Boston Thus, Tom Shay's practice was likely to only enter names of people when he had a phone number to enter, and he didn't obtain Alfred Trenkler's phone number and business card until he lied to him about a business opportunity in July 1991. There was no other, nor earlier phone number listed for Alfred Trenkler.

John Cates testified that he did not know about the 1986 Quincy Hoffman artillery simulator until Alfred Trenkler told him about it in November 1991, because of the police searches on 5/6 November. Said Cates, "...*he told me about a prank that happened in 1986 that that had caused some problems and was, I guess eventually dismissed, that it was a 4th of July type firework burning.*" (TT 9-102) Cates said that Donna Shea had asked Trenkler to play a prank on someone at a fish company.

Cates' recollection of Alfred's contacts with Tom Shay in the summer of 1991 was the same as at the Shay trial, as was his recollection of their (Cates' and Trenkler's) time together over the weekend of 25-27 October 1991. Those recollections were correct.

Under cross-examination by Terry Segal, John Cates described Alfred's car as "*beat up*" and rusty and had a WBCN [a Boston FM rock 'n' roll radio station] decal and an antenna on the back, and he agreed with Segal's characterization of it as an "*eyesore.*" (TT 9-121) Also, he said that Alfred, whom he called "*Al,*" as did Alfred's friends, purchased groceries for both of them and that his driving Cates to and from work was part of his contribution to their combined expenses.

Segal then asked John Cates more about what Alfred Trenkler said under questioning by Paul Kelly, about the 1986 Quincy device and the judge upheld Paul Kelly's objection due to hearsay. Terry Segal argued the point and the judge explained it to the jury, that the prosecution could obtain that testimony because it involved a hearsay exception such a state of mind or admissions against penal interest, but the defense, which has the ability to call the defendant to testify, doesn't have that ability. Said Judge Zobel, although "*he* [Kelly] *can do that, you can't offer it for the defendant. That's the rule.*" (TT 9-129) Still, the truth about the first meeting between Tom Shay and Alfred Trenkler in June 1991 had been presented to the jury by the prosecutors' "hostile" witness, John Cates.

Richard Brown was the next witness for the prosecution. Like John Cates, he was unemployed at the time of the trial. Frank Libby established that ARCOMM had, at peak times 6-7 part-time employees, but that Brown and Alfred Trenkler were the only two full-time employees. The Christian Science Church project was the first major project for ARCOMM, and it lasted about seven months, through the end of 1991.

Brown repeated his Shay trial testimony that he saw Alfred Trenkler with Thomas A. Shay over a weekend in 1990 when Trenkler was living and working at ATEL. Brown identified Shay from a photo array and remembered driving him somewhere on the Sunday of that weekend. This was the same testimony as given in the Shay trial, but slightly more definite on the identification of Tom Shay.

Richard Brown described the ATF searches of ARCOMM, and Frank Libby showed some sympathy, as he asked, "*Fairly unpleasant to be hit by federal agents?*" and Brown responded, "*Yes.*" (TT 9-158)

Brown said that he asked Alfred Trenkler how he met someone like Thomas A. Shay, and the response was, "*He told me that he just met him on a corner or someplace and that he felt bad for him. He didn't have any friends and that's how he ended up exchanging numbers or he gave him his number and business card.*" (TT 9-162)

Richard Bown said that Alfred Trenkler had told him about drawing a block diagram of a bomb at the request of ATF agents, and that the agents hadn't taken it with them, so he, Alfred, shredded it.

Brown was asked about the end of the ARCOMM relationship in February 1992 and a conversation he had in December 1991 with Alfred Trenkler at the Weymouth office in the presence of Donna Shea. Brown said that he urged Alfred Trenkler to cooperate with the investigation and tell the investigators if he knew anything about it, and Trenkler appeared to be thinking about the suggestion.

Judge Zobel called a recess, for witness testimony at least, with Brown to come back in the morning for cross-examination.

During the ensuing bench conference, Frank Libby tried again to argue for the admissibility of statements by Tom Shay. Terry Segal argued that "*this is like six bites at the apple, your Honor....*" and the judge agreed, saying, "*we're having no further argument on this issue.*" (TT 9-168)

The trial adjourned at 1:00 p.m.

Next day's headlines: None

25 26 27 28 29	1 2 3 4 5	8 9 10 12	15 16	22 23 24	29
X X X X X	X X X X X	O O O O	O O	O O O	O

Day 10: Friday, 5 November

Terry Segal cross-examined Richard Brown and sought to impeach his credibility. He asked Brown if he remembered telling Segal last summer, of 1993, that he had been present when Alfred Trenkler drew the diagram for the ATF agents. Brown did not remember making that statement. Terry Segal had memoranda from two people in his office, one of them his investigator for the Trenkler case, but Judge Zobel would not allow the memoranda to be introduced, apparently due to the extra time required, nor to bring either of the people to testify as to what they heard. During the investigation, it was established that Richard Brown had had several head injuries and his memory was impaired. If Terry Segal had been able to introduce that evidence, Brown's testimony could have been minimized, especially his refreshed recollection of seeing Tom Shay and Alfred Trenkler together in the fall of 1990 - which didn't happen. Once again, judicial economy trumped truth.

Important as it was, Terry Segal did not question Richard Brown about that important identification of Tom Shay as being the person he saw with Alfred Trenkler at ATEL over one weekend in 1990, and for whom he gave a ride to the "T". An important part of such cross-examination would have been the ATF report of 10 December 1992 by Agent Thomas D'Ambrosio that Brown "said that he now wasn't sure Shay was the person he gave a ride to, from ATEL in Boston to the 'T'."[4] Perhaps Segal didn't believe he could successfully shake the false scenario that Shay and Trenkler's relationship began one or two years previous to 1991, or that he didn't think it was important. John Cates had recently testified that, to his knowledge, the acquaintance began in June 1991. It was important to challenge that false scenario, a long term Shay-Trenkler relationship, which was supported only by Brown's testimony and by the next two witnesses, Edward Carrion and Paul Nutting.

Carrion was examined by Paul Kelly and the testimony was the same as in the Shay trial. Under cross-examination, Terry Segal asked Ed Carrion what a "*shunt*" was, as Carrion had had previous electronics experience, and Carrion replied, "[A] *Shunt is a device in which you would either turn on or turn off the device.*" Responded Segal, "*It's not like a switch, but it's some sort of a diverter of electricity?*" and Carrion answered, "*Diverter of electricity, but it also can be used as a switch.*" Terry Segal asked, "*Is it a common term in electronics?*" and Carrion said, "*Most of the time, yes.*" (TT 10-44) The prosecution didn't object, as Edward Carrion certainly was not qualified as an expert in electronics, so Segal was able to make his point, which would be useful later.

Carrion's most damaging testimony to Alfred Trenkler was the testimony, as with the Shay trial, where Carrion said that he have given Tom Shay rides to Whitelawn Avenue in Milton "*three or four times*" in the summer of 1989 and that he identified Alfred Trenkler from a photo array as the person from Whitelawn, whom he had previously seen twice. (TT 10-33). Those two times were in the company of Tom Shay in the area known as "*the Block*". (TT 10-37) However, Mr. Segal did not ask Carrion any questions about the claimed rides or the identifications. Carrion was not asked about the common sense problems with his testimony. Why, Segal might have asked, would Carrion give rides to Tom Shay, a man with whom he had had an ongoing relationship to take him to see another alleged lover? Did Carrion give rides to other friends to go see other friends and then leave them at those destinations? Did Tom Shay ever tell Carrion how he was transported home after being in Milton? Also, Segal might have asked Carrion where else he drove Tom Shay to meet such lovers. To Wellesley? To Winchester? To Weymouth? Only to Whilelawn Ave. in Milton? Segal might have asked why he gave Shay such rides at all? Why not tell Tom Shay to take the bus or subway and Trenkler could meet him? Why would Shay ask Carrion to drive him 3-4 times to the same home in Milton? Was Carrion aware of any contact between Tom Shay and Alfred Trenkler in 1990 or 1991? Were there any rides to Trenkler's residences over that period at ATEL or Quincy?

Regarding the claimed sighting of Shay and Trenkler together at "*the Block*", Segal did not ask questions normally asked about such claimed identifications, such as the time of day, the weather, and the distance from which the identification was made. Alfred Trenkler wrote in 2007, "*It goes beyond unlikely that Ed Carrion saw me with Shay, Jr. in 'the Block.' It is impossible. I have never hung out at, stopped at or spoken to anyone in 'the Block,' ever.*" Segal did not ask Carrion about his previous statement on 27 February 1992 to the ATF that the Alfred Trenkler he saw had a mustache. It was obvious to the jury that Trenkler did not have a mustache at the defense table, but that would not have been persuasive enough. Segal would have needed to present evidence during the defense case about Alfred Trenkler's facial hair, or lack of it, during the late 1980's. He could have asked every one of the upcoming defense witnesses, "*Did Alfred Trenkler ever have a mustache during your acquaintance with him after 1980?"* As Edward Carrion was not asked about the mustache, that issue was never raised. In his "Testimony" in Appendix B, Tom Shay stated that the man with the mustache was Ralph Pace and not Alfred Trenkler. One goal of cross-examination is to show that the version of the truth presented by a witness is either wrong or questionable and on the issue of the date of origin of the Shay-Trenkler acquaintance, the cross-examination of Edward Carrion failed.

Eyewitness evidence is called "direct evidence" in the law, and circumstantial evidence is called "indirect evidence". The implication of the labels is that direct evidence is more reliable than indirect evidence, but that's often not the case. In 2007 it's known that eyewitness evidence, often by victims of crime, has caused approximately 75% of the 200+ wrongful convictions which have been reversed by the Innocence Project since 1989. At Alfred Trenkler's 1993 trial it was thought that eyewitness identifications were more reliable, so Carrion's identification, and the upcoming Paul Nutting identification, were more powerful then than they might be considered now. The next witness showed how identification mistakes could be made.

Frank Libby examined Mrs. Nancy Shay and asked about being abused by Thomas L. Shay, her former husband. Judge Zobel asked at a bench conference, *"May I ask why we're getting into this. I mean, you have established over and over again Mr. Shay's feelings about his father."* (TT 10-53) The issue, said the judge, was Shay's state of mind about his father, and not whether he actually saw any abuse in the family or not. It was how he felt about it that counted.

Terry Segal added, *"I would say they tried the Shay case once. This isn't the Shay trial. And my client is on trial here."* (TT 10-54) Then there was unresolved discussion whether Mrs. Shay was a "hostile" witness, and thus, whether Mr. Libby could ask leading questions. Her son was just convicted and sentenced to 15 years 8 months in prison for trying to kill his father, her ex-husband.

Frank Libby then asked her, *"Do you see the individual you now know to be Alfred Trenkler in the courtroom today?"* and, instead of saying "Yes" as the prosecution expected, she said, *"This is the first time I've seen Alfred Trenkler."* (TT 10-62) This answer must have stunned Frank Libby because the prosecution had used her descriptions of a man on two occasions in different places, she believed to be Alfred Trenkler, in the trial of her son. It's known by many that eye-witness identification is often erroneous, but it's not often that a mother will testify at her son's trial and state a belief that her son's alleged co-conspirator was with him in her house - when in fact it wasn't Trenkler, the alleged co-conspirator, at all. Frank Libby tried to change her mind by referring her to her previous descriptions, *"And the man on the couch that you threw out that evening was this man, Alfred Trenkler, wasn't it?"* Mrs. Shay held fast and responded, *"No, I swear to God that isn't the guy that was there."* (TT 10-71) If Alfred Trenkler had testified at Tom Shay's trial, and if Mrs. Shay had been allowed to stay in the courtroom and see him, Mrs. Shay would likely have made the same non-identification at Tom Shay's trial. It might have made the difference in the jury's verdict. Unfortunately, she was left with the burden of knowing that her incorrect identification of Alfred Trenkler from ATF photos as being the man in her condo with Tom Shay in October of 1991 was one of the pieces of the puzzle that the Shay jury put together to convict her son. This change in her testimony was never used in any of the Shay appeals as a reason for a retrial or reversal, but it should have been.

On cross-examination, Nancy Shay said she had never received a phone message from Alfred Trenkler, nor ever seen him with her son, Tom.

On redirect, Frank Libby tried again, but failed, to shake her in-court non-identification of Alfred Trenkler.

A bench conference began with the defense's request for the completed raw data forms for the five other matching bombings which came out of the EXIS system and which matched the 1986 Quincy and 1991 Roslindale devices. The prosecutors resisted, saying that it was privileged as being like an attorney's work-product; but Judge Zobel saw through that argument and said simply that computer reports are only as good as the data input into them. She asked the prosecutors to see what they could do to furnish the requested documents.

Then she pressed for a faster schedule, and persuaded the prosecution not to have two ATF agents come and testify to basically the same events. Terry Segal then said, again, that he expected to take five to seven days and the Judge said, "*See what you can do to cut it down.*" (TT 10-86) The scheduling problem was that the holidays of Veterans Day and Thanksgiving were coming and Judge Zobel had work-related travel plans. Also, a juror had an upcoming divorce hearing in Dedham, but the judge noted that a call from her Federal court to the state probate court could likely assist in changing that morning hearing to an afternoon hearing or achieve other scheduling relief.

Terry Segal insisted he had always said his case would take 5-8 days, and that "*I have an important case that I have to put in, your Honor.*" (TT 10-88) Unfortunately, he later used only three days to present the defense's case. It's not known how much of that reduction of Trenkler's defense was due to Judge Zobel's pressure to minimize the length of the trial.

Paul Kelly then examined Paul F. Nutting who was the first witness in the Alfred Trenkler case who had not already testified in the Thomas A. Shay case. Nutting said he first met Alfred Trenkler in the 1980's and had seen him 3-6 times since then. He also recognized Thomas A. Shay, as he saw him on the "People are Talking" show on gay teenagers and had seen him two more times since, once in Provincetown. Another time was at the Blue Hills reservation when he saw Tom Shay alight from "*a small, white car*" [TT 10-94] driven by Alfred Trenkler in the Spring of 1991. Later, he refined the description to say that it was "*a small white car in disrepair*" and "*it wasn't completely white. There may have been rust spots or primer paint or --.*" [TT 10-95]

Scott Lopez cross-examined Nutting and asked, "*I believe you testified that you saw a car sometime in 1991?*" to which Nutting responded, "*That's right.*" Then Lopez asked, "*Do you recall if that was in June of 1991?*" (TT 10-96) which was a surprising question since Nutting had already said it was in the spring of 1991, and while June is technically mostly in the spring, it's commonly thought of as summer. The distinction is important because Alfred Trenkler has stated many times that he first met Tom Shay in June, and not before. If Paul Nutting believed that his identification happened before June, then the driver he identified was not Alfred Trenkler. Lopez established that Nutting saw Alfred Trenkler and Tom Shay together only that one time, possibly in June 1991. In fact, they were never at Blue Hill Reservation together.

However, Lopez did not challenge Paul Nutting on an obvious problem with his testimony which was that he had told ATF Agents Dennis Leahy and Victor Palaza on 7 April 1993, only six months before, that, according to Dennis Leahy, "he knew Al

Trenkler and Tom Shay (the younger) and had seen them together in the Blue Hills area several times probably in the 1989/1990 time frame. Mr. Nutting said that the Blue Hills area was a known gay hangout for free sex. Mr. Nutting said that he thought that Al always drove, usually in a blue pickup truck and that sometimes they [Trenkler and Shay] would separate in the Blue Hills and sometimes they would stay together." Alfred has never owned a blue pickup truck and he had only owned his off-white Toyota since September of 1990.

   When Alfred Trenkler learned that Paul Nuttting was going to be a government witness, he did not know who he was and asked to see a photograph of him. There was a Nutting family which provided catering services to the Milton Hoosic Club and inquiries were made to see if there was a connection to Paul Nutting, but there wasn't. When Nutting testified, it was the first time Afred Trenkler had ever seen him and that visual contact confirmed Alfred's belief that he had never met Paul Nutting.

   The next Government witness for Frank Libby to examine was Thomas D'Ambrosio, a Boston-based ATF agent, who also did not testify at the Shay trial. He described how he was working at the ATF's satellite office with the Boston Police Dept. Homicide Unit on Monday evening, 4 November. He had the report from the Quincy Police Dept. of the 1986 device with Alfred Trenkler's name in it, and looked through the photocopies of the pages of Thomas A. Shay's address book for the name of Alfred Trenkler and found it on the first page. The book was alphabetized by first name.

   Then D'Ambrosio looked for more information about Alfred Trenkler and drove to the Milton Police Dept and then to 7 Whitelawn Ave at 9 p.m., but no one appeared to be at home. The next day, 5 November, the ATF and Boston Police Dept. interviewed Donna Shea, whose name was on the 1986 Quincy report, and that evening he and other officers searched John Cates' apartment at 133 Atlantic Street in Quincy, where Cates and Trenkler lived.

   Alfred Trenkler answered the door with jeans and a shirt on and talked with the gathered officers, and the agents searched the apartment for about an hour. Agent D'Ambrosio said that they asked Trenkler if they could go with him to the ARCOMM offices in Weymouth and Trenkler agreed, but he didn't have a functioning car. The ATF provided transportation. After Alfred Trenkler found his keys to the office and a pack of cigarettes, the eight officers and Alfred left for Weymouth which D'Ambrosio said was a 10 minute drive. However, Alfred Trenkler recalls that the trip to ARCOMM took 20 minutes, because they first went to his disabled car in Quincy on Mechanic Street. where a carpet sample was removed. Perhaps because Terry Segal did not feel the omission was important or because he didn't notice D'Ambrosio's error, he did not question him.

   At ARCOMM, Alfred Trenkler said of the 1986 device, according to D'Ambrosio, "*that it utilized a large firecracker type device, that it would never have harmed anybody, and that it was not intended to harm anybody.*" (TT 10-121) D'Ambrosio said he asked Trenkler, in the presence of Special Agent Dennis Leahy, to sketch a diagram of the 1986 device and Trenkler did so. D'Ambrosio said that Trenkler, "*... was very cooperative and seemed willing to provide me with the information that he was asking for.*" (TT 10-122)

   Then the officers and Trenkler talked a little about the technology of remote controls and D'Ambrosio said that his interest was not really in the 1986 device but in the 1991 Roslindale Bomb, and Trenkler "*acknowledged that.*" (TT 10-124) D'Ambrosio continued, "*So I then said to him, 'If I told you that the bomb that detonated in Roslindale also utilized remote control, but rather than a large firecracker type device, it utilized dynamite, how would the wiring of the diagram you just drew for me be different.'* " (TT 10-124) Then, according to D'Ambrosio, Alfred Trenkler allegedly drew a second diagram. Testified D'Ambrosio, the second diagram "*was essentially the same, beginning with a power source wired to a switch which was then turned wire* [sic] *to a radio receiver. At that point, he diagramed [sic] what he described as two blasting caps which were then inserted into two sticks of dynamite.*" (TT 10-125)

Frank Libby asked Agent D'Ambrosio, "*Now, did you consider at the time that Mr. Trenkler was drawing this for you, did you consider that to be significant?*" and D'Ambrosio responded, "*When he completed the diagram, I did consider it very significant,*" (TT 10-125) in part because he knew by that time that the 1991 Roslindale Bomb had at least two blasting caps in it.

Alfred Trenkler's own recollection of that exchange is different, but he was not able to present it at his trial because he took his lawyer's firm advice not to testify. He wrote years later to a friend, Mark Brodie,

"*They told me that they knew about the 1986 incident, that they knew it was a prank. They told me that if I would draw a diagram of what I did in 1986, it would show them that what I did then was so different from the '91 device, it would show them that I had nothing to do with the '91 device. I knew that I had nothing to do with this horrible incident and so I drew what I remembered of the '86 device. I figured that it would be beyond coincidence that my '86 firecracker device would in any way compare to the '91 device that had killed a police officer. After drawing a simple block diagram of what I remembered of the '86 device, ATF agent D'Ambrosio and Agent Leahy both looked at the drawing, handed it back to me, at which point I threw it away in a waste paper basket. Agent D'Ambrosio then asked me to draw a similar diagram if it contained two sticks of dynamite and at least two blasting caps set off by remote control. I told them that I've never seen dynamite or blasting caps and would have no idea how they went together and would not be able to draw it. He then told me to take a guess, that maybe it could help them find the guilty party. I told them that they were not going to set me up by doing anything so stupid, that I would not even 'fathom a guess.' D'Ambrosio said that was ok, they were just asking for my help.*"

In 2007, Alfred wrote again about that disputed part of the search and Agent D'Ambrosio's and Leahy's testimony.

"*Dennis Leahy testified that he and Agent D'Ambrosio asked me to diagram the '86 device which I did. The agents then said they asked me to draw the '91 device which they said I did. Dennis Leahy then said he wanted to take some tools and needed to have me sign a receipt. Leahy proceeded to write out the receipt by hand on the same pad of paper I allegedly had just drawn the '91 diagram. Leahy retained the receipt.*

Agent Leahy also testified that at my office was only one table and a couple of chairs and on the table was a single pad of lined yellow paper.

The theory was, if I had drawn a diagram of the '91 device on the only pad of paper in my 82 Broad Street office and it had been removed, the impression of that drawing would have been on the next piece of paper that agent Leahy took with

him, upon which was written the receipt for the tools Leahy was removing from my office.

In other words, the receipt the government had would still have the impression of whatever was written immediately before the receipt. Terry Segal asked agent Leahy if anyone had tried to lift the impression off of the receipt. Agent Leahy stated that he did not know or was not aware of how to lift impressions from paper - of course not - the only impression would be of the '86 diagram and only the '86 diagram - I never drew the '91 diagram. Further, I told the agents I had no idea how the '91 device was put together since I had nothing to do with it.

In fact, none of the agents ever asked me to draw the '91 device. I was only asked if I had any ideas how the '91 device may have been assembled to which I answered no...."

Alfred recalled in 2007, too, *"The night the ATF and Boston police were at my office, the morning of November 6, 1991, we all left together. I did not shred the '86 drawing until the next day. In fact, the '86 diagram was on that table all day. I did not go to work until the 7th, a Thursday. I had taken the 6th off since the agents had kept me up until almost 3:00 in the morning."*

Another problem with the claim that Alfred had drawn a diagram of the Roslindale Bomb, was that Thomas Waskom testified that the bomb did not have sticks of dynamite, but had approximately 3-5 pounds of packed ammonia dynamite, wrapped in a page of a magazine, with two or three detonators imbedded within.

D'Ambrosio's trial testimony continued. The investigating officers left ARCOMM about 1:30 a.m. after giving Alfred Trenkler a receipt for items that were taken. Agent D'Ambrosio testified that he forgot to obtain the page with the diagram of the 1986 and 1991 devices. He told other officers about the alleged drawing of the 1991 bomb, and also, later, told Richard Brown, who, prior to that conversation, had not heard previously of the diagram of either device.

Then the officers asked Trenkler if they could search his portion of his parents' garage at 7 Whitelawn Avenue, Milton. D'Ambrosio said that Trenkler was concerned about awakening his parents, and D'Ambrosio tried to accommodate by saying that they could go in one car, and *"we would not make a lot of noise, in* [sic, and] *that, if by chance we woke his parents, he could tell them anything he wanted to, he could make up a story as to who we were."* (TT 10-131) Thus, the agents showed they were quite able and willing to make up a story if it helped them achieve their objective. The two agents with Alfred were D'Ambrosio and Dennis Leahy and they stayed at the garage for about 20 minutes.

Taking Alfred back to his apartment, the agents decided, according to D'Ambrosio, to ask if they could search his car, and he agreed. The car was parked in downtown Quincy where Alfred left it, because it was disabled. The agents searched the vehicle and cut a sample of the trunk carpet, with Alfred's permission, for testing for traces of explosive. Then, on the way home, they stopped and Alfred left their vehicle to purchase a pack of cigarettes. The agents left Alfred at 133 Atlantic Street around 2:30 a.m.

Again, according to Alfred Trenkler in 2007, the ATF version had the search of the car out of sequence; but it was his recollection against that of several ATF agents and their version was backed up by a report. If Alfred Trenkler had testified, he may have recounted the exact routes which were taken, as he gave the directions to the ATF agents and may have, thereby, persuaded the jury that the ATF agents were mistaken. However, such shaking of the ATF version could not happen without Trenkler's testimony.

The items which were collected from the four Trenkler locations were sent to the ATF laboratory in Maryland and there was no connection made for any of them to the Roslindale Bomb. The report of the searches on 5/6 November was prepared by the Boston police.

On 20 November, D'Ambrosio and Dennis Leahy talked with Richard Brown at the ARCOMM office in Weymouth. The next day, D'Ambrosio had a telephone conversation with Brown, as was noted above in the discussion of Richard Brown's testimony. On the stand D'Ambrosio next described his role in the searches of 31 January 1992 of Trenkler's parents' home, and ARCOMM. There was also a new search of John Cates' apartment in Quincy. D'Ambrosio arrived with four other officers at the ARCOMM location around 8 a.m. and left at about 1:30 p.m. Items were taken for analysis, and the results were that there was no connection for any of them to the Roslindale Bomb.

Agent D'Ambrosio then described his next contact with Alfred Trenkler which was on 4 February 1992 in the ATF Boston Field office. D'Ambrosio joined Trenkler and Agent Leahy in a conference room and said to Alfred Trenkler that, *"we have learned of inconsistencies in his statements relating to his acquaintance with Tom Shay, Jr.. He told me that he has had, since that time, he had time to think about it and that he recalled first meeting Tom Shay, Jr. in the summer of 1991. He remembered that date specifically because his roommate John Cates was on vacation."* Libby asked about the month, and D'Ambrosio said, *"I believe he said it was July 1991."* (TT 10-143) [John Cates had testified earlier in the Trenkler trial that his vacation was between 9 June and 18 June 1991. (TT 9-96)] That should have been very helpful testimony to Alfred Trenkler with respect to the time period of his acquaintance with Tom Shay, as it was consistent with the truth.

Terry Segal cross-examined, and clarified that there were four ATF agents who searched the ARCOMM office on the morning of 6 November, and four Boston police detectives, and Officer Thomas Tierney from the Quincy Police Dept.

Then Segal asked about the second diagram and D'Ambrosio's testimony that Alfred drew a second diagram, of the hypothetical design of the 1991 Roslindale Bomb with two blasting caps. As the information about the two detonators was not yet public, Segal asked, *"Either he was the bomber or he took an awfully lucky guess, am I right?"* (TT 10-153) and D'Ambrisio agreed, and no doubt the prosecutors were pleased, too. Rather than characterize the two detonators as an *"awfully lucky guess"* he could have characterized it as a very typical and safe guess for a single bomb. Electronic engineers always think of backup plans and options in case of a problem. Two blasting caps is a good idea, as recommended by the military manuals on IED's, and not an *"awfully lucky guess."* By Segal's setup of a choice, the jurors chose later to believe that it was actually NOT a lucky choice but that Trenkler was a Bomb Maker. The choice may have been forced on them right there, in part.

Terry Segal sought to avoid that Hobbesian choice by arguing that the diagram didn't really exist at all and that ATF Agent D'Ambrosio was lying, which is always hard for a jury to accept, or simply mistaken. D'Ambrosio agreed that once he realized the next day that he had forgotten to bring the diagram page, he didn't think to try to draw his own recreation of the 1991 diagram. Also, he agreed that Boston Police Detective

McCarthy's report of the search at ARCOMM didn't mention the 1991 diagram. And he agreed that Agent Leahy filled out the receipt of items taken on the same desk as Trenkler was using to draw the 1986 diagram, and allegedly the 1991 diagram; and that the first mention in a police report of the diagram page was a 17 January 1992 ATF report, 2 1/2 months later.

Agent D'Ambrosio also agreed that when Alfred Trenkler came to the ATF offices on 4 February 1992, he did not ask Trenkler about the diagram page, nor the 1991 diagram. He didn't, for example, ask Alfred Trenkler to draw another one. D'Ambrosio agreed that he never contacted Alfred Trenkler to ask him to make another such drawing, as he allegedly did on 6 November, and the first time that D'Ambrosio tried to draw his own recreation of what Alfred Trenkler allegedly drew was in May 1993 when preparing for court hearings on preliminary matters in the current case against Alfred Trenkler.

Agent D'Ambrosio agreed that during the meeting at the ATF office on 4 February 1992, Alfred Trenkler told him "*that he was innocent in this matter.*" (TT 10-165)

Going back to the search on the morning of 6 November, Agent D'Ambrosio agreed that Richard Brown was not at the ARCOMM office at that time. Then, Terry Segal, rushed by Judge Zobel to finish the cross-examination quickly so the trial could adjourn by 1:00 p.m., showed Agent D'Ambrosio an enlarged copy of the diagram he drew on in May 1993 which was D'Ambrosio's recollection of what the Alfred Trenkler's diagrams of the 1986 and 1991 devices looked like. Then Segal directly challenged D'Ambrosio's veracity by asking, "*Isn't it true, sir, all he drew was the '86 diagram which was ancient history because you knew it already?*" to which D'Ambrosio responded, "*That's not true.*" Continued Segal, "*And isn't it true that the piece of paper, you left on the table that morning, only contained the '86 diagram and not the '91,*" to which D'Ambrosio replied again, "*That's not true.*" (TT 10-169) The exchange had the makings of a Perry Mason moment, but D'Ambrosio's answers were predictable and the effect was probably to encourage sympathy from the jury for the badgered witness.

Frank Libby had a few minutes left for redirect, and he led D'Ambrosio to agree that it was he, Frank Libby, who asked D'Ambrosio to try to recreate the alleged Trenkler drawing in Mary 1993. While agreeing that the drawing was not perfect, the ATF agent insisted that what Trenkler drew for him and Agent Leahy had two blasting caps. Without finishing D'Ambrosio's testimony, the court adjourned at 1:00 p.m.

Next day's headlines:

Boston Herald: "AGENT: SUSPECT DREW DIAGRAM RESEMBLING FATAL BOMB" by
  Ralph Ranalli

25 26 27 28 29	1 2 3 4 5	8 9 10 12	15 16	22 23 24	29
X X X X X	X X X X X	X O O O	O O	O O O	O

Day 11: Monday, 8 November

Frank Libby continued his redirect-examination and established that one reason Agent D'Ambrosio didn't go back and ask Alfred Trenkler for the diagram was that he did not want to alert Trenkler to how significant D'Ambrosio thought such a diagram of the 1991 device might be.

D'Ambrosio said that he had told Richard Brown in his face-to-face interview on 20 November 1991 that Alfred Trenkler had drawn two diagrams for him on the night of 5/6 November. The next day, when D'Ambrosio talked with him by phone, "*and asked* him if he had any conversation with Mr. Trenk;er since I had left the day before. And he told me that he had and that Mr. Trenkler told him that he wasn't worried about the diagram [page, and] that he had destroyed it." (TT 11-6)

As that was obviously hearsay, and having explained to the lawyers that it would be allowed as a state-of-mind exception to the hearsay rule, Judge Zobel explained to the jury, "*Members of the jury, this evidence cannot prove that Mr. Trenkler in fact destroyed it, the diagram. It can only, as we recounted by this witness, it can only show that Mr. Brown said something for the purpose of showing what Mr. D'Ambrosio's state of mind was and why he did not go back. That's all this testimony can prove.*" (TT 11-6) Of course, however, the jury heard the statement and they were free to interpret it as they wished and they appeared to have concluded that Alfred Trenkler did destroy the diagram page, regardless of whether it had one or two diagrams on it.

On recross-examination D'Ambrosio agreed that Richard Brown had also told him that Alfred Trenkler didn't seem particularly concerned about the diagram page.

All the controversy about the missing diagrams by Alfred Trenkler must have seemed odd to the few people in the courtroom who knew that Tom Shay had drawn a diagram of a bomb, with a location for batteries and ON and OFF switches. The police did retain that diagram, but they had no interest in presenting it to Shay's jury because it was a childlike drawing. It would have been just a little harder to convince the Shay jury to convict the person who drew such an amateurish diagram. It's not clear why Shay's defense team didn't introduce the diagram.

Also on this day, the defense filed a "*Motion in limine to Exclude Admission of EXIS Computer Evidence.*" The motion argued that "*an adequate foundation for admission of the EXIS computer evidence can not be established in this case. Specifically, introduction of the EXIS computer evidence is prohibited by the hearsay rule, best evidence rule, and authentication rules.*"

The next witness for the Government was Michael Coady, aged 28. Questioned by Paul Kelly, Michael Coady testified that he was a "*companion*" of Alfred Trenkler from 1980 to 1983, from when he was of the age of 15 and 1/2, in 9th grade, until the age of 18. Coady said they took trips out of state together. "*The first trip was to California for approximately eight or nine days.*" (TT 11-12) "*The second trip would have been to Fort Lauderdale, Florida, for a spring break; and the third trip, a ski trip for about four days, I believe.*" (TT 11-13)

The alleged trips to California and Florida were by air and Coady paid for no part of expenses. Coady said that he and Trenkler stayed in a hotel in California and at the home of a friend of Trenkler's in Florida. Paul Kelly asked Coady if Trenkler provided other items and Coady said, "*He supplied me with basically anything [I] wanted, clothes, cars, moneys, furnishing, furniture for my apartment.*" (TT 11-14) Coady said that Trenkler provided him with two cars, and also paid for his driver's education course. The first car was a 1977 or 1978 Thunderbird, which he said was worth about $5,000.

Terry Segal objected to this testimony on the grounds that it was irrelevant, and the Judge was also concerned. She permitted the evidence, *de bene*, or tentatively, "*conditional subject to its being connected to the* [sic] *having to do with this case. Let's do it fast.*" (TT 11-14/5)

Coady continued that Alfred Trenkler was living with his parents at the time, but Coady never met them. He said that Alfred Trenkler took him to his work sites, "*Yes, one was in Andover. *It was a tower, a receiving tower, where he had put some devices on; several locations to that effect, where he would drive me to maybe Plymouth, Duxbury, to climbing towers, to Rhode Island, to the same thing, towers."* (TT 11-15/16)

Then Paul Kelly asked, *"Did any of these job sites have any storage areas, to your memory sir?"* (TT 11-16) on the theory that with access to a storage area, Alfred Trenkler could have built the 1986 device in one of them, and the 1991 device, too.

None too soon, Terry Segal objected strongly, and there was a bench conference and Paul Kelly explained the other evidence that Coady was going to provide, including the use of magnets and the detonation of a firecracker. Segal responded, *"The point is, he's putting in all this evidence of trips and cars with this witness, and there is no evidence that he's going to put as to Mr. Shay. This is highly prejudicial. Because then, the jury is unfairly going [to] assume: Well, he must have provided all those things to Mr. Shay; and therefore, he made the bomb. Mr. Kelly can argue all he wants, that he made the bomb or didn't with Mr. Shay. But to put this evidence in is unfairly prejudicial, since he can't link up the similar evidence - -"* (TT 11-20)

Judge Zobel allowed Kelly to proceed, but not with any more testimony about sheds that Trenkler may have had access to in the 1980's.

Paul Kelly returned to the witness and asked about Trenkler's hobbies, and Coady stated, *"He was very much interested in remote control and electronics, gadgetry... He used to have a remote control [toy] Jeep in his Jeep that I used to play with."* (TT 11-22) Coady testified that the toy Jeep was a Tyco toy, which Coady said he was sure of because he took it later. Kelly asked, *"Did you ever know the defendant to possess any magnets of any kind, Mr. Coady?"* (TT 11-23) and Coady said *"Yes"*, in the big Jeep. Asked to elaborate, Coady said, *"Sometimes I was there for hours. So I went with the Jeep, to keep busy, I went through his box of supplies. At that point I found several magnets, a quarter size, with a hole in the middle, and shavings across the top. I remember the magnets because I took two of them and put them on my shoe - - on my coat string, and I kept them as well."* (TT 11-22)

Asked about Alfred Trenkler's interest in fireworks or explosives, Coady testified, *"At one time when we were out, I'm not sure exactly where it was, it was a nighttime, in a remote area, with people he had known, friends of his with, me along with him, we were out, had a bonfire going, things like that. And he ran across the field and set something up and then came back and it exploded."* (TT 11-23). Asked to describe further, Coady said, *"Just a massive explosion, I could not hear for several hours...."* (TT 11-23) Coady said he was familiar with fireworks, and this explosion was larger than a *"cherry bomb,"* adding, *"It was the loudest explosion I've ever heard in my life."* (TT 11-23)

Then the inquiry shifted, with Kelly asking if Coady had ever gone with Trenkler to the Blue Hills Reservation, and Coady said that he had been there several times with Trenkler, but *"That didn't begin until after our acquaintance, after our friendship."* (TT 11-24) Coady said he'd been there twenty times with Trenkler. Coady said that he, not Trenkler, had ended the relationship.

In a development almost as stunning as Michael Coady's testimony was the brevity of Terry Segal's cross-examination. He established that Coady's testimony was about events several years previous and that Coady knew that Alfred Trenkler was skilled in electronics. Third, and lastly, he asked if Coady knew that Alfred Trenkler went to Thayer Academy and Wentworth Institute, and Coady replied, *"I'm not aware of his educational background."* (TT 11-25] There was no inquiry about the alleged facts, some of which could have been verified through other sources. For example, were the alleged two cars registered and insured? Was parking a Thunderbird two blocks away enough to prevent parents and others to wonder what this young man was doing with a Thunderbird? Where did he drive this vehicle to? Is it possible for a teenager to possess a Thunderbird and not be seen by a lot of people driving it? Did he ever take Alfred Trenkler for a ride? Any friends for rides? To where? Where did he get the car serviced and inspected? Most importantly, what was his birth date, and thus how old was he when he knew Alfred Trenkler.

Michael Coady's testimony was loaded with false information, but there was no further inquiry about the claimed California trip. In 2007, Alfred Trenkler explained that he had been to California once in his life. In 1980 he and a friend, David King from Gilsum, New Hampshire, had an opportunity that young people dream of: to drive across the country. In November or December 1980, before Alfred began work for the Archdiocese of Boston, he and King flew to Los Angeles, where King use to live, to drive King's car back to New Hampshire. Mike Coady was definiitely not on that trip.

There was no further inquiry about the alleged Florida trip, which did not occur, either. Alfred Trenkler had been to Florida only twice in his life and neither trip was with Michael Coady. The first was in the early 1960's when Alfred's grandmother, Josephine Johnson Barnum Suter, took him to Florida to see his mother ice skate. The other trip was in September 1990 when Alfred took a two week vacation from ATEL in Florida. It was during that trip that Videocom tracked him down and told him about the Christian Science Church satellite project. In the early 1980's when Michael Coady claimed that Alfred Trenkler took him to Florida where they allegedly stayed with a friend of Trenkler's, Alfred Trenkler had no friends who lived in Florida.

There was no further inquiry about the claimed skiing trip. Alfred had never been skiing with Michael Coady, whether on a trip alone or otherwise. Further, Alfred Trenkler does not believe that Michael Coady knew how to ski.

There was no further inquiry by Terry Segal about trips to Alfred's work sites, which did not occur. There was no further inquiry into the claim of an explosion at a party, which did not occur.

There was no further inquiry about a toy car or magnets in Alfred's Jeep, and there were no such magnets nor toy car, either.

The jury was left to surmise that all of what Coady said was true, regardless of how many years previous it was. Perhaps Terry Segal either thought some of Coady's story was true, or perhaps he felt it was so preposterous that the jury would discount it. Perhaps he thought that his "*Motion to Strike*" the testimony would effectively delete it from the trial record, but the jury heard all of it. Perhaps he felt that if he questioned Michael Coady too much about his allegations, that he, Segal, would be delving into matters which he had already persuaded Judge Zobel to order be excluded, i.e. the alleged solicitation of teenage males. Alfred wrote in 2007 that "*Terry's strategy was not to make a big fuss over Coady to show that 'we' were not concerned with this character. He came off as an off-the-wall sleaze bag wearing a bright purple suit jacket.*" Unfortunately for Trenkler, the jury believed enough of Coady's story, and they apparently felt that clothes did not make the man. Terry Segal should have been concerned about every bit of false information which was heard or seen by the jury. A thorough cross-examination would have taken much of a day, and it should have been done.

Declining to make a strong cross-examination was a risky gamble and the loser of the gamble would not be Terry Segal; it would be Alfred Trenkler. A strong cross-examination would have shown the Michael Coady to be extremely unreliable; and it would have put the entire prosecution's case up for closer scrutiny. Almost everything Michael Coady said about his relationship with Alfred Trenkler was untrue.

A key issue was Michael Coady's age when he first met Alfred Trenkler, as it was damaging for the jury to hear that he was allegedly 15 when he met Trenkler in 1980. It should have been a high priority for the defense to challenge the date of the first meeting of Coady and Trenkler. Alfred Trenkler recalls that they met at Blue Hills Reservation in 1983, when Coady was 18 or 19, and he was using his brother Bill's ID which showed him to be older.

Alfred Trenkler has estimated that the value of the gifts Mike Coady claimed that Trenkler had bestowed on him in the early 1980's could have been about $23,000. Alfred also recalls that in 1981 his part-time income was $600.00 and because of his disabling hepatitis in 1982, his income for that year was only $12,000. In 1983, his income was $6,400, for a total over three years of $24,000. With such a low income, the claimed gifts to Michael Coady seem preposterous.

If Michael Coady had been successfully challenged by cross-examination on every claim, the jurors might ask, if the prosecutors can believe this totally unreliable witness without much verification, what about the other witnesses they have presented to us?

The next witness for the Government was Dennis Leahy, a Special Agent for the ATF in its Boston office. Examined by Paul Kelly, Agent Leahy found Mr. Thomas L. Shay to be always cooperative and helpful with the investigation. On 5 November, Leahy and Detective John McCarthy of the Boston Police Dept. knocked on the door at the apartment of Alfred Trenkler and John Cates. Agent Leahy and Boston Detective Peter O'Malley talked with Trenkler most of the time during the one hour search of the apartment. Leahy testified that "*Mr. Trenkler asked if we were there about his phone call, which I had no idea what he was talking about. And he went on to talk about someone was taking photos in the neighborhood or doing something in the neighborhood.*" (TT 11-37)

The jury might have wondered why the defendant would have called the Quincy Police Department that fall and call attention to himself if he was in the middle of a conspiracy to kill the father of an acquaintance. It was a point that was never made for the jury.

O'Malley and Leahy asked Alfred Trenkler about the 1986 device and "*He became visibly red. His jaw was clenching.*" (TT 11-40) Shortly thereafter Trenkler asked if the police were going to arrest him, and the officers said no. Agent Leahy said that Alfred Trenkler was cooperative, and agreed to take the officers to his place of work. Leahy said that Trenkler knew a Quincy detective in the search team, Officer Thomas Tierney, who had alerted the Boston Police and ATF to the 1986 device, and so Trenkler rode in a Quincy cruiser to the ARCOMM office in Weymouth. Trenkler didn't know of Tierney's role in forwarding the information to Boston until the trial. There are a lot of pivotal points in this case, prompting the rhetorical question, "What if?" something had been just slightly different. Here, the question might be asked, what if Thomas Tierney had not made his hunch that the 1986 Quincy incident appeared to be similar to the 1991 Roslindale Bomb? Then the police and ATF questioning of

Alfred Trenkler would have been just like the questioning of the other people in Tom Shay's address book, and there would have been no "signature" issue and no EXIS database issue and, likely, no trial for Alfred Trenkler.

Agents Leahy and D'Ambrosio sat at a table with Trenkler, who described the 1986 device, "*It was a remote control, had batteries, had a magnet, had tape, he said duct tape. It had a military tank simulator as the main charge. He went on to describe it in some detail.*" (TT 11-47) According to Agent Leahy, Agent D'Ambrosio asked him to draw a schematic diagram of the 1986 deviced, and then asked if Trenkler could draw a diagram of what the 1991 Roslindale Bomb might have looked like.

The agents asked about Thomas A. Shay and Trenkler said "*He said where he met him, in Boston, over near, I think it is Boylston Street; how he met him, I think he met him in the White Hen Pantry over there. And we asked him how friendly were they. He said he had only given him a ride a couple [of] times, that he had never been inside his apartment at Atlantic Ave., although -- excuse me he had driven him to the apartment, near it several times.*" (TT 11-50)

Then Agent Leahy described the assurances they gave to Trenkler to allay his concerns about disturbing his parents if they went to 7 Whitelawn Ave for a search of the garage. The assurances were the same as described by Agent D'Ambrosio, except that Leahy provided the cover story, "*...if his parents woke up, we would say we were employees of his, and we [were] just getting some tools for an early morning job....*" (TT 11-51) One wonders if the jurors wondered if the ATF agents could have made up the 1991 diagram story just as easily as they were willing to make up the "employee" story at the Wallace's garage.

Agent Leahy explained that he didn't write his report of the events of 5/6 November as he normally would have done because the Boston Police were in charge; but in mid-January it was decided that the investigation would be led by the ATF. At that point, it was discovered that there was no report about the events of 5/6 November, so Agent Leahy prepared his report on 17 January 1992.

Then Agent Leahy testified about his role as team leader of the 31 January 1992 search of Trenkler's parents' garage. He described how Detective Fogerty of the Boston Police advised Trenkler not to talk with the search team, because he now had a lawyer and said, "*Well take his advice and don't say anything.*" (TT 11-59) Nonetheless, Alfred Trenkler, being the friendly conversational person that he is, and because Leahy was not talking directly about the case, talked with Agent Leahy about several topics including the 1986 device, "*and it led into a discussion of the explosives in general. And he discussed how the blasting caps have a shunt on them. He discussed how the two leg wires can act as an antenna. He discussed how explosives if they are placed neck to each other can -- when one explodes it can cause the other to explode, which is known as a sympathetic detonation.*" (TT 11-61)

Regarding remote controls on such a bomb, Agent Leahy said, "*He told me it was unreliable to use a toy car because sometimes the toy cars can go straight ahead and, then, without any command at all it will turn right or left. So that, basically, they are inexpensive and not as reliable.*" (TT 11-62)

Agent Leahy testified, "*I discussed where he was working, at the Christian Science. And he had stated that he had been in the Radio Shack across the street maybe four times. That would be 197 Mass. Ave. He stated that he made purchases there.*" (TT 11-62)

Agent Leahy said that their discussion about Tom Shay was the same as before, except that Trenkler said that Shay had been inside the apartment in Quincy, "*watching TV*" (TT 11-63) and that he, Trenkler "*had spent the weekend with Shay, Jr. at Atell.* (sic, ATEL) *He had forgotten to tell us the previous time I talked to him.*" (TT 11-63/4) Leahy said that Alfred Trenkler told him that "*Shay, Jr. hated his father.*" and "*He said that he had driven him to Shay, Sr.'s house once.*" (TT 11-63)

Agent Leahy said that Trenkler "*was being very cooperative. He also allowed a consent search of his car. And he was talking very freely. He was very cooperative. So I asked him if he'd mind drawing a diagram again of the 1991 bomb, and he refused. He said he had spoken to an attorney, that* [sic, he] *wouldn't do it.*" (TT 11-64) and Leahy reported that Trenkler became "*flustered for a minute or two*" during the discussion about the diagram. (TT 11-65)

Trenkler and his parents signed consent forms for searches of Alfred's room in the house, and his car.

The next contact between Agent Leahy and Alfred Trenkler was by phone on 3 February which Trenkler initiated in order to obtain the return of business-related documents taken during the 31 January searches. He needed them for his business. The conversation turned to Tom Shay. "*He talked - - I think I asked him when he first met him* [Shay] *again. And he said that he had first met him in June of '91. I asked him if he was sure, and he said he was, because his roommate was in Europe at the time and that's how he could recall when he met him. You know, I went over where did he meet him again. Went over if he gave him rides again, where he gave him rides to. And I think this time he said he gave him a ride to Rhode Island, that he gave him a ride to Winthrop,*" (TT 11-69) and that Tom Shay had been in his apartment once, and again, "*that Shay, Jr. hated his father.*" (TT 11-69) and that he did not know about Thomas L. Shay's lawsuit until he read about it in the newspaper.

The next day, Alfred Trenkler came to the ATF office to pick up copies of documents and Agent Leahy led him to a conference room and then retrieved the documents and Trenkler, "*leafed through the documents. And he started complaining, he said: 'I need more than this.' I said: 'That's all we have.' He said: 'I need --' he started naming business files: 'I need this file, I need that file.' And I said: 'Well, that's all we're prepared to give you.' He said: 'Well, I want them...'*" (TT 11-71)

They sat down and the conversation continued for about two and one-half hours, despite, Leahy's reminding Trenkler that he had an attorney. "*And I went on to give him my standard: 'You know, we know you did* [it]. *If you cooperate we'll bring it to the attention of the U.S. Attorney and the Court...'*" (TT 11-72) Asked about Trenkler's response, Agent Leahy said, "*He looked at me. He said: 'I'm not going to make up' - - and he stopped, and he just looked down at his papers.*" (TT 11-72) Agent Leahy asked Trenkler for his thoughts about the crime, and "*He said he had two theories, and that one of them was that Shay, Jr. did it,*" and Trenkler would "*put money on it.*" (TT 11-72)

Then Agent Leahy described the final part of the conversation as Trenkler was leaving, "*The final thing he said to me was - - I'm not positive of the exact words, but he said: 'If we did it, then only we know about it. How will you ever find out and if neither one of us talked?'*" (TT 11-73) In contrast to the cooperative demeanor during the earlier part of the 2 1/2 hours, Leahy described Trenkler's demeanor at the end as "*arrogant.*" (TT 11-74)

Alfred Trenkler's recollection of that conversation is understandably different, and again, it was unfortunately not presented to the jury. Most importantly, Alfred's recollection of the "*If*" statement is that he said, "*If neither one of us did anything why would one say the other did anything?*" With the change of only a few words, the meaning and tone of the statement changes completely. Also, Alfred states that he did not say "*would put money on it*" that Tom Shay built the bomb. Instead, he recalled in 2007 that he said to Dennis Leahy, "*I'd put money on it Shay Sr. did the bombing to bolster his lawsuit.*" It was an idea that defense lawyers Nancy Gertner and Terry Segal later supported. Alfred's second theory was that the defendants in Mr. Thomas Shay's civil lawsuit were involved in the Roslindale Bomb.

Alfred remembers that Dennis Leahy was asking Alfred to help ATF "get" Tom Shay, saying "*You know, Al, I once read a book. I can't remember the name of it. But in it a man committed a murder and got away with it for many years until the man confessed the murder to a friend. The friend turned around and told authorities and the man was convicted of the murder. I'm telling you this because you can either sit back and wait to be convicted of murder or you can be the first one in the door, get creative and help us get Shay. Once the door closes, that's it. No deals.*" Alfred wrote that he responded, "*If I have nothing to do with this and Shay knows that I have nothing to do with this, why would one say the other did anything?*" It was a sincere response to a provocative request, as would come from any innocent citizen who is asked to help investigate an alleged co-conspirator.

Then the direct examination by Paul Kelly shifted to Leahy's participation in the arrest of Tom Shay in San Francisco in March of 1992.

At a bench conference Paul Kelly asked for the "*fourth motion for reconsideration*" of his efforts to get Tom Shay's admissions into evidence in this Trenkler trial.

Then Paul Kelly asked Agent Leahy a few questions about the consistency of Alfred Trenkler's answers to his inquiries about his whereabouts on 28 October, saying, "*On one occasion* [he] *told me he was at Videocom, a store, a place of business in Dedham. On another case* [sic] *occasion, he told me at the Christian Science Monitor, working. On another occasion, he said he was at ARCOM. He wasn't consistent.*" and not consistent about whether Tom Shay had ever been to his apartment, either, nor about rides Trenkler had given to Tom Shay. (TT 11-77) Paul Kelly was permitted by Judge Zobel to ask one question about the rides and he asked, "*When you first questioned him about the subject of rides, did he tell you that he had given him a ride to Rhode Island, for example?*" and Leahy said "*No, at first he did not.*" (TT 11-78) This claim of inconsistent statements is hard to defeat when one party to conversations is entering information into reports and the other party is not creating simultaneous reports or recordings, and later, when challenged to recall the events, declines to testify. However, Alfred Trenkler never drove Tom Shay to Rhode Island, so there never was a statement by him that was inconsistent. The suggestion of Rhode Island surely arose when Alfred Trenkler said he had driven Tom Shay to Randy Stoller's in Attleboro, which is adjacent to Rhode Island, and when Alfred was on his way to a business meeting in Rhode Island, but he had never driven Tom Shay to Rhode Island. Instead of being an inconsistent statement to a government agent, the incident illustrated a misunderstood recollection by that agent of a conversation.

Terry Segal began his cross-examination by asking Agent Leahy about the initial suspects, and the one new name was Richard Brown. Not explored in the courtroom was Brown's police record in Quincy for having blown up a phone booth with an explosive.

Agent Leahy said he was not familiar with the use of the term "*shunt*" in electronics, nor in medicine, but then he remembered that doctors had installed a shunt, to act like a drain, when his own appendix was removed. Segal could have explored further Dennis Leahy's apparent belief that anyone with knowledge of communications electronics, e.g. antennas and static discharges, would also necessarily be knowledgeable about explosives.

He acknowledged that one of the files that Alfred Trenkler may have requested was the MIT file and another was the Christian Science file, which were not insignificant customers. Also, he acknowledged that Trenkler offered to talk with Shay, Jr. on behalf of the Government, and that, on the other hand, he was concerned, in Segal's words, "*that the Feds would fabricate evidence against him.*" (TT 11-95)

Segal's cross-examination ended abruptly when he asked Agent Leahy if his memory of the claimed Trenkler diagram was "*much better on November 5th, than it was in May 1993*" when D'Ambrosio and Leahy recreated a drawing? Leahy replied, "*Yes, sir, that's why --* " and Terry Segal cut him off, saying, "*I'm asking you if you can answer my question, and I have no further questions.*" (TT 11-97) He didn't ask Leahy for further clarification about his other damaging statements such as the claimed conversation when Trenkler was "*arrogant*" or the claimed inconsistency of other statements. All of those claimed inconsistencies could have been carefully examined. Cutting off a witness is not an action designed to show a jury that the lawyer is interested in getting as much truth into the trial as possible.

Leahy's claim that Alfred Trenkler had told him that Tom Shay had been with him on a weekend at ATEL should have been challenged. Did Leahy, for example, ask Tom Shay any questions about that claimed weekend? Unchallenged, and supported by Richard Brown's testimony that he saw Shay at ATEL, the jury was left to believe that it was true.

Leahy's recollection that Alfred Trenkler had told him that he made purchases at the 197 Mass. Ave. Radio Shack should have been re-examined on cross. Since his days at Wentworth Institute, Alfred had made several purchases there including the purchase in October or November 1991 of an audio plug for his car stereo. The presentation of such purchases to the jury would also help them understand the claimed familiarity of Radio Shack salespeople with Trenkler.

Regarding Leahy's claim that Alfred Trenkler told him that Tom Shay hated his father, Segal could have asked whether Trenkler might have said to him that Tom Shay said to him that his father didn't want his son around when the father's friends were around, due to Tom Shay's coming-out appearance on "People are Talking."

At points like these, with no other means of challenging false prosecution testimony, the defense should have reconsidered its decision not to have Alfred Trenkler testify. Terry Segal said in 2007 that his reason for the no-testify decision was to keep the focus on the government's weak case, rather than permitting the prosecution to divert attention to the life of Alfred Trenkler. However, the perceived weakness is a relative measure, compared to the strength of alternative representions of truth. In the absence of a presentation to the jury about the life, work and character of Alfred Trenkler, the prosecutions "weak" case became relatively strong.

On redirect, Paul Kelly established that Agent Leahy thought that Trenkler's knowledge of shunts was significant because, *"I felt that a layperson would not know about shunts on blasting caps."* This again blurred the understanding of Trenkler's knowledge. He knew about shunts, as would any first year electronics student, but he knew nothing about blasting caps. Leahy's testimony continued, *"There were different types,* [and a layperson] *would not know a lot about leg wires, blasting caps,* [and that] *you could get static electricity from blasting caps;* [a layperson] *would not know there's a short propagation that could set off explosives that are near other explosives."* Also Leahy clarified how the diagram of Trenkler's ideas about the possible design of the Roslindale Bomb was solicited, as Trenkler was *"asked to assume that it was a remote control device and he built it."* and to assume that dynamite was used, but he wasn't told about blasting caps. (TT 11-98/9)

Terry Segal had no questions for recross-examination.

The next Government witness was William Lanergan, a detective in the Quincy Police Department. He was one of the investigators of the 1986 device, along with Detective Tierney. At his first interview with Alfred Trenkler on Wednesday 3 September 1986, Tierney said that Trenkler said, *"...that we must consider him* [Trenkler] *a good suspect in that particular case we were investigating because he was an electronics engineer and he also repaired microwave ovens."* and that *"if anybody could get an M-80 device, he could go to Chinatown, anybody could buy that kind of stuff."* (TT 11-110) whereupon Lanergan testified that he responded, *"I told him we didn't* [yet] *mention any type of device."* (TT 11-111) Alfred Trenkler, who has never repaired microwave ovens, did not initiate the subject of fireworks. Detective Lanergan was at Trenkler's apartment investigating the apparent fireworks explosion at the Wojtasinski's.

On 4 September 1986, Trenkler was asked to come to the Quincy Police Dept. where he initially told Lanergan, *"...a story about an unknown male party who contacted him and wanted him to make a device for him."* (TT 11-114/5) Refreshed by his own report, Lanergan said that Trenkler had told him that the man was going to pay him. Lanergan told Trenkler that he didn't believe that story, and then Trenkler decided to tell the truth, and told him how he made the 1986 device, and Lanergan described it for the court, and then Alfred Trenkler admitted that there was no unknown man; as he had made the device, as a prank, for Donna Shea who *"wanted, to as he put it, scare the shit out of the Wojtanski* [sic] *brothers."* (TT 11-119) The brothers were the owners of the Capeway Fish Market, where Donna Shea formerly worked. After Alfred Trenkler finished explaining his role, he asked if he could leave the police station, as he stated that his grandmother had died; and Officer Lanergan said *"No"* and placed him under arrest for possession of an "infernal machine," i.e. a bomb.

Lanergan was asked if he saw Alfred Trenkler later, and he said that he did see him at a grocery store, and about three years later at a Chinese restaurant in North Quincy in 1989. The story was explained, so it could be shown that Lanergan bore no ill will toward Trenkler. Lanergan said, *"I learned from Mr. Trenkler when he was bidding on a job to do some kind of a security surveillance at the restaurant and he asked me not to mention the previous incident."* (TT 11-125) Lanergan didn't.

Cross-examination by Terry Segal was very brief, and established that Lanergan was not one of the original two officers who responded to the 1 September 1986 explosion. More importantly, Terry Segal did not ask about other occasions when Officer Lanergan saw Alfred Trenkler. In particular, he did not ask about their meeting on

Sunday, 27 October 1991 at the "Egg and I" Restaurant on Hancock Street in Quincy where Lanergan was eating lunch with four other uniformed Quincy police officers and Alfred was sitting with John Cates. After Alfred and John finished, he went over to the officers' table and said hello to Officer Lanergan. As this chance meeting was within the time period that the Asst. U.S. Attorneys claimed that Alfred Trenkler had placed the Roslindale Bomb underneath Mr. Thomas Shay's car, Terry Segal might have asked Officer Lanergan what he thought of Alfred Trenkler's demeanor on that day. Then the jury could have contemplated whether such a described demeanor was that of a man who was about to place, or already had placed, a bomb with the intent to kill someone. Coincidentally, in 2007 on the door of the "Egg and I" restaurant was a poster for the "*15th and final*" annual "William E. Degan Memorial Road Race" which was initially run in September 1993 in memory of U.S. Marshal Degan, a former Quincy resident, who was killed at Ruby Ridge, Idaho in 1992.

At the time of the 1991 Roslindale Bomb, Detective Lanergan was skeptical of any connection to Alfred Trenkler and didn't think it would be helpful to forward any reports to Boston about the 1986 incident. Detective Thomas Tierney disagreed and sent copies from his own personal records.

After Detective Lanergan's testimony, there was a bench conference about the upcoming tight schedule. One of the prosecution's proposed witnesses was Stephen Scheid on the EXIS database, but Paul Kelly said, "*That's Mr. Libby's matter. I know nothing about this EXIS system.*" (11-127) A six-minute segment of the Channel 56, Marinella-Shay interview was ready to be shown to Judge Zobel and to Mr. Segal to be sure there were no further objections before showing it to the jury.

Examined by Paul Kelly, the next witness for the Government was Robert Francis Craig, former roommate and employee of Alfred Trenkler for four-and-a-half years from 1985-1989. Craig was from Milton and attended Milton High School and was 31 years old, and lived at the time of the trial in Boynton Beach, Florida. Craig said that Alfred Trenkler had assembled the 1986 device out of a toy car in Donna Shea's parking lot, and that he, Craig, helped him assemble it. He thought that Alfred acquired the remote control toy from Radio Shack.

Asked who designed the 1986 device, Craig said "*There was no design. All is what* [sic] *you needed was a 12-volt charge. He said it was Alfred's idea and the intent was to scare someone.*" (TT 11-142) Robert Craig was not familiar with the name of Todd Leach, but his memory was refreshed by his grand jury testimony. Then he remembered that Leach was Donna Shea's nephew and that "*he might have gone to the Radio Shack with them, I'm not sure,*" but he, Bob Craig, was not present during the "*shopping trip.*" Terry Segal did not object to the hearsay nature of the "*might have gone*" testimony nor did Judge Zobel caution Mr. Craig to only testify about what he knew.

Paul Kelly, on his own, tried to get more specific and asked, "*When you say you were aware ot it, then, what do you mean sir?*" Craig replied, "*I just remember somehow that he was with him.*" [TT 11-145]

Craig said that sometime after the Quincy explosion, Alfred told him about it, and that he had placed the device under the Capeway Fish Truck, but then remembered to go back to the truck and clear a safety switch; and then he set it off. Trenkler had told him that the remote control transmitter needed to be within 60 yards of the explosive device for it to work. The only error in that recollection of the detonation was that the

M21 Hoffman was placed along the left side of the Capeway Fish truck, and not underneath.

On cross-examination Terry Segal established that Craig knew that Trenkler's parents were "*fairly affluent*" and that Trenkler sometimes asked them for money, if he was short. (TT 11-154) Segal established that Donna Shea, who could be intimidating, asked Alfred to assemble the Quincy device. Craig stated that he never went on any trips with Alfred and Todd Leach anywhere, whether to purchase something or otherwise. Finally, Craig understood that it was Donna Shea that supplied the Hoffman M21 artillery simulator, for Alfred then to assemble into a remote control device.

Without being challenged by a Terry Segal cross-examination or by contradictory testimony from Todd Leach's mother, MaryAnn Leach, or from his aunt, Donna Shea, or from Alfred Trenkler, the jury now had heard from two witnesses that Todd Leach participated in the purchase of pieces for the 1986 device. It was very damaging, as it fit into the prosecutors' claim that Alfred Trenkler used surrogates, and even worse, young boys, to acquire parts for nefarious devices.

There was no redirect, and the jury was adjourned, and then there was a bench conference, primarily about scheduling the last days of the trial.

Judge Zobel asked about a planned defense witness, David McGarry, who Segal expected would say that he was at the Plymouth House of Correction at the same time as Trenkler and David Lindholm (the upcoming inmate informant for the Government) and that Trenkler didn't say anything to him, McGarry, for three or four months. Judge Zobel said that would not be admissible because it was hearsay. She said, "*The Government can put on evidence that you cannot. This is not tit for tat.*" (TT 11-157) While she didn't explain further, the problem is that a prosecutor can enter into evidence of admissions by a defendant as an exception to the hearsay rule. However, there is no exception to the hearsay rule for a defendant to try to enter into evidence the statements of other people about what that defendant said that was not an admission. The available alternative for defendants is to take the stand and testify about what she or he did or said. That would not be hearsay. Actually, for David McGarry to say that there was no conversation would not be hearsay either, as it would be testimony about conduct.

Segal also said he needed him to counter the Government's expected witness named Mallick, but Judge Zobel said that Mallick would not be testifying. In an apparent balancing effort between the prosecution and defense, Zobel said she would not issue a subpoena for McGarry to come in.

Frank Libby and Paul Kelly said that the Government could not produce the raw reports that went into the EXIS database for the five bomb incidents which were reported to be similar to the 1986 Quincy and 1991 Roslindale Bomb. Scott Lopez said there must be a misunderstanding about what was requested, as those reports, and even the data input forms at EXIS, surely exist. The matter was unresolved, but it did not appear that the defense would be getting the reports. For that reason and others, the relationships among the lawyers were frayed.

Judge Zobel strenuously sought to complete the case and send to the jury before Thanksgiving, which would come on Thursday, 25 November, and she offered to conduct the trial all day on Thursday, November 11, which was Veterans Day. Originally, that was planned to be a day off, and Mr. Segal said he might have trouble getting witnesses who otherwise were planning to be available on Wednesday or Friday, but not Thursday. The matter was left open.

Then came a critical question. Judge Zobel asked, "*Is the defendant going to testify?*" and Terry Segal answered, simply, "*No.*" (TT 11-165] That was that. The most important evidentiary issue for the trial was addressed and dismissed with one word. The decision for Alfred not to testify was made even before the trial started at a meeting with Jack Wallace, Terry Segal, Scott Lopez, Matt Feinberg and Brenda Sharton. Alfred brought the subject up and recalls "*the concern was that not only would Kelly and Libby try to twist whatever I may have said to government witnesses or to ATF agents, but the subjects Judge Zobel barred the government from delving into were now fair game. AUSA's Kelly and Libby could ask about drugs, sex and rock and roll just to let the jury hear the questions. It did not matter if the questioned events or accusations occurred or not, Kelly and Libby would be allowed to put the thoughts into the jurors' minds.*"

That pre-trial decision was apparently unaffected by the course of the trial where damaging testimony was made about Alfred Trenkler, with no one to dispute it but him. The incorrect testimony would later come from others, too, but the decision for Alfred not to testify was apparently cut in stone, despite the growing risk of unchallenged testimony against him. The prosecutors could delve into any relevant matters they wished and the jury could be delivered messages indirectly about Alfred Trenkler even if direct testimony on those issues was prohibited by Judge Zobel. The prosecutors were already twisting what information they had, and Alfred Trenkler needed to testify to set the record straight, or at least to tell the jury that there was another side to the story.

Next day's headlines:

Boston Globe: "BOMB TRIAL WITNESS CALLS DEFENDANT AN EARLY SUSPECT" by Matthew Brelis

Boston Herald: "FED: BOMB SUSPECT PUT BLAME ON SHAY" by Ralph Ranalli

25 26 27 28 29	1 2 3 4 5	8 9 10 12	15 16	22 23 24	29
X X X X X	X X X X X	X X O O	O O	O O O	O

Day 12: Tuesday, 9 November

Testimony in the court began immediately, with the direct examination of Francis Hankard, retired chief of the Massachusetts Crime Laboratory. He had special training in explosives at the FBI school, and was the Assistant Chief of the Crime Lab in 1986 when the 1986 Quincy device was analyzed. The lab analyzed 600 fires and 200 instances of explosives or fireworks a year. Hankard remembered the Quincy case, but not the details of the 3-page report he wrote, which was admitted into evidence.

Under cross-examination, Hankard said that his office had done about 100 "*examinations*" in explosion cases a year during his 40 years, or 4,000. Segal asked if there was anything in the report which said where the 1986 device was placed *vis a vis* the truck where it exploded. Frank Libby objected, but Judge Zobel reminded him that he placed the report into evidence. Mr. Hankard's response was "*No,*" and that the report said that the device was placed "*on* [the] *truck.*" [TT 12-17] Also, Mr. Hankard agreed that the report did not indicate how the "*aluminum colored*" tape was used with the 1986 device.

The next Government witness, examined by Paul Kelly, was Todd Leach, aged 17, who said that he had known Alfred Trenkler most of his life, through his aunt, Donna Leach Shea. To the question "*did you spend any time with the defendant while your aunt was not around?*" he responded, "*Yes, sometimes I would go to the store, yes.*" (TT 12-23) Asked what he knew about Alfred Trenker's business at the time, and bearing in mind that he was 11 years old in 1986, he said, "*...him and my Aunt Donna were in business together.... I think they were put* [sic, putting] *up satellite dishes.*" (TT 12-23)

Asked about his role in building the 1986 device, Leach said, "*I remember taking a speaker magnet from a speaker*" at the request of Al Trenkler.[5] (TT 12-24) He testified that at the time, he was in the parking lot of his home and he did not know for what purpose the magnet was intended. "*I remember I was on my way to the store with Al. He asked me to run over and get some magnet out of a speaker that was in the corner parking lot. There was much trash in the corner parking lot.... Yes, he had those speakers and he told me to run over, get the magnet out of it and rip it apart.*" (TT 12-25) Prior to that instruction, Leach said that he did not know that magnets were incorporated into voice speakers. The parking lot was at the Weymouth public housing project where he lived.

Leach described the speaker he ripped apart as being made of "*fake wood*" and the magnet was round and silver and about six inches across, and about one inch thick, and a black substance around the outside edges. Also he said that Al Trenkler took him to a Radio Shack in Quincy, to which he had never been before "*to get some wires and stuff.*" (TT 12-27) He thought that Trenkler's roommate, Bob Craig, was in the car with him and Al.

Leach said, "*Al gave me a list and told me to go in and read off the list if I couldn't read it or whatever, to get the stuff, and then I went in and I couldn't read all of* [the] *stuff off* [sic] *and understand what it said, so I handed it to* [a] *guy. And then Al came in.*" (TT 12-30) Leach explained further the interaction with the "*guy*".

Q "*What is the next thing you remember?*"
A "*Al started talking to the guy.*"
Q "*Just tell us what you heard.*"
A "*They were just talking about what kind of parts he needed, and the guy asked Al jokingly if he was making a bomb; it was just jokingly.*"
Q "*And how did the defendant react what* [sic] *the clerk joked with him about making a bomb.*"
A "*Just, you know, like I think he said, yes, almost joking around.*" (TT 12-31)

Leach then said that was the first time that he had any idea that what Trenkler was building was the 1986 device.

Paul Kelly asked, "*... in the fall of 1986, do you remember anything about a remote control car?*" and Leach responded, "*I remember Al playing with a remote control car in the parking lot.*" (TT 12-31] Again, the referenced parking lot belonged to the Weymouth public housing project where he lived.

Kelly asked, "*Do you have any memory, sir, of any discussion about any, any rigging of the remote control car that might be necessary in construction or whatever they were building?*" and Leach responded, "*I remember Al saying something to Bob* [Craig] *about it, that it should only go forward or it should only go in reverse or something like that.*" (TT 12-33) Leach described what the 1986 device looked like and said there was "*a little black box and a little white and gray box, like a rectangular box or something.*" (TT

12-33] Asked about the use of a light bulb in the device, Leach testified, "*I remember seeing a little, teeny light bulb that went on when he flipped the switch and went off when he turned it off, or whatever.*" (TS 12-34)

Leach said that he saw solder in the device. When it was put together, Leach described it as being about 12 inches across and four inches thick. The final "*shape was more like* [a] *rectangle than a ball of tape.*" (TT 12-38)

As to the installation of the device, Leach said, "*I heard somebody say that they put it underneath by the gas tank.*" (TT 12-39) There was no objection, but it was clearly hearsay, and not from anyone in particular. In fact, according to Alfred Trenkler in 2007, the 1986 device was attached to the left outside frame of the Capeway Fish Company truck, and not underneath. Alfred Trenkler reminded his attorney of this important distinction several times during the trial, but as the decision not to have Alfred testify had already been made, there was no way to get Alfred's understanding of the construction and placement of the M21 Hoffman Artillery simulator into evidence.

Terry Segal began his cross-examination by pointing out that the 1986 Quincy explosion occurred around 2:00 in the morning on 1 September, and the 11 year-old Todd Leach would likely have been in bed sleeping. Sarcasm appeared to be irresistible, but there was nothing else. Segal asked Leach if he was aware of a reward or if he was aware that his aunt, Donna Shea, had asked Alfred Trenkler to make the 1986 device and the prosecution successfully objected.

Terry Segal knew that a private investigator working for Nancy Gertner and Tom Shay had previously interviewed Todd Leach's mother, MaryAnn Leach who was also the sister of Donna Shea. In that interview, MaryAnn Leach said that her young son had no role in the purchase of materials for the 1986 device. Also, MaryAnn had told the investigator that her son, Todd, had spoken with her several times about his desire to get the reward money so that he could assist the legal defense for his uncle, John Shea who was in prison. Segal did not use his understanding of that interview in his cross-examination of Todd Leach, nor did he seek to call MaryAnn Leach as a witness to impeach her son's credibility. Nor did he call Donna Shea who also knew the truth of the Radio Shack purchase of the Tyco toy car. Also, Terry Segal had read the substantially similar grand jury testimony of Todd Leach, along with Alfred Trenkler's frequent comments, "*Not True.*" The most important "*Not True*" issue was Todd Leach did not accompany Alfred Trenkler and Donna Shea when they purchased the remote control car the week before the 1 September 1986 incident. Thus, there was no list, and no conversation with a salesperson about making a bomb. The purchase was for a toy car at Radio Shack, and not dynamite, and no Radio Shack employee who wanted to keep his job would ask customers if they were planning on building a bomb. Also, Alfred had never taken Todd Leach in his car anywhere, and Todd was at home at the time of the 2:00 a.m. detonation of the 1986 device. Alfred had no independent relationship with the 9-10 year old Todd Leach, except that he was the nephew of his friends John and Donna Shea.

According to Alfred Trenkler in 2007, it was young Todd Leach who told Alfred in 1986 that his uncle, John Shea, had recently discarded stereo speakers into the trash dumpster and that they were a source for magnets.

Terry Segal's cross-examination consisted of only the innocuous questions about Leach's age, his bedtime, his knowledge of the reward and his relationship to Donna Shea, and those questions took about two pages in the transcript. He was overly confident that the jury would find Leach's testimony to be not credible, if not incredible.

Segal did not note that Todd Leach had described the Radio Shack purchases as "*wires and stuff*" and described plastic boxes, which perhaps not coincidentally, were part of the 1991 Radio Shack purchases, and did not say anything about the purchase of a remote control toy car. The official police report of the 1986 device described the use of scrap wires, not new wires, and did not mention plastic boxes. Thus, Todd Leach had testified to have purchased items from Radio Shack which were not in the 1986 Quincy device and he did not describe the Radio Shack purchase of the only item in the 1986 device which actually was from Radio Shack. How many 10 year old boys would have omitted the description of a purchase of a remote control car? Also, he recalled that Bob Craig was with Alfred Trenkler and him during the trip to Radio Shack, but Bob Craig had just testified that he was not on such a trip.

On redirect Paul Kelly reaffirmed that Todd Leach was not interested in the reward. Even if he had been, payouts for such rewards are rare, and in this case, none was ever made. On recross, Segal asked if Todd Leach remembered what kind of car Alfred Trenkler drove in 1986 and Todd Leach said that he didn't. Terry Segal asked no further questions, and the jury was, once again, left with a choice:

A. Believe all of Todd Leach's testimony

B. Believe part of it.

C. Believe none of it.

Terry Segal hoped that the obvious problems with Leach's testimony, and with Coady's and Nutting's, would lead the jury to "C," but it was a risky hope. In fact, some of Leach's testimony was true, such as his role in breaking apart a discarded stereo speaker to retrieve the magnet, and seeing Alfred Trenkler play with the toy car in order to determine its transmitter's range, before cannibalizing it; but that wasn't incriminating as Alfred Trenkler had admitted from the beginning that he built the 1986 device.

Why didn't Terry Segal challenge every single statement by Todd Leach that implicated Alfred Trenkler? Did he feel constrained by the tight schedule imposed by Judge Zobel? If so, that was that a legitimate reason not to aggressively cross-examine Todd Leach? If the prosecution could take the time to present such testimony from such a witness, the defense could certainly take the time to refute every allegation. It appears that Segal was increasingly appalled by the incredible witnesses presented by the prosecution and felt that even questioning them might make it seem like he thought the jury would even be tempted to believe any part of Leach's story, or Michael Coady's story. However, some of each's story was true, and the challenge was to sift out the wheat from the chaff. Instead the jury was thrown both to digest and its indigestion produced a wrongful conviction.

What did the jury think of the non-cross-examination? It appears from the verdict that they chose either "*A*" or "*B*," perhaps using something like the adage, "*Where there's smoke, there's usually fire.*" There was smoke, and a little flame of truth, and the rest was still untrue smoke.

One of the difficulties for Terry Segal and Alfred Trenkler was that there was little time for them to talk. Alfred was at his parents' home under house arrest and was able to visit Segal's office only one to two times a week before the trial. During the trial, he would talk with him by phone each day before the trial, but after each trial day he had to be escorted home. A major problem with the phone calls was that Alfred believed that the ATF was listening to all of them, even though the wiretap authorizations had expired. His stepfather, Jack Wallace, had seen AFT agents working at a phone company junction box into which ran the Wallace's phone lines within days of Alfred's release on bail on 2 August 1993. Terry Segal had brought this concern to Judge Zobel's attention, but she dismissed the fears as unwarranted, as the ATF had no judicial authorization to resume the wiretapping which had been terminated in 1992.

Alfred Trenkler's belief that his parents' phone was wiretapped was strengthened by a sequence of events that began with Alfred's reading the ATF report of its interview of Paul Nutting where Nutting said that he had seen Trenkler and Tom Shay in Trenkler's blue pickup truck at the Blue Hills Reservation. During his house arrest period, Alfred had discussed this observation with Terry Segal and told Segal that he, Trenkler, had never owned a blue pickup truck and had own no car other than his 1979 white Toyota in 1990 and 1991. At Trenkler's trial a few months later, Nutting's description of the vehicle he saw being driven by Trenkler change from a blue truck to a white small car in "*disrepair,*" which description perfectly fit Alfred's car. On the other hand, the ATF agents could simply have told Nutting the make and color of Trenkler's car.

Before Stephen Scheid testified on the EXIS database, there was a bench conference and Scott Lopez argued strongly in support of the defense motion to exclude such testimony. He said, "*And it's our position, your Honor, that the EXIS computer and the information contained within that computer is nothing more and nothing less than totem pole hearsay*" and without any available exception, such as the business records exception. (TT 12-44) Lopez noted that the Government had been unwilling or unable to provide the source documents for the data that was input into the EXIS database. Lopez said that because the Government will seek to show that a computer had determined that among 14,000 bombings in the U.S., the two in Quincy and Roslindale are very much alike, the effect on the jury would be very prejudicial.

Frank Libby argued that the EXIS data was reliable and also that the defense should not have waited until the middle of this trial to ask for the basic documents.

Judge Zobel heard both sides and ruled that Scheid's testimony could be admitted. She said, "*I do believe it is hearsay,*" (TT 12-48) but that it can be admitted under the business records exception. Also, she agreed with the prosecution's claim of lateness, "*...I would regard it as unfair to raise this issue* [of the request original documents of the 5 remaining culled bombings] *at this point in the trial where the government's entire case has been based in part on this.*" (TT 12-49)

Given that ruling, Terry Segal asked for a limiting instruction to the jury and Judge Zobel guessed what he wanted, "*Well, what I would tell the jury is that this is being offered, not to show that just because Mr. Trenkler did something like this once, he would do it again. However, it is to show that he knows how to make bombs, that, and perhaps on the intent, since there - - I mean, do you really want me to tell the jury that?* (TT 12-50) She said that something like that might be more harmful than helpful, but if Mr. Segal wanted such an instruction, he should draft it and present it to her. Segal's apparent willingness to state that Alfred Trenkler knew how to make bombs was not only harmful, it was untrue. Alfred Trenkler had never built a bomb in his life, and certainly not one with dynamite and blasting caps. What he had done in 1986 was to take an existing military noise simulator with the two wires sticking out, and likely with instructions on the casing saying "12 volts," and remotely deliver those 12 volts from two six-volt batteries without hurting anyone. That was not the work of a Bomb Maker.

The jury then entered, and after the judge's apology that the testimony was resuming before the jury's "*goodies*" of coffee and doughnuts arrived. She assured them that the coffee would remain hot until the first break, after Stephen Scheid's direct testimony.

Stephen Scheid was questioned by Frank Libby about EXIS, the Explosives Incident Data Base. Scheid explained how the database works, just as he did in the Shay trial and how he searched for the incidents between 1979 and 1991 and asked a series of winnowing questions and came up with seven bombs with similar characteristics. The jury was left to conclude that since two of the seven, out of 14,252 were from Massachusetts and since Alfred Trenkler admittedly built one, that he built the other.

After direct examination, Judge Zobel announced that the trial would not be conducted on Thursday, 11 November, Veterans' Day, but that she still hoped to have the case in the jury's hands before Thanksgiving.

Scott Lopez cross-examined Scheid and quickly established that EXIS is not a comprehensive database, because there are no legal requirements that all relevant incidents in the U.S. be reported to ATF by all law enforcement agencies. He showed how crucial the questions or queries were to the results. For example, if the query had been "*Futaba*," or "*Rock Star*" the 1986 Quincy device would not have appeared. If the query had been for "*Tyco*" or "*trucks*" then the Roslindale Bomb would have been excluded. In sum, there were 18 factors which were not common to both devices, but the queries which produced the match involved five factors which WERE common to both devices. Stephen Scheid agreed that the data for the 1986 Quincy device was not entered into the EXIS database until after 28 October 1991.

On redirect, Frank Libby established that there were not many mistakes that were found in the data submitted for EXIS, and under recross, Stephen Scheid agreed that there had been some mistakes. Scheid's testimony was left substantially unshaken as it supported a computer's "conclusion" that the same person built the 1986 Quincy device and the 1991 Roslindale Bomb even though Scott Lopez showed that the computer's decisionmaking was entirely controlled by Stephen Scheid.

It was as if the EXIS database were asked to determine if two children of the same parents were identical twins on the basis of five criteria: that both individuals had two arms, two legs, one head, two eyes, one nose and one mouth. With those five queried items, the EXIS computer would conclude, "Twins!" despite the contrary, but unsubmitted data that the individuals had different hair color, different eye color, and different sexes, among 15 other differences. After such a computer conclusion, would a jury still find that the two individuals were identical twins?

Next to testify for the Government was the ATF explosives expert, Thomas Waskom. Frank Libby was advised by Judge Zobel that he could directly examine Mr. Waskom for 23 minutes before the day's recess. Waskom said that he had worked on more than one thousand explosives cases and about 70 cases where the bombs were reconstructed and there were two "*signature*" cases where he believed that more than one bomb was made by the same person, and with the same "*signature.*" One was the current Trenkler case and the other a series of bombings in Alabama.

As Frank Libby questioned Mr. Waskom about his decision process in reaching his conclusions about the similarity of the 1986 Quincy simulator and the 1991 Roslindale, Waskom adroitly noted that he read the reports of the defense expert, Denny Kline, whom he respected. It's always a good tactic to show respect for one's opponents. Waskom graphically stated that the power of the M21 Hoffman artillery simulator was not to be discounted, "*If they put one in their hand and function it, their hand is going to be gone.*" (TT 12-139/40)

The trial recessed at 1:00 p.m.

Next day's headlines:

Boston Globe: "*BOMBING CASE WITNESS CITES 1-IN-14,000 TIE*" by Matthew Brelis

Boston Herald: "*TEEN CLAIMS HE BOUGHT PARTS FOR SUSPECT IN '86*" by Ralph Ranalli

25 26 27 28 29	1 2 3 4 5	8 9 10 12	15 16	22 23 24	29
X X X X X	X X X X X	X X X O	O O	O O O	O

Day 13: Wednesday, 10 November

Judge Zobel began a bench conference by saying that she had reviewed the proposed sections of the Channel 56 tape and would allow all of it to be shown to the jury, "*except for one sentence in which Mr. Shay talks about how he's non-violent. Because I know that to be untrue on other evidence that was elicited at the sentencing hearing. And I'm allowing it both as being state of mind evidence, and thus not hearsay, and hearsay evidence that is admissible as a statement, a declaration against penal interest and corroborated. Every one of the statements has substantial corroboration. And for that reason, I'm allowing it and your* [Mr. Segal's] *objection is noted.*" (TT 13-2]

As shown in Chapter 6 herein, and despite Judge Zobel's claim of "*substantial corroboration,*" every single statement that Thomas A. Shay made in that videotape that connected Alfred W. Trenkler to the 1991 Roslindale Bomb was false. Somehow, because of the separation of the trials, or because neither Alfred Trenkler nor his lawyers were actively present at the Shay trial, and because of Alfred Trenkler's several decisions not to testify before Judge Zobel, it was not made known to Judge Zobel nor the media how false Shay's statements were. Of course, Trenkler's legal team was not successful in Trenkler's trial either. Judge Zobel made clear that she would disallow parts of the tape that she felt were untrue, and Terry Segal and associates failed to meet that burden.

Why was that? Should they/could they have subpoenaed Tom Shay for the purposed of inquiring into those statements? Could they have sent him *a "Request for Admissions*" or another type of interrogatory as is done in civil trials? Could they have sued in civil court for defamation in some way? Whatever the possibilities, there were not enough and if there were other techniques available, Terry Segal did not use them. Thus, the tape was prepared for showing to the jury - and available to them again during their deliberations. As has been said, a picture is worth a thousand words and that tape was worth several thousand to the prosecutors. The rest of the trial saw the use of approximately 336,000 words.

Almost as damaging would be a one-minute video of an M21 Hoffman being placed underneath a 55-gallon drum and sending the barrel 20 feet into the air. The prosecutors sought to show the video to the jury to show that an M21 was powerful and to counter the testimony in court that Alfred Trenkler viewed the 1986 Quincy device as a prank.

Arguing strongly against the showing, Terry Segal said, "*Here's my objection. I saw this tape yesterday. Under 403(1)* [Federal Rules of Evidence], *it is unfairly prejudicial.*" (TT 13-10] Judge Zobel asked "*Why?*" and Segal responded, *"I'll tell you why. In the first place, Mr. Waskom has testified that this M21 can blow off a hand.*"

"*Why is that prejudicial?*" returned the judge, and Segal argued, "*One, I've cross-examined a lot of things, but I've never cross-examined a tape with somebody speaking on it.*" (TT 13-10) He continued, "*But more importantly, this shows a demonstration not of an M21 under a truck, which is what the government's theory is in this case, this shows an M21 under a barrel, being shot up. That has got nothing to do with this particular case. And they are doing the same thing that you permitted them to do with the transmitter, which was closer. You're taking something that's unrelated and trying to apply it. If they had done a demonstration under a truck, which is what this is all about, they claim, I can see it.*" (TT 13-10) Segal made one error in implying that the M21 was detonated under the Capeway Fish Market truck. Instead, it was placed along the side of the truck.

Frank Libby said they wanted to counter Trenkler's view, as expressed to Agent D'Ambrosio, that the 1986 device was a firecracker prank.

Losing the argument, Terry Segal said, "*Your Honor, we saw this tape yesterday for the first time* [arguing this type of trial unfairness was effectively used by the prosecution the previous day, re: the requests for the EXIS raw data]. *I'm not in the business of production. I think this is a trial by production, if you permit something that is so prejudicial -- .*" Judge Zobel said she would allow it. (TT 13-13)

What Terry Segal didn't argue, and hindsight is admittedly 20/20, was that, as was stated during Bob Craig's testimony, Donna Shea had given the M21 Hoffman to Alfred Trenkler. Trenkler had little idea about its possible power, judging from its size and purpose, and could only guess that a noise simulator should not be too dangerous. Intent is important in the law, and there was testimony that the 1986 Quincy device was intended as a prank. There was also testimony that the Quincy device did no harm to property or person. That the M21 COULD have caused greater harm should not have been the standard, and even if more harm had been done, that was not Alfred Trenkler's intent and not the result.

Right after showing the video, Waskom repeated the same point about the 1986 device, "*It wasn't intended to hurt anyone from the reports I read. It was intended to cause a disturbance, put fear in another person.*" (TT 13-18) Then Thomas Waskom repeated the opinion he stated at the Shay trial, that "*the materials used in the 1986 and the materials used in the 1991 show one person built both devices.*" (TT 13-19) Waskom also attached some importance to the claim that the builder of both devices had someone else purchase materials, "*in a sense the builder separates himself from the crime by going through other people.*" (TT 13-15)

Under cross-examination by Terry Segal, Thomas Waskom agreed that his testimony in the Trenkler case was the first time he had testified in court on a "*signature*" issue. Waskom worked on one other signature case, involving five bombs in Alabama in 1972 and four in 1989. Each of the five bombs was a pipe bomb and each contained a typed extortion letter, and had other similarities making the bomb "*signatures*" obviously similar.

Returning to the issue of the size of the 1986 device, Waskom conceded that if held in one's hand, "*a cherry bomb would also cause similar damage to the hands* [as would be caused by an M21 Hoffman]." (TT 13-34/5) Terry Segal cross-examined Thomas Waskom extensively on the differences between the 1986 and 1991 devices, just as was done in the suppression hearings, but he did not shake Waskom's opinion that the the same person built both of them. The jury later agreed.

Frank Libby then examined the next Government witness, Peter Turowska, of the Quincy Police Dept. who participated in the investigation into the 1986 Quincy device. His short testimony presented the claim that the 1986 Quincy device was attached underneath the body of the Capeway Fish Market's truck. However, according to Alfred Trenkler in 2007, as noted earlier, it was attached on the left side frame of the truck, in front of the rear wheel. It would have been attached on the side of the body of the truck, but it was made of aluminum and the magnet would not affix the simulator to it. Also, the device was round and only about six inches in diameter and three to four inches thick.

Under cross-examination by Terry Segal, Turowska stated that he saw no damage to the truck from the 1986 Quincy device. Segal did not challenge Turowska's statement that the bomb was underneath the truck even though Alfred Trenkler had reminded him several times of its positioning. It was an important distinction as Stephen Scheid used "underneath vehicle" as one of his queries.

Prior to the next witness, William David Lindholm, Paul Kelly read to the jury a stipulation by the defense and the prosecution, Government Exhibit 67, "*The parties to this action hereby stipulate as follows: The defendant Alfred Trenkler was indicted on Wednesday, December 16th and arrested later the same day, agreed and stipulated by counsel.*" (TT 13-78) The purpose of the stipulation was to reduce the trial time it would have taken with witness testimony to establish for the jury the timetable for Alfred's encounters with William David Lindholm. .

Lindholm, age 43, said he graduated from "*Milton High School in 1968 and then attended college in Charlestown, Boston University and Suffolk University for approximately four years, from 1968 to approximately 1972.*" (TT 13-79) He was in the "*marijuana business*" from 1969 to 1988 and was convicted of conspiracy to distribute marijuana and income tax evasion in 1990 and sentenced to 97 months imprisonment which would bring his release sometime in 1997.

In 1992 he was incarcerated in the Federal Correctional Institution (FCI) in Big Spring, Texas, and was, according to Paul Kelly's question "*brought back to Massachusetts to be questioned about other matters relating to or arising out of your own conviction; is that fair to say.*" (TT 13-82) On Thursday, 17 December, 1992, he was brought to the Federal Courthouse in Boston, the site of this trial of Alfred Trenkler, for questioning. That evening he was taken to the Plymouth County House of Correction. After arrival, he was first taken to the intake unit, and then went to the orientation unit, which Lindholm described as "*one general dormitory study type living area in approximately - - I would say approximately 22 bunk beds in this area, and a shower area and a bathroom area at one end of the living unit. When I first went there it was very noisy. The lights are on 24 hours a day. There are two different sets of lights. They would turn one set down late in the night.*" (TT 13-83/4) He said the noise was excessive and the room was smaller than Judge Zobel's courtroom, and had approximately 44 inmates. The racial balance was mostly Black and Hispanic and four Caucasians; and he met Alfred Trenkler.

Testified Lindholm, "...*I couldn't sleep at all because of the noise and being in a new environment and not feeling very well. And I got up and I went to the bathroom end of the unit and moistened a towel to put on my forehead because I wasn't feeling well. After that, I still couldn't sleep and I observed Alfred Trenkler sitting at a picnic table, which would be the best characterization.*" (TT 13-85/6) They engaged in small talk conversation.

Lindholm said that six or seven inmates were in the orientation unit over the weekend, as most were transferred into the general population. He was released on Monday, 21 December around noon. Lindholm was in the unit all day Friday, 18 December, but Trenkler was not there during the daytime hours, because, Lindholm believed, he was in Boston being arraigned or had a bail hearing.

Paul Kelly asked for Lindholm's observations on how Alfred Trenkler was getting along in the unit, and Lindholm answered, "*He was having some slight difficulty with some of the other inmates.*" Terry Segal objected for relevance, but the Judge allowed Lindholm to continue his answer, "*... Some of the inmates were asking him to clean himself up a little bit.*" (TT 13-87/8)

On Saturday the 19th, testified Lindholm, he had breakfast with Alfred Trenkler and Learned learned that they both were brought up in Milton. After learning that Alfred attended Thayer Academy and Milton Academy, Lindholm said to Trenkler, "*And my father when he was a young man attended Thayer Academy and Milton Academy and Brown [sic] and Brown University. And we talked, you know, about Thayer Academy and Milton Academy. And we also, he also brought to my attention that he lived on Whitelawn Avenue, and I lived on Whitelawn Avenue approximately 1961 to 1962, for one year.*" (TT 13-88/9)

He continued, "*...and I asked him about what happened to the people what owned the property that my mother and I lived at. He told me that, to the best of his recollection he then, [sic] Mrs. Dunning and son (ph.) [sic] were both deceased at that time.*" (TT 13-89)

Lindholm answered, "*Yes*" to Paul Kelly's leading question, "*Is it fair to state, Mr. Lindholm, that you offered the defendant some free advice on a number of matters based on your own experience and your own understanding of the law?*" (TT 13-90) For example, continued Lindholm, "*we discussed how it's beneficial for a defendant to actively participate in his own defense strategy during the trial.*" (TT 13-90)

Asked Paul Kelly, "*Now, at this point on Saturday the 19th of December, did the defendant tell you that he was not guilty of the charges, that he was innocent of the charges?*" and David Lindholm replied, "*Yes, he did.*" (TT 13-91)

On Sunday, 20 December Lindholm testified that "*Trenkler stated to me that he couldn't understand why Mr. Shay [Tom Shay] would be implicating him in this case.... He stated that he did not think that Mr. Shay would testify against him or on behalf of the Government, and I told him that I [sic, it] was most fortunate that that would be very damaging to his position if Mr. Shay did testify.*" (TT 13-91)

Asked about where Trenkler said he met Tom Shay, Lindholm testified, "*...he stated that he met Mr. Shay at a bus stop across from WBCN studio near the Fenway Park Drive area in Boston...*" and "*that he knew him approximately two years.*" (TT 13-97) Lindholm said he became aware of Trenkler's sexual orientation based upon "*his conversations with me about his relationship with Mr. Shay.*" (TT 13-97)

Lindholm said that no one overheard these conversations with Trenkler because "*We would walk towards the end of the unit where there was a wall approximately four or five feet in height that segregated the bathroom end of the unit from the living end of the unit, and there wasn't anybody really around that area.*" (TT 13-93)

AUSA Paul Kelly asked David Lindholm what Trenkler may have said about Radio Shack, and Lindholm testified "*that it was -- the Government had knowledge that some components were purchased from a local Radio Shack distributor, a retailer.*" (TT 13-94) Said Lindholm, "*I stated that it was rather careless that anybody that might be involved in building a device such as this would go to their local Radio Shack retailer and purchase this type of equipment as opposed to going out of state or out of New England,*" and he said that Alfred Trenkler responded that "*... yes, that was an accurate observation, and it was regrettable.*" (TT 13-94)

Lindholm said that Alfred Trenkler told him about the 1986 device late on Sunday afternoon, 20 December, or early evening, and they continued to talk. That night, they were at the end of the orientation unit and talking quietly, with Trenkler saying, "*Even if I did build the bomb, I did not place it on the car... Then he paused for a moment and said, so I built the bomb. I built the bomb. I don't deserve to die or spend the rest of my life in prison for building this device.*" (TT 13-96)

Lindholm continued, "*He stated that the two bomb squad officers were foolish and negligent for not wearing body armor at the time that they were examining this device, and in essence that it served them right for what happened to them. It wasn't his fault.*" Asked whether Trenkler made the last comments with "*any sadness or remorse,*" Lindholm replied, "*None.*" (TT 13-96) Asked about Trenkler's demeanor, Lindholm said, "*He was very cold, calculating and disparaging toward the officers.*" (TT 13-97) Lindholm said that he then told Trenkler "*...that he should not repeat that statement to anybody else he might encounter. It could potentially be very damaging to him.*" (TT 13-97) The best advice that Lindholm could have given to Alfred Trenkler would have been, "**and you shouldn't be talking with me, either, because I know that the way to get a reduction in sentence is to inform on another inmate to help the government get a conviction**." (emphasis added)

About the device, Trenkler was said by Lindholm to have said, "*We talked about C 4 explosives and mercury switches and remote control devices. We -- he stated, I asked him what he thought the distance would be for a remote control switch in terms of activating the device, and he thought it would be approximately 50 yards in distance.*" (TT 13-97)

Regarding Tom Shay, Lindholm said that Trenkler said, "*At one point he stated that he thought that Mr. Shay was HIV positive, and - -.*" (TT 13-97) Also Trenkler "*made a number of remarks about Mr. Shay in a jealous vein.*" (TT 13-98)

Lindholm said they talked further about Tom Shay, as Lindholm had spent an hour with him in the lockup in the Federal courthouse where he formed the opinion that "*I didn't think that Mr. Shay was capable of putting batteries in a flashlight. And he [Trenkler] agreed with me in terms of his [Shay's] lack of technical ability.*" (TT 13-98)

The conversation allegedly shifted to politics and the prosecution and how newly elected President Bill Clinton would be appointing new U.S. Attorneys. Trenkler allegedly said, "*He stated to me that he had some information that you, Assistant Attorney Paul Kelly, would be leaving this office to pursue some other legal career..,*" and that Trenkler "*had a definite dislike for you.*" Lindholm continued, "*He stated that you* were an insidious prosecutor, and that you - - he had an enormous dislike for you personally." (TT 13-99)

David Lindholm denied that he any agreement or deal with the prosecutors for any benefit for this testimony and that he was offended by Trenkler's lack of remorse. Lindholm said that in prison he had reformed his values "*in terms of how they live one's life and the decisions they make, knowing the difference between what's wrong and what's right, what's illegal and legal.*" Lindholm testified, "*... it was a correct thing for me to be here to relate to the Court what I know about what happened and what statements he made to me about what happened.*" (TT 13-101)

Terry Segal cross-examined, and Lindholm acknowledged that he had read the *Boston Herald* while he was at the Plymouth House of Correction, and that he had read that Trenkler came from Milton. Of articles shown to him, Lindholm remembered reading only the *Herald*'s Trenkler case article of 19 December 1991. Lindholm thought the Whitelawn Ave. house he lived in with his mother from 1961-62 was #22 Whitelawn and that it was owned by the Dunn family and they had an apartment in the home. However, Lindholm's mother, Mary L.Lindholm was reported in the Milton Voter List to be living at 34 Hollis Street from 1959 to 1967 and then at 494 Granite Ave until 1972. From 1972 to 1992, his mother was listed in the Milton Residents' List as living at 174 Brush Hill Road, and that was the address from which David Lindholm registered to vote in 1972 until he moved to Hull in 1992. There was no gap in the Milton Town records for the Lindholms living a year on Whitelawn Ave.

Returning to the 18 December *Boston Herald* article, Segal paused and said, "*Well, we'll get to Saturday.*" and Judge Zobel asked, "*Do you have any other questions?*" and after Terry Segal replied "*Yes,*" Judge Zobel said, "*Well, let's keep asking them.*" (TT 13-108)

Segal asked Lindholm, "*Didn't you tell, Mr. Trenkler over that weekend that you had offered to help any inmate incarcerated on federal charges,*" and Lindholm agreed, "*In terms of advice, yes.*" Segal continued, "*...didn't you state* [to Trenkler] *that you always disliked the Federal government, being a product of the 60s, and that you would offer help to any inmate who was incarcerated on federal charges?*" To which Lindholm replied, "*I stated that I had had an adversarial relationship with the federal government due to the business of selling marijuana for all those years.*" (TT 13-108) It's unclear why Segal attempted to show Lindholm's hostility to the government, as Segal was generally trying to show that Lindholm was working **with** the government to entrap Trenkler.

Lindholm agreed that he had dropped the appeal of his criminal conviction on 15 December 1992, but was not asked why, and that he was in Boston on the 17th to provide information to the U.S. Attorney about other people in the illegal drug business. Terry Segal asked him if in December 1992 he "*understood that after one year goes by in that sentence, the only way your sentence could be reduced is if you supply new information to the Government; is that correct?*" and Lindholm replied "*Yes.*" (TT 13-112) That understanding came directly from Rule 35(b)(2)(c) of the Federal Rules for Criminal Procedure which provides that after one year of sentencing, the government may request a reduction of sentence for an inmate who provides "*information the usefulness of which could not be reasonably have been anticipated by the defendant until more than one year after sentencing and which was promptly provided to the government after its usefulness was reasonably apparent to the defendant.*" Segal seems to have presumed that the jury understood that no inmate could expect relief pursuant to that rule unless other appeals were dropped, which is the most likely reason for Lindholm's dropping of his appeal on 15 December. The Federal Rule does not require that appeals be dropped, but the prosecutors may have requested it. In any case, Lindholm likely knew he had a deal before he met Alfred Trenkler, and he certainly knew afterwards, and before Trenkler's trial, that he could make a deal.

Lindholm recalled telling Trenkler that Trenkler's case could set a precedent in the First Circuit because it might be a death penalty case.

Lindholm said he told Trenkler that the 1986 incident "*was a serious problem that he had, that it could be viewed as a prior bad act.*"

Shifting to other subjects, Segal asked, "*Didn't he tell you that he had a cousin over at Fidelity that was going to refer you to a high tech company for work?*" and Lindbolm answered, "*He stated to me that he had a cousin that from time to time gave him referrals for his skills for his skills with electronics.*" (TT 13-115) Continued Lindholm, "*He was very optimistic about his monetary future.*" Lindholm said that Alfred Trenkler said that he was innocent. (TT 13-115)

Lindholm said that while he was in a cell with Tom Shay and six or seven others, he did not talk with Shay at all.

Terry Segal asked Lindholm about his motivation for testifying, and Lindholm denied that he even hoped that his testimony would help reduce his remaining 65 months of his sentence. He agreed that he was debriefed about his prior drug activities twice in Springfield before the 17 December meeting with the U.S. Attorney's office in Boston.

Finally, and dramatically, Lindholm responded to another question about his motivation for testifying, "*I'll go on the record to say that I'm not going to ask for any benefit, rewards, [or] inducements any time in the future.*" (TT 13-124) William David Lindholm was then excused with his story unshaken.

Then the jury was shown the six-minute video containing excerpts from the 17 October 1992 Channel 56 interview by Karen Marinella of Tom Shay. Announced Judge Zobel, "*Members of the jury, what you're about to see is a small excerpt of an interview given by Mr. Thomas Shay, Jr. to a reporter from Channel 56.*" [TT 13-126] Included in the excerpt were a few sections from the full interview as was played for the Shay trial jury on Day 16, Tuesday, 20 July. Below are the portions of the interview played for the jury in the Alfred Trenkler trial:

TOM SHAY: "*Today is October 17, 1992. It is almost one year after the death of Jeremiah Hurley and the maiming of his partner Francis X. Foley, a year after a bomb exploded and left one officer dead and one destroyed for life, two families destroyed without ever having any chance of repair until the builder of that device and conspirators are behind bars for life.*

I, Tommy Shay, am guilty of something in that case, but do not know what. I don't have the average 20 year male history. From age 5 to 18, I was in the Department of Social Services care."

KAREN MARINELLA: "*Okay. Now, let's get into some of that a little bit. You - you - you said that you are guilty of something in this case....*

Mm-hmm. But you helped purchase the equipment for this bomb. You're admitting that."

SHAY: *"I'm admitting that, but not to the fact that I was helped* [helping?] *to purchase stuff to build the bomb....*

... and I'm always, you know, like the Radio Shack clerk on Mass. Ave. recognized me. I don't know why he recognized me...."

MARINELLA: *"What kinds of things were you buying? Tell me.*

SHAY: *A toggle switch, a[n] AA battery holder, wires, you know, electrical supplies."*

MARINELLA: *"Explosives? Did you buy--"*

SHAY: *"No-"*

MARINELLA: *"-explosives?"*

SHAY: *"I didn't buy no explosives. Nope.... purchased all kinds of stuff, but everything - there's only two things that I purchased that were inside that explosive device that killed Officer Hurley and -"*

MARINELLA: *"What were those two things?"*

SHAY: *"The toggle switch and the AA battery holder... On the 28th, at about twelve o'clock, I started to piece things together and after my jailing at the Dedham House of Correction and my release, I thought it was time for me to get out of here because I just didn't want any involvement. I was scared. My youthfulness came back into me, and I was scared like a little boy, and I just needed to get out of there. I didn't want any part of it because I had nothing to do with it. I did have something to do with it, but the knowledge of what happened was nothing, no part of it.."*

MARINELLA: *"So you went to California."*

SHAY: *"So I went to California, the reason I used James Kehoe's military ID, the military ID was expired, I cannot be charged with that charge of using a military ID. The reason I used it is because of the new name and his ID was 22 years old. I was 20 at the time and that was, you know, bar time for me... My guiltiness is knowing who did it or thinking about who did it after the bomb and then fleeing - ."*

MARINELLA: *"Mm-hmm."*

SHAY: *"-not to tell anybody."*

MARINELLA: *"Right."*

SHAY: *"That's my guiltiness... But once the - once the purchase came through from Radio Shack, and I found out that, I'm the one that built - built, excuse me - purchased part of the built - building, then I - it kind of hit me. You know?"*

MARINELLA: *"Mm-hmm."*

SHAY: *"A man's dead out there. There are five children and a wife lost forever, family destroyed. Never mind another family destroyed. I don't know if Francis X. Foley can ever put his life together. I hope he does, but nobody will ever be able to put their life together until the streets are safe again."*

MARINELLA: *"Mm-hmm."*

SHAY: *"I feared that."*

MARINELLA: *"What do you need to do?... Well, you've told me many times that you hated your father."*

SHAY: *"No, no, no, no-"*

MARINELLA: *"-for-"*

SHAY: *"-no, no, no. For what?"*

MARINELLA: *"You've told me many times on the phone-"*

SHAY: *"No, I- I never-"*

MARINELLA: *"-that you felt-"*

SHAY: "-that-"

MARINELLA: "-deserted as a child unloved-"

SHAY: "Deserted and unloved-"

MARINELLA: "And you hated him."

SHAY: "-not hate. That's not hate. Hold on. Then I got to go back on my words here because-"

MARINELLA: "Okay-"

SHAY: "-I never said I hated my father. Hate - hating someone as taking a gun or a bomb to them is two different things. You know? Hate, that's - a dislike, I should say. I should have used my words better when I talked to you-"

MARINELLA: "Okay."

SHAY: "-whenever I said that be dislike him for deserting me and my mother, you know, back when I was five years old."

MARINELLA: "All right. I'm going to pursue this a little bit here. Bear with me. Thousands of children in this state are abused sexually, emotionally, physically every year in this state. They don't go out and build bombs."

SHAY: "No comment. I have - I can't think of anything to tell you. I just poured out my heart today and here you are again. The light's going dim, too."

MARINELLA: "This isn't - a lot of people are going to hear this, Tom, and I have to ask these questions, and they're going to say this is hard to believe. This is hard to believe, A, that this kid went out and bought all this stuff and had absolutely no knowledge that this was going to be come a bomb."

SHAY: "That's my story."

MARINELLA: "They're finding it very hard to believe right now. Why should we believe this?"

SHAY: "Well, I-"

MARINELLA: "Well, tell me -"

SHAY: "-can't say anything, anymore"

MARINELLA: "I'm here. Tell me why we should believe this."

SHAY: "I - I can't say anything no more. You know? I just told you and if they don't believe it..."

MARINELLA: "You're going to change that light?"

SHAY: "You don't believe me. That's all right."

MARINELLA: "I have to ask these questions, Tom. I mean, I mean, I .. how many things have - have we talked about the past few months that perhaps haven't happened yet or perhaps the truth was stretched a little bit? I mean, you've told me from day one you knew nothing about this from day one, and now this is a complete turnaround, so I have to ask you why I should believe this now. I have to. Tell me."

SHAY: "I don't have an answer for you. Maybe I do have an answer for you. My friends have been dumped on. My family has been dumped on. I've been dumped on. I saw no reason to cooperate with anybody and tell them what was going in or what I thought or anything until it comes down to me."[6] [TT 13-126]

There was no comment by anyone after the playing of the tape. The jury was just left to absorb it, with no clarification about what parts were true and what parts were known to be false. For example, Shay said that two of the items he purchased were in the Roslindale Bomb. In fact, there was never any proof that any of the six items purchased on 18 October was in the Roslindale Bomb. It was claimed that a toggle switch, of the same model as the toggle switch he claimed to have purchased was in the Roslindale Bomb, but being of the same model is not the same as being the same actual switch. There was nothing in the Roslindale Bomb debris from a Radio Shack AA batter holder. (To read most of the transcript along with Alfred Trenkler's comments, see Chapter 3)

Judge Zobel then explained to the jury that she was trying to extend the hours of one or two trial days in order to get the case to them before Thanksgiving, and then the jury was excused.

Terry Segal asked about his motion and memo regarding the requested testimony of Jay Flynn, the attorney who took over responsibility for the Thomas L. Shay Dedham Service Center case from Alan Pransky, and Judge Zobel said, *"I think it very unlikely that Mr. Flynn will testify."* (TT 13-128)

The trial adjourned at 12:59, until Friday, 12 November, as Thursday, 11 November was Veterans' Day.

It was the worst day of the trial for Alfred Trenkler with the Lindholm testimony and the Tom Shay interview with Karen Marinella. The falsity of the Tom Shay statements was reviewed in Chapter 3. Below are several corrections to the unchallenged untruths from Lindholm's testimony about his conversations with Alfred Trenkler. First, it must be noted that Alfred Trenkler recalls that the total duration of his few conversations with David Lindholm *"amounted to all of 10 minutes,"* according to Alfred in 2007. It was David Lindholm who initiated the few conversations with Alfred Trenkler.
- Alfred Trenkler was having no problems with other inmates.
- No inmates were asking that *"he clean himself up a bit."*
- Alfred did not have breakfast with David Lindholm on Saturday morning.
- Lindholm's father did not attend Thayer Academy nor Milton Academy, and probably not Brown University.
- It's extremely unlikely that Lindholm ever lived on Whitelawn Ave., although he did live in Milton during his high school years.
- Alfred Trenkler did not state to David Lindholm any opinion about whether Tom Shay would or would not testify for the Government against him.
- Alfred Trenkler did not tell David Lindholm that he had met Tom Shay at a bus stop in the Fenway area, as that was not true. In fact, there was no such bus stop in the Fenway.
- Alfred Trenkler did not tell David Lindholm that he had known Tom Shay for *"approximately two years,"* as he had met Shay in early June 1991. By the middle of December 1992, that was 18 months previous.
- Alfred Trenkler had no discussion with David Lindholm about the wisdom of the purchasing components for a bomb at a local Radio Shack.
- Alfred Trenkler did not build the Roslindale Bomb.
- Although he did not say it to David Lindholm in those words, it is true that Alfred Trenkler doesn't *"deserve to die or spend the rest of my* [his] *life in prison for building this device"* as he had absolutely nothing to do with it. Alfred wrote in 2007, *"I had said to Lindholm, in response to his telling me that the '86 act could end up giving me the death penalty that, 'so I built the '86 device, [and] I paid for that incident, [and] I don't deserve to die or spend the rest of my life in prison for some harmless prank I pulled in 1986.' "*
- Alfred Trenkler never said that Officers Hurley and Foley were *"foolish."* Alfred had

worked closely with police and fire departments and respected their work.

- Alfred Trenkler never asked Lindholm not to repeat anything he said over that entire weekend in December 1992.
- Alfred Trenkler did not discuss with David Lindholm "*C 4 Explosives*" nor mercury switches.
- Alfred Trenkler did not tell David Lindholm that he thought that Tom Shay was HIV positive, but he did say that ATF agents told him that Shay was HIV positive.
- Alfred Trenkler was never jealous of or jealous for Tom Shay, with whom he was merely acquainted for a few hours in June and July 1991.
- Alfred Trenkler never expressed a dislike for Asst. U.S. Attorney Paul Kelly.

Unfortunately, it was David Lindholm's testimony that the jury heard, without the balancing testimony of Alfred Trenkler, and without any defense witnesses who could testify further about David Lindholm's stay at the Plymouth County House of Correction in December 1992. The jury did not learn that Lindholm's nickname in the prison system was "little stories" because of his alleged snitching, or "testilying," against other inmates. Because of this label and reputation, Lindholm had to be moved from prison to prison in order to reduce the likelihood that inmates would know about his reputation. This was likely the reason that he was in Texas rather than in a prison closer to New England.

Next day's headlines:
Boston Globe: "*MAN SAYS TRENKLER ADMITTED BOMB ROLE*" by Matthew Brelis
   He wrote of Lindholm's testimony: "*A Quincy engineer admitted building a bomb that killed one Boston police bomb squad officer and wounded another, then coldly blamed the victims for failing to wear protective gear while examining the device, a government witness told jurors....*"
   The article said that parts of the Marinella interview were played to the jury.. "*He* [Shay] *refused to testify against Trenkler but yesterday jurors saw excerpts of a WLVI-TV (Ch. 56) interview with Shay in which Shay admitted he bought a toggle switch and battery holder at a Radio Shack and the parts were used in the bomb.*"
Boston Herald: "*FELLOW JAILMATE TESTIFIES SUSPECT IN BOMBING SAID HE BUILT EXPLOSIVE*" by Ralph Ranalli

25 26 27 28 29	1 2 3 4 5	8 9 10 12	15 16	22 23 24	29
X X X X X	X X X X X	X X X X	O O	O O O	O

Day 14: Friday, 12 November
Judge Zobel opened the court by denying Terry Segal's motion to call Maurice Flynn, which was to be for the purpose of impeaching the testimony of Richard Brown as the proffered testimony because "*this is not a case where the contradicting testimony goes directly to the guilt or innocence of the defendant.*" (TT 14-2) Flynn would have testified that Richard Brown's testimony that Alfred Trenkler had told him about drawing a diagram at the request of officers on the night of 5/6 November 1991 was contrary to Brown's statement to Flynn that Brown had actually been at ARCOMM at the time.
   Judge Zobel said she would read Terry Segal's motion to strike the testimony of Michael Coady. The motion, filed on 8 November, before Michael Coady's testimony,

requested that Coady's testimony relating to Trenkler's alleged "*solicitation of teenage males as sexual partners, including his willingness to provide them with money, drugs and other material goods, and the performance of personal favors to induce and/or maintain the relationship*" be excluded. [TT 5-135.] As was typical of motions in this trial, the stated reason for the Motion was that the allegations were irrelevant and unfairly prejudicial and there was zero corroborating evidence to back up his statements. It would probably not have made a difference to Judge Zobel's response to the current motion, but it still would have been useful for the defense to add that the allegations were untrue and without foundation.

As happened at the Shay trial, the final Government witness was retired Boston Police Officer Francis Foley. Examined by Paul Kelly, his testimony closely paralleled that in the earlier trial. As stated in this book about the use of Foley's testimony in the Shay trial, it was unfair for the prosecution to be able to put the wounded victim of the crime on the stand at the end of the prosecution's case where it served no purpose other than to inflame the emotions of the jury. A serious cross-examination might have seemed to attack the victim, or even blame him; so Terry Segal asked no questions. He might have inquired, for example, about the 600 bomb cases a year investigated by the Boston Bomb Squad. One question might have been how many of those are sent to ATF to be entered into the EXIS database and who makes that decision. It might be that the Bomb Maker's real signature has appeared in other Boston bombs, but hadn't been recorded. Another question might be how many of the 600 cases a year involved signature issues, or simply bombs made by the same person. However, Francis Foley was not there to provide testimony about the Bomb Squad or as an expert about bombs; he was there to inflame the jury.

So concerned was Terry Segal about the impact of Foley's testimony that he filed a Motion with the Court beforehand to request that members of the Hurley and Foley families be asked to leave the courtroom before Foley's testimony in order to avoid prejudicial emotional outbursts. Judge Zobel denied the Motion.

The Government's case ended and the trial moved immediately into the defense's case, without fanfare or introduction. The first few defense witnesses gave alibi testimony for Alfred Trenkler for 18 October and the period 25-28 October 1991. Defense attorney Scott Lopez examined Joseph Pelphrey, security manager for the Christian Science Church. Pelphrey agreed that the security logs at the church showed that unnamed ARCOMM employees worked at the Church on Thursday, 17 October 1991 and on Saturday, 19 October, but there is no surviving record of them working on the 18th at the Christian Science Center.

On cross-examination Paul Kelly established that although the names of one or two other ARCOMM employees or sub-contractors were on the logs for the 17th and 19th, the name of Alfred Trenkler was not. Alfred Trenkler was actually there on both days, despite the absence of clear confirmation in the logs. His own personal calendar shows that he was there.

Scott Davis, a Senior Buyer in the Purchasing Dept. for the Church, was the next defense witness. On direct examination by Terry Segal, Davis said that he met with Alfred Trenkler and Richard Brown on 3 September and 25 September 1991, giving them Purchase Orders for rooftop antenna installation work with contract prices of $10,300 and $27,406, respectively. The work was to be completed by the end of October, and it was.

The next defense witness was Mark Romboli, an accountant, who first met with Richard Brown on 11 October at the ARCOMM office in Weymouth. Romboli's testimony relied upon his "*daily plan*," pages of which were entered into evidence. Brown and Romboli scheduled a followup meeting for Thursday, 17 October, but Richard Brown did not show up, and Romboli waited an hour.

The rescheduled meeting was held on 18 October, the day of the Radio Shack purchase by JYT SAHY at 2:36 p.m., but Richard Brown did not show for that meeting either. Romboli waited for about a half-hour and then called Alfred Trenkler's pager, at 11:36, and Trenkler arrived at the office between 11:40 and noon. In his date plan, Romboli wrote of his work that day at ARCOMM, "*It says that I reviewed invoices and cash disbursements with Al T. Its [sic] says I had discussions with Al. T. on various points ranging from setting up the company, business plan, financial operations, bank accounts, et cetera.*" (TT 14-16) Romboli left around 2:00 p.m.

While at ARCOMM, Romboli observed, "*The place was being fixed up. They were trying to get it ready to open up. It was being painted. There was a lot of work going on, carpentry work, et cetera.*" (TT 14-47)

During cross-examination, Paul Kelly established that Romboli could have left the ARCOMM offices between 1:45 and 2:15.

Romboli sent ARCOMM a bill for $817.50, but only $272.50 of that was ever paid. Paul Kelly seemed eager to show that ARCOMM was not the best-run company. Earlier, regarding the failure of Richard Brown to make the appointemnt for 17 October, Kelly asked, "*Between an hour to an hour and a half, you waited for these guys on the 17th, and they did not show?*" (TT 14-51) Mistaken appointments are not unusual, and it's not known how the mistake of the 17th was made, but Richard Brown, Alfred Trenkler and the ARCOMM team were on the roof of the Christian Science Administration building in Boston all that day.

The next defense witness was Robert Davidson, who formerly owned Davidson Distributing, a supplier of materials for ARCOMM. He was examined by Brenda Sharton. Davidson would deliver items to ARCOMM, but occasionally Alfred Trenkler would come to his office, which was also in Weymouth. Davidson remembered one such pickup on 28 October 1991, and he had a copy of a check from Alfred Trenkler for $32.50 on that date. With his memory of the date of that visit refreshed by the dated Invoice and ARCOMM check, he recalled other details of that meeting, which occurred between 1:00 to 2:00 or 2:30. He remembered that Trenkler came with Richard Brown in Brown's Lincoln Continental and they talked about the antenna on that car which came from Davidson Distributing. Unfortunately, the defense did not present to the jury a large size blowup of Alfred's actual schedule for that day, nor for other days either. With such evidence, the jury would have seen that Alfred Trenkler was more like them - working hard at a job, without the time or inclination to be trying to kill the father of young disturbed man he barely knew.

The cross-examination by Frank Libby established that Davidson was friendly with Trenkler, but did not have any kind of a social relationship with him or Brown.

Then Scott Lopez examined David Fardy, who worked at "The Design Shop" which engineered and built custom parts. He said he was working with one of his fellow "Design Shop" workers, Peter Cataldo, and with Al Trenkler installing a microwave antenna onto a previously installed mast at the Christian Science building on 17

October 1991. He said they worked most of the day on the Christian Science roof, 7:00 a.m. to 3:30 p.m., and his bill for "The Design Shop's" services on that day was paid.

Cross-examined by Frank Libby, David Fardy said he had known Alfred Trenkler since the 1980's and that they had ridden in Trenkler's Jeep in the woods.

Nurdan Cagdus was then examined by Terry Segal, and he confirmed that he was working on the roof of the Christian Science Church with Al Trenkler and two others on 17 October 1991. One event remembered from the 17th was that the team ordered pizza from Domino's and Cagdus ran down about 30 flights of stairs because the freight elevator was slow.

On 18 October, Nurdan Cagdus said that he and Alfred Trenkler went to an "*all-time check cashing*" machine in Quincy to cash his ARCOMM check. (TT 14-80) The check was for $245 for several employees including Alfred Trenkler, but because Cagdus had identification the check was made out for him.

On 19 October, Cagdus said that ARCOMM, including David Flaherty, Rich Brown and Alfred Trenkler, was back on the Christian Science roof either removing or erecting scaffolding.

Nurdan Cagdus received another ARCOMM check on that day, 28 October, and he went with Alfred Trenkler to cash it in South Boston, and Alfred Trenkler went with him. Afterwards they went to another microwave dish satellite project and did some work. He said that he was at the ARCOMM office in the morning, along with Rich Brown and Alfred Trenkler.

Paul Kelly cross-examined and established that wage payments to Cagdus were "*under the table*" and that withholding taxes were not deducted. He said that he worked for ARCOMM for one or two months. Cagdus was uncertain about what days of the week were 18 and 28 October.

Terry Segal conducted his redirect examination, but during Kelly's recross, Terry Segal asked if he could have two more questions. The judge denied the request, "*I thought we finished after the second round, and this is the second round.*" Mr. Segal then tried again, "*That's right. Can I get one question?*" and the judge's response was, "*Thank you Mr. Cagdus, you are excused.*" (TT 14-100) Begging for justice should not be necessary in the courts of the United States of America.

The next witness was David Millette, who was examined by Brenda Sharton, and he described the dinner party at his house in Dorchester on the night of Saturday, 26 October, with Alfred Trenkler, John Cates and others. Cates and Trenkler were there from about 6-7:00 p.m. to 2-3:00 a.m., when Millette fell asleep.

Paul Kelly questioned Millette about his recollection of the date of the Saturday, 26 October dinner party and established that Millette and John Cates were friends and lovers in Texas before coming to Boston. He established that David Millette was homeless at the time of the trial, but the Judge did not permit further questioning in that direction.

On recross-examination Paul Kelly tried to show inconsistencies between Millette's grand jury testimony and at trial, and the exchanges became testy. Kelly asked if Millette remembered all the questions Kelly asked him at the 9 April 1992 grand jury proceeding and Millette responded, "*The only way for me to know that is to ask me every question and you can tell by* [my] *responses whether I remember every one. I cannot state whether I know every question you ask me because you asked me every question.*" and Kelly responded, "*The only reason you're making that speech, sir, is you don't remember every question I asked you do you?"* (TT 14-111/12) That questioning continued, over the objection that it was argumentative, and finally Judge Zobel said, *"I do believe, Mr. Kelly, you're arguing with the witness."* (TT 14-113)

Scott Lopez questioned the next witness, Philip Colwell, who lived at 44 Eastbourne Street, across the street from 39 Eastbourne. He said that approximately two weeks before the 28 October explosion, he saw someone approach 39 Eastbourne at about 11 p.m. close enough to trigger the outside light sensor, which turned the lights on at Mr. Thomas L. Shay's house.

Paul Kelly established that Mr. Colwell was talking with his former girlfriend in his car on that night two weeks before the explosion and Kelly asked, *"Nothing more than that* [i.e. talking]" and Judge Zobel cautioned him, *"You needn't get into that Mr. Kelly."* (TT 14-121) Kelly then established that Mr. Colwell's recollection of the man who triggered the lights was more detailed when he talked with detectives on 28 October, than at the current trial.

Terry Segal then examined Brian O'Leary who had done carpentry work for Alfred Trenkler on the Christian Science project. On 16 December 1992, [transcribed as 16 October, but the day of Alfred Trenkler's arrest was 16 December] he was working with ARCOMM on *"setting up a satellite down link and running a cable and various assorted work.... It was right there in those few days that I was working there that he was arrested."* (TT 14-129)

Frank Libby cross-examined and established that Brian O'Leary had come to Libby's office in March of 1992 and, in the presence of a Federal agent, they talked about O'Leary's relationship with Alfred Trenkler going back to the 1980's. They first met when Trenkler would get gas for his Jeep in Quincy at the station where O'Leary worked.

Among the projects that he worked on with Alfred Trenkler was a 180 foot tower in Rhode Island. Kelly established that O'Leary introduced several people to Alfred Trenkler, including Robert Craig, later Trenkler's roommate, Richard Brown and Andy Robinson. Finally, Kelly established that O'Leary came to the U.S. Attorney's office at the request of Boston Police dectective Frank Armstrong, and that afterward, O'Leary called Alfred Trenkler to let him know.

Before Terry Segal examined the next witness, Edward Alvaro of Channel 25-TV, there was a bench conference, partly about Segal's motion to strike part of the Coady testimony. Terry Segal had argued, *"My concern is, and the reason for this motion is, over my vigorous objection, is I think we went through the back-door by putting on evidence that he* [Trenkler] *was living with a 15-year old giving him gifts. That's the same sort of thing your Honor ruled out."* (TT 14-146) Unfortunately, Segal did not say, as he could have because it was not before the jury, that there was absolutely no truth to Coady's allegations of travel to California, Florida and skiing. Also, unfortunately, Segal mischaracterized Coady's testimony, as there was no allegation that Trenkler was *"living with a 15-year old"* in the usual sense of the phrase. Judge Zobel said she would review Coady's testimony but she was left with the impression, as were the prosecutors, that the allegations were true - just unfairly prejudicial. Terry Segal could not avoid his strategic error in failing to comprehensively cross-examine Mike Coady and failing to offer evidence, such as Coady's use of false identification cards and Alfred Trenkler's own testimony, to impeach Michael Coady's testimony.

Ed Alvaro testified that he met with Alfred Trenkler to ask him to bid on a project for installing two microwave satellite antennas. Prior to this testimony, in a bench conference, Judge Zobel was firm about not wanting a lot of testimony about Trenker's ongoing work projects.

On cross-examination by Frank Libby, Mr. Alvaro said that he knew Alfred Trenkler from his work with Boston Catholic Television, well before 28 October 1991. As with other defense witnesses, the prosecution asked if the witness was appearing voluntarily or by subpoena. The apparent basis for the question was to lead the jury to the conclusion that people who appeared for the defense voluntarily were biased in favor of Alfred Trenkler. These questions were not asked of the prosecution's witnesses. Also asked of all the defense witnesses but three, two examined by Brenda Sharton and one by Scott Lopez, was one of the prosecution's early questions, "*Are you married?*" It's not known why that question was permitted by Judge Zobel, except perhaps out of habit; but the question is irrelevant and it supports the view that the prosecution was anti-gay.

Brenda Sharton examined the next defense witness, Frank Cavallo, a vice-president for Videocom, a Dedham company that provides satellite communications services. His customers were the networks such as ABC, CBS and ESPN who would send to Videocom signals through fiber optics or microwave and then Videocom would distribute the programs around the world by satellite. He had known Alfred Trenkler for five to seven years and had used his services to install satellite dishes.

The relationship was strictly business and Trenkler had done approximately 20-40 installations over 5-7 years at approximately $4-5,000 each for the service, not including the hardware. Larger dishes cost more, with a nine-meter dish in the $10-15,000 range. Cavallo had recommended Alfred Trenkler to other business people.

Cross-examination was by Frank Libby who established that Frank Cavallo would probably not have come to testify if he had not been supoenaed. Such a statement would seem to help Alfred, as Cavallo's testimony was helpful, and if he wasn't doing it as a loyal friend, that made it more credible.

The next defense witness was Roderick Kennedy, a private investigator and former FBI agent, who worked as a private investigator for the Trenkler defense. Examined by Brenda Sharton, Kennedy was paid to determine the time required to travel by car from the ARCOMM office in Weymouth to the Radio Shack store at 197 Mass. Ave. in Boston. He took the same route on four successive Fridays, as 18 October 1991 was a Friday. His first trip was on 15 October 1993 and the average time for the four trips was 27 minutes.

Frank Libby asked, on cross-examination "*Was a former FBI agent required to do that [timing project] in your mind?*" (TT 14-173) Ms. Sharton's objection was sustained. Libby established that Terry Segal helped him establish the route, but he didn't know if Alfred Trenkler had any input into the decision.

On redirect, Brenda Sharton established that the route Kennedy used for his four timed trips was not the route suggested by Terry Segal. Kennedy had taken several trips beforehand to establish the fastest route, and Segal's suggested route was slower.

At the end of the day, Judge Zobel announced that she hoped the defense's case would be closed by the following Tuesday, 16 November, and then there would be a break and closing arguments would begin on the following Monday, 22 November, three days before Thanksgiving on the 25th. The trial adjourned at 1:47.

25 26 27 28 29	1 2 3 4 5	8 9 10 12	15 16	22 23 24	29
X X X X X	X X X X X	X X X X	X O	O O O	O

Day 15: Monday, 15 November

Moving beyond the alibi defense, the first witness on Day 15 was the defense's explosives expert, Denny Kline, but before that there was a bench conference about two issues. First, Judge Zobel denied the defense's motion to strike a portion of Michael Coady's testimony. She said she had just received the defense's motion to strike the "signature" testimony of Thomas Waskom, but she hadn't yet read it. That motion to strike argued that there was a chain of custody problem with the debris from the 1986 device, because the policeman, Leo Voigt, who retrieved it was deceased. Thus, it could not be proven that the debris analyzed by the State Police actually came from the 1986 device.

"What else?" asked Judge Zobel. (TT 15-1) Terry Segal raised the issue of Frank Libby's expected question to Denny Kline of whether he talked to Alfred Trenkler about the design of the 1986 device. Segal was opposed to allowing Frank Libby to ask that question because it would *"highlight"* for the jury the defendant's exercise of his constitutional right not to testify in this case. Segal felt if important to repeat his earlier statement that *"He's not going testify in this case. I'm making a flat unequivocal statement."* (TT 15-4) From the transcript, the words appear like a bravado challange, as if Terry Segal was saying, *"HA! I think the prosecution's case is so weak that my client isn't even going to dignify the case with his own testimony. That's how confident we are."*

Terry Segal then examined Denny Kline, a former FBI agent and explosives expert who was retained by the defense in the Trenkler case. While in the FBI, his major investigations included the Pan Am Flight 103 explosion over Lockerbie, Scotland, and other airplane bombings. Kline had performed about 200 investigations and has testified for the prosecution in some other cases. Coincidentally, in 2007, the only man convicted in the Lockerbie bombing won a second chance to appeal in his claim of a wrongful conviction based on an allegedly inaccurate identification by a retail store owner of a purchaser of clothes on December 7, 1988. The trial court had not been told in that case that the store owner had seen a photo of the defendant a few days before the positive identification.

Denny Kline testified that he did not talk with Alfred Trenkler about the design of the 1986 device. In terms of the truth-seeking purpose of a trial, it's again unfortunate that court rules discouraged an expert from talking to the actual designer of the 1986 Quincy device. Such communication could have been sterilized by use of a third party and documents. Alfred Trenker had always been open about his role in the 1986 incident and it was harmful to the trial that he was not able to describe for the jury or his own experts what he had done in 1986. Judge Zobel said she would think about the issues.

Denny Kline defined "*signature*" as "*simply a term that is applied to the principle in bomb investigations that suggest that an individual who makes the bomb makes the bomb in the same way using the same components and putting those components together in basically the same way.*" (TT 15-10) He continued, "*... it takes singularly unique features in consideration in making a determination about a signature identification, certainly.*" (TT 15-11)

Kline said that he had done "*signature*" analyses or comparisons in 350 cases with the FBI. These cases involved international and domestic terrorist groups, and such groups as motorcycle gangs. He had testified in about 15 cases involving the signature issue. He found single signatures or sufficiently common characteristics to establish signature in several cases. He described those characteristics, such as the time of day of explosions, or presence of a letter, in several major cases such as those involving the FALN, a Puerto Rican nationalist group (175 bombings), and a Croation terrorist organization (12-15 bombings), and Omega 87, and anti-Castro Cuban group (135 bombings). The Omega 87 bomber left notes with his bombs and always used an expensive Helbros pocket watch, costing about $100, rather than the less expensive Westclox watch.

Then Mr. Kline explained his task on behalf of Alfred Trenkler, to compare the 1986 Quincy device to the 1991 Roslindale Bomb. He said that comparisons were difficult because of the meager information available about the 1986 Quincy device, and because they occurred five years apart and because there were only two devices. Here again, even the defense's own expert was hampered by the rules of legal representation. There should have been some way, in addition to his actual testimony, for Alfred's knowledge about the 1986 device to have been communicated to the jury.

Kline's opinion was, "*Due to the absence of unique similarities and the preponderance of dissimilarities, I personally could not make an opinion that there was a signature identification that existed between the '86 bomb and the '91 bomb.*" (TT 15-20) Then the defense introduced Defendant's Exhibit 150 which was Kline's reconstruction of the 1986 Quincy Hoffman M21 device.

Then Terry Segal questioned Denny Kline about several elements of each bomb:
- Main charge - different
- Initiator/detonator - different
- Fusing system - different
- Firing system - different
- Battery use - different
- Battery connections to wires - different
- Use of toggle switches - different
- Wires - different
- Container - different
- Magnets - different
- Adhesives - different
- Removal of charge wrapping - different

Denny Kline was asked whether, "*in your opinion, do these two devices exhibit a different level of sophistication or knowledge about explosives?*" And he answered, "*Yes, they do.*" (TT 15-30]

He continued, "*Well the basis for that opinion begins with just a visual observation of the two devices. This device* [1986] *is kind of crudely put together with materials that are, that are kind of readily available, almost at the spur of the moment kind of thing. Where, this device [1991] was built by a person who was rather calculating, precise, who used components that were easy to assemble. This device certainly would be more efficient. That would be one of the ways that I would consider there was a difference in criminal sophistication, if you will, in this."* (TT 15-30)

Kline was asked about the level of bombmaking sophistication of the 1991 device. First, answered Kline, the presence of two detonators was a clue. *"Secondly, is the fact that in this device, the bomber did not solder-connect the detonator leg wires. And the reason that, that someone who knows about making bombs doesn't solder-connect those leg wires, is that he's afraid that heat or friction or, or shock could cause an accidental explosion of that detonator. He's going to handle those detonators with a little caution. And he's not going to be playing around with a soldering iron in those cases. I think most bomb technicians would agree with that.*

In the '86 device, however, the maker of this bomb did solder-connect his, his electrical circuit into the wires that lead into the element that causes this bomb to explode. So, there is a different level, a different mindset, if you will, between how these two bombs were put together in that regard." (TT 15-33)

Kline disagreed with Thomas Waskom's view that presence of wires *"twisted, soldered and taped"* made a difference because it's commonly done. Similarly, the use of duct tape was widespread, and the fact that both devices were underneath the body of a car was too common, too. However, according to Alfred Trenkler in 2007, the M21 Hoffman device was not placed underneath the Capeway Fish Market truck. It was placed on the left outside frame of the truck. Thus, there was even less similarity between the two devices than Kline thought. If a car was a target, then many bombs were placed underneath, reasoned Kline. He didn't believe that the fact that round magnets were used in both devices was significant, either. In 1986, the speaker magnet was probably just available. It could have been rectangular or square. The shape of the magnet doesn't make any difference. In other words, it was just a coincidence that the magnets in both the 1986 and 1991 devices were round.

He disagreed that the use of toggle switches in both bombs was significant because they're commonly used, and they were used quite differently in the 1986 Quincy device compared to the 1991 Roslindale Bomb. Similarly, because there were no lamps in any circuit in the 1991 bomb, there was no issue of a signature use of light bulbs.

Denny Kline disagreed with Thomas Waskom's conclusion that the presence of remote control was an issue of signature. Again, Kline said that remote control was so common as to say little about the builder of a device. Of the seven bomb incidents distilled from EXIS, five were not a part of the instant case. Of the remaining five, Kline looked closely at the 1980 attempted bombing of the Cuban Ambassador in New York and an attempted 1980 bombing in Hialeah, Florida. Each of these bombing incidents had common qualities, such as *"underneath vehicle,"* (thus making the same mistake about the 1986 device) and Futaba receivers, but there was no indication that they were made by the same bomber, nor that that they were made by the same bomber as the maker of the 1991 Roslindale Bomb.

Denny Kline conducted the battery longevity test for a Futaba receiver that the defense had asked the prosecution's witnesses, Cynthia Wallace and Thomas Waskom, about earlier in the trial. Kline inserted four AA batteries into a standard, recently purchased Futaba receiver, but later model than in the 1991 bomb, and found on two tests that the four batteries lasted about 22 hours each time. This was an extremely important finding and Kline's words are worth repeating, "*I repeated this test twice. And on both occasions, approximately the same amount of time, 22 hours, was all that these batteries would function or last after that single toggle switch or rather, the slide switch was turned on.*" (TT 15-52)

If the test was accurate, this means that the slide switch on the 1991 Roslindale Bomb must have been turned on, and the Futaba receiver activated, no earlier than 2:00 p.m. on Sunday, which was one hour **after** Thomas L. Shay found the device when moving his Buick back into his driveway. The additional challenge for law enforcement should have been to determine when that slide switch could have been activated and by whom.

Carrying the analysis in a different direction, the batteries would have to have lasted at least 27 and one-half hours for a bomber to have placed the Bomb underneath Mr. Shay's car before he drove on his errands on Sunday morning, 27 October. To place the bomb underneath the car in the dark, before dawn on Sunday morning, it would have to have been done at least four more hours earlier, thus lengthening the longevity requirements for the four AA batteries. This testing would make impossible one of the government's theories that the bomb was attached to the Buick around 8:00 p.m. on Saturday evening, 26 October, which was a full 40 hours before the explosion.

A few years after the trial, Jack Wallace called a salesperson in a Boston-area hobby shop which sold Futaba receivers, to learn more about the receiver and the salesperson said that the ATF had been to his store looking for receipts for Futaba units. After looking up the partial FCC ID code retrieved from the bomb debris, the salesperson told Jack Wallace said that the Futaba receiver in the 1991 Roslindale Bomb, was an older model receiver, as Denny Kline had told Terry Segal back in 1993. What wasn't known, however, was that the older model was an electricity hog, and that it would likely use up the power in the double AA batteries in about two hours. If so, or if even close to that number, the search for the person who armed the bomb on Monday morning would shrink considerably.

It seems extremely unlikely that someone would have come to 39 Eastbourne in broad daylight on a narrow dead end street and reached underneath the Buick while it was parked on the street on Sunday morning 27 October to place the bomb or activate it or both. This question of the timing of the activation of the Roslindale Bomb was very important. After 1 p.m. on Sunday, when Mr. Shay found the bomb in his driveway, the only person who knew its whereabouts for the next 23 hours was Mr. Shay himself. During that period, only Mr. Shay would have been the person to activate the bomb, and the only reasonable intent would have been to make it look like someone was trying to kill him.

Terry Segal sought to introduce into evidence a chart that summarized Denny Kline's comparison of the New York and Hialeah, Florida and 1991 Roslindale Bombs and there was objection. Said Judge Zobel, "*Good try.*" (TT 15-53) He was able to get it entered as Defendant's Exhibit 160 for identification.

Terry Segal tried to ask the question, "*Mr. Kline, from your experience in bombing investigations which led to arrests, what has been the result of searches of the defendant's homes and businesses?*" (TT 15-51) The prosecution's unexplained objection to that question was sustained and Segal had to settle for the already-known fact that there was no physical evidence that linked Trenkler to the 1991 Roslindale

Bomb. Fortunately for Segal and Alfred Trenkler, the answer to his question came in an answer to a convoluted Frank Libby question a few minutes later in the trial.

Terry Segal did not ask Denny Kline about his conclusion in a pre-trial 8 June 1993 affidavit that that *"the use of remote control devices is not considered rare in the United States....In fact, in April, 1980, I was involved in the examination of a radio controlled bomb that utilized Futaba components, a toggle switch as its trigger, a high explosive main charge, and two (2) detonators. The components were mounted on a board and secured with duct tape, black plastic tape and adhesive, and utilized two (2) ring magnets to attach the device to the underside of a vehicle. I have also had the occasion to personally examine and am aware of other cases involving Futaba radio controlled devices."* The jury would have benefited from hearing that remote control devices were not rare and from hearing that Denny Kline had had direct experience investigating a bomb that was far more similar to the 1991 Roslindale bomb with its two detonators and Futaba receiver remote control, than the 1986 M21 Hoffman artillery simulator.

Frank Libby cross-examined Denny Kline and sought to portray Kline as an expert in terrorism by groups or political terrorism, but not individual bombs. He asked, *"Nothing terrorist of any kind involving the Roslindale bombing, true?"* and then, *"No terrorist aim or goal of any kind associated with the 1991 Roslindale Bombing"* and Denny Kline replied, *"Not that I'm aware."* [TT 15-59] It seemed unfair that the prosecution should argue at this point with its question that terrorism was not involved, when it had argued successfully at Alfred Trenkler's arraignment that he was a *"domestic terrorist."* Magistrate Bowler had used that argument in denying bail the previous Christmas Eve and said that she agreed that Alfred Trenkler was a *"domestic terrorist."* Now, at trial , and after achieving its goal of pre-trial incarceration for Alfred Trenkler, the prosecution argued that there was no terrorism.

Libby then asked about Kline's objectivity, *"And you say, sir, that Mr. Trenkler is not your client?"* (TT 15-64) Denny Kline had made the point that he worked for Terry Segal, rather than directly for Alfred Trenkler. Libby then referenced earlier testimony by Denny Kline where he testified that he was working *"on behalf of Mr. Trenkler."* (TT 15-64) which is not the same as a *"client"* relationship. Nonetheless, Libby persuaded Denny Kline to agree that he *"mispoke"* on that issue. This effort by Frank Libby to show bias by the expert seems unfair. Kline was qualified as an expert by the Judge and the prosecution did not object. No one asked the ATF agents or the Boston policemen who their client was. Libby's attack should have been restricted to the quality of Kline's analysis, rather than hammering on claimed bias, and the legal distinction of whether his client was Alfred Trenkler or for his attorney.

The hypocritical side of Libby's attack was that the prosecutors had also tried to retain Denny Kline as their expert, but their communications to him were late by a few days. Their efforts were an indication of how well respected Kline was in the explosives field.

Then Judge Zobel interrupted testimony to say that, after thinking about it, she denied the defense motion to strike portions of Thomas Waskom's testimony.

Denny Kline disagreed with Thomas Waskom's conclusion that the large round magnets from the 1991 Roslindale Bomb were necessarily magnets from an audio speaker. They could have been, but not necessarily.

In response to Frank Libby's question during cross-examination that the 1991 Roslindale Bomb, if detonated, *"would reduce the area of the driver's seat to rubble,"*

Kline gave his opinion on the estimated impact, if detonation were complete, *"It would more than likely penetrate the side of the driver's [sic], where the driver's sitting, throw fragmentation up through there. If the windows were closed, it would probably blow the windows out. Fragments would go through the roof, blow it out. It would produce a significant amount of damage."* He testified that the explosion likely, *"could kill the driver."* (TT 15-72)

Frank Libby went ahead with his question about whether Denny Kline talked with Alfred Trenkler, this way, *"So when you asked Mr. Trenkler, your client, where the 1986 toggle switch was, in this circuit or that circuit, what did he tell you?"* (TT 15-86) Terry Segal objected, but Judge Zobel denied the objection. Then Denny Kline answered that he had not talked with Alfred Trenkler at all, at the request of his lawyer, Terry Segal, in order to ensure that Kline's knowledge about the 1986 device was the same as the prosecutors, and limited to the available reports. Segal persuaded Trenkler that anything that Trenkler would say about the 1986 device would be discounted as biased through self-interest. The difficulty with that strategy, together with the apparent decision that Alfred Trenkler was not going to testify, was that there was no way to present to the jury the details of the actual 1986 device. Libby asked more leading questions about what Alfred Trenkler could likely tell anyone about the 1986 device, but Judge Zobel forbade further inquiry, per the earlier discussion at a bench conference.

Then Frank Libby asked Denny Kline if he violated his confidentiality requirements as an FBI retiree by using FBI documents for his own use as a consultant, whereupon there was an objection and a bench conference. Terry Segal thought it unfair that Frank Libby had originally said he would oppose Kline's discussion of FBI investigations such as the Cuban Ambassador bombing attempt without documentary backup. So Kline pulled documents from his own files at home and brought them. Judge Zobel permitted Frank Libby to continue to try to portray Kline as person who violated federal law to bring those documents to court. Denny Kline said he didn't realize there might be a problem with his use of those documents as he did.

Frank Libby questioned Denny Kline about the identification of the toggle switch, and Kline agreed that the contact points of the Radio Shack 275-602 are *"distinct to that model."* [TT 15-108] Libby continued, *"And you understand, sir, that in this case, there is an absolute match between the toggle switch which was employed in the '91 device and the toggle switch which was depicted on the Radio Shack Receipt?"* [TT 15-108] Denny Kline responded, *"I agreed with the identification that ATF made that the toggle switch used in the '91 bomb was in fact a Radio Shack toggle switch of the same model that I did not speak of."* [TT 15-108]

An important issue for Denny Kline was that no physical evidence was found which would link Alfred Trenkler to the 1991 Roslindale Bomb. He said, *"I would submit to you that in almost every case that I've investigated, whether it be a terrorist group or an individual bombing, when we have reconstructed the bomb, whether it be an attempted bombing or it be an actual bombing, and conducted searches in connection with that bombing investigation, in every case that I have personally been involved in, physical evidence was collected and identified and helped us to establish that that individual was in fact the bomb maker of those bombings."* (TT 15-111) The conviction of Alfred Trenkler was to be the first exception to Kline's experience.

This was a point that should have been more helpful to Alfred Trenkler, but it wasn't exploited. The defense said nothing in the trial about the fact that none of the fingerprints on Mr. Shay's car belonged to Alfred Trenkler. Unfortunately, there was no testimony about any of those fingerprints, especially those underneath the car, and Alfred Trenkler did not even know about the existence of the unidentified 17 prints until long after the trial. The defense did not emphasize enough that the electronic sniffer found no evidence of dynamite at any of the Trenkler search locations. Kline's point went beyond such absence of evidence, in that for cases involving explosives, it was more unusual than in other types of cases not to find such physical evidence in the cases where the actual perpetrator was found and convicted. The reason was that the chemical traces of explosives are very powerful and easy to trace, if they are present at all. Again, Kline said, "*in* **every** *case that I have personally been involved in, physical evidence was collected and identified and helped us to establish that that individual was in fact the bomb maker of those bombings.*" (TT 15-111) [emphasis added]

Seeing that Kline's answer was, or could have been very helpful to Alfred Trenkler, Frank Libby asked whether that answer to a difficult and complicated question with tiers of assumptions, "*was not responsive to my question was it?*" Mr. Segal objected and Judge Zobel permitted Libby to ask the question, and Denny Kline said he believed his answer was responsive. Then Frank Libby asked more provocatively, "*Did you intend that answer to benefit anyone, sir?*" Terry Segal objected again, and the Court sustained his objection. (TT 15-111)

Frank Libby finally challenged Kline's credibility once more by waving his $200/hr fee to the jury and establishing that Kline had already billed the defense $10,000 and would bill more. No one asked how much the ATF agents were paid, nor the Boston Police officers, nor how much it was costing the taxpayers to pay for underwater robots to search for bomb debris in a Quincy quarry or to take a boat to search the ocean.

Frank Libby did not cross-examine Denny Kline on his key finding that the four AA batteries would have lasted only about 22 hours once the fusing circuit was activated. That would come with the prosecution's rebuttal case.

Mr. Segal asked that the defense mockup of the 1986 device be treated the same way in evidence as the prosecution's mockup of the 1991 device.

The next defense witness was William McNamara who was examined by Scott Lopez. McNamara was Manager of video transmission services at the Christian Science Church in 1991 and thus worked with Alfred Trenkler on the installation of antenna dishes. The church wanted to connect its Norway Street building to its Soldiers Field Road facility and to the Videocomm facility in Dedham by microwave transmission, and to replace its use of the existing fiberoptic cable. They could own the antenna dishes whereas the fiberoptic cable was leased. Paul Kelly and then the judge did not want extensive questioning on why the antenna dishes were placed on Christian Science roof, as it was enough to know that the work was deemed necessary.

The work had come to Alfred Trenkler and ARCOMM because Bill McNamara had called Frank Cavallo at Videocom to get a recommended installer for the dishes, and Cavallo recommended Alfred Trenkler. McNamara decided to contract the work to ARCOMM in July 1991. That work was done to McNamara's satisfaction, and he talked with Alfred Trenkler about more installations that would have grossed approximately $150-200,000 for ARCOMM.

Paul Kelly said the prosecution had no questions, and Mr. McNamara was excused. The government did not want to spend any more time with a witness who appeared to contradict a major part of the case against Trenkler, that he was running a failing business and built the bomb in the expectation of getting a share of the inheritance from the still-in-litigation lawsuit by Mr. Thomas L. Shay against Ber-Giam, Inc. Alfred Trenkler recalls that Paul Kelly made an aside comment around that time about the *"fancy shmancey microwave project that Trenkler was building."*

The trial was adjourned at 12:54 p.m.

Next day's headlines:

Boston Globe: *"EX-AGENT: BOMB UNLIKE EARLIER TRENKLER WORK"* by Paul
  Langer The article stated, *"With seven members of the Boston bomb squad
  sitting in the spectator section and glowering at Kline yesterday, the former FBI
  bomb specialist said... Shay has refused to testify in Trenkler's trial, but the
  federal court jury has been shown a tape of a television interview in which Shay
  admits he bought a toggle switch, similar to one believed to have been used on
  the fatal bomb, for Trenkler."*

Boston Herald: *"EXPERT DOUBTS LINK BETWEEN '86 & '91 DEADLY EXPLOSIVES"*
  by Ralph Ranalli. The article begins, *" A defense bomb expert testified
  yesterday that there is not enough evidence to conclusively link a 1986 explosive
  device built by Alfred Trenkler of Milton and a 1991 bomb that killed a Boston
  Police bomb squad officer in Roslindale.*

  *But federal prosecutors hit the testimony of former FBI bomb expert Dennis Kline,
  suggesting his analysis was more appropriate to terrorist attacks than domestic
  bombings like the one Trenkler is accused of masterminding."*

25 26 27 28 29	1 2 3 4 5	8 9 10 12	15 16	22 23 24	29
X X X X X	X X X X X	X X X X	X X	O O O	O

Day 16: Tuesday, 16 November

Josephine Wallace, mother of Alfred Trenkler was the last witness for the defense. Before her testimony, Brenda Sharton read to the jury a stipulation agreed by the parties, *"In October of 1991, the total number of passenger vehicles registered in the Commonwealth of Massachusetts was 4,174,756. Of those registered vehicles approximately 2,100,000 had license plates which consisted of three numbers followed by three letters."* (TT 16-2) This stipulation seemed to dilute the impact of James McKernan's testimony that the license plate of the unknown car he saw on Eastbourne Street on Monday morning, 28 October, had a three-number-three-letter license plate. Ruth Leary's Mazda also had a license number with the same pattern.

Examined by Brenda Sharton, Josephine Wallace said she was a real estate broker and before that she was a professional ice skater, after having won a national ice skating championship.

She said that she had never met Tom Shay, nor had he ever called their home. She said that Alfred had never stayed overnight during 1991, but she was not questioned about the years 1989 and 1990. That would have been helpful to challenge Edward Carrion's testimony that he brought Tom Shay to the Wallace's home 3-4 times. Josephine Wallace could have been asked if anyone ever came to the home to visit with Alfred. She could have been asked if Alfred ever brought anyone to the home in the years 1989-1991, and did any such people stay overnight?

Mrs. Wallace was not asked about Alfred's facial hair, i.e. the presence or absence of a mustache. She would have stated the he didn't have a mustache since a short-lived effort in the 1970's. She was probably the best opportunity, short of Alfred's own testimony, to thwart the testimony by Edward Carrion, but the defense didn't seek to present those truths to the jury.

On cross-examination, Paul Kelly asked whom among Alfred's friends Josephine Wallace had met. She had known Brian O'Leary and Richard Brown, but wasn't sure if she had met Robert Craig, Alfred's former roommate. She had never met Michael Coady or Todd Leach. Paul Kelly's last question was whether Alfred had ever seved in the "United States military," and his mother responded that he had not. It's not known why he asked that question, but it seemed likely intended to discredit Alfred before the jury.

Brenda Sharton had no questions on redirect, but she might have continued Paul Kelly's strand of questioning and confirmed that Mrs. Wallace had never met Edward Carrion, nor heard his name. The defense did not exploit that question and answer to Mrs. Wallace about Alfred's non-service in the military, with the observation that Alfred could not therefore have learned any techniques in the military about how to build bombs, including the idea to attach multiple detonators to multiple sticks of dynamite. Mrs. Wallace was then excused.

The defense rested. Now gone was Alfred's chance to speak for himself before the jury. He would be stuck with the picture of him as conveyed by others, and it wasn't a nice picture. Whether by design or unintentionally, the jury did not know, for example that Alfred Trenkler had volunteered to take a lie detector test before his lawyer at the time persuaded him not to do so. Nancy Gertner was able to tell the Shay jury that Tom Shay had made such an offer, so Trenkler should have been able to do so, too. The jurors probably wondered during the trial how the man in the suit at the defendant's table could be as monstrous a person as had been pictured by the prosecution and its witnesses, but if he, Trenkler, was not willing to speak for himself and not willing or able to counter what others said. Then what was the jury to believe?

In rebuttal, the prosecution called two witnesses. The first was ATF agent Thomas D'Ambrosio who had "*been sitting in the back of the courtroom throughout the trial, with other agents and members of the Hurley and Foley families,...*" Kelly did not ask how much that was costing the Government. (TT 16-12)

On Friday 29 October, and before the testimony of Roderick Kennedy, but probably after the prosecution knew that a driving time test had been done, D'Ambrosio and ATF Agent Dennis Leahy tested the driving time from the ARCOMM offices in Weymouth to 197 Mass Ave. in Boston. D'Ambrosio took the shorter route and the trip took 18 minutes and 20 seconds, and Dennis Leahy took a longer route and it took 20 minutes and 12 seconds. As he had testified earlier in the trial, Roderick Kennedy's average time was 24 minutes.

Under cross-examination by Terry Segal, D'Ambrisio was asked how many miles was his route, and he didn't know. Terry Segal suggested 14 miles, and retraced with D'Ambrosio his route. Unfortunately, he didn't do the math, as 14 miles in 18.33 minutes would have meant an average speed of 45 miles per hour which sounds high considering the traffic light stops. However, D'Ambrosio also testified that Agent Dennis Leahy traveled a longer route and it still took less time than Roderick Kennedy. But consider the probabilities, of why Alfred Trenkler would rush from the ARCOMM office in Weymouth to a Radio Shack in downtown Boston on a Friday afternoon to purchase the only item which was claimed to be in the 1991 Roslindale Bomb - a Radio Shack #275-602 toggle switch. And to meet with Tom Shay in the process and give him a list? It was an unlikely scenario. Also, Alfred Trenkler didn't need to purchase a toggle switch, as he already had several in his collection of parts and tools, but that important point was never presented to the jury.

On redirect, Paul Kelly quarreled with Terry Segal about Segal's asking more questions of Thomas D'Ambrosio about his route than he asked Roderick Kennedy about his route. It brought a few light moments when the examination and cross-examination in the U.S. District Court descended to questions and answers about stop signs and traffic lights, but it did not match the required dignity of the courtroom and the trial process and the seriousness of the instant case.

If a similar question of the driving time from Point A to Point B were to arise in another case today, the courts might resort to MapQuest on the Internet, if it could be qualified as a reliable resource. MapQuest in 2007 calculated the ARCOMM/Radio Shack distance as 15.86 miles, including the 12.6 mile leg of the Southeast Expressway, which would take a law abiding driver 24 minutes. The route recommended by the computer appeared to be the same as taken by ATF Agent D'Ambrosio.

The second and last Government rebuttal witness was Albert Gleason, a consultant in explosives, who worked for ATF until 1986. Prior to his testimony, the defense objected because it wasn't in the nature of rebuttal evidence. Judge Zobel then convened a bench conference to determine the planned content of Gleason's testimony, and explained to the jury, "*Members of the jury, when counsel offers rebuttal evidence, what they are entitled to do is to cover issues that the defense raised that weren't properly part of the case in chief. I mean, for example, this business about the mileage. That was something that came up in the course of the defense. It is appropriate for the government to offer rebuttal. I wish to see counsel to find out whether this* [Mr. Gleason's testimony] *is proper rebuttal or whether they should have done it as part of their case in chief.* " (TT 16-33)

The prosecution argued that Denny Kline brought the issue of terrorist bombs into the case and as that was new, the prosecution should be able to have a rebuttal witness. Most of the discussion was between Judge Zobel and the Asst. U.S. Attorneys. Said Judge Zobel, "*I don't understand it to be new defense evidence. The defendant called an expert and gave an opinion. You tried to shake that opinion, you being the government, on the grounds that this guy's expertise is in terrorist bombs, not in ordinary bombings. And now, you want to put on an additional expert to say that ordinary bombs are different from terrorists' bombs. But you were the one who raised it in cross-examination; they didn't raise it.*" (TT 16-45) The issue at the bench was one fairness in the game rather than whether any additional truth or facts might emerge which might be helpful to the jury. The issue was also ironic, as the prosecution had labeled Alfred Trenkler as a "domestic terrorist" before the trial.

Judge Zobel did permit Mr. Gleason to testify on the life-of-batteries issue as that was new, although the defense had asked prosecution witnesses Cynthia Wallace and Thomas Waskom about conducting such a test early in the trial.

Albert Gleason maintained that Denny Kline's battery test was invalid because the act of testing drained the batteries more than would have been the case if the device had been left alone. Without the testing, he was asked if the batteries would have lasted longer, and he responded, "*Mostly likely certainly would, yes.*" (TT 16-50)

Terry Segal's cross-examination tried to show Gleason's bias by noting that he was a former ATF agent until 1986 and that he was being paid $62.50 an hour and had spent many hours on the case. Segal didn't focus on the merits of Gleason's analysis, just as Frank Libby did not when cross-examining Denny Kline. The life-of-batteries issue could have been extremely important and it's unfortunate that more analysis could not have been done by the defense and by the prosecution before the trial. If it had been done ten times, using a procedure which perhaps Albert Gleason and Denny Kline could agree on, wouldn't that make a difference?

Thomas L. Shay found the device at 1:00 p.m, Sunday, 27 October which was 23 hours before detonation. He returned from his Sunday morning travels at approximately 11:30 a.m. which was 24.5 hours before detonation and left for those travels at 8:30 a.m. which was 27.5 hours before detonation. Suppose, for example, the average of those ten trial runs of the batteries had been 22 hours, 26 or 30 or even 36 or more. If the battery life had been as long as 40 hours, then the Government's theory of an 8 p.m. placement in the South End Saturday night would have been possible. Most of those results would have led to different conclusions about when the bomb could have been placed under Mr. Shay's car or when, if at all, the slide switch could have been turned on. It would seem unlikely for a person to place the Roslindale Bomb underneath Mr. Shay's car earlier in the weekend and then return to flip "on" the slide switch to turn on the Futaba receiver, all before 1:00 p.m. Sunday.

In other situations, such as the building of a house, or development of a new business, when it's discovered that more information is needed in order to solve a critical problem, there may be a halt to construction or some other development to ensure that the problem is solved. However, in a criminal trial, the clock is inexorable. The trial must go on, even if there is substantial risk of a verdict flawed by lack of information or truth. In the words of Tom Shay, there are times when one wishes one "*could turn back the hands of time....*" (TS 9-88) and wait for the necessary information.

Upon the end of Albert Gleason's testimony, the evidence portion of the trial ended on that Tuesday, 16 November and the jury was dismissed until the following Monday, 22 November.

Then the lawyers and the Judge discussed the final steps. Terry Segal had filed a motion to acquit Alfred Trenkler. Starting with Count 2, he said, "*there is absolutely no evidence in this case from which a reasonable jury looking at this evidence in the light most favorable to the government can conclude Mr. Trenkler received any dynamite.*" (TT 16-52) Judge Zobel responded, "*I don't think that's entirely true. If the jury, if the jury believes, for example, Mr. Lindholm's testimony, then they can infer from that that he must have received the dynamite. You can't very well build a bomb without dynamite....*" (TT 16-52) It was an interesting example for Judge Zobel to use for she knew what the jury likely did not know, which was that inmate informers were notoriously unreliable and that they would say almost anything to reduce their sentences. In the years since the trial, it's been shown that jailhouse snitches were used to convict many of the two hundred-plus inmates exonerated by DNA evidence.

Segal responded to Judge Zobel's dynamite comments, "*All right*" and challenged the conspiracy evidence, and Judge Zobel returned, "*Same thing on conspiracy.*" (TT 16-52) And later, "*a reasonable jury can determine that there is evidence beyond a reasonable doubt, I believe, on every one of the three counts."* (TT 16-52) Thus, the motion was denied.

Then there was discussion about the judge's charge to the jury with the major question being how would this charge differ from her charge to the Shay trial jury. They agreed to submit proposed sections to her on Monday morning at 8:30 and also that the main closing arguments would be an hour, and the Government's rebuttal fifteen minutes. The trial adjourned at 10:26 a.m.

Next day's headlines:

Boston Globe: "JUDGE DENIES TRENKLER MOTION" no byline.

Boston Herald: "REGIONAL: SIDES REST IN FATAL BOMBING" no byline. "...But U.S. District Judge Rya W. Zobel severely limited the testimony of Florida-based expert Albert Gleason. Gleason said that only one of Kline's tests on a mock-up of the bomb was 'neither valid nor scientific.'

Closing arguments in the case are scheduled for Monday because Zobel must attend a judicial conference."

25 26 27 28 29	1 2 3 4 5	8 9 10 12	15 16	22 23 24	29
X X X X X	X X X X X	X X X	X X	X O O	O

Day 17: Monday, 22 November

Before the discussion of proposed instructions to the jury, Judge Zobel noted that Alfred Trenkler was not in the courtroom, as was his right, but Terry Segal waived that right and they proceeded with the bench conference. The defendant had the right to be present at all the discussions among lawyers, including bench conferences, but he didn't realize that.

Scott Lopez presented draft charges for the jury on four issues and the first was the use the jury could make of the knowledge that Alfred Trenkler built the 1986 Quincy device. Judge Zobel noted, *"I must say... it strikes me as somewhat unusual for somebody to build a bomb to cause harm to a third person in order to vindicate the rights of a friend."* (TT 17-6) While she was surely talking about the 1986 device, the same reasoning applied even more so to the 1991 Roslindale Bomb as there was no harm to any person intended in 1986.

An initial question for the jury, Judge Zobel stated, was whether they would believe Thomas Waskom's testimony that the 1986 device and the 1991 Roslindale Bomb were made by the same person. Amidst the argument, she returned to the nuts and bolts of the discussion, *"The question is: What shall I tell [the] jury?"* (TT 17-7) She addressed Frank Libby, *"Just answer my question: If there is no signature, if the jury disbelieves Mr. Waskom, then how can -- what should I tell them? I mean, I think it's a two-step process. No. 1, is there signature? If not -- I mean , if yes, it's easy, if not, then how can the jury use the 1986? You say knowledge of electronics and bomb building. What else?"* (TT 17-8) Other proposed instructions covered the issue of circumstantial evidence and the problem of guilt by association. The discussion moved to what to say about Thomas A. Shay's conviction, and the lawyers seemed content with what Judge Zobel said at the trial's opening: that he was convicted on some of the charges. There had been no suggestion during Alfred's trial that the conviction of Tom Shay was a mistake. In 1993, in the early days of DNA exonerations, the concept of wrongful convictions was still remote, and comfined to the State courts.

The jury entered, and Frank Libby began the Government's closing argument by reviewing the horror of the explosion and then, "...*you've heard that some months later, it was one man's opinion that these officers on that day were foolish, negligent, that it served them right what happened to them. Those words, ladies and gentlemen, as you've learned were the words of this man, the defendant, Alfred Trenkler, one of two men charged in the indictment before you.*" (TT 17-20) Hearing that statement must have made Alfred Trenkler sick and already made him realize that he had made a terrible mistake to take the strong advice of his attorney not to testify.

Frank Libby put himself in the role of the the Bomb Maker, "*He's tested his circuitry, ladies and gentlemen, with a test bulb. And when it's ready, all I've got to do is move this slide switch and it's ready for action.*" (TT 17-26) However, there was no evidence in the case of the use of a light bulb, but it was Libby's way of bringing a second item, of the six purchased, from the 18 October 1991 Radio Shack purchase. Sure, a light bulb could have been used to test the circuits, but there was no evidence to say that it was.

Then Libby reviewed the life of Tom Shay and said it was "*beyond dispute*" that he hated his father, and made many statements about his role; and he was convicted in this same consipiracy. Libby made the connection that may have not been made before for the jury, which was that the 18 October Radio Shack purchase occurred on the same day as the angry confrontation with Ed Carrion at Carrion's apartment. Guilt by coincidence. Libby reminded the jurors, "*You'll also recall, interestingly, that Mr. Carrion testified to Shay, Jr.'s interest in body building magazines.*" (17-33) Is there something wrong with being interested in body building and therefore in body building magazines? Guilt by coincidence. Libby reviewed extensively the evidence against Tom Shay - but this was the trial of Alfred W. Trenkler.

When returning to Trenkler, Libby said "*He lived in the basement apartment with John Cates. You recall the illegal basement apartment in Quincy.*" (TT 17-36) It was as if living in a basement apartment which a landlord had not properly registered made someone more likely to seek to kill another person, but that was the Asst. U.S. attorney's apparent argument.

Libby reviewed the unchallenged testimony of Todd Leach about the speaker magnet and the Radio Shack purchase; and the testimony of Michael Coady, also unchallenged.

Libby reviewed the evidence from several sources that Alfred Trenkler had known Tom Shay for about two years, and not merely since June 1991 as Trenkler had claimed, through the testimony of John Cates and Dennis Leahy. Again, Alfred Trenkler must have wanted to jump up from his chair and give the jury the truth.

Frank Libby replayed the videotape of Tom Shay describing to Karen Marinella his purchase at Radio Shack, and then repeated David Lindholm's unchallenged statement that Alfred Trenkler had said that making a purchase so close to his work site was "*regrettable.*" (TT 17-50) The jury was reminded of the rest of Lindholm's incriminating testimony, too.

In closing, Libby made his final appeal to emotion rather than reason, though he clothed it in terms of "*truth.*" He said, "*... there are two fundamental truths in this case. One is that two families have suffered grievous losses, and the City of Boston lost the valuable, invaluable services of two highly skilled bomb technicians. The second is there can be no fault associated with these two dedicated brave men.*" (TT 17- 54) Of course, the defense could agree to those same two truths, but those two truths had nothing to do with the guilt or innocence of Alfred W. Trenkler.

Terry Segal began his closing statement by noting the observation of the defense expert, Denny Kline, that the police always found physical evidence in the homes and workplaces of guilty bombers - and there was none found in this case. Then he said what needed to be said, "*Al Trenkler is an innocent man, ladies and gentlemen. I said that in the opening a month ago, and I submit to you nothing in this last month has changed that.*" (TT 17-57)

He reviewed the problems with the Government's "*four or five attempts*" to fill in the gaps left by the absence of physical evidence, "*the so-called 1991 diagram, Agent Leahy's interviews, Mr. Lindholm, Mr. Waskom's attempt to make the signature identification comparing '86 and '91 and the EXIS computer.*" (TT 17-58) Of those, Segal said that Trenkler simply never drew a diagram of the 1991 bomb. Regarding Trenkler's visit to the ATF office to retrieve business documents on 4 February, Alfred Trenkler offered to "*wear a wire to talk to Mr. Shay for you?*" (TT 17-63) Was that an offer from a guilty man?

Terry Segal addressed one of the primary obstacles to a not guilty finding, "*Enter Mr. Lindholm. I submit to you, ladies and gentlemen, his testimony is inherently unreliable and not worthy of belief.*" (TT 17-64) Unfortunately, Segal had not already completed the information checks on Lindholm's father which indicated that he attended neither Milton Academy nor Thayer Academy and probably not Brown University either. Lindholm had lied to Alfred Trenkler about his father and lied to the court as well. An alternative explanation is that Lindholm's father had lied to him. Either way, it all made for an extraordinary coincidence in the Plymouth County House of Correction to have two men with connections to Milton, Massachusetts, Milton Academy and Thayer Academy. It was an odd instance of Lindholm's overkill, as the coincidence of the residence in Milton would have been enough to "bond" the two men.

Calling Lindholm a "*three day wonder*" for having met Tom Shay and Alfred W. Trenkler over three days, Segal noted that Lindholm said to the jury that the only way to get your sentence reduced, after one year from conviction was to supply new information to the government. That's what Lindholm was doing for the government's drug cases until he found Alfred Trenkler. Then Segal made a prediction, contrary to Lindholm's statement to the jury that he would not seek any benefit in return for his testimony. Said Segal, "*Imagine if you're Mr. Kelly, though, sitting at your office one day soon, you get a phone call, this is Mr. Lindholm, do you remember me? I'm the fellow who was rehabilitated after about a year, I provided some new information, I want you now to reduce that sentence.*" (TT 17-67) Four months later, Lindholm's lawyer did exactly as Segal predicted, and wrote a letter to Paul Kelly asking for help in reducing Lindholm's sentence; and Paul Kelly provided that help.

Terry Segal pulled apart Thomas Waskom's theory of a common signature between the 1986 M21 Hoffman device and the 1991 Roslindale Bomb, both on common sense grounds and relying upon Denny Kline.

Segal then addressed the motives that Paul Kelly claimed in his opening statement, "*..friendship, sexual friendship and financial...*" (TT 17-72) But there was no evidence of either motive entered into the case.

Segal said the EXIS system was designed to assist in investigations, not to find signatures among bombmakers. He said the Scheid queries were biased and manipulated, as, for example, the "*under vehicle*" criterion, which was not on the official reports about the 1986 incident. It would have been helpful, of course, if Terry Segal could have referred to Alfred Trenkler's testimony that the 1986 device was not placed underneath the Capeway Fish truck at all, but along the left side.

Referring to Denny Kline's test of the four AA batteries showing a probably power supply for 22 hours, Segal said that "*the government's theory in the case is that this device was put on the automobile on Saturday night, 40 hours before it detonated. Do you honestly believe those batteries lasted 40 hours?*" (TT 17-46)

Regarding Tom Shay, Segal said, "*I suggest Mr. Libby in his closing statement did an excellent job implicating Shay, Jr., and a terrible job implicating my client.*" (TT 17-76) Segal argued that Tom Shay was guilty, and "*there is no evidence that Al Trenkler helped him in any way. It's one thing to know another person, it's another to go around building a bomb for another person.*" (TT 17-77)

Segal apparently conceded that Alfred Trenkler knew Tom Shay before June 1991, saying, "*The government's evidence shows Al Trenkler knew Tom Shay, Jr. before 1991.*" (TT 17-77) but he tried to minimize the period length of the relationship. Perhaps he thought it was too much to try to deny more of the government's evidence, but Alfred Trenkler told Terry Segal and his team that he first met Tom Shay in June, 1991. Period.

Terry Segal asked the jury to "*Look at the address book. There are stars next to certain names of real good friends. See if Mr. Trenkler has a star in that book.*" (TT 17-77) He didn't. This seemed to be an excellent point, but it wasn't explained to the jury during the trial. Even if Tom Shay didn't testify, someone else could have testified who knew Shay well enough to confirm that the starred names were his better friends. In fact, Tom Shay put his rating system in the first page of his address book. "*Star is the best. Circle is Great. Squaring Good Friend. Plus Sign is Good.*" Al Trenkler did not have a circle, or a square or a plus sign. Another indication about how Tom Shay used his address book is that the next name after Al Trenkler, was Alan Pransky and his father was under "*D*" for "*Dad Shay*" Of the 31 names in his book, one had a circle, one had a square and two had plus signs and none had a star. Shay's use of his address book was another good reason to firmly request Tom Shay's testimony at Alfred's trial.

Then Terry Segal reviewed the defense's case, and noted that Denny Kline had a large amount of experience and mostly worked for the prosecutors. The Trenkler case was only his second case working for a defendant. Kline had testified in 15 signature cases and for Thomas Waskom, this was the first.

Segal said that the Government didn't make a mockup of the 1986 device because it was so different from the 1991 Roslindale Bomb, and indeed it was.

Segal did not allow Denny Kline to talk with Al Trenkler about the construction of the device, because if he had, the Government would have attacked it and said that it was self serving. Perhaps though there was a way around that problem, again knowing that hindsight is 20/20. Alfred Trenkler had already drawn a diagram of the 1986 device, so it wasn't as if drawing another one would have incriminated him. It was acknowledged that he did it. Perhaps Kline could have been commissioned to create a mockup without input from Alfred Trenkler and have Alfred do another diagram and also do a verbal description and then compare them. Perhaps that work could have been done under the watchful eye of an independent person.

Terry Segal effectively noted that the 2:36 p.m. time of the Radio Shack receipt meant that Tom Shay, if it was Tom Shay, entered the store around 2:12, because he took five minutes before Mr. Armbrister talked with him, and another 15 minutes before coming to the counter with his items and then four minutes to total up the transaction, for a total of 24 minutes. There was no way that Alfred Trenkler could have driven to Boston to get there by 2:12, as he was with his accountant in Weymouth until 2:00 or 2:15 or 2:30.

Segal described Alfred's alibi evidence for 18 October and for the weekend of 25-27 October and for Monday 28 October. He could not have been purchasing parts for a bomb, nor planting a bomb nor lying-in-wait to transmit a deadly "detonate" signal during those periods.

Regarding the Government's claimed financial motive for Alfred Trenkler, Segal noted that the completed Christian Science project and the anticipated projects would have brought in over $100,000 from that one customer alone.

Near the end Segal said, "*Ladies and gentlemen, the government has the burden of proof. They must prove this beyond a reasonable doubt, not beyond a reasonable suspicion, a reasonable speculation, a reasonable association, because I submit that's what this case is, guilt by association.*

He knew Shay, he was [allegedly] *gay, he was involved in '86, he worked near Radio Shack, he had a small car, he knew this fellow Coady ten years ago.*" (TT 17-86) That was the only mention of Michael Coady's testimony, which was damaging as it was unanswered by Alfred Trenkler.

Terry Segal completed his statement by noting the inscription inside the U.S. Justice Dept. building: "*The United States always wins when justice is done to its citizens.*" (TT 17-88) He concluded, "*I respectfully submit, ladies and gentlemen, when you return a verdict of not guilty in this case, you will be doing justice.*" (TT 17-88)

Paul Kelly then gave the Government's rebuttal closing statement. There was no physical evidence found of Trenkler's involvement because he was very clever. By implication, therefore, Kelly was saying that all the other people who Denny Kline described as having a physical connection to their bombs were not very smart.

Kelly said that Trenkler DID draw his idea of what the 1991 bomb would look like, and to think otherwise is to accuse the veteran agents of perjury.

Paul Kelly said that Terry Segal admitted, in his opening statement, that the Radio Shack toggle switch purchased on 18 October "*was inside the bomb.*" (TT 17-91] It was true that Terry Segal stated "*That's not in dispute that that toggle switch was purchased and the same number matched the bomb debris.*" (TT 2-36) However, that mistake does not make it true. There was simply no evidence that the toggle switch contacts which were found at 39 Eastbourne Street came from the toggle switch purchased on 18 October 1991.

Kelly noted that the Government never claimed that Trenkler was at the Radio Shack when Tom Shay purchased the parts, and thus, Segal's efforts to show an alibi were a "*smoke screen.*" (TT 17-92) That was a shade disingenuous as the Government worked hard to show a *modus operandi* that Trenkler had others make his bomb-related purchases for him. The use of Todd Leach's allegation of being sent into a Radio Shack store was one reason that Judge Zobel permitted the introduction of all the 1986 incident evidence, because it showed a pattern.

Regarding the placement of the bomb underneath Mr. Shay's car, Kelly said, "... *the most reasonable inference is that it was attached sometime between 6 o'clock on Saturday night the 26th and probably 6 o'clock the next morning.*" but Kelly discounted Alfred Trenkler's alibi of being with friends at a dinner party. "*Ah, the Dorchester dinner party. How convenient.*" (TT 17-92)

Kelly addressed the credibility of two individuals: David Lindholm and Denny Kline, an interesting combination. Kelly repeated Lindholm's promise (to be broken four months later) that "*He's received no promises, no rewards, no inducements for coming forward, and he will not ask for any in the future.*" (TT 17-93) Kelly noted that there is corroboration for part of Lindholm's story. For example, he did know where Alfred Trenkler went to school. However, it's a rare lie that isn't wrapped together with some truth. In this case it was wrapped in newspapers, as Lindholm could have easily read the biographical information about Alfred Trenkler from the newspapers.

Then Kelly attacked Denny Kline for his using government documents while doing his own $200/hour consulting work. Also, Kelly claimed that Kline's expertise was with terrorists' bombs and not individual bombs. That was another disingenuous distinction to make as Paul Kelly had called Alfred Trenkler a "*domestic terrorist*" at his 18 December 1992 bail hearing. Finally, he noted that Terry Segal had warned the jury against finding "*guilt by association,*" and then essentially asked the jury to do just that, "*Now that this is over, ladies and gentlemen, what associations of the defendant have we learned about?*" (TT 17-98) He said they included Tom Shay and Michael Coady, and the purchase of a $4-5,000 car for him. And the association with David Lindholm which Kelly said was "*one that I'm sure he regrets.*" (TT 17-99) On that latter point, he and Alfred Trenkler would be in total agreement, but for different reasons. The jury then left the courtroom for a brief recess and returned for the judge's instructions or charge.

Judge Zobel reminded the jurors that she was "*the judge of the law, but you are the judges of the facts.*" (TT 17-101) And that no higher court would be overruling them on the facts.

She explained the types of evidence and the types of witnesses and how to evaluate the reliability and credibility of evidence.

She continued, "*And finally, consider all the evidence. Draw reasonable inferences. But do not guess. Do not speculate. That you may not do. And I urge you to use your common sense as you go about sifting the evidence in reaching your verdict.*" (TT 17-109) She explained that the opening and closing statements of the attorneys were not evidence.

Regarding the defendant's rights, she said, "*A defendant in a criminal case is presumed to be innocent, which means really much more than that, it means that the defendant is innocent. He is innocent until the government proves him guilty. And that means that a defendant does not have to prove his innocence, he does not have to offer any evidence whatsoever, he does not have to take the stand and testify in the trial. And you may draw no inference of guilt from the fact that this defendant did not testify. He did offer evidence, and the evidence is before you, and it should be considered by you in reaching your verdict. But there are many reasons why a defendant might choose not to testify, including, very simply, that he can just say to the government: You, Government, have accused me. Now, you, Government, prove my guilt.*"

But you may draw no inference of guilt from the fact that this defendant chose not to testify in this case.

Now, the government has to prove him guilty beyond a reasonable doubt. Proof beyond a reasonable doubt is not, is not, proof beyond all possible doubt. It is not proof to a mathematical certainty. Proof beyond a reasonable doubt is proof that leaves you firmly convinced of the defendant's guilt...It is doubt based on reason and common sense....It's not sufficient for the government to establish a probability, even a strong one, that the defendant is guilty....If you view the evidence in this case as reasonably leading to one of two conclusions, either that the defendant is guilty or that the defendant is not guilty, then you cannot convict. You must find the defendant not guilty." (TT 17-113)

Judge Zobel reminded the jurors of what she said in the beginning about Tom Shay, that *"he was convicted on some but not all of the counts,"* and that the jury should ignore that conviction when considering the evidence in the Alfred Trenkler trial. (TT 17-115) That was probably a request the jury found hard to abide just as it was likely hard to avoid drawing inferences about Alfred Trenkler's decision not to testify.

Regarding the conspiracy count, she said that the Government *"does have to prove that there was some agreement between Mr. Shay and Mr. Trenkler to achieve the object of the conspiracy as set forth in the indictment."* (TT 17-126)

She concluded and the prosecution and defense were satisfied with the charge and the trial was adjourned for the day at 12:45 p.m.

Next day's headlines:

Boston Globe: "TRENKLER JURY HEARS CLOSING ARGUMENTS" by Matthew Brelis The article began, *"Alfred W. Trenkler was a cold, calculating engineer who used his knowledge and skill to build a bomb for his occasional lover Thomas A. Shay, federal prosecutors said yesterday in closing arguments in U.S. District Court.*

Boston Herald:" JURY HEARS CLOSING ARGUMENT IN CASE AGAINST ALLEGED FATAL BOMBER" by Ralph Ranalli. Excerpts from the article: *"Federal prosecutors called accused bomber Alfred Trenkler a 'cunning' but 'cowardly' killer yesterday, but his defense attorney insisted his client was an innocent man caught up in the rush to find a police officer's murderer....Trenkler is charged with masterminding the Oct. 28, 1991, bombing ... as a favor to friend and lover Thomas A. Shay, the man's son. Libby said the government had proved its case against Trenkler by showing that he had a history of building bombs and doing favors for younger lovers. 'His string of relationships with younger males give you an insight into his later deadly relationship with Thomas Shay,' Libby said."* This was a quote from Libby's closing statement in the courtroom.

25 26 27 28 29	1 2 3 4 5	8 9 10 12	15 16	22 23 24	29
X X X X X	X X X X X	X X X X	X X	X X O	O

Day 18: Tuesday, 23 November

The day began with Mr. Segal waiving Alfred Trenkler's right to be present when the judge sent the jury off to its deliberations, whereupon the jury entered the courtroom and was then dispatched to its work. Terry Segal said to the judge, *"In future sessions, I would like the defendant here, if possible."* (TT 18-2) And Judge Zobel agreed, but said that she had hoped Segal would waive Trenkler's right this morning so she could get the jury started. One logistical problem was that Trenkler could not be brought into the courtroom until all the jurors were in the courthouse, so as to avoid a chance meeting in the hallways or elevator. The intended effect of such a practice is to prevent any close human contact between a defendant and jurors, and this practice worked double damage to Alfred Trenkler because of his decision not to testify.

At 10:35, the jury sent a request to the judge for a copy of Quincy Detective Lanergan's notes from his conversation with Mr. Trenkler, but Terry Segal objected to sending them. The notes had not been entered into evidence and were only used to refresh Lanergan's recollection while on the stand. Judge Zobel agreed to not send them, and to simply tell the jury that they were not in evidence. The request was an indication of the jury's interest in Trenkler's attitude and response to law enforcement - and Trenkler, and Terry Segal, too, must have again wondered if the decision not to testify was the correct choice.

As already promised to the jury, Judge Zobel did send them a copy of her charge.

The jury indicated that it would be ceasing its deliberations at 4:00, and the question for the judge and lawyers back in the courtroom was what to say about Wednesday, the day before Thanksgiving, i.e. how long to deliberate, if they needed more time. One juror was overheard to be concerned about cooking her two turkeys and another had a 3:00 flight to catch on Wednesday.   The jury returned to the courtroom before leaving, and was asked about the Wednesday schedule. Knowing of one juror's flight at 4:00 (not 3:00), a juror suggested deliberating until 2:30 on Wednesday and all agreed.

Next day's headlines: None

25 26 27 28 29	1 2 3 4 5	8 9 10 12	15 16	22 23 24	29
X X X X X	X X X X X	X X X X	X X	X X X	O

Day 19: Wednesday, 24 November

Before the jury arrived, Judge Zobel referred to a letter from one of the jurors about the charge to the jury about reasonable doubt. She said she did it correctly, and the letter came too late in any case, and would be filed. Again, expedience trumped the search for truth. As the definition of "reasonable doubt" was very important for a juror to know, one wonders what would have been the problem with a further discussion between the judge and the jury about the term. As the phrase, "reasonable doubt" was so important to the outcome of the case, why not poll each juror to ensure that each was comfortable with his/her understanding of the standard?

At 2:24 the jury returned to the courtroom and was dismissed until the following Monday. For Alfred Trenkler and his family, it was not to be a Happy Thanksgiving.

Next day's headlines:

Boston Globe: *"JURY REMAINS OUT IN BOMBING TRIAL"* no byline

25 26 27 28 29	1 2 3 4 5	8 9 10 12	15 16	22 23 24	29
X X X X X	X X X X X	X X X X	X X	X X X	X

Day 20: Monday, 29 November

At 2:11, the jury sent a question to the judge about circumstantial evidence, which was read aloud, "*One, we are having difficulty weighing the difference between and relative importance of direct and indirect, paren, or circumstantial, end paren, evidence. Would it be possible for us to receive a clarification of these concepts vis-a-vis the law?*

How tight does the web of circumstantial evidence have to be?" (TT 20-3) At 2:33 the
jury came to the courtroom to hear Judge Zobel's answer, which was developed after
20 minutes of discussion and debate among her and lawyers over 12 transcript pages.
Judge Zobel told the jury in 426 words, *"First, I see the question as in two parts. And
the answer to the first question which is, is there a difference in relative importance, the
answer is, no. As I told you during the charge, where Perry Mason always says, oh, it's
just circumstantial evidence, Perry Mason is just plain wrong. There is no difference in
the weight that may be given to direct or circumstantial evidence.*

*The second part of the question asks for clarification of the concept of circumstantial
evidence in the context of this case. Let me tell you, first, that the government has the
burden of proving each element of each of the three offenses charged beyond a
reasonable doubt. In deciding whether the government has proven each element beyond
a reasonable doubt, you should consider all of the evidence, and you may draw from all
of the evidence, reasonable inferences, viewing the evidence in its totality. Understand
that you cannot draw inferences from inferences, but you have to draw inferences from
facts that you find. Now you may draw an inference from a single fact. And the example
that counsel suggest, which I confess I had not heard before, is the famous example of
the turtle on the tree stump. If you walk in the woods and it is shown, the witness
testifies, that there was a turtle on a tree stump three feet high, then you may infer from
that that somebody put the turtle there because we know, at least in this example we
know that turtles can't climb trees. So this is an inference drawn, an inference that
somebody put the turtle there, drawn from the single fact that there is a turtle on tree
stump. Or inferences may be drawn from a series of facts.*

*If the witness were to tell you that the witness observed footprints in the snow going
toward the house and observed a newspaper by the back door, and then observed
footprints going away from the house, that is a series of facts from which you may infer
that the newspaper person came and delivered the newspaper.*

*So you may draw inferences from a single fact, you may draw inferences from a series
of facts that you find, but you may not draw inferences from inferences.*
Does that help?

*You may now continue your deliberations. And I am aware of Part 2 of your note which
says that you anticipate ceasing deliberations at 6, and will at that time excuse you, if
you do not have a verdict before then. Thank you."* [TT 20-15/17]
The jury returned to its deliberations at 2:37 p.m.

About 5:15 the jury returned after a total of 66 hours of trial and 21 hours of
deliberations with its verdicts of guilty on all three counts. The members of the jury
were polled, and then, after expressing her appreciation for their work, the judge
released them at 5:23 p.m. Unfortunately, the members were not polled for any
specific questions which might have clarified their results. How could they, for
example, have concluded that Alfred Trenkler acquired explosives when there was no
evidence that he had ever purchased, acquired or possessed explosives? The only way
the jurors could have come to that conclusion was after they inferred that he was
involved in the conspiracy and then that since he was the smarter of the two, that he
"must have" been the one who acquired the dynamite. That would appear to be a good
example of what Judge Zobel told the jury it could not do, which was to draw an
inference from an inference.

The U.S. Marshal was instructed to take charge of the defendant, and a disposition hearing was tentatively scheduled for 15 February 1994.

Alfred was immediately incarcerated and sent to the Hillsborough County Jail, New Hampshire, as a Federal Government prisoner. Alfred wrote long afterwards on 16 June 2006, *"It was rather interesting that I was placed in an orientation unit and while I was watching TV, whether by mistake or not, David Lindholm was brought into the same unit, sent to the cell I was assigned to and by the time I was going to confront him he had turned around and walked back to the door and was let out."* One wonders what each would have said to the other.

Below are presented two tables to summarize the truth as presented by the prosecutors and Alfred Trenkler's defense team, and then in the second table, and as a preview to the remainder of the book, the truth which has subsequently become known.

Table 1.

THE TWO COLUMNS OF TRUTH AS PRESENTED TO THE JURY;
IT CHOSE THE LEFT COLUMN, BEYOND A REASONABLE DOUBT.
(Table 2, below, provides Alfred Trenkler's Truth as developed or revealed after the trial.)

PROSECUTION'S TRUTH

ALFRED TRENKLER'S TRUTH

Roslindale Bomb
-Alfred Trenkler built it
-Alfred Trenkler acquired explosives.
-Built it for Shay's affection.
-Built it for the money, as business was failure
-Was placed and armed sometime **before** daylight on Sun., 26 Oct.

-Toggle switch was Radio Shack Model 275-602
-Toggle switch was purchased by Tom Shay on 18 Oct. 1991.

-Had knowledge of Roslindale Bomb because drew diagram for Leahy and D'Ambrosio.

1986 M21 Hoffman
-Showed Trenkler's interest in bombs
-Similar in design to 1991 bomb
-Similar modus operandi to 1991.

-No. Was busy at work all fall. Alibis.
-No. No linking physical evidence found.
-No. Only an acquaintance.
-There was no such interest, and Trenkler's business was successful
-Receiver batteries would have been dead by Monday, noon. Must have been armed **after** discovery by Thomas L. Shay, Sun. Maybe, as late as Monday morning.
-Not disputed.

-No. But even if he did, Alfred Trenkler didn't incorporate it into the Roslindale Bomb.
-Did not draw such a diagram.
.

-It was a one-time prank.
-Not similar.
-Not similar. Denied having Todd Leach

purchase parts in 1986 or having Tom Shay purchase parts on 18 October 1991.

EXIS database
-showed similarities of 1986/1991

-Garbage in, garbage out. The results all depended upon the questions and the way data was entered.

Thomas L. Shay
-Intended murder victim.
-Didn't know about black box.

-Not by Alfred Trenkler.
-Thomas L. Shay's version of events did not make sense.

Tom Shay
- 2-3 year relationship with Trenkler

-Acquaintance began in June 1991 and ended in August.

-Relationship was sexual
-Shay hated father.
-Shay told Trenkler of hatred for father
-His statements were believable

-Not disputed.
-Not disputed.
-Not disputed.
-Statements were unbelievable, but not admitted for their truth, so were not cross-examined or challenged. His other false statements were not admissible as per any exception to hearsay rule.

-Had met with and conspired with Trenkler in September & October

-Not challenged, due to lack of Trenkler testimony.

Richard Brown
-Saw Trenkler and Shay together at ATEL in 1990. Gave ride to Shay.

-Not sufficiently challenged.

Edward Carrion
-Took Tom Shay to 7 Whitelawn several times in 1989.

-Not sufficiently challenged.

-Saw Trenkler and Shay together at "The Block," before 1991.

-Not sufficiently challenged.

Todd Leach
- Purchased parts for 1986 device Showed modus operandi of having other person purchase items.

-Not sufficiently challenged.

Paul Nutting
-Saw Tom Shay and Alfred Trenkler together at Blue Hills in Spring, 1991.

-Not sufficiently challenged.

Michael Coady
-Showed Trenkler's interest in young boys. Taken to California, Florida and

-Not sufficiently challenged.

skiing trip.
-Taken to party where large firecracker   -Not sufficiently challenged.
  was exploded by Trenkler.
- Saw magnets and toy Jeep in   -Not sufficiently challenged.
  Trenkler's Jeep.

William David Lindholm
-Lived one year on Whitelawn Ave   -Whitelawn challenged, but residence
  in Milton.   in Town of Milton was correct.
- Father went to Milton & Thayer   -Not challenged.
  Academies and Brown Univ.
-Trenkler admitted building bomb   -There was no such admission.
-Trenkler showed arrogance toward   -Not challenged.
  police victims.
-Lindholm trying to reform self.   -Lindholm expected a deal for testimomy.

Other reasons for conviction
-Shay was already convicted as co-conspirator in two-person conspiracy.
-Trenkler did not testify at any hearings, nor the trial.
-Trenkler did not have friendly witness, or recording of his conversations with
  investigators.
-Trenkler's lifestyle and alleged homosexuality.

Table 2.

<u>WITH THE RIGHT HAND COLUMN OF TRUTH NOT PRESENTED TO THE JURY, OR AS
LEARNED AFTER THE TRIAL, WITH CORRESPONDING PROSECUTOR ALLEGATION.</u>

Roslindale Bomb
*Toggle switch was Radio Shack Model   * Toggle switch contacts may have come
  275-602   from another brand switch, but such
                                           switch has not been found.

*Was placed and armed sometime   * Later it was learned that the Futaba
  before daylight on Sun., 26 Oct.   receiver was an older model, allowing only
                                           two hours of battery life. Thus, arming would
                                           have been required on or after 10:00 a.m.
                                           Monday morning.

1986 M21 Hoffman
*Similar in design to 1991 bomb   *Not similar. Not placed under 1986 truck.
*Similar modus operandi to 1991.   *Not similar. Never, for example, had
                                           another person buy parts for him. He and
                                           Donna Shea purchased the toy car
                                           together in 1986, and not with Todd
                                           Leach. No connection to the 18 October
                                           1991 purchase either.

EXIS database
*showed similarities of 1986/1991

* First Circuit Court of Appeals said it was error to introduce at Trenkler's trial, but error was "harmless" beyond a reasonable doubt.

Thomas L. Shay
*Didn't know about black box.

*He likely had black box in hand in car on Monday morning, per testimony at Shay trial by Evelyn and Robert Pirello and by Eleanor McKernan. Tom McKernan had seen Thomas Shay at Z-Lock/"Sound Securities" with black object in hands. None was called to testify at Trenkler trial.

Tom Shay
* 2-3 year relationship with Trenkler

*Acquaintance began in June 1991 and with four hitched rides in Jun/July and one accidental meeting in August. Alfred Trenkler was trying to distance himself from Tom Shay after July.

*Relationship was sexual
*Acquaintance was not sexual

*Shay hated father.
*Strongly disputed. Tom wrote letter to father in October.

*Shay told Trenkler of hatred for father
*Shay did not describe nor show such feelings to Alfred Trenkler

*His statements were believable
*Statements were unbelievable, and the prosecutors knew that. Shay trial was reversed to allow psychiatric testimony of his lying disorder.

Richard Brown
*Saw Trenkler and Shay together at ATEL in 1990. Gave ride to Shay.

*Did not happen. Did not meet Tom Shay until June 1991.

Edward Carrion
*Took Tom Shay to 7 Whitelawn several times in 1989.

*Didn't happen. Shay has never been to Whitelawn. Trenkler was not living there in 1989. He was living in Hull until Feb. 1990 when he moved to S. Boston, and later to Quincy.

*Saw Trenkler and Shay together at "The Block."

*Didn't happen. Trenkler has never been to "the Block," except when driving through. Man with mustache was Ralph Pace.

Todd Leach
*Showed modus operandi of having

*Alfred Trenkler never purchased anything

other person purchase items.

with Todd Leach, a young boy in 1986. Was never with him alone and never took him shopping anywhere. Alfred Trenkler was with Donna Shea when SHE purchased TYCO toy car for the 1986 device.

Michael Coady
*Showed Trenkler's interest in young boys. Taken to California, Florida and skiiing trip.
*Taken to party where large firecracker
.

*No interest in young boys. Never went to California, Florida or on a ski trip with Mike Coady.
-Did not happen.

* Saw magnets and toy Jeep in Trenkler's Jeep.

-Alfred Trenkler never had magnets in his cars and no toy Jeep's either.

William David Lindholm
*Lived on Whitelawn Ave in Milton and father went to Milton & Thayer Academies and Brown Univ.

*Whitelawn challenged, but Milton residence was correct. Father did not attend or graduate from any of the named institutions.
*There was no such admission.
*None was shown.

*Trenkler admitted building bomb
*Trenkler showed arrogance toward police victims.
*Lindholm trying to reform self.

*Lindholm expected a deal for testimomy, and his sentence was subsequently reduced by 55 months to 42 months.

Next day's headlines:
Boston Globe: "TRENKLER IS CONVICTED IN FATAL BOMBING" *by Matthew Brelis*
Excerpts from the article:
"Alfred W. Trenkler, a Milton native who was educated at exclusive private schools, was found guilty by a federal jury yesterday...Foley, seated in the front row of US District Court Judge Rya W. Zobel's courtroom, embraced family members and law enforcement officials as Trenkler's mother sat sobbing across the aisle.... Trenkler, 37, was portrayed by assistant US attorneys Paul V. Kelly and Frank A. Libby, Jr., as a cold, calculating engineer who built a remote control bomb...for his lover, Thomas A. Shay....'My feelings were a lot more adamant about Trenkler,' Foley said. 'He was the one who was and is capable of making this device. He's the one I'd be afraid of....' They [prosecutors] alleged Trenkler built the bomb to maintain his relationship with Shay and to get money for his failing telecommunications business....

'It was all circumstantial evidence and very hard to come to a decision,' said one juror who spoke on condition of anonymity. 'We took many votes.' The juror said the evidence about the 1986 bombing was 'very decisive in the jury's finding.' The juror said some members found Lindholm's testimony to be very important while others did not...

US Attorney Donald K. Stern praised Kelly and Libby and the cooperative investigation conducted by Boston police and the [ATF]."

<u>Boston Herald</u>: "BOMB-MAKER GUILTY IN COP'S DEATH" by Ralph Ranalli
Excerpts from the article:
"Alfred Trenkler, who prosecutors called the 'sinister' mastermind behind a 1991 bombing that killed Boston police officer Jeremiah Hurley, was found guilty of the crime yesterday in federal court.

'I'm hysterical, I don't know if I could even put it into words,' Hurley's widow, Cynthia, said last night. 'It's great just to finally put it to rest and finally have justice served.' Hurley called the effort of police and federal investigators - who one official estimated put in '10 to 12 man-years' of work on the case - a 'tribute' to her husband's memory....

Trenkler's mother wept at the verdict, and left with his stepfather without commenting to reporters. Foley said he 'felt bad for what he (Trenkler) put them through.. He doesn't need my forgiveness, but I don't hate anybody,' Foley added.

'But I don't understand it and I don't condone it. It was only a matter of yards from a school. What if five or six little kids had picked it up?' "

END NOTES
_____

1. Justice John Paul Stevens, 6 August 2005, in a speech to the American Bar Association. He was commenting on the large number of wrongful convictions which have been found in death penalty cases.
2. These charges came from Alfred Trenker's former friend, Donna Shea. Reported Thomas D'Ambrosio and Dennis Leahy on 15 November 1991, "Ms. Shea said that Alfred Trenkler was gay and that Trenkler was doing cocaine and young boys." Also, the report continued, "Trenkler frequented the Blue Hills and rest area's, picking up young 14-15 year old gays."
3. Judge Hiller Zobel made another ruling in the civil case which wasn't overruled by his wife. In their investigation of the case, the newspapers found medical and psychological records of Mr. Thomas L. Shay in the case files in the court, and Judge Zobel granted his attorney's, Jay Flynn, motion to impound those records. They had been left unintentionally open to the public. <u>Boston Globe</u>, "SON SAYS BOMB MEANT FOR HIM", 1 November 1991.
4. The date of this supplemental report may be incorrect. Agent D'Ambrosio reported that he and Agent Dennis Leahy interviewed Richard Brown on 20 November 1991 and Agent Leahy wrote a report on 4 December 1991. Then D'Ambrosio's report states that "on the following day 11-21-92" he re-interviewed Richard Brown by phone That supplemental report was dated 10 December 1992 both by D'Ambrosio with a typewritten date, and by his supervisor, Victor Palaza, in handwriting. It seems likely that the reference to the date in the report of the followup telephone call was actually 21 November 1991,and not 1992. In any case, the report was not referenced at Trenkler's trial.
5. According to Boston Detective Francis Armstrong's 10 March 1992 report, Donna Shea had testified at the grand jury that Todd Leach had used magnets from an automotive transmission when helping Alfred Trenkler assemble the 1986 Quincy device.
6. The portions of the tape played for the jury are not contained in the transcript. The portions were identified in a letter from Paul Kelly to Scott Lopez on 8 December 1993 by highlighting sections of the WVLI transcript of the entire interview.

Chapter 9: AFTER THE TRENKLER VERDICT: APPEALS AND APPEALS (30 November 1993 to 30 August 2002)

> *When we determine that justice has not been*
> *served by an indictment or a conviction, we have*
> *an obligation -- legal, moral, and ethical -- to act*
> *decisively to correct the injustice."* [1]
> Suffolk County District Attorney Daniel Conley, 2004

On 4 December 1993 the Boston Police Relief Association held its 123rd annual awards banquet. According to the *Boston Globe* article, "*2 BOSTON OFFICERS, 1 SLAIN, HONORED WITH AWARD,*" 33 officers were honored for outstanding police work. Medals were awarded to the widows of officers killed on duty, and Cynthia Hurley was there for Jeremiah Hurley, Jr., two years after his death.

On 6 December 1993, Terry Segal filed two motions for relief from the judgment of guilty. Counting the trial as Request for Justice I, or RFJ I, Segal's "*Motion for Judgment of Acquittal*" was RFJ II. Other future RFJ's will be the upcoming court appeals or letters to a Judge or, finally, political requests to the Federal Government. Terry Segal's RFJ II requested that Judge Zobel turn aside the jury's guilty verdict because it was unjust, and not supported by the evidence. Sometimes judges do take this dramatic step, but most of the time, these Motions are created and denied as a perfunctory matter of routine. Wrote Segal in the Motion, "*The government's case, which was based on circumstantial evidence that the defendant was the builder of the 1991 bomb, was totally absent of any evidence from which a rational jury could infer that the defendant acted with knowledge of and in furtherance of the aims of the conspiracy or substantive counts alleged.*

1. Specifically, there was insufficient evidence of any conspiracy to commit the substantive counts alleged (COUNT I). In short, there was no evidence that defendant knowingly and willfully combined, conspired or agreed with Thomas A. Shay, Jr. to commit the substantive offenses of (1) receipt of explosives in interstate commerce with the knowledge and intent that the same would be used to kill, injure or intimidate Thomas L. Shay, Sr. or damage and destroy his real and personal property, including his automobile...

2. There was no evidence that defendant and Thomas A. Shay , Jr. even came to a tacit agreement regarding Thomas L. Shay, Sr....

3. There was also no evidence that defendant affixed the explosive device to the undercarriage of Thomas L. Shay's 1986 Buick; and

4. There was no evidence that Thomas A. Shay affixed the explosive device to the undercarriage of Thomas L. Shay's 1986 Buick.

5. There was also no evidence that Thomas A. Shay solicited the assistance of defendant in a plan to kill his father as alleged.

6. There was also no evidence that defendant agreed to construct the remote-controlled explosive device, knowing the same would be used by Thomas A. Shay, Jr. in an attempt to kill, injure or intimidate his father.

7. There was also no evidence that on or about October 27, 1991 either defendant or Thomas A. Shay, Jr. affixed said explosive device to Thomas L. Shay, Sr.'s automobile as

alleged.
*8. There was also no evidence that defendant or Thomas A. Shay, Jr., in or about
October, 1991, received in interstate commerce explosive materials with knowledge and
intent that said explosive materials would be used to kill, injure or intimidate Thomas L.
Shay, Sr., or cause damage and destruction to his 1986 Buick automobile ....
WHEREFORE, defendant requests this Court to set aside the verdicts rendered in this
case and enter a judgment of acquittal on all counts."*

The media response was minimal. The <u>Boston Globe</u>'s no-byline article, *"TRENKLER
SEEKING ACQUITTAL, 2D TRIAL,"* was 58 words long. There was none in the <u>Boston
Herald</u>.

Judge Zobel's 21 January 1994 response was brief. *"Denied,"* she wrote by hand on
the bottom of the first page of the Motion. Alfred Trenkler's <u>Request for Justice II</u> had
failed.

Alfred's <u>Request for Justice III</u> was Terry Segal's *"Motion for a New Trial,"* also filed
on 6 December 1993, with the reasons listed below, which were similar to those in the
Motion for Acquittal. The general difference was that this motion focused on judicial
error:

*"1. Defendant was substantially prejudiced and deprived of a fair trial by the Court's
erroneous admission of the evidence relating to the 1986 incident ...
2. The Court erred by failing to strike the opinion testimony of Thomas Waskom on the
signature issue...
3. The Court erred by failing to exclude and strike the testimony of Michael Coady...
4. The Court erred by failing to grant a mistrial after opening statements based on Mr.
Kelly's reference to statements by Thomas Shay, Jr...
5. The Court erred by failing to preclude the government's remote control bomb
demonstration during the testimony of Thomas Waskom as highly prejudicial...
6. The Court erred by failing to sustain defendant's numerous and continuing objections,
and permitting the admission of each and every statement by Thomas Shay, Jr. at trial
where this court excluded other statements by Thomas Shay, Jr. as 'inherently
unreliable' by quoting the government's own expert at Thomas Shay, Jr.'s sentencing
hearing that Shay was not to be believed....* [This objection included generally, but not
explicitly, the statements in the Channel 56, Karen Marinella videotaped interview with
Tom Shay.]
*7. The Court erred by failing to sustain defendant's objection, and permitting the
admission of a video-tape concerning a M-21 Flash Simulator during Thomas Waskom's
testimony...
8. The defendant was substantially prejudiced and deprived of a fair trial by the Court's
erroneous admission of the EXIS computer evidence where an adequate foundation was
not established, and where the evidence should have been ruled inadmissible pursuant
to the hearsay rule, best evidence rule, and authentication rules.....
9. The Court erred by prohibiting defendant from calling Maurice Flynn to testify to prior
inconsistent statements by the government's witness, Richard Brown, where Mr.
Brown's testimony was material to the government's circumstantial case....
10. The Court erred by prohibiting defendant access to the lab notes of Ms. Cynthia
Wallace relative to her forensic identification of dynamite....
11. The Court erred by prohibiting defendant from calling Mr. Kelly as a witness to
testify to statements by Shay, Jr. which were inconsistent with guilt pursuant to*

defendant's timely motion before trial where the Court admitted into evidence statements by Shay, Jr. consistent with guilt.

12. The Court erred by refusing to give the jury an instruction, in response to the jury's question on circumstantial evidence, that if the circumstantial evidence and the inferences therefrom were consistent with both guilt and innocence, the defendant was entitled to an acquittal.

13. The Court erred in denying defendant's motion for acquittal made at the conclusion of the government's case and at the conclusion of the evidence.

WHEREFORE, for all the reasons set forth above, defendant respectfully requests that this Court grant him a new trial."

Judge Zobel's response was an efficient, handwritten *"Denied"* on 21 January 1994. Thus ended Alfred Trenkler's <u>Request for Justice III</u>.

The rules of the adversarial legal system in the U.S. have evolved over centuries. For every procedure and rule, there have been debates in many judicial opinions and articles and books. Regarding retrials, only the defendant can request a new trial, because of the Constitutional prohibition against being twice tried for the same offense. The grounds for new trials must arise from mistakes by the court. Thus, Terry Segal did not file a Motion or a New Trial because HE had made a mistake, as the government would not want to spend the money and put the victims and their families through a new trial, for something that was the fault of the defendant's attorney. If such a motion were written, Mr. Segal might have written:

"1. The defense erred in not requesting the testimony of Dr. Robert Phillips to testify about Tom Shay's propensity to lie, consistent with the diagnosed infirmity, "pseudologica fantastica" Also, the defense erred in not presenting an expert in the field of voluntary false confessions.

*2. The defense erred in not offering the testimony of the defendant, Alfred W. Trenkler. At the time of trial, the risks of prejudicial attacks on Mr. Trenkler seemed to outweigh his ability to present the truth in this case. My own overconfidence in an acquittal led me to give him erroneous advice not to testify at his trial, or at any of the other proceedings. Attached to this Motion is the substance of the testimony, in Question and Answer, deposition-like format, which Alfred Trenkler might give. (See Appendix A of this book.) The **www.findlaw.com** columnist, Julie Hiller, believes that the question of whether a defendant should testify can be summed up with the advice that 'defendants should testify unless they have a long record. The jury wants to hear from them.'[2] Alfred Trenkler's 1986 prank and automobile infractions were far from constituting "a long record," and I should have encouraged him to testify.*

3. The defense erred in not joining the government's subpoena to Tom Shay to testify. While the government was confident that Tom Shay would incriminate Alfred Trenkler, the defense is at least as confident that he would have been unable and unwilling to do so, and, in fact, would have told the truth. That truth is that neither he nor Alfred Trenkler were involved in the Roslindale Bomb in any way.

4. The defense erred in not pursuing the identification of the Futaba receiver, whereby it would have been determined by the retrieved FCC [Federal Communications Commission] identification number, that the receiver was an older, power-hungry model that would have exhausted its batteries in two hours, instead of the 22, as was presented in court.

5. The defense erred in not insisting on the examination of the layers of black electrical tape found amidst the Bomb debris, after our expert, Denny Kline, had stated at a meeting that he had seen a fingerprint between layers of that tape.

6. The defense erred in failing to thoroughly cross-examine each of the witnesses who claimed to have identified Alfred Trenkler as being in the company of Tom Shay, prior to June 1991. Richard Brown, Edward Carrion and Paul Nutting were three of those witnesses, and their testimonies were incorrect on that crucial point.

7. The defense erred by failing to thoroughly cross-examine Michael Coady and Todd Leach. Their testimony was so incredulous to me, that I made the fateful assumption that the jury would also have a similar reaction, and totally disbelieve them.

8. The defense erred by not presenting more thoroughly alibi evidence and character witness evidence on behalf of Alfred W. Trenkler. He was thoroughly and otherwise occupied on 18 October and the entire month of October to have had any role in the Roslindale Bomb.

9. The defense failed to present the testimony of Evelyn Pirello or Eleanor McKernan who would have testified as they did in the Shay trial about Mr. Thomas L. Shay carrying a black box upon his return from errands on Monday morning, 28 October.

10. The defense erred by failing to bring to the court's attention its strong opposition to the leaks to the media by anonymous members of the prosecution's law enforcement team. Since the identification of Alfred Trenkler as a suspect, and the public release of information about his sexual preference, and the relationship to Tom Shay, the Boston newspapers have repeatedly mischaracterized him. Similarly, the press often presented the prosecution's view of evidence and our defense team was reluctant to present facts and views because of our overly strict view of the bar rules against waging a court battle in the media. We should have either sought the Court's assistance in stopping the prosecution's 'unnamed sources' or fought the battle with them equally in the media.

11. The defense erred by not objecting strongly enough to the admission of any part of the Karen Marinella-Tom Shay interview tape. Every statement that Tom Shay made in that tape which implied that Alfred Trenkler had any role in the Roslindale Bomb was false. On the other hand, after the Court admitted portions of the tape, I could have urged the Court to admit the entire tape and to request the examination of Karen Marinella and to use other evidence to impeach the credibility of Tom Shay. In addition, I could have agreed with AUSA Paul Kelly to a stipulation that what Tom Shay said pursuant to his proffer agreement, at that point, was mostly false.

12. The defense did not display a video tape of a 1986 Buick Century, with a mockup black box attached by magnets, traveling over the speed bumps in McDonalds and Burger King restaurants where Mr. Thomas L. Shay said he had traveled on Sunday morning, with the black box underneath his car for the entire morning. The videotape showed that the box likely would have fallen off the Buick, or been crushed, at the "bumps" at either fast food restaurant. It was not presented at trial because of its poor quality, but despite that drawback, it still would have made the point for the jury.

13. The defense erred, generally, because it failed to convey to the jury the overall view that Alfred Trenkler is perfectly innocent of any role in the Roslindale Bomb."

Of course, such a document was never filed for several reasons. Among them, the rules don't provide for new trials because of defense counsel mistakes, unless they rise to the level of incompetence; and Terry Segal was a very competent lawyer and his work for Alfred Trenkler was good in several ways. The problem was that it wasn't good enough, in the face of a bizarre set of circumstances and a determined investigation and prosecution; and two innocent men were convicted.

On the other hand, as the U.S. Attorney's office won the case, it was not going to request a new trial, either, even though it, too, felt the court had made mistakes, such as refusing to admit the photo identification by Dwayne Armbrister of Tom Shay at Radio Shack.

On 14 January 1994 Alfred Trenkler completed an "*Affidavit in Support of Motion on Appeal in Forma Pauperis,*" which, if approved, would enable him to retain for his appeal a lawyer provided by the government, just as was done for Tom Shay. Alfred stated in the form that he earned $200 in his last month of employment, the month of December 1992, at least through the middle of 16 December, and that he had $300 in a bank account. Alfred was painfully aware that his parents had spent over $300,000 for the legal fees of Terry Segal and all of it was for nothing. Further, Alfred Trenkler was in a worse position legally than when Terry Segal was retained. He was now subject to be sentenced to life in prison for crimes he didn't commit.

Imagine what such a circumstance might mean in other areas of life. Imagine going to a doctor and paying, without insurance, $300,000 for heart surgery and learn afterwards that the heart problem was worse than when the treatment began. A good doctor would apologize for the bad result and maybe stay with the case without further charge in an attempt to achieve the expected improvement. Alternatively, the patient could, ironically, consult a lawyer about suing for malpractice. However, in both the medical and legal professions, errors and mistakes are not always indicators of malpractice. Alfred's fate would likely have been avoided with another lawyer with a different, and proactive, legal strategy.

Alfred and his family struggled about what to do next, and how to pay for it, and one option was to pursue public assistance. Despite the disaster of using a high-priced defense lawyer, the alternative to the "*in forma pauperis*" petition, was to find a high-priced private appellate attorney, and that was what Alfred's parents did. It would eventually mean the depletion of a substantial portion of their life savings and assets, but they had to do everything they could to free Alfred from his conviction for crimes he didn't commit.

On 6 February 1994 Alfred Trenkler turned 38 years old. He was still in the Federal section at New Hampshire's Hillsborough County Jail because on 21 January, Judge Zobel had denied his Motion to be moved to the Plymouth County House of Correction, pending final sentencing on 8 March.

Sentencing for Alfred was scheduled for 24 February 1994, but the U.S. Attorney's Office requested a postponement until 8 March, and the defense agreed.

Preparing for that earlier date, 29 friends and relatives of Alfred wrote to Judge Zobel urging leniency. All were incredulous that Alfred could have been convicted of such crimes. Several noted that Alfred would never intentionally harm another human being, and that his desire for financial gain was minimal. Retired Massachusetts Superior Court Judge George Hurd, a neighbor of the Wallaces, wrote, "*Alfred never struck Beth and me as possessing the criminal intent to commit the crime for which he stands convicted.*" Unfortunately, these character traits were not presented to the jury, and the jury had long been excused before this information came to the court,

Letters were also sent by members of the Hurley and Foley families which described movingly the grievous losses they had suffered. From Cynthia Hurley, the widow of Jeremiah Hurley, came these comments in a letter the previous September:

"October 28, 1991, a beautiful fall day, back to work after a week long Caribbean cruise. All was well at work, glad to get back into the swing of things. At 11:30 a.m., I receive a call from my husband, Jerry Hurley, asking me how I was and how was getting back to work. I started to tell him and he received a call from the dispatcher to go to Roslindale. He said I have to go see you tonight. One (1) hour later a police officer was standing at my desk telling me there had been an accident, nothing serious I was told, just come with me. And the nightmare begins. How can you put in words the emotional impact. First of all to my husband, I can't even imagine the pain and suffering, he had so many injuries. He still had time and presence of mind to worry about his partner and others at the scene also. His concern for his family, wanting us to know how much he loved us. He was a wonderful human being. Everybody loved him and his beautiful smile. He never had a bad thing to say about anyone or anything. His love and kindness was reflected in his family. He was the greatest husband, always caring and sharing, nothing bothered him. He was my life, love and best friend. We shared so much happiness. Especially watching our four children grow. Jerry was a great father and grandfather. They are all denied having their father around to love and care for them. Things in our lives will never be the same. We've tried to put our lives back together as he would have wanted us to do. But the loneliness is almost unbearable sometimes. Having difficulty concentrating, making decisions I never had to make alone, sleepless nights, trying to be strong and supportive to my family. I know they are grieving also and it is very hard sometimes to understand what they are feeling and they what I am feeling."

For surviving members of families it's usually birthdays and other holidays which bring back memories. For the Hurley family, there were also the unscheduled, unpredictable but certain reminders with each new killing of a Boston Police officer. The 6 February 1994 *Boston Herald* carried Maggie Mulvihill's story, "*TRAGEDY STRIKES TOO OFTEN*," about the killing of Detective Berisford Anderson. He was the first to die in 1994, but the article recounted the chronology of recent deaths, including that of Jeremiah Hurley.

The month of February saw another coincidence in Boston's legal community, as the former U.S. Attorney, A. John Pappalardo, went to work in Nancy Gertner's law firm of Dyer, Collura and Gertner. The firm was still representing Tom Shay. Gertner had been nominated to become a U.S. District Court judge during Tom Shay's trial in July 1993, and would later take the oath of office in April 1994. After Pappalardo was asked to leave his position as U.S. Attorney in November 1993, and was replaced by Donald Stern, he was nominated by Governor William Weld to be a Superior Court Judge in Massachusetts. However, Pappalardo's nomination was destined to fail at the Governor's Council because of high-powered criticism from several people. Some were angry that former State Senator Joseph Timilty had been prosecuted and convicted for a minor real estate irregularity in an effort to get him to testify against bigger fish. Also, there was anger that he was arrested at his home early one morning in front of his wife and children on 27 January 1993, when his attorney had requested a voluntary surrender without theatrics. That was only six weeks after Alfred Trenkler's needlessly theatric arrest by armed agents. By coincidence, the Wallaces knew the Timilty's. On the other hand, one Governor's Councillor was pleased with Mr. Pappalardo and planned to vote for him. He was Edward Foley, brother of the injured

Boston Policeman Francis Foley. Despite that support, Pappalardo withdrew his application and signed on with Dwyer, Collura and Gertner.

On 22 February, Pamela Lombardini, a Probation Officer of the Probation Office of the U.S. District Court sent a draft Presentencing report to Terry Segal and the prosecutors for review and comment. As part of her preparation, she interviewed Alfred Trenkler. These reports are used by judges in determining appropriate sentences. She wrote, "... *the presentence report is used by the Federal Bureau of Prisons to determine the institution in which the sentence is to be served, the defendant's classification within the facility, his ability to obtain furloughs, and his eligibility for programs within the institution.*"

Excerpts from the 24 page report are below:

"*Offense Conduct,*" which appears to represent the prosecution's theory of the crime, including features that were not mentioned at the trial.

"- *Trenkler met Shay Jr. while frequenting gay clubs, including the Ramrod Lounge in Boston. Shay Jr. and Trenkler became friendly and had a relationship which continued thereafter until the fall of 1991.*

- *In late September or early October, 1991, Shay Jr. decided to kill his father. His motive was both personal... and financial.*

- *Shay, Jr. knew that ... Trenkler had been involved in building a remote-controlled explosive device in 1986.*

- *At the time, Trenkler was involved in yet another struggling electronics business.*

- *Trenkler proceeded to design and construct a relatively sophisticated remote controlled explosive device. Trenkler alone obtained the dynamite and blasting caps...*

- *On October 18, 1991 and acting at Trenkler's direction and with a 'shopping list' prepared by Trenkler, Shay Jr. purchased, among other things, a toggle switch...which, as Shay Jr. later conceded on a videotaped news interview... was integrated into the firing circuit of the deadly device.*

- *Sometime on October 26 or 27, 1991, the bomb was affixed to the undercarriage of Shay Sr.'s automobile... Trenkler sought to maximize: 1) the prospects of, first, targeting Shay Sr. alone in his automobile... and then killing him on triggering the device: and 2) making good his escape from the vicinity of the blast, likely while driving behind Shay Sr. on the highway or lying in wait, in an automobile nearby... In this fashion Trenkler also sought to minimize the prospects that the device would be detected ... Trenkler failed, however, to take into account the potential for dislodgement of the device...*

- *Together with Shay Jr., Trenkler planned for and intended to kill Shay Sr. with a powerful bomb.*

- *In December, 1992, while in custody at the Plymouth County House of Corrections... Trenkler made the acquaintance of David Lindholm... whose father was a graduate of both Milton Academy and Thayer Academy. Trenkler began to seek out Lindholm... In the course of these conversations, Trenkler confessed to Lindholm that he had built the 1991 bomb.* [Alfred's sharply different version of those conversations is in Chapter 4.]
Victim Impact

- *Foley described Trenkler as coming from a 'fine upbringing, with 'good schooling', who has proven to be 'totally self gratifying'. He feels that Trenkler had to contemplate what he was doing, when building the bomb. Foley also stated that Trenkler is a bright man who is quite talented in the field of electronics, unlike Shay, who is incapable of such detail. Foley feels more animosity toward Trenkler than toward Shay because he feels that Shay is a confused and disturbed person.*

- *Foley wonders how Trenkler, not emotionally involved with Shay, Sr., could assist in his attempted killing. Without Trenkler, Shay would not have had the capability to kill his father in this manner. Foley considers both Trenkler and Shay to be terrorists."*

Francis Foley is correct to wonder how Alfred Trenkler could have participated in such a scheme without any emotional involvement with Mr. Thomas L. Shay. Alfred Trenkler did not know Mr. Thomas Shay and knew nothing about him. Thus, not only did he have no emotional involvement with Tom Shay, he had no emotional involvement with Mr. Thomas L. Shay, either. With no involvement, he had no interest in harming Mr. Thomas L. Shay or anyone, for that matter; and Alfred Trenkler didn't participate in any way in the building or placement of the Roslindale Bomb. Officer Foley's intuition was correct, but his faith in the work of law enforcement overcame his intuition.

In the *"Acceptance of Responsibility"* section, Ms. Lombardini presents correctly Alfred Trenkler's claim of innocence as presented in this book. Thus, there was no acceptance of responsibility for the Roslindale Bomb.

She wrote that the crimes for which Alfred was convicted carried a maximum punishment of death or life imprisonment, but did not mention that a jury recommendation was required before imposing either of those maximum sentences.

On 1 March 1994, Terry Segal filed *"Objections of Defendant, Alfred Trenkler, to Presentence report."* Generally, he objected to the report's portrayal of the case beyond, or contrary to, the evidence presented in court.

- *"The evidence did not establish that they* [Tom Shay and Alfred Trenkler] *had a 'relationship;' they were merely acquaintances."*
- Judge Zobel had stated at Tom Shay's sentencing hearing *"that there was no evidence that Shay, Jr. 'intended to kill his father.' "*
- *"There was absolutely no evidence at either trial on this factual issue."* [of Shay's knowledge of the 1986 device.]
- *"...the evidence at trial established that Trenkler's business was very successful during the Fall 1991 time frame, and that defendant was involved in a $38,000 project for the Christian Science Church."*
- *"... there was no evidence as to when, or by whom, the explosives were obtained."*
- *"There was no evidence that at the time of Shay, Jr.'s Radio Shack purchase he was 'acting at Trenkler's direction' 'with a shopping list prepared by Trenkler.'"*
- *"... there was no evidence at trial that defendant placed the device on the car, or was aware, beforehand, where the device was to be placed."*
- *"There was no evidence that 'Shay, Jr. or Trenkler planned for* [sic] *and intended to kill Shay, Sr.'..."*

There were other corrections recommended by Terry Segal, but there was no objection to Pamela Lombardini's analysis of the maximum possible sentence, or her failure to mention the jury's required role in establishing such a sentence.

Also on 1 March 1994, AUSA's Paul Kelly and Frank Libby wrote a six-page response to Pamela Lombardini. They urged a maximum sentence for Alfred Trenkler, and objected to Ms. Lombardini's *"downward adjustment"* recommendation for a sentence because Alfred Trenkler didn't intend to kill Jeremiah Hurley. Wrote Kelly and Libby, *"This result is a patent absurdity,"* and argued that if one builds a deadly bomb, one is responsible for deadly results.

They, too, did not cite the required role of the jury in the consideration of a maximum penalty for the crimes for which Alfred Trenkler was convicted.

Also on 1 March, Terry Segal submitted a "*Sentencing Memorandum*" which argued that the "*most analogous*" crime to that for which Alfred Trenkler was convicted was involuntary manslaughter, and the statutory guidelines were for 51-63 months imprisonment. However, Segal wrote "*Defendant submits ... although his conduct was reckless, there was no evidence that <u>his conduct</u> caused the unintentional killing in this case.*" And later, "*...the evidence supports a finding that defendant's construction of a bomb was reckless.*" The problem for a lawyer in this sentencing process was whether to continue to argue that one's client is totally innocent and risk angering the sentencing judge or argue that, given the conviction, that the defendant's commission of the crime was in such a manner as to warrant a minimum punishment; and Segal apparently chose the latter course. Segal sought to tread a thin line of admitting the construction of a bomb, but denying the placement of the bomb, because "*there was absolutely no evidence suggesting that this defendant placed the bomb in a position which could injure or kill...*" However, there was no physical evidence that he built the bomb either. Statements by others constituted the only evidence.

Perhaps Terry Segal could have written that "*The defendant is as innocent now as he was when convicted, thus any punishment would be unjust. A finding of innocence, against the jury's verdict, is the best possible ruling by the court. In the absence such a ruling, if the minimum sentence for involuntary manslaughter is the minimum possible for the crimes for which defendant was convicted, then that is the sentence which the court will have to impose, as unjust it will be. Alfred Trenkler is perfectly innocent.*"

On 2 March, Pamela Lombardini released the final 40 page PreSentence Report (PSR), which included a 16 page Addendum with her responses to the objections to the PSR by the prosecutors and the defense. She made a few minor changes in the report, but where the objections by the defense were complicated, she wrote, "*The defendant's objection has been relayed to the Court via this addendum.*" Thanks to her interview with Alfred Trenkler, this report was the first opportunity Judge Zobel had to read Trenkler's version of his acquaintance with Tom Shay and the best opportunity to read about his post-college living arrangements, which had previously been described as being almost transient.

On 7 March, Paul Kelly and Frank Libby submitted the 19-page "*Government's Sentencing Memorandum*" and an addendum which was submitted by letter the following day. The *Memorandum* concluded, "*Imposition of a life sentence is the only just result.*" There was no mention of the requirement that such a sentence could only be imposed upon a recommendation by a jury.

On 8 March came the Disposition Hearing. Tom Shay had been sentenced to 15 years and 8 months and the law enforcement community was furious. What would be the sentence for Alfred Trenkler, the alleged "*mastermind*" of the Roslindale Bomb, using the Ralph Ranalli's term, and which would creep into Tom Shay's Appeal Brief the following week? On the morning of the hearing in the *Herald*'s, "*CONVICTED BOMBER SEEKS TO HAVE HIS SAY IN COURT*," Ralph Ranalli wrote, "*Convicted Roslindale Bomber Alfred Trenkler wants to speak 'for approximately 60 minutes' at his sentencing hearing today in federal court, according to a letter from his lawyer.*"

Judge Zobel began the hearing by considering the objections of both sides to the Presentencing Report. Regarding the relationship between Alfred Trenkler and Tom

Shay, she ordered that the defense's requested description of that relationship be entered into the Presentencing Report. That didn't necessarily mean that she agreed that it was true that Alfred Trenkler and Tom Shay had a minimal acquaintance, but it became part of the record of the case.

Frank Libby argued for the prosecution for a maximum sentence of life in prison because Trenkler's crimes were analogous to first degree murder. He said, "*Your Honor, this, all told, is a classic example of lying in wait. Lying in wait. Not a gun. It's not a knife. It's a bomb. It's configured in such a way to permit the individual whose thoughts lie behind this deed to stand some distance away, pick his time and place to detonate this instrument of death, allow him to get away from the scene and leave no connection with the crime.*" (TTH 6-16]

Terry Segal argued that there was no pre-meditation on Alfred Trenkler's part - again assuming that he did anything at all. Looking at the verdict as the jury was given no specific questions to answer, said Segal, "*I submit the jury could have inferred from that that Mr. Trenkler was somehow involved in this, in the scheme to, or conspiracy to, blow up Mr. Shay's vehicle, or to give Mr. Shay a device that he could use to do something and Mr. Trenkler had no idea how it was going to be used.*" (TTH 6-24) This idea might be compared with Tom Shay's statements to Karen Marinella that he purchased items for Alfred Trenkler, but that he, Shay, had no idea how they were to be used.

After a short recess, Judge Zobel gave some of her views on the jury's verdict. "*I think the verdict on Count 2, viewed fairly, I think, imports a finding that the defendant acted with a premeditated design to effect the death of a human being....I must for sentencing purpose[s] independently ascertain the defendant's state of mind and determine his conduct; and I do so according to a preponderance of the evidence standard, not beyond a reasonable doubt.... I am persuaded by the evidence that he was the designer, that he was the builder of this bomb, and that he knew what damage it could do, and that he participated in placing it not merely under the car, but under the driver's seat of the car. This evidence permits the inference, which I draw, that Mr. Trenkler intended that the bomb kill Shay, Sr.; and under the doctrine of transferred intent, he is responsible for the death of Mr. Hurley...*" (TTH 6-27]

Terry Segal argued that where Tom Shay was given a 15 year and eight month sentence, it would be "*totally unfair*" to sentence Alfred Trenkler to life in prison, given the absence of any physical evidence and the only direct evidence being the dubious claims of William David Lindholm. (TTH 6-31]

Then Judge Zobel addressed Alfred William Trenkler, "*Mr. Trenkler, do you wish to be heard?*" and he responded, "*Yes I do, your Honor.*"[TTH 6-31]

Alfred Trenkler then spoke to the court and the audience for the first time since he said to a Boston TV camera person on 16 December 1992, "*I am an innocent man. I had nothing to do with this case.*"

Since 16 December 1992, Alfred Trenkler had been told what to do and say, and what not do and say by his lawyers. The term "*told*" is used because the technical term "*advised*" is not correct. The lawyers were part of the system which would determine his fate and he was advised to leave it to them, the highly paid professionals. "*Trust us*" and "*pay the bills*" was the message. As Alfred was not paying the bill personally, he dared not jeopardize the faith of his parents by taking too strong a position against Terry Segal's strategic decisions. After all, he understood belatedly that one of the reasons for his predicament was that he had already said too much to the ATF agents. Rather, it wasn't that he said too much, it was that he had said it without any friendly witnesses, or recording devices, so that the only written records of his statements were from the ATF.

Now, on 8 March 1994, after more than a year in jail, and the significant prospects for many, many more years in prison, Alfred was ready to speak out in what will be called here his <u>Request for Justice IV</u>, or <u>RFJ IV</u>. Here is Alfred Trenkler, *"Your Honor, I stand here before you an innocent man, mistakenly accused and convicted for a heinous crime I did not commit.*

I am not this cowardly cold-blooded killer that I have been labeled. I in no way, shape or form played any part in this horrible incident. I respect life, all life: man, animal, insect and plant. I could not, I would not, even contemplate any plan of any sort that would cause the loss of life to any human being, whether known or unknown to me; less contemplate the destruction of property.

I am not a violent person. I have no history of violence. In fact, I joined volunteer groups throughout the years in conjunction with police that made efforts to make our streets and neighborhoods a safer place.

I may have pulled some pranks in my days, but who hasn't? But nothing that threatened life or limb or damaged property.

I am a hard-working American citizen. Every cent I ever earned came from honest, legitimate work through high school years and after college, up until the day of my indictment.

Your Honor, I have lived this case for more than two years, the first case -- the first year in shock and disbelief watching my life being torn apart in the media based on the ravings of an unstable teenager by the name of Tom Shay, Jr., a person I barely knew for mere hours out of my life; further, by allegations by authorities via the media.

The second year of my indictment, studying discovery materials every waking hour seven days a week, trying to understand how I could be accused of this horrible, senseless crime. In fact, I have read and reviewed countless times a stack of information ten feet high, the majority of it concerning Tom Shay, Sr. and Tom Shay, Jr., and a small fraction pertaining [to] myself. I know this material inside and out. I know more about Tom Shay, Sr. and Tom Shay, Jr. than I care to know about any other human being.

As an engineer I tried to look at it as factors of a machine to find the combination of factors that make it operate one way and not the other, such as character, education, background, habits, ethics -- everything. When I view the combination of available facts and the analysis thereof, I seriously question the outcome of these events and why, based on obvious facts, other courses of action were not followed and why these illogical choices have been made that affect us all, based not on factual information, but rather on opinion and theory to form circumstance and inference.

When investigators and attorneys retire for the night or enjoy the weekends away from the job, their minds are not working on this case to the degree my family and I have been. We have had the time to analyze this information, without public pressure, in a logical, concise manner considering all the factors. We have taken into account the information produced by the Boston Police, the ATF, and the universe of information surrounding those be snared in the net that had been cast out into the water.

It is abundantly clear that the government chooses to ignore the obvious, simple, logical answers to this riddle based on fact, answers that are right in front of all of us but chosen to be discarded. Instead, this case was tried and based on opinion and groundless theories, completely negating the facts discovered by the Boston Police within minutes, within hours, within days of this tragic event that point in a totally different direction, ignoring motive, opportunity and intent, preparation, plan, knowledge, identity, or absence of mistake or accident; based on facts pointing in one direction and developing theories based on opinions, absent any facts to possibly support them pointing in a totally opposite direction.

Why does the government choose to take all the information generated by the Boston Police, who publically [sic, publicly] stated their observations pointing in one direction, and discard this important information and take under their wing the original suspect with motive and intent supported by fact, transporting him from suspect to victim to prosecution witness, and never question evidence as seen in this courtroom that proves this man is part of a coverup on his own behalf?

There were originally many suspects, but within three days these people with proven motives are discarded and I, with no proven motives, was put at the top of the list supported by nothing but theories and opinions.

I have proof of my innocence. The government has theory of my guilt.

Your Honor, before I go on, I must address the real victims of this crime. It is with a heavy heart I address the Hurleys and the Foleys.

Mrs. Hurley, you and your family have suffered an enormous loss emotionally and physically. You have lost a husband and a friend. Your children have suffered the loss of a father.

Officer Foley, you have suffered injuries. You have lost a friend and a partner and a profession you enjoyed. As a result your family also has suffered.

We have all suffered losses at the hands of some misguided individual or individuals, and I share the grief and pain you are suffering. I extend my condolences to all of you. Any loss of life is remorseful to me.

I, along with my family, have lost many a family member, as well as friends of our family. I personally have lost many of my best friends over the years. I know what it is like, the finality of it all. I'm sorry for your losses, your pain and your suffering.

I can only imagine how you all must feel with me, the accused and convicted, speaking before you; but we must take into account that revenge is a strange animal, something that causes us to develop blinders that cause us to miss or avoid facts along the way to satisfy our desire for revenge. It's sad to say that this is what has occurred here.

To you, Mrs. Hurley and your family, to you, Officer Foley and your family, I am a Christian. I cannot lie. As I stand here before you, I swear to God I played absolutely no part in this horrible crime. An equally horrible mistake has been made. I am an innocent man who thus far has been paying for the sins of another. This is not me. I have a great regard for life and could never participate in anything such as I have been accused. An enormous error has been made.

Throughout the years I have known and worked beside those in Civil Service in the ranks of police and fire in the communities I have resided. I have much respect for those in uniform and the risks they take in the course of their duties. However, my friends behind their badges have turned their backs on me. My world has caved in. I am so alone. The country I know and love has turned against me and I have done no wrong.

I hope I can spark a glimmer of doubt in your mind as to my alleged participation in this affair, that one of you will question the outcome here, that one of you would want to be sure the streets are indeed rid of a dangerous person. For as long as I am standing here or incarcerated somewhere, a man or men will wrongfully be guaranteed freedom to walk amongst those in freedom, allowed to get away with the sin of murder, and I will be paying for those sins though I have not sinned.

This man is living in freedom in one of our neighborhoods. This man must be brought to justice. He is a danger to us all. This man has been dancing to the music for over two years. Isn't it time he paid the piper? Is it ever too late to do the right thing?

I beg all of you to open your minds and walk with me for a while and ask yourselves in your hearts if you really believe I could do what I have been accused of doing.

God bless you all and may the Lord be with you.

I would like to give you a brief history of my background now. I was born in Boston, Massachusetts, February 6, 1956; raised in Milton, Mass. by my mother and father, the Wallaces, along with my stepbrother David Wallace.

I enjoy a loving family and have throughout these years, and especially throughout these hard times. We have always been a close family.

As for education, I attended Milton Academy in Milton, Massachusetts; Park School in Brookline, Massachusetts; Thayer Academy in Braintree, Massachusetts; graduated in 1975. I went on to college attending Wentworth Institute in 1976, 1977, 1980 and 1981; and I took night courses at Northeastern University, 1978 and 1979.

As for employment, I have always been gainfully employed working at various companies, nights, weekends, and summers during my high school years earning money toward my college expenses.

After college I began my full-time employment starting with Analog Devices in Norwood, Mass., in 1978 to 1979; and Boston Catholic Television in Newton, Mass., 1981 to 1987; and its sister company, Television Production and Services in Newton, Mass., 1981 to 1985. I was self-employed at AWT Associates from 1987 to 1988, and at ATEL in South Boston, 1989 to 1991; at Cambridge Electronic Trans, in Jamaica Plain, Mass., for the MBTA, February of 1991; and Global Technology Research Corporation [GTRC] in Framingham and Hopedale, Massachusetts, March through June of 1991; and a co-venture with Richard Brown at ARCOMM, June of '91 to February of '92.

Outside of work I kept busy with many volunteer causes serving my community. I was a volunteer at Mayor White's march against drug abuse; a volunteer member of the American National Red Cross, taking courses with the Milton Police and Milton Fire Departments and working with the Milton Fire Department during emergency operations. I assisted with evacuations during the Chelsea fire in the '70s.

A member of Massachusetts Safety Squad, a local volunteer response group assisting the Boston Police and Boston Fire Departments in the Hyde Park area; a member of the Massachusetts Chapter of React, a nationwide disaster response group, working with the Massachusetts State Police and the Civil Defense; a member of the Friends of Blue Hills, assisting the MDC Police and surrounding fire departments.

I assisted with the formation of the Fenway Community Watch Group, working with the Boston Police, the MDC police, Northeastern University, Zach Communications out of Hopkinton, Mass., who also provided communication support for the Boston Marathon, and coordination with citizens in the Fenway/Back Bay area.

I also did volunteer light and sound work for the Milton Music [sic, Hoosic] Club in Milton, Massachusetts, donating the proceeds to Milton Hospital and other charitable causes. I also volunteer for many church activities in my community. I'm also a supporting member of Green Peace, the ASPCA and John Walsh's WSPA.

As for my hobbies and other activities, I am an avid skiier in the winter, a tennis player in the summertime, and I enjoy staying home and relaxing, reading a book or watching TV.

I also design useful products, some of which I had prototyped and was preparing to patent before my world was taken away.

Mostly I enjoy the quiet company of a close friend or friends.

As for my residences, I lived with my parents until 1982, briefly living in Boston in 1982, and returning home because of hepatitis until 1984.

From 1984 to 1988, I lived in the Quincy area with a friend of mine and a neighbor, Bob Craig, from Milton. In 1989 we moved to Hull, Mass., and then in 1990 I resided in South Boston. September of '90 to September of '92 I lived in Quincy with my roommate, John Cates.

Contrary to rumors, I am not some desperate, sex-starved maniac soliciting the likes of Tom Shay, Jr. or any human being. I do not buy friendship; I earn it based on mutual trust. I have a small, close group of friends that I am proud to know and share with my family.

I lead a simple life. I am not hung up on material wealth. I have no use for jewelry, fancy cars or fancy furnishings.

I have no hangups. I do not gamble. I own no weapons. I hold no grudges. I am not a violent person. I do not possess the capacity to bring harm onto anyone and have no history of physical violence.

I'm a giving human being. I'll give a friend a hand. I will give back to my community what help I can. If someone's hurt, I'll offer assistance. If I witness a wrong, I will take steps to correct it. If I find someone needs a ride within reason, I'll provide it.

I am a hard-working American citizen with developed lifetime skills earning a legitimate living with a bright future. I am not a transient. I have always lived in the South Shore community, paying rent, whether by cash or barter, with deep established roots.

As for my sexual orientation, I have never confirmed or denied whether I'm heterosexual, bisexual, or homosexual. It is not something I discuss or honestly know. I guess I would call it interesting. But ever since the worldwide concern for AIDS in the '80s and the long list of other social diseases, I have voluntarily abstained from any sexual behavior, short of long-term monogamous relationships, of which I have had a few.

The bottom line is throughout my life sex has been a very insignificant part of my life. I hold more important my platonic relationships that last a lifetime and my life-long studies in electronics and, of course, the love of my family.

Of the two monogamous relationships I had, John Cates was the second since 1985. We had met through friends while I was on vacation from ATEL in 1990. We cohabitated starting in September of 1990 and had the same type of friends, hard-working people with roots in the local business community. Though we had an open relationship, we chose not to be apart short of work. We lead and share the same lives, working hard and enjoying the peace of each other's company. We got along so famously we were inseparable. After working hours we would stay home together, my roommate composing his music and I catching up on paperwork. We would socialize together, go skiing together. We did everything together. But most of all we led a peaceful, uneventful existence together, accompanied by a canine pet.

It was sort of uncanny how well we got along together. We had a long trusting, long-term relationship that continues to this day, something I would never jeopardize for anything, never mind for the likes of which I have been accused. We had no financial problems. We would share the rent. I would take care of the groceries and transportation, an even split after all was said and done.

During our entire relationship there were no other people involved with either John Cates or myself. We shared the concerns of all the deadly diseases and we had our friends that were platonic relationships. We were simply two people growing in wholeness. Tom Shay, Jr. was not any part of me or John Cates, simply someone that happened to cross our paths at different times in different places, with John Cates years ago, and with myself in June of 1991; and with both the same circumstances. Tom Shay, Jr. just happened to be someone that John Cates and I were [acquainted with], separated by time and location -- I'm sorry.

Of the large percentage of the Boston population that has met or talked to Tom Shay, Jr. with the myriads of backgrounds, I just happened to have a crazy coincidental crazy background of the prank, which is all this case is, a weird coincidence. Never mind the coincidence that Tom Shay, Jr. was recognized from his nationwide appearance on a talk show by many people back in 1990.

It has been stated that I ran a string of unsuccessful businesses and that I was running yet another struggling electronics business during this alleged conspiracy. First of all, I don't know exactly what makes up a string of anything. I myself owned only one business for 18 months, 1987 to 1988, catering to Northeastern and Boston University, literally handed to me by Boston Catholic TV, my former employer; successful until these universities experienced such a drop in enrollment, making it difficult to for me to survive. I chose to close up shop.

The alleged struggling electronics company, my second that I coventured into with Richard Brown, called ARCOMM, was founded in 1991. The venture sprung from my knowledge of the Christian Science Monitor project, which I learned back in 1990 while at ATEL, and other projects I had learned about over the years; combined with Richard Brown's learning of other projects gleaned from his employment in sales at another electronics company in Weymouth, Massachusetts. However, no commitments were made until June of 1991, the time we had learned the Christian Science Monitor project was a go. But let's take a look at this failure.

July, our first project for Marcus Communications in Connecticut, grossing $6,000, for one radio tower job, giving an estimate of $150,000 for several smaller tower jobs.

August, small projects with Videocom and ATEL, my former employer, grossing $4,500. And through ATEL I gave a bid to Wang Computer in Lowell, Massachusetts, for my life [sic] project, for $35,000.

September, the Christian Science Monitor projects [sic] begins. We completed a helicopter lift on September 26th. We received $12,500 down payment on September 1st of that month, giving estimates of $75,000 to Christian Science Monitor for future work after this project was completed; giving an estimate to Frank Camarlo (phonetic,[actually Cavallo]) of Videocom for $15,000 for a Christian Science Monitor backup satellite dish; discussion with Videocom, the chief executive officer, for a facility move estimated at $150,000.

October we continued at Christian Science Monitor, completing the second helicopter lift on October 13th, receiving from Christian Science Monitor another $18,000. We discussed more projects with Christian Science Monitor, giving estimates of $50,000 in the month of October; discussing with Ed Alvaro (phonetic) of Channel 25 $25,000 in future projects.

Richard Brown entered a bid with Quincy Civil Defense for $20,000. MIT called us to set up meetings for more projects that I couldn't handle until November because we were swamped during the same time of this alleged conspiracy.

November, we continued at Christian Science Monitor.
I gave bids to MIT for $43,000, repair a system for MIT saving them $7,300.

December we continued at Christian Science Monitor, Christian Science Monitor giving us a final payment of $10,400. Quincy Civil Defense gives ARCOMM $20,000 dollars. We won the bid.

So for a summary of the figures. July, we gross $6,000, giving job estimates of $150,000. August, we gross $4500 giving job estimates of $35,000. September, we gross $12,500, giving job estimates of $240,000. October, grossing $18,000, giving job estimates of $95,000. November, grossing $650, [sic, should be $6,500] giving estimates of $43,000. And December, grossing $30,400. For a total of July to December bank deposits of $72,050; $563,000 in estimates; averaging $12,000 a month in deposits. July to October deposits of $41,000, and estimates of $523,000.

September and October alone, but during the time of this alleged conspiracy, we had $30,500 in deposits and $335,000 in estimates.

As for overhead, other than insurance, subcontractors and resale equipment, we had none until October 8th when we rented our office in Weymouth. But right here a question comes to mind: If the company was struggling so badly, how or why on earth would we be renting an office, paying six months rent up front and completely remodeling this office in October, halfway through this alleged conspiracy when it's *alleged the company is struggling and in desperate need of money?*

These figures come from documents possessed by the government. In fact, Rich Brown stated the company was terminated not because of failure but because of the ATF's constant harassment and not until 1992.

Now think of this for a moment. I am working at the Christian Science Monitor in the middle of a $40,000 job. Part of my job required the use of a helicopter on September 26th and October 13th of 1991 to lift heavy equipment. As Mr. Libby can identify, this is no walk in the park exercise. This event must be announced and cleared with the Boston Police, to which Rich Brown and I personally notified Paul Davies of arson headquarters, the Boston Fire Department, which Rich Brown and I personally notified through Rich Brown's father, Chip Brown of the Boston Fire Department, the FAA and Logan Airport, notified by Wiggins Airways; not to mention that during these two lifts there were hundreds of spectators.

Does it make any sense that five days after a highly visible, highly documented helicopter lifting operation, in between two days when my crew and I were working at Christian Science Monitor, namely, the 17th and 19th of October, 1991, a place where I have access to any number of toggle switches or micro switches that would be completely untraceable, as well as an electronics supply that rivals Radio Shack, that I would send Tom Shay, Jr., a man that appeared on nationwide TV in 1990, to a Radio Shack across the street from the Christian Science Monitor with a shopping list, less have a need to, to purchase electronic parts that not only would people at that store identify Tom Shay, Jr. as purchasing, but would leave a traceable paper trial and perhaps a surveillance photo of Tom Shay, Jr. making this purchase? This makes no sense at all. Does any of this make any sense at all, with the figures my clients mentioned, both in payments and estimates of future projects, that I would have a need to do something that would jeopardize this success and my personal relationship with John Cates, that would risk the lives of people I don't even know, that would risk my life and reputation allegedly for money offered by some unstable teenager that I gave some rides to and barely knew?

Please give me some credit. The deposits in the bank alone equate to what is alleged Tom Shay, Jr. was offering for this misdeed. The future projects known to me as of October of '91 were worth more than $100,000 more than Tom Shay, Sr.'s total lawsuit.

I deal with reality. I deal with high-level executives in Fortune companies landing legitimate contracts. Just what the heck would I have a need to deal with some street person for? This is absurd.

As for my personal finances, as with any company you start, you take a cut in pay to invest in your company. Rich Brown and I agreed to $1,000 a month each. July to December we each received $6,000, plus my tort case that Mark Cosgrove testified to for $6,000, receiving $12,000 from July to December. I was by no means strapped. I own my car. I possess no credit cards. I owe no loans. My only obligation was a $3,600 IRS bill on which I was making monthly payments, something I would not damage, intimidate, injure or kill for. Just where is this urgent need of money? Not to mention the fact if I did need money, I could borrow from my family, I which I had done in the past and was welcome to do again.

I would have to be suffering from severe dementia to jeopardize my success dealing with company executives to participate in an illegal scheme of any kind with some transient that hangs around the streets of Boston, a city where I am employed, a city where I had the misfortune to meet Tom Shay, Jr.

I guess putting yourself in the open can draw both desirable as well as undesirable results. I just never ran into any bad results until I met Tom Shay, Jr. I must have been living on borrowed time.

Your Honor, at the very least, I hope I have shed some light on who I am, showing some of the inaccuracies and misstatements about me, the conflicts to these accusations about me. What takes me aback is the ease to which the government has to point the finger at someone like me, making all sorts of accusations based on opinions and theories. Though I have proof these accusations are false or inaccurate, backed by witnesses, documentation, photographs and bank statements, the government somehow wins by saying my facts do not hold a candle to their mere opinions and theories, though they have no evidence to back what they say.

I have been accused of the most horrible of crimes, death to one human being, and serious injuries to another. I wish I had the answer to this crime, but I do not. I have remorse for those affected, but I cannot claim responsibility for what I am not responsible for.

I am a Christian. I cannot lie. And when I stand here and swear to God I am innocent, I am telling the truth. I in no way, shape or form played any part in this crime, any more than anyone in this courtroom. I could never do anything that would have a remote chance of injuries to any living thing.

I am lost with this helpless feeling, with the knowledge that whoever is responsible is out there on the street, and others that surround this person know of their participation. This person or persons count on me being convicted and sentenced, ensuring their freedom, paying with my life for their sins. While they dance in freedom, I rot behind bars. I have this fear that the more time that goes by the less of a chance the truth will be found. I may well pay for their evil deeds for the rest of my life.

Unless something is done soon in efforts to find those responsible, those responsible will be allowed to get away with the murder of Officer Jeremiah Hurley, injuries to Francis Foley, and the pain to both families, as well as the wrongful, mistaken incarceration of me and the pain my family also suffers.

To quote Edmund Burke, 'All that is necessary for the triumph of evil is that good men do nothing.' But if everyone believes I truly did this crime, and no attempts are made to re-evaluate this investigation, to admit mistakes were made, this could very well be my end.

I stand here to tell you that something has gone wrong. This case went askew from the early days, avoiding the concrete and searching the abstract. Nothing physically links me to this crime. No witnesses link me to this crime. No motive was proved to link me to this crime. No intent was demonstrated to link me to this crime.

The only link to this crime are statements from the government. The Boston Polices [sic] statements point in a totally opposite direction.

As is clear from both trials, Tom Shay, Sr. had an overwhelming motive of

$400,000, stemming from a previous explosion, whose stories conflict with the Boston Police and the ATF, who transgresses from victim to suspect to prosecution witness against his own son within three days.

As soon as the ATF took over within days of the '91 incident, all the Boston Police uncovered -- including documents; witnesses; evidence, physical and circumstantial; and statements -- that all point in a direction far removed from me, are thrown away, discarded. I am targeted based on Tom Shay, Jr. having my pager number and a few pieces of paper from 1986 describing an incident that was totally dissimilar, that did no damage, caused no injuries, contained no dynamite, involved an explosive equivalent to fireworks, dismissed because of its lack of seriousness, and at this point of the investigation had not even been analyzed yet, compared with the '91 incident that contained three sticks of dynamite and blasting caps that killed and injured [sic] that were still being collected from Eastbourne Street.

From that day forward the ATF was going to make me fit the puzzle that made up this crime even if the pieces had to be forced to fit. Over one year was spent trying to make these pieces fit the puzzle, overlooking or discarding anything that showed my innocence or the guilt of others.

We usually see only the things we are looking for, so much so that sometimes we see them where they are not. This is the case we have here.

To assist the government in making me fit this puzzle, the government relies on an inmate by the name of David Lindholm, a man with a sordid past of drugs, lies, tax evasion, tax and bank fraud; a typical man the Boston Police would enjoy seeing behind bars for life; the only man on the face of this earth who is a federal inmate transferred from Texas to this courthouse, coincidentally placed in a cell with Tom Shay, Jr., the babbling brook that has a habit of talking to every inmate he contacts. Coincidentally he [Lindblom] was transferred the next day to Plymouth House of Correction, because he missed his bus elsewhere, where I just happened to be held prior to a bail hearing.

Coincidentally, Mr. Lindholm was ill, just like Larry Plant was with Tom Shay, Jr., coincidentally the only federal inmate on the face of this earth that alleged [sic] lived on my street in my home town, a confirmed lie.

Coincidentally, Mr. Lindholm's father [sic, Lindholm further] testified his father attended Milton Academy and Thayer Academy, two schools I attended, which we found out he has never attended those particular schools. And, coincidentally, those two facts were contained in newspapers which were, coincidentally, at Plymouth House of Correction while Mr. Lindholm was there; i.e., all my personal information was available without Mr. Lindholm ever talking to me.

Coincidentally, Mr. Lindholm just happens to hear me tell him what I have told no other human being and have vehemently denied to everyone on this planet, and right after I had been warned by my attorneys not to talk to anyone in jail about anything; i.e., jail is a haven for reward or deal seekers.

This was the government's star witness in this case, developed within the first three days of my indictment. Why does this not seem at all suspicious or, at least, a little bit coincidental, that I would tell a total stranger something that I have denied to my family and closest friends and, coincidentally, almost word for word what

Larry Plant stated Tom Shay, Jr. told him.

Another point, when Mr. Lindholm made up his little story, he now risks injury or death at every prison he is placed. He's labeled a snitch. No one risks their life for nothing. Mr. Lindholm had an incentive. Mr. Lindholm's new drugs [sic] of choice is freedom, the dearest thing in the world. He knows how to deal for it. Alfred Trenkler is his ticket.

Mere statements are made concerning my background by the government based only on theory and opinion. I am said to be running a failing and struggling company. But what was used to gauge this failure or struggle? There are no signs of failure or struggle. Success was proven with cold hard facts and figures that don't lie, including my clients that testified to current and future projects.

In fact, Richard Brown stated the company did not fail because of anything other than the ATF's harassment. Our only struggle was what color carpet to buy for our office in October.

I am said to be in need of money personally. Just what need was this? None was demonstrated. I was comfortable. I may not be rich, but what's wrong with that? Money doesn't mean anything to me.

But it seems just in case that theory would not hold water, more theories were developed: that I sympathized with Tom Shay, Jr. over his father's rejection and hostility or that I wanted to get close to Tom Shay, Jr. by killing his father. This is totally absurd. No one is worth killing for. I have a life, a profession, a stable relationship. I live in reality.

Meeting Tom Shay, Jr. was a total coincidence. He was simply at a place where I and John Cates had visited before. All I ever did was give this Tom Shay, Jr. a few rides in my car and hand him a business card. I had absolutely no involvement with this person. I simply handed him a business card for the gain of new possible business relationships that Tom Shay, Jr. said he knew. But after my brief encounters with Tom Shay, Jr., my goal was to avoid this person. He had a psyche that said 'Stay away,' an embarrassment to admit to know.

The government did not show any relationship with Tom Shay, Jr., especially during this alleged conspiracy. Tom Shay, Jr. was a typical street person with no apparent attributes, except to scrounge rides and attempt to make friends. However, he tried too hard to be liked and would go overboard to be accepted. As soon as one got to know Tom Shay, Jr. was the time you wanted nothing to do with him.

I'll put it to you this way: Tom Shay, Jr. was like a stray dog that you'd see in front of your favorite store. You might give it a pat. You might feed it a snack. It might follow you home. But you don't keep it as your pet. You don't know its past. You send it on its way to wherever it came from.

I am accused of being a domestic terrorist that has cold bloodedly killed and injured based on a prank from my past in for someone known to me for many years, a device from which there was no harm or damage and none intended, a device that was equivalent to and made a noise like a large firecracker, a device of which there are no remains, compared to and said to match a sinister device from which death and injuries resulted, a device that contained three sticks of dynamite, surrounded by motives of lawsuits, intimidation, destruction, death and injuries.

How much more unfair could this be? These two devices are as different as night and day. The 1986 [device] is obviously a prank device not made for damage. The 1991 device is obviously a sinister device for damage and injuries surrounded by a totally different set of circumstances and motives and intent. These devices were totally different in purpose and construction. How can the intent and state of mind be possibly said to be the same? It's like comparing fireworks thrown by someone's front lawn versus three sticks of dynamite thrown by someone's front door. The former makes a noise. The latter blows the front of the house in.

Your Honor, I could go on for hours with comparisons revealing all the errors in this case. But from what I have observed, this incident demonstrates the importance of honest intelligence in a world where the concept of deterrence is predicated on the assumption that men with their fingers on the trigger have accurate information. At the onset the Boston Police did have accurate information, but this was distorted and deleted from this case. In substitution of this information was nothing more than inaccurate opinion and theory and accusations and inferences.

I have always felt we didn't believe in sacrificing innocent people because it might help some higher goal. This is still the United States. The deliberate incarceration of an innocent man by the government stains every citizen. Justice should be served. Punishment should be imposed, but on the guilty, not the innocent. We have a wonderful system of justice, but there are mistakes. There are bad decisions. I must stand up to the injustice in this case. My life, my reputation, my freedom is on the line.

I still have hope, since the courts have an obligation to protect society as well as the individual from wrongful prosecution. I have this awful feeling that innocence or guilt has little to do with what's going on here. All that seems important is just winning this case.

To sense what I have gone through put yourself in my shoes for a moment. You are accused of a heinous crime. People against you -- people you respect and worked for or known -- let me start over again, please.

Put yourself in my shoes for a moment. You are accused of a heinous crime against people you respect and have worked for or known; put through a trial, accused of things that were never proven, listening to people you never laid eyes on putting you in places you never were with people you barely know, saying you made statements you never made; convicted and jailed an innocent person, awaiting sentencing and you've done no wrong; and you are helpless to correct this.

Your Honor, I am the sacrificial lamb who has been wrongfully accused of committing a heinous crime that another is responsible for. Whoever did this enjoys freedom at my expense. This is not just. This is wrong. Is it now up to me to solve this case or suffer forever in this living hell I am forced to bear?

Sentencing me is not the solution. It does not close the book on this case. It is a continuance of a horrible mistake. I realize you are bound by your responsibilities. I just wonder when this mistake will be corrected.

I am reminded of a story Dennis Leahy of the ATF told about a man who got away with murder. The years went by and this man was never caught, until one day he confided in a person he had known over the years. This person told all. The *murderer went to jail. Is this my story? Do I have to wait for someone's mistake to be absolved?*

Your Honor, I know I'm reaching, but is it not better to concede to mistakes that have been made and acquit or sentence me and find out down the road that the government made a mistake and convicted the wrong man? The truth will not be hidden forever. It will surface, and, I pray to God, sooner than later.

I have said my piece. I am at your mercy. Please search your soul for the answer Thank you, your Honor." (TTH 6-32/59)

Did any believer in Trenkler's guilt in the courtroom, especially Judge Zobel, give any credence to this statement by Alfred Trenkler? On the defense side, had the mistake of not having Alfred testify already become apparent? Wouldn't he have made a good impression on the jury? How many people in the courtroom were saying to themselves, *"Why didn't all that information get presented to the jury?"*

Judge Zobel then spoke and concluded with her sentence, *"Mr. Trenkler has argued forcefully against the verdict of guilt, but I must act on the basis of the verdict rendered by the jury. I accept that verdict.*

Counsel has cited Mr. Trenkler's nonviolent nature in support of an argument for departure; but this was, as the evidence showed, not the first, not the second, but the third bomb. And the second one was not exactly a firecracker, at least as I heard the evidence.

It is true that Mr. Trenkler does not have a prior record to speak of. It is true that there was little direct evidence of guilt, but the jury did find guilt and did so on the basis of circumstantial evidence which was strong, indeed.

The defendant also argues in the papers that were submitted that the guidelines specifically encourage downward departure, quote, if the defendant did not cause the death intentionally or knowingly, end quote. That's from the guidelines....

The fact that there is a difference or there will be a difference in the sentences between the two defendants is the result of the differences in their conduct and their state of mind as I have found it to be.

This was a horrendous crime. An absolutely innocent person doing his job was literally blown apart and another seriously injured and maimed. The letters of the Mr. Foley and members of his family and those of the daughters and sister of Mr. Hurley speak eloquently of their loss and their pain. I have also read and considered the letters of Mr. and Mrs. Wallace's friends on behalf of Mr. Trenkler. They too speak of a close and loving family and they too speak of the losses that that family is now suffering. I have, of course, considered the statements of counsel and Mr. Trenkler and the written submissions.

On the basis of all of these, I find it inappropriate to depart down, and I sentence you to imprisonment for your life on Counts 2 and 3, which sentences are to be served concurrently; to imprisonment for a period of 60 months on Count 1, which is to be served concurrently with the sentence on Counts 2 and 3. You are to pay a special assessment of $150; that is, $50 on each count.

Under the circumstances, I do not believe supervised release is appropriate, and I shall impose neither fine nor restitution... You have the right to appeql from this judgment of conviction and sentence, and I have allowed the defendant's motion for leave to proceed on appeal in forma pauperis....

Mr. Marshall, the defendant is now in your custody under sentence of the court." (TTH

Judge Zobel's reference to three bombs must have been a shock to Alfred Trenkler and Terry Segal, until they considered Michael Coady's virtually unchallenged testimony about Alfred setting off a large firecracker at a party, which was a completely untrue statement. There was insufficient cross-examination of Coady and many others, and Alfred's side of each story was not heard.

Terry Segal's apparent strategy of ignoring Mike Coady's testimony on the grounds that it was preposterous was a complete failure. Even Judge Zobel, who had seen a lot of tall tales from her side of the witness stand seemed to have believed the firecracker party story. Did she believe everything else that Michael Coady said? It appears to be the case.

Ralph Ranalli wrote the _Herald_'s page 5 story, "*CONVICTED BOMBER GETS LIFE - OFFICERS' FAMILIES APPLAUD STIFF SENTENCE.*" The article described Trenkler's "*long, sometimes repetitious speech in which he outlined his life. He accused federal prosecutors of ignoring evidence that he said implicated Shay's father.*" Said Boston Police Commissioner Paul Evans, "*I think the most culpable person was Trenkler. I think without his skill and expertise, Officer Hurley would still be alive...*" Said Cynthia Hurley, "*I don't think it will ever be over for us, but this is certainly a happy day for us.*"

The Request for Justice IV had failed, as Alfred was sentenced to two life terms by Judge Zobel, and Judge Zobel alone, without the recommendation from the trial jury.

Judy Rakowsky wrote the _Boston Globe_'s article, "*BOMB-MAKER GETS LIFE IN PRISON FOR 1991 BLAST THAT KILLED OFFICER.*" She referred to Tom Shay as Trenkler's "*co-defendant*" as compared to Ranalli's terms, "*friend and lover,*" and caught Trenkler's description of Shay as "*a stray dog outside a store.*" She quoted Paul Evans, "*We're not talking revenge here... We're talking justice,*" and Cynthia Hurley, "*I didn't appreciate his comments to me,*" and Francis Foley, "*I don't need his sympathy.*" The _Worcester Telegram and Gazette_'s story from the Associated Press was headlined, "*MASTERMIND GETS LIFE IN FATAL BOSTON BOMBING.*"

Even if the verdict were just, everyone knew that there would be an appeal, as there usually is after a criminal conviction. In most of them, it seems safe to say, the defendant actually committed the crime or was involved in some way.

For a few, the defendant is perfectly innocent, and Alfred William Trenkler was one of those.

Shortly after the sentencing, Alfred was transferred in the custody of U.S. Marshals to the Allenwood Federal Prison in White Deer, Pennsylvania which was the nearest Federal prison to Massachusetts with the high level of security which Trenkler was deemed to require. As a highly skilled electronics engineer who was convicted of building a bomb, Alfred was designated a high security risk. Since his conviction and pending the sentencing, he had been imprisoned at the temporary Federal facility within the State of New Hampshire's Hillsborough County House of Correction, near the city of Manchester.

Also sent to Allenwood for life about the same time was CIA counterspy Aldrich Ames whose duplicity had sent at least ten Soviet citizens to their deaths for spying for the U.S. Intriguingly, one reason why Ames' eight years of selling secrets to the U.S.S.R. was not caught sooner, was that he had passed two lie detector tests. Another spy at Allenwood was John Walker, Jr. who, like Alfred, was serving two life terms-plus. A third CIA-related inmate was Edwin Paul Wilson who was convicted in 1983 of smuggling weapons to Libya. Part of his defense was that he was a CIA employee at the time and his actions were pursuant to CIA orders. However, the CIA denied at Wilson's trial that he was an employee. In 2004, a Federal judge ordered Wilson released after a document was obtained which showed that Wilson was, in fact, a CIA employee.[3] Thus, his 1983 conviction was a Federal wrongful conviction.

Also on 15 March, Terry Segal filed Alfred Trenkler's "*Motion for Appointment of Counsel to Proceed on his Appeal to the United States Court of Appeals for the First Circuit from the Judgment and Sentence of the District Court.*" He had already filed his Notice of Appeal to the First Circuit, which is comprised of New England and Puerto Rico, minus Vermont and Connecticut. This appeal was Alfred Trenkler's <u>Request for Justice V</u>.

On 17 March, Alfred wrote to Congressman Joseph Moakley to ask his assistance in placement in a prison nearer to home so his family could be closer to him and so he could work more effectively with his lawyers. He stated, "*This was a horrible crime that I have been sentenced for, however, I maintain my innocence. This is a total travesty of justice. I have been set-up as a scapegoat to pay for a crime I did not commit. My family has been devastated by this entire nightmare.*"

Also on 17 March, Alfred Trenkler wrote to the Court of Appeals to inquire whether he could secure the appellate services of Dana Curhan, a fellow Thayer Academy alumnus, but of the class of 1977, two years behind Alfred, but Attorney William A. Brown was appointed by the Court to represent him. However, on 2 May 1994, the First Circuit allowed Brown to withdraw, as Alfred's parents had retained Morris Goldings, a well-known Boston lawyer and partner in the firm Mahoney, Hawkes and Goldings. In addition to the considerations they faced after the indictment when deciding whether to retain private counsel or accept the publicly funded attorney, Alfred and his family were uncomfortable with their understanding that Brown was a friend of Paul Kelly. Such friendships between prosecutors and defense lawyers are not unusual, but lawyers are more comfortable than others with the boundaries they draw between their professional and personal lives.

On 1 April 1994, 23 days after Alfred Trenkler's sentencing and unbeknownst to Trenkler's attorneys, the attorney for William David Lindholm, Roger Cox, wrote to Paul Kelly to ask for what Lindholm had told the Trenkler court and jury he would not ask for: a reduction of his sentence. Wrote Cox, "*Nevertheless, his* [Lindholm's] *assistance was extraordinary. It was forthright, honest and compelling, and of immense value in strengthening the prosecution against Mr. Trenkler. While Mr. Lindholm provided this assistance to the United States without any* [explicit] *expectation of benefit, I believe that it is my duty, as his counsel, to secure whatever benefit I can for him. There may be no enforceable legal obligation on the part of the Government to assist Mr. Lindholm, but I believe that fairness requires that your office seriously consider filing a motion before Judge Woodlock recommending that Mr. Lindholm's sentence be reduced because of his substantial assistance. It is simply the right thing to do.*"

On 12 April, Paul Kelly reminded Roger Cox of Lindholm's promise in open court, where Lindholm said "*I'll go on the record to say that I'm not going to ask for any benefit, rewards, inducements any time in the future,*" but asked Cox to confer with Lindholm and get back to him if they wish to do the obvious, i.e. present such a request to Judge Woodlock. On precisely the same day, 12 April, Roger Cox wrote back a hard copy letter and said that he had already conferred with Lindholm and that he wished to proceed. Well, of course. The result was Motion, pursuant to a Federal Rule of Criminal Procedure 35(b), to Judge Woodlock by Paul Kelly and Frank Libby on 19 July 1994 to reduce Lindholm's 97 month sentence by 24 months. Because the matter was filed in the case of U.S. vs. William David Lindholm, there was no procedural requirement that Trenkler's attorneys be notified, but it would have been the correct and fair step to take.

On 6 June, Morris Goldings filed "*Defendant-Appellant Alfred Trenkler's Designation of Appendix and Statement of Issues.*" The 13 issues stated by Goldings' Associate lawyer, Amy Axelrod, were the same as those raised by Terry Segal in his "Motion for a New Trial," with the 13th being "*Whether the Court erred in denying Defendant's Motion for Acquittal made at the conclusion of the Government's case and at the conclusion of the evidence?*" There was no explicit reference to the Karen Marinella-Tom Shay interview, or to William David Lindholm. Nothing was said about the ability of the District Court to sentence Alfred Trenkler to life in prison without a recommendation from the trial jury. There was nothing to indicate that the Roslindale Bomb's toggle switch contacts may have come from a source other than Radio Shack, and nothing to indicate awareness that the Futaba receiver was an older, energy-hog model. The truth about these last two technical matters had not yet been discovered.

Far away in White Deer, Pennsylvania in the land of the 1978 film, "*The Deer Hunter,*" Alfred Trenkler was trying to help. He sent Morris Goldings a 50-page handwritten letter with ideas about factual and legal arguments, saying, "*Dear Morris, How goes the battle? I hope all this material gets to you in time to be useful for the appeal. I have included other issues that we never discussed and wonder if these are issues that we can bring up or that stand out enough for the appeals court to take notice.*" Unfortunately, there were few issues that Alfred could hang his hat on. From now on the focus was to be on legal errors rather than on his innocence or guilt.

On 10 June 1994, the *Boston Herald* carried Ralph Ranalli's front page story about Francis Foley's role in the filming the previous summer in Boston of the movie, "*Blown Away,*" starring Jeff Bridges, Lloyd Bridges and Forrest Whittaker. The headline was "*EX-COP SETS PAIN ASIDE TO WORK IN BOMB FILM.*" Frank Foley was cast in the non-speaking role as "*Lt. Frank Foley.*" His costume was his former police uniform which he hadn't worn for two years.

On 21 June, Moira Downes wrote in the *Herald* about the first awarding of a scholarship in Jeremiah Hurley's honor. In "*SLAIN OFFICER'S MEMORY LIVES ON WITH SCHOLARSHIP,*" she wrote that Cynthia Hurley presented the $500 award to Erin Dalia, 12 years old, a student at St. Anne's Elementary School in Readville. Said Mrs. Hurley, "*Through these scholarships, Jerry's memory will live on forever.*" Continued the article, "*Three scholarships, now in their second year, have been set up in Hurley's name. They are available to students at St. Anne's school, children of Boston Police Department bomb technicians and Knights of Columbus members. The recipient must exemplify the 'spirit' of Jeremiah Hurley.*" We hope that this book also exemplifies the spirit of Jeremiah Hurley, and that he would not have abided any wrongful conviction which came to his attention.

On 30 June, there was a benefit showing in Boston of the film "*Blown Away,*" and the film began with the dedication "*This film is dedicated to the memory of Boston Police Officer Jeremiah J. Hurley, who died in the line of duty... Oct. 28 1991.*" The film was released nationwide the next day. Peter Gelzinis wrote the column in the *Boston Herald*, "*IN DEATH, HUB OFFICER'S HEROIC ACTIONS FORGOTTEN*," which was about another recently-killed policeman, John Mulligan, who, coincidentally, had come to the aid of Jeremiah Hurley and Frank Foley on 28 October 1991.

On 1 August 1994, the full 73 page appeal for Alfred Trenkler, with a 7 volume Appendix, was filed. The argument focused entirely on three of the 13 issues mentioned earlier: the admission of evidence of the 1986 Quincy incident, the introduction of the queries from the EXIS database, and the admission of Tom Shay's statements. A new issue was that the "*Prosecution engaged in numerous instances of misconduct which improperly influenced the jury and unfairly prejudiced Trenkler.*" Two of those "numerous" instances were that the prosecution made a "*prejudicially inflammatory its opening statement*" and that "*the prosecution introduced evidence that it had previously represented that it would not introduce.*" It's not known why the other issues were discarded.

In the "*Statement of the Facts*," despite the earlier efforts by Terry Segal to suppress the evidence and statements taken on the night of 5-6 November 1991, Goldings wrote, "*With Trenkler's permission, and with Trenkler's full cooperation the agents searched Trenkler's residence, the premises of his business, his parents' garage and his car.... Several items were seized... but the Laboratory's analyses did not make any findings which would link any of Trenkler's items to the bomb.*"

About Lindholm, Goldings wrote, "*Although Lindholm testified that he had no agreement with the Government to testify,* [he] *thought rehabilitation was an important goal for the penal system, and that his testimony 'was a correct thing ... to do....'* Lindholm also understood, however, that 'the only way* [his] *sentence could be reduced* [was] *if* [he] *suppl[ied] new information to the Government.' *" Goldings did not know, but should have been informed, that two weeks earlier, on 19 July, AUSA's Paul Kelly and Frank Libby had filed the Motion with Judge Douglas Woodlock to reduce Lindholm's sentence.

Regarding the introduction of the evidence of the 1986 device for the purpose of showing the same signature, Goldings argued, "*In sum, whether one considers each device's individual components or each device as a whole, the two devices show a marked disparity in the use of the generic components, and in the techniques necessary to assemble them.*"

In addition to arguing that it was error to introduce the 1986 evidence, the appeal argued that the error was "*not harmless error.*" Citing a previous decision by the First Circuit, Goldings said the standard for "*harmless error*" was that "*it is 'highly probable' that the error did not contribute to the verdict.*" In support of that view the brief argued "*There is no question that,... the evidence of the 1986 incident contributed to the jury's verdict.*" Goldings quoted a document by the prosecutors where they stated that "*the evidence as to the 1986 bombing ... represents the centerpiece of the Government's case in chief.*"

Regarding the EXIS database, the appeal argued, as Terry Segal had before, that it was hearsay and not covered by any exception to that rule, and the entering of the 1986 information after 28 October 1991 was particularly suspect. Also, continuing the pattern of argument, the error was harmful, and "*like the carnival magician, the EXIS computer evidence creates the illusion of trustworthiness. In a society that places great value on computer derived information, it is highly probable that the jury accepted blindly the apocryphal EXIS 'statistics' and relied upon them without question to convict the Defendant. A trial where the result can - and did - lead to a sentence of life imprisonment should not be infected by a process more like a Nintendo game. "*

Addressing statements by Tom Shay, the appeal stated the jury knew that Shay had been convicted, and that admitting any of his statements violated Alfred Trenkler's Sixth Amendment right to confront witnesses against him. Goldings presented nine such statements which were introduced to the jury through the testimonies of Detective Miller Thomas and cellmates Robert Evans and Larry Plant. At the end of the list was No. 10, which merely stated that *"Channel 56 reporter Karen Marinella interviewed Shay....Portions of Shay Jr.'s statements given in the videotaped interview were introduced at trial,"* without specifically naming the harmful statements.

Argued Goldings, *"The statements did more than prejudicially spill over to Trenkler; they prejudicially engulfed him in Shay Jr.'s guilt and deprived him of the opportunity to cross examine Shay Jr."* Then Goldings quoted the Supreme Court in the case <u>U.S. v. Dworken</u>, *"A defendant is entitled to have the question of his guilt determined upon the evidence against him, not on whether a codefendant or government witness has been convicted of the same charge."* Again, Goldings faced the difficulty of whether to concede that Shay was guilty or whether to maintain that all of Shay's incriminating statements were caused by his "pseudologia fantastica" ailment or as is called here, his "voluntary false confessions."

In the last major argument, Morris Goldings addressed the alleged prosecutor misconduct. In the prosecution's opening statement, Paul Kelly stated that *"you will hear that Shay, Jr. told investigators that he wasn't the one who built it, that he wasn't the one who got the dynamite, that he wasn't the violent one. "* Said the appeal, *"Here the Prosecutor's remarks exceeded the bounds of ethical conduct and were the first in a series of improprieties. Compelled to make sure that the tenuous evidentiary link between Shay Jr. and Trenkler was established in the minds of the jurors, the Prosecutor deliberately employed Shay Jr.'s inflammatory statements knowing that he might not testify, and in direct contravention of the district court's order."* Further, despite objections by the defense, Judge Zobel did not try to correct the damage by giving the jury a *"curative"* instruction. Thus, reasoned Goldings, the opening comment *"poisoned the minds of the jurors"* which damage was *"compounded"* by the subsequent admission of Shay's inculpatory statements.

The second source of claimed prosecutor misconduct came with the questioning of Michael Coady, despite Judge Zobel's order that there was to be no evidence submitted to the jury of Trenkler's alleged solicitation of teenaged males as it would be unfairly prejudicial. Despite the order, and despite the prosecutors' representation that it would not delve into that forbidden area, Coady was asked about the trips to California and Fort Lauderdale when Coady was between 15 and a half and 18. Important as that legal argument may have been, the irony was that Mike Coady was actually 18 or 19 when Alfred Trenkler met him and that there were no trips to California, Florida or snow covered mountains.

The Morris Goldings appeal concluded *"For the foregoing reasons and authorities, this Court must vacate the conviction of the Defendant-Appellant Alfred W. Trenkler and order a new trial."*

On 30 August 1994, the prosecutors filed a motion with the First Circuit *"to schedule the above-captioned cases* [Shay's and Trenkler's appeals] *for argument on the same date before the same appellate panel.*" Paul Kelly and Frank Libby argued that the two appeals arose out of the same basic facts and that it would save judicial resources if the same three-judge panel considered both cases.

Tom Shay's attorneys, Amy Baron-Evans and Kathy Weinman, opposed the consolidation of the two cases because the primary reasons for the convictions of Shay and Trenkler were different: They argued that Shay was convicted by his own statements and the Radio Shack receipt, and Trenkler was convicted by the evidence of the 1986 device. Baron-Evans and Weinman argued that the claims of error were different, too, in that Shay claimed that the exclusion of Dr. Phillips' psychiatric testimony was error and "*Trenkler did not attempt to introduce expert psychiatric testimony regarding the reliability of Shay Jr,'s statements, did not attempt to introduce Shay Jr.'s prior inconsistent statement, and did not seek special instructions regarding the reliability of Shay Jr.'s statements. Accordingly, Trenkler's appeal has nothing to do with any of those issues... Shay Jr.'s state of mind, of course, was not at issue in Trenkler's trial, and is not an issue in Trenkler's appeal.*"

It's unclear beyond these differences what Baron-Evans and Weinman feared from the consolidation. Were they thinking that Trenkler was really guilty while their own client was innocent, and that the association of Shay with Trenkler on appeal would taint Shay's appeal? Given that it was Tom Shay's web of lies that contributed substantially to the conviction of Alfred Trenkler, Shay's attorneys might have sought to do what was helpful for Trenkler as well as for Shay. However, a lawyer's responsibility is first to his or her client, with truth and justice being further down the ladder. This conflict was most apparent when they persuaded Tom Shay not to testify at Trenkler's trial.

If both sets of lawyers had taken the position that both of their clients were perfectly innocent, which was, in fact, the truth, they might have been more successful in the trials and appeals. As it was, each defendant appeared to be pointing to the other, when they weren't pointing to Mr. Thomas L. Shay.

Unfortunately for Alfred Trenkler, Shay's argument persuaded the First Circuit to schedule the hearings for Tom Shay and Alfred Trenkler on different days, and before different panels, with the one exception that Chief Judge Juan Torruella was on both panels.

On 26 September 1994, Paul Kelly and Frank Libby filed the Appellee Government's 60 page Reply Brief, together with an additional 100 page Appendix, which supplemented Morris Goldings' seven volume Appendix.

In their statement of the "Facts of the Case," Kelly and Libby described in some detail the meeting of Alfred Trenkler and William David Lindholm at the Plymouth County House of Correction, and Lindholm's subsequent testimony of Trenkler's admission that he built the Roslindale Bomb. The Lindholm testimony was not part of the argument, which responded to the four parts of the argument of the Appellant Alfred Trenkler. As with the restriction of cross-examination to the issues raised during direct examinations of witnesses, a reply brief in an appeal responds to the claims of error by the appellant; and need not expand further with explanations of why the lower court verdict was a good one.

AUSA's Paul Kelly and Frank Libby did not state in their brief that David Lindholm was scheduled to be released four days later, on 30 September, after receiving a 55 month reduction in his 97 month sentence. Nor did they disclose their own 19 July

Motion to Judge Woodlock requesting a 24 month reduction. He ordered the 55 month reduction on 3 September. Legal rules did not require such notice because Judge Woodlock was acting on Lindholm's original 1990 criminal conviction, which had nothing to do with the Roslindale Bomb case. However, given the obvious importance of Lindholm to the Alfred Trenkler case, some informal notice should have been given. Judge Douglas Woodlock had more than doubled the request by Paul Kelly, perhaps because the judge was informed by others in the U.S. Attorney's office of Lindholm's commitment to testify at any upcoming proceedings against the Boston mobster, Whitey Bulger, should he ever be found and returned for trial. Paul Kelly's Affidavit in support of the Government's 19 July 1994 Motion for reduction of sentence did not mention the claims by Alfred Trenkler that Lindholm lied about the claimed Trenkler admissions precisely to obtain a reduction in sentence. It's not known whether Judge Woodlock inquired further about the circumstances of Lindholm's testimony in the Trenkler case. Did he, for example, discuss the request for reduction of sentence with Judge Zobel? It's doubtful and probably prohibited by an otherwise well-intentioned rule against such judge-to-judge communications, except in open court.

In Argument I, Kelly and Libby said the admission of the evidence of the 1986 device and the EXIS database information was proper, and that the District Court took special care in extensive pre-trial hearings to establish that the 1986 and 1991 devices were sufficiently similar. A key issue in any appeal is the "*standard of review*" that will be applied, which varies depending upon the nature of the claimed error. With respect to the claim that the 1986 and EXIS evidence was improperly introduced as evidence, the prosecutors stated that the standard of review is that "*A factual determination made by the trial court in any preliminary hearing is subject to reversal only if **clearly erroneous***." (Emphasis added for the standard of review.)

Regarding the EXIS database, Kelly and Libby addressed in a footnote an issue the appellate judges would find crucially important, "*Even assuming arguendo some error in admitting the EXIS evidence, it was harmless,*" because there was other evidence linking the 1986 and 1991 incidents, and other evidence pointing to the guilt of Alfred Trenkler and Tom Shay.

The second major appellee argument, about the admission of Shay's statements, was that they only showed Tom Shay's state of mind and none of them directly implicated Trenkler.

The third argument was that the prosecutors did not engage in any misconduct in the opening statement about Shay's statements, because there was no order not to do so, contrary to appellant's allegations. Regarding Michael Coady's testimony, the prosecutors wrote, "*At no time during his testimony did he mention anything about sexuality, homosexuality, or drugs.*"

Concluded the prosecutors, "*For the foregoing reasons, this Court should affirm the judgment and conviction below.*"

On 12 October 1994, Morris Goldings filed a "Reply Brief" in response to the above Appellee Brief by Paul Kelly and Frank Libby. Wrote Goldings with more heat than light, "*The Government attempts to overcome the inadequacy of its legal and factual argument in support of the admission of the 1986 incident with an array of misleading characterization of the record and of the evidence....*" Later, he wrote, "*The Government disingenuously fails to reveal that Waskom's opinion on the issue of modus operandi is based in its entirety upon hypothetical facts posed to him by the government.*"

Getting to the merits, the "Reply Brief" insisted that the 1986 and 1991 devices were different and "*idiosyncratic*" in many ways, and Judge Zobel's finding of similarity was wrong. Regarding the admission of Shay's statements, Goldings argued that even though Paul Kelly and Frank Libby didn't mention Alfred Trenkler by name, the jury knew that Shay had been convicted and that there was only one other indicted co-conspirator; thus the jurors understood who Tom Shay was talking about, and thus Trenkler was subject to "*guilt by association.*"

On 13 October 1999, Scott Lopez from Segal and Feinberg wrote to Amy Axelrod at Alfred's appellate law firm, Mahoney, Hawkes & Goldings, about a conversation he had with Amy Baron-Evans of Tom Shay's defense team. "*Apparently, Shay claimed that he had been involved in the theft of a substantial amount of munitions from Fort Devens and that he sold these munitions to IRA sympathizers who were involved in a plot to assassinate President Clinton. What is most interesting about Shay's story is that it was convincing enough to cause a Secret Service agent named Grzesiuk to interview him about this matter. Not surprisingly, it turns out that Agent Grzesiuk was unable to corroborate any of Shay's story and [was] not even able to confirm that any munitions from Fort Devens were missing. In short, the agent, who has a background in psychology, concluded that Shay made the entire story up....*

First, if true (which is quite unlikely) it indicates that Shay may have access to explosives. This undercuts the government's theory that the Roslindale Bombing was a two person conspiracy. It also seems to me that these new statements are as much against Shay's penal interests as his statements about the Radio Shack purchase. In both cases, he made up the story because he wanted someone to pay attention to him.

Second, and more importantly, if untrue (which is likely) it seems to me that these statements may be more advantageous to Al. Specifically, this 'new' evidence, which was not available at the time of trial, would tend to show the total unreliability of Shay's statements. Moreover, since Shay's other statements were vital to the government's burden that a conspiracy existed, it seems that admission of these new statements could lead to an acquittal." Nothing about the Fort Devens munitions affair was ever brought to a judge's attention in either the Shay or the Trenkler cases. It might have been used in a Shay retrial, but the statements were made after 28 October 1991.

The hearing of Alfred Trenkler's direct appeal at the First Circuit was held on 6 December 1994. The three judge panel was composed of Chief Judge Juan Torruella, and Judges Norman Stahl and Frank Coffin. Although cassette recordings were made of the hearing, no transcripts were created in the absence of a request from either side. The cassette recordings have subsequently been discarded as part of a normal record retention/discarding process. Only the *Boston Globe* covered the hearing the next day, with the article on page 65, "*LAWYER APPEALS BOMBING VERDICT.*"

On 6 February 1995 Alfred Trenkler turned 39 years old.

On 18 April 1995, the *Boston Globe* published a photo, captioned, "*IN HER FATHER'S FOOTSTEPS,*" of Leanne Hurley, a daughter of Jeremiah Hurley, at her swearing-in as a new Boston Police Officer.

In May 1995 Attorney Amy Axelrod, of Morris Goldings' firm, wrote to Warden Holland at Allenwood to ask that Alfred be considered for a tutoring job through the prison library, instead of his current position working for UNICOR, the prison industry officer furniture maker.

The First Circuit issued its decision on 18 July 1995, and for Trenkler, it was a heartbreaking 2-1 vote upholding the verdict. Judge Norman Stahl wrote the majority opinion and noted the heavy reliance by the government on the testimony by William David Lindholm, who, he said, *"testified that he had not received nor discussed receiving anything from the government in return for his testimony."* It does not appear that any of the judges knew at the time of the 6 December 1994 oral argument that Lindholm had been released 10 weeks earlier, on 30 September 1994, a full 55 months early from his 97 month prison sentence. Neither Alfred Trenkler nor his attorneys nor the media knew anything about the requests for early release and the actual release.

Judge Stahl observed, *"On cross examination, Trenkler's counsel made only a minimal effort to impeach Lindholm, raising matters unrelated to his testimony implicating Trenkler."* Judge Stahl's observation was particularly painful to Alfred. Not only was Terry Segal publicly criticized for not thoroughly cross-examining David Lindholm, Segal's advice not to testify also contributed to the free ride for Lindholm's story.

In 1988, when sending materials about the case to his friend, Mark Brodie, who worked at CBS Television, Alfred wrote, *"I had requested Segal to subpoena inmates from the Plymouth County House of Correction where Lindholm and I had been held in order to show that Lindholm was lying. ...these inmates would have shown that beyond the 5-10 minute conversation I had with Lindholm, there was no other interaction between myself and Lindholm. Lindholm had remained in bed almost the entire time he was there in fact it had been rumored that he had AIDS and everyone, including me, avoided him like the plague. These inmates would have testified that I constantly proclaimed my innocence and that Lindholm would spend his day reading newspapers in bed, something that Lindholm had denied. The newspapers contained the same information that Lindholm is testifying that I told him. I was prejudiced in that I had available witnesses to corroborate my avoiding Lindholm and my proclamation of innocence. I had no other way to obtain these witnesses without the assistance of my attorney.... My attorney refused to subpoena and or interview these inmates that would have impeached Lindholm."* Also, wrote Alfred, his attorney had instructed him not to discuss the case with anyone in jail, and Alfred, unlike his co-defendant, was following those instructions.

Returning to Judge Stahl's opinion and its statement of the facts, the damage of Todd Leach's virtually unchallenged testimony, and the absence of any testimony from Alfred Trenkler, was evident. Wrote Judge Stahl, *"Testimony at trial established that Trenkler purchased some of the electrical components for the Quincy bomb from a Radio Shack store. On one occasion, Trenkler sought to obtain needed components by sending [Donna] Shea's eleven-year-old nephew into a Radio Shack store with a list of items to purchase while Trenkler remained outside. Shea's nephew, however, was unable to find all the items, and Trenkler eventually came into the store to assist him."* None of that was true. That is, Todd Leach made no purchases and was never sent into any store, Radio Shack or otherwise, to buy anything for Alfred Trenkler. Once again, Alfred would suffer dearly for Terry Segal's failure to cross-examine Todd Leach enough to shake his false testimony.

The damage of the Marinella tape was also evident as Judge Stahl wrote, *"Shay Jr. admitted purchasing the switch during a taped television interview, portions of which the government introduced at trial."* Continuing the damage of the Leach testimony, including the "*list*" as an example of *modus operandi*, Judge Stahl stated about the

1991 Radio Shack purchase, "*Furthermore, a sales clerk at the Radio Shack testified that prior to purchasing the switch, the person who bought it had browsed in the store for several minutes, appearing to shop for items written on a list. The sales clerk also testified that he recalled seeing Trenkler in the store on two or three occasions during the fall of 1991.*" As Alfred Trenkler could have testified at the trial, he has been a long time Radio Shack customer and he has saved 97 receipts from 11 stores. Incredibly, unless one believes in the adage about returning to the scene of a crime, Alfred Trenkler purchased 6 1/8" plugs (stock number 42-2387) for $3.65 at the 197 Massachusetts Avenue store on 1 May 1992. The other purchase at that store was on 4 May 1990. Thus, it should not have been probative of anything that Alfred Trenkler was recognized by sales staff at the 197 Mass. Ave. store.

Judge Stahl mentioned the version of the 4 February 1992 meeting at the ATF where "*after Leahy ended the discussion, Trenkler announced arrogantly upon leaving the ATF offices that 'If we did it, then only we know about it. How will you ever find out . . if neither one of us talk?'*" Once again, the damage from the decision not to have Alfred Trenkler testify was substantial. If the trial transcript had contained Alfred Trenkler's version of that statement, "*If neither one of us did anything why would one say the other did anything?*" the appellate judges would likely have taken a different view. Even without Trenkler's testimony, Terry Segal could have shown that the alleged statement was unlikely on its face because no one could work together with Tom Shay on anything and have any assurance that he would not talk about it. Even with his total of 8.5 hours of acquaintance with Tom Shay, Alfred Trenkler knew that Tom Shay was, to put it mildly, conversational and unreliable.

Regarding the admission of evidence about the 1986 device, the majority said, "*We agree with the government that the Quincy bomb evidence has 'special relevance' on the issue of identity and that the district court did not abuse its considerable discretion in admitting it.*" After listing some of the similarities, they noted that "*even Trenkler's expert witness, Denny Kline, testified at the pretrial hearing that, in light of these similarities, 'there is a possibility, a **probability,** that maybe **there is a connection** between the maker of these two bombs.'*" (emphasis in original)

The two judge majority was troubled by the substantial number of differences between the two devices, but the question remained, "*could a reasonable jury have found it more likely than not that the same person was responsible for both bombs,*" and the judges agreed that such a finding was reasonable. However, the problem was not to determine who built both devices, as it was already known who built the 1986 device. The problem was whether the knowledge of the identity of the builder of the 1986 device could be used to determine the identity of the builder of the 1991 Roslindale Bomb. The two judges thought that was reasonable, despite all the differences and despite their views about EXIS. The distinction is the difference among coincidence, connection and causation.

Regarding EXIS, he wrote, "*Because we believe that the government clearly failed to establish that the EXIS-derived evidence possessed sufficient 'circumstantial guarantees of trustworthiness,' we hold that the district court abused its discretion in admitting the evidence....Although we agree with Trenkler that the district court erred in admitting the EXIS-derived evidence, we nonetheless find the error harmless beyond a reasonable doubt. Initially, we note that substantial evidence, beyond Trenkler's participation in the Quincy bombing, supported a finding that he had built the Roslindale Bomb. Principally,*

David Lindholm convincingly testified that, in fact Trenkler had actually admitted building the Roslindale Bomb. Other admissions by Trenkler made to various law enforcement officers inferentially corroborated Lindholm's testimony, specifically Trenkler's sketch of the Roslindale Bomb, drawn shortly after the explosion and conspicuously featuring two electrical blasting caps."

Again, Judges Stahl and Coffin relied upon Lindholm's testimony without knowing that he had been released the previous September upon the prosecutors' recommendations. Also, they did not know Lindholm had testified falsely, or at least incorrectly, that his father went to the same schools as Alfred Trenkler.

This reference to the diagram is another example of where Alfred's testimony would have been helpful. He insists that he never drew a second diagram, after drawing a diagram of the 1986 device. If he had testified, it still would have been two officers against a defendant, but 2-1 odds are better odds than 2-0.

Judge Juan Torruella's strongly worded dissent, presented below in part, gave Trenkler hope. The judge addressed several matters, including the EXIS database and the claimed admission heard by William David Lindholm. He was the one judge among the three who was already familiar with the overall case as he shared the unanimous opinion in the Tom Shay appeal that exclusion of Dr. Robert Phillips' testimony in the Shay trial was probably an error, and sent the case back to Judge Zobel for further clarification of her rulings on that issue.

TORRUELLA, Chief Judge, (Dissenting).

In my view, the erroneous admission in this case of evidence derived from the EXIS computer database violated the defendant's Sixth Amendment right to confront witnesses against him. Contrary to my brethren, I do not believe that this error was harmless beyond a reasonable doubt. I therefore dissent.

Based on this analysis, Scheid told the jury that, out of the 14,252 bombings and attempted bombings reported in EXIS, only the Roslindale and the Quincy incidents shared all the queried characteristics.

For a jury reviewing otherwise weak circumstantial evidence (In support of its motion in limine to admit evidence of the 1986 incident, the government described this evidence as "the centerpiece of the Government's case in chief.") of defendant's guilt (see infra), this is powerful stuff -- tangible, "scientific" evidence which seems to conclusively establish that the same person who made the Quincy device in 1986 made the Roslindale Bomb in 1991. Unfortunately, as the majority concedes, the reports from which the EXIS information is derived are utterly unreliable, thus rendering its conclusion equally unreliable, and, as will be shown, completely misleading. For three related reasons, I disagree with the majority's conclusion that admission of the EXIS-derived evidence was "harmless beyond a reasonable doubt." First, the EXIS-derived evidence plainly influenced the district court's decision to allow the government's motion to admit evidence of the Quincy incident, under Fed. R. Evid. 404(b), to show that the same person must have built the Roslindale Bomb. Second, the EXIS-derived evidence was very powerful and very misleading. Third, the other evidence against Trenkler was not "overwhelming," as is required under our precedent.

The majority assumes, without deciding, that Trenkler's Sixth Amendment right to confront witnesses against him was violated by introduction of the EXIS-derived evidence. Supra n.22. As the majority recognizes, constitutional cases are governed by a stringent harmless error analysis -- a conviction cannot stand unless the effect of the evidence is "harmless beyond a reasonable doubt." (citations omitted here)

In a footnote, he said, "The majority properly holds that the EXIS-derived statement -- that out of more than 14,000 bombings and attempted bombings in the EXIS database only the Roslindale and Quincy incidents shared the specific queried characteristics -- is inadmissible totem pole hearsay. That is, it was based on a host of out-of-court statements (the 14,252 underlying reports submitted by unknown authors) offered in court for the truth of the matters asserted therein (the characteristics of those bombings)."

The opinion continued, "The majority also alludes to a potentially more pernicious problem concerning the EXIS-derived evidence. The majority notes that the database entry for the Roslindale incident lists approximately twenty-two characteristics describing that incident, but Scheid, inexplicably, chose only to query ten of those characteristics. The majority notes that there is nothing to suggest that these ten characteristics are more important to a bomb signature analysis than any of the other characteristics not chosen. Scheid offers no reason why he chose to query only certain generic characteristics instead of the more specific characteristics of the Roslindale Bomb, which would be more evincing of a "signature." For example, the Quincy device would not have been a match if Scheid had queried any of the following characteristics of the Roslindale Bombing: Futaba antenna, Rockstar detonator, use of dynamite, nails, glue, 6-volt battery, slide switch, paint, magazine page, or black electrical tape. The majority leaves the implication unspoken. I will not be so discreet. The obvious implication is that Scheid chose the particular characteristics in an attempt to find a match with the Quincy device. This implication is enforced by the fact that, according to Scheid's own testimony, the Quincy incident was not entered into the database until after the Roslindale incident. ...

The majority thinks these concerns go more to the weight of the evidence than to its admissibility; to the contrary, they go directly to the question of whether the evidence has particularized guarantees of trustworthiness under the Confrontation Clause. They demonstrate that it does not. Because the reports upon which the EXIS evidence is based are inherently and utterly unreliable, the EXIS evidence itself is inherently and utterly unreliable, and Trenkler's Sixth Amendment right to confront the witnesses against him was violated. See Wright, 497 U.S. at 805. The question then becomes whether this error was harmless beyond a reasonable doubt.

Under the harmless beyond a reasonable doubt standard, we must vacate the conviction if there is "some reasonable possibility that error of constitutional dimension influenced the jury in reaching [its] verdict." citing United States v. Majaj, 947 F.2d 520, 526 n.8 (1st Cir. 1991) and other cases.

As I see it, there are three related reasons why admission of the EXIS evidence cannot be considered harmless beyond a reasonable doubt. First, it is clear to me that the district court relied on the improper EXIS evidence in its decision to allow the government to present evidence of the Quincy incident to the jury to prove identity under Rule 404(b).

At the hearing on its motion in limine to admit evidence of the Quincy incident under Fed. R. Evid. 404(b), the government presented the testimony of Scheid, regarding the EXIS computer analysis, and the testimony of the government's bomb expert, Waskom, who testified that, in his opinion, the Quincy and Roslindale devices were so similar that they must have been built by the same person. In turn, Trenkler presented expert testimony that the devices were too different for anyone to be able to determine if they *were built by the same person. After hearing this evidence, the district court concluded that "the similarities (between the two incidents) are sufficient to admit the evidence under the rules established . . . by the First Circuit."*

*The majority states that, based upon its review of the record, it is convinced that the EXIS-based evidence "was not a critical factor in the district court's decision to admit the Quincy bomb evidence for purposes of identity. The EXIS-derived evidence was merely cumulative, corroborating the testimony of the government's explosives expert." Supra pp. 39-40. Yet the record demonstrates that the district court judge thought otherwise when she decided to admit evidence of the 1986 Quincy incident. In her oral opinion on the government's motion, the district court judge began by summarizing the testimony of Waskom, and then stated: "**Adding to this evidence**, the statistical evidence from the EXIS system, I am persuaded that the two devices are sufficiently similar to prove that the same person built them, and thus relevant to the issues in this case." (emphasis added[in original]). The district court judge did not say that the EXIS evidence "corroborated" Waskom's testimony. She stated that, when she adds the EXIS evidence to Waskom's testimony, she becomes convinced that the two devices are sufficiently similar. It is plain that the district court judge relied on the EXIS evidence to form the critical final link between the two devices. Indeed, in arguing its motion, the government chose to first present the EXIS evidence and then to present the Waskom testimony, suggesting that it intended the latter to corroborate the former. The district court's erroneous determination that the EXIS evidence was admissible led not only to the jury hearing that evidence, but also to the jury hearing Waskom's testimony with respect to the two incidents. I cannot agree, therefore, that admission of this evidence was harmless beyond a reasonable doubt.*

The second reason that admission of the EXIS evidence cannot be considered harmless is that this type of "scientific" evidence is too misleading, too powerful, and has too great a potential impact on lay jurors, to be disregarded as harmless.

The EXIS-derived evidence was, in the best case scenario, unintentionally misleading, and, in the worst case scenario, deliberately skewed. Scheid testified that, in entering information about the Quincy incident into the EXIS database, he relied solely on a laboratory report prepared in 1986 by investigators from the Massachusetts Department of Public Safety. This report does not state that the Quincy device was attached to the underside of the Capeway truck. Rather, it refers only to an "[e]xplosion on truck." Somebody must have given Scheid further information about the Quincy explosion because he entered "under vehicle" as a characteristic of the Quincy incident. The majority acknowledges these facts but, inexplicably, makes no comment. See supra n.8. These facts are important for three reasons.

First, they illustrate the fallibility of the underlying reports. How many of the other 14,232 reports had similar defects? Second, they illustrate how easily one wrong or incomplete entry can affect a query result. If Scheid had actually followed the report, the Quincy incident would not have matched the Roslindale Bombing because Scheid's query entry was for a bomb "under vehicle." Finally, these facts indicate that the EXIS test was skewed (whether intentionally or unintentionally) to find a match between the Quincy and Roslindale incidents.

The EXIS-derived evidence is also misleading because it focuses the jury's attention on the trees instead of the forest. By focusing on similar minor aspects between the two devices -- e.g., duct tape, magnets and soldering -- the majority completely brushes aside the fact that the central and most important ingredient in the two devices is fundamentally different. The central ingredient in a bomb, one would think, is the explosive content (in much the same way that the central ingredient in a high-performance car is the engine). The Roslindale Bomb used two to three sticks of dynamite -- a very powerful explosive. The Quincy device used an M-21 Hoffman artillery simulator, which is a device used by the military to simulate, in a safe fashion, the flash and noise of artillery. The simulator is, in effect, a firecracker-like device; it has nowhere near the strength of dynamite. In stark contrast to dynamite, a simulator is not designed to cause physical or property damage. Indeed, while the Roslindale device created an explosion large enough to kill, the Quincy device caused no visible damage to the truck it was placed under. Equating the two devices is like equating a BB gun with a high caliber rifle.

The misleading nature of the EXIS-derived statement is compounded by the nature of its source, and the way in which it was presented to the jury. Not only is it rank hearsay evidence, it is hearsay evidence wrapped in a shroud of "scientific" authenticity. This is not a paid government expert testifying that, in his opinion, the two devices were built by the same person; this is a computer declaring that the two devices were built by the same person. Computers deal in facts, not opinions. Computers are not paid by one side to testify. Computers do not have prejudices. And computers are not subject to cross-examination. Moreover, the chart of the EXIS queries performed by Scheid, and the printouts of the results of those queries, were introduced into evidence and presented as exhibits to the jury.

Consequently, the jury had this misleading, physical evidence with them in the jury room during deliberations. Does it not stand to reason that the lay juror will accord greater weight to a computer's written findings than to the testimony of a government expert witness? The common-sense answer is, of course.

The majority decision in this case not only defies common sense, it is also contrary to our precedent. (citations omitted here)

The third reason that admission of the EXIS evidence is not harmless beyond a reasonable doubt is that the other evidence against Trenkler was not "overwhelming." See Clark, 942 F.2d at 27. The majority points to a conglomeration of other testimony in support of its conclusion that there was "substantial evidence" of Trenkler's guilt, independent of the Quincy incident. The test, of course, is not whether there is "substantial evidence" of Trenkler's guilt but whether there is "overwhelming evidence" of Trenkler's guilt. The two standards are qualitatively and quantitatively different. In any case, I will begin by addressing Trenkler's "statements" to government agents.

ATF Agent D'Ambrosio testified that he asked Trenkler to draw a sketch of the Quincy device, which Trenkler did. D'Ambrosio then told Trenkler that the Roslindale Bomb also used remote control, but that, rather than a firecracker type device, it used dynamite. D'Ambrosio asked Trenkler how, in light of these facts, the wiring diagram he had just drawn for the Quincy device would have been different for the Roslindale Bomb. D'Ambrosio testified that Trenkler then drew a diagram which showed two blasting caps inserted into two sticks of dynamite. The majority considers this significant evidence of Trenkler's guilt because the fact that the Roslindale Bomb used blasting caps had not been publicly disclosed. The majority fails to note, however, that D'Ambrosio actually testified that at least two blasting caps were used in the Roslindale Bombing. Thus, Trenkler's drawing of only two blasting caps was not an exact match. Moreover, the jury heard evidence that Trenkler had extensive knowledge of both electronics and explosives, so it is not necessarily significant that Trenkler was able to reconstruct an aspect of the Roslindale Bomb, particularly considering the information concerning the bomb provided to Trenkler by D'Ambrosio. Trenkler merely identified that blasting caps were a likely way in which a bomb of this size and power would be constructed. In the absence of any testimony that the use of blasting caps is unusual or unique (a proposition which is highly unlikely), the jury could only speculate as to the significance of the drawing.

The majority also finds significance in ATF Agent Leahy's testimony that Trenkler said to him: "If we did it, then only we know about it . . . how will you ever find out .... if neither one of us talk?" The majority paints this statement in a confessional light. This testimony may or may not have been of some circumstantial relevance to the jury (although standing alone, of course, it would not be sufficient to sustain a conviction). But, upon review, when the court is looking for "overwhelming evidence of guilt," one would think the court would not have to resort to this sort of an ambiguous, taunting statement. Similarly, the court notes that there was evidence that Trenkler and Shay knew each other, and that Trenkler had knowledge of both electronics and explosives. While the jury might consider this type of circumstantial evidence relevant, it can hardly be said that it does much in the way of providing "overwhelming evidence" of defendant's guilt. Cf. <u>United States v. Innamorati</u>, 996 F.2d 456, 476 (1st Cir. 1993)

The majority relies most heavily on the testimony of David Lindholm, who testified that Trenkler confessed to building the Roslindale Bomb. But Lindholm had some serious credibility problems which make his testimony "shaky," to say the least. Lindholm testified that he met Trenkler while Lindholm was serving a 97-month sentence for conspiracy to distribute marijuana and tax evasion. He further testified that he was in the marijuana business from approximately 1969 through 1988, and that he did not pay any income taxes during that time. Lindholm also testified that, in order to secure bank loans to purchase property during that period, he showed several banks false income tax returns. On the basis of Lindholm's shady past alone, the jury might have completely disregarded his testimony. But Lindholm also had some less obvious credibility problems. The circumstances of his meeting Trenkler strike me as a little too coincidental. On December 17, 1992, after a year and a half incarceration in Texas, Lindholm is brought back to Boston concerning certain unspecified charges related to his conviction. He is then placed in the orientation unit at the Plymouth House of Correction where he meets Alfred Trenkler, who is being held in connection with the Roslindale Bombing. The two subsequently discover that they have an extraordinary amount in common. First, they are both from the town of Milton, Massachusetts. Second, Trenkler attended Thayer Academy and Milton Academy, and Lindholm's father also attended Thayer Academy and Milton Academy. Third, they both lived for a time -- overlapping by one year -- on White Lawn Avenue in Milton. Based on these commonalities, and Lindholm's generosity in sharing his knowledge of the criminal justice system with Trenkler, they form a friendship. Trenkler then, allegedly, confesses to Lindholm that he built the bomb.

In my view, a reasonable juror might question whether Lindholm was placed in the orientation unit by the government for the purpose of obtaining a confession from Trenkler. If so, that juror would likely wonder what Lindholm got in return. Not surprisingly, Lindholm testified that he had no agreements with the government and that he did not receive any promises or inducements for his testimony. He did testify on cross-examination, however, that he knew, when he provided the information about Trenkler to the government, that the only way his 97-month sentence could be reduced was if he supplied new information to the government.

We do not know how much weight the jury gave Lindholm's testimony, but we do know that, at least on paper -- for we did not observe his demeanor at trial -- Lindholm had some significant credibility problems. Consequently, I cannot conclude beyond a reasonable doubt that the jury would have believed his testimony; particularly in a case such as this where there is absolutely no physical evidence tying Trenkler to the bombing. Cf. _Coppola_, 878 F.2d at 1571

The only evidence coming near that level of reliability was the improperly admitted EXIS evidence. Absent the EXIS-derived evidence, the government's case against Trenkler consists of a smorgasbord of inconclusive circumstantial evidence and an inherently unreliable alleged jailhouse confession. Faced with this sort of evidence, a reasonable jury would probably look for some sort of tangible evidence upon which to hang its hat. The EXIS-derived evidence was just that. Because it was the only ostensibly conclusive evidence tying Trenkler to the crime, it may have been the clincher for the jury. See _Coppola_, 878 F.2d at 1571. It was therefore not harmless beyond a reasonable doubt.

A horrible crime was committed in which one police officer was killed and another seriously injured. Society rightfully demands that the guilty be apprehended, tried, and punished. But the distinguishing feature of our legal system is that even those charged with grotesque crimes are guaranteed certain constitutional rights intended to ensure that they receive a fair trial. Unfortunately, and with all due respect to my brethren, I believe the defendant's right to a fair trial was violated when the government was permitted to introduce the highly prejudicial evidence derived from the EXIS computer database. Because this error so severely violated defendant's Sixth Amendment right to confront the witnesses against him, and because the remainder of the evidence against him was not "overwhelming," I dissent.

Even this critical dissenting opinion had significant erroneous statements. While Judge Torruella argued persuasively that the entry of "_under vehicle_" by Mr. Scheid was faulty because the police report did not say "_under vehicle_," Judge Torruella still believed, in the absence of Alfred's testimony or other evidence at the trial, that the device was placed under the Capeway Fish Market truck. Judge Torruella did not know that the Trenkler case was the only criminal case where the EXIS database had been used to try to show "signature," and it hasn't been so used since that trial either. Also, Judge Torruella appeared to believe Thomas D'Ambrosio's testimony that Afred Trenkler did, in fact, draw a diagram of the 1991 device based on D'Ambrosio's description. Finally, none of the Appeals Court judges knew about David Lindholm's early release from prison in return for his testimony against Alfred Trenkler. Their lack of knowledge was important for two critical reasons. First, it showed that there was a _quid pro quo_ for Lindholm's testimony against Alfred Trenkler despite Lindholm's and the prosecutors' denials. Second, the failure of the prosecutors to inform Trenkler's counsel of the Motion for early release, and of Lindholm's actual release, and failure to tell the Appellate Court in a document or at the December 1994 appeal hearing of the release, and even their failure to inform the Court upon the publication of its opinion was egregiously wrong. Such an insult to the interests of truth and fair play should have resulted in some judicial remedy such as reversal of the verdict, or of the appellate opinion, or at least a rehearing of all the issues.

After the 2-1 decision, it was rumored that one reason for Judge Torruella's strong dissent was the he thought he was originally writing the majority opinion to overturn the conviction, but that one of the other two judges changed his mind. It seems likely that if that other judge had known about the Lindholm early release, he would not have changed his mind about the unfairness of the trial and verdict for two reasons. First, it showed that there was a post-trial reward for Lindholm's testimony despite Lindholm's denial and despite his promise not to seek such a reward, even if a pre-trial agreement was not proven. Second, the act of concealment, of Lindholm's early release, by the Office of the U.S. Attorney would have, or should have, offended the judges.

Now, after the two appeals in the Roslindale Bomb case, there was a 3-0 vote of the First Circuit to overturn or question Tom Shay's conviction and a 2-1 vote to uphold Trenkler's. As a major reason for Trenkler's conviction was the conviction of Tom Shay, one can argue that Trenkler's should have been overturned when Shay's was overturned; but the grounds were different. Still, with the judges voting 4-2 against the convictions of both men, in a sense, our confidence in the correctness of Trenkler's continued incarceration should be shaken. The one appellate judge to hear both appeals, Judge Torruella, voted to overturn both of them.

Nevertheless, Alfred Trenkler's <u>Request for Justice V</u> failed.

The 20 July 1995 <u>Boston Globe</u> reported the appellate decision in "*APPEAL IS DENIED IN FATAL BOMBING*," and noted that there was a dissenting opinion, but that the majority found the evidence of Trenkler's guilt "*overwhelming.*"

Also on 20 July the tragedy of Waco, Texas was brought home to readers of the <u>Boston Globe</u> as a woman from Dorchester described for a Congressional Committee in Washington the deaths of her Harvard Law graduate husband and four of her children. After the failed initial ATF raid on the compound on 28 February 1993, Sheila Martin left the compound and planned to return to her family. According to the article, "*SIEGE STILL FRESH FOR DORCHESTER NATIVE*," she said at the hearing, "*We need to know the truth about what happened.*"

On 1 August 1995, Morris Goldings filed Trenkler's <u>Request for Justice VI</u>, with the First Circuit, which was a "*Petition for Rehearing and suggestion for Rehearing en banc of the Defendant-Appellant.*" A request for an 'en banc' hearing meant to have the case considered by entire Court of 9 appellate judges. Essentially, it was an appeal from the 2-1 decision against the first appeal. The issue posed to the full Appeals Court was, "*Whether the district court abused its discretion in admitting under the residual hearsay exception evidence derived from the EXIS computer database as it was rank hearsay violative of the Defendant's Sixth Amendment Right of Confrontation, and whether the admission of such tainted evidence was not harmless beyond a reasonable doubt.*" Even at this late date, Goldings did not yet know of the 30 September 1994 release of Lindholm, nearly a year earlier. If he had known, the legal issues would surely have been included in the Petition for hearing *en banc*.

On 31 July 1995 Ralph Ranalli wrote in the <u>Herald</u> of the tightening web of witnesses against Whitey Bulger and on that list was William David Lindholm. The article, "*MOB BUDDIES READY TO ROLL ON WHITEY & SALEMME*," told of "*a former drug trafficker who will testify that a gun was put to his head during a dispute with Bulger.*" Wrote Ranalli, "*Official sources said investigators have scored a double coup by convincing convicted marijuana trafficker and Milton native David Lindholm to become a government witness in the case. ... As a bonus for the government, Lindholm's cooperation has also knocked formidable defense attorney Richard Egbert out of the case... when prosecutors told U.S. District Court Judge Mark L. Wolf that Lindholm, another one-time Egbert client , would testify.... Lindholm is no stranger to helping federal prosecutors. In 1993, he helped convict Roslindale Bomber Alfred Trenkler... "*

Now the Trenkler and Shay defense lawyers could see, perhaps, the reason that Lindholm had been brought to Boston to meet with the U.S. Attorney's office in December, 1992. Despite his reliance on "*official*" though unnamed sources, Ranalli didn't reveal what Alfred Trenkler would consider the really important news about Lindholm, which was the news of Lindholm's release from prison.

On 1 August 1995, the *Boston Globe* carried its own story about the drug investigation with a dramatic article by Judy Rakowsky headlined "*WHITEY BULGER TIED TO DRUG DEALING IN S. BOSTON*". This slant on the headline was big news in Boston, because Bulger's image was that he was that he was a defender of the South Boston neighborhood against the drug traffic, which he reportedly detested. The fifth paragraph of that article stated, "*Besides* [Paul] *Moore, convicted drug dealer R. David Lindholm of Milton is expected to testify that he was forcibly taken to an East Boston meeting with Bulger, where a gun was pointed at his head.*"[4] Then the article made a surprising but obscure announcement, "*Lindholm was reportedly released from federal prison 37 months into an 8-year sentence and testified against convicted bomb builder Alfred Trenkler in the Boston bombing case in which a Boston police officer was killed.*"

Eight days later Alfred Trenkler's <u>Request for Justice VII</u> began on 8 August 1995 to the First Circuit Court of Appeals with a "*Motion to Remand*" by Morris Goldings. Given the revelation about Lindholm's release, Goldings reminded the court of its recent opinion in the Trenkler appeal which stressed the importance of Lindholm's testimony to Trenkler's conviction, and asked the First Circuit to send the case back to Judge Zobel's U.S. District Court for a hearing on why Lindholm was released early and whether that early release was related to his testimony in the Trenkler case and whether there was an undisclosed "*agreement, explicit or implicit, between the Government and Lindholm or whether there were any promises or inducements from the Government.*" The response of the First Circuit came on 25 August and it was brief. Wrote Chief Judge Torruella, and Judges Coffin and Stahl, "*Defendant's motion raises issues of concern, which could merit a hearing. However, the proper forum for such a hearing is before the district court upon motion of a new trial. The motion* [before the First Circuit] *is therefore denied.*" <u>Trenkler's Request for Justice VII</u> had failed.

Also on 25 August the First Circuit Court denied Trenkler's request for an *en banc* hearing of his direct appeal. The motion was considered by Judges Torruella, Cofffin, Selya, Cyr, Boudin, Stahl and Lynch, and the decision stated, "*...and the suggestion for the holding of a rehearing en banc having been carefully considered by the judges of the Court in regular, active service and a majority of said judges not having voted to order that the appeal be heard or reheard by the Court en banc*" the petition was denied. The undisclosed vote may have been close, as Torruella and Boudin voted on 22 June 1995 to overturn Tom Shay's verdict with a remand for consideration of the exclusion of the testimony by Dr. Phillips, and Torruella had dissented in the 2-1 decision against Alfred Trenkler's appeal. It was not stated whether the Court knew about the multi-level Lindholm deception of the Court. Perhaps the judges believed that the suggestion of <u>RFJ VII</u> to go back to the District Court was enough, but it wasn't. As it was the First Circuit Court of Appeals that was deceived by the unannounced early release of David Lindholm, that Court should have provided a remedy, whether it be an *en banc* rehearing of the case, or delegation to a single justice. In any case, Trenkler's <u>Request for Justice VI</u> failed.

On 26 November, the *Globe* carried Kevin Cullen's story about the retirement of the Boston ATF's Agent-in-Charge, Terry McArdle, "*FACING TRANSFER, ATF HEAD DECIDES TO LEAVE.*" As part of ATF's post-Waco shakeup, McArdle was reassigned to head the Miami office, but he chose to stay in New England. He cited the 1991 Roslindale Bomb investigation was among the "*best work of the agents he supervised,*" and that "*the bombing investigation, in which ATF agents, Boston police and federal prosecutors worked as a task force, was the quintessential partnership.*"

On 22 December 1995 Morris Goldings filed with the U.S. District Court Alfred Trenkler's <u>Request for Justice VIII</u>, which was a "*Motion for a New Trial, or, in the Alternative, for an Evidentiary Hearing.*" There were three grounds for the Motion:

1. That the revelation of Lindholm's release was a new development, which affected the trustworthiness of his testimony at Alfred Trenkler's trial.

2. The Court of Appeals had ruled on 22 June that the exclusion of Dr. Phillips' testimony from the Tom Shay trial was "*clear error.*" Thus, the absence of Dr. Phillips' testimony at the Trenkler trial also required a new trial.

3. That the Court of Appeals had ruled that the introduction of the EXIS evidence was erroneous, but that it was harmless error because of the strength of the other evidence.

4. The "*other evidence*" was now shown to be unreliable. In addition to the Lindholm testimony now being questioned, the admission of Tom Shay's out-of-court statements should no longer be considered trustworthy. "*Because this Court precluded Shay Jr. from introducing at his trial expert psychiatric testimony that his own statements were the unreliable product of a recognized mental disorder called 'pseudologia fantastica,' Trenkler's trial counsel believed it would be futile to seek to introduce the same or similar testimony as to Shay Jr.'s statements at Trenkler's trial.*" Attached to the Motion was an Affidavit by Terry Segal supporting that argument.

5. Finally, if a New Trial were not granted, Goldings asked for an evidentiary hearing to consider the issues he raised.

On 6 February 1996 Alfred Trenkler turned 40 years old.

On 12 February 1996, AUSA Paul Kelly and Frank Libby filed an 8-page "*Opposition to Defendant Alfred W. Trenkler's Motion for a New Trial,*" which was supported by a 6-page affidavit by Paul Kelly and 29 pages of exhibits.

The prosecutors noted that "*the granting a new trial is an extraordinary remedy and that 'Courts disfavor new trials, and exercise great caution in granting them.' *" citing a court case. They wrote that there was a four-part requirement for a new trial based on newly discovered evidence: "*that the evidence was: (1) unknown or unavailable at the time of trial, (2) despite due diligence, (3) material, and (4) likely to result in an acquittal upon trial.*"

Paul Kelly and Frank Libby argued that there was no agreement with William David Lindholm about a reward for his testimony. However, as Lindholm testified at Trenkler's trial, the way to get a sentence reduced is to provide information to the government and everyone knew that. Since Lindholm did receive a substantial reduction in his sentence as result of his testimony in Trenkler's trial, what difference should it make that there was no prior agreement to provide that benefit? Knowing of the potential for that benefit through the clear language of Rule 35(b), an inmate informer may distort the truth to achieve that benefit whether or not there is a formal agreement to provide it.

Regarding the testimony of Dr. Phillips, the prosecutors argued that Terry Segal should have sought to introduce Phillips' testimony in the Trenkler trial as a way of precluding the admission of Shay's out-of-court statements. However, as he didn't do so, Trenkler should not now be permitted to do so. Also, in a footnote, they argued that the issue of the Phillips testimony in Tom Shay's trial was still pending before Judge Zobel, and she might still determine that it was not error to exclude his testimony.

In White Deer, Pennsylvania, Alfred Trenkler was serving his sentence, and trying to help his defense team. Two of his fellow inmates sought to help with affidavits. On 23 May 1996, Frederic Trainor, Inmate #86374-011, completed a short Affidavit, which stated:

"2. I state that Alfred Trenkler has consistently and unwaveringly maintained his innocence of the crimes he was charged with and subsequently convicted of.

3. Alfred Trenkler's closest association has been with myself and one Mark O'Berg, and that at no time during our association has he in any way inferred or alluded to anything other than absolute innocence of criminal charges; nor has he, to my knowledge, had opportunity or reason to confer or confide with or in any other inmates or prison staff concerning his case."

Less polished was Mark O'Berg's handwritten statement with a similar message:

"I, Mark O'Berg, #03890030, under penalty of perjury swear that the following is a true and correct statement to the best of my knowledge

Since January 1995 I have known Alfred Trenkler here at USP Allwd [Allenwood]. Basically, he is my closest friend and confidant and I his. Since I have known him, he has vehemently denied any participation in the Roslindale, Mass. bombing. I have on numerous occasions played the 'Devil's advocate' to Alfred to see if the innocence he proclaims is truth. It is.

On many, many, many occasions Alfred has talked about the Gov't getting another paid informant to lie against him in any upcoming trials. This is a major worry for him as there are any number of people most eager to make some type of deal for providing information, even if it's false information.

Like I said earlier, Alfred is my closest friend and confidant. We spend the better part of each day together except while working. And he has never said anything other than 'I am innocent.' When others try to steer the conversation towards crimes particularly his, he always walks away, stating, 'I do not want to know or hear this.'

If anyone refutes this, I refute them. They, not Alfred are blatant liars. (And must need burn in the everlasting fires of Hell.)"

On 7 October 1996 Jack Wallace wrote to the new Chief Judge of the U.S. District Court, Joseph Tauro, to ask for his help in obtaining a decision from Judge Zobel regarding Alfred Trenkler's "*Motion for a New Trial*" which had been filed the previous December (RFJ VII) after the Court of Appeals had remanded to Judge Zobel in August Trenkler's plea to the Appeals Court for a new trial. (RFJ VI) At the time, the three and one-half years of wrongful incarceration seemed like a lifetime and they were hopeful that a favorable judicial decision would free Alfred and them from their nightmare.

However, it was not to happen.

Jack had attached a letter by Josephine Wallace which she and he had written after the November 1993 conviction. After summarizing the legal deficiencies in the case she wrote, "*Our family and friends know Alfred. He is a good and gentle person who has been victimized by the very system that is supposed to protect him, our judicial system. We will continue to fight for Alfred's freedom and to eradicate the terrible wrong that has been done to him. My faith in the judicial system will only be restored when the real truth emerges and the guilty party is found and brought to trial. In the meantime, an innocent man has been incarcerated for life for a crime he didn't commit.*"

In September 1996, ATF Agent Jeff Kerr was called by Donna Shea. He reported, "Shea stated that she was arrested by the Weymouth Police for being in possession of eleven packets of cocaine. Shea stated the cocaine didn't belong to her and that she was being set up by the Weymouth Police Department. She stated that she could not go to jail because of her children and her husband's approaching wrap-up on a current prison term." Her husband was John Shea, a Milton friend of Alfred Trenkler who was convicted in 1992 of attempted murder and kidnapping. Those charges arose after a well-publicized incident in 1991 when he took two women out in his boat and threw them overboard five miles from shore when they refused his sexual advances. Fortunately, another boater came by and saved the two women from drowning or hypothermia. There was some evidence, too, that Shea had also turned around to rescue the two women.

Kerr's report continued, "On or about October 2, 1996, I was again contacted by Shea.... She stated she would kill the Weymouth Police Officer and herself if she had to go to jail.

Shea further stated she had information that a woman by the name of Ramona 'LNU' [Last Name Unknown], who sat on the jury that heard the Trenkler case, was known to her as well as to Trenkler. She stated she was going to go out with a bang if she was going to be sent to jail. She stated she would call Trenkler's attorney and provide this information. She stated she was very angry that nobody helped her get her husband out of jail after she had helped with the Trenkler investigation and that she would pay people back." [The help that she was referencing included the locating of four prosecution witnesses: Mike Coady, Bob Craig, Todd Leach, and Paul Nutting. Not only did she refer the ATF to these people, it's believed that she also talked about the case with them prior to their grand jury and trial testimonies. She brought James Harding to Alfred and worked with Harding to record Alfred's statements. She also testified twice before the grand jury, but did not testify at either Roslindale Bombing trial.]

"On October 8, 1996 Special Agent William Murphy and I interviewed one Donna Shea at her residence in Weymouth, Massachusetts.

Shea stated that approximately twelve years ago, her friend Nancy Tolmie would on occasion contact Shea in order to obtain cocaine for personal use. Shea stated when she received these requests, she would contact Alfred Trenkler, who distributed cocaine and that Trenkler would come to her home to conduct sales. Shea stated that during this time frame, on three or four occasions Tolmie arrived with another woman. Shea stated she knew the woman's first name was Ramona but did not know her last name. She stated when asked, that she had no memory of Ramona 'LNU' being present in the room when Trenkler sold cocaine to Tolmie.

Shea stated she never saw Ramona 'LNU' purchase drugs from Trenkler nor anyone else. ...

Shea stated that she never heard Trenkler refer to or directly address Ramona by either her first or last name nor does she remember Ramona 'LNU' referring to or talking to Trenkler using either his first or last name.... She stated that since Trenkler didn't know or have dealings with Ramona back then, it is unlikely that Trenkler knew who she was during the trial.

On October 18, 1996 I had a follow-up telephone conversation with Shea. Shea now stated that on two or three occasions she remembers Tolmie coming to her house accompanied by Ramona 'LNU.' She stated that on the two or three occasions that Ramona 'LNU' accompanied Tolmie to her (Shea's) residence, Tolmie purchased drugs from Trenkler. She stated that the transactions were conducted in her basement apartment. She now stated that Ramona was present in her room when the transactions were conducted.

On October 28, 1996 I telephonically interviewed one Nancy Russell, formerly Nancy Tolmie. Present for the conference call interview was ATF Special Agent John Mercer.

Ms. Russell stated that she indulged in regular use of cocaine powder from approximately 1984 through a part of 1987...

Ms. Russell stated she met Ramona Walsh through common friends. She stated that she saw Ramona Walsh approximately once every three weeks during 1985 and 1986....

Ms. Russell stated she bought cocaine on approximately forty to fifty occasions from Donna Shea....at Shea's residence.... She stated that she never brought Ramona Walsh with her to Donna Shea's home. ...

On October 29, 1996 I interviewed Ms. Russell at her place of employment...Ms. Russell stated that in re-thinking her past, she believes she purchased cocaine from Donna Shea on more than the approximately fifty times she initially recalled....

Lastly, Ms. Russell stated she may recall Donna Shea mentioning somebody by the name of Al but she never met him nor knows who the person is."

During this controversy but on a different dimension of the Roslindale Bomb case, a memorial stone was dedicated to Jeremiah Hurley, Jr., in Wolcott Square in Hyde Park[5]. The inscription read, "*Taking the first step with a good thought, the second with a good word, and the third with a good deed, I enter paradise.*"

On 1 November, AUSA Frank Libby wrote to Judge Zobel about the issue of Ramona Walsh's alleged acquaintance with Alfred Trenkler. He repeated the charge that Walsh had come to Donna "*Shea's house to buy cocaine, allegedly supplied by Trenkler.*" He argued that whatever the relationship, there was no injustice because Ramona Walsh had been only an alternate juror and was dismissed before deliberations began. He wrote that he had talked several times with Alfred Trenkler's lawyer, Amy Axelrod, who worked in Morris Goldings' law firm. Also, there had been no contact with Ms. Walsh herself, so as to avoid violating the "*First Circuit proscription against attorney-initiated post-trial contact with jurors.*" Libby wrote that "*The only claim of juror misconduct even remotely cognizable from Shea's (contradictory) allegations is failure, on the part of Ms. Walsh to disclose her prior knowledge of Trenkler,*" and he reminded the Judge that in response to her questions at the trial, Walsh and the other potential jurors said that they did not know Alfred Trenkler, although she did acknowledge knowing potential witnesses, including Donna Shea. Walsh was an employee of the Quincy District Court.

On 19 November 1996, Morris Goldings filed, together with an 11-page Memorandum, a "*Motion for Judicial Inquiry into Possible Juror Misconduct and for a New Trial,*" which can be called Trenkler's <u>Request for Justice IX</u>. He wrote that "*Without judicial investigation, it is unclear whether the alternate juror, Ramona Walsh, failed to disclose during the <u>voir dire</u> that she knew Trenkler, whether she communicated that fact (and possibly other information) to the deliberating jurors and whether that extraneous information affected the deliberating jurors to such an extent that they failed to keep an open mind and render a verdict based solely on the evidence.*"

On 16 December, Frank Libby wrote another letter, including the charge against Alfred Trenkler, "*that Defendant and Ms. Walsh were together in the same room on one or more occasions in the early 1980's when Defendant sold cocaine to one Nancy Tolmie/Russell, then a friend of Ms. Walsh's.*" Lost in the legally significant controversy about whether Ramona Walsh actually knew Alfred Trenkler was the allegation that Alfred Trenkler sold cocaine to anyone. In fact, he did not, and his lawyers should have aggressively made that point. His use of cocaine was explained by Pamela Lombardini in the Pre Sentencing Report, "...began using cocaine at age 23 or 24, used it on occasion until 1987 at which time he began using it weekends. He stopped using cocaine in 1989 when he saw what the drug was doing to his friends. The defendant has used no other drug [other than marijuana which he smoked "a few times weekly until his arrest on the instant offense."] The report could also have noted that Alfred Trenkler did not sell drugs either.

Frank Libby argued in his letter that nothing need be done because it "deals solely with one [alternate juror] who played no role in the outcome of Defendant's (meticulously fair) trial. For this reason, it falls far short of the threshold showing which must be met before any juror may be disturbed through post-verdict interrogation."

On 4 February 1997, Judge Zobel denied Alfred Trenkler's "*Motion for a New Trial*" based on the exclusion of the Dr. Phillips' testimony in the Shay trial and the Lindholm early release. Judge Zobel said that Terry Segal had his opportunity to attempt to introduce the Phillips testimony, and he didn't. Period. Regarding Lindholm, Judge Zobel stated, "*... the record is devoid of any evidence to suggest that Lindholm's early release was the result of anything other than an arrangement made subsequent to the trial (by several months) between Lindholm and the government based on Lindholm's cooperation in the Trenkler trial.*" The fact that David Lindholm did get a very real benefit from his testimony didn't matter to Judge Zobel unless he had beforehand made an actual agreement for such a benefit. She did not see that Federal Rule 35(b) was such an "*arrangement,*" Thus, Alfred Trenkler's <u>Request for Justice VIII</u> failed. The <u>*Boston Globe*</u> briefly covered the story on the 8th, "*NEW TRIAL DENIED FOR BOMB CONVICT.*"

On 6 February 1997 Alfred Trenkler turned 41 years old.

On 13 February 1997 Morris Goldings filed a Notice of Appeal with the First Circuit of Judge Zobel's denial of the "*Motion for a New Trial or Evidentiary Hearing.*" This was his <u>Request for Justice X</u>, which appealed the denial of the <u>Request for Justice VIII.</u>

On 22 May 1997 Judge Zobel denied the Motion for further inquiry into the Ramona Walsh allegations, i.e. RFJ IX. She repeated Donna Shea's report that "*Trenkler, the alleged supplier of the cocaine, may have present in the room*" when Donna Shea sold cocaine a friend of the juror, Ramona Walsh. There was no indication that Ramona Walsh knew who Alfred Trenkler was. After noting that the alleged transactions were 12 years previous, Judge Zobel denied the Defendant's motion, saying that "*Such speculative and incredible claims do not trigger a duty on the part of this court to investigate the alleged juror misconduct any further.*" It would have been helpful if Alfred Trenkler's alleged sales of drugs could have been included in Judge Zobel's list of "*incredible claims.*"

On 4 June 1997, Morris Goldings filed an appeal, RFJ XI, of the denial by Judge Zobel of further inquiry into the juror misconduct issue. It was unfortunate that Alfred Trenkler's desperate pleas for justice were led down these odd paths at great legal expense without much consideration of the truth of the original case. Goldings' goal, as was the case for other appellate lawyers, was to find the key to the appellate lock in order to gain a new trial. Any key would do.

While Alfred Trenkler continued to struggle for justice, his chief accuser, William David Lindholm, had moved on to a new career, and to Hull, Mass. another town where Alfred formerly lived. The 25 July *Boston Globe* reported that he was a self-described "*consumer advocate,*" according to his business card and was using an unorthodox tactic of business persuasion, the picketing of several RE/MAX realty franchises. The article by Richard Kindleberger, "NEW PLAYER IN RE/MAX CASE: DRUG DEALER TURNED GADFLY," featured Lindholm's curious role in a dispute between the RE/MAX corporation and a purchaser of the Back Bay, Boston RE/MAX franchise. On several occasions in June and July Lindholm allegedly recruited fellow picketers from the Pine Street Inn, a homeless shelter in Boston. On one occasion he picketed an "Open House" in Sudbury, 30 miles west of Boston, which was being marketed by a local RE/MAX realtor. Lindholm's dispute with corporate RE/MAX apparently arose because the husband of the Back Bay franchisee, Michael Carucci, was an alleged money launderer and connected to Stephen "the Rifleman" Flemmi, against whom Lindholm was to testify in Federal Court. RE/MAX had apparently permitted Carucci to work as a realtor, but not Lindholm. In the meantime, Lindholm was said to be working as a $10/hour house painter. Still, he was free, and Alfred Trenkler was not. A court enjoined the picketing on 28 July.

On 8 August 1997, Morris Goldings filed a brief with the First Circuit Court of Appeals which combined both RFJ X (on the issues of Phillips and Lindholm) and RFJ XI (the issue of the juror misconduct)

On 17 September, AUSA Kevin McGrath filed a 57-page Appellee Brief for the U.S. Attorney's office.

On 5 November 1997, there were oral arguments at the First Circuit Court of Appeals. Attending the hearing were Jack and Josephine Wallace who had been, thus far, through six years of torment and enormous monetary and emotional cost. It probably appeared ominous to them that two of the three judges were Frank Coffin and Norman Stahl, who constituted the majority in the 2-1 denial of Alfred's direct appeal in July 1995.

Jack Wallace wrote a "*Memorandum*" on 20 November to First Circuit Judges Juan Torruella, Bruce Selyea, Frank Coffin, Norman Stahl, and U.S. District Court Judges

Joseph Tauro and Rya Zobel, and Assistant U.S. Attorney Kevin McGrath, Morris Goldings and David Beck and finally to Alfred Trenkler as well. He asked rhetorically how his stepson, Alfred Trenkler, could be in prison for life on the testimony or statements by Tom Shay and William David Lindholm, whose prison nickname was reportedly "*Little Stories,*"[6] and Lawrence Plant. Then Jack Wallace condemned the use of the EXIS database and the 1986 Quincy incident at Alfred's trial. He wrote, "*Alfred was in essence convicted for a crime in 1993 based on evidence of a prior unrelated incident in 1986 which had been dismissed....*"

He enclosed a copy of a six-page document he wrote, "*Case for Reasonable Doubt in Support of Alfred's Complete Innocence.*" Beginning with the Judge Torruella's observation that "*There is absolutely no physical evidence tying Trenkler to the bombing,*" Wallace listed the problems with the case, beginning with the use of the EXIS database, and then David Lindholm's testimony and other issues. He concluded his impassioned essay, "*Alfred and his family have steadfastly maintained his total innocence in this horrible crime for which he was unjustly convicted and sentenced to life imprisonment. We are confident that these facts support our feelings that Alfred's conviction should be overturned.*"

On 17 November, the <u>Boston Globe</u> reported that 69 names of Boston Policemen killed during duty would be carved into a stone wall at the Police Dept's new headquarters on Berkeley Street in Roxbury, Boston. Jeremiah Hurley's name was the 66th, wrote David Arnold in "*FOR 69 FALLEN OFFICERS, A PLACE OF HONOR.*"

On 17 December 1997 Jack Wallace sent an additional "*Memorandum*" to the same judges and other addressees as on the 20 November Memorandum. This was about the similarities he saw between the two government informers, Larry Plant against Tom Shay, and William David Lindholm against Alfred Trenkler. What Jack didn't know was that the problem of the unreliability of jailhouse informers was well-known to judges and law enforcement people. They accept the dirtiness of dealing with inmates because of the high value of convicting accused people who might otherwise escape justice. Alfred Trenkler, in the minds of many employees of the U.S. Government, was one of those people worth snaring. What Jack also didn't know, and many of the addressees probably suspected but didn't yet know, was that jailhouse informers have been one of the major sources of wrongful convictions in this country, as they have been measured since 1989.

Concluded the loyal and determined stepfather, "*I have complete confidence in the innocence of my stepson, Alfred Trenkler, in the crime for which he was unjustly convicted and sentenced to life imprisonment.*

Alfred has been incarcerated for four (4) years and nine (9) months; it is a miscarriage of justice that Alfred is serving a life sentence for a crime he did not commit.

Alfred has been victimized by the very system that is supposed to protect him, our judicial system. It is time for that system to eradicate the terrible wrong which has been done to him."

On 14 January 1998, Jack Wallace sent a third "*Memorandum*" to the same distribution list as his 20 November and 17 December 1997 "*Memoranda*" described above. Jack summarized the injustice of William David Lindholm's testimony to convict Alfred Trenkler. He enclosed 10 pages of newspaper articles about Lindholm's anticipated testimony against Whitey Bulger and others, and asked "*After reading what I have outlined, how could anyone consider William David Lindholm a credible witness?"* Jack Wallace's *"Memorandum"* was sent before learning of the First Circuit' decision, which had been issued one week earlier, as described below.

On 6 January 1998 the First Circuit denied Trenkler's appeal with no dissent. Judge Norman Stahl who wrote the 11 page unanimous opinion for himself, Judge Bruce Selya and Judge Frank Coffin. The Court found no abuse of discretion by Judge Zobel regarding the Ramona Walsh controversy, given that the original informant, Donna Shea, had contradicted herself *"by admitting that defendant did not know 'or have any dealings with' Walsh during the relevant time period."*

Regarding David Lindholm, Judge Stahl said that *"Perjury allegations should prompt a new trial when the court is 'reasonably-well satisfied that the testimony was false and that, without the false testimony, the jury 'might have reached a different result.' "* [citing a case] He continued, *"The district court rightly observed that nothing in the record indicates that Lindholm perjured himself or that his early release from prison was the result of a deal made prior to the trial that the government failed to disclose."* It appears that Morris Goldings did not tell the Appeals Court either in his brief nor in oral argument that Lindholm's testimony about his father attending Thayer Academy and Milton Academy was false. However, Lindholm's testimony may not have been lies if his father falsely did tell him that information, and that he attended Brown University as well, but that should have been the subject of some judicial or investigative inquiry. Alfred Trenkler and his family and lawyers knew in 1994 that Lindholm's father attended neither Milton nor Thayer Academies, and it was determined via the Internet in 2007 that no one named Lindholm was in the Brown University alumni directory, although Lindholm's father may have been deceased by that time. Goldings also did not present Lindholm's false claim of the one-year residence on Whitelawn Ave.

In this appeal, Alfred Trenkler was again thwarted by his failure to testify at his trial. The best first step in claiming that David Lindholm lied would have been Trenkler's own testimony. The testimony of his fellow inmates at Plymouth County House of Correction over the period 16-20 December would have been helpful, too. The suspicion of a possible dark deal between the prosecutors and Lindholm was not enough.

As for the testimony of Dr. Phillips, the First Circuit opinion stated, *"That the district court excluded the testimony in Shay Jr.'s trial and that defendant's trial counsel believed that it would be futile to offer it in light of the prior trial do not excuse him from making the offer. The decision of defendant's trial counsel in this case not to offer the testimony may have been part of his reasonable trial strategy; although some of Shay Jr.'s statements were not favorable to Trenkler, some of his admissions supported Trenkler's defense. Thus, trial counsel may have determined that it would be unwise to risk discrediting Shay Jr.'s admissions, even for the sake of discrediting his statements about the existence of a co-conspiracy between Shay Jr. and defendant."* Thus, rather than believe Terry Segal's affidavit about his reason for not requesting Dr. Phillips' testimony at Alfred Trenkler's trial, Judge Stahl chose to speculate on his trial gaming strategy. Even though the First Circuit was well aware by this time of the importance of Dr. Phillips' testimony in the reversal of Tom Shay's trial, it was quite willing to accept Alfred Trenkler's two life sentences because of his lawyer's mistakes. In the legal system, it is the client who suffers the mistakes of the lawyers and the judges, both of which groups still get paid regardless of the outcome, and freely go home every night. Alfred Trenkler's <u>Requests for Justice X</u> and <u>XI</u> had failed.

On 6 February 1998 Alfred Trenkler turned 42 years old.

On 7 May 1998, Alfred Trenkler sent a packet of about 170 pages of information to his friend and Thayer Academy classmate, Mark Brodie, who worked at CBS in New York in the hopes that his case would be aired on "*60 Minutes*" or another national television program. Alfred raised several issues when trying to explain how he was wrongly convicted, including:

- His trial lawyer, Terry Segal, failed to call as a witness Allan Kingsbury, the Radio Shack employee who had initially recalled the purchaser(s) of the six items listed on the 18 October 1991 receipt as being a "Middle Eastern man."

- My attorney had prohibited me from corresponding, meeting or conversing with my hired bomb expert. In doing so it was to ensure that I gave no input to the expert's analysis of my prior bad act. However, my expert, Denny Kline, in trying to show a dissimilarity between my prior act and the '91 bombing, had given my prior act device attributes and features that never existed, namely 1) Twisted soldered and taped wires and 2) slide switch. Nowhere in the 1986 device evidence was there any mention of the "twisted" aspect of wires. While there was no evidence of twisted, soldered and taped wires in the '91 device evidence room when my bomb expert, private investigator and attorney had gone to inspect the bomb remains on multiple occasions, it was only after my bomb expert had signed an affidavit stating, wrongly that the 1986 evidence had twisted soldered and taped wires unlike the 1991 device, that the government would "suddenly" produce a "twisted, soldered and taped" wire and the government now saying that, bolstered by Kline's error, that this "twisted" aspect showed a "unique style" of attaching wires to each other thus, a "signature trait". Without Kline's wrong analysis of the 1986 device, this would have been one thing less to show a similarity between the 1986 device and the 1991 device. This was a fatal error on the part of my attorney and bomb expert. For some reason, since Kline did not see "twisted wires" in the 1991 device, he puts them in the 1986 device, again, the "twisted" aspect of the 1986 device was never mentioned in the 1986 report as well as the fact that the author of the 1986 report had deceased prior to the 1991 bombing. There was no way for either Kline or Waskom to base their finding that the 1986 device contained "twisted wires", further, Kline had placed a "slide switch" in the 1986 device but had no basis for doing so since nowhere in the 1986 report was there any mention of the presence of a "slide switch" being used and the only person that could have verified this was deceased. There was no way for either Kline or Waskom to know whether or not the "twisted" aspect or "slide switch" ever existed. Further, there were no photos, schematics or any physical remains of the 1986 device other than a list of parts that had been recovered and that there was the presence of tape and solder, therefore, there was no way, other than guessing, of knowing how the 1986 device designed or what method of connecting wires beyond the 1986 report stating that there were solder and tape.

None of these details had ever been published, therefore, never available, therefore, could not have been determined short of ESP. I was prejudiced in that my attorney and bomb expert would actually guess instead of simply stating that there was no way to ascertain details beyond what was available in the 1986 report, therefore, not enough evidence available for signature analysis.

These "guesses" the government would use to their full advantage and most likely was the evidence that had allowed my prior act into trial.

Another point, if it is useful, during the hearing on whether to admit the 1986 "prior act" evidence, my attorney requested that I remain out of the procedure, something I had told him might be important for me to be present for, since I knew that my attorney Segal would be snowed by the experts' knowledge in electronics as well as the AUSA Frank Libby who also had a background in electronics. I felt that I could have assisted my attorney since I had a vast background in electronics and would have been able to combat whatever they tried to "snow" the judge with.

Another witness whom Terry Segal failed to request to testify was Mary Anne Leach who would have impeached her son Todd Leach which would have negated the government's "similar M.O. [Modus Operandi]" theory. Todd Leach testified that in 1986 I had sent him into a Radio Shack to purchase items for the 1986 device. The government used this testimony to say that my M.O. in 1986 was the same in 1991 by saying that codefendant Shay Jr had been sent into a Radio Shack by me to purchase parts that had been used to "assist" the builder of the 1991 device, showing a signature M.O. to the 1986 device. Mary Anne Leach had been interviewed by a P.I. who was working for codefendant Shay's attorneys. She stated that her son had told her that he was going to 'lie for the government' in order to obtain the reward that had been offered in this case, up to $65,000.00, in order to bail his Uncle John Shea out of jail. She also stated that her son was never in a car with me or my roommate, Robert Craig, and that he had never left her house with anyone but herself or a family member. (Leach was unemployed at the time and was always home to watch her children as well as the fact that her son was only 9 years old in 1986) [Actually, he was 10 during the summer of 1986, using the birthdate of 14 November 1975 from the 31 March 1993 ATF report, but Alfred's point remains valid.]

Mary Anne Leach also stated that the 1986 'prior act' was entirely Donna Shea's idea, in fact, the simulator used in the 1986 device was owned by Donna Shea, Leach's sister, given to Donna Shea some years prior to the 1986 incident. Donna Shea had 'stored' the simulator at Mary Anne Leach's house but had wanted the simulator to show me and to 'get me to find a way to set it off'. This witness was available and willing to testify. This witness's statements are available from Shay Jr's law firm and or P.I. 'Emmett [Sheehan].' My attorney knew of these statements but had not informed me until after my trial. This would have been impeachment evidence of a government witness used to establish M.O. as well as a witness that would have weakened the government's theory that I had some 'secret source' for explosives and had simply chosen to use dynamite in 1991 versus 'choosing' a simulator in 1986. This witness would show that I did not 'choose' a simulator to set off in 1986 to intimidate someone that Donna Shea was having an argument with, instead, Donna Shea chose me to set off a simulator that she had been given some years prior to the 1986 act and something I had not been aware of until 1986."

Continuing his analysis for Mark Brodie, Alfred described other witnesses who could have/should have been called to challenge the government's case. Specifically:

- Evelyn and Robert Pirello who would have testified as they did at the Shay trial about seeing Mr. Thomas L. Shay carrying a black box on 28 October when he emerged from his car at 39 Eastbourne.

- Tom McKernan, who "*had told* [Boston] *police that he had seen Shay within 20 minutes of the bombing coming out of a local gas station bathroom with something in his hands. Later Tom McKernan would* [reportedly] *tell the ATF that he saw Shay Sr. leave the gas station with 'nothing in his hands.'* "

- John Doering, owner of Rolling Wrench Garage, "*was available to testify and would have shown that Shay Sr. was lying about being afraid of driving his car because he, Shay Sr., thought that there might be more bombs under his car. Doering stated to police that Shay Sr. was not driving his neighbor's car, a gray Mazda, on October 28th, but in fact, Shay Sr. was driving his Black Buick, on which the bomb had been allegedly attached. Doering also stated that when he, Doering, mentioned that what Shay Sr. says he 'found' in his driveway might be a bomb, that Shay Sr. simply laughed at the 'bomb' comment of Doering's. Doering also displayed a knowledge of magnets similar to those used on the 1991 bomb as coming from old auto transmissions and indicated that he used to have some of them on an empty shelf behind his desk. He also had knowledge of the other type of magnets that were on the 1991 bomb as being used in the autobody business that Shay Sr. just happened to be in.*

- Shay Sr.'s girlfriend, Mary Flanagan, had stated to police that Shay Sr. was paranoid of 'Lewis and Jeff'* [Louis Giammarco, Jeffrey Berry] *out to harm Shay Sr., in fact, she had stated to a Dr. Weiner, a psychiatrist that she and Shay Sr. were seeing in relation to Shay Sr.'s ongoing lawsuit, that Shay Sr. would always check under the hood and seat of his car before using it for 'something' that Lewis* [Louis] *or Jeff might have put there. She had also stated to police that Shay Sr. had put extra locks on the doors and windows of her house and had motion lights installed around the outside of her house. On the day of the bombing, Flanagan says to police, 'is he hurt, did he get him?' in reference to Lewis and Jeff. Flanagan would have shown that Shay Sr. was lying when he testified that he never said he was afraid of Lewis* [Louis] *or Jeff, and that Shay Sr. had predicted the manner and placement of 'something' that would kill or injure Shay Sr. and that his only enemies were Lewis* [Louis] *and Jeff. This would have shown that either Shay Sr. was concerned that Lewis* [Louis] *and Jeff were after him showing their 'guilt' or that Shay Sr. was simply forecasting the 'bombing' and staging this '91 device to 'bolster' his ongoing lawsuit that has a possible yield of $400,000.00 which, coincidently, Shay Sr.'s attorney in the ongoing lawsuit had informed Shay Sr. that the insurance company did not believe any of Shay Sr.'s story... that Shay Sr. was injured or that he was so paranoid of the people that he is suing that he cannot work, two weeks prior to this bombing.*

On over 50 occasions, Dr. Weiner had reported that Shay Sr. stated that he was convinced that Lewis[Louis] *and Jeff were out to injure or kill Shay Sr. Dr. Weiner was a psychiatrist hired by the insurance company that Shay Sr. was suing - the question I have is, can this particular psychiatrist testify in my trial in that the psychiatrist was being used to "verify" Shay Sr.'s problems stemming from a prior* explosion at the hands of the people he was suing? None of these witnesses, who were all available, had given Grand Jury testimony as well as being on record via police and ATF Field reports, were called by my attorney, all of which would have aided in the impeachment of Shay Sr. as well as the possible guilt of Shay Sr. and pointing the blame away from me and toward Shay Sr. who had almost all of the attributes that the government stated that I possessed but were never able to prove. After all, Shay Sr. was the one that was running a 'failing business' and had the demonstrated motive and intent in having a successful lawsuit, shown by the insurance company's psychiatrist, the many police reports filed because of Shay Sr. constantly reporting events that he had attributed to "Lewis [Louis] and Jeff", Shay Sr.'s girlfriend that would have shown Shay Sr.'s absurd behavior, Shay Sr.'s history of many successful lawsuits, Shay Sr. 'predicted' the placement of the bomb under the seat of his car, Shay Sr.'s paranoia had suddenly increased in the Fall of 1991, the bombing had occurred two weeks subsequent to Shay Sr.'s attorney informing him that the insurance company did not believe any of his stories. Shay Sr.'s girlfriend, Mary Flanagan, telling police that Shay Sr. had a gambling problem that she had recently 'paid off'."

Alfred stated to Mark Brodie there was insufficient effort to investigate other leads in the case, e.g. that the ATF failed to search the home of Arthur Shay, the brother of Mr. Thomas L. Shay. Also, there had been no attempt to separate the seven layers of electrical tape which had been found as a bomb fragment, in order to locate fingerprints, or DNA.

Alfred continued,"- I had requested the Christian Science Monitor Security Log for the month of October to check the dates I had been working at the site. (I had a contract with Christian Science Monitor's World News program, installing microwave transmitter and receiver systems for their world wide news distribution system. I was the consultant, engineer and installer for Christian Science working under my company ARCOMM) Christian Science security, represented by Joseph Pelphry, informed me that the 'log was lost' and that no other copies were available and was not in their computer system. What was strange was the fact that out of all the years of records kept, only October of 1991 was missing. But stranger still was the fact that the US government had given me a partial copy of the log in question. Missing from the log was a key date, October 28, 1991, that I maintain would have shown that I was working at Christian Science at 12:00 PM on October 28th, 1991, the same day and time that the government would try and place me in Shay Sr's neighborhood lying in wait to set off the 1991 bomb.

Logically, if Christian Science informs me that the October Log is missing and the government later gives me a partial copy, the government must have taken the log in question and withheld the key dates from my defense. In fact, the government had given me the log for October 18th, 1991 that had shown that I was not working at Christian Science that day, and sending Shay Jr into the Radio Shack across the street. But the most crucial date was conveniently 'missing'."

Alfred wrote to Mark Brodie that one reason for not calling all those witnesses was that Terry Segal had said that the defense was running out of money, or going over the predicted budget.

Finally, Alfred said that Terry Segal had "*informed me that he had spoken to a US Marshal who had informed my attorney* [Segal] *that inmate Lindholm had not been 'accidentally' sent to the same prison as where I was. In fact, the U.S. Attorney's office had specifically instructed the Marshal's service to send Lindholm to Plymouth...*" Unfortunately, Terry Segal did not record the name of the U.S. Marshal and when he was asked about that conversation later, he was non-committal.

Despite Brodie's efforts, CBS did not produce a program about Alfred Trenkler's case.

On 18 June 1998, the new Boston Police HQ was dedicated, with its memorial wall, and it was reported by Marcella Bombardieri in the *Globe*'s article, "*SLAIN HUB OFFICERS SALUTED AT POLICE STATION DEDICATION.*" She quoted Cynthia Hurley, "*Anything we can do to keep our husbands' memories alive is wonderful.*"

On 5 January 1999, Alfred Trenkler filed a Motion for *Habeas Corpus* on his own, or pro se, to set aside his conviction, with the statutory reference to 28 United States Code 2255 on the ground that "*Petitioner's Constitutional Right to Effective Assistance of Counsel was denied him by the actions of his Trial Counsel.*" The Motion was filed in U.S. District Court in Boston. Trenkler argued in his supporting memorandum that Terry Segal's failure "*to attempt to introduce the expert testimony of Dr. Phillips was an act of ineffective assistance of counsel...This act of ineffectiveness prejudiced Trenkler as the jury may well have been influenced to reject the statements of Shay if they would have known of the mental disorder from which Shay suffered and the effects of that disorder upon his statements.*" Alfred Trenkler concluded, "*... Petitioner prays that this Court will grant his petition and find that he received ineffective assistance of trial counsel, vacate the conviction in this case and grant him a new trial.*"

Assisting him in this Petition, termed here the Request for Justice XII, was Joseph M. Kalady, a "Senior Research Analyst" of the Illinois firm of "Legal Research Ltd" which assists prison inmates with pro se legal papers. Kalady sent the Petition to the District Court and a copy to Morris Goldings as well.

On 6 February 1999 Alfred Trenkler turned 43 years old.

On 20 April 1999 AUSA Kevin McGrath filed a "*Memorandum of Law in Opposition to ... Petition to Vacate Sentence.* He argued first, that such a 2255 Petition must be filed within one year of the time when his conviction became final, or August 1994, or within one year of the enactment of AEDPA, the Antiterrorism and Effective Death Penalty Act of 1986 or 23 April 1997.

Next, argued McGrath, Trenkler did not identify the Shay statements which were introduced against him, nor establish whether those statements were consistent with "pseudologia fantastica," as Dr. Phillips' testimony would have addressed. Also, Trenkler had not established whether Terry Segal's decision not to attempt to introduce Dr. Phillips' testimony was due to a tactical decision, for which Trenkler was responsible. McGrath pointed out that Terry Segal conceded Shay's guilt in Segal's opening statement, and thus attacking his inculpatory statements later would have been inconsistent.

He continued, "*Trenkler entirely fails to sustain his burden of establishing that the decision not to offer the testimony of Dr. Phillips, even if error, substantially affected the outcome of the case, particularly given that Shay's statements did not directly implicate Trenkler and given the independent overwhelming evidence of Trenkler's guilt, including his own admissions of responsibility for the bombing.*" There were never any admissions by Alfred of any involvement in the bombing. There was only a claim of an admission by William David Lindholm, a federal inmate, who received a substantial benefit in return for his testimony against Alfred Trenkler.

Trying to leave no stones unturned, Jack Wallace wrote to Barry Scheck at the Innocence Project at the Cardozo Law School at Yeshiva University in New York. Unfortunately, because there was no DNA yet detected in the Roslindale Bomb case, Scheck wrote back on 18 August 1999 to say that the Innocence Project could not help.

On 24 October 1999, Tom Shay wrote from his Federal prison in Bradford, Penn., to Jack and Josephine Wallace, whom he knew only by name, and by seeing them attending his trial as spectators. He wrote: "*Dear Sir/Madam, I would like to know if you would be interested in filing some paperwork that would help your son & myself in the event we strike gold. Your son is innocent! I can prove it! Would you be willing to pay to have me given a lie detector test? I will take it if it can be arranged. Also some Freedom of Information Act papers need to be filed. I will go into the details if your* [sic] *interested.*" The proposed lie detector test was not arranged, but it would have been interesting to see if a polygraph would work with a sufferer of "pseudologia fantastica."

On 6 February 2000 Alfred Trenkler turned 44 years old. The previous year saw the last visit from his friend John Cates, who found the visits very difficult to stomach.

On 20 February Tom Shay wrote another letter, typewritten this time, to the Wallace's, declaring Alfred's innocence, asking for their help. He wrote, "*Attorney Goldings and I met on Monday February 21, 2000 and we had a good conversation, and I have a good feeling within my heart that based on that conversation Al will win his appeal.*

Attorney Goldings and myself talked about how I can help Al and we came up with two possible ways, the first is for me to take a polygraph and the second, is to read through case files and make notes. I will do whatever in my power to help show that Al is innocent.

Though Al and I were just acquaintances, we weren't really friends. He is my co-defendant and he is innocent.

I am asking you for one hundred and seventy-five dollars and fifty cents as I need to purchase new glasses...

Thanking you in advance for allowing me to talk with you. Sincerely, Thomas Shay."

On 1 April 2000 the "Discovery Channel" featured the Roslindale Bomb case in its series, "*The New Detectives.*" This program was about the ATF with a semi-fictionalized re-enactment called "*A FEDERAL OFFENSE.*" The ATF's Jeff Kerr, Cynthia Wallace and Stephen Scheid explained their roles in solving the Roslindale Bomb case. Ironically, the name on the 18 October Radio Shack receipt was said to be "Ashy," yet another variation of "Shay." There were errors in the program, but at the end it stated correctly, "*Alfred Trenkler's resolve never weakened. He never talked and he was sentenced to life in prison.*" Missing from the program was any mention of the David Lindholm testimony.

On 18 April 2000, Judge Zobel denied Alfred Trenkler's 2255 Petition, and his Request for Justice XII, because it was filed late.

On 16 May 2000 Morris Goldings filed an appeal, called here Request for Justice XIII, of Judge Zobel's 18 April denial of Alfred Trenkler's 2255 petition. The First Circuit responded on 5 July that it could not consider Trenkler's appeal until he had obtained from the District Court a "*certificate of appealability.*" The Court ordered Trenkler to file such a certificate or file an explanation of the effort taken to obtain that certificate, and keep filing such reports every 30 days until it's been obtained, or a decision has been made by the U.S. District Court not to issue a certificate of appealability. Trenkler applied for such a certificate on 21 August and on 9 November Judge Zobel granted the application, with a handwritten note, "*Although I adhere to my view that the petition is time-barred, petitioner's tolling arguments are not frivolous. Accordingly, the application is granted as to these issues.*"

On 16 June Jack Wallace wrote to Morris Goldings a five page handwritten letter about the absence of physical evidence. He concluded, "*It is so obvious that the government and the ATF came up with nothing on Alfred. Alfred serving a life sentence is a disgrace to our justice system.*" Jack and Alfred's mother, Josephine Wallace, had to struggle with the need to live a normal life with the knowledge that Alfred was wrongly in prison. It was not a dilemma that any other Milton parents faced.

How does a parent talk to a wrongfully convicted son on the phone at one moment and then go shopping the next? Or go out to a restaurant? Or resume any other normal activity? For the parents of the vast majority of the 2 million people who are in jail or prison in this country, and who actually committed crimes, these questions are hard enough. For the parents of the wrongfully convicted, they are vastly harder.

For the friends of the Wallaces, there was inevitable awkwardness. What do you say to a friend whose son is in a high security Federal prison instead of in a high-rise office building in Boston or New York where the sons of many Milton parents worked? "*How's Alfred?*" For the friends who wrote letters to Judge Zobel and who attended Alfred's trial, their dilemma was what to do next? The message that the lawyers gave to the Wallaces was to keep sending them money so they could make their arguments against other lawyers before new lawyer-judges.

Mostly, the Wallaces struggled privately and declined the awkward offers of friends. Sometimes, though, their rage at the system would lead them to seek help from the other institution in our society which holds itself out as being interested in the truth: the media. Jack Wallace would call and write whomever he could. Sometimes, he would get a sympathetic ear, and that might lead to the interest of another person, but the usual result was no further investigation of the facts and no story. To the readers and viewers of the Boston media, and listeners, too, Alfred Trenkler had virtually disappeared. Even to Alfred's friends and most friends of the Wallaces, the result seemed fixed in stone. Said one family friend in 2006, "*I thought that was done. I thought that it was over. Now you're telling me that he's innocent?*"

In August 2000, in advance of Morris Goldings' anticipated appeal, Jack and Jo Wallace sent out a form letter to several reporters, "*as you have written articles in the past about my stepson, Alfred Trenkler.... Mrs. Wallace, Alfred's mother and I have always maintained our complete and total confidence in Alfred's innocence in the horrible crime for which he was unjustly convicted and sentenced to life imprisonment. ... We now have compelling evidence which, combined with other evidence in the past, supports our confidence in Alfred's innocence and presents an even more compelling challenge to the government's weak case. We would appreciate your reviewing the enclosed motion based on the new evidence... If you have any questions, please call my wife, Jo or myself.*" The press release did help, and at least one reporter, Shelley Murphy, did interview the Wallaces for her story about the upcoming filing of the

On 10 August 2000 Morris Goldings filed a "*Motion for a New Trial, or, in the Alternative, for an evidentiary hearing,*" referenced here as <u>Request for Justice XIV</u>. There were three grounds for the motion which claimed new evidence:

1. That the Radio Shack corporation had established that the 18 October 1991 Radio Shack receipt was not a valid receipt, and

2. That Thomas A. Shay had stated in an interview with Morris Goldings at Shay's place of incarceration in Pennsylvania that Radio Shack employee, Dwayne Armbrister's, testimony about Shay's alleged 18 October 1991 purchase was incorrect and biased, and

3. That a witness, John Bowden, had come forward to impeach the credibility of William David Lindholm.

Then the Motion "*discussed*" the three claims:

1. Radio Shack is owned by the Tandy Corporation, and one of its Associate General Counsels completed an affidavit which stated that "*none of the information on sales receipt No. 098973 matches any information contained in Radio Shack's general journal for store No. 01-1021 on October 18, 1991.*"

2. The content of the interview between Morris Goldings and Tom Shay is not available, but it probably paralleled a letter which Tom Shay sent to Morris Goldings on 6 December 1999. Of course, Goldings was subject to the same "Selective Truth Temptation" that Paul Kelly and Frank Libby suffered when talking to Tom Shay: the temptation to pick the statements he wanted to believe were true. Excerpts from Tom Shay's letter are below:

"*I was virtually coerced by my former attorneys to plead guilty* [before the anticipated second trial in 1998]. *I, Mr. Goldings, am truly innocent and your client is also innocent. There is actually no sure way to prove our innocents* [sic] *except by tearing down the house of fragile cards, one by one. I want to file two motions in the court. The first is ineffective counsel to the court. By law suite* [sic] *the filing fees will cost about $600. I had 3 attorneys and I'm filing against two as the third, a friend and non-partner of the firm, was also coerced into coercing me to plead guilty. She was basicly* [sic] *forced, to force me to play ball & save the firm $! Before I plead* [pled guilty], *my mother Nancy Shay..., my sister Paula Shay... and my other sister, Amy Lerner* [sic, Lenar]... *They were with my attorneys in a conference room speaking to me on a speaker phone while I was at Plymouth County Jail, Oct-98. Throughout the conversation* [the assumption] *was my known innocents* [sic]. *My lawyers said it was better this way. My sister Nancy who lives with my mother, did not want me to plead guilty. She was also present at the conference call. An hour before I plead guilty, I met an old attorney of the firm who was then & is now still a Federal Judge* [Nancy Gertner] *and I told her I was innocent. She said she knew and she gave me a hug....*" Goldings requested that Tom Shay be brought to Massachusetts to testify and be cross-examined.

3. Below is the 22 April 1998 Affidavit of John J. Bowden concerning William David Lindholm:

"*1. I am currently a federal inmate being held at USP Allenwood, White Deer, PA 17887.*

2. While at USP Allenwood, I met [a man], *who I now know as Alfred Trenkler who was convicted in November of 1993 for the "Roslindale Bombing".*

3. While I was being held in the Middleton County Jail in Middleton, Massachusetts between July 1992 and May/June of 1994, I had met William David Lindholm, another federal inmate.

4. I knew from the media that Lindholm was testifying against Alfred Trenkler, in Trenkler's ongoing trial.

5. In a number of conversations I had with Lindholm, it had become apparent that Lindholm had ties to my home town of Revere, Massachusetts through Lindholm's drug dealing past.

6. I asked Lindholm what the deal was with his testifying against Trenkler. Lindholm said that he thought Trenkler was guilty and that the FEDS would convict Trenkler anyway.

7. I asked Lindholm if Trenkler actually admitted to participating in the Roslindale Bombng. Lindholm stated that it really did not matter, the FEDS are convinced Trenkler did the bombing, that Trenkler was scum and deserved to be behind bars. He stated that if it wasn't Lindholm saying that Trenkler had admitted to the bombing, someone else would do it for the government and Lindholm was not going to pass up this chance for him to make a deal to get out of jail, not to mention the advantage of the coincidence that Lindholm had lived in the same home town as Trenkler.

8. ... He then stated that if the government did not come through with Lindholm's release, Lindholm would write Trenkler's attorneys and tell that he lied for the government and suffer the perjury charges.

9. I asked Lindholm how he was so sure he would be released, what kind of 'deal' the government gave him. He told me to look up Rule 35(b) in the Federal Rules of Criminal Procedure, something that Lindholm said that I could use to my advantage.

10. This summarizes the content of the conversations I had with William David Lindholm.

11. I have been given no promises, rewards or inducements for this affidavit or any future testimony concerning William David Lindholm."

The affidavit seemed to parallel Lindholm's testimony about Alfred Trenkler, in that both Bowden and Lindholm had a common interest in a town or city, Revere and Milton, and that Lindholm had given Bowden some legal advice. The key difference was that Bowden had no apparent incentive to create this affidavit, apart from his prison acquaintance with Alfred Trenkler and interest in truth, whereas Lindholm's interest in his testimony was to secure a reduction in his sentence. Considering that difference alone, Bowden's prison informer statement should have been more credible than Lindholm's, but the legal system was not to view it that way. [A photocopy of the Bowden Affidavit is in Appendix E.]

On 9 July 1998, another inmate, Thomas Conley, completed a handwritten Affidavit on behalf of Alfred Trenkler. He said,

"This is an affidavit written on behalf of Al Trenkler. My name is Thomas Young Conley III, DOB 10/20/71...

As long as I have known Al, since Nov. '96, I've talked with him many times concerning his case. He has done nothing but complain about the lies used to convict him, complain about the evidence withheld by the government which would prove his innocense [sic] and constantly profess his innocense [sic]. From the papers he has shown me, and what he has told me, I believe he is not guilty of the crime. However, this is not the purpose of this affidavit. The purpose of this Affidavit is to swear under oath that Al has denied all ties to this crime, and has never admitted doing it to me or anyone I know. He always professes his innocense [sic]. So if a convict from USP Allenwood tries to get a departure by saying Al confessed to this crime, to them, they are lying! This is the truth as I know it."

On 16 August 2000, the <u>Boston Globe</u> caught the story of Morris Goldings' "*Motion for Retrial*," with the article, "*NEW TRIAL SOUGHT IN 1991 BOMBING- LAWYER SAYS KEY EVIDENCE IS 'BOGUS'.*" Written by Shelley Murphy, who had moved from the <u>Boston Herald</u>, the lengthy article included an interview with the Tandy Corporation lawyer, Robert Blair, whose affidavit was the basis of the 'bogus' receipt claim. He conceded that since the claimed transaction was several years previous, and since not all stores reported all transactions correctly, the receipt may still have been valid. Ms. Murphy also interviewed Jack and Josephine Wallace whose behind-the-scenes work for their son over the previous seven years had not been noticed by the media. "*They had no proof that Alfred built that bomb*," said Jack Wallace, Alfred's stepfather. U.S. Attorney Don Stern said, "*Trenkler received a fair trial and is exactly where he should be for a very long time. It's regrettable that the families of the police officers have to go through another round of litigation and relive the horror of a regrettable crime.*" He did not acknowledge the possibility of a wrongful conviction.

On 18 August, Shelley Murphy wrote the <u>Boston Globe</u>'s thorough followup article, "*'BOGUS' EVIDENCE REBUTTED IN 1991 FATAL BOMBING CASE.*" Former ATF Agent Dennis Leahy described how the original receipt was found after receiving many pages of corporate documents from Tandy Corporation in November 1991. It was from those documents that the trail led to the 197 Mass. Ave store. Murphy described the other challenge to the Goldings' motion which was that in October 1998 Tom Shay had pled guilty and specifically admitted that he had purchased the items on 18 October 1991.

On 25 August 2000, the <u>Patriot Ledger</u> 's Dennis Tatz wrote that paper's first independent examination of the case, after previously publishing several articles from the Associated Press. The article was entitled, "*CONVICT SEEKS NEW TRIAL IN 1991 FATAL EXPLOSION: POLICE OFFICER DIED, ANOTHER WAS MAIMED.*" It addressed all three parts of Morris Golding's "*Motion for a New Trial*," and Tatz quoted Jack Wallace extensively, who "*said while everyone realizes the police officers' families have suffered, his family has also gone through an ordeal believing in his stepson's innocence and his wrongful conviction. 'What about the injustice?' he asked. 'Is it fair to have a son in jail for a crime that he didn't do?'*"

On 11 September 2000 AUSA Kevin McGrath responded to Morris Goldings' "*Motion for a New Trial*" with a 26 page "*Memorandum*" and a 59 page Appendix. First, he argued that the Motion was time barred because such motions must be filed within three years of a verdict, i.e. by 29 November 1996. Most of the memorandum contained a summary of the ever-longer "*Procedural Background*" of the case and a "*Statement of Facts*" beginning with the 28 October 1991 explosion.

Regarding the Radio Shack receipt, McGrath argued that the prosecution had also used Tandy Corporation's corporate records and the receipt was valid. Also, Shay had admitted purchasing the toggle switch in his Karen Marinella interview and also his 1998 plea agreement where it was stated, "*On October 18, 1991, Defendant purchased certain electrical components, including a toggle switch, needed for the construction and testing of the explosive device. ... Trenkler built a remote controlled explosive device consisting of dynamite, blasting caps, and other materials, including the toggle switch that Defendant had purchased from Radio Shack on October 18, 1991.*"

McGrath said there was insufficient documentation of the claims about Shay's statements. As McGrath did not appear to have the Bowden Affidavit, as it was inexplicably not attached to Morris Goldings' Motion, he was responding to the Motion's general claims. Perhaps the absence of the affidavit was because Morris Goldings was already suffering from the stress of the upcoming unraveling in December 2000 of his multi-million dollar thefts from his other clients.

McGrath concluded that the claimed new evidence would not likely result in an acquittal upon retrial, the standard of review to follow, and that the Motion should be dismissed without a hearing.

On 26 September 2000, after being given permission by the court, Morris Goldings filed a "*Reply*" to McGrath's "*Opposition*" and argued that the testimony at the requested hearing of John Bowden was the best way to examine the credibility of his Affidavit, as it related to the important issue of William David Lindholm's testimony at Alfred Trenkler's trial.

On 10 November, the *Worcester Telegram and Gazette* reported on the 9 November hearing on the "*Motion for a New Trial*." The article, from the Associated Press, was headlined "*LAWYER CLAIMS NEW EVIDENCE WILL FREE MAN CONVICTED IN POLICE BOMBING CASE*," and reported that Morris Goldings said, "*We claim his innocence... This is a case, not just of 'not guilty,' but of innocence.*" Unfortunately, the article continued the false label of Alfred Trenkler being the "*sometime lover*," of Tom Shay.

On 28 December 2000, Judge Zobel denied the "*Motion for New Trial*" stating that the Radio Shack records available at the time of trial showed that the 18 October 1991 Radio Shack receipt was valid, and that the proposed testimony of Tom Shay would conflict with his sworn testimony at his plea agreement hearing, and that the proposed testimony of John Bowden was not supported by an Affidavit or other reliable documentation. The last deficiency must have been frustrating to Alfred Trenkler, because John Bowden's original affidavit was signed on 22 April 1998. Trenkler's Request for Justice XIV had failed.

Morris Goldings, who had worked with the Wallaces and for Alfred Trenkler since the initial 1994 appeal, had succumbed to greed which led to his embezzlement of approximately $17 million of clients' funds. On 29 December 2000, the managing partner of his law firm, James Cox, wrote to Alfred Trenkler about the problem with a soft spin, "*I write to inform you that our partner, Morris Goldings, has very recently become disabled. His condition prevents him from practicing law, and he has retired from the firm.*" After conviction in the courts where he practiced law as a highly regarded lawyer and Harvard Law graduate, he spent three years in Federal prison, and then moved to Florida where he was teaching law-related subjects to university undergraduate students. His former partners, Bruce Edmands and Richard Jacobs, had recommended that the Wallaces and Alfred find a new appellate lawyer, which led them to James Sultan and Charles Rankin of the firm, Rankin and Sultan. While the Wallaces and Alfred were generally pleased with Morris Goldings' work for Alfred, until the last hearing, and while they had not entrusted him with any investment funds, his disgraceful collapse was not a reassuring development.

The Patriot Ledger was the first with the story, on 29 December, "*TIME RUNS OUT ON TRENKLER'S APPEAL: ALLEGED BOMB MAKER CLAIMED NEW EVIDENCE.*" Reporter Dennis Tatz again sought the views of Alfred's family, and Jack Wallace responded," *We have proof that he didn't do it... Why should there be a deadline on the truth?*"

On the 30th, the *Boston Globe*'s 9-line article was headlined, "*CONVICTED 1991*

BOMBER LOSES BID." Seeing that headline was Jack Wallace's first news that Judge Zobel had denied the "*Motion for New Trial*." After a phone call to Morris Goldings' firm he learned of Goldings' disgrace and why he hadn't heard earlier about the decision.

On 8 January 2001 Edmands and Jacobs, of Morris Goldings' former law firm, filed an appeal with their "*Brief for Petitioner-Appellant*" with the First Circuit Court of Appeals on the issue of whether Alfred Trenkler's 28 USC 2255 Petition (Habeas Corpus) was correctly time-barred by Judge Zobel. This appeal is denominated here as RFJ XV, and it was the followup to RFJ XII, regarding the claimed failure of Terry Segal to attempt to introduce testimony by Dr. Phillips. They argued that the time period should have been "tolled" or the clock should have been stopped, because Trenkler was waiting for ruling in another of his motions, and that Federal inmates should be subject to a more lenient standard regarding timely-filing requirements.

Frustrated with the Morris Goldings' collapse and with the judicial system in general, Jack Wallace wrote a five page letter on 16 January 2001 to the Chief Judge of the U.S. District Court in Boston, William Young. Mr. Wallace argued for the recently-denied "*Motion for a New Trial*," and was particularly aggrieved at the failure of Attorney Goldings' to include John Bowden's Affidavit in the Motion and failure to mention it at the oral hearing. Wallace posed one of the central questions in the case of why some statements of Tom Shay - the incriminating statements - were acceptable to the courts, but that the other statements were not. He was referring to Tom Shay's recent statements that Alfred Trenkler was innocent.

Also he posed a question which is posed in this book, "*...how can there be a time limit on the truth? Why should an innocent man waste away in prison for the rest of his life for a crime he did not commit?*" Referring to the disparate sentences for Shay and Trenkler, and the retrial, which became a plea agreement for Tom Shay, Jack Wallace cited authority, "*As Boston College Law School Professor Robert M. Bloom states in referring to another case involving co-defendants, 'One is convicted with basically the same witnesses and is getting a new trial. What's the public to think? It looks like the appearance of an injustice if the other doesn't get a new trial as well.*" There, Wallace hit a major theme of this book and the Campaign for Justice for Alfred Trenkler, which is that the "*public*" has an interest in justice and that it's not just a game for lawyers to play. Jack Wallace enclosed a copy of a six-page summary he had written about the case, "*The Case for Reasonable Doubt in Support of Alfred's Complete Innocence.*" Jack Wallace wrote a subsequent handwritten letter to Judge Young on 3 February 2001 in response to seeing newspaper articles about uncovering corruption in the FBI and justice for wrongly convicted people. He wrote, "*We all deserve a better and fairer treatment from the judicial system - the very system that is supposed to protect Alfred Trenkler.*"

On 6 February 2001 Alfred Trenkler turned 45 years old.

Judge Young replied to Jack Wallace's letter on 14 February 2001, saying that he had forwarded the letter to Judge Zobel, with whom he would be unable to discuss any aspects of Alfred's case.

On 20 February 2001, James Sultan and Charles Rankin, filed an appeal, RFJ XVI, with the First Circuit of Judge Zobel's denial of Alfred Trenkler's "Motion for a New Trial," RFJ XIV, based on the three claims of the Radio Shack receipt, Tom Shay's statements and John Bowden's Affidavit. The new lawyers had been retained by Alfred and his parents, after Morris Goldings had to withdraw due to other difficulties with his practice of law. The First Circuit replied with an Order stating that the deadline for Sultan's appeal was 8 February 2001, but gave Sultan until 28 March to present an explanation for the delay or why the deadline was not as the First Circuit understood. Sultan responded on the 28th with a request for understanding by the Court of the confused and "*unique circumstances*" involved in Morris Goldings' departure, and the retaining of new counsel, and reliance on an oral statement by a court clerk regarding the appeal deadline.

On 6 April 2001, three judges of the First Circuit, Juan Torruella, Levin Campbell and Norman Stahl voted to dismiss the appeal "*for lack of jurisdiction*", due to the missing of the time deadlines for appeal. Said the Court, and quoting an earlier First Circuit case, "*reliance on the advice, statements or actions of court employees cannot trigger the* [unique circumstances] *doctrine, whether appellant is or is not pro se.*" Thus, the First Circuit denied RFJ XV which was an appeal of RFJ XII.

On 21 May 2001, Alfred's father, Freddie Trenkler, died in California. The obituary in the *New York Times* did not list his imprisoned and only son, and namesake, among his survivors. Freddie Trenkler had not seen Alfred since the 1980's as their relationship had evolved into an annual phone call on Christmas. Such was the effect of being a continent apart and being divorced long ago from Alfred's mother and being devoted to his present wife and daughters.

Death was also on Alfred's mind as he read of a U.S. Supreme Court decision about capital punishment which seemed to say that it was not unconstitutional to execute innocent people. As one innocent person against whom the U.S. Attorney had been considering pursuing the death penalty, Alfred was interested.

With legitimate anger, he wrote a letter to the *Boston Globe* which wasn't published:

"*Factoid: The U.S. Supreme Court has stated that it is constitutionally legal to execute an innocent man.*

If the government is at ease sentencing innocent citizens to the ultimate sentence, death, based on tainted evidence, jail-house informants selling their testimony for freedom, 'testilying' by police and government agents as well as prosecutorial misconduct including the withholding of exculpatory evidence, you can understand and believe that anything less than a death sentence would be governed by an even lesser standard.

Today it would appear that one has a better chance at freedom if one is actually guilty since one can be a useful tool for the government. Innocent citizens have nothing to offer and have become expendable. Just ask Joseph Salvati[7] and Peter Limone[8] or Bobby Jo Leaster,[9] ask them, ask me.

I am currently serving Two Concurrent life sentences because of the words of a Twenty ton marijuana smuggler, Million Dollar bank defrauder and Twenty year tax evader turned government mouthpiece who, in efforts to 'rehabilitate' himself, was given his freedom for testifying that I admitted to the building of the October 1991 Roslindale Bomb, an admission and a crime I continue to vehemently deny. By the government 'making' me guilty and 'winning' this case all but guarantees the freedom of those actually responsible for this crime that I wrongfully continue to pay for. Sound familiar?

Fairness and convictions based on legitimate investigation and actual versus manufactured evidence has taken a back seat to the winning of cases at any cost, outcomes have become more important than procedure. It is true that someone must pay for crimes against humanity, but should the innocent?

There are heinous crimes against society where emotions are in overdrive and the pressure to attach a name and a face to the miscreant, but does the need to place blame, to seek revenge, warrant the wholesale exclusion of our rights to a fair process?

We can't hold the government to be infallible but we can ask that it is responsible. The question is when."

On 3 July 2001, Rankin and Sultan filed for a "*Writ of Certiorari*" to the U.S. Supreme Court, which was essentially an appeal, but the Court was not required to hear it. This was <u>RFJ XVI</u>, and the issue posed to the Court was "*whether the lower court erred when it held that the doctrine of unique circumstances is available only when incorrect information about the deadline for filing a notice of appeal is conveyed by the district court judge herself, rather than by the district court's clerk.*" With this ancillary question the Roslindale Bomb case was again a long way from 39 Eastbourne Street and the question of who built it. In September 2001, and likely at the request of the U.S. Attorney in Boston, the U.S. Solicitor General, Theodore Olson, filed an opposition to Trenkler's "*Petition for a Writ of Certiorari*" on 1 September 2001. The "*Brief in Opposition*" was written by Asst. Attorney General Michael Chertoff, who later became an Appellate Judge with the Third Circuit Court of Appeals in Pennsylvania, and is now the Director of the U.S. Dept of Homeland Security. Olsen's wife was killed 10 days later when her American Airlines Flight #77 crashed into the Pentagon.

On 26 September 2001 Catherine Hinton, of Sultan and Rankin's firm, wrote a 36 page "*Memorandum to Trenkler File*" in order to "*set forth a review of the entire file, evaluate the merits of potential claims to be made, and make recommendation for future action.*" She reviewed procedural history of the case and all the possible claims, including several which were being pressed by Jack Wallace. However, she concluded that they were barred for various procedural reasons, primarily because they were too late. She concluded that "*It is unfortunate that so much time has gone by since the verdict and that so many claims were botched by Goldings' firm.*"

On 9 October 2001, the U.S. Supreme Court denied Alfred Trenkler's petition, and his <u>RFJ XVII</u> failed.

Meanwhile <u>RFJ XV</u>, the appeal to the First Circuit of the denial for lack of timely filing of Trenkler's request for 28 USC 2255 relief, "Habeas Corpus", continued. The Appeal was filed originally by Bruce Edmands, in the transition after the departure of Morris Goldings, and James Sultan and Charles Rankin filed their 43-page appeal brief with the First Circuit in March 2001. On 10 May, Special Assistant U.S. Attorney David Mackey and AUSA Kevin McGrath replied with their 39-page brief supporting the denial of Trenkler's petition for lack of timeliness. On 2 August, Charles Rankin replied with a 9-page "*Reply Brief.*" The issue of a time deadline was getting a lot of attention, far away though it was from other deadly questions at 39 Eastbourne Street such as the time at which the Roslindale Bomb was placed underneath Mr. Shay's car.

On 16 October 2001 a three judge panel of the First Circuit Court of Appeals denied <u>RFJ XVI</u>. Judge Kermit Lipez, writing the opinion for himself and Judge Bruce Selya and Chief Judge Michael Boudin, stated that Alfred Trenkler's "*Motion for a New Trial*" on the three grounds of the receipt and the Shay and Bowden affidavits was simply filed too late and they would not overrule Judge Zobel's determination that there was insufficient reason to warrant a waiver of the time limitation rules.

The next day's _Boston Globe_ reported simply, "*BOMBMAKER IS REFUSED A NEW TRIAL.*"

Thus, as can be seen below, during the period after his trial until 29 August 2002, Alfred Trenkler had requested justice seventeen times, and had lost every time. The most important near-miss was Judge Torruella's dissent in the 2-1 Court of Appeals Decision on 18 July 1995.

On 6 February 2002 Alfred Trenkler turned 46 years old.

On 30 August 2002, Tom Shay was released from Federal Prison which left Alfred W. Trenkler alone to continued paying for someone else's crimes.

REQUESTS FOR JUSTICE

No.	Court	Date	Description
I	Dist.	25 Oct 93	The Trial of Alfred Trenkler
II	Dist.	6 Dec 93	Motion for Acquittal by Terry Segal
III	Dist	6 Dec 93	Motion for New Trial by Terry Segal
IV	Dist	8 March 94	Alfred Trenkler's Pre-sentencing presentation
V	1st Cir	15 Mar 94	Appeal to the First Circuit of Denial of Request For Justice I
VI	1st Cir	1 Aug 95	Request for Rehearing by the First Circuit, of RFJ V, the denial of RFJ I
VII	1st Cir	8 Aug 95	Motion to the First Circuit to order Remand to District Court on issue of Lindholm's reduction of sentence and effect on Trenkler trial testimony.
VIII	Dist.	22 Dec 95	Motion for New Trial or Evidentiary Hearing at U.S. District Court on the Dr. Phillips and Lindholm issues.
IX	Dist.	19 Nov 96	Motion for Judicial Inquiry into Juror Misconduct/Evidentiary Hearing
X	1st Cir	13 Feb 97	Appeal to First Circuit of Denial by Judge Zobel of RFJ VIII. (X merged with XI)
XI	1st Cir	5 Jan 99	Appeal to the First Circuit of Denial by Judge Zobel of RFJ IX. (XI merged with X)
XII	Dist.	12 Jan 99	Trenkler's pro se Motion for a New Trial on the basis of ineffective counsel, 2255
XIII	1st Cir	16 May 00	Goldings' appeal of Judge Zobel's 18 April 2000 denial of RFJ XII.
XIV	Dist.	10 Aug 00	Motion for a New Trial based on newly discovered evidence, the alleged fabrication of the Radio Shack receipt, and evidence re Lindblom. Denied by Judge Zobel.
XV	1st Cir	8 Jan 2001	Appeal by Bruce Edmands to the First Circuit of the denial by Judge Zobel of XII, the 2255 motion.
XVI	1st Cir	20 Feb 01	Appeal by James Sultan of Judge Zobel's Denial of new Trial, RFJ XIV.
XVII	Sup Ct	3 Jul 01	Petition to U.S. Supreme Court by Rankin and Sultan of First Circuit denial of RFJ XVI, due to timeliness.

END NOTES

---

1. Suffolk County [Mass.] District Attorney Daniel Conley in Op-Ed in _Boston Globe_, 19 March 2004.

2. In email from Julie Hiller to the author, 20 March 2007.

3. Edwin P. Wilson was no relation to Joseph Wilson, the U.S. diplomat who was sent to Niger by the CIA to ascertain the truth about the claim that Iraq had attempted to purchase uranium from that country.

4. A 2003 newspaper account stated that the gun incident was not just a pointing of a gun at Lindholm's head. Wrote Andrea Estes in a 19 July 2003 _Boston Globe_ article, "SUIT AGAINST BULGER, FLEMMI SEEKS $20M", When Lindholm balked at paying, according to the complaint, Bulger fired a shot past his head. Bulger, who fled to avoid racketeering charges in 1995, then allegedly placed a single bullet in the gun's chamber, spun the cylinder, and snapped it closed. He then placed the gun to Lindholm's head and 'without a moment's hesitation,' pulled the trigger." Estes' article was about Lindholm's lawsuit against the U.S. Government and Whitey Bulger and Stephen 'The Rifleman" Flemmi to recover the money extorted from Lindholm before his 1990 conviction. Flemmi's nickname came from his service in the Korean War as a rifleman. Most riflemen of that war discarded their job titles upon returning to civilian life, but Flemmi kept it.

5. Wolcott Square is only a half mile from the large industrial building at 1605 Hyde Park Avenue, which formerly was occupied by Union Paste Company, which was owned by the author's mother's family until the 1970's.

6. Coincidentally, David Lindholm's mother's sister was named Alice Liddell, whose namesake was Alice P. Liddell, who was the "Alice" of Charles Dodgson's (Lewis Carroll's) "Alice's Adventures in Wonderland."

7 Joseph Salvati and Peter Limone were convicted in 1968 in a Massachusetts state court of a 1965 gangland murder. Years later, FBI files were uncovered that showed the the FBI was aware that its informant and primary witness against Salvati and Limone and two others Joseph Barboza was lying. Salvati and Limone were paroled in 1997, after more than 30 years in prison, after their convictions were found to be wrongful. In 2007, their civil lawsuit against the Federal Government for $100 million was heard by U.S. District Court Judge Nancy Gertner and in August 2007 she awarded the four plaintiffs $101.7 million. It was Joseph Barboza's attorney, John Fitzgerald, whose car was bombed in 1968.

8. See End Note #6 above about Joseph Salvati and Peter Limone.

9. Bobby Jo Leaster was wrongly convicted of a 1970 murder and served 15 years in Massachusetts prisons before finally being exonerated, thanks to nine years of pro bono effort by lawyers Robert Muse and his son Christopher.

CHAPTER 10: AFTER THE VERDICT, THOMAS A. SHAY: APPEALS 28 July 1993 to the Present

> *The truth is incontrovertible.*
> *Malice may attack it.*
> *Ignorance may deride it.*
> *But in the end, there it is.*[1]
> Winston Churchill

For Tom Shay, the legal wheel of fortune was to be more kind. After the verdict, Nancy Gertner filed the twin Motions for Acquittal and for a New Trial. These two motions are filed almost automatically after criminal convictions and they are almost automatically denied, but sometimes they give the trial judge the opportunity to correct his or her own mistakes in the trial before going "upstairs" to an appellate court. Trial judges do not like to be reversed by appellate courts.

On 4 August 1993, the *Boston Globe* reported that Nancy Gertner had filed on 3 August a "*Motion for Hearing On Extraneous Prejudicial Information*" with Judge Zobel to consider whether the jury was improperly influenced by newspaper reports of the trial.. Reported the short article, "*MEDIA ROLE CITED IN SHAY APPEAL*," Gertner cited stories in the *Boston Herald* and the Matthew Brelis' story in the *Boston Globe* on 28 July 1993, "*US PROSECUTORS TURN TO SHAY CODEFENDANT*," which reported that jurors expressed the wish that they could have seen the evidence which they understood had been suppressed. (see Chapter 6's "*Next Day Headlines*" for 27 July.) The U.S. Attorney argued against that Motion with the primary argument that the jury had observed, even if not heard, many bench conferences and it was logical for the jury to surmise that some of those conferences were about whether legal rules permitted the introduction of evidence. Also, argued the Asst. U.S. Attorneys, the jury knew that it was not told the whole story about some events, such as the "*incident*," at 39 Eastbourne in May 1988 when Tom Shay stole money and valuables. Judge Zobel denied the Motion.

On 28 September, Judge Zobel denied Tom Shay's "*Motion for a New Trial*" and "*Motion for a Judgment of Acquittal,*" both filed on 3 August.. The legal standard for a New Trial, according to the Federal Rule of Criminal Procedure 33, was whether a new trial was "*required in the interest of justice,*" and whether there were one or more errors sufficient to prejudice "*substantial rights*" of a defendant. Shay's defense team had argued that those errors included:

1. the exclusion of the testimony of Dr. Robert Phillips
2. the exclusion of the offered testimony by Fred Burke, Scott Critcher, William McPhee and David Shilalis offered to show the unreliability of Tom Shay's statements.
3. the instruction to the jury about the requisite intent for a finding of guilty.
4. the instruction to the jury about the terms, "*aiding and abetting.*"
5. the instruction regarding the voluntariness of Tom Shay's statements to the police.
6. the court's decision not to allow a bifurcated trial, with the second phase to consider the claim of insanity.
7. the court's decision to exclude medical testimony regarding the "diminished

capacity" of Tom Shay.

8. the court's decision not to declare a mistrial after Dwayne Armbrister's expansive answer to a "yes or no" question."
9. the court's decision to admit Alfred Trenkler's statements to Dennis Leahy about "shunts" as declarations against penal interest.
10. the playing of a portion of the Channel 56 interview where Tom Shay stated that Dwayne Armbrister had recognized him, even though the court had excluded Armbrister's own testimony about such identification.
11. the decision not to sequester the jury.
12. the decision to sustain the Government objection to a question to John Cates about the allegation that a police officer had urged him to "*be creative*" about cooperating with the police in order to qualify for part or all of the reward.
13. the instruction to the jury about Mrs. Nancy Shay's prior inconsistent statements.

The Motion for Acquittal pursuant to Rule 29 of the Federal Rules of Criminal Procedure argued that the evidence in the trial was insufficient to support the jury's verdict. In particular, Shay's defense team argued that:

1. there was insufficient evidence of a conspiracy.
2. there was insufficient evidence that Tom Shay aided and abetted Alfred Trenkler.

On 1 October, Nancy Gertner filed a 46-page "*Sentencing Memorandum*" which argued that by acquitting Tom Shay of Count 2, the count about explosives, the jury did not intend that he be punished for a homicide. Also, she noted Tom Shay's personal history, which "*could not have been more tragic. His was the prototype of the dysfunctional family -- alcoholism, abuse, severe neglect -- leading to a suicide attempt at age five. And, perhaps even worse, his story is also the prototypical story of the state not only failing to rescue him, but dramatically multiplying his pain -- he was exposed to sexual abuse in state institutions at an early age, infected with a sexually transmitted disease at the age of eleven.*"

Gertner's theory of Shay's culpability was that he "*acted recklessly in communicating his history of abuse and neglect to Trenkler and purchasing a toggle switch, unknowingly where an ordinary person under the same circumstances would have realized the consequences...*" It's not clear whether Nancy Gertner believed these statements or whether she was accepting the jury's verdict as a given and trying to interpret it as best she could for her client's interests.

One of the unfortunate assumptions of Gertner's "*Memorandum*" was that she assumed Alfred Trenkler's guilt, even before his trial. For example, in arguing for a lighter sentence for Shay, she argued, "*Because Shay Jr. was 'substantially less culpable than the average participant,' and lacked knowledge or understanding of Trenkler's activities, his offense level should be decreased...*" There was no room, it seemed, for the helpful word, "*alleged.*"

In response, the prosecutors' "*Sentencing Memorandum*" urged that Shay's crimes be considered to be analogous to first degree murder. Reasoned Paul Kelly and Frank Libby, if the bomb had killed Mr. Thomas L. Shay, as intended, there would have been no question of the proper punishment. The prosecutors recommended a life sentence for Tom Shay.

On Wednesday, 6 October the sentencing hearings began for Tom Shay. At this hearing, Nancy Gertner was able to present the testimony of Dr. Phillips who had diagnosed Tom Shay as suffering from "pseudologia fantasica." In the main trial, his testimony was not permitted as it was offered for the issue of Shay's guilt or innocence, rather than to help determine the appropriate sentence. Matthew Brelis wrote in his 7 October _Boston Globe_ article, "*LIGHTER SENTENCE URGED FOR MAN CONVICTED IN BOMB SQUAD OFFICER'S DEATH*," that Dr. Phillips testified that Shay "*has an identity disorder that makes him incapable of long range planning or thinking about the consequences of his actions.*" Dr. Phillips said that Tom Shay " '*is a dysfunctional* [man] *with a long history of dysfunction and average to low-average intelligence,*' He said Shay has a combination of psychological and physiological problems that create '*significant aberrant behavior... His family and developmental history is extraordinarily aberrant,*' he said. Phillips said that when Shay was 7 years old he attempted suicide. At 11, Shay contracted gonorrhea after being abused at Nazareth Home in Jamaica Plain, according to court documents.*" AUSA Paul Kelly cross-examined Dr. Phillips and tried to show that Tom Shay's flight to California showed some capacity to plan ahead.

On 8 October 1993 came the second day of the disposition hearing with testimony by the government's medical witness, Dr. Martin Kelly. During the initial discussion of Dr. Kelly's qualifications, it appeared that Nancy Gertner did not have a copy of his resume with the "*yellow highlighted*" sections as did others at the hearing. Even in such a serious hearing, humor was permitted as she stated, "*My copy is not highlighted, your Honor. I am shocked and appalled.*" Frank Libby then gave her another copy and announced, "*You are no longer shocked and appalled.*" (TS 10/8/93 p. 7) Humor can be dry in Federal court.

Dr. Kelly, with no stated relation to AUSA Paul Kelly, said, after interviewing Tom Shay for several hours and after reviewing "*four linear feet*" of records, "*that he does have the capacity to deliberate and premeditate.*" (TS 10/8/93 20)

He was asked by Frank Libby about Dr. Phillips' diagnosis of Tom Shay as suffering from "*pseudologia fantastica*" and Dr. Kelly said it was less of a disease and more simply a "*Latinization of someone who is a bragger and a BS-er and a self-aggrandizing individual.*" (TS 10/8/93 25) Also, "*he has no disease that would prevent him from telling the truth if he was so motivated.*" (TS 10/8/93 26)

The prosecution's opinion of Dr. Phillips' views came later from Paul Kelly who said, "*Dr. Phillips I think described Tom Shay as telling tall tales with little foundation in fact as being talkative with little substance to the content of his speech. It is my suggestion to this Court that the same label and description can be put on the testimony of Dr. Phillips.*" (TS 10/8/93 120)

During cross-examination, Nancy Gertner asked Dr. Kelly to consider Tom Shay as a potential patient, apart from the criminal proceeding, and Dr. Kelly responded, "*Tom Shay would need to be in an institution for a very long time...He had a mixed personality disorder with antisocial, narcissistic, histrionic, sadomasochistic features...It reflects itself in self-aggrandizing behavior.*" (TS 10/8/93 72/73)

Dr. Kelly was excused and the prosecution then argued for a life sentence, and the defense for leniency. Judge Zobel said, "*I am simply not persuaded by the trial evidence that he intended to kill his father.*" (TS 10/8/93 122) She added that in any case, the jury found Shay not guilty of the explosives count. Judge Zobel considered the presentencing report of the U.S. Probation Dept. and the recommendations of the prosecution and the defense and the moving oral and written Victim Impact Statements, by members of the Hurley and Foley families. Perhaps because Tom Shay had said in the Karen Marinella interview, "*Also, I have a book coming out,*" Judge Zobel said she was "*concerned about the possibility that Mr. Shay may make some profit from the story being told on television or otherwise;*" but she said she did not have any statutory authority to avoid that possibility. (TS 10/8/93 136)

Then, Tom Shay was asked by Judge Zobel, "*do you wish to address the Court before I impose sentence?*" He replied, "*No, No, your Honor.*" (TS 10/8/93 135) It's not yet known why he chose, uncharacteristically, to say nothing, but it was another lost opportunity to speak the truth, and where there was no threat of cross-examination. Tom Shay could have told the court what happened and how he wove the web of lies he could not escape. He could have explained his statements to the police and the media. He was not incapable of telling the truth. It was perhaps an indication of the shock he felt at the conviction which was directly attributable to his previous statements. Then Judge Zobel sentenced Tom Shay to 188 months (15 years 8 months) in prison for Count 3, the intent to destroy an automobile and 60 months on Count 1, for Conspiracy, to be served concurrently. The sentence was longer than the accumulated total of all of his previous institutionalization.

Judge Zobel said in her own finding of fact that the prosecution did not prove that Shay intended to kill his father, so the maximum sentence under federal guidelines was the 188 months sentence, by reference to the standard for second degree murder.

After the sentencing, his attorney, Amy Baron-Evans said Shay would not be making any comments pending his appeal. It appeared that the conviction had finally shaken Tom Shay's impulse to call reporters.

The next day, on 9 October 1993, the newspapers conveyed the police reaction to the Shay sentence. The <u>Boston Globe</u> headline read, "*SHAY SENTENCE ANGERS POLICE - FATAL BOMB BLAST DRAWS 15 1/2 YEARS.*" The story by John Ellement about the sentencing showed the considerable anger by police at the sentence. Said the "*Boston Police Superintendent in Chief Paul Evans, 'Today I think we heard that the life of a dedicated Boston police officer is worth 16 years. My reaction, on behalf of the department, is one of bitter disappointment....It's an insult to every working police officer in the commonwealth.'*" One reason for the police anger may have been the 8-12 year sentence given in Massachusetts Superior Court two days earlier for Katherine Ann Power, for her role in the bank robbery in 1970 which led to the killing Boston Police Officer Walter Schroeder. Coincidentally, the gun shots which killed him were heard at the home of Mr. Thomas and Nancy Shay a few months before Tom Shay was conceived.

U.S. Attorney A. John Pappalardo announced that he would appeal the sentence. "*He is a ticking time bomb,*" Kelly said of Shay, "*set to kill some other innocent victim.*" However, as sentences are discretionary decisions by judges within statutory boundaries, and since Judge Zobel's decision was within those boundaries, a successful appeal was unlikely. Nonetheless, on 15 October 1993, the prosecutors filed a "**Motion to Correct Judgment,**" and it was opposed by Tom Shay's defense team on 26 October and denied by Judge Zobel on 1 November 1993. By that time, the direct appeal was well underway, and that would eventually lead to a new sentence for Tom Shay.

On 12 October the defense team filed a Notice of Appeal with the First Circuit Court of Appeals on the main case and also on the denials of its "*Motion for Judgment of Acquittal,*" "*Motion for a New a Trial,*" and of the sentence.

The previously mentioned 15 October _Boston Herald_ Op-Ed by Beverly Beckham[2] was opposed to the 15 1/2 year sentence for Tom Shay, "_SHAY SENTENCE FLIES IN THE FACE OF LAW AND JUSTICE._"

"It took federal prosecutors two years of dogged detective work to piece together the Shay case. It took two years of bucking the odds, of doing the right thing, not the easy thing.

Then they won, but they lost anyway. A jury brought in a verdict which a judge defiantly ignored.

Thomas A. Shay Jr., 21, was convicted in July of conspiring to plant a bomb under his father's car. A jury found, beyond a reasonable doubt, that Shay had conspired to murder his father; that he planned to use explosives to kill him; and that these explosives were to be attached to his father's car....

Last week U.S. District Court Judge Rya Zobel thumbed her nose at the law by ignoring the jury's findings. She determined, despite the evidence, that Shay never intended to kill his father, ('His conduct with his father is inconsistent with an attempt to kill his father.'), and sentenced him not to life without parole, but to 15 1/2 years, the federal sentence for second degree murder. Subtracting for time already served plus 53 "good time" days a year, this means that Thomas Shay Jr. will be free at age 33.

From day one the court has coddled this criminal. He had public defenders working for his defense, courtesy of taxpayers. Throughout the trial, Shay had the edge. Critical physical evidence linking Shay to the explosion was ruled inadmissible by the judge, but cloying testimony about Shay's childhood was allowed. At the sentencing hearing, it was four more hours of talk about the defendant's mental problems, with hardly a word about the psychological problems the victims and their families endure.

What's remarkable, however, is that despite all the intentional obfuscation and legal maneuvering that went on in the course of Shay's trial, the jury waded through it and found Shay guilty as charged.

They believed the evidence: Shay's own testimony that he purchased the toggle switch found inside the bomb, and that he knew the toggle switch was a mechanism for a bomb. They listened, and they deliberated, and they determined that Shay knowingly, willfully and intentionally involved himself in a conspiracy to kill his father by means of a bomb.

But in the end it was all a waste of time, money and energy. For Zobel, in seconds, negated everything: two years of tedious police work, months of pre-trial skirmishing, five weeks of trial and the jurors' careful deliberations. The verdict the jury delivered required that Shay spend the rest of his life in jail. But the verdict didn't matter to Zobel...."

The next challenge for Tom Shay was whether to testify at Alfred Trenkler's trial, which he probably wanted to do. However, in his view, the possibility that such testimony could lead to perjury charges and even more imprisonment led him to refuse to testify during a series of legal maneuvers. The final decision was made before Judge Zobel during Alfred Trenkler's trial on 3 November. He and his lawyers had calculated that the resulting prison term from criminal contempt charges, if any, would still be less than the potential increased imprisonment from possible perjury charges.

On 11 December, Ralph Ranalli wrote in the _Boston Herald_ of the upcoming criminal contempt hearing for Tom Shay for his refusal to testify, "PROSECUTORS: SENTENCE BOMBER FOR CONTEMPT." Still confident that Shay would have testified against

Trenkler with their favored version of the truth, prosecutors sought a stiff additional sentence for Tom Shay who *"had previously fingered Trenkler [his 'lover'] as the bomb builder to investigators and the media."*

On 14 December, Judge Zobel sentenced Tom Shay to an additional 45 days in prison for his refusal to testify in the trial of Alfred Trenkler. Said the <u>Globe</u> headline, *"CONVICTED BOMBER GETS EXTRA TIME."*

On 24 December 1993, the *"Living"* Section of the <u>Boston Globe</u> carried the article, *"HELMS LAYS DOWN THE LAW."* Columnist Alex Beam wrote that Helms *"has held up the nomination of lefty lawyerette Nancy Gertner to the federal bench. And yet this may be an instance where Helms, to invoke the fashionable vocabulary of moral relativism, is doing the right thing. In two separate proceedings in Boston, Gertner counseled her client, convicted cop killer Thomas Shay, to disobey US District Judge Rya Zobel's order to testify against his lover and partner in crime, one Alfred Trenkler. Already sentenced and immunized by Zobel from further prosecution, Shay refused to testify on advice of counsel, meaning Gertner. Zobel found him in contempt and added 45 days to his formidable 16-year-long reservation in federal hostelry. After one of the court hearings, Gertner said she had ceased to represent Shay after she was nominated to the federal bench in October. Her opponents charged that this was merely a convenient fiction to avoid the opprobrium of advising a client to disobey a federal judge who might soon become one of her colleagues. Gertner now says she takes responsibility for all actions in the Shay case and that she never advised him to disobey Zobel; she merely explained to him that he risked a perjury charge if he testified against his partner in crime."*

For Tom Shay's main case, his 78-page Appeal Brief to the First Circuit was filed by Kathy Weinman and Amy Baron-Evans on 18 March 1994. It succinctly summarized: *"The case against Shay Jr. essentially consisted of the statements he had made to the police, to the media, and to prison inmates after the explosion."* The appeal brief contained five arguments:

1. That Judge Zobel erroneously excluded the proffered testimony of Dr. Robert Phillips on the issue of Tom Shay's propensity to lie. They argued that Dr. Phillips' *"testimony was especially compelling in this case because Shay Jr.'s pathology of falsely admitting he did something wrong solely to call attention to himself, no matter how bad the circumstances, is the reverse of the jury's common experience."* Although Judge Zobel had prohibited the testimony because the jury did *"<u>not need</u> expert evidence on the issue of the defendant's credibility"* (TS 16-4/5) the proper standard to apply was whether such expert testimony <u>would assist</u> a jury in its work, and cited the recent 1993 U.S. Supreme Court case <u>Daubert v. Merrill Dow Pharmaceuticals</u>. Weinman and Baron-Evans concluded this section by stating that Tom Shay had a constitutional right to present a defense and call witnesses in his behalf.

2. That Judge Zobel erred in excluding the testimony of Tom Shay's former attorney, William McPhee, on the issue of his sending Tom Shay a copy of the Radio Shack 18 October receipt before Shay mentioned it to police investigators. What was excluded from the jury, after the prosecutor's objection, was Tom Shay's statement to McPhee that it was the first time he had seen the Radio Shack receipt. The brief argued that without this testimony, the jury could have concluded that Shay knew about the Radio Shack receipt because he was the purchaser. This issue was important, said the brief, because the Radio Shack receipt was the only piece of physical evidence which linked Tom Shay to the Roslindale Bomb. Intriguingly, Weinman and Baron-Evans noted in a

footnote that the purchaser could have just as likely been Mr. Thomas L. Shay as Tom Shay. It was, after all, the last four digits of Mr. Shay's phone number the digits of which were transposed on the receipt rather than those of Tom Shay's own phone or of Tom Shay's mother in Quincy where he lived.

3. That Judge Zobel erred by not instructing the jury as requested by the defense, "*inviting the jury to look critically and indeed even skeptically at Shay Jr.'s statements.*" Included in "*Requested Instruction No. 10*" were the statements: "*In deciding whether the statements are reliable, you may consider other statements made by Mr. Shay* [Tom Shay] *which are inconsistent with those the government contends indicate guilt.... you may also consider his reputation for truth-telling among people who knew him... You may also consider all of Mr. Shay's statements in order to determine whether any of them can be believed as an accurate reflection of what he knew, or, on the other hand was a product of suggestibility or a tendency to fabricate....If you determine that Mr. Shay's statements are not reliable, you should disregard them entirely.*" Instead of those instructions, Judge Zobel instructed the jury to "*consider all the statements you believe that the defendant made and the context in which he made them. Consider, also, whether they are corroborated by independent evidence in the case.*" Concluded this section, the brief stated that "*The lack of both expert testimony and instructions on this central issue* [of Tom Shay's statements] *was devastating.*"

What wasn't said was that the defense was also crippled by its inability to introduce into evidence many, many more of Tom Shay's statements. Because they were not admissions, or otherwise admissible as exceptions to the hearsay rule, none of those other fantasy fabrications could be introduced. As the defense did not see legal error by Judge Zobel, this problem was not presented to the Appeals Court, but a legal problem it was. Suppose, for example, that a defendant has made 100 statements, 10 of which are incriminating, and it's known that of the other 90, 45 are totally false and 30 are substantially false. Does it make sense that a jury could be told only of the 10 incriminating statements and none of the others? That's what the rules of evidence apparently allowed, as applied in this case. The other reason for the lack of his unreliable statements to be seen by the jury was that the defense had decided not to have Tom Shay testify. This was the other example of how the adversary trial system was unable to deal with the voluntary false confession case. If Tom Shay had testified, the prosecution would have been in the unusual position of defending the defendant's credibility and the defense would have been trying to attack it - a position they were unwilling to take so directly.

4. That Judge Zobel erred in excluding other psychiatric evidence offered by the defense. Kathy Weinman and Amy Baron-Evans argued that Judge Zobel misunderstood the defense's withdrawal of a complete "insanity defense" as meaning that it would not be presenting expert testimony on Tom Shay's diminished mental capacity to form the intent to commit the alleged crimes. Even though the prosecutors had prepared to rebut the anticipated defense expert testimony by Dr. Phillips, Judge Zobel excluded it saying that it would be unfair to the government as the trial had already begun and the prosecution didn't have time to prepare.

5. That Judge Zobel erred in her excessively long sentence for Tom Shay, who, argued the brief, was a "*minimal or minor participant,*" which under Federal law required a lowering of punishment from the standard recommended in sentencing guidelines. Weinman and Baron-Evans wrote, "*Since Shay Jr. contributed almost*

nothing to the crime and Trenkler was its mastermind and perpetrator, a downward adjustment was warranted." It was neither necessary nor fair for the defense to concede Alfred Trenkler's guilt since Tom Shay's own incriminating statements were a substantial reason for Trenkler's conviction and the defense knew the unreliability of those statements. The Shay defense team could have used the protective phrasing such as in their previous paragraph, "*The court's findings... were as follows*" or "*The jury determined...*" or "*alleged mastermind.*"

Curiously, the appeal brief said nothing about the arguably inconsistent verdicts. How could a man be found in Count 1 guilty of conspiring to commit the offense of "*receipt of explosives in interstate commerce*" and then be found not guilty of Count 2 which said that "*defendants herein, did receive in interstate commerce certain explosive materials, including dynamite and detonators....*" When Nancy Gertner responded immediately after the announcement of the guilty verdicts that the verdict was "*perplexing,*" she was right.

As the jury was not given the option of answering specific questions about the facts of the case, we are left to guess. Did the jurors find "Not Guilty" on Count 2 because they believed that Alfred Trenkler was the person who acquired the explosives and detonators? That would still be inconsistent with 1/2 of the conspiracy charge, and, worse, it would be a conclusion which was totally without any foundation of evidence. That is, there was no evidence, zero evidence, that either Tom Shay or Alfred Trenkler had purchased or otherwise acquired explosives or detonators. The jury did hear ATF Agent Dennis Leahy's testimony that Tom Shay said to him, "*I'm not the one who built it. I'm not the one who placed it. I'm not the one who got the dynamite. I'm not the violent one.*" (TS 14-89) It was interesting that such statements were permitted as they were hearsay, but the defense was apparently content that its client's denial of involvement was admitted as evidence, and the prosecution was content that the implication had been made that even if Shay didn't get the dynamite, at least one member of the two-person conspiracy did get the dynamite. Thus, the jury appears to have found Tom Shay not guilty of Count 2 on the basis of that denial, and thus assumed that Trenkler was the acquirer of the explosives, but still found Shay guilty of the conspiracy to receive explosives. Unfortunately, the jury, or even just the foreman, wasn't returned to the courtroom to be asked some questions about the verdicts.

It may have been that the jury felt it could find Tom Shay guilty of conspiracy if he participated in some, but not all, of the alleged "*overt acts.*" Judge Zobel had explained in the "Charge" that if there was agreement in the conspiracy to receive explosives, it was enough thereafter that only one member of the conspiracy committed the overt acts. The problem with the jury's apparent conclusion is that there was no physical evidence in either trial that Alfred Trenkler had ever purchased, acquired or possessed explosives or detonators related in any way to the 1991 Roslindale Bomb.

On 6 May 1994, the Assistant U.S. Attorneys filed their own, coincidentally enough, 78 page brief, not including appendices. They argued against every point made by the defense and that the conviction should be affirmed. In the "*Statement of Facts*" they wrote that the 18 October 1991 Radio Shack "*receipt did not merely reflect a combination of coincidences,*" as most of their case could be described, but that Tom Shay had admitted making the purchase. For the appellate court, Paul Kelly and Frank Libby were able to simply repeat Tom Shay's statements to Karen Marinella just as if he had been an honest law abiding citizen. Once admitted, a courtroom statement is a courtroom statement even though it was presented in a non-cross-examined videotaped interview with a journalist.

They stated that Dwayne Armbrister had testified that he had seen Alfred Trenkler in that same Radio Shack store in September and October, as if such testimony supported their proof. This issue wasn't an important part of the argument, but wouldn't it have been easier for Trenkler to have simply purchased a toggle switch himself, if he had actually been in that Radio Shack store or any other? As Trenkler had his own collection of toggle switches in his parents' garage, going to great lengths to acquire a new one, using another person to act as a "front," seems illogical. The prosecutors use of the Radio Shack purchase goes back to the Todd Leach testimony in the Trenkler trial allegedly showing a pattern of having others do the purchasing - again showing the problem with not sufficiently cross-examining his testimony, nor putting Alfred Trenkler on the stand.

They stated that Alfred Trenkler "*was experiencing a rather difficult financial situation in 1991*" and cited Richard Brown's testimony in the Shay trial. They did not remind the Appeals court of the considerable testimony in the Alfred Trenkler trial that ARCOMM was doing well in 1991 and had expectations of several more contracts. However, because this testimony was in the other trial, the prosecutors were not bound to refer to it, nor to temper their support for the contrary argument.

The prosecutors stated that the duct tape roll found in Alfred Trenkler's parents' garage was missing a 15-foot strip of tape approximately 1 7/8 inch wide, and that duct tape "*consistent in composition and construction*" with what was used in the Roslindale Bomb. However, duct tape was a very commonly available item, and there was never proof that the bomb contained duct tape from that roll. Nevertheless, in their appeal brief, the prosecutors stated it as one of the facts in their case.

They quoted the Tom Shay statement from the Karen Marinella interview that "*I got a ride home to Quincy from him and he was a student at Wentworth Tech....*" and said that statement was consistent with Richard Brown's testimony. However, they didn't note that the testimony was inconsistent with the fact that Alfred Trenkler hadn't been a student at Wentworth Institute since the 1970's. Thus, the appeals court was given a weighted slice of the "*Facts.*"

The worst distortion of the facts came with the presentation of Mrs. Nancy Shay's observations at Shay's trial. The prosecutors said, "*Nancy Shay, testified that within 30 days of the bombing, she came home to her Quincy residence one night to find a man, whom she described as 5'8" tall, approximately 140 pounds and balding, asleep on her couch, while her son slept on the floor nearby. This physical description matched that of Trenkler, and her son later told her that the man she had seen and ordered to leave the house -- was, in fact, Trenkler.*" The problem with this representation was that the prosecutors knew very well that at the Trenkler trial, Nancy Shay testified, after seeing Alfred Trenkler in the courtroom, that she had never seen him before in her life. Perhaps they persuaded themselves that they were bound only to observe the truth as presented in the trial and not the truth outside the trial, but it was an incorrect interpretation of prosecutorial ethics. It should never be permitted for any lawyer, whether a prosecutor or defense lawyer, to state a falsehood to a court.

On 22 September 1994 Tom Shay wrote a four page letter to Jefferson Boone about establishing a "*Tom Shay Defense Fund*" with approximately $8,000 from checks which Tom had sent to him. The Defense Fund was to be a "*non-profit organization established under the Massachusetts Revenue Service code 501(c)(3),"* and Tom wanted a Post Office box and checking account established. Shay continued, *"I want a* [to] *copyright the Tom Shay Support Group, and Defense Fund. I want to run ads for volunteers and support in the 'in' gay and lesbian news weekly, 158 Shawmut Ave. Boston, Mass. I want it run in 'Bay Windows' also. Now we are down to 5 thousand. I want a fundraiser hired, who will work for nothing, work out of his pocket and he gets a percentage. You know how it works. Find a friend a public accountant, C.P.A. to work with us, Pref. Gay. I want a synopsis written by you about my life leading up to the events* [i.e. the Roslindale Bomb], *my goals of a support group, which will go on to help gays in similar situations as mine. Innocent men and women in jail. I want at least a two page synopsis writ*[ten] *and I want both gay papers to print it. We are now down to $4,500. Send me $1,500... so I can buy stamps, copies, etc. Send it ASAP. We need a coordinator for the Group and a meeting place. Maybe a friend of yours is out of work. Now we are down to $2,500. Deposit it and wait and see what happens. I think once we have a group that grows and believes, the bank account will grow. We should shoot to raise $250K for investigators....*

I am sending you my new flyer also, which I think brought this $8,200 in to us.... Help me Jefferson. I know it will work. It's not a scam. I am a true gay innocent man."

In 2007 Jefferson Boone recalled that the checks were invalid and Tom's plans were dashed. This effort to arouse public support began shortly after his conviction when Tom wrote to many of his acquaintances and asked for help. One artist in Bowdoinham, Maine, Carlo Pittore, wrote to Jefferson Boone in response to Tom Shay's letter to him to ask for more information about the case and the needs for funds. Tom Shay was smart in some ways, and with some different strokes of fate and luck, he might have been a community organizer. Also, he would have begun the public campaign for justice for himself and Alfred Trenkler twelve years before the 2006 establishment of the Alfred Trenkler Innocent Committee.

On 22 June 1995, more than a year after the filing of briefs, the First Circuit Court of Appeals agreed with Tom Shay's appeal. Judge Paul Barbadoro wrote the unaminous opinion for himself, Chief Judge Juan Torruella and Judge Michael Boudin. They remanded the case to District Court Judge Rya Zobel for her to reconsider her previous exclusion of Dr. Phillips' testimony regarding *"pseudologia fantastica."*

The Court cited four statements by Tom Shay as being the most damaging to his case:

1. The statement to Detective William Bridgeforth that he wished he *"could turn back the hands of time and make it not have happened,"*
2. The statement to reporters about the remote control of the bomb, before police had told him about that aspect of the Roslindale Bomb's design,
3. The statements to Karen Marinella, and
4. The statement to Larry Plant that *"I'm the one who killed the Boston cop."*

The First Circuit Court stated simply, *"...we conclude that the district court erred in excluding Dr. Phillips' testimony... "* After observing that *"common understanding conforms to the notion that a person ordinarily does not make untruthful inculpatory statements,"* the Court said that *"Dr. Phillips would have testified that, contrary to this common sense assumption, Shay Jr. suffered from a recognized mental disorder that caused him to make false statements even though they were inconsistent with his apparent self-interest.*" Interestingly, because Dr. Phillips testimony would turn the reason for the "against penal interest" exception to the Hearsay Rule on its head, the defense could later argue that not only should Dr. Phillips be permitted to testify, but that the statements against penal interest for a person suffering from "pseudologia fantastica" should not be admitted as exceptions to the Hearsay Rule because they lacked sufficient motivation to be truthful. Looking at it another way, if one knows that most statements by a person are untrustworthy, and the Hearsay Rule aims at excluding untrustworthy statements, does it make sense to utilize an exception to the Hearsay Rule to admit any statements by that person?

Judge Barbadoro wrote that the exclusion of Dr. Phillips' testimony did not necessarily require a retrial. Instead, the case was remanded to Judge Zobel to further evaluate the testimony and such considerations as whether, as the prosecutors argued, "*Dr. Phillips does not sufficiently fit the facts of the case and because the potential prejudice resulting from his testimony substantially outweighs its probative value.*"

Significantly, the Court stated that "*if the district court determines on remand that Dr. Phillips should have been permitted to testify, the exclusion of the testimony cannot be considered 'harmless error'. Although not all erroneous exclusions of evidence are harmful, where the exclusion 'results in actual prejudice because it had a substantial and injurious effect or influence in determining the jury's verdict,' reversal is required.*" (quoting an earlier First Circuit case, US. v. Legarda.)

Regarding the William McPhee testimony, the Court said Judge Zobel did not err because the defense didn't give her enough information about the expected testimony. As for the claimed error in the instruction to the jury about the credibility of Tom Shay, the Court said that Judge Zobel covered that territory well enough.

The Court addressed a key problem for Tom Shay's defense by noting, "*Shay Jr.'s principal trial theory was that he was uninvolved in the bombing. Nevertheless, prior to trial, he filed a notice.... of his intention to offer expert testimony on the subjects of insanity and diminished capacity.*" While not saying so, that was an indication to the appellate court, as it was to Judge Zobel, that, in fact, Shay was involved in the Roslindale Bomb, but that he was too mentally ill to be criminally responsible for his actions. When Nancy Gertner announced that she was withdrawing the planned insanity defense, she didn't explicitly retain the option of continuing with a "diminish capacity" defense. On the 12th day of the trial, when she attempted to introduce such evidence through Dr. Phillips, Judge Zobel said that it was too late in the trial as the prosecutors would not have a chance to adequately prepare to cross-examine. The First Circuit upheld Judge Zobel's decision.

The Court did not address the sentencing issue, perhaps because it anticipated, though did not require, a retrial.

On 23 June 1995 Judy Rakowsky wrote the story for the *Boston Globe*, "*TRIAL REVIEW ORDERED IN FATAL BOMBING CASE.*" She quoted Jeremiah Hurley's daughter Lisa, "*It's never ending.*" The article said, "*Boston Police Sgt. Robert O'Toole, a former partner of the slain officer, said the decision means delayed closure for everyone who mourns him.... Nonetheless, O'Toole said, 'We have faith in the judicial system, and if we need to march back up there for a retrial we will go forward because we have a good case and it's the right thing to do.'*"

On 31 October 1995 Judge Zobel issued a "*Procedural Order*" which noted that the two sides in the case interpreted the First Circuit's order differently, and asked the two parties whether a further hearing was necessary. Her view was that she could, without a further hearing, make a determination about Dr. Phillips' testimony, and resolve the uncertainties of whether the "*potential prejudice of the testimony outweighs its probative value*" and whether the proposed testimony "*fits the case.*" However, she gave the parties until 20 November to give her their recommendations.

In apparent response and apprehension that Judge Zobel would rule in Shay's favor, AUSA Paul Kelly and Frank Libby filed a "*Motion for Clarification as to Scope of Remand*" with the First Circuit. They argued that "*the district court's* [procedural] *order too narrowly circumscribes the appropriate scope of the remand.*"

On 27 December 1995, the same three judges of the First Circuit responded to the prosecutor's request for clarification and wrote, "*The government argues in its motion for clarification that the district court construed its authority on remand too narrowly. We agree. We did not determine whether the proposed testimony satisfied Rule 702's other requirements. Nor did we limit the district court's power to consider the question on remand. Thus, the government's motion is granted.*" This government victory may remind the reader of the adage, "*Be careful what you wish for...*"

On 2 and 3 April 1996 Judge Zobel held a hearing on the issue of admissibility of Dr. Robert Phillips' expert testimony about Tom Shay. Reported Ralph Ranalli of the *Herald* in "*COP-KILLER SAID TO HAVE LYING DISORDER,*" on 3 April, "*Phillips said that pseudologica* [sic] *sufferers are different from most liars in that they do not lie for conscious gain, but because of a deep psychological need and that they also tell lies that get them into trouble.*" Ranalli reported that AUSA Paul Kelly pressed Dr. Phillips to admit "*that he did not check whether many of Shay's statements were actually true...*" Paul Kelly knew very well that many of Tom Shay's statements were false or a "*hoax,*" in Kelly's own words. One slight bit of good news for Alfred Trenkler was that Ralph Ranalli referred to him in this article as Shay's "*friend*" rather than "*friend and lover.*"

Paul Langner wrote the 3 April 1996 article for the *Boston Globe*, "*BOMBER'S ATTORNEY SEEKING NEW TRIAL.*" He said that Tom Shay's new attorney "*is trying to show that self-incriminating statements Shay made to a television reporter and statements made to fellow jail inmates and to police are not to be believed.*"

On 14 August 1996 Jack Wallace wrote to Judge Zobel to congratulate her on being named Director of the Federal Judicial Center in Washington, and more importantly to him, to urge her to issue a decision on the issue of the admissibility of Dr. Phillips' testimony. This was a decision "*that could affect Alfred.*"

On 14 September 1997 Paul Langner wrote a followup article for the *Boston Globe*, "*NO RULING ON NEW TRIAL FOR SHAY,*" and stated that it had been 15 months since Judge Zobel had conducted the 3 April 1996 hearing on the issue of the admissibility of the Dr. Phillips evidence. Shay's new attorney, William Kettlewell, noted the change in lawyer roles on the case, saying, "*usually the prosecution tries to depict my clients as hopeless, incorrigible liars. Now when I try to make that claim for Mr. Shay, the prosecutors insist that he told the truth.*"

Finally, 27 months after the first remand from the First Circuit and 21 months after the second, Judge Zobel issued her opinion on 24 September 1997, regarding the admissibility of Dr. Phillips' testimony. She interpreted her task as to determine whether the offered testimony was "*reliable and relevant.*" She found it to be both.

However, she left to the First Circuit the question of whether to order a new trial, even though the First Circuit opinion on 22 June 1995 said that the error could not be considered "*harmless error*" and that its correction would require reversal.

A week later, on 1 October 1997, the newspapers picked up the story. For the *Boston Globe*, Patricia Nealon and John Ellement wrote the article, "*BOMBING CASE MIGHT BE RETRIED*," and reported the comments of Tommy Nee, the president of the Boston Police Patrolmen's Association. "*This is lunacy... We'd be dismayed that there is the potential that the families will have to live through this great injustice again... They've gone through their period of closure. They've kind of put this behind them. This is nuts.... Zobel has admitted to making a mistake... It is our belief that the only mistake that was made was when the young man was not put in jail for the rest of his life. He's a threat to society.*" Shay's lawyer, Bill Kettlewell, being more proactive with the media than Shay's previous lawyers, and Trenkler's lawyers, said, "*The psychiatric testimony...* [offered an alternative explanation to jurors whose common sense told them that] *no one incriminated himself unless he's guilty.*" The *Patriot Ledger*, based in Quincy, the city of residence of both Shay and Trenkler in 1991, carried the Associated Press story with the headline, "*JUDGE ADMITS ERROR IN CAR BOMB CASE.*"

Ralph Ranalli's 1 October article in the *Boston Herald*, "*REVERSAL MAY MEAN NEW TRIAL FOR BOMBER*," added that the new U.S. Attorney, Donald Stern, said that his office was ready to retry the case. In this article Ranalli referred to Alfred Trenkler as Shay's "*accomplice.*"

The next day, 2 October, Ralph Ranalli wrote the follow-up article in the *Boston Herald*, "*NEW TRIAL COULD SPELL TROUBLE FOR CONVICTED BOMBER, COP KILLER.*" For this article about the possibility of a harsher sentence after a second trial, only prosecution-oriented sources could be found. Frank Libby, who had left the U.S. Attorney's office to go into private criminal law practice with Paul Kelly, said, "*It's my personal view that a new trial presents this defendant with clear potential for greater peril,*" he said. The article explained that a U.S. Supreme Court case, <u>North Carolina v. Pierce</u>, held that accused people should not be punished by harsher punishment after a second trial, but Ralph Ranalli quoted unnamed "*legal observers*" who said that a new judge for the second trial could interpret the U.S. sentencing guidelines differently, and Donald Stern said Shay should be sentenced to life in prison. Another exception to the <u>Pierce</u> rule was that additional punishment could be given if additional incriminating evidence was discovered and then used in a subsequent trial.

On 20 October 1997, the U.S. Attorney's office filed a Motion with Judge Zobel for reconsideration of her decision, and a hearing was held on 2 December. That morning, the *Boston Globe* published Patricia Nealon's article, "*MOTION FILED TO BLOCK BOMBING RETRIAL.*" AUSA's Kevin McGrath and David Apfel, and Special Assistant U.S. Attorney, Frank Libby, had filed the Motion which urged the judge to change her mind "*before the court proceeds any further down the path toward a retrial of this tragic case with the inevitable pain that would cause for the victims' families.*" In none of the articles about retrial was there a mention of the pain that might continue to be suffered by either Shay or Trenkler if they were entirely innocent.

The day after the hearing, on 3 December 1997, Patricia Nealon covered the story for the *Boston Globe*, as headlined, "*RETRIAL FOR SHAY HINGES ON PSYCHIATRIC EVIDENCE.*" The article stated, "*Former federal prosecutor Paul V. Kelly, who prosecuted Shay and is now in private practice, said allowing the psychiatric testimony could set a 'dangerous precedent'.... In every case in which you have a defendant who made an [incriminating] statement, you open the door for bringing in a hired-gun psychiatric expert to basically pitch this theory, which I continue to maintain is classic junk science," Kelly said. Hurley's widow, Cynthia, who attended yesterday's hearing in US District Court with [her] family and several members of the Boston Police Bomb Squad, is troubled by the prospect of a second trial. 'The last thing my family needs is 16 more weeks of a trial,' she said. 'There's just no closure for us.' Special Assistant US Attorney Frank A. Libby Jr. argued that Zobel, after holding the hearing, now has information that the appeals court did not -- namely, that Phillips was not prepared to say that Shay's disorder caused him to lie. While Shay may have been 'a kooky, wacky, nutty kid that speaks all over the map,' Assistant US Attorney David J. Apfel said, he did not exhibit an 'uncontrollable urge to spin a web of lies.' "*

On 16 January 1998, Judge Zobel announced her decision that the testimony of Dr. Phillips should have been admitted at the 1993 Shay trial. Wrote Patricia Nealon for the *Boston Globe*, "*NEW TRIAL LIKELY FOR BOMBING CONVICT - JUDGE STANDS BY EARLIER DECISION.*"

The prosecutors appealed Judge Zobel's decisions to the Court of Appeals for the First Circuit and on 1 April 1998, the same three-judge panel of the First Circuit Court decided, *per curiam*, to "*affirm the District Court and remand the case for a new trial.*" Said the *Boston Globe* headline for the 11-line article, "*NEW TRIAL ORDERED IN '91 BOMB DEATH.*"

Despite all the previously unsuccessful efforts to negotiate a plea agreement with the unreliable Tom Shay, the prosecutors tried again. This time, they were facing pressure from the victims' families and from the police not to have a retrial. Not only would a retrial drag everyone back through a case they wished to forget, there was no guarantee that a guilty verdict would again come from a jury. One difference in the prosecutors' favor, however, was that Alfred Trenkler had been convicted so Shay would now be in the same position as Alfred Trenkler was in November, 1993 - on trial for being the second member of a two-person conspiracy where the other member of the conspiracy had already been convicted. Thus, there were incentives on both sides for a plea agreement.

In August 1998 Edwin Gaeta returned to the Roslindale Bomb story as he was in the new Federally-contracted Donald Wyatt Detention Center in Rhode Island, along with Tom Shay, who was awaiting retrial. It appeared that it was Gaeta who had encouraged Tom Shay to contract to write a book two years previously, and Amy Baron-Evans was reminded that she had written to Gaeta "*that there would be no book deal and to leave Tom alone.*" In a 12 August 1998 "*memo to file*" she noted that Tom Shay and Edwin Gaeta were at Allenwood together for 2 1/2 years. Now, at Wyatt, it appeared that Gaeta was protecting Tom from other inmates. Bill Kettlewell and Amy visited with Tom Shay, who wanted to be transferred back to Middleton. Also, he requested that his attorneys file Motions for bail for him while awaiting trial, and he could live with his mother at her new home. Regarding the prosecutors' offer of a plea bargain with a twelve year sentence, Tom's reply was to tell them to "*stick it.*" He said that his defense team should seek the testimony of Louis Guzman of New York, who would "*say that he was Tom's lover, not Trenkler.*" Amy wrote that Tom's older half-sister, Jeanne, visited with him recently and passed on the word that none of his sisters was speaking with Mr. Thomas L. Shay, presumably because of his role in convicting his only son, but also perhaps because of their suspicion that he may have had a role in building the Roslindale Bomb.

Amy Baron-Evans' "*Memo to File*" stated that Tom discussed Ed Carrion's relationship and said that Ed Carrion gave him rides to his mother's at 26 Belvoir Road, but not to Trenkler's home, contrary to Carrion's testimony at Shay's and Trenkler's trials. Amy Baron-Evans wrote, "*We promised Tom that we'd get on a regular visiting schedule, and that next week, we'd bring the paperwork (now on Susan's desk) to discuss all the evidence he has been thinking about over the years that we can present this time.*" One wonders whether he or his attorneys were also reconsidering whether he should testify this time, too.

After meeting with Tom Shay, Amy Baron-Evans went to meet with Edwin Gaeta. Tom had said that Dennis Leahy had also talked with Gaeta when Gaeta was in Massachusetts. According to Tom, she wrote, "*Gaeta says he has a friend whose name is something like Ian Murdock. [Later, he was identified as Ian Medoff.] He is a body builder and was a bouncer at a straight bar in Peabody. Gaeta claims that in 1990 or 1991, this person told Gaeta that Tom Shay came to that bar ... and asked him out of the blue to build a bomb.... Tom believes Gaeta believes this guy. (I believe Gaeta is making the whole thing up.) Gaeta says he is 'going to tell the truth.' Leahy allegedly asked him to testify before the grand jury and told him that they wanted evidence of premeditation.*"

Amy Baron-Evans indicated her skepticism about the story because Tom Shay doesn't patronize straight bars. Regarding Trenkler, she wrote that Gaeta "*said he believes Tom when he says Trenkler had nothing to do with it because he [Gaeta] met Trenkler once on a van and Trenkler said to him, 'If you know anything please help me.' He said that several months before the explosion, Tom tried to contract with one of his people, a wrestler, to build a remote control device, he specifically asked for a remote control device.*" Did the wrestler subscribe to *MuscleMag International*? Might the person trying to make such a contract have been someone other than Tom Shay?

On 18 August 1998, Kathy Weinman wrote a memo to Amy Baron-Evans, Bill Kettlewell and "DG" after her telephone call with David Apfel and Kevin McGrath of the U.S. Attorney's office. The AUSA's were interested in negotiating the plea bargain, but that was set aside, pending more discussions with Tom Shay. David Apfel then said that he was aware of Amy Baron-Evans and Bill Kettlewell's visit the previous week to Wyatt Detention Center, because Edwin Gaeta had called the U.S. Attorney's office.

Weinman wrote, "*David Apfel reported that Gaeta told him that Tom Shay said there were plea negotiations going on. He said that the lawyers are encouraging him, but that Tom is resisting because he wants to be on TV. Gaeta said that he also talked to Tom Shay about Alfred Trenkler. He had been in prison with Trenkler and had spent about one hour with him. Gaeta is convinced that Trenkler had nothing to do with the bombing. Gaeta shared this with Tom Shay and Amy. Tom Shay agreed that Trenkler was not involved in the bombing. Tom had acknowledged his own involvement. In addition, Tom said that he can say anything because he has this great card in his hip pocket, pseudologia fantastica.*"

Kathy Weinman talked with Morris Goldings about Edwin Gaeta and sent copies of his news clippings to Goldings. Also, David Apfel left Morris Golding a phone message about Gaeta. The next day, on 19 August 1998, Morris Goldings traveled to see Edwin Gaeta, who was surprised to see him. Wrote Goldings in his own "*Memo to File*" Gaeta repeated the same story to Goldings about the contract to kill Mr. Thomas L. Shay for $10,000. Wrote Morris Goldings, *"Mr. Gaeta did reiterate that on several occasions Mr. Shay said that Al Trenkler was innocent. Mr. Gaeta prefers not to be involved, but would testify (if his testimony would be admissible) to save Al Trenkler as an innocent person from spending the rest of his life in jail."*

Morris Goldings apparently believed Gaeta's story as he wrote, *"I hope to hear from Mr. Gaeta again, as to his ability to disclose the name of the person whom Mr. Shay propositioned for the $10,000 explosive device would be of great importance."* Mr. Goldings apparently did not consider the question of where Tom Shay would find such an amount of money, as he did not have sufficient money to fix his teeth, or pay rent.

Then Goldings wrote, *"I told Kathy Weinman in a telephone conversation this afternoon that I had met Mr. Gaeta and that Mr. Gaeta had implicated her client. Kathy had earlier in the day refused to allow me to speak with Mr. Shay."* Once again, Tom Shay's attorneys were blocking Tom from talking with Trenkler's attorneys. Fortunately, Tom Shay's concern about what he had done to Al Trenkler appeared to have outweighed his interest in following his lawyers' orders; and he met with Morris Goldings, anyway.

If such conversations had been permitted in 1991, this double tragedy of wrongful convictions may have been avoided. Of all the instances in the Roslindale bomb case where legal rules have blocked the search for truth, the inability of the defense teams for Tom Shay and Alfred Trenkler to work together is one of the worst. As Tom Shay's statements were a substantial reason for the indictments and trials in the first place, why shouldn't Terry Segal have been able to interview him? When did Shay really meet Alfred Trenkler? Did Alfred Trenkler ever ask Tom Shay to purchase anything? If yes, then When? Where? Why shouldn't Nancy Gertner have been permitted, if not encouraged to interview Alfred Trenkler? What did Tom Shay really tell Alfred Trenkler, if anything, about his father or about his father's civil lawsuit or about anything in his life? Wouldn't each attorney and each client have been assisted by learning as much as possible about the truth? It should be that it always helps a defense lawyer to know the truth. One tactic that lawyers use to help them know the truth is to suggest to their own clients that they take a lie detector test. While they may present the proposition to their client as an effort to bolster the version of the client's story, another motivation for the lawyer is to verify that it's actually true. In some cases, when faced with such requests by their own lawyers, clients have come forward with the truth, and their lawyers were better prepared to defend them.

Morris Goldings closed with, *"I have called David Apfel for more information and also to see if the government will join me in attempting to determine the accuracy of Mr. Gaeta's report of Mr. Shay's statements."* Later, Amy Baron-Evans obtained a U.S. District Court Subpoena to the Wyatt Detention Center for any available records of telephone calls and visits to Edwin Gaeta, in order to determine the identity of the alleged bar bouncer who allegedly was asked to build the Roslindale Bomb.

In September 1998, Alfred's half-brother, David Wallace, began purchasing toggle switches which were similar to the Radio Shack #275-602. After looking at toggle switches at an electrical supply company in Quincy, he went to the U-Do-It Electronics store in Needham, and purchased a Philmore Model #30-219 toggle switch and the threads of the screws seemed to be similar to those of the Radio Shack #275-602. A few years later, a friend of the Wallace family took apart the Philmore switch and believed that he had found the contacts to be even more similar to those found in the bomb debris, than those from the Radio Shack #275-602. However, in 2007 the author disassembled several Radio Shack #275-602's and one Philmore #30-219, and the #275-602 contacts resembled those in the Roslindale Bomb and the contacts in the #30-219 did not. The discrepancy may have been due to the different disassembly dates together with possible design changes in the switches.

David also showed to a professor at Wentworth Institute a copy of the 18 October 1991 Radio Shack receipt and the professor stated that the six purchased items were typical for a student project at Wentworth. That is, all six parts were used in typical student projects, which is significant because the prosecutors in the Roslindale Bomb cases claimed that Tom Shay made the six piece purchase, but only one item of the same model type of the #275-602 toggle switch was used in the Roslindale Bomb.

Before Tom Shay's upcoming guilty plea hearing, David Wallace met with Kathy Weinman and told her of his discovery of a similar switch.

On the afternoon of 29 October 1998, Judge Edward Harrington conducted the guilty plea agreement hearing for Tom Shay. The morning's newspapers predicted the result. "*GUILTY PLEA EXPECTED AFTER COURT OVERTURNS BOMBING CONVICTION*" said the *Globe*'s article by Patricia Nealon, which reported that the retrial for Tom Shay had been previously scheduled for 19 January 1999. "*ONCE-TRIED BOMB SUSPECT SEEN MAKING DEAL,*" said the *Boston Herald*, with Ralph Ranalli again describing Alfred Trenkler as Tom Shay's "*lover.*"

At the hearing, AUSA David Apfel led the prosecution's effort, together with Kevin McGrath and Frank Libby. William Kettlewell led the defense's side, assisted by Amy Baron-Evans and Kathy Weinman. Thus, all the leading players were different from the trial proceeding.

Judge Harrington asked Tom Shay if he wanted to file the plea, and Shay responded affirmatively. Then the judge asked why the government was asking for a reduced sentence from 188 months to 144 months. The unspoken reason, as with all plea agreements is that it was a negotiated deal to save the government the time and money, and risk of losing, in a retrial. AUSA David Apfel's response was that whereas Tom Shay didn't accept responsibility for the crimes in 1993, he now was doing so. The 12-year sentence was predicted to result in 10 years in prison, assuming time deductions for good behavior.

Then Judge Harrington returned to address Tom Shay and asked a number of questions to determine the validity of the plea, including the last question, "*Is the plea that you're entering here today entirely free and voluntary.*" (P. 10) Before answering, Tom Shay consulted his attorney and then was asked again, and he replied, "*Yes, your Honor.*" Those at the hearing must have wondered. Did he say to Bill Kettlewell then or earlier, "*But I didn't do this?*" If he had, his attorney would have been obligated to notify the judge, or rationalize that Shay's decision was his decision alone to make.

In the criminal justice system the plea-bargain system is often conducted with a wink and a nod, as innocent people plead guilty in order to avoid the risk of being convicted for the instant crime or other crimes. In those cases, their lawyers rationalize what is happening as being just in some way. The judges profess not to know what is really happening. Was this plea agreement for Tom Shay one of those sham agreements for an innocent man? One of his considerations was surely a look at what happened to his acquaintance, Alfred Trenkler, who was in prison for life. There is little doubt the prosecutors advised Shay's attorneys that they would seek a life sentence in a retrial. Tom Shay had been advised by Jefferson Boone that the sentence for a retrial could be no greater than what was imposed at the first trial, but Shay was not sure whom to believe.

On the other hand, Tom Shay had been in prison since 1992, and the ten years would be completed in fewer than four more years. To Shay, it was a deal worth signing, despite its unfairness to someone whose crimes were really the lesser crimes of lying to a law enforcement officer and possibly perjury. Of course, there have been very few convictions of people who were lying as they incriminated themselves in a crime. For example, there have been no perjury charges against John Mark Karr who voluntarily and wrongly confessed to killing Jon-Benet Ramsey.

Then Judge Harrington asked AUSA Apfel to summarize the evidence that the U.S. Attorney's office would have introduced if the case had gone to trial. He responded:

"First, that in the fall of 1991 in the District of Massachusetts defendant Thomas Shay conspired and agreed with an individual named Alfred W. Trenkler to commit certain offenses against the United States, including receipt of explosives in interstate commerce with the intent and knowledge that the explosives would be used to damage and destroy a Buick automobile owned and operated by Shay's father Thomas L. Shay, Sr.

Second, that the defendant Thomas Shay and Alfred Trenkler agreed that they would use a remote controlled explosive device in furtherance of their conspiracy.

Third, on October 18 of 1991 defendant Thomas Shay purchased certain electrical components including a toggle switch needed for the construction and testing of the explosive device. And defendant Shay purchased these components at a Radio Shack located at 197 Massachusetts Avenue here in Boston.

Fourth, in October of 1991 Alfred Trenkler built a remote control explosive device consisting of dynamite, blasting caps and other materials including the toggle switch that defendant Thomas Shay had purchased from Radio Shack on October 18 of 1991.

Fifth, on or about October 27 of 1991 in the District of Massachusetts, the explosive device was affixed to the undercarriage of the 1986 Buick automobile owned and operated by Shay, Sr., Thomas Shay's father. The Buick automobile was used by Shay, Sr. in interstate commerce and in activities affecting interstate commerce.

Finally, the sixth point that Mr. Shay is prepared to agree to is that on October 28, 1991, the explosive device exploded killing Boston Police Bomb Squad Officer Jeremiah Hurley and seriously injuring his partner Boston Police Bomb Squad Officer Francis Foley.

The evidence in the case would conclusively show all of those facts." (P. 11-12) Upon further questioning and several *"Yes, Your Honor*[s]," Tom Shay agreed to Mr. Apfel's presentation of the facts. Then Judge Harrington asked Shay's lawyer, William Kettlewell, *"Counsel, do you know any reason why the court should not accept any plea of guilty?"* and he answered, *"No, Your Honor."* (P. 13)

It is the view of this book that most of the presented facts were false. The number of people in that courtroom on that day who believed those facts to be false is unknown. Mrs. Nancy Shay was there and she believed them to be false. Jack Wallace, stepfather of Alfred Trenkler, believed them to be false. In 2007 Tom Shay stated in a *"Motion to Vacate the 1998 Guilty Plea"* that he told his attorneys that he was innocent and that they coerced him into pleading guilty. One specific conversation with his declaration of innocence was in a 1998 conference call with his attorneys, with him at the Plymouth County House of Correction and his lawyers and his mother and sister in Boston. Coincidentally, Jefferson Boone visited Tom Shay immediately afterwards.

Then the court heard from the victims' families. Speaking on behalf of the families were Doris Hurley Halliday, sister of Jeremiah Hurley, and his daughter, Lisa, and widow, Cynthia, who said, "*Seven years ago today, I was planning my husband's funeral. It's been an agonizing seven years.*" Regarding the plea agreement, she said, "*I want everybody in this room to realize that we did make the -- my family and I agree to accept this plea for a lesser sentence. We could not sit through another trial.*"

Also, she said to Tom Shay, "*...I hope in your remaining years of your sentence you can get the help and the repentance (ph.) that you need.*" (p. 20) That wish for help made an impression on Tom Shay, because Cynthia Hurley was one of the people who still believed that Tom Shay was really guilty. Nine years later on 5 August 2007, Tom Shay recalled what she said almost word for word in a letter, "*I hope that you will get some help, wherever you go.*"

Then Judge Harrington, a former U.S. Attorney, imposed the sentence on the standing Tom Shay, and said, "*Although you are only going to have to serve twelve years for this vicious and heinous offense, you are going to have to live your whole life with the realization that you have killed a man, a father, and a police officer. Innocent.* [sic] *Was only doing his duty. Just to live with that has to be punishment enough.*" (P. 22-3) In addition, after prison Shay had to serve five years of supervised release.

In fact, what Tom Shay had to live with was that he was substantially responsible, by his statements and actions, for his own wrongful conviction and for the wrongful conviction of Alfred Trenkler. Someone else, or some other people, were responsible for the death of Jeremiah Hurley and the maiming of Francis Foley. Tom Shay explained later why he pled guilty, "*Jeff Boone will recall the conversation we had when I was at Plymouth '98, in which I told him Kettlewell & Weinman said 'that I would get life if I didn't take the deal', that they were looking on me as if I were their child and even though they knew I was innocent, innocent people can get convicted twice and the deal was best. Boone told me that the judge was bound by what Judge Zobel had sentenced me and he didn't understand why Kettlewell & Weinman felt that way. Kettlewell & Weinman pressured me and made me feel a new trial was hopeless and if I took the new trial they would not give me a good defense.*" Shay repeated that story in a 5 August 2007 letter. Jeff Boone does recall the conversation and continues to maintain that Shay should not have pleaded guilty in 1998.

The one final matter AUSA Apfel presented to the judge was the "*concern on the part of the government, on the part of the victim* [sic] *families that Mr. Shay not profit in any way from his conduct in this case.*" Judge Harrington asked the parties to prepare an agreement to avoid that result. After Tom Shay agreed that he would not appeal, the hearing was adjourned.

The headlines captured the story. It was "*MAN GETS 12-YEAR TERM IN BOMB DEATH OF OFFICER,*" in Patricia Nealon's article in the Boston Globe, and "*BOMBER GIVEN REDUCED SENTENCE AFTER ADMITTING ROLE IN '91 KILLING.*" in the Boston Herald's article by Ralph Ranalli. Cynthia Hurley said to Patricia Nealon, "*We're looking for some kind of closure, which we're never going to get, but this is a start.*" Ranalli described Tom Shay as "*finally admitting his role,*" but there was no assurance that this statement by Shay was any more reliable than the others. Ranalli said that the bomb fell off the Buick owned by Tom Shay's "*estranged father,*" but they weren't estranged on 28 October 1991. The _Patriot Ledger_ ran an Associated Press article, _"QUINCY MAN PLEADS GUILTY AT RETRIAL IN '91 BOMB PLOT."_ No one was quoted in any article as suggesting that Shay may have been lying again and that the struggle, and lack of closure, would continue because one or both of the convicted men were possibly, probably, or certainly innocent. That change of perception would have to wait.

Judge Harrington's concerns about Tom Shay's interest in a book deal, whether profitable or not, were not far from the mark. On 8 July 2001, Tom Shay wrote to Boston Police Dept. Chief Hussey the following letter:

"I am writing to you sir because I was told you are a man of honesty & integrity. Please Bare with my spelling and Diahdine [sic] _I am partly responsible for the death of Officer Hurley and maiming of Officer Foley. I am directing this letter to you Because you personally know Mrs. Hurley and Officer Foley. Recently I have been offered a large sum of money to do a book deal. I would like to offer those rights to Block St._[sic] _and me or anyone from using my name to make money. There's more But I don't want Mrs. Hurley to suffer any longer. Sir, I need your Suggestion on what I should do. Al Trenkler is innocent. My father, Thomas L. Shay and his attorney Alan Pransky are my real codefendants. We were the ones involved. The bomb was only meant to do property damage not to injure to persons. It's a big puzzle, But one I can put together which would make sense. I am willing to help you Build a case or Keep Quiet. I will do either for Mrs. Hurley. The Decision is yours. In October of next year I will be released after 10 1/2 years of prison. I would like to request two things. No revenge from Boston Police to me physically. To Be able to apologize privately to officer Foley and to Mrs. Hurley. To go on and live a quiet life. I make this offer to you, what you do with it is up to you. Please respond when you can. Please do confer with Mrs. Hurley as she doesn't want anyone to make money off her husband's death."_ [A copy of Tom Shay's letter is included in Appendix E.]

For supporters of Alfred Trenkler, such a letter probably looked promising, as it said that Alfred was innocent. On the other hand, this is a symptom of the STT (Selective Truth Temptation] as Tom Shay also said he was partially involved. Was he still seeking publicity and controversy? Was there an offer of a book contract from anyone? How to extract truth from Tom Shay? Mistrust, **and** verify.

On 10 September 2001 AUSA Kevin McGrath forwarded a copy of the letter to Trenkler's attorney, Charles Rankin, and a copy to Shay's most recent attorney, William Kettlewell. McGrath wrote that the letter "contradicts Mr. Shay's signed plea agreement, as well as his guilty plea, in which he admitted to conspiring with Alfred Trenkle to build the bomb..." Significantly, McGrath stated that "the government has requested [to Kettlewell] the opportunity to speak with Mr. Shay should he wish to be debriefed regarding the claims raised in this letter. Should the government subsequently learn of any exculpatory evidence as a result of any such meeting, it will be promptly disclosed to you." [A copy of McGrath's letter is included in Appendix E.]

On 29 January 2002, Tom Shay sent from the Ray Brook Federal Correctional Institution in upper New York State an extraordinary New Year's greeting with a handwritten salutation to _"Mrs. and Mrs. Trenkler."_ It was a printed letter written _"To family and friends"_ like the Christmas card letters people send to update friends and relatives of family events during the previous year, and Tom sent it to many others.

Tom Shay, now 29 years old, proudly announced attaining his GED with a score of 258 out of a possible 300. He listed his education hours spent on other subjects, including, "*Heart Savers/CPR (12 hours), Victim Impact (80 hours), Anger Management (100 hours), Ceramics (60 hours) and Culinary Arts (250 hours).*" He stated, "*Upon my release I will seek to further my education by applying for a school loan and attending college. I hope to enroll in various Business Management, Accounting, Real Estate and Photo Journalism* [courses]."

Then came the subtitled section "*Legal Matters*" where he wrote, "*In 1999* [sic, it was 1998] *I plead guilty to a crime I did not commit. But like my former attorney, Nancy Gertner who is now a federal judge said, sometimes the outcome of a trial is not always just or right, however much we want them to be. I realize some of my family and friends were upset that I plead guilty. What you have to realize is that this is my life and as an innocent man already convicted and sentenced once in the past, I was not willing to roll the dice and play with my life while my attorneys are advising that I plead guilty or take the chance of spending my whole life in prison. I accepted defeat and stood meek.*

Recently, I had a visit from my attorney, Amy Baron-Evans... I spoke with her about my co-defendant, Alfred Trenkler, who is innocent and is serving a life sentence. We had a good conversation about all the possible scenarios of how to help Al win his appeal." However, it did not appear that she advised Tom Shay to tell the truth to Alfred's appellate defense teams or to the U.S. Attorney's office.

Tom's New Year's greeting continued, "*Also recently, I have asked for a change of venue for my Supervised Release, and as it has been a bridge over troubled waters thus far, I am hoping to not have to return to the Boston area. I want to start a new life in a new city....*" He reviewed the status of his mother and sisters with hopeful comments about each, and continued, "*My Release and the Future: My release date is August 30, 2002. I plan to join a good church, become a swimming member of the local YMCA, volunteer at a local homeless shelter and do what sons are supposed to do and that is to take care of my mother.... I end this newsletter with a wish that this New Year be a special one to all of you. This coming birthday and the holidays that follow will be my first in the free-world in almost 12 years. I hope that I can celebrate them all with you. Lots of Love, Thomas A. Shay.*"

It was an extraordinary document for Tom Shay to prepare and send, whether he was involved with the Roslindale Bomb or not. He said he wasn't.

The August 2002 issue of *Boston Magazine* reported on the Roslindale Bomb case and the upcoming release of Tom Shay. Written by Walter Alarkon and headlined, "*BOMBER'S AWAY - CULPRIT IN COP CASE COMES HOME,*" the short article quoted Cynthia Hurley, who was then the President of "Massachusetts Concerns of Police Survivors," and who said, "*Definitely he didn't get what he deserved, but September 1 is coming whether you like it or not.*" Francis Foley commented, "*I wish he had gotten more time, ... but I'm not going to sit around and worry because of him.*" Concluded the article, "*Alfred Trenkler, 46, who actually built the bomb, is serving life in prison.*"

On 30 August 2002, Thomas A. Shay was released from Federal Prison, and began the last part of his sentence, which was five years of "supervised release." Sentenced for a total of 12 years, plus the 45 days for contempt, he completed his sentence after serving a total of 10 years, 5 months and 24 days since his 24 March 1992 arrest in San Francisco. He had spent approximately eight years at Allenwood, but neither saw Alfred Trenkler, nor communicated with him in any way during that period.

On 10 May 2003, Tom Shay was in the newspapers again, but this time he didn't seek out additional publicity. He was living with his sister, Paula, on Washington Street in Quincy and a dispute arose and Tom Shay allegedly fled to the bathroom as she was chasing him with knives. Fortunately, Tom Shay brought his cell phone with him, and he called his parole officer from the bathroom. Dave Wedge wrote the story for the _Boston Herald_, "*EX-CON'S SISTER ALLEGEDLY THREATENS HIM WITH CLEAVER.*" The Quincy police came to the home and arrested Paula Shay. The article summarized the Roslindale Bomb case and described Alfred Trenkler as being Tom Shay's "*lover and cohort.*"

John Ellement's story in the _Boston Globe_'s "*MAN IN 1991 BLAST TAKES SISTER TO COURT,*" said that Paula Shay was being detained at the Framingham State Prison for Women and that Tom Shay had obtained a restraining order against her.

In April, 2005 he was ordered to live in a half-way house, Coolidge House, in Cambridge, due to unspecified parole violations. However, he was reportedly dissatisfied there and left in May.

On 27 June 2005, the _Boston Globe_ carried the Associated Press story, "*POLICE BOMBER ARRESTED ON PAROLE VIOLATION.*" Tom Shay had left Coolidge House and had moved to Durham, New Hampshire, where he had signed a one-year lease for an apartment. However, with the distinctive Massachusetts license plate, "WASSUP," the Durham police found him easily once they were given a tip to search for him because of an outstanding arrest warrant for violating his probation or "supervised release."

On 22 July 2005, Lisa Fleisher of the _Boston Globe_ reported that Tom Shay had been ordered to return to Coolidge House and ordered to spend an additional year on supervised release because he had lied to his probation officer about his whereabouts. In the article, "CONVICT RETURNED TO FACILITY - INVOLVED IN PLOT THAT LED TO DEATH OF POLICE OFFICER," Fleisher wrote that Tom Shay read a statement to Judge Rya Zobel and called his probation officers his "*guardians*" and "*protectors.*" He continued, "*Everyone of these officers have been hand-picked, the best apples from the orchard, to protect society and me from myself.... It scares me a little to think that I will be out in the world one day, alone and unprotected.*" The article reported that he said he longed "*to feel real love... and live an ordinary life.*" In addition to the additional year of supervision, through 1 September 2008, he was given a six-month suspended sentence for violating his parole and was ordered to stay at Coolidge House for four months. If he didn't he would have to serve the six-month sentence in prison. "*He needs structure,* ' said Zobel, who was the judge in Shay's original case. '*I do think he needs a great deal of encouragement.*' " Finally, Fleisher reported that David Wallace, half-brother of Alfred Trenkler, and "*who maintains Trenkler's innocence, traveled from his home in Maine yesterday to attend the hearing, hoping to hear something that might exonerate his brother.*"

Laurel Sweet wrote the _Boston Herald_'s story of the hearing, "*BOMBER WHO KILLED HUB COP FREE AGAIN.*" She captured one Shay quote more completely, "'*I'm a piece of wood adrift,*' Thomas Shay, 33, told Zobel in a candy-coated plea for mercy. '*I want to give and feel real love. I want to live an ordinary life.*' " The article continued, "*Assistant U.S. Attorney Lisa Asiaf reminded Zobel: 'This is an extremely serious case that resulted in the death of a police officer.' But Zobel snapped, 'We don't have to go back to that.'*" Sweet also interviewed David Wallace and his wife, Judy Lloyd, and wrote, "*They don't believe Trenkler or Shay is guilty of the bombing.*" This was the first time that any Boston newspaper article had carried the suggestion that Tom Shay was completely innocent of any involvement with the Roslindale Bomb.

On 28 July 2005, the weekly _Roslindale Transcript_ reported the story in an article by David Harris, "_BOMBER GETS SUSPENDED SENTENCE._" He interviewed Frank Foley who was also at the hearing, "_He's a sick individual.... I think his parole should have been revoked. The judge should have a little more compassion for the Hurley family. It's almost like they're trying to make him a victim._" Tom Shay probably was a victim, many times, of the State and Federal governments. The compassion that should have been shown for the Hurley family may well have been to avoid the evidence-thin prosecution of Tom Shay and Alfred Trenkler in the first place. Instead of building a case on an improbable foundation, investigators and prosecutors could have followed the real clues.

On 18 October 2005, Tom Shay was arrested by Northeastern University police when he was soliciting massage business. The police had set up a sting after a few students had complained. A struggle erupted during the arrest and Shay was tackled by a policeman. Later, Tom Shay said, "_If I hadn't run, I would haven't been arrested._" The story of this arrest attempt was not publicized at the time, but it was included in a 7 June 2007 article by Michele McPhee in the _Boston Herald_, "_Transexual cop killer hunted in Bay State._"

The Northeastern University incident led to a conviction for Assault on a police officer in Boston Municipal Court and a two and one-half year sentence. Representing him as a court appointed lawyer was Lawrence Fallon, Jr. who, coincidentally, had previously provided legal services for Alfred Trenkler's company. The sentence was suspended, partly because Shay had already been sentenced in Federal Court on 19 October to an additional six months in Federal custody for violation of the terms of his probation. He served that time in the Plymouth County House of Correction.

On 2 April 2006, the _Boston Herald_ columnist and radio talk show host, Howie Carr, wrote about a letter he had received from Tom Shay, who was still in the Plymouth County House of Correction. Headlined, "_YOU DON'T SHAY.... CON COWBOYS UP FOR WHITEY,_" Howie Carr quoted parts of Tom Shay's letter to him, "_You once wrote an article about me, my sexual preference and a gay bar... Who gives you the right to bash an American idol... Sal Mineo may have had sex with anybody, Whitey Bulger, Rock Hudson, James Dean or even you, but who's {sic} business is it. Who cares if Whitey Bulger had contact with gay men? ... Your intention may be at the request of the embattled FBI to flush out Whitey...Like James Dean, Rock Hudson, Anthony Perkins, Robert Reed, Ellen DeGeneres, Sal Mineo is an American idol, a personality that showed us grace and entertained our lives._"

On 17 April 2006 Tom Shay was released from his six month Federal sentence. On the previous 10 January he had written to Judge Zobel to seek her assistance in obtaining his release by 23 March, thanks to time credits for good behavior. He wrote, "_Thank you for your time, strength and patience into this matter. Hope your New Year was pleasant. Sincerely, Thomas A. Shay. P.S. Please give my regards to Judge Gertner._" However, his effort was only minimally successful, as he was released only two days before the six month date of 19 April.

He went to Spencer, Massachusetts with the support of a network of church-based friends. There, he attended Bible classes and provided youth counseling. He had rented his own room, and worked in a supermarket, but not for long. In July 2006, as reported in Michele McPhee's 7 June 2007 article, there was an incident in Spencer where police responded to a report that Tom Shay had stolen money from two boys in a home shared with Shay. When the police arrived, Tom Shay was gone.

Also in July 2006, Jack Wallace successfully contacted Tom Shay and facilitated an interview of Shay by Dennis Tatz of The *Patriot Ledger*. The result was a substantial contribution to Tatz's front page "LEDGER UPDATE" article in the 7 August edition of that newspaper. [See the next chapter.] During that same visit to Massachusetts, Tom Shay visited his mother, Nancy, but that was to be the last visit for a while. He then left the state for Illinois in fear of being arrested for outstanding state and/or Federal warrants. From his experience of being caught in San Francisco in 1992, Tom was well aware of how communications to home can lead to arrest; so he communicated rarely with his family. In Illinois, he made a living buying and selling objects on the street and on "Craig's list," on the Internet.

In the Spring of 2007, the U.S. Marshals staked out the duplex with the homes of Shay's mother and a sister in the hopes of arresting Tom. The news of their efforts made front page news in the 7 June 2007 *Boston Herald* article noted earlier. The article was also in the *Roslindale Transcript,* a weekly newspaper owned by the *Boston Herald*. Said Boston Patrolmen's Association President, Tom Nee, "*The system has failed when dirtbags like this can still walk the street after killing a Boston police officer.... It's shameful.*" Tom Shay had six warrants outstanding for his arrest. The first was a Federal warrant for violation of the conditions of his "supervised release" as extended in 2005 by Judge Zobel.   The other five warrants were from the Commonwealth of Massachusetts:

18 October 2005. Assault and Battery on a police officer - the Northeastern University incident in Boston. Even though he had already served his Federal time for that offense, it was still listed with the U.S. Marshals as an outstanding warrant.

13 May 2006. Larceny in East Brookfield, Mass.

29 June 2006. Contributing to the delinquency of a minor in Spencer, Mass.

5 July 2006. Possession and distribution of a Class C substance.

20 July 2006. Failure to appear at East Brookfield District Court regarding the above three warrants.

In Illinois, the word reached Tom that the television program, "America's Most Wanted" was preparing publicly to open a search for him. His 1992 fantasy was perhaps about to come true. Tom Shay was using a different name, but he calculated that even in a large city, someone would recognize his six foot five inch frame; so he decided to return home and give himself up.

On Monday, 16 July 2007, Tom Shay was arrested at his mother's and sister's duplex in Quincy by the U.S. Marshals and local police on the outstanding warrants. The police were at the home about a domestic disturbance complaint arising from arguments between Paula Shay and her half-sister Amy, who lived upstairs. Concerned that the police would take away her newborn child, Paula Shay told the police that her brother, Tom Shay, was in the house; and he was apprehended. He had been there a few days and had called his former attorney, Jefferson Boone, to inquire about turning himself in. Boone had advised Shay that if he were to come to Boone's office, Boone would quietly turn him over to the U.S. Marshals without prejudicial media coverage. Tom never made it to Boone's Brighton office.

The *Boston Herald* carried the story on front page. Together with his photograph was an image of a letter he had written to the *Herald* which was contemptuous of the police for not catching him, but also it implied that he would soon be giving himself up. Partially obscured, the letter contained these statements, "*I know who committed the offense, and I guarantee you it wasn't Alfred Trenkler. He is an innocent man.*"

A probation revocation hearing was held by Judge Rya Zobel on Tuesday, 24 July, with many uniformed officers present.[3] The three charges against him were for breaking the terms of his probation or supervised release, because of alleged state criminal offenses, failing to meet with a mental health counselor and failing to meet with a probation officer.

She found that his actions in Spencer with two minors who believed they were purchasing cocaine were, by a preponderance of the evidence, sufficient cause to revoke his probation. This finding came despite the conclusion of the State Police laboratory report that the white powder found on a CD case was not a controlled substance. Shay's failure to meet with his mental health provider and failure to meet with his probation officer were conceded.

Judge Zobel stated that Tom Shay was no longer an appropriate candidate for probation and she sentenced him to 33 months in prison, after which there would be no probation. He was returned to the Plymouth County House of Correction, under contract with the Federal Government, where he began serving his sentence. About two weeks later, he was transferred to the Donald Wyatt Detention Center in Rhode Island where he awaited transportation to a longer term prison in New York or Pennsylvania. During one visit to her son, Nancy Shay summarized his plight with a verbatim quotation from Sir Walter Scott, "*Oh what a tangled web we weave, when first we practise to deceive!*"[4] She learned it from the Dominican nuns at the now-demolished Rosary Academy in Watertown in the 1950's.

On 19 August 2007 Tom Shay wrote a letter to the Office of the U.S. Attorney in Boston to claim his innocence and that he had been coerced by his attorneys in 1998 to plead guilty. He said that attorneys William Kettlewell and Kathy Weinman told him that he could be faced with life in prison if he chose to face a new trial. Also, he wrote that his attorneys assured him that "*by pleading guilty, it no way implicated Alfred Trenkler in any way.*" Afterwards he had learned that his plea did include a specific statement of Trenkler's guilt. His letter concluded, "*It may be too late to say I am innocent, because laws and statutes don't allow me to appeal. But I cannot stand by while Alfred Trenkler hangs in the wind. He IS INNOCENT.*"

In mid-September 2007, Tom Shay filed a Motion in U.S. District Court to overturn his 1998 guilty plea and conviction on the grounds that it was coerced. Shay stated that he was advised by his attorneys, William Kettlewell and Kathy Weinman, that he faced life in prison if reconvicted by a jury at a new trial, but they knew that the Supreme Court decision of <u>North Carolina v. Pierce</u> precluded such an outcome.

END NOTES

---

1. British Prime Minister Winston Churchill during a radio address on 16 June 1941. By that time, Britain had been at war with Germany for almost two years.

2. In the Summer of 2006, I called Beverly Beckham and asked her if she would be interested in an update on the Alfred Trenkler story; and to see if she would consider information that Alfred Trenkler was innocent. By our agreement, I sent her some materials by email, along with the address of Alfred's

website. I did not hear from her again, but sent her an e-copy of an earlier version of this Manuscript Edition of _Perfectly Innocent_ in July 2007.

3 While the Boston police officers and ATF agents were permitted to wear their "statements," the author was not permitted to bring his briefcase into the courtroom because it had pasted on both sides two sets of bumperstickers with only the names of websites on them, www.singleglobalcurrency.org and www.alfredtrenklerinnocent.org." The briefcase went unnoticed at Alfred Trenkler's 4 April 2007 hearing.

3. The quote comes from _Marmion_, Canto vi Stanza 17. 4

> *"I don't know if you recall my case,*
> *but you sentenced me to two (2) concurrent life*
> *terms in March of 1994."*
> Alfred W. Trenkler in 1 December 2005 letter to Judge Rya Zobel.

After the 30 August 2002 release of the man whose statements were substantially responsible for his wrongful conviction, Alfred Trenkler was even more aware of the injustice inflicted upon him.

On 3 October 2002, and desperate for anything to unlock the prison doors, his attorneys filed a "*Petition for Habeas Corpus*", pursuant to 28 USC 2241 on the grounds that the definition of "interstate commerce" as used in his trial, had been slightly changed by a U.S. Supreme Court decision; and that therefore the statutory prohibition for the crime for which he was convicted no longer applied to him. This was his <u>Request for Justice XVIII</u>. The case name was <u>Alfred W. Trenkler v. Michael Pugh</u>, Warden, USP-Allenwood and it was prompted by the U.S. Supreme Court case of <u>United States v. Jones</u>, 529 U.S. 848 (2000), "*which significantly heightened the requirements for proving the interstate commerce element, thereby removing the conduct for which Trenkler was convicted from the ambit of 844(i and 844(d) which were the sections proscribing criminal interstate purchases of dynamite.*" In that case, allegedly involving arson at a residence and not used as a commercial building, the Supreme Court held that because the home was not used commercially in interstate commerce, federal jurisdiction would not apply. The case was one of the few times since the 1930's where the Supreme Court has drawn a line between what falls inside and outside interstate commerce for criminal jurisdiction purposes. The filing attorneys were Catherine Hinton and James Sultan of Rankin and Sultan and the necessary local Pennsylvania Attorney, Ronald C. Travis, because the Motion was filed in the U.S District Court for the Middle District of Pennsylvania. For Alfred Trenkler, the issue was whether Mr. Thomas L. Shay's 1986 Buick was properly designated as being part of interstate commerce, after <u>Jones</u>.

On 13 January 2003 on behalf of the U.S. Attorney for Masschusetts, AUSA Kevin McGrath filed a 54-page "*Memorandum of Law in Opposition to Alfred Trenkler's Petition for Writ of Habeas Corpus.*" His primary argument was that "*... Trenkler's claim that Jones requires that his conviction under 844(d) be overturned is baseless. Trenkler fails to cite a single case subsequent to Jones in which a defendant has even attempted to argue that Jones has any bearing on the scope of 844(d) and no court has so held.*"

On 6 February 2003 Alfred Trenkler turned 47 years old.

On 10 February 2003, Catherine Hinton and James Sultan filed a Reply Brief and on 7 March 2003, U.S. District Court Judge Richard Conaboy ordered that Alfred Trenkler's Petition be dismissed. Judge Conaboy stated that "*Trenkler's reliance on Jones is misplaced... [and] he is unable to show that a change in the substantive law since his conviction has negated the criminal nature of the conduct for which he was sentenced.*" <u>RFJ XVIII</u> had failed.

In his denial of Alfred Trenkler's Petition for Relief in Pennsylvania, <u>RFJ XVIII</u>, Judge Conaboy wrote compassionately about Alfred Trenkler's situation. He wrote that he was aware of "*the stark difference between the life sentence imposed on the Petitioner and the 12 year sentence imposed on his co-conspirator following a plea agreement in the latter instance. Such perceived disparity may be what impels the Petitioner to repeated litigation. Other than the obvious human emotional response, this should not and did not play any role in the Court's* [Judge Conaboy's court's] *disposition of this case.*"

Also, when he was distinguishing the facts of one previous case, Judge Conaboy explained the relevance of the Third Circuit Court's Dorsainvil case, "*Fundamental to this approach* [in Dorsainvil] *was the fact that a petitioner could claim that he was actually innocent of the crime for which he was convicted.*" Then he quoted a U.S. Supreme Court case, Bousley v. U.S., " *'It is important to note in this regard that 'actual innocence' means factual innocence, not mere legal insufficiency.'* "

Then Judge Conaboy delivered an astonishing comment, "***In this case, Trenkler failed to present any evidence that he was actually innocent of the crimes for which he was convicted.***" (emphasis added here) What was not effectively presented to the judge, and what he missed, was that Alfred Trenkler had been claiming innocence since his indictment, but the legal system had lost sight of that demand, as he struggled to find legal hooks to effect his release. [A copy of the quoted sections of Judge Conaboy's opinion is included in Appendix E.] Since that decision, the U.S. Supreme Court has issued another important opinion on the issue of a judge's role in the face of a claim of "actual innocence." In the 2006 case of House v. Bell, Warden, the court said the standard is whether, "*had the jury heard all the conflicting testimony - it is more likely than not that no reasonable juror viewing the record as a whole would lack reasonable doubt* [as to the guilt of a defendant]. In other words, the standard for judges to act in favor of a defendant subsequent to a conviction was whether there was enough evidence of actual innocence that no reasonable juror could convict beyond a reasonable doubt.

Judge Conaboy also struck at another characteristic of the legal system: too many words. He noted in his 19-page opinion that "*the parties submitted unnecessarily lengthy briefs*" in the case. The "*Memoranda of Law*" before him from both sides totaled 114 pages. In the appeal to the Third Circuit the Briefs, including Appendices, totaled 354 pages, and the Court of Appeals decision was 8 pages.

He concluded while quoting from the Dorsainvil case, "*It would not be a 'complete miscarriage of justice' to deny relief in this case.*" Thus, Alfred's petition was denied not because he's guilty, and not because there is a miscarriage of justice, but because there was insufficient showing of a "***complete*** miscarriage of justice." (emphasis added here.) Alfred's RFJ XVIII had failed.

On 5 May 2003, Attorneys Hinton and Sultan appealed Judge Conaboy's decision with a 66-page Appeal Brief with the Third Circuit Court of Appeals, which is responsible for Pennsylvania. This legal effort is labeled here RFJ XIX. On 4 June, Kevin McGrath filed a 66-page Reply brief, to which Hinton and Sultan filed on 18 June an 18-page Reply Brief.

On 3 September Alfred Trenkler wrote Catherine Hinton a letter, forwarding information about cases involving sentences for crimes prosecuted under the same statutes as his. Importantly, he brought to her attention a new issue that the Federal statute under which he was sentenced, 18 USC Section 34, provided, at the time and before being amended, that a life sentence, or death, could only be given if the jury recommended such a sentence. Otherwise only a term of years could be given, up to the remaining life expectancy of the defendant. Alfred wrote, "*It is obvious that Judge Zobel did not have the authority to hand down a life sentence in my case. Why Terry Segal and Morris Goldings never mind the Appeals Court never noticed such a plain error and abuse of discretion on the part of Judge Zobel is beyond me. The question now is, how do we bring this to the attention to the Appeals Court to remand for resentencing in Zobel's court?*"

Alfred learned of this sentencing problem from a widely publicized case in Boston, U.S. v. Barone. In that case in early September 2003, U.S. District Court Judge Mark Wolf was anticipating resentencing Pasquale Barone because his original life sentence was erroneous. The problem was that the jury in that case had deadlocked on the Count which carried the life sentence. The error had been uncovered during consideration of the successful claim by Barone that the prosecution had withheld exculpatory evidence. The *Mass. Lawyers' Weekly* covered the story on 29 September with the headline, "ERROR DISCLOSED IN MOBSTER'S SENTENCE," and on 4 October, Barone was resentenced.

On 18 December 2003, Third Circuit Court of Appeals Judge Thomas Ambro wrote the unanimous 5-page opinion for himself and Judges Fuentes and Garth, which affirmed the decision by District Court Judge Conaboy. He concluded "*Jones does not decriminalize the conduct for which Trenkler was convicted.*" RFJ XIX had failed.

On 30 January 2004 Alfred Trenkler's attorneys filed RFJ XX, a "*Petition for Panel Rehearing and for Rehearing En Banc....*" On 13 February 2004, 14 Circuit Judges of the Court of Appeals for the Third Circuit denied the Petition for rehearing. Not only was there not a majority, but not one of the judges voted in support of Alfred Trenkler's petition. Notably included among the 14 were Judge Samuel Alito, now a U.S. Supreme Court Justice, and Michael Chertoff, now the head of the U.S. Dept. of Homeland Security. Probably Judge Chertoff should not have joined in the opinion as he wrote a brief for the U.S. Government opposing Alfred Trenkler's "*Petition for Certiorari*" in an earlier appeal, RFJ XVII in 2001. Given the one-sided decision, the conflict was not worth pursuing.

On 6 February 2004 Alfred Trenkler turned 48 years old.

On 13 May 2004, Catherine Hinton and James Sultan filed a 30 page "*Petition for Certiorari*" for relief at the U.S. Supreme Court. This was RFJ XXI. They argued that "*Trenkler has presented a cognizable and non-frivolous claim that the Jones decision significantly heightened the requirements for proving the interstate commerce element, thereby removing his alleged conduct from the ambit of 844(i) and 844(d)....* Trenkler's petition for habeas corpus was erroneously dismissed for lack of jurisdiction, in a manner which conflicts with the law of this Court, the Third Circuit's own precedent, and decisions of several other circuits."

The U.S. Supreme Court denied the "*Petition for Certiorari,*" and RFJ XXI had failed.

Alfred and his parents retained another lawyer to bring the illegal sentence claim, Dana Curhan, who was the same appellate attorney, and fellow Thayer Academy alumnus from the class of 1977, Alfred had requested to retain during his 1994 effort to obtain a government-funded lawyer for his initial appeal. On 24 August 2004, Curhan filed a "*Petition for a Writ of Mandamus*" to the First Circuit Court of Appeals to order U.S. District Court Judge Rya Zobel to vacate Alfred Trenkler's sentence because it was issued without a recommendation of the jury, which the statute, 18 USC Section 34, then required. His Petition is numbered here as RFJ XXII.

On 6 February 2005 Alfred Trenkler turned 49 years old. His good friend, John Cates, would die this year of liver cancer, the origin of which was traced back to his severe case of hepatitis B before meeting Alfred in 1990.

On 16 February 2005, First Circuit Court of Appeals Judges Michael Boudin, Juan Torruella and Sandra Lynch denied Trenkler's Petition for a "*Writ of Mandamus*" in a two sentence opinion: "*Petitioner seeks, through a petition for writ of mandamus, to vacate his two life sentences. We deny the petition for writ of mandamus because to allow it would be effectively to negate the stringent gatekeeping restrictions on second or successive 2255 petitions.*" Thus, you only get one bite at the apple, no matter how just the cause may be. Procedure and efficiency had trumped justice. Alfred must have felt that prison door slamming ever more firmly as Judge Torruella did not dissent, as he had so eloquently done in the initial direct appeal ten years earlier. RFJ XXII had failed.

On 14 May 2005, Dana Curhan filed a Petition for "*Writ of Certiorari*" with the U.S. Supreme Court, RFJ XXIII, and it was denied on 20 June 2005.

The long struggle for justice was losing steam, but Jack Wallace and Alfred kept trying.

On 1 November 2005, Jack Wallace wrote to U.S. District Judge Edward Harrington to provide him supplemental information about his 28 October 1998 Disposition Hearing for Tom Shay's guilty plea bargain. That the letter came more than seven years after Shay's final sentencing is an indication of the feelings of desperation among Alfred's family and supporters.

Wrote Jack, "*I am writing to you to rebut Mr. Apfel's remarks in response to your question regarding the evidence the government would have introduced were the case have gone to trial.*

David Apfel, AUSA, who represented the government at the hearing is the same David Apfel who informed Alfred Trenkler's attorney, Morris Goldings, that Tom Shay told several government agents that Alfred had nothing to do with the bombing.

He told Morris to do with it [the information] *what he wished whereupon Morris called Kevin McGrath, AUSA, with the information and asked Mr. McGrath what he was going to do about it. His response was that he wasn't going to do anything.*"

Then Jack Wallace reviewed the evidence presented by David Apfel at the Shay disposition hearing, and argued that much of it was unproven or false. He continued,

"*Tom Shay now admits that the government convinced his attorneys that he could get life imprisonment if the case went to trial. He said he was coerced by his attorney to plead guilty or take the chance of spending his whole life in prison.*

Apparently both parties ignored double jeopardy, and the Supreme Court case, North Carolina vs Pierce, which states that a defendant cannot be punished for seeking a new trial by a harsher sentence the second time around.

Shay's attorneys were told by Terry Segal, Alfred's attorney, that our bomb expert, Denny Kline, said the remains of the toggle switch were not from Radio Shack. (See enclosed.) [Enclosed was a copy of Denny Kline's initial preliminary report, which was sent to Terry Segal on 22 April 1993.]

I hope that this letter clarifies the facts that were used against Tom Shay, and which adversely reflected on my stepson, Alfred Trenkler. I should have responded sooner, but

[we] *have been pursuing appeals with the District Court, the Court of Appeals and the Supreme Court, all of which were denied without addressing the merits of the case."*

On 1 December 2005, Alfred Trenkler wrote the letter below to Judge Zobel, for his Request for Justice XXIV. He wrote to her directly because he had read of Federal Judge Mark Wolf's self-correction of a sentencing mistake. Also, Alfred knew that there was no statutory authority for his two life sentences and that the First Circuit must have been in error, or that it was just the wrong forum, when it denied Dana Curhan's Petition for a Writ of Mandamus to order Judge Zobel to resentence him.

Dec. 1, 2005
White Deer, PA

Hon. Rya W. Zobel
U.S. District Judge
Moakley Federal Courthouse
One Courthouse Way
Boston, MA 02110

Re: U.S. v. Alfred W. Trenkler
D.C. Case No. Crim. A-92-10369-Z
Statutorily Barred Life Sentences

Dear Judge Zobel:
I am writing to you as a matter of last resort. I don't know if you recall my case, but you sentenced me to two (2) concurrent life terms in March of 1994. Recently, upon researching the statutes I was convicted under, it is apparent that, absent a recommendation from the jury, you were without jurisdiction to independently impose life sentences as a matter of law. Hence, this letter to you.

The applicable statute, 18 U.S.C. §34, which is part of §844 (d) and §844 (i) , as it read in March of 1994, specifically provided that a sentence of life could only be imposed upon the recommendation of the jury following a jury trial. Since the matter of punishment was never presented to the jury, the statute prohibits the court from independently imposing a life sentence. As a result, the sentence I am currently serving is, in fact, an illegal sentence, because it was not permitted by law under the statute in effect at that time.

In trying to see how this could have occurred, I turned to the PSI report. There, the probation dept. even overlooked the mandatory requirements of the statute and mistakenly stated that you could impose a life term. It is apparent that no one, including the USPO, the AUSA, my defense counsel, nor the Court, realized that the statute then in effect prohibited a life term without it so being recommended by the jury. Accordingly, the Court could only impose a term amounting to a number of years and not life.

Recently, in a case of similar impression, Judge Wolf resentenced a defendant who was in the similar predicament. That case, U.S. v. Barone, was widely publicized and upon reading about it, that is what prompted me to research the sentencing issue in my case. In the Barone case, just as in mine, everyone involved failed to notice the sentencing error. The only significant difference in the two cases is that Barone's life sentence was the result of a calculation error, whereas the error in my case is simply that the statute was not adhered to.

Relevant to all of this is the fact that the applicable statute was later amended to allow the court to independently impose a life sentence, but that does not apply to me. This later change in the law, may have contributed to perhaps why the Court of Appeals failed to see this plain error on direct appeal.

Judge Zobel, I am not an attorney and am not well versed in the law. However, I feel the primary responsibility of correcting this illegality falls upon you, the sentencing court. Especially so since you failed to follow the mandatory statutory requirements of 18 USC §34, as contained in §844(d) and (i). In light of the amount of time that has lapsed since my 1994 sentencing and the fact that my appeals process has ended, I feel my only avenue of legal recourse is to now bring this to your attention.

Absent any action on your behalf, perhaps the only other remedy available would be to move the local district court in a habeas action to discharge me from custody since, without question, I am in fact serving a sentence that was not authorized by law. I don't know if that is the proper way to proceed or not, so I will defer to you, by way of this letter, to make any sentencing correction that you would deem appropriate in light of this revelation.

Thank you for taking your time to read this and I await your response.

Sincerely
Alfred W. Trenkler /s/
No. 19377-038 1-B
U.S. Penitentiary
P.O. Box 3000
White Deer, PA 17887

enclosures: 3
cc: U.S. Attorney
Wm. G. Young, Chief Judge
Mark Wolf, District Judge
Dana Curhan, Esq.
Scott Lopez, Atty
Terry Segal, Atty
Ken Chandler, Boston Herald
John D. Wallace

On 21 December 2005, Tom Shay wrote from the Plymouth County House of Correction to Jack and Josephine Wallace. "*Dear Jack & Joe* [sic], *Just wanted to thank you for the paper & pen money. Hope you will have a merry Christmas. A Better one next year when al comes home. Let's do our best to work on his behalf. I will start writing in the first week of January. I will write everything I know. If you feel uncomfortable without his permission, please ask Al if I can have a prison photo of his. I will look at it every day I write. If not, I will understand. But let me know either way. Tommy XXXXX*"

On 6 February 2006 Alfred Trenkler turned 50 years old, the last birth anniversary reached by Jeremiah Hurley, Jr. If Alfred Trenkler remains in prison, his life can be said to have ended, too. Everybody, and probably including the Bomb Maker, agrees that the death of Jeremiah Hurley was a tragedy and a waste. There remains strong disagreement about whether Alfred Trenkler should remain deprived of his right to the pursuit of happiness as a free man. At age 50, after a career as a policeman, just at the time that the country was learning about the epidemic of wrongful convictions, one wonders what Jeremiah Hurley would say about Alfred Trenkler's case. If he had survived, like Francis Foley, would he be open to dialogue? To the pursuit of truth?

Alfred came close to dying in those first months of his 51st year when his heart began slowing down. On several occasions in 2005 he had gone to the prison infirmary for treatment for arythmia or irregular hearbeat attacks. On 2 March 2006 he had an attack that the prison hospital identified as a "total block" that lowered his heartbeat to 20 beats per minute and falling. He was rushed to the Susquehanna Health Services in Williamsport where a pacemaker was inserted. Dr. Burks told him that he had been within minutes of dying. The pacemaker sends an electronic impulse to his heart to force it to beat whenever the natural signals fail. Every three months, the pacemaker gets a checkup within the prison by placing a magnet (ironically) with various sensors next to his chest and then transmitting data over a telephone to Williamsport. Once a year the magnet device is hooked up to a computer and the frequency of the triggering of the pacemaker's use over the previous year is transmitted; and the remaining life of the battery is analyzed. As of September 2007, that annual checkup had not yet occurred and Alfred has no idea how often the device has fired, or saved his life. Every 7-10 years the entire pacemaker, located just underneath his skin, is replaced, depending upon the actual number of firings. The electrical engineer is thankful for the availability of such a device, but believes that his 14 years of wrongful imprisonment were the primary reason for the failure of his physical health.

In the Spring of 2006, the efforts in support of Alfred Trenkler expanded to the Internet with the same goal as this book, which is to bring to the people of the U.S. and the world the story of Alfred's wrongful conviction. A central tenet of the transformed Campaign for Alfred was that correcting wrongful convictions is an obligation of all citizens and not just the lawyers who run the judicial system. The judicial system is part of the political process and, despite sanctimonious protests of being uninfluenced by politics, the judiciary must listen to the people.

Supporters organized the Alfred Trenkler Innocent Committee with its first meeting with Alfred at Allenwood in June 2006 during the annual visit by his parents. The Committee later took the initial step of securing a post office box and then began the more complicated process of securing recognition as a bona fide non-profit organization.

Also on 28 June 2006, Jack Wallace, on behalf of Alfred Trenkler, filed a "*Motion for a court order to review the evidence the ATF has from Mr. Trenkler's trial.*" This Motion can be labeled Alfred's <u>RFJ XXV</u>.

The motion stated, "*The motion is to make arrangements for a fingerprint expert, Richard Whalen... and myself to examine all of the evidence the ATF has in its possession. The purpose is to take photographs and fingerprints of the remnants of the*

1991 Shay bomb and all other evidence in the ATF's possession. Please order the ATF to preserve all of this evidence from the Trenkler trial.

The reason for my request is as follows:

Cynthia Wallace, ATF forensic chemist, incorrectly identified the two contacts found in the bomb debris as coming from a switch exclusively made for Radio Shack.

We purchased a competitive toggle switch - Philmore No. 30219 - to compare with the Radio Shack, Model #275-602. The two switches are identical with one major exception - the contacts of the competitive switch matched the contacts of the ATF evidence; the contacts of the Radio Shack switch did not match." Jack Wallace had enclosed photos of the toggle switch contacts of the Roslindale Bomb and of a Radio Shack #275-602 and a Philmore #30-219 and believed that they supported his claim that the Roslindale Bomb contacts were not from a #275-602.

On 7 August 2006 Dennis Tatz of the _Patriot Ledger_ wrote a front page article about the case, "*LEDGER UPDATE: BOMBER'S CONVICTION DECRIED - IMPRISONED QUINCY MAN UNJUSTLY CONVICTED, SAYS ANOTHER MAN LINKED TO DEADLY CRIME.*" Excerpts from the article are below:

Since his arrest for building a bomb that killed a Boston police bomb squad officer and badly injured another in 1991, former Quincy resident Alfred Trenkler has insisted he is an innocent man.

Now, in an exclusive interview with The Patriot Ledger, Thomas Shay, Trenkler's convicted accomplice, says that overzealous prosecutors wrongfully went after Trenkler when they should have been looking at other suspects.

"Every day he spends in jail is an atrocity," said Shay, 34, whose conviction was later overturned. "Alfred Trenkler is innocent. He has been innocent since day one."

"It was convenient to nail me," Trenkler, 50, said during a recent telephone interview from the Allenwood Federal Penitentiary in White Deer, Pa.

"My saving grace is that I had nothing to do with it. It keeps me sane. I hope the truth comes out sooner than later. I had nothing to do with this."

Federal prosecutors alleged that Trenkler, an electrical engineer, conspired with Shay to kill Shay's abusive father, who also is named Thomas Shay.

The younger Shay admitted his guilt in a plea agreement after he was initially convicted in federal court. That conviction was overturned because U.S. District Judge Rya Zobel refused to allow a psychiatrist to testify in Shay's defense when he was on trial.

Shay, ...said someone else planted the bomb at his father's home in Roslindale. The younger Shay made that statement in connection with a lawsuit his father had filed asserting that his hearing was damaged in 1987 when dynamite exploded in a barrel at a Dedham auto body shop where the elder Shay had rented space.

The elder Shay told doctors before and after the deadly explosion at his home in Roslindale that he feared the defendants in the suit wanted him dead, according to court papers.

But court documents also show Thomas Shay believed his father was responsible for the bomb because he wanted to pressure the defendants to settle the suit while making it appear he was on a hit list....

Evidence showed that the elder Shay, then 47, was living on money from settlements in other personal injury claims at the time of the "Roslindale Bombing."

The elder Shay's $400,000 lawsuit was at a standstill because the insurance company believed he had been faking his injuries, according to court papers.

The younger Shay, whose early years were spent in the custody of the state Department of Social Services, said prosecutors made too much of the brief homosexual encounter between him and Trenkler.

"When I heard they were focusing on Al, I said that was impossible," Shay said. "What motive could he have?

"Alfred Trenkler is the exact opposite of me. Where I came from a bad home, Alfred Trenkler came from a good home. Where I was jobless, he had his own company. Where I had little friends, he had many friends."

Despite defense insistence in 2000 that new evidence in the case could help clear Trenkler, Judge Zobel refused to schedule a hearing. The judge ruled that the three-year time limit for an appeal prohibited her from giving Trenkler a new trial....

[Jack] Wallace maintains that a forensic chemist for the U.S. Bureau of Alcohol, Tobacco and Firearms incorrectly testified that two contacts found in the bomb debris came from a toggle switch made exclusively for Radio Shack. Wallace said there is proof that the switch contacts used in the bombing came from a Radio Shack competitor. "The incorrect identification of the toggle switch caused other members of the prosecution team to offer testimony or statements which were incorrect," he said.

The defense had also fought unsuccessfully for the court to hear from another Allenwood inmate, whose testimony allegedly called into question the truthfulness of a key witness at Trenkler's trial. The witness, David Lindholm, said that Trenkler admitted to him that he had built the bomb. He said the admission came while both men were being held at the Plymouth County jail.

The article [a copy of which is in Appendix E] was a welcome change in media coverage for Alfred Trenkler. The single most significant error in the article was Tom Shay's statement that there had been a brief homosexual encounter between him and Alfred Trenkler. There was none, but Alfred's family was so pleased with the article that no request for correction was made, lest they appear ungrateful. However, the level of the relationship between Alfred Trenkler and Tom Shay was a crucial piece of the prosecution's case, and the stronger the relationship, the more believable was the possible motive. The correction in the media of its perception of the Trenkler/Shay acquaintance would await another day or website or book.

Also Tom Shay made unpublished statements in his interview which may not have been truthful either. For example, he said that one reason he pled guilty in 1998 was to protect his mother whom, Shay said, was threatened with death by his father. After his remarkable, and remarkably truthful, New Year's Greeting message of January 2002, was *pseudologia fantastica* a lingering problem?

Often when a regional newspaper, such as The *Patriot Ledger* publishes a story of larger interest to the metropolitan Boston area, the two Boston daily newspapers will pursue the story. However, no Boston newspapers picked up the lead from Tatz's article.

In August, Attorney Joan Griffin of the national law firm, McDermott Will & Emery, contacted Alfred and the Wallaces as she had been asked by Judge Zobel to examine the facts and law raised by Alfred's December 2005 letter to Judge Zobel. If there was merit in the claim of an illegal sentence without the recommendation of the jury, then Joan would file a Motion with the Court for her appointment as counsel for Alfred and for Judge Zobel to consider vacating the two life sentences and resentencing Alfred according to the statutory requirements at the time.

Those initial organizing steps of the Alfred Trenkler Organizing Committee were put on hold so as not to disrupt the judicial process. As had happened several times in the past, all hope for justice for Alfred was focused on a single Motion or Petition, which in this case was Judge Zobel's handling of that request. She had already done more than was expected, as the First Circuit had denied exactly the same claim, when made by Attorney Dana Curhan, in RFJ XXII. That is, she could have ducked the issue in his letter and not responded at all, or had a clerk respond with a letter that she was bound by the unanimous 16 February 2005 decision of the First Circuit denying the illegal sentencing claim.

Alfred's family began hoping that the resentencing would result in a sentence for "time served" or for only a small amount of time in addition to the 14 years already served.

On 6 November 2006 Joan Griffin filed the "*Defendant's Petition and Motion for a Writ of Coram Nobis and/or Audita Querela, and Request for Appointment of Counsel and Further Briefing.*" A copy of the Petition was sent to the U.S. Attorney's office, but there was no response from the prosecutors. The motion urged the correction of "*an error of the most fundamental character.*"

Joan Griffin stated that despite the long post-conviction legal history of the case, the sentencing error had not been corrected, but that the ancient *Writ of Coram Nobis* could be used by Judge Zobel. The Motion stated, "*The writ of coram nobis is 'an unusual legal animal that courts will use to set aside a criminal judgment . . . under circumstances compelling such action to achieve justice,'* " quoting from a 1999 First Circuit Court of Appeals case, United States v. Barrett.

On 15 November 2006, Judge Zobel approved the Motion with a handwritten decision, "*Motion for Appointment of counsel allowed. The government shall file a responsible pleading on or before 1/5/07.*" That date passed without any response from the U.S. Attorney's office. Perhaps that omission meant that the law was clear to the prosecutors, too, and there was no disagreement regarding vacating the original sentence and then resentencing? For wrongly convicted people and their families, hope springs eternal.

As it was highly likely that the U.S. Attorney would oppose any reduction in Alfred Trenkler's two life sentences, Judge Zobel sought to ensure that there was no misunderstanding. On 26 January 2007 she issued a formal "*ORDER,*" which stated, "*... To date the government has not responded. Unless it submits a responsive pleading by February 2, 2007, the court will decide the matter without opposition.*" That day came and went without response from the U.S. Attorney.

On 2 December 2006, Boston Police Officer Denise (Kraft) Corbett died, and on 5 December Michele McPhee, Police Bureau Chief of the *Boston Herald*, wrote that Denise Corbett's apparent suicide by gunshot was at least indirectly caused by her continued distress at seeing the 28 October 1991 explosion, and fearing renewal of courtroom testimony if one or both cases required retrial. Also, she may have felt that her two-way radio may have set off the 1991 explosion, as was subsequently rumored, even though that was never shown to have been the cause and no police report indicates that she was making a radio transmission at the time of the explosion. At

Tom Shay's trial, she explicitly responded "*No*" to Nancy Gertner's question, "*Did you receive any transmissions prior to the time the bomb went off?*" (TS 4-86].

On 6 February 2007 Alfred Trenkler turned 51 years old.

On 20 February, Judge Zobel decided, "*Both because the petition is unopposed and based on the merits, I grant the writ and order petitioner to be delivered to this court for resentencing*" on 4 April 2007. She continued, "*Clearly, Trenkler continues to suffer the collateral consequences of the sentencing error. He will likely die in prison while serving the two invalid life sentences imposed by this court. Had the error not occurred the maximum possible legal sentence would offer him the possibility of leaving prison in his lifetime.*" She cited a case which held that the maximum sentence under the statute in effect in 1994 was a term of years "*less than the defendant's life expectancy.*"

The U.S. Attorney's office clearly received this order because on the 21st it filed an 8-page "*Motion to Stay Order of February 20, and for Leave to File a Response to the Petition for a Writ of Coram Nobis.*" After five pages of the history of the case, the Motion sought to explain its lack of response to Joan Griffin's Petition and the two orders by Judge Zobel by noting that the lawyers who had previously handled the long-running case were no longer working in the office and that the transition of the case to a newly assigned AUSA was not effective.

Signed by AUSA James Lang, the "Motion" said that the U.S. Attorney was "vigorously opposing the petitioner's efforts to reduce his sentence." He wrote that "Because the defendant stands convicted of conduct that resulted in the death of one Boston Police officer and to the serious injury to another, the case is too important to the deceased victim's family, to the surviving victim, and to the public at large to warrant resolution of the <u>coram nobis</u> petition without the Court having the benefit of briefing by the government."

Judge Zobel responded quickly with an order on 22 February that denied the request for a stay, but gave the prosecutors until 7 March to file an Opposition to her order. She clarified one source of possible misunderstanding, which was that she "*did not immediately vacate the sentences, but left that to the date of resentencing.*" Pointedly, she said the government's response "*shall focus on the issues raised by the petition, namely the illegality of the sentence and the propriety of the procedural vehicle chosen to raise the issues. It shall abjure any arguments irrelevant to these issues including specifically any matters pertaining to the underlying crime.*" She concluded, "*Pending further order of the court, the date for resentencing, April 4, 2007 stands.*"

The *Patriot Ledger* was the first to break the story, on 21 February 2007 with the article by Susan Reinert, "JUDGE: BOMB-MAKER WRONGLY SENTENCED TO 2 LIFE TERMS." On 22 February, the *Ledger*'s Dennis Tatz wrote a follow-up story about the response from the U.S. Attorney's office, "ATTORNEYS FIGHT NEW RULING IN BOMB CASE." The article stated, "*In a statement, U.S. Attorney Michael Sullivan admitted his office had unintentionally failed to respond to two court orders about Trenkler's illegal sentence claim.*

'The government has successfully opposed at least four earlier post-conviction challenges by Trenkler, and it was always our intent to do so in this instance.' Sullivan said.'Additionally, we have begun an immediate internal review to determine how the office failed to comply with the court's orders. Without question, this is a matter that is deserving of our highest attention and this failure is unacceptable.'"

By the 28th, the Boston papers took notice, too. Suzanne Smalley and MacDaniel wrote the _Boston Globe_'s article, "_SENTENCE TOSSED IN OFFICER'S SLAYING - U.S. ATTORNEY MAKES PUBLIC APOLOGY._" There were no comments from the lawyer or family of Alfred Trenkler. The article stated that Boston Police Commissioner Edward Davis had sent a memo to all Boston Police officers about the case. "_It frustrates me that the persons responsible for the murder of Officer Hurley continue to victimize the victims and their families and refuse to take responsibility for their crimes._" The comment could be reversed as well, by noting that the U.S. Attorney and ATF continue to victimize the victims and their families by not yet taking responsibility for the wrongful convictions of Tom Shay and Alfred Trenkler.

Commissioner Davis was not unaware of the problem of wrongful conviction as he was a detective in 1983 who arrested Dennis Maher in Ayer, Mass., for three rapes on the basis of flimsy clothing descriptions. Dennis Maher was convicted of the three rapes and imprisoned until freed in 2003 thanks to DNA and the work of the Innocence Project. Wrote _Boston Globe_ columnist Brian McGrory on 24 October 2006, "_WAITING FOR LEADERSHIP,_" Edward "_Davis has never expressed regret or remorse or just about anything at all_" about that wrongful conviction.

The _Boston Herald_'s 28 February article about the Trenkler resentencing was more dramatic, "_FED FLUB MAY FREE COP KILLER - JUDGE TO RESENTENCE BOMBER NOW SERVING TWO LIFE TERMS._" The _Boston Herald_'s Police Bureau Chief, Michele McPhee, wrote that Trenkler "_could be released from a federal prison on a technicality._" Boston Police Patrolmen's Association President Thomas Nee said, "_We're very upset that a technicality within the law has reopened a very dark day and a very difficult time for Officer Hurley's family, Officer Foley's family, and Boston police officers. Alfred Trenkler should never be allowed out of jail in his natural life._" There was no mention in the article of the dark days for Alfred Trenkler's family, nor any comment from them, nor of any effort to reach them or Alfred's attorney.

On 5 March 2007 Michele McPhee's "_Police Beat_" column was titled, "NO EVEN BREAKS FOR COP KILLERS, PLEASE." She wrote, "_It is unclear what will happen to Trenkler when he shows up in Zobel's court on April 4, but the city should say a collective prayer that she sends him back to his cell for good._" The article did mention that Alfred Trenkler's supporters had established a website in support of his claims of innocence.

On 7 March, the U.S. Attorney's Office filed a 51 page "Opposition to Trenkler's Coram Nobis Petition and Motion for Reconsideration of the Court's February 20, 2007, Memorandum and Order Granting a Writ of Coram Nobis to Reopen Sentencing"

Filed by Assistant U.S. Attorneys Randall Kromm, Dina Michael Chaitowitz, Timothy Feeley and James Lang, on behalf of U.S. Attorney Michael Sullivan, the Motion begins by saying that "Trenkler is not entitled to the relief he seeks. Trenkler's petition establishes no valid basis for merits review of his long-delayed claim." The Government argued that a "_Writ of Coram Nobis_" was not appropriate in this case and that Trenkler's time for appeals had expired. Only in a footnote, #15 on page 37, did the AUSA's make their claim that the sentencing error should be ignored and that he had not shown "actual prejudice" for his failure to protest the illegal sentence in 1994.

On 8 March Judge Zobel scheduled a "status conference" for lawyers in the case only, for Wednesday, 28 March. Before that conference, Joan Griffin and Corey

Carlsberg responded to the Government's "Opposition" with a 9-page "Opposition" of their own on 21 March. Among other arguments, they wrote, "*The United States Attorney is the representative not of an ordinary party to a controversy, but of a sovereignty whose obligation to govern impartially is as compelling as its obligation to govern at all; and whose interest, therefore, in a criminal prosecution is not that it shall win a case, but that justice shall be done. As such, he is in a peculiar and very definite sense the servant of the law, the twofold aim of which is that guilt shall not escape or innocence suffer. He may prosecute with earnestness and vigor -- indeed, he should do so. But, while he may strike hard blows, he is not at liberty to strike foul ones. Berger v. United States, 295 U.S. 78,88 (1935).*

Society wins not only when the guilty are convicted but when criminal trials are fair; our system of the administration of justice suffers when any accused is treated unfairly Brady v. Maryland, 373 U.S. 83,87 (1963).

The heart of the Government's argument is that Alfred Trenkler should bear the burden, a heavy one, the rest of his life in prison for the Government's error in successfully urging the Court to sentence Mr. Trenkler to two life sentences despite the fact that it lacked authority to do so. The Government argues that Mr. Trenkler should bear this burden because he and his attorneys missed previous opportunities to bring this error to the court's attention. The Government's hard-line position on deadlines missed by Mr. Trenkler contrasts sharply with the leniency it claims for itself, in its filing of its opposition, despite missing three deadlines to respond to Mr. Trenkler's initial petition. But far worse is the Government's modus operandi in this and other cases of placing the blame, and the consequences, of its own mistakes on the accused and the convicted. It is the Government which prosecuted Mr. Trenkler and which sought an illegal sentence after his conviction. The Government forgets its duty to all citizens, including those accused and even convicted of crimes, to ensure justice under the law.

The Government's position is not merely a bad faith attempt to win at all costs, rather than uphold the law; it is incorrect. Despite filing a 51-page brief, the Government buries in a footnote its response to the heart of the Court's decision allowing the petition. In footnote 15 of its Opposition, the Government acknowledges First Circuit case law permitting resentencing where, as here, the Government had requested and permitted the Court to impose a sentence where it lacked authority to do so and where remanding the case would require only a simple resentencing, grounds correctly relied upon by this Court in allowing the petition. The Government relegates its discussion of these cases to a footnote because it has no response to the Court's reasoning that issuance of the writ in these narrow circumstances is appropriate.... "

On 26 March, the *Boston Herald*'s Police Bureau Chief, Michele McPhee, wrote forcefully about the upcoming hearing and the relation of the Roslindale Bombing to the recent suicide of Denise (Kraft) Corbett, "*In the days before Boston police officer Denise Corbett died, she had become obsessed with explosions - including the one that changed her life forever. She asked her mother to mail back to her the envelope stuffed with yellowing newspaper clips with horrific headlines like:*

"Bomb Blast Kills Police Officer."

The articles were all about the dynamite planted in a Roslindale driveway that killed BPD bomb squad officer Jeremiah Hurley and maimed his partner, Francis X. Foley, on the afternoon of Oct. 28, 1991.

But when Denise Corbett took her own life Dec. 2, she became the second Boston police officer to die as a result of that merciless 1991 explosion.

On April 4, U.S. District Court Judge Rya Zobel will consider whether Alfred Trenkler should serve any more time for Hurley's death. He was never charged or convicted in the death of Corbett so many years later, though his bomb killed her just as surely as it killed Hurley.

This month, Zobel vacated Trenkler's two life sentences, after U.S. Attorney Michael Sullivan missed a deadline to respond to briefs in the case.

Zobel freed the other man convicted in the case, Thomas Shay, after just nine years. But nothing less than life is acceptable for Trenkler. Not to the Boston Police Department. Not to Police Commissioner Ed Davis. And not to the Hurley, Foley and now Corbett families.

"There is not a doubt in my mind that the stress of that event contributed to Denise Corbett's death,"Davis said yesterday. "The stress of that day wore her down."

In the weeks before she died, Corbett began to watch gory war movies. Then she started writing checks to Iraq war veterans maimed in bombing attacks. Many mornings she was jerked awake by nightmares.

All of it was a reaction, said her husband Mark Corbett, also a Boston cop, to the idea that she may be called to testify in a court hearing for Trenkler.

"She was terrified that she would be dragged back through it," he told me last week in an interview at his family's Walpole home, which is festooned with crayon-scrawled pictures drawn by the youngest of the couple's five children. Two of the youngest are severely autistic.

"During that trial, she was up all night, every night. It was so hard for her, looking at the Hurley family and Foley family in the court room," he said.

Denise Corbett was a rookie police officer taking a statement from the bomb's intended target, Thomas Shay, in a Roslindale driveway when the bomb built by Trenkler and planted by Shay's son exploded. The blast hurtled her to the ground and pelted her with debris.

Hurley died in her arms begging her to tell his wife, Cynthia, that he loved her. She desperately tried to save Foley's eye, applying pressure with a towel.

Her tearful testimony about that day is unforgettable to veteran cops who attended the trial of Trenkler and Shay.

"It was really, really bad," Denise Corbett testified in 1993, just weeks after she gave birth to her daughter. "There was blood everywhere."

As her testimony grew even more graphic, Hurley's widow and two of their five children fled the courtroom crying. Corbett's own voice was shaking with tears as she went on.

"They wanted to know how each other was doing," she testified.

Last Dec. 2, the trauma she suffered that day became too much and she took her own life. Her husband found her in their car parked outside.

Now Corbett, who has lost 25 pounds since his wife's death, is facing life without his 'angel.' Their children are facing life without their mother. And their financial picture worsens with each day Mark Corbett cannot return to work.

Zobel thought a paltry nine years behind bars was appropriate for Shay, even after he violated probation upon his release. Let's hope that Trenkler is not treated with such leniency.

Perhaps before she makes any decision, Zobel should attend the Friends of the Corbett Family Fundraiser at Moseley's in Dedham this Saturday night - which is open to anyone who wants to help the fallen cop's family. I'll even buy Zobel's $20 ticket so she can see firsthand how the Boston Police Department is now dealing with the loss of two fine BPD cops at the hands of Alfred Trenkler and Thomas Shay."

Everyone, and probably including the Bomb Maker, whomever he may be, agrees that the Roslindale Bomb caused untold misery, and the damage and pain continue. Unfortunately, the strong emotions arising from that bomb have been channeled toward the wrong people, Tom Shay and Alfred Trenkler. If the real maker(s) of the Roslindale Bomb had been found and convicted, there would be little or no continuing controversy.

On 27 March 2007 Dina Michael Chaitowitz, the Chief of the Appeals Unit of the U.S. Attorneys Office, filed another "Opposition" from the Government. She began, 'The petitioner Alfred Trenkler has moved the Court to strike..... The government opposes this motion.

1. Trenkler asserts that the government's opposition was filed in 'bad faith', and that the Court should not only 'strike it in its entirety,' but also 'admonish' the government that it has an obligation to do justice. While we believe this hyperbole is unhelpful to the Court with respect to the legal issues it must resolve, we feel we must respond...."

On 28 March the attorneys met with Judge Zobel and presented their arguments orally, and then the schedule for the 4 April hearing was planned. Afterwards, the two sides exchanged another volley of memoranda on the resentencing issue and there was also an Aflred Trenkler request that he be allowed to wear street clothes during the hearing. Judge Zobel ordered that he be permitted to wear clothes brought to the courthouse by his brother..

Scheduled in Courtroom #12 for 45 minutes, the 4 April hearing took one and a half hours. Judge Zobel began with a short statement that everyone is required to follow the rules, including judges, and then, *"Accordingly, I now vacate the sentence...."*

AUSA James Lang, for the U.S. Attorney's office, urged Judge Zobel to delay her resentencing decision until the Government could appeal the issues to the First Circuit Court of Appeals, and Judge Zobel quickly denied that request, saying *"We will proceed now."* Then AUSA Lang argued that Trenkler's and Shay's trial attorneys had waived the need for a jury recommendation on the sentence, by accepting the fact that death was caused by the 28 October 1991 explosion, in their Motion to eliminate the redundancy in the original five-count indictment. He argued that Alfred Trenkler should be resentenced to life in prison for all the reasons that applied to the original sentence, especially the death of a police officer.

Leanne Hurley Teehan spoke of the terrible personal loss suffered by the Hurley family, especially her mother and widow, Mrs. Cynthia Hurley. The daughter continued that *"I often try to see the other side of things,"* which was a good sign, but then she addressed Alfred Trenkler directly and told him of all the harm *"you have caused..."* and she noted the arrival of grandchildren that Jeremiah Hurley would never see. She urged Judge Zobel to resentence Alfred Trenkler to life in prison. Otherwise, *"you will be letting a terrorist loose."*

Jeremiah Hurley's partner, Frank Foley, spoke of the need and hope for closure and that when he read that the U.S. Supreme Court had denied a recent Trenkler appeal that the end of such litigation and reminders would be near. He noted that Alfred Trenkler had no relationship with "*the intended victim*," Mr. Thomas L. Shay, yet he methodically constructed and tested the 1991 Roslindale bomb. "*I don't believe he has any kind of conscience,*" and called Trenkler a "*terrorist and a coward.*"

Trenkler's lawyer, Joan Griffin, argued that the maximum sentence should be 10 years, or time-served, because the jury could have found Alfred Trenkler guilty only by a determination that he intended to cause property damage to Mr. Thomas L. Shay's car. She reminded Judge Zobel of her charge to the jury to that effect. She argued that the Government could have prosecuted Alfred Trenkler for first degree murder, but chose to prosecute for lesser crimes, and thus should be prohibited from now seeking a sentence for a more severe crime than was prosecuted.

Continuing on the theme that the Government must be consistent in its approach to the Roslindale Bomb case, she said that at Tom Shay's plea-bargained resentencing, the Government stated that there was no intent to kill Mr. Shay, and "*The Government cannot have it both ways.*" Among the effects of Alfred Trenkler's life sentence, Griffin said that he was forced to live with "*the worst of the worst.*"

AUSA Lang responded that Alfred Trenkler was himself "*the worst of the worst.*" With her final response, Attorney Griffin said that Judge Zobel is bound by the statutes which set the maximum sentences. Then she described two letters to the judge in support of Alfred and gave them to the clerk. She did not mention nor present to the clerk the 15-page letter, plus Exhibits, (See Appendix E) to Judge Zobel from the author of this book which described Alfred Trenkler's actual innocence. The "Exhibits" in the letter include:

A - Images of toggle switch contacts, and two pages of Denny Kline's preliminary report to Terry Segal *[In 2007 the author disassembled several Radio Shack #275-602's and one Philmore #30-219, and the #275-602 contacts resembled those in the Roslindale Bomb and the contacts in the #30-219 did not. The discrepancy between his observations and the images in this "exhibit" may have been due to the different disassembly dates together with possible design changes in the switches.]*

B - John Bowden Affidavit regarding William David Lindholm. John Bowden is now a free man and continues to stand by the truth in his 1998 affidavit. Asked about whether such an affidavit is consistent with Charlestown neighborhood's legendary "code of silence", Bowden responded quickly that the code doesn't apply when speaking in support of someone's innocence, i.e. Alfred Trenkler.

C - 7 August 2006 Front Page Article in *The Patriot Ledger* of Tom Shay interview.

D - 10 November 1992 Memo to File by Paul Kelly with Alfred Trenkler annotations.

E - 11 May 1993 Paul Kelly Letter to Nancy Gertner, with Alfred Trenkler annotations.

F - Transcript of sections of 17 October 1992 interview of Tom Shay by Karen Marinella, with Alfred Trenkler comments.

G - 7 March 2003 Order of Judge Conaboy dismissing Alfred Trenkler's Motion for Habeas Corpus

H - 8 July 2001 Letter from Tom Shay to Chief Hussey of the Boston Police Dept.

I - 10 Sept. 2001 Letter from AUSA Kevin McGrath to Charles Rankin, Atty for Alfred Trenkler.

On Attorney Griffin's recommendation, Alfred decided on the day of the 4 April hearing that the letter would not be submitted to Judge Zobel at the time she was calculating the proper resentencing period. It was mailed to Judge Zobel afterwards.

Judge Zobel asked Alfred Trenkler if he wanted to speak and he barely rose from his chair to say, "*I thank your Honor for bringing me here for resentencing.*" He had planned to make a statement similar to his presentencing statement in 1994 but was advised not to do so, in order to avoid angering the judge, or even the spectators who mostly in uniform as a statement of their support. Also, Alfred was very tired from the three sleepless days of bus travel from Allenwood Prison to a Philadelphia facility on 2 April and then to Brooklyn on 3 April, and then to Rhode Island and Massachusetts on the morning of the 4th. Thus was lost another opportunity to explain to the judge, the victims' families and other officials in the audience and to the media that he was totally innocent. For the public to be persuaded of the innocence of a person, they need to hear that person make the case, just as he did at his 1994 sentencing hearing.

At the conclusion of the statements and arguments, Judge Zobel resentenced sentenced Alfred Trenkler to 37 years in prison, and he was quickly escorted out of the courtroom With time off for good behavior, at the rate of 54 days per year, that would mean that he might be released before he is 69 years old, on 7 July 2025. Since 1987 there has been no parole in the Federal prison system. Thus ended Alfred's <u>Request for Justice XXIV</u>, and it was the first of the 24 which was at least partially successful. Thirty-seven years is a long time, but it isn't life, and he now had a good chance to come out alive. If all his Requests for Justice fail over the next 18 years, he will be released in 2025.

He was returned that same day to the Wyatt Detention Center in Central Falls, Rhode Island, and expected to be transported shortly back to Allenwood Prison. However, the sentencing paperwork from the court to the U.S. Marshals was mislaid, and it was not until Monday, 21 May that a new set of sentencing orders was mailed to the U.S. Marshal Service. He hopped into the bus to Allenwood, via the Metropolitan Detention Center in Brooklyn, NY, on Thursday, 24 May. The silver lining of his longer-than-expected stay in Rhode Island was that he could see visitors he hadn't seen in 14 years, and he could see his family more often as well. The visiting schedule permitted three 55 minute visits per week and he saw more visitors in those seven weeks than he had seen in the entire 14 years to date at Allenwood.

During his two week stay at Brooklyn, he fell on his wet cell floor and hurt his wrist. On Thursday, 7 June Alfred was taken back to Allenwood, but to a different cell. Back "home," he returned to his job of inspecting office furniture produced by the prison factory, and to his 1-2 hours, 6 days a week, of stationary bicycling. Back "home" he could obtain the quarterly checkup of his pacemaker.

Being "home" with all his paper records meant he could complete his application to the New England Innocence Project (NEIP) for assistance in overturning his wrongful conviction. The New England Innocence Project is an affiliate of the New York Innocence Project headed by Barry Scheck and Peter Neufeld, and it has secured exonerations for 10 New England men between 1997 and 2007, with the most recent being in 2004. The application was mailed on 25 June, and then Alfred began a final review of the manuscript of this book.

The NEIP application was rejected on 29 June by the "Intake Coordinator" because Alfred had stated on the application that he was represented by counsel. What he didn't say was that his lawyer, Joan Griffin, was his court-appointed lawyer only for the purpose of securing and defending a legal sentence. After the 4 April hearing, that work consisted only of defending Judge Zobel's granting of a "*Writ of Coram Nobis*" against the appeal to the Court of Appeals by the U.S. Attorney's office. As the U.S. Attorney had appealed the reduction of Alfred's sentence from two life terms to 37 years, Joan Griffin was appealing the 37 year sentence. That appeal was filed on is Alfred's RFJ XXVII. In any case, Joan Griffin's work had nothing to do with Alfred's wrongful conviction claim, and it's hoped that the NEIP will reconsider its prompt rejection of Alfred's application.

On 17 July, Alfred Trenkler filed a 28 U.S.C. 2255 *"Application For Leave to File a Second or Successive Motion to Vacate, Set Aside or Correct Sentence"* to the U.S. Circuit Court of Appeals, which was his <u>Request for Justice XXVIII</u>. He based his motion on five grounds:

1. That codefendant Tom Shay now states that Alfred Trenkler is innocent,
2. The toggle switch contacts from the Bomb debris were not correctly identified at trial as being from Radio Shack, and that they really came from a competitor,
3. The defense's bomb expert, Denny Kline, had observed fingerprints on the electrical tape recovered from the Roslindale Bomb,
4. The actual Futaba receiver model from the Roslindale Bomb was older than was used at the trial for testing, and it consumed batteries in two hours, instead of the 22 hours as stated at his trial, and
5. The Government possesses exculpatory evidence of Alfred Trenkler's actual innocence.

On 6 September, that Court certified the Motion to the District Court, *"but without prejudice to summary resolution by the distict court if further information required from Trenkler or tendered by the government so warrants."* Circuit Court judges Judges Boudin, Selya and Lipez saw their role as to *"determine whether Trenkler has made a prima facie showing of newly discovered evidence that a reasonable fact finder aware of such evidence would not have convicted him."* They continued, *"Trenkler has alleged under oath new forensic evidence that, if established, could well be substantial"* and then noted that *"exculpatory statements by a co-defendant are less impressive."*

On 28 September, the Alfred Trenkler Innocent Committee posted on his website the full text of Version 8 of the manuscript of <u>*Perfectly Innocent*</u> with the dual goals of soliciting feedback to ensure that the book contains the truth, and also to inform stakeholders (investigators, prosecutors, families of the victims, judges, jurors and the media) that the conviction of Alfred Trenkler, and Tom Shay were wrongful convictions. This publication can be called Alfred's <u>RFJ XXIX</u>, as it is an open plea for justice.

In October 2007, Alfred is expected to file a 2255 Motion with the U.S. District Court to vacate his 1993 conviction. That Motion will be called <u>RFJ XXX</u>.

REQUESTS FOR JUSTICE

<u>No.</u>	<u>Court</u>	<u>Date</u>	<u>Description</u>
XVIII	Dist.(PA)	3 Oct 02	Petition for Habeas Corpus due to redefinition of Interstate Commerce.
XIX	3rd Cir	5 May 03	Appeal of denial of XVIII.
XX	3rd Cir	30 Jan 04	Petition for En Banc rehearing of XIX.
XXI	US S.Ct	13 May 04	Petition for Writ of Certiorari, for denial of XX.
XXII	1st Cir	24 Aug 04	Petition for Writ of Mandamus to U.S. District Court.

XXIII US S Ct 14 May 05   Petition for Writ of Certiorari, for denial of XXII.

XXIV Dist Ct   1 Dec 05   Letter from Alfred Trenkler to Judge Zobel regarding legality of sentence. Resentenced on 4 April 2007.

XXV Dist Ct. 18 Jun 06   Motion for examination of the ATF evidence, by Jack Wallace. It is still pending.

XXVI New England Innocence Project

15 June 07 Application for assistance from NEIP, headquartered in the Boston law firm, Goodwin Procter. It was rejected three days later.

XXVII 1st Cir.   Trenkler's appeal of the 4 April 2007 sentence of 37 years.

XXVIII 1st Cir.18 Aug. 07 Motion for Habeas Corpus, 28 U.S.C. 2255. Certified to U.S. District Court on 6 September.

XXIX The public 28 Sept 07 Printing of 100+ copies of Version 8 of the manuscript of the book, *Perfectly Innocent.*, and posting on website.

XXX   Dist. Ct. __ Oct. 07 The Motion to the U.S. District Court to vacate the 1993 judgment.

Chapter 12: Conclusion

> *"I don't think it's idealistic or quixotic to say that the truth still matters."* Al Gore, 2007[1].

This book was almost titled *The Perfect Legal Storm* or *The Imperfect Legal Storm*, with a nod to Sebastian Junger's best-selling book, *Perfect Storm*. In that book, many bad weather elements came together all at once to form a unique and terrible storm. In the Roslindale Bomb cases, most of what happened had been seen before, but perhaps not all at once. Wrongful convictions in the Federal courts are rare, but this one saw a stormy brew of the following:

Aggressive detectives who fell victim to the Selective Truth Temptation, and heard and recorded what they wanted to hear and record.

Prosecutors who set their sights on suspects and evidence which then began to appear that was not seen before.

Witnesses who stepped forward to say things about people, even former friends, for unknown reasons.

Decisions by good people trying to do what was right by previously accepted standards and rules, but which frustrated the search for truth in these cases.

The tornado twist for all this was the "voluntary false confessor," Tom Shay, who wove a web of stories to contribute to the perfect legal storm.

Two juries found Tom Shay and Alfred Trenkler guilty beyond a reasonable doubt of working together to kill Mr. Thomas L. Shay, although Judge Zobel later found that Tom Shay did not intend to kill his father. Of the two or three jurors who talked with Mathew Brelis of the *Boston Globe* after the Alfred Trenkler trial, one said that the evidence of the 1986 device was very important while another said that the Lindholm testimony was believed important by some jurors, but not by others. Other jury members have not yet come forward with explanations of their votes for guilty, so we are left to surmise the reasons.

At one level, Shay and Trenkler were convicted because prosecutors prosecuted, and they usually win their cases. There is a common expression that prosecutors are so powerful within a grand jury room that they can indict a ham sandwich. The success rate for prosecutors in criminal trials is not as high, but they win in 85% of the federal murder trials.[2] The conviction rate is higher because most cases do not go to trial, as the defendants plead guilty, often with the threat of jailhouse snitches to testify if trials are demanded. In the Roslindale Bomb cases, the prosecutors had an extra advantage, in that a policeman was killed and another was seriously wounded. In such cases, investigators work extra hard to find evidence and prosecutors work extra hard to prepare strong cases. The two juries had a special burden to give guilty verdicts to the two men the prosecutors said were responsible for that most serious of crimes.

Below are reasons in approximate descending order of importance, why the juries voted for guilty for the two counts for Tom Shay and all three counts for Alfred Trenkler.

Tom Shea

Statements to the media
Statements to law enforcement
18 October Radio Shack receipt
Acquaintance with Alfred Trenkler
Possession of Alfred's pager number
Reason to resent father
Desire for the money
Failure to testify

Alfred Trenkler
Tom Shay already convicted in the same two-person alleged conspiracy
The 1986 incident in Quincy
Testimony of William David Lindholm
Statements of Tom Shay on videotape
Testimony of Michael Coady, Todd Leach and Paul Nutting
18 October Radio Shack receipt
Alleged drawing of diagram of 1991 device as drawn subsequently by ATF agents
Failure to make a persuasive case for alternate suspects or scenario.
Failure to testify

Each participant in the Roslindale Bomb trials has his/her own theory as to what broke the case against the defendants. Terry Segal told Alfred and his parents early in the litigation that if the prosecutors were allowed to present evidence to the jury of Alfred's role in the 1986 Quincy incident that the case was likely to be lost. The prediction had a way of keeping expectations low, and they were not exceeded. Jim Karolides said in 2007 that "[t]*hey convicted Alfred Trenkler on that diagram,*" referring to the diagram of the 1991 bomb that the ATF agents drew but claimed that Alfred Trenkler had originally drawn and discarded. Karolides believes that the diagram was never drawn, but "[w]*ho is going to believe an agent will lie?*"

Below are listed the reasons why both Tom Shay and Alfred Trenkler are innocent. First are listed the reasons common to both and then separately.

Both Men
1 No history of violence
2 No interest in the money from Mr. Thomas Shay's lawsuit
3 No relationship beyond a brief acquaintance from hitchhiked rides, and no
    meeting nor substantive phone call since August 1991
4. Alternate suspects not sufficiently investigated
    a. those related to Mr. Thomas L. Shay's gambling debts.
    b. Mr. Thomas L. Shay
    c. Jeffrey Berry and Louis Giammarco, the civil case defendants.
    d. those who contracted to build bomb (Gaeta/Medoff)
    e. the actual victims of Mr. Thomas L. Shay's domestic abuse (former wife and
        stepdaugthers), rather than those who witnessed it, including son, Tom Shay.
5. Fingerprints underneath Mr. Thomas L. Shay's Buick did not belong to either
    Tom Shay or Alfred Trenkler.

6. Fingerprints between layers of electrical tape not analyzed, and do not belong to either Trenkler or Tom Shay.
7. The Roslindale Bomb's toggle switch contacts could have come from switchers other a #275-602 Radio Shack toggle switch, and Alfred Trenkler had no need to purchase a new switch, as he had dozens in his personal collection.
8. Longevity of batteries in old Futaba receiver likely 2 hours, not 22.

Tom Shay
1. Loved his father and wanted to be closer to him.
2. Not a violent person. As his uncle Arthur said in 2007, Tom "*was not that kind of guy* [who would be involved in the Roslindale Bomb] *He is innocent.*"
3. If involved, he would have told someone, if not the media, hints of his role.
4. His inculpatory statements were prompted by reasons other than guilt.
5. He was not a typical Radio Shack customer and 18 October receipt was not his.

Alfred Trenkler
1. Career beginning to take off. Many projects in queue.
2. No physical evidence linking him to crime.
3. No involvement in the 18 October Radio Shack purchase.
4. 1986 device was a fluke, one-time event and not similar to 1991 bomb.
5. No knowledge of Shay's father or feelings toward him.
6. No history of being abused as a child and no interest in obtaining redress for the alleged abuse of Tom Shay by his father, about which he knew nothing.[3]

The double tragedy of death and wrongful conviction arising from the 1991 Roslindale Bomb continues, as Alfred Trenkler remains in prison. His sentence has been reduced to 37 years, but that is still close to a life sentence; as he will likely not be released until 2025 when he will be 69 years old.

Who was really responsible for the Roslindale Bomb? Unfortunately, we don't know. Given the unreliability of statements made in police reports and even of testimony in court, there is no string of consistent facts and testimony which make clear sense and which are not contradicted by some other fact or testimony.

One way to get to the truth is to ask subsidiary questions, just as can be put to juries. In fact, some uncertainty in this case would have been avoided if the two juries had been asked specific questions. Judge Zobel gave an example of one question at Tom Shay's 1993 sentencing when she stated that she did not believe that Tom Shay intended to kill his father, which led to the relatively short sentence. So that might have been a question for the jury when it was sent to deliberate, "*Did Tom Shay intend to kill his father?*" Here are a few questions which might help get us closer to the truth of the Roslindale Bomb case.

1. Was the Roslindale Bomb built
   A. to kill Mr. Thomas L. Shay, or
   B. to make it look like it an attempt to kill Mr. Shay?
   A. If meant to kill Mr. Shay, who would want to kill him? There was little evidence that anyone disliked him enough to want to kill him or even harm him physically. He was a small time gambler, but was thought to have kept his

gambling debts under control. Some people were dissatisfied with his auto body work on their cars, but that was not an unusual problem, and not many such disputes across the U.S. ended with the customer killing the auto body person. By October 1991 Jeffrey Berry and Louis Giammarco viewed Thomas L. Shay as a nuisance as his lawsuit was taking time and costing them legal fees, but there was little serious risk that he would win any substantial amount of money. Even if Mr. Shay did win, it likely would be covered by insurance. It would likely be settled for some nuisance value amount of money, just as had all of Mr. Shay's other lawsuits. And it was.

The idea that Tom Shay would want to kill his father was just not supported by evidence of his activities that fall, nor of his general inability to plan ahead and then remain silent. Sure, he had reason to dislike his father, which erupted after he realized that his father was pointing his finger at him, but lots of sons, and daughters, too, have reason to dislike their fathers. However, while Tom Shay had reason to dislike his father, that's not the same as actual dislike and there was no evidence of actions or even words which showed such a dislike. Yes, sons and daughters have been known to kill their fathers, but it's almost always for a more obvious and immediate reason than distant ineffective parenting and the remote possibility of inheriting the proceeds of a doubtful lawsuit.

If someone really intended to kill Mr. Thomas Shay, there were easier and more reliable ways to do it. Even if the decision had been made to use a car bomb, it would have been relatively easy to hook the device up to the car's own electric system such as the brake lights. When the brake pedals were pushed, the bomb would explode.

It is almost a certainty that the Roslindale Bomb was not planned to be detonated by a remote control radio somewhere in the vicinity of 39 Eastbourne Street. It's a dead end narrow street with many small houses close together. As the trial testimony showed, neighbors do see things from time to time and it would have been unreasonable for the Bomb Maker, or agent, to be near that street at the time of detonation. If there was a plan to detonate the bomb with remote control at all, it must have been elsewhere. For example, the Bomb Maker might have planned to follow Mr. Shay in his black Buick and then detonate the bomb somewhere on a road or parked.

One question which was never answered was why Louis Giammarco completely failed the lie detector test. After that failure his lawyer then stepped in and stopped all questioning. Should that have been the end of the story? What are the usual explanations for innocent people failing lie detector tests? One explanation is that lie detectors are unreliable and many people who have taken such tests have registered "false positives" and been completely truthful. On the subject of lie detector tests, it's been maintained here that it was a mistake for Alfred Trenkler not to take such a test as he originally agreed with Peter O'Malley to do. If he had failed, he could have done little worse that Louis Giammarco who quickly understood that the matter was serious and stopped talking with the police. On the other hand was it a mistake for the ATF not to ask Mr. Thomas L. Shay to take such a lie detector test? What about the efforts have such a test for Tom Shay?

We don't know as much as the prosecution thought we knew about the case. For example, was it possible that the bomb might not have been intended for Thomas

L. Shay at all? Maybe it was attached by the Bomb Maker to Shay's Buick when it was parked in the South End of Boston on Friday night, 25 October and was intended for someone else.

B. If intimidation was the goal, who would want to intimidate Mr. Shay? And toward what direction of behavior? Usually, such a threat of harm is associated with something that the "Intimidator" wants, or does not want, the "Intimidatee" to do. One such intent would have been the idea to deter Mr. Shay from pursuing his lawsuit, but, again, by October 1991, it was not going well for Mr. Shay, so there was little need to stop him from proceeding. The easiest way to stop the lawsuit was the same way most such nuisance law suits are stopped - by settling them for their nuisance value. Everyone in the case knew this, and it was eventually settled in the summer of 1993 for such nuisance value, $27,000.

Making a device that looked like it was a bomb intended to kill or intimidate seems most likely. Unfortunately, if this theory is correct, the Bomb Maker made a device too realistically close to being a bomb intended to be used against someone, and it exploded. The leading person who might have an interest in making it look like he was a target was Mr. Shay himself, followed in intensity by his children. Such a *faux* bomb would have validated his paranoia that someone might try to kill him or even might plant a bomb under his car as he is said to have predicted to a psychiatrist. Thus, he might not have appeared so paranoid if his fears were shown to be entirely realistic. Such a bomb might have made it look like Berry and Giammarco really were dangerous people and that the 1987 incident was part of their pattern of behavior. This "look like" option would explain why Mr. Thomas L. Shay appeared to be comfortable later putting the device near his daughter's outdoor play set, as he wouldn't have thought the black box to be dangerous, or because he had not yet turned on the slide switch.

It could explain the question about his early statements that he had thrown the black box to the ground a couple of times. He may have actually done that, or he may have just said that he did that. As with the driving to the Rolling Wrench Garage and the car-lock store on the morning of 28 October, his statements about tossing the box may have been intended to show his ignorance of what the black box could possibly be. He may never have tossed the box to the ground at all, but, instead treated it very gently, and told the police he had treated it roughly in order to show his purported ignorance. One unforeseen outcome of his telling Officers Foley and Hurley that he had tossed the black box to ground was that they were led to believe that the bomb was not movement-sensitive, as it may well have been. Or they may have thought it was a hoax.

Whoever built it may have reassured Mr. Shay that it wouldn't go off accidentally, or as the possible builder, Mr. Shay may have reassured himself.

Mr. Shay testified that he didn't tell Mary Flanagan about the device before the explosion because he was having a running argument with her. However, another reason might have been the idea that if she had seen it first, she might have thought it was related to Mr. Shay's frequently stated paranoia and not treated it carefully; but if the police were to come and take it away and later report back that it was **real**, then Mary Flanagan would have taken the story more seriously.

One difficulty with this intimidation-without-explosion theory is that the bomb would have had to be built 100% antiseptically so that if the Bomb was disarmed and disassembled, no one could have determined who built it. If the actual Roslindale Bomb had been deactivated before explosion, it would have been vastly easier to find the sources of the receiver, the dynamite, the toggle switch and even the wood and ballpoint pen draftlines. Thus, it may have been the intent of the Bomb Maker that the bomb not be detonated so as to cause harm to Mr. Shay or anybody else, but that it be detonated at some harmless point after its seizure on 28 October 1991. Sometimes, when disassembling is deemed to be too dangerous, the Bomb Squad takes a device to a safe place and detonates it so as to remove the danger. If that was the foreseen outcome, then the debris would have been less helpful in determining the identity of the builder.

Thomas L. Shay had some training in the Army National Guard and may have learned some basics there about detonators and dynamite, but not about wiring batteries together in series or in parallel. It was thought that his brother, Arthur Shay, had more such training as he served in Viet Nam. However, Mr. Arthur Shay recently stated that his service in Viet Nam was with a water purification unit. Perhaps Thomas L. Shay knew Dennis Owen, the man arrested in June 1991 for threatening his roommate and who had several models of bombs in his apartment.

There are so many questions about Mr. Thomas L. Shay's actions on the weekend+ of 25-28 October 1991 that even he may not know all the answers. For example, as he was an experienced auto body technician, why did he not know immediately that the black box was unusual, and not part of any alarm system or any part of a normal car that he had ever seen before? For a person who was afraid that someone was trying to kill him and who had taken several precautions around the house and who looked regularly underneath his cars for suspicious objects, was it a coincidence that something looking like a bomb finally appeared underneath his car?

One of the questions to ask is why did he park his Buick in the driveway on that particular weekend, when his usual practice had been for Mary Flanagan to park her car in the driveway and for him to park on Eastbourne Street.

Was it a coincidence that the Roslindale Bomb was placed underneath Mr. Thomas Shay's Buick on Saturday or Sunday, 26 or 27 October, the days after the car had been returned from the loan to Louis Rotman? Was it placed by Mr. Shay himself, or was someone watching Mr. Shay's routines very closely? And who knew which car belonged to Mr. Shay?

Was it a coincidence that the method used to try to kill or intimidate Mr. Shay, or make it look like such attempts, was a bomb when the foundation of his lawsuit was an explosion almost exactly four years earlier? Or that Mr. Shay had told his psychologists that he was afraid to start his car lest it explode? Or that the 1987 Dedham Service Center incident occurred at around noon? Or that Mr. Shay allegedly said to a psychologist that he was convinced that a bombing would occur in 1991?

What would investigators have thought if the 1987 incident had involved draining brake fluid from Mr. Shay's car and the 1991 incident also had involved the draining of brake fluid? Was there a pattern there which led to Jeffrey Berry and Louis Giammarco, or was there an intent by the builder of the Roslindale to make it look like there was such a pattern?

Thomas L. Shay may have had the black box with him when he drove to Rolling Wrench on Monday morning, but he may not yet have decided how to get it to the police. Maybe driving around with the device might have looked too nonchalant, so he may have hid the fact that he had it with him that morning. When he returned to 39 Eastbourne after his morning travels he may have, indeed, had the box in his hands as Evelyn and Robert Pirello believed, and as Eleanor McKernan observed that same morning. Tom McKernan may actually have seen Mr. Shay with the box at the "Sound Security" store. While Mr. Shay might have initially intended to bring the box to the police station, he might have decided later that the best way to involve the police was to put the device on the driveway in between the GTO and the van/truck and go to the Police Station to report it. He could have assumed that the police Bomb Squad would handle the device carefully and perhaps even blow it up at a remote firing range. If that had happened, then no one would have been hurt and it may have given him a little leverage in his lawsuit against Dedham Service Center. Also, there would have been no forensic disassembly to trace the origin of the bomb.

On the last day of its deliberations in Alfred Trenkler's trial, the jury asked its question "*How tight does the web of circumstantial evidence have to be?*" (TT 20-3) The jurors were surely thinking about the web that pointed toward Alfred Trenkler, but they might also have asked or been thinking about the web that pointed toward Thomas L. Shay. That web included a stronger motive than the evidence showed that his son, Tom Shay, may have had to build and place the bomb to increase the likelihood of success for his lawsuit. There was no evidence of Alfred Trenkler's alleged motive. Mr. Thomas L. Shay had access to the crime scene, whereas Tom Shay had been advised to stay away from 39 Eastbourne Streed, and Alfred Trenkler had never been there, and didn't know where Mr. Shay lived, and didn't even know his name. If the jury even agreed that one "*web of circumstantial evidence*" pointed toward Mr. Thomas L. Shay, how could it have concluded that the other web, which pointed toward Alfred Trenkler was the correct web beyond a reasonable doubt?"

Given all his vague answers at both trials, and all the other circumstances in the case, it seems likely to his family that Mr. Thomas L. Shay knows more about the Roslindale Bomb than he has previously disclosed.

2. Who built the Roslindale Bomb?

The evidence was that the woodwork of the Roslindale Bomb device was more expert than the bomb itself, with its grossly excess amount of voltage. The Bomb Maker used a ball point pen to draw the lines for sawing the wooden pieces. I have used a ball point pen for such line markings when a pencil was not immediately available, so there was nothing special about it being a pen-drawn line as compared to being pencil-drawn. Woodworkers draw such lines commonly, but there was no evidence that Mr. Thomas L. Shay or Tom Shay or Alfred Trenkler built anything of wood using such lines. There was not one such piece.

How did Mr. Shay cut the wood that was used for the window jams to ensure that no one broke into his house? Investigators had reported that Mr. Shay had a woodworking ship in the basement, and that there were several scraps of wood in his yard on 28 October 1991. Arthur Shay, the brother of Thomas L. Shay was reportedly more skilled at woodworking, and he had more military training and skills than his brother, as Arthur had been to Vietnam. When the police went to the Rolling Wrench Garage on 10 March, they interviewed John Doering and Arthur Shay, but the report of Arthur Shay's interview is not available, yet, to the author.

The Roslindale Bomb was spray-painted black and Mr. Thomas Shay had an opened can of spray paint in his garage and he had professional spray painting equipment for his work.

We know that the bomb was built sometime after the publication of the July 1991 issue of *MuscleMag International*, so it was likely built for one of the purposes above. That is, it wasn't built at an earlier time for some other person for whatever reasons, but not used; and given to someone which led to its getting to 39 Eastbourne. The arrest of Dennis Owen in June 1992 showed that there are people who built such devices from time to time. Maybe one of his devices was sold to someone which led to 39 Eastbourne, but there wasn't much time between July 1991 and 28 October 1991 to allow for such coincidences. That is, someone wanting such a device and someone having such a device already built was an unlikely coincidence.

On the 28th, Thomas L. Shay may have been as shocked as everyone else about the explosion, because if he was involved, he didn't expect it to explode. To look realistic, yes, but not to explode. While it was assumed by some that he was in some kind of shock after the explosion because he appeared to be the target, he could have just as easily been in shock because he was now responsible for the serious injury of two policemen, and he came close to severely injuring himself, too.

3. What about the 18 October 1991 Radio Shack Receipt? Of all the evidence in the case, this seems to be one of the hardest to explain. Was it the Mother of All Coincidences in this case? Perhaps like the entire Roslindale Bomb case itself, we may never understand the exact truth about it. It's unlikely that Tom Shay was the purchaser because he said nothing about Radio Shack until his attorney, William McPhee, sent him a copy of the Radio Shack receipt in May 1992 and Tom Shay then spun it into his web of explanations. There are too many unknowns about the receipt to make it a conclusive piece of evidence. Why "S A H Y?" Google reports 770,000 "results" for the word "SAHY," with many of them being names of people from Eastern Europe. Why "J Y T?" What was the "5100?" In 1991 there were approximately 34 sets of telephone numbers for Boston, and there were several other variations of the last four digits of Mr. Thomas Shay's phone number, 7380. The Radio Shack Receipt had 3780, but the real number could have ended in 3708, 7308, 3709, 8370, 0378, etc. for a total of 24 different combinations. Thus, in the Boston area, there were 816 (34 X 24) possible phone numbers which might have been accurately or inaccurately given to Dwayne Armbrister on 18 October. If one considers that many Radio Shack customers purchase items outside of their own home city, then the number of possible phone numbers rises dramatically. Of the 97 Radio Shack Receipts which Alfred Trenkler has in his files, none was for a Radio Shack in Milton because there was none. Some were from Quincy where he did live in 1990-1991, but most of the 97 were in cities and towns where Alfred Trenkler never lived, such as Braintree or Cambridge.

If a toggle switch was needed for the Roslindale Bomb, what were the other five items on that receipt used for? Why the different type fonts for the information printed on the receipt? What about Mr. Blair's inability to find the receipt in the Tandy corporate computer system in 1998? What about Allan Kingsbury's initial recollection that the purchaser was a "Middle Eastern" man? What about the coincidence (?!) that the manager of the 197 Mass. Ave Radio Shack Store was the roommate of a former lover of Tom Shay, who was, by 18 October, very angry with Shay?

Tom Shay said many things to many people about that receipt, once he learned of its existence, and most of them were false. He told a story to Karen Marinella. He told investigators that he remembered that receipt in Trenkler's car. He told William McPhee that he hadn't been in a Radio Shack since 1989 when he purchased a fog horn in Revere with Ralph Pace. (It might be useful to ask Ralph Pace, what, if anything, he and Tom Shay ever purchased together anywhere, but Mr. Pace cannot be located. Radio Shack doesn't sell any item known as a fog horn, but it does sell items which make loud noises like horns.)

It is not claimed here that any of the investigators, or any of the Radio Shack employees fabricated any part of the receipt. It's possible, but unlikely. If one or more investigators had conspired with Dwayne Armbrister or others to fabricate any part of the receipt, the conspiracy would come apart as some point, just as it's believed here that if there had actually been a conspiracy between Tom Shay and Alfred Trenkler, some concrete evidence of it would have emerged - but none has.

There are too many unknowns for that receipt to remain an important piece of evidence against Tom Shay.

One possible explanation is that the receipt was really for Thomas L. Shay and that he gave his own phone number, but that doesn't explain the "JYT" first name or the "5100" address. It's not known if his photo was included in the photo arrays shown to Allan Kingsbury and Dwayne Armbrister.

Finally, if the toggle switch used in the Roslindale bomb was not a Radio Shack switch, then the 18 October Radio Shack receipt would become totally irrelevant. Then, all the questions about the coincidences would still be interesting, but academic.

4. Guilty or Not Guilty?

Jefferson Boone summed up his former client's case this way in a 2006 email: *"The whole case against Tommy was smoke, mirrors and innuendo, seasoned with Gay-bashing. There was no real evidence, other than his own self-aggrandizing, half-witted statements to the press."* Boone believes that Tom Shay is totally innocent and believes that Nancy Gertner believed that too. At the 2007 national conference of the Innocence Network, a coalition of Innocence Projects well-known for their DNA-related exonerations, Federal Judge Nancy Gertner stated publicly that she continues to believe that she had a client who was convicted but whom she believes to be innocent. At least one member of the 150 person audience knew that she was talking about Tom Shay.

Now, near the end of the main text for the book, readers can again examine how they might vote as if on the jury. Where are you on this first scale of involvement in the Roslindale Bomb, or innocence expressed as a percentage.

Percent (%) of certainty of involvement

```
0--.1--1--10---20---30---40---50---60---70---80---90--99--99.9--100
|-----------------------NOT GUILTY----------------------------| |GTY|
```

And where are you, reader, on this second chart, as you complete the segment of the sentence beginning with: "Alfred Trenkler....."

0%	- did not build the "Roslindale Bomb" with total certainty. NOT GUILTY
.1%	- did not build the "Roslindale Bomb" w/ near total certainty. NOT GUILTY
1.0%	- did not build the "Roslindale Bomb" with much certainty. NOT GUILTY
10%	- very likely did not build the "Roslindale Bomb". NOT GUILTY
20%	- probably did not build the "Roslindale Bomb". NOT GUILTY
30%	- might not have built the "Roslindale Bomb". NOT GUILTY
40%	- possibly did not build the "Roslindale Bomb". NOT GUILTY
50%	- undecided. Don't have an opinion. NOT GUILTY
60%	- possibly did build the "Roslindale Bomb". NOT GUILTY
70%	- might have built the "Roslindale Bomb". NOT GUILTY
80%	- probably did build the "Roslindale Bomb". NOT GUILTY
90%	- very likely did build the "Roslindale Bomb". NOT GUILTY
99%	- did build the "Roslindale Bomb", with much certainty. NOT GUILTY
99.9%	- did build the "Roslindale Bomb", beyond a reasonable doubt. GUILTY
100%	- did build the "Roslindale Bomb", absolutely, with total certainty. GUILTY

Is there anyone who has read this book who believes that if a retrial were held that either defendant would be found guilty beyond a reasonable doubt? At the 99.9% and 100% levels?

5. <u>Who was Responsible for the Wrongful Convictions</u>?
There were one or two people responsible for this entire tragedy, the deaths of Jeremiah Hurley and later Denise Kraft Corbett and the maiming of Francis Foley. The people responsible were the Bomb Maker and perhaps another person, but, for those who responded with "Not Guilty" above, we don't know who they are.

The responsibility for the wrongful convictions is easier to establish as it belongs to those who investigated, prosecuted, defended and judged the case, including those on appellate courts who are expected to steer the justice system clear of wrongful convictions. The responsibility also belongs to those who established the statutes and rules which governed the jurisdiction, prosecution and trial of Tom Shay and Alfred Trenkler.

By wrongly convicting Alfred Trenkler and Tom Shay, the justice system failed those two men as well as Officer Foley and the Hurley and Foley families and the country. The justice system has been patiently crafted over centuries to do justice, and it should be troubling to the best legal minds in the country that even with the best legal expertise in Boston, Alfred Trenkler and Tom Shay were still found guilty beyond a reasonable doubt. Jim Karolides summarized the source of the problem by noting that the two men were caught in the *"legal system"* and not a *"justice system."*

At each level in the case one or more people could have performed his/her role better, but no one factor guaranteed its result. It was a perfect legal storm, where all the factors came together to drown the innocents in a sea of inference and coincidence.

Once Paul Kelly and Frank Libby had Alfred Trenkler in their sights, *"looks like a monk"* as Libby repeated, they saw an increasingly evil man. Normal characteristics were turned into evil. Allegedly gay men became predators. People who exploded firecrackers became bombers. Pranks became crimes.

They also showed their disbelief in the deterrence of the justice system. Even though the 1986 Quincy charge against Alfred Trenkler was dismissed, Alfred Trenkler still was chastened by the experience and showed absolutely no interest in firecrackers or other explosives during the subsequent years. As his mother said in her 19 November 1991 interview, he had not been in any trouble with the police since that incident. In his case, the legal system worked - but the prosecutors had no confidence in it. It was as if attaching a remote control radio device in 1986 to a pre-packaged U.S. Army artillery simulator, with two wires sticking out and inviting an electronic connection, was an addictive experience. It was not.

COSTS The costs of the Roslindale bomb are large. Incalculable was the human loss of Jeremiah Hurley and the near loss of Francis Foley. Another cost was the stress on those who were near the case of the Roslindale Bomb. One was the now-deceased Boston Police officer Denise Corbett, formerly Denise Kraft, who may have felt that it was her hand-held radio that detonated the explosion when she was calling to her dispatcher.

The total monetary cost of the crime now exceeds several million dollars. First, there was the loss of one officer's life and the maiming of another and all their lost wages and taxes. The public cost components are the costs of the investigation by the Boston Police and the ATF and the prosecution by the U.S. Attorney's Office, as well as that office's work on the several appeals. Also included are the costs of the trial judge and jury and all the appellate judges in both cases. Tom Shay's defense was provided by tax dollars and was expensive, even if not at the initially approved rate of $200 per hour for Nancy Gertner.

Alfred W. Trenkler and his family chose to tap their savings and other resources in order to pay for Alfred's legal struggle. Through 2007, that total came to more than $650,000, with a 2007 present value of close to $1 million. Ironically, the cost of legal representation for the one shadow of a victory for Alfred with his 2007 resentencing was borne by the taxpayers.

At approximately $30,000 per year, the cost of imprisoning Tom Shay for 10 years, and Alfred Trenkler for 14 years, so far, is approximately $720,000. Of course, if the real Bomb Maker had been found, this cost would not have been avoided, but it would have been more fairly spent.

Other costs included the lost wages of Alfred Trenkler and those of his former part-time employees over 14 years.

<u>WHAT IF's</u>. Other "What if's" can be considered in the case. "What if" this didn't happen, or that not happen?   For Alfred, the most significant were:

1. "What if" he had not offered to give Tom Shay a ride on that rainy June night?
2. "What if" he had told Donna Shea in 1986 that the idea of detonating the M21 Hoffman was a stupid idea, and the satisfaction of throwing fright into the owners of the Capeway Fish Market was not worth the risks that the explosion might hurt someone in the construction or detonation?
3. "What if" he had continued with his first instinctive response to the investigation, i.e., "*I have nothing to hide*," and he had testified at his hearings, and before the grand jury and and at his and Tom Shay's trial?
4. "What if" the defense had looked more closely at the contacts of the Bomb's toggle switch?
5. "What if" the defense had successfully forced the Boston Police Dept. to reveal the results of its analysis of the fingerprints underneath Mr. Shay's Buick?
6. "What if" the tests of an older model Futaba receiver had been done before the Roslindale Bomb trials?
7. "What if" the judges and defense lawyers had known at the December 1994 oral hearing that David Lindholm had already been released from prison the previous September?
8. "What if" Terry Segal had sought to present the testimony of Dr. Robert Phillips' instead of assuming that such a request would be denied, just as it was at the trial of Tom Shay?

There are many other "What if's."

<u>GENERALLY</u>. At some point, the question needed to be posed: Can one be tough on crime, and supportive of strong punishment for the maker of the Roslindale Bomb and still be in favor of justice for Alfred Trenkler and Tom Shay? The challenge of this book and the Campaign for Justice for Alfred Trenkler is to persuade many people that the two positions were not inconsistent. More than most people, members of the law enforcement community and victims of crime and their families should be concerned that innocent people are not punished as collateral damage in their strong efforts to avenge the death of someone close to them. Police and prosecutors have extraordinary powers and they should not be wielded without extreme care.

Every aspect of the U.S. legal system has been developed as a delicate balance between competing and worthy values such as:

the state's need to prosecute criminals vs. the rights of citizens' and the presumption of their innocence, and

the government's interest in reducing the cost of justice vs. the defendant's interest in a full hearing of all the evidence, as many times as it takes.

One of the rules or assumptions or customs in criminal litigation is that defense lawyers don't take every opportunity to proclaim their clients' innocence. Thus, courts sometimes wonder and contribute to the expectation that it might make a difference. In Pennsylvania Judge Conaboy observed that Alfred Trenkler "*failed to present any evidence that he was actually innocent of the crimes for which he was convicted.*" The doctrine of "actual innocence" has crept into legal decisions as a reason for justifying the waiving of procedural rules. So caught up are the appellate courts in the procedural niceties of court cases that they had felt too far distant from the real issue of guilt or innocence. In Alfred's case, we can expect to hear the term used more often in the future, as the courts will be asked to reconsider the case yet again. Then, the struggle will be between "actual innocence" and those who seek judicial economy and its corollary, "finality." The reason for shutting the door on some appeals is the fear that if it wasn't done, prisoners would be appealing forever and ever. However, that fear is almost groundless.

In Massachusetts, there is a state criminal procedure rule 30(b) that "*the trial judge may grant a new trial at any time if it appears that justice may not have been done. Upon the motion, the trial judge shall make such findings of fact as are necessary to resolve the defendant's allegations of errors of law.*" There is no comparable rule, yet, in the Federal Rules of Criminal Procedure. However, as was seen with the 4 April 2007 resentencing of Alfred Trenkler, the courts can find ways to deliver justice when they are convinced of what is right.

Other possible legal reforms could include a thorough re-examination of the question of a defendant's right to testify. If a defendant has some contribution to make to the presentation of truth to a jury, then there ought to be some way for that truth to be presented. In the Shay and Trenkler trials, both defendants were persuaded by their lawyers that the prosecutors would unfairly turn their lemonade testimony into lemons, even though, as argued in this book, their testimony would likely have been truthful, and certainly would have been helpful to the juries, in any case. The rules in the system that discourage the presentation of truth, or which encourage the presentation of mis-information to the jury ought to be re-examined.

One reform might be to encourage a more careful *voir dire* of defendants before they waive their right to testify. Such a *voir dire* would be similar to what is done now to ensure that defendants pleading guilty are doing so completely voluntarily. When advised by a defense lawyer that the defendant will not be testifying a judge could ask the defendant, outside the hearing of the jury, questions such as the following:
- Are you aware that you have a constitutional right to testify?
- What are your reasons for not testifying?
- Do you understand that while the prosecutors may question you about matters relevant to the crime, they may not question you about irrelevant matters?

The goal of such questions is to assist the defendant in deciding affirmatively to testify. In the process, and in the instances of a defendant's declining to testify, the judge will learn fully the reasons for such refusal and be satisfied that justice would be served by such non-testimony. If the reasons for not testifying include fear of some cross-examination questions by the prosecution, then perhaps the judge can reassure the defendant that some questions cannot be asked because of irrelevance or the hearsay rule or other evidentiary rule. If an area of questioning is permissible, the judge can, perhaps after discussion with the prosecutor, determine the exact scope of questions in that area.

The importance of the right to testify was shown in the before the First Circuit Court of Appeals *habeas corpus* case of Dwayne Owens which was decided on 12

April 2007. [Cases 05-1784 and 05-1785] One claim brought by Owens was that his lawyers did not adequately advise him of his right to testify. That is, they advised him not to testify, which advice he accepted; but they did not fully explain that it was **his** decision and that it was an important right he had. The appeal was successful on that and other grounds, and was remanded to the U.S. District Court for further hearings on the actual advice given to Owens. Said his former attorney and public defender, Miriam Conrad, "*Obviously there are things that I messed up that I could have done, should have done differently, and Mr. Owens should not pay the price for that.*" That echoes the foundation of this book which is that Alfred Trenkler should not have to pay the price for mistakes made by police, prosecutors, judges and his own lawyers.

The purpose of the appeal system is to catch errors in trials which may tend to make the trial unfair to either side. At the core of the desire to make the trial fair is the underlying assumption that a criminal trial seeks to determine whether the investigator's and prosecutor's selection of the alleged perpetrator is correct.

It was Justice Felix Frankfurter who contributed a short statement to the general wisdom that the courts should not convict innocent people by saying that it is better that ten guilty people go free than one innocent person be found guilty under the American/British system of justice. He did not mean that such a ratio is satisfactory, however. That is, as there are some people in our society who believe that too many guilty people are allowed to escape justice, with O.J. Simpson being the most famous recent case, those same people may believe it's okay to convict some innocent people in the effort to reduce the number of guilty-but free people.

Such thinking seems to have led to a reversal of the ratio, and the view that it's acceptable that for every ten actually guilty people to be convicted, it's acceptable that one innocent person be included. While there is no precise way to know how many innocent people there are in U.S. jails and prisons, some of the estimates approach that 10 percent figure. At least that 10 percent did not commit the crimes for which they are currently incarcerated. Many of those, of course, did commit other crimes for which they were not convicted.

In the recent history of exonerations of wrongful convictions, there have been very few exonerations for those convicted in Federal Courts. One long-standing claim, but without exoneration, has been maintained by former U.S. Army Green Beret, Dr. Jeffrey MacDonald, who was convicted by a military court of killing his wife and children at Fort Bragg, Carolina in 1970. Another case referenced in this book was the exoneration of former CIA Agent Edwin Wilson who was convicted in 1983 of arms trafficking after the CIA had denied in writing, and wrongly, that he was a CIA employee or operative. However, just because such Federal wrongful convictions are rare does not mean that they do not happen. One reason for the low number of Federal exonerations is that Federal courts rarely see trials for murder or rape and thus rarely see DNA evidence. It can be expected that the percentage of wrongful convictions in non-DNA cases is just as high as where there is DNA, perhaps 1-3% of all convictions in the U.S. Alfred Trenkler's conviction and Tom Shay's convictions were two of those wrongful convictions.

My view is that Tom Shay and Alfred Trenkler are **innocent with nearly total certainty (99.9%)**, and that's a big 180 degree difference from the legal system's verdict of **guilty beyond a reasonable doubt**.

The way forward is to seek the truth, and talk to everyone who might be willing to present the truth, including those who testified at the trials of Tom Shay and Alfred Trenkler and those who did not. In the coming days, weeks and months, everyone should pursue the truth and be open to accepting it, even where it conflicts with then currently held views. The truth **SHOULD** set Alfred Trenkler free.

On 6 February 2008 Alfred Trenkler will be 52 years old.
On 6 February 2009 Alfred Trenkler will be 53...
On 6 February 2010 Alfred Trenkler will...
On 6 February 2011 Alfred Trenkler...
On 6 February 2012 Alfred...
On 6 February 2013...
On 6 February ...
On 6...
On...
...

END NOTES

1. In an intereview with Al Gore on National Public Radio, 24 May 2007. The focus of the interview was Gore's new book, _The Assault on Reason_.
2. US Department of Justice, "Criminal Case Processing Statistics", Summary findings, at www.ojp.usdoj.gov/bjs/cases.htm
3. For a case where a killing occured in substantial part because of the desire for revenge against an alleged rape and abuse by the stepfather of a friend, and where motiivated by abuse within his own family, see the case of Eric Windhurst in New Hampshire. He was convicted of a 1985 killing of the stepfather of Melanie Paquette. _Portland Press Herald_, 16 June 2007, page B8.

CHAPTER 13. CAMPAIGN FOR JUSTICE FOR ALFRED TRENKLER

When the truth is found to be lies
You know the joy within you dies.[1]
Jefferson Airplane, 1967

Alfred Trenkler has struggled for 15 years for justice within the legal system. His 5 December 2005 plea for resentencing, <u>RFJ XXIV</u>, was the first that gave him some relief from injustice, with the 4 April 2007 sentence of 37 years instead of two life terms; but that's not enough. He must be given complete justice and exoneration will surely follow.

As has been seen in the book, the legal system seeks to achieve judicial economy through "finality" for its verdicts, and that goal often outweighs the search for the truth. In the cases of Alfred Trenkler and Tom Shay, finality can never be achieved at the cost of a wrongful conviction and continued imprisonment of an innocent man.

It has been argued here that Alfred should have been encouraged, in the interest of truth and justice, to testify and participate more in his defense. The success of his December 2005 letter to Judge Zobel, which was created and sent without assistance from attorneys, shows how individuals can achieve a measure of justice on their own. One doesn't have to be a lawyer to achieve justice, but it's almost always recommended, if affordable.

What is needed now is a broad campaign approach to achieve justice for Alfred Trenkler, including the use of lawyers and the courts. This is true for Tom Shay as well, but the primary focus of this book and of the Alfred Trenkler Innocent Committee is on the wrongful conviction of Alfred Trenkler because will remain in prison until 2025 unless exonerated.

Justice can be achieved via one of two intertwined routes, directly to the Federal Courts, or through the U.S. Attorney and U.S. Department of Justice.

1. Persuade the Federal Courts to invoke extraordinary methods to reverse the 1993 conviction, or otherwise overturn it., or
2. Persuade the U.S.Attorney to inform the U.S. District Court that the convictions of Tom Shay and Alfred Trenkler were wrongful, or probably wrongful or even possibly wrongful.

a. If *wrongful with substantial certainty*, the U.S. Attorney could inform the court that it wishes to drop the prosecution of Alfred Trenkler, in which case the reversal of the conviction would almost be automatic.

b. If *probably wrongful*, the U.S. Attorney could file a Motion for a New Trial with the reasoning that even though the U.S. Attorney still believes in the guilt of Alfred Trenkler, enough doubt has emerged as to warrant a retrial where a jury can fully evaluate the case.

c. If *possibly wrongful*, or if needing a more thorough evaulation, the U.S. Attorney can establish an independent commission or seek other outside assistance to evaluate the case more fully and make recommendations to the U.S. Attorney. Such a revaluation would be expected to produce either an endorsement of the original guilty verdict beyond a reasonable doubt or a determination that the conviction was "wrongful with substantial certainty" or "probably wrongful."

1. <u>The Federal Courts.</u> Despite the tightening by Congress in recent years of the rules allowing further judicial review of convictions and sentences, the courts still have the inherent ability to achieve justice. Judge Zobel's use of the Writ of *Coram Nobis* to correct her previous sentencing error is a good example of such power. This judicial power comes from the old English Courts of Equity which were less formalistic than the Law Courts. Now, their functions are merged, but the Federal Judicial judges still retain their "equitable" powers to do what is right.

The apparent strength of the scientific evidence in the Trenkler case made conviction appear more winnable and thus may have had the effect of moving other evidence more closely in support of conviction. Thus, the more careful examination of the physical evidence is critical to Alfred's exoneration. The current *habeas corpus* Motion to the U.S. District Court will hopefully lead to that re-examination of the physical evidence.

In addition to the scientific evidence, every witness who appeared at the trial, and even those potential witnesses who didn't, needs to be re-interviewed. For example, for those who testified before the grand jury and the trial in the hopes of winning part of the $65,000 reward money, their testimony was made more prosecution-friendly by the understanding that Alfred might well be convicted. For William David Lindholm, for example, he was said by another inmate to have commented that since Alfred Trenkler was guilty anyway, it didn't make much difference who informed on him; as someone was surely going to be found to do it.

If re-interviewed amidst the prospect of exoneration, the perspective of witnesses may be different. One witness has told Alfred's half-brother, David Wallace, that he will recant his testimony if he is promised immunity from prosecution from perjury at the trial and grand jury.

2. <u>The U.S. Attorney</u>.

The advantage of seeking to work with the prosecutors is that they are part of the executive branch and are appointed by the Presdent, together with the U.S. Attorney General. The required level of U.S. Senate approval has been a contested issue of late. Thus, U.S. Attorneys are subject to proper political influence. The term "proper" is used here, as the country is currently awash with charges of improper firings of U.S. Attorneys. By "proper" influence, we mean the ability to address the government with information and grievances and the right to be heard, as a voter and citizen. A citizen should be able to present facts to a U.S. Attorney at any time about a case and that U.S. Attorney should evaluate those facts and always carefully consider whether his or her actions, or those of his/her predecessors were correct. The doors should always be open to the office of a U.S. Attorney, even if they are not always open to a judge's chambers.

Every fair means of persuading a government official can be used to help persuade a U.S. Attorney, as compared to a judge who can only be persuaded by carefully filed legal papers and on-the-record oral presentation.

In the Trenkler case, it is hoped that the U.S. Attorney for Massachusetts, soon to be vacant with the departure of Michael Sullivan to Washington, D.C. to become the new Director of the Bureau of Alcohol, Tobacco and Firearms, will appoint an Asst. U.S. Attorney or an outside attorney or group of attorneys and citizens to carefully examine the facts.

a. After such an evaluation if the U.S. Attorney is persuaded that a wrongful conviction occurred then s/he can file a Motion with the U.S. District Court to dismiss the charges.

b. If not certain about the case, then a new trial can be requested.

c. To assist in the evaluation of the above, the U.S. Attorney can appoint an independent commission to ascertain the important facts about the case and make findings of fact and recommendations. The most recent national use of a commission to conduct a comprehensive review of a complex problem was the Iraq Study Group's work on the Iraq War. In Massachusetts, one well-known effort was the Ward Commission's review of corruption in Massachusetts construction projects in 1980.

The most famous such re-examination of a criminal case in Massachusetts was in 1927 when Harvard President A. Lawrence Lowell chaired a commission to investigate the cases of Nicola Sacco and Bartolomeo Vanzetti. Although the Commisson's affirmation of the guilt of the two men is not an especially good omen for Alfred Trenkler, the establishment of such a Commission would still be a good step. Given the improvements in forensic science since the Sacco and Vanzetti case, such a commission should produce a more authoritative result. It should be able to hear testimony under oath and to subpoena witnesses.

The Campaign for Justice for Alfred Trenkler can be said to have begun at Alfred Trenkler's on 17 April 1992 when he was arrested at the instigation of the ATF for a business check which bounced in Rhode Island. However, the campaign's tactics were subordinated in the first months and years to the work of lawyers in the U.S. District Court, the Courts of Appeal and the U.S. Supreme Court. The lawyers' mantra was that this was a legal problem and that if the family would pay the lawyers, justice might be achieved.

Alfred's stepfather, Jack Wallace, valiantly struggled to bring the wrongful conviction of Alfred to the attention of the media, judges and a few politicians, but the doors were closed. He was likely dismissed as being long on love for Alfred, and short on substance, but the substance was there, for those willing to listen, look, think and question.

In the spring of 2006, Alfred and his family sensed that public exposure of the wrongful conviction must be achieved in order to gain public support, and that the campaign should be more organized - hence the establishment of the Alfred Trenkler Innocent Committee and the website, www.alfredtrenklerinnocent.org.

A fundamental idea behind the campaign is that in a democracy, justice is more than the province of lawyers and the police and courts. While most lawyers prefer that the process of correcting a wrongful conviction belongs in the courtroom, the corrective process sometimes requires more than that, as in this case. All citizens in a democracy have a responsibility to seek justice. The closer one is to a crime and the investigation process, the higher is the responsibility.

The obligation to do justice in a Federal case extends to all those who can influence our national government, which means everyone in the U.S., and even people and organizations outside the U.S. Campaigns for justice for wrongly convicted people necessarily involves everyone related to the case, plus thousands of people who had no earlier connection to it at all. As with a political campaign, what is needed is volunteers, organization and money. Every witness needs to be revisited, and every fact re-explored and the word must reach as many citizens as possible.

Below is a discussion of the role of the stakeholders or interested groups in this case and how they can help to achieve justice and the truth in the Roslindale Bomb case.

ALFRED TRENKLER. For 15 years he has been nearly invisible to everyone but his few lawyers and family members. Because there are no Federal prison facilities in New England, he has been in a high security Pennsylvania facility for his entire sentence. He has learned to live in a restricted environment, far from the free lifestyle he once led. Even though he has developed routines to deal with his circumstances, his fury and frustration with the legal system has increased with every courtroom loss and every year of captivity.

In the renewed Campaign for Justice, Alfred will be asked to campaign harder for himself. While he has worked closely with his stepfather, Jack Wallace, and with the lawyers who his family was able to afford, Alfred was not able to campaign on his own, with a few exceptions. For example, he did write one letter to the _Boston Globe_ in 2001, as noted in

Chapter 11, but it wasn't published; and he waited for and worked on the next legal development.

The best example of what he can do was his 1 December 2005 letter to Judge Zobel which led to her resentencing hearing on 4 April 2007.

What is needed now is for Alfred to campaign full-time for his freedom, even if he is behind bars. That means writing letters and more letters to newspapers, other media, politicians, academics and everyone who might be able to help. He will be writing with a few basic statements:

1. I am perfectly innocent, and was wrongly convicted in 1994 of crimes

    in which I had no role.

2. Here are the reasons why my case warrants your attention

    a. No physical evidence linked me to the 1991 Roslindale bomb.

    b. I had no knowledge of Mr. Thomas L. Shay prior to 28 October 1991, and didn't even know his name nor where he lived nor anything about his treatment of his son, Thomas A. Shay.

    c. The 1986 device was a prank gone too far, and not the work of a murderous bomber.

    d. Tom Shay implicated himself and me in several "voluntary false confessions" such as was seen in 2006 by John Mark Karr in the JonBenet Ramsey case, He sought the attention that his statements brought to him; but the collateral damage was his and my conviction.

    e. A critical piece of evidence, a toggle switch, was identified at my trial, and that of my co-defendant as being exclusively a Radio Shack #275-602, but it probably wasn't. It makes a difference, because the prosecution's cases relied heavily upon a Radio Shack receipt for the purchase of a #275-602 in Boston, 10 days before the 28 October 1991 explosion.

    f. etc, etc. as presented in this book....

3. I need your help, and contributions.

4. For more information about my case, see the website of the Alfred Trenkler Innocent Committee, at www.alfredtrenklerinnocent.org and the book, Perfectly Innocent, the current draft of which is available online at the website.

THOMAS A. SHAY. Tom Shay's 35th birthday was on 4 November 2006. Like many people, he now understands more about the entire case than he understood in 1991-1993. He made some helpful statements to Dennis Tatz of *The Patriot Ledger* in August 2006, and in his August 2007 letter to the U.S. Attorney and his Motions to the U.S. District Court. We need to hear more from Tom Shay, and all of it must be truthful. Appendix B presents the testimony of Tom Shay as he might have given it in 1992. That testimony clarifies his non-role in the Roslindale Bombing, and his subsequent statements and actions.

Hopefully, he will have the opportunity to come forward and answer the questions in his own words and swear to his statements under oath.

Since his capture in July 2007, he has helped the writing of this manuscript with comments, corrections and edits, and has begun his own fight for exoneration.

VICTIMS AND FAMILIES

The HURLEY FAMILY. The Hurley family was most devastated by the Roslindale Bomb and they have the greatest interest in punishing the person or persons who built and planted the bomb. Unfortunately, they have been misled into thinking that Tom Shay and Alfred Trenkler were responsible and they've resented the recurring appeals from both men. Hopefully, one or more members of the family will want to know the truth behind the investigation of the Roslindale Bomb and raise his or her voice to demand further investigation. The Hurley family and the family of Alfred Trenkler and his supporters in the Alfred Trenkler Innocent Committee want the same results from this case: Justice, Truth and Closure. For 14 years, the Hurley family has sought to properly grieve for Jeremiah Hurley and then move on, but the recurring appeals of the Shay and Trenkler cases have kept opening the wounds. The way to achieve the closure both sides seek is to support a complete investigation of the case and if that supports the innocence of Alfred Trenkler, he should be exonerated and then the search should resume for the real Bomb Maker.

The FOLEY FAMILY. Francis Foley also has an interest in justice, and has implied that he doesn't fully accept the guilty verdict against Alfred Trenkler. At the end of the Shay and Trenkler trials, he was quoted in newspaper articles as being perplexed by the motives of the two men, and was especially puzzled by Alfred Trenkler, as he had a comfortable upbringing, and he had no known connection to Mr. Thomas L. Shay. Hopefully, Mr. Foley will read this book and ask questions about the case and return to his hunch that it just didn't make sense for a man like Alfred W. Trenkler to have built the Roslindale Bomb. Mr. Foley's hunches have been right all along. The conviction doesn't make sense.

The CORBETT FAMILY. Denise Kraft Corbett's death in December 2006 is considered by her family to be an indirect result of her presence at 39 Eastbourne Street on 28 October 1991 and her involvement in the investigation. Over the subsequent years, the image of the bomb and the expectation of renewed appeals and investigations were said to have haunted her and led to her suicide.

Given the harm and hurt already caused to the Hurley, Foley and Corbett families, it may seem that asking them to help correct the ensuing injustice is asking too much. They didn't ask for the harm and hurt to be inflicted upon them. However, the police and prosecutors have asked for, and received so far, the support of the victims and their families for the wrongful convictions. The families thought, of course, that they were supporting justice and valid convictions. It doesn't seem inappropriate, therefore, to ask respectfully for their help in pursuing truth and in correcting injustice as it was achieved in their names.

One of the better known examples of the role of a member of a victim's family toward a person exonerated for the crime against the family member came with the exoneration of Ray Krone in Arizona. He was the 100th of the 200+ Innocence Project's exonerees and was on death row for most of his 10 years in prison for the murder of a woman he knew. The effort to secure his release cost about $100,000, which came from a wealthy relative and the efforts of two hardworking lawyers. When he was released in 2002, he greeted the mother of the murdered victim and said to the writer of the 23 February 2003 _Parade Magazine_ cover story, "_She was hugging me and apologizing for hating me and asking my forgiveness. I told her that I understood why she hated me and that I never held it against her. She hated the murderer, and that wasn't me._"

The families of the victims of the PAN AM Flight 103 have been very organized and one outspoken father, Dr. Jim Swire, has been consistently calling for truth and justice instead of mere revenge. He said, "_I attended every day of the trial at Camp Zeist and saw every moment of evidence. In that time, I was converted from believing the two Libyans must be guilty to believing they were scapegoats in an international game._" Dr. Swire is calling for a full inquiry into the entire case.[2]

In the case of the Roslindale Bomb, considerable public anger has been directed at Alfred Trenkler, when it should more properly be directed against the person who built the Bomb.

It's hoped that one or more members of the Hurley and Foley families will make contact with the Alfred Trenkler Innocent Committee and even Alfred Trenkler himself in order to better evaluate for themselves the evidence in the case and the character of Alfred Trenkler.

FURTHER VICTIMS: FAMILIES AND FRIENDS OF TOM SHAY AND ALFRED TRENKLER.

For some family members and friends, the convictions of Tom Shay and Alfred Trenkler were accepted as being correct. Tom Shay was thought to be crazy enough to think of such a thing as the Roslindale Bomb. Alfred Trenkler's electronics skills often mystified his friends and they were led to believe that the Roslindale Bomb required such skills. Also, Alfred's lifestyle and recreational drug use led some friends to believe that he had irreparably descended down the slippery slope toward crime. Those friends were sucked into believing the government's case and there was no public effort to pull them in the other direction. Now, with the substantial probability that both men were perfectly innocent, it may be difficult for Alfred's former social and business friends to question their previous willingness to believe the government. To assuage such feelings of emotional guilt, Alfred has a message for his extended family friends: "*Welcome back.*" It's very important to Alfred that his friends return to communicate with him and support his Campaign for Justice.

Included among the friends of Alfred are his future friends who are attracted to this cause. Alfred welcomes all of them. Others will be his fellow alumni from the schools he attended: Milton Academy, Park School, Thayer Academy and Wentworth Institute. At each institution, a certain loyalty to fellow alumni and to the school is cultivated. Such loyalty is tested in the matter of an alumnus who is convicted of a serious crime, but it should at least be sufficient to enable some alumni to take a look or a second look at the conviction. It doesn't take much examination to see that there was much amiss in the convictions of Alfred Trenkler and Tom Shay.

Thayer has a student Amnesty International chapter which seeks to assist wrongly imprisoned people overseas, so it's hoped that this activity will lead to an active interest in a wrongly imprisoned alumnus in the U.S. Also, Alfred's brother, David Wallace, graduated in 1981 and Alfred's most recent appellate attorney, Dana Curhan, graduated in 1977. One of the strong supporters for Federal compensation for exonerees Joseph Salvati and three others was Massachusetts Congressman William Delahunt, a 1959 Thayer Academy graduate. With all these connections to Alfred Trenkler and the cause of justice, and with the growing awareness of the wrongful conviction, Thayer's support is sure to grow.

JURY MEMBERS FROM BOTH TRIALS. The jurors in the original trials were asked to make judgments based on incomplete information and they did their work conscientiously; but the verdicts were mistaken. What do people do in other situations when they make mistakes? They try to correct them. It is hoped that some of the jurors in the Shay and Trenkler trials will step forward and question what they did in 1993.

Members of a jury are asked to come together for a relatively short time, usually measured in hours and work as a team with 11 other people and decide on whether a defendant committed a crime and should be punished, sometimes very severely.

Jurors are then encouraged to walk away from their jury duty as if it never happened. Jurors are told in some states to say nothing to the press about their case. Judge Zobel told the Shay and Trenkler juries that they could talk to the media, but she urged them not to. It's better, she might have said, to preserve the illusion of justice than to get into the messy details which often lead to Motions for Retrials. The mantra continues from those who do not wish to disturb the "finality" of justice that the system must be efficient and if convicted defendants really knew what was said in a jury room about them and about their cases, there would be many requests for new trials. Now that it appears, from the DNA exoneration work by the Innocence Project, that 1-5% of guilty verdicts are actually wrongful convictions of defendants, maybe the doors will be opened to more retrials, and thereby reducing that intolerable result.

Sometimes, jurors step aside and do the right thing as they have the right to do. There was a case in Pennsylvania where a juror believed in the innocence of a defendant and that his legal representation was poor, and held out as long as he could for a "Not Guilty" verdict. As many jurors do in such a position, he eventually gave in to the other jury members and voted for "Guilty." Afterwards, however, he felt badly about what he had done, or not done, which is an emotion felt widely enough in the legal system to be called "jurors' remorse," that he contacted the defendant/now felon, and hired a new lawyer for him. The new lawyer secured a retrial and the defendant was found "Not Guilty" by a new jury.

This was very unusual for a jury member, but entirely legal and entirely moral and entirely correct. It should happen more often.

In Georgia, Marie Manigault was the jury foreperson in the Genarlow Wilson trial and she announced the verdicts of "Not Guilty" on the more serious charge of rape, and "Guilty" on what she and other jurors believed was the less serious charge involving oral sex. When the judge pronounced a sentence of 10 years in prison, Ms. Manigault and the other jurors reacted with shock, tears and anger. Manigault immediately became a strong proponent for justice in that case, and has continued that commitment to this day, with legislative lobbying and media interviews. In June 2007 a judge ordered Wilson released as the punishment did not fit the crime, but the Georgia Attorney General appealed the order, and Wilson remains in prison, with his promising college academic and athletic careers remaining on hold.

In Norfolk, Virginia, four men were convicted of the 1997 rape and murder of a woman after one trial and three guilty pleas based upon their confessions. The detective who achieved the confessions has been disciplined, but the case might have been forgotten if the real killer, already in prison for life, had not been subsequently identified; and he gave a real confession. One juror, Paul Weitz, wrote to the _New York Times_ (2 Sept 2007) about his experience, "*I am relieved that there were some good people who kept this and the other cases alive so that the courts could get closer to the true story of that horrible rape and murder.*" In a subsequent telephone interview he said that he was "*very upset*" at the "*miscarriage of justice*" and that he "*felt betrayed by the prosecutors,*" because they knew about several key problems in the case they were presenting to the jury. Weitz has assisted the lawyers who are seeking a complete pardon from the Virginia governor, even though the mother of the victim continues to believe that the original convictions were correct. Weitz's support has helped secure justice for the "Norfolk Four."

For the Shay and Trenkler trials, any jury member can come forward and speak publicly about the case, and work as hard as they can for justice. For those who have questions now, or in 1993, about the case, they should be able to search out the truth and are encouraged here to do so. If the Alfred Trenkler Innocent Committee does not have the answers, the jurors should be able to ask more questions about the case and/or to contact a judge and/or the U.S. Attorney's office to express his/her concern about the wisdom of his/her jury's verdict. Any juror can join the Alfred Trenkler Innocent Committee and every juror is welcome to correspond with Alfred Trenkler and visit him in prison. If a juror expresses interest in visiting, such visits are permitted by the U.S. Bureau of Prisons. During trials, jurors are introduced to the defendant during the empanelment process, but they prevented from coming physically close to defendants in the hallways and elevators. After a claimed wrongful conviction, it's just that kind of human contact that is very helpful when a juror considers whether to help overturn his or her own earlier decision to convict.

As the jury verdicts in the Shay and Trenkler trials took juries 13 and 21 hours, respectively, to decide, there were surely jury members who were hesitant about the verdicts. In what other temporary work, with zero skill and experience requirements, can people make a decision in so little time with so much effect? Whatever those jurors have felt during the next 14 years, they are now invited to come forward and seek answers to questions they had at the time, and to their newly developed questions, too.

Finally, the jurors in both trials need not feel guilty (pun noted) for what they did in 1993. The prosecution was aggressive and seemed to prove a good case. The defense lawyers were good, but they didn't know what we know now about the case in general and in particular about the true source of the toggle switch and the true energy consumption of the actual Futaba receiver. The defense lawyers also didn't work with each other sufficiently to truly understand the minimal relationship between their two clients. Here were two very dissimilar men accused by the U.S. Government of conspiring to try to kill the father of one of them. It wasn't a good way to develop trusting teamwork between Tom Shay and Alfred Trenkler to defeat the prosecutors' charges.

Now, in 2007, the jurors have another opportunity to take a longer look and to pursue the truth wherever it leads them. Hopefully, several jurors will begin that search and come forward anonymously or openly. Once jurors learn of Alfred's continuing claim of innocence and of this book, and of the website, it is hoped that they will follow their consciences and seek the truth. For those who come to see their 1993 votes for convictions as mistakes, working to seek the truth will assist them in dealing with their feelings of responsibility.

In May 2007 the _Bangor Daily News_ published a "Reporter Query" to ask that members of a jury in a 1984 murder conviction to contact the reporter who was doing a story about the case. One week after publication, four jurors had responded, and maybe the pursuit of truth will be enhanced. When truth-seeking reporters in Boston seek the views of the jurors in the Roslindale Bomb case, it's hoped that they will respond, and that they consider the information now available about the case, that was not available to them at the trials.

WITNESSES. The witnesses for the defense, or those who testified to facts which supported the defense, must wonder how it was that the person they knew or the facts they saw were woven into a conviction. For the witnesses for the prosecution who testified about facts that were used to convict a person claiming wrongful conviction, the burden is greater, and the difficulty of seeking the truth is greater, too. Among the prosecution witnesses, there is another dividing line, between those who made an honest mistake in their testimony and those who intentionally misled the prosecution and the jury for whatever reason. It's the assumption in this book, until proven otherwise, that every false fact given to the jury was a mistake, rather than the result of intentional lying. For some in the Trenkler trial, a simple, "_I must have confused him with someone else._" may be all the change from testimony that is needed.

It's hoped that those witnesses who wish to change some parts of their testimony will come forward with information about the changes and send them to the U.S. Attorney's office or to Judge Zobel, or to the Alfred Trenkler Innocent Committee, or to all three.

JUDGES. Judges have an obvious interest in justice. In the U.S. they are the referees between the opposing sides. While they make important decisions about evidence and the flow of a trial, they rarely ask questions of witnesses or of lawyers. In Europe, judges are more aggressive in the search for the truth. One of the better known examples of such judicial involvement was the campaign to bring the Mafia to justice in Southern Italy and Sicily.

Judge Rya Zobel was the primary judge in the Roslindale Bomb cases, but Judge Edward Harrington conducted the Guilty Plea for Tom Shay in 1998. Judge Douglas Woodlock reduced the sentence of David Lindholm; and Judge Magistrate Marianne Bowler made several pre-trial decisions in both trials. Each judge has the power to revisit earlier decisions and make changes, if necessary. For example, Judge Zobel could reverse her earlier denial of Alfred Trenkler's Motion for a New Trial, and order one now. Each judge can also appoint attorneys to represent Tom Shay or Alfred Trenkler, just as Judge Zobel appointed Joan Griffin to represent Trenkler for his resentencing request.

PROSECUTORS. The prosecutors in a wrongful conviction case can be approached with the truth and asked to help. It is in their interests to assist in the correction of a wrongful conviction case at the earliest possible moment. The longer the resistance to valid claims of the truth, the less the prosecutors or former prosecutors will appear to be on the side of justice.

Paul Kelly and Frank Libby prosecuted both of the Roslindale Bomb cases. It can be argued that they played the game well, and they won, but the rules of the game were unfairly applied. They suffered from STT, the Selective Truth Temptation, and brushed aside information which conflicted with their views of how the Roslindale Bomb was conceived, constructed, placed and detonated, and by whom.

Since the trials, other Asst. U.S. Attorney's, e.g. Kevin McGrath and James Lang, have fought to keep Tom Shay and Alfred Trenkler in prison on the basis of what they thought were valid convictions, but they too can re-explore the truth in this case.

It must be every prosecutor's nightmare to lead a jury to convict an innocent person. The proper resolution is not to suffer that nightmare further, but to stop its continuing damage to all the victims of the Roslindale Bomb and lead the way toward reopening the case and finding the real Bomb Maker(s).

DEFENSE LAWYERS. What should lawyers and former lawyers do for their clients who were wrongly convicted? Jefferson Boone has openly declared that Tom Shay is completely innocent of any involvement in the original crime and has offered to help in any way he can. When the 1998 plea bargain was struck for Tom Shay to plead guilty, Jefferson Boone felt that Tom had been persuaded incorrectly that he could have been sentenced to more prison time than previously sentenced if he had gone ahead with a retrial.

There were many lawyers involved in the two cases. For Tom Shay they were, in roughly chronological order: William McPhee, Jefferson Boone, Francis O'Rourke, Nancy Gertner, Amy Baron-Evans, William Kettlewell and Kathy Weinman. For Alfred Trenkler they were: Martin Cosgrove, Terry Segal, Scott Lopez, Brenda Ruel Sharton, William Brown, Morris Goldings, Amy Axelrod, Charles Rankin, James Sultan, Catherine Hinton, Ronald Travis, Dana Curhan, Joan Griffin and Corey Salsberg.

What are their obligations to correct an injustice? Perhaps one or more of them actually believe that Tom Shay and/or Alfred Trenkler is guilty. Can they say that publicly? No, they cannot, because that would violate the attorney client privilege. So the lawyers who remain silent about their clients are the ones who believe they were guilty, and the ones who speak up are the ones who claim innocence? It's a difficult dilemma.

Still, it doesn't seem right that a lawyer could be paid a fair and substantial fee to defend a client against unjust accusations by a democratic government and then LOSE and walk away. If an auto body mechanic, to take a randomly selected profession, charged $3,500 for repairing a post-accident car, and the repair left the car looking far worse than when the service began, wouldn't the $3,500 have to be returned, or for the further repair to achieve the goals of the original repair? Ironically, it would be lawyers and judges who would enforce such a moral obligation.

A lawyer who loses a criminal case for an innocent client can reason that, well, the client must have been lying to the attorney or to the jury and judge. In Alfred Trenkler's case there was no testimony in court by the defendant, so who would know what the client really did tell the lawyer? Sometimes a lawyer who loses a criminal case for an innocent client is saved by the happenstance that the judge or prosecutor or even the jury made a mistake so serious as to require a reversal and sometimes a new trial.

What is a lawyer to do when his innocent client is found guilty? I remember talking with one former Maine defense lawyer who went on to become Attorney General for Maine who still felt badly that one of his innocent clients was convicted and that client was still in prison, but there was nothing that he felt he could do. He did nothing, but he could have helped a lot by continuing to urge the courts to re-examine the case and promoting the kind of campaign presented in this book.

What was Terry Segal, or Scott Lopez, to do? Give part of his fee back? That would have been a helpful, but seldom seen, gesture. Perhaps either lawyer could have written to Judge Zobel or to the Appeals Court, or to the U.S. attorney about his perceptions of the case outside of court. Thus far, Terry Segal's response has been professionally correct, which has been to decline to explore with the author in detail how the wrongful conviction occurred. However, he has provided comments on an earlier version of this manuscript.

Nancy Gertner and Amy Baron-Evans are in a slightly different position because the U.S. Government paid for Tom Shay's legal fees, but their obligation was still to pursue justice. Should it end when the innocent client goes to prison? Or even when he is later released into "supervised release?" Nancy Gertner's subsequent appointment to the Federal Bench makes her future assistance to Tom Shay even more problematic. So far, her public statement of her continued belief in Tom Shay's innocence is powerful support for him, given that she could easily have ducked the issue and said, as would most judges in her position, that *"I'm now a judge and cannot discuss previous cases."* Hopefully, she will continue to do what she can, consistent with legal and judicial ethics.

THE MASSACHUSETTS BAR ASSOCIATION, AND THE COMMONWEALTH OF MASSACHUSETTS Bar Associations across the country provide "Continuing Legal Education" for lawyers, and in many states such continuing education is required. It is in the enlightened self-interest of attorneys to encourage the delivery of high quality legal services. It is part of the overall effort to achieve quality control.

Lawyers are required to carry legal liability insurance which assists clients who are victims of legal malpractice, but what if the legal services provided met a reasonable standard of quality, but which resulted in a wrongful conviction? It's not known how many of the 200+ DNA-related exonerees around the country have recovered any damages from their lawyers professional liability insurers. The likely answer is very few.

In Massachusetts, the Supreme Judicial Court administers the Clients Security Board which makes payments to clients from whom lawyers have embezzled money. The clients of convicted embezzler and former Alfred Trenkler attorney, Morris Goldings, likely received some compensation from this fund.

Like many states, Massachuetts has a Victims of Violent Crime Compensation Fund which provides up to $25,000 to crime victims. Is the imprisonment of an innocent person a violent crime? Even if not, the effects are often just as disabling.

The New England Innocence Project (NEIP) is supported primarily by one law firm in Boston, Goodwin Procter, and lawyers from other firms volunteer to provide *pro bono* legal services as are needed. There is no official link to the bar association or the state and no comprehensive or public reporting of statistics is given. The NEIP has not yet joined the other Innocence Projects in the U.S. which have begun to accept non-DNA cases.

The Commonwealth of Massachusetts also now has a statutory system for compensating wrongfully convicted people, based upon a formula multiplied by the number of years in prison. The maximum payment is $500,000.

What is missing from the above array of services to ensure that justice is fairly administered, is a system to assist those who **claim** wrongful conviction. While some people believe that almost all prisoners claim innocence, that's not true, as the real percentage is about 5%. For those 5%, in prison and indigent, it is very difficult to prove a wrongful conviction.

One of the unfortunate side effects of the success of the New York-based Innocent Project DNA-related exonerations of 200+ people over the past 20 years is it's tempting to believe that the problem is almost solved, and that the Innocent Projects are the solution. The problem is that DNA is involved in only about five percent of felony crimes. Assuming that wrongful convictions occur in DNA-related, but untested, crimes as often as they do in non-DNA-related crimes, there are nineteen wrongfully convicted people who should be exonerated.for every exoneree who was lucky enough to have an available DNA source at the crime scene. Thus, over the past 20 years, we should have seen the exonerations of at least 3,800 more prisoners, if the non-DNA exoneration could have matched the DNA exoneration rate. In truth, the 200+ exonerations to date have only scratched the surface. It's been estimated that the wrongful conviction rate is somewhere between one-half and seven percent, but if it's only one percent, there would be 20,000 among the country's two million prisoners.

In the case of Alfred Trenkler and Tom Shay, no DNA has yet been identified, although there may be traces of DNA amidst the fingerprints between the layers of black electrical tape which have yet to be analyzed. Without DNA being indentified, so far, the New England Innocence Project is not assisting Alfred Trenkler and Tom Shay, so they are left with the other 95% who claim wrongful conviction but for whom there is no DNA.

Some states have created Innocence Commissions which bridge the gap between those claiming innocence and those who are actually considered by the courts for exoneration. North Carolina created the country's first Innocence Inquiry Commission in 2006 after seeing a number of exonerations of wrongfully and usually poor people. Five of the eight commissioners will vote on applications for exoneration and a majority vote will send the application to a three judge panel which must vote unaminously to exonerate an inmate.

A similar commission has functioned in Great Britain since 1997 and it has referred 300 of the 8,500 applications to a similar judicial panel. Of those 300, about 200 have been reversed.

A leading advocate for the wrongfully convicted is Professor Sam Gross of the University of Michigan Law School. He said, "*The innocence commission is a response to the fact that our system doesn't have a process for reevaluating the innocent or guilt of somebody who has been convicted.... There's a hole in the middle of the process.*"[3]

Alfred Trenkler and Tom Shay are presently within that hole. As the Campaign for Justice for Alfred Trenkler proceeds, one goal will be to create an Innocence Commission for Federal inmates across the country. A helpful early step will be for Massachusetts and the other states to create such a commission.

INVESTIGATORS FROM THE BOSTON POLICE AND ATF. Most of the investigators have moved on to other jobs or other roles, but each of them can help in some way. If Alfred Trenkler and Tom Shay did not build the Roslindale Bomb, then the investigators who were pursuing other leads were more likely right than they were given credit at the time. Perhaps they have information or ideas which may lead to the actual Bomb Maker. In 1991, these investigators were nudged aside as the seemingly clear appearance of the name, "Al Trenkler," in Tom Shay's address book, and the evidence of the 1986 device. Then came the Radio Shack receipt on 18 October 1991, together with the Radio Shack toggle switch. Then came the claims of William David Lindholm. It's always hard to argue with success in any organization. If the Tom Shay/Alfred Trenkler plot idea was going to solve the Roslindale Bomb case, then those with other ideas had other work to do. There's always room for one's hunches to be wrong.

Those investigators can come forward with their ideas, either quietly within their former departments or publicly to the media.

Even the investigators who became convinced early in the investigation that Alfred Trenkler and Tom Shay were guilty are welcome to now re-examine the evidence and reconsider their solutions. It is better to recognize a mistake sooner rather than later.

OTHER LAW ENFORCEMENT OFFICIALS. There is enormous loyalty among law enforcement officials to other law enforcement officials, but for some, that loyalty does not go the extent of supporting wrongful convictions. Most, however, will not get that far as they decline to listen to the other side. For one sergeant, upon hearing about this book and the Campaign for Alfred, the choice was easy, "*I can see that you're very concerned about someone who kills cops.*" My unconvincing response was, "*I AM concerned that the person who built the Roslindale Bomb is still free and unpunished.*" The officer's concluding comment was, "*I don't want to talk with you about this case.*"

For a few special law enforcement people, working on the Campaign for Alfred is an opportunity to cleanse the sheet of any taint which arose from this case. If Alfred Trenkler is, indeed, guilty, then these volunteer investigators and campaign workers can help uncover the truth. On the other hand, if Alfred Trenkler is clearly innocent then he should be released and then the police can resume their search for the real Bomb Maker.

MEDIA. The media, and primarily the newspapers, played some role in the conviction of Tom Shay and Alfred Trenkler. First, they gave uncritical coverage to Tom Shay who gave several press conferences and seemed to love their spotlighted attention, to the detriment of the truth. There wasn't much fact checking after those press conferences.

Second, the media attached the labels of "*lover*" to Tom Shay and to Alfred Trenkler without asking Alfred Trenkler the simple question of whether it was true. The other label was "*mastermind*" which conjured up images of the creation of Frankenstein, but was not realistic or accurate.

Third, the newspapers made frequent use of unnamed law enforcement sources for material for their articles. If the informants were not willing to be identified, their information should have been refused.

Now, in 2007, the media have a chance to redeem themselves. While the weight of current news and deadlines is heavy, the story of the wrongful convictions of Tom Shay and Alfred Trenkler deserves to be told, especially considering the role of the media in the original convictions.

Almost any publicity about a case of claimed wrongful conviction is good publicity. If the publicity exposes true facts, they are useful. If untruths are publicized, then they can be corrected, and the controversy might inspire further interest. Either way, the truth slowly emerges, but 14 years is a long time for the truth to emerge. Thirty-seven years is an even longer time.

A core value for the media is the pursuit of the truth, and that is what is needed here.

CITIZENS. Every citizen can help with the achievement of justice in the Roslindale Bomb case. Every citizen can write or call his/her state representatives and senators and U.S. Congressmen and U.S. Senators, and U.S. Attorney, and U.S. Attorney General and the President of the United States about this case. Every citizen can write or otherwise contact the media and ask questions about the case publicly. Every citizen can write to Alfred Trenkler, too, and to the Alfred Trenkler Innocent Committee and ask questions and even provide information where it might be helpful. There are many, many people in Massachusetts and New England who have information about the Roslindale Bomb case which can be helpful.

To be most effective, such efforts should be organized and the work of the Alfred Trenkler Innocent Committee is described below.

The Campaign for Justice for Alfred Trenkler will end not just with his exoneration, but with the re-investigation of the entire case with the goal of finding the real Bomb Maker. The identity of the Bomb Maker may never be shown beyond a reasonable doubt, but knowing who probably made it will be more satisfying to the victims' families than not knowing at all. O.J. Simpson was convicted by a civil jury of killing his wife Nicole and her friend. He didn't go to prison, but he lost much of his wealth and his reputation. He was deprived of his freedom to resume a normal life, which is part of what prison does.

Every citizen, and every member of each stakeholding group described here can contribute money, as every democratic campaign requires money.

STRATEGY AND TACTICS. What can be done? The Campaign for Justice is being led by the Alfred Trankler Innocent Committee and it works in parallel with lawyers who are helping Alfred within the court system. The strategy is to view the work to exonerate Alfred Trenkler as a comprehensive political campaign and not just as a legal problem for lawyers to solve.

For tactics, the Committee will do anything that's reasonable and respectful to bring Alfred's case to the attention of the Federal Government and to the citizens of the U.S. in order to persuade the U.S. Government to correct its mistaken wrongful convictions of Alfred Trenkler and Tom Shay.

The writing of this book and the creation of the website, www.alfredtrenklerinnocent.org, are two parts of the Campaign for Alfred Trenkler, and its efforts to present the truth. Through the writing of this book, and the creation of the website, we now know far more about the case than was known at the time by either the prosecution or the defense. There is less wiggle room now for the unknown. Also, because we have the testimony from the trial, we know which facts are disputed and, after 14 years, have a better idea of how to inquire about them.

There is more information in this book and on the website about the case than was known by any of the participants before its publication, because no one had access to everything, and we still don't. For example, the prosecution had not seen, before the creation of the website many of Alfred Trenkler's own statements about the case and his interpretations of his own life and actions. Now, with everyone given a chance to see the documents and the evidence, perhaps a different view of the case will emerge at the office of the U.S. Attorney for Massachusetts.

WHAT CAN INDIVIDUALS, INCLUDING ALL THE STAKEHOLDERS ABOVE, DO? Even when seeing injustice, most citizens assume incorrectly there is nothing that they can do, as the lawyers have convinced others that justice is their special province - even when they get it wrong.

Below is a list of actions citizens can take to correct an injustice.
- Learn about the case. Alfred's website has a large amount of material on many pages, but a review of the documents on the Home Page should give a good sense of how the wrongful convictions of Tom Shay and Alfred Trenkler occurred. For those who have further questions, the rest of the website has a large number of documents and even some recordings. Further questions can be addressed to the Alfred Trenkler Innocent Committee, either by U.S. mail or by clicking on the CONTACT link on the website.
- Talk with others about the case. It's a good way to clarify one's own thinking, and one never knows who will know someone involved in the case who might make a difference or who will talk to someone else and so on. In the Spring of 2007, one Alfred Trenkler supporter mentioned the case and Alfred Trenkler's name to a retired Boston Fire Department officer, expecting to hear nothing in response or to hear a mild admonition, such as *"ought to throw the keys away."* Instead the fireman responded, *"Trenkler was railroaded."* A lot of people in the Boston area believe that to be the case, and we need to bring them together to fully understand why they believe he was railroaded and also to seek their contributions and other assistance. We need to organize these people into a political campaign. The retired fireman was a welcome addition to the Alfred Trenkler Innocent Committee, as is his strong belief in truth and justice.

- <u>Join the Alfred Trenkler Innocent Committee</u>. All it takes to join is to send an email address to the contact address on the website. For those who do not have an email address, ask a friend with a website to allow you to use his or hers, and then the friend can print communications from the Committee. Within the organization, members learn more and more about the case and about more opportunities for action, such as letterwriting to individuals or newspapers or calling others for contributions or other support.

THE WORK OF THE ALFRED TRENKLER INNOCENT COMMITTEE.
The Committee acts on its own and coordinates the work of members to do the work described below:
   o Obtain media coverage of the case in order to bring to the public the truth about the Roslindale Bomb case.
   o Seek the interest and cooperation of local, State and U.S. Government officials, with the overall goal of persuading the U.S. Attorney to reopen the case.
   o With the assistance of a private investigator, re-investigate as many of the important facts as possible and present that evidence in a judicially acceptable manner such as personal affidavits and reports from accredited forensic laboratories.
   o Seek the involvement of stakeholders in the Campaign for Justice for Alfred Trenkler, which is also a Campaign for Justice in the entire Roslindale Bomb case.

To accomplish this work, the Alfred Trenkler Innocent Committee is guided by several principles.
1. We are polite and respectful to everyone, including those thought by some to be responsible for the wrongful convictions in the Roslindale Bomb case.
2. We assume, until proven otherwise, that the wrongful convictions occurred due to mistakes and misunderstandings during the investigation and prosecution of the Roslindale Bomb case, where the revelation of the truth sometimes was not the first priority.
3. We seek the truth and will follow it wherever it leads.
4. We seek closure of the case as soon as possible so that the victims affected, including Alfred Trenkler, can move on with their lives. Final closure will come when the real Bomb Maker is found.

BEYOND THE ALFRED TRENKLER CASE:
   To reduce wrongful convictions to an absolute minimum, there needs to be structural changes in the legal and judicial systems in the U.S.
   The standard for evidentiary and trial procedure decisions within a trial ought to aim for the generation of truth. Judicial economy ought to be relegated to a lesser role.

There have been proposals over the years for making jurors more effective and more knowledgeable, such as recruiting jurors with business experience for commercial cases, etc., but those efforts have faltered. One technique that is gaining support is to encourage jurors and grand jurors to ask more questions on their own. In the I. Lewis "Scooter" Libby trial, Judge Reggie Walton encouraged jurors to ask their own questions. The procedure was that jurors would write their questions, and then the judge and the lawyers would consider the correct form for the question to ensure its overall propriety within the trial. For example, one juror asked why former _New York Times_ reporter Judith Miller kept her interview records in grocery shopping bags.

Most judges discourage such questioning and lawyers get paid by their clients to do the questioning. At the trial of Tom Shay, Nancy Gertner had a different plan for jurors' questions, saying, "*And if at the end of this process you still have questions that have not been answered, then you have reasonable doubt.*" [TS 4-27] It's likely that now, as a Federal judge herself, Nancy Gertner would support a larger role for the jury in the pursuit of truth. Back in 1993, the prospect of jurors asking questions wasn't an issue. Now, with our increased awareness of the possibilities of wrongful conviction, it is inexcusable for a jury to begin and complete its deliberations while it has relevant questions which could be answered by participants in the trial. If the answers are unavailable, the jury can be told why the question cannot be answered.

Another concern was raised in Carol Leonnig's _Washington Post_ article about the juror questioning in the Libby case, "*The whole practice has been controversial among attorneys on both sides -- worried about losing control of the points they hope to score with each witness's testimony -- who argue quietly with Walton at the bench over what can be asked.*"[4] While the lawyers may prefer to control the questioning, the article stated that Walton has told them that it is important for the jurors to be able to probe the things they want answered. He has allowed jurors in his courtroom to ask questions for several years, a rare practice that is slowly becoming more common among some judges. About 15 percent of state courts and 8 percent of federal courts permit jury questions, and three states require that questions from jurors be allowed: Arizona, Colorado and Indiana.

Other laws need to be changed, such as the Federal Rules of Criminal Procedure, which needs to adopt a rule like Rule 30(b) of the Massachusetts state courts, which permits an inmate to make a claim to a judge for justice at any time. By that rule, justice trumps procedure, as it should. In Massachusetts state courts, several wrongfully convicted people have been exonerated by application of that rule. If the Federal Rules of Criminal Procedure had a similar rule in 1993 and thereafter, Alfred Trenkler would likely be a free man today. The Federal Court mistakenly convicted Alfred Trenkler, but, as Judge Zobel showed with

Alfred's resentencing in 2007, the courts are able to correct their mistakes if procedural rules permit reexamination.

It is time for justice in the Roslindale Bomb case.

END NOTES

1. "Somebody to Love" by Jefferson Airplane, 1967. In the album *Surrealistic Pillow*.
2. "Swire urges Salmond to order full inquiry," from Scotland on Sunday, 24 June 2007.
3. "North Carolina Creates at new route to Exoneration," The *Christian Science Monitor*, 10 August 2006.
4. "Jurors' Queries Yield Insights -- And Laughs - Judge in Libby Case Among Few Allowing Such Practice," By Carol D. Leonnig, *Washington Post*, Thursday, February 1, 2007; A13 at
http://www.washingtonpost.com/wdyn/content/article/2007/01/31/AR2007013101940.html?referrer=emailarticle

www.ingramcontent.com/pod-product-compliance
Lightning Source LLC
Chambersburg PA
CBHW081456200326
41518CB00015B/2280